Dedicated to those giants
upon whose shoulders we stood
to see beyond the crowds —

But especially to the memory of:
EDGAR SHEFFIELD BRIGHTMAN,
a philosopher's philosopher.

But when all is said, this work of mine can help no one who has already fixed his philosophy and his philosophical method, who has thus never learnt to know the despair of one who has the misfortune to be in love with philosophy.

(Edmund Husserl)

TABLE OF CONTENTS

PREFACE

Plato believed that philosophy was not for the masses; however, it is the authors' earnest hope to render philosophy both pleasurable and comprehensible to the layman. Two reasons exist for this desire: the first is to enrich the nonphilosopher's perspective with the wealth of value philosophy affords; the second is to initiate recruits to an exciting new world of thought.

Whether or not you are a philosopher, (or have studied philosophy), you have undoubtedly philosophized, since everyone does, whether he has consciously planned it, or is totally unaware of it — even the philosophical renegade who rebels, saying that he refuses to philosophize or accept any philosophy whatever is, in effect, entertaining and practicing a philosophy. Inasmuch as this is the case, it would prove far more desirable to engage in philosophical pursuits, consciously, deliberately, and preparedly, thereby deriving the utmost from so rich a culture which is afforded to man.

Not all philosophy is of equal difficulty, nor equivalent in value; moreover, various areas of philosophy are of such diverse character that personal preferences will early and quickly be evidenced. The same holds true for professional philosophers, attracting them to differing fields of specialty — from logic to political theory. In the present work, the more difficult realms of philosophy are reserved for the latter half of the book, allowing the reader a gradual preparation for entrance to the profundities of philosophy.

Serving somewhat as an appendix for reference purposes, there is at the end of the book an outline of philosophers, arranged chronologically, and according to schools of philosophical thought, with brief valuable data, such as, dates on vital statistics, important books published, ideas, etc. To date, the authors have not seen a publication of this nature, and have provided it for the philosophical novitiate who is constantly inquiring respecting such data. Its value, however, is not limited to the needs of the beginner, but is of appreciable value to the professional, since no man is a walking encyclopedia.

A glance at the table of contents (Part 6) will readily indicate that major philosophical schools of thought have been amply treated, but what may escape detection is the fact that many affiliated schools have also been dealt with, such as Critical Realism, under Neorealism; Instrumentalism, under Pragmatism; Neo-Scholasticism, under Neo-Thomism, etc.

The present work shares the same objective as a former book of one of the authors, *Systems of Ethics and Value Theory*, an attempt to provide a thorough summary, explanation, and critical evaluation of classics in philosophy, with the author's explanations richly interspersed with quotations from the classics, the hope being that the reader will benefit from significant inflections of the classic philosophers speaking for themselves, along with the guide provided in the present exposition.

There is no better encouragement to entice an individual into the world of philosophy than the Socratic injunction: "The unexamined life is not worth living;" thus, with this in mind, we wish you a rich new experience on your philosophic journey.

William S. Sahakian

Beacon Hill,
Boston, Massachusetts.

ACKNOWLEDGMENTS

Grateful acknowledgment is hereby made to the following publishers and authors for their kind permission to include copyrighted material in the present volume: The Macmillan Co. for Alfred North Whitehead, *Process and Reality,* Edwin Holt, *The New Realism,* Henri Bergson, *Matter and Memory;* The Free Press of Glencoe for Max Scheler, *Ressentiment;* Cambridge University Press for F. R. Tennant, *Philosophical Theology;* Clarendon Press, Oxford, for Aristotle, *Nicomachean Ethics* (tr. W. D. Ross), Epicurus, *Extant Writings* (tr. C. Bailey), Epictetus, *Fragments;* Routledge & Kegan Paul Ltd. for L. Wittgenstein, *Tractatus Logico-Philosophicus* (tr. Pears and McGuinness); The Royal Institute of Philosophy for W. P. Montague, "Story of American Realism" in *Philosophy;* The Vision Press for M. Heidegger, "Metaphysics," "Essence of Truth," in *Existence and Being;* Student Christian Movement Press Ltd. for M. Heidegger, *Being and Time;* Harper & Row, Publishers Inc. for M. Heidegger, *Being and Time* (American rights), S. Kierkegaard, *Purity of Heart* (tr. D. V. Steere); George Allen & Unwin Ltd. for Adams and Montague, ed., *Contemporary American Philosophy;* Charles Scribner's Sons for Jacques Maritain, *The Person and the Common Good;* Holt, Rinehart and Winston, Inc. for H. Bergson, *The Two Sources of Morality and Religion, Creative Evolution;* and John Dewey, *Logic: The Theory of Inquiry;* Joseph F. Wagner, Inc. for Fr. Lumbreras, "The Twenty-four Fundamental Theses of Official Catholic Philosophy" in *Homiletic and Pastoral Review;* Mr. Kenneth W. Sorley and Mrs. Geoffrey Bickersteth for W. Sorley, *Moral Values and the Idea of God;* Doubleday & Co., Inc. for Étienne Gilson, *Elements of Christian Philosophy,* Bertrand Russell, *Wisdom of the West;* The Ronald Press for Edgar S. Brightman, *Person and Reality;* Prentice-Hall, Inc. for Edgar S. Brightman, *A Philosophy of Religion;* Henry Regnery Co. for Martin Heidegger, *Existence and Being* (U. S. rights); *The Review of Politics* for J. Maritain, articles appearing in "The Person and the Common Good;" Boston University Press for A. C. Knudson, *The Philosophy of Personalism;* Princeton University Press for S. Kierkegaard, *The Sickness unto Death, Concluding Unscientific Postscript,* and *Either/Or;* Dover

Publications, Inc. and Victor Gollancz Ltd. for A. J. Ayer, *Language, Truth and Logic;* Philosophical Library, Inc. for Jean-Paul Sartre, *Being and Nothingness* and *Existentialism,* Jean Wahl, *Existentialism;* Beacon Press for John Dewey, *Reconstruction in Philosophy,* Max Scheler, *Philosophical Perspectives* and *Man's Place in Nature;* George Braziller, Inc. for R. B. Perry, *Present Philosophical Tendencies;* Liveright Publishing Corporation for Sigmund Freud, *The Future of an Illusion;* The World Peace Foundation for Immanuel Kant, *Eternal Peace* (tr. W. Hastie); Barnes & Noble, Inc. and Routledge & Kegan Paul Ltd. for Hans Vaihinger, *The Philosophy of 'As If'* (tr. C. K. Ogden); Random House, Inc. for Jacques Maritain, *Existence and the Existent,* and *The Basic Writings of St. Thomas Aquinas* (ed. Anton C. Pegis).

Part One: EPISTEMOLOGY — Knowledge and Proof of the Truth

I

EPISTEMOLOGY

The Study of Knowledge

Epistemology, although a foreboding-sounding term of Greek origin, etymologically means simply 'knowledge,' or more accurately, the *study* of knowledge. Many persons are acquainted with the study of logic but few realize that it is a branch or subdivision of epistemology. Epistemology embraces a wider area of learning than does logic whose scope is defined as the study of correct thinking, whereas epistemology includes the study of knowledge in general. Typical questions which epistemologists seek to resolve are: What is the nature, extent, and scope of knowledge? Is knowledge possible? How much knowledge is possible for a human being to grasp? What is the source of knowledge?

Although psychologists also have an interest in the nature of human thought, it is to be distinguished from logic, the study of valid thinking. The psychologist's scope is restricted to the manner in which people do in fact think as well as labeling types of human thought, whether or not valid. For example, a psychologist may describe a subject's thinking as paranoid because the individual cannot escape the obsessional thought that people are persecuting him but nevertheless the psychologist refrains from expressing judgments of value regarding such behavior. On the other hand, the philosopher, whose task it is to express value judgments, states whether or not paranoid thinking is good or bad, true or false, desirable or undesirable, etc. Not only is the distinction drawn above the basic difference between the science of psychology and the study of philosophy, but also it delineates philosophy from all other sciences. Philosophers evaluate; they state whether a person, his behavior or character, is good or bad, right or wrong, beautiful or ugly; in fact, this is precisely the way *Plato* defined philosophy, namely, the study of the true, the good, the beautiful. Scientists refrain from evaluations since they consider the practice unscientific, and rightly so. On occasion, when scientists inject value judgments into their studies, they no longer speak as scientists but as laymen, or allegorically, they don the garb of the philosopher and become philosophers of science or just plain amateur philosophers along with other lay philosophers.

Definition of Philosophy.

In consequence of the foregoing discussion, perhaps this would be an appropriate place to discuss the definition of philosophy. Tradition has it that the term originated with an ancient Greek philosopher named *Pythagoras,* widely known for the discovery of the theorem which is identified by his name, the Pythagorean theorem. The term 'philosophy' is essentially a contraction of two Greek words: 'love of wisdom'; although it still carries that connotation, it may technically be defined as "the critical evaluation of all the facts of experience." The key term in this definition is 'evaluation' since only philosophers evaluate, while scientists describe facts as accurately as they possibly can with the aid of scientific instruments, experimentation, etc.

I. CRITERIA OF TRUTH

Proof: Its Test and Validity.

In all disciplines, but particularly in philosophy, it is necessary to reason accurately and cogently, inasmuch as philosophy is the pursuit of truth, independent of and unhampered by presuppositions, bias, prejudice, or any other type of foregone conclusion. The philosophical spirit is essentially one of freedom; a critical spirit occasioned by wholesome doubts without which the pursuit of truth would be hampered. The philosopher's penetrating and uncompromising desire for truth is such that despite whatever cost or injury it may cause to cherished beliefs, he will, nevertheless, follow wherever it leads. The fetters of falsehood must be shed regardless of consequences; truth is the paramount consideration, capable of setting one free.

Success in philosophical adventure presupposes a system of proof sufficiently adequate to detect truth of whatever nature: moral, scientific, religious, etc. It now becomes desirable to discuss the various systems of proof, or criteria of truth, as they are called. Actually, many criteria of truth are employed by philosophers and others, but not all are of equal value or validity, nor does it follow that better criteria enjoy a wider circulation or acceptance, particularly by the general public. The task falls to the philosopher who must analyze and evaluate with utmost critical scrutiny all available criteria capable of distinguishing truth from error.

It would lie beyond the scope of an introductory book in philosophy to examine and evaluate at length every criterion of truth which has been utilized by individuals, consequently we shall have to rest content with a treatment of the more widely used criteria despite the relative weaknesses of some. Those selected for consideration are: (1) Naive Realism, (2) feeling, (3) custom, (4) tradition, (5) time, (6) intuition, (7) revelation, (8) instinct, (9) majority, (10) plurality, (11) *consensus gentium* (unanimous opinion), (12) authority, (13) correspondence, (14) Pragmatism, (15) loose or mere consistency, (16) rigorous consistency, (17) coherence.

Naive Realism.

Those who adhere to this criterion of truth, namely *James McCosh, Thomas Reid,* and other Scottish philosophers, believe that reality is precisely as it appears to the senses; for example, the desk before me is merely the brown object which my eyes perceive, not an imperceptible concourse of atoms in motion which the atomic physicist conceives it to be. The Naive Realist seeks to simplify reality by repudiating the claims of philosophers and scientists who complicate it with their contentions that reality is composed of unseen atoms, matter, ideals, etc. The trees, sky, sunset, desk, etc., are exactly as the senses depict them to be, for this and nothing else is truly real. In a sense, this is the philosophy of the 'man on the street,' an adherent of the proverbial 'man from Missouri' who will not believe in an object unless he can see it, for 'seeing is believing.'

The philosophy of Naive Realism sprang up as a reaction to the complex philosophies which were in existence during the last couple of centuries. Philosophies which treat metaphysics (the study of ultimate reality) are usually most complicated and at times inscrutable. As a reaction, Naive Realists sought to eliminate what they believed was a needless complication of philosophy.

Naive Realism, most vulnerable to criticism, crumbles without much critical provocation. Essentially a philosophy of reaction to existing metaphysical philosophies, it reverted to the opposite extreme of oversimplification in its concept of proof and reality. One can readily find serious objections and contradictions in the philosophy of Naive Realism; for example, a straight stick in water appears bent, but merely because it appears bent does not mean it actually is, yet this is the contention of a Naive Realist. When one looks at a pair of train tracks as they recede into the distance, they appear to converge as if they were touching, but this is obviously not the case for when one travels down those tracks, he soon learns that they are equally parallel at any point along the line. The Naive Realist in his eagerness to simplify matters has compounded already complicated problems.

Qualities perceptible to the senses are usually not ultimately real, since reality is imperceptible; for example, reality is composed of atoms, but atomic substance is unobservable by the senses, nor are sound waves, electricity, light waves, infra-red and ultra-violet waves, x-rays, etc., subject to sense observation, yet they are considered realities of science. According to this philosophy, sound frequencies above or below the level of human hearing would have to be denied any reality whatever.

Feeling.

Although feeling is the criterion of truth associated with the masses, many intelligent individuals unwittingly, and even consciously, appeal to it as a test of truth despite the fact that they are fully aware of its gross inadequacy. Most persons seem to go through life feeling their way through, as it were. The average person does not stop to assess rationally the nature and quality of his food intake, that is, he does not order his food in a restaurant with a view to food value, such as the proper number of calories or the amount and kind of vitamins, proteins, minerals, cholesterol content, etc.; he merely checks the menu for cost, his wallet, his appetite, and then commences ordering by *feeling,* which if not the sole test, is at least the most influential and decisive.

Many individuals, consciously or unconsciously, appeal to the criterion of feeling when they bet on the races (for this is the nature of a 'hunch'), while others use feeling when spending great sums of money in the selection and purchase of securities in the stock market; still others use feeling as the conclusive test in the choice of a marriage partner. It is unnecessary to multiply examples any further; it should be obvious by now to the reader that although feeling appears to be a feeble test of truth, its use is widespread even among scientists and philosophers who, in seeking a little relaxation and recreation, often will go by feeling in arriving at a decision; for example, such a person might say to himself that he feels like going to the theatre tonight instead of the baseball game or bowling.

Feeling is an inadequate criterion of truth on a number of serious counts: in the first place, feelings are usually vague and ill-defined; often one never really knows how he feels; feelings ordinarily lack preciseness. Secondly, feelings often conflict with one another; many persons have mixed feelings on a number of subjects. An illustration of this is the mother, who at her son's or daughter's wedding is both tearful and joyful, yet not at all certain as to her feelings. However, the most serious objection is that feeling is quite sterile and useless in almost every instance of scientific and philosophical research; for example, how is one to produce spacecraft or discover the cure of cancer or heart disease solely through feeling?

Custom and Tradition.

Custom is by many used as a criterion of truth, particularly in matters pertaining to morals, politics, dress, etc. The average person does not dress purely for functional or aesthetic reasons, for these are of secondary value to fashion which is dictated by custom or the prevailing vogue of the moment. It is most embarrassing to wear evening dress in day-time when shopping for groceries regardless of the fact that evening dress is both beautiful and functional, giving warmth and covering to the body.

Unlike philosophers generally, the majority of persons do not rationally arrive at the moral principles to which they adhere; usually they merely follow the injunction: 'When in Rome, do as the Romans do.' In other words, they bow to custom as the criterion of moral right.

Tradition, akin to custom, differs principally in respect to temporal priority, that is, traditions are customs which have been preserved for generations, and consequently have deeper roots and greater cogency.

Neither tradition nor custom is a valid criterion of truth, for one need only consider the customs and traditions of savages to realize that many of them are totally without foundation or validity. Although it is traditional in some ancient societies to place a wife alive in a funeral pyre with her deceased husband, it does not prove that the practice is right.

Time.

For a number of persons, time is regarded as an excellent test if not a final one. Often prompted from loyalty, a Christian will, without giving serious thought to the matter, say: 'I know that my religion is true because it has stood the test of time.' The intimation, that Christianity is true but all other religions false, is made without realizing that Christianity is a relatively young religion as religions go: Judaism, Hinduism, and some other living religions of the world antedate Christianity by a considerable margin.

If time were a reliable test of truth, then many obviously false superstitions would be validated since a number of them have won adherents and have been practiced for thousands of years. Very few, if any, current superstitions are modern innovations. One major reason invalidating time as a good test of truth is the fact that erroneous ideas can be propagated for hundreds of years as is evidenced by belief in superstitions, magic, occult, etc.

Intuition.

Since it carries different connotations for different persons, intuition is not easily definable; some persons equate it with feeling, while certain philosophers understand it to be a type of dynamic thinking which penetrates deeper than logic. The philosopher *Borden Parker Bowne* said that life is deeper than logic, implying that there is more to understanding life than logic alone. The brilliant psychiatrist *Carl Jung* defines intuition as thinking which is done on the level of the unconscious, while the noted French philosopher *Henri Bergson* considered intuition as a dynamic process of thought which penetrated the static limitations of logic.

For present purposes, intuition is defined as 'truth which comes from one knows not where.' For example, a scientist may awaken in the middle of the night with the solution to his problem which has perplexed him for months. An inventor, such as Thomas Edison, may suddenly awaken from deep sleep in which he, without any logical explanation, is given the idea that illumination may be obtained electrically from an incandescent lamp, the truth of which is verified in the laboratory.

Assuming the above to be true, nevertheless one is still not in a position to claim that intuition is a conclusive test of truth or even qualifies as any test whatever. In the first place, if intuition were a test of truth, little progress would be made since by the time mankind stood around waiting for intuitions, disastrous results such as famine, disease, etc. could overtake him. In the second place, it is doubtful that intuition is any sort of criterion at all, since strictly speaking, intuition is not a test of truth but rather a source of truth, as is evidenced in the case of the invention of the electric incandescent lamp. Verification was not ascertained during the actual intuitive experience for there was no possible way of knowing whether or not the lamp would work; its operation was unknown until tested in some nonintuitive manner such as a laboratory demonstration. Apparently, the laboratory test was the true criterion, not the intuition, which in the final analysis, is not a criterion of truth, but at best, a source of truth.

Revelation.

Many religious persons, such as the distinguished philosopher *Kierkegaard* and other religious Existentialists of the school known as Neo-Orthodoxy, consider revelation to be a conclusive test of truth.

Revelation, as a criterion of truth, may be defined as, 'truth which comes from God, the source of all truth.' This criterion resembles intuition, but differs only as to the nature of the source, whereas intuition is the belief that 'truth comes from we know not where,' revelation is the belief that 'truth comes from God.' Technically, both are sources of truth, not tests, consequently, whatever was said of intuition in this respect, maintains for revelation, except that in the case of revelation the source is known, namely, God.

To demonstrate that revelation is not a test of truth, but rather a source, one need only become acquainted with the countless numbers of revelation-claims, as they are called, before various churches authenticate them as valid, but this process of verification is, ultimately, the criterion. That is to say, when a person believes that he has had a revelation from God, he is expected to offer evidence in its behalf before the church will acknowledge it; such techniques of proof then become the criterion of all truth, including even revealed truth.

Traditional Christianity has employed a number of criteria to test the various revelation-claims which have been called to its attention. One such test is morality: an immoral revelation is *ipso facto* presumed to be erroneous. *St. Thomas Acquinas* asserted that God would never issue a revelation which contradicted the laws of logic. Authority is another test utilized in determining authentic revelations; for example, whatever Jesus, St. Paul, or St. Peter taught would be considered valid revelations by virtue of the very fact that such authorities are considered inspired. Nevertheless, in the last analysis, it must be concluded that revelation is a source of truth, not a test.

Instinct.

As a criterion of truth, instinct has found many proponents among the ranks of psychologists such as *Freud,* and philosophers such as *Santayana.* It is believed that what is instinctive must by virtue of that fact be true since nature deemed it so; for example, if an organism has an instinctive thirst for water, then water must exist; if one has an instinctive need for sleep, then sleep must be a reality; if an organism has an instinctive drive for the opposite sex, then members of the opposite sex must exist for the purpose of fulfilling the instinctive urge.

A searching evaluation of instinct as a test of truth would reveal a number of difficulties: First of all, the notion of instinct is vague, ill-defined, and scientifically difficult to support. Secondly, the objective of most instinctive behavior is difficult, if not impossible, to ascertain. Thirdly, psychologists and others encounter a wide range of discrepancy concerning the number and kinds of instincts. Fourthly, even granting the validity of instincts, scientific and philosophical enterprise would be limited to the point of virtual stagnation since the acquisition of human knowledge would be limited to the instinctive, whereas most scientific and philosophical knowledge thus far acquired by man lies beyond the bounds of instinct.

Majority, Plurality, Consensus Gentium.

In democratic organizations, regardless of whether the institution is a nation, church, club, etc., the final test of truth is 'majority rule.' Democratic organizations may invoke the advice of experts, such as scientists and other authorities before taking any vote, but in the last analysis the issue is resolved on the basis of majority decision. Most democratic deliberations are not even resolved on the basis of a majority, a simple *plurality* usually sufficing; furthermore, the simple plurality may diminish to a still less degree when one considers that only a plurality of those voting is necessary in many instances. The reasoning which underlies this criterion in the minds of many is: 'Seventy million Frenchmen can't be wrong.'

Although a majority decision is democratic and the most desirable method of resolving questions in the political realm of life, it is hardly adequate in determining issues in science, philosophy, etc. How ludicrous it would be to take a vote in order to decide the cause of a lethal disease or a problem in nuclear physics! Most issues cannot be resolved on a democratic basis, particularly when an advanced degree of training is necessary, such as in matters pertaining to medical cures, scientific truths, etc.

Furthermore, majorities have often been proven wrong and have had to reverse their decisions; merely because a majority renders a decision, it does not necessarily follow that it is by virtue of that fact, true.

A *consensus gentium* is a unanimous majority opinion; some individuals maintain that if every person holds to the truth of a belief, it is *ipso facto* true. *Cicero*, thoroughly in accord with this criterion, wrote "that concerning which the nature of all men agree is necessarily true."[1] A psychologist once asserted that since everyone believed in immortality, then precisely for that reason it must be true; in a sense it becomes instinctive, hence true.

Not only do the objections directed against instinct as a criterion of truth maintain here as well but it is evident that what is universally believed in is not necessarily true even if one were successful in obtaining such thorough and extensive data. For example, during the

[1] *De Natura Deorum*, i. 16.

Middle Ages it was universally accepted that the sun revolved about the earth, but with the appearance of the heliocentric theory of the universe, it became apparent that the opposite was true, namely, that the earth rotated around the sun. Aproximately during the same period, it was equally believed that the earth was flat but as is known today, it is global or even 'egg-shaped.' For everyone to believe in an object as real does not make it true, a criterion other than *consensus gentium* is necessary to determine its validity.

Authority.

Men such as *St. Thomas Aquinas* have long regarded authorities as excellent criteria of truth and currently authorities are still used extensively to prove a point or resolve an issue whether it be a religious, scientific, or legal one. For example, Biblical truth, since it rests principally on the inspiration of the Bible, is mainly supported on the basis of religious authority. A court case in which a lawyer seeks to prove that his client was physically injured will enlist the services of a competent authority in medicine to testify to that effect, and in both of these cases the voice of authority is respected as strong supporting evidence.

Valid reason exists for accepting authority as a criterion of truth; it rests on the premise that authorities have been thoroughly trained in their fields, and have acquired a degree of competence and success; accordingly one may justifiably conclude that when an authority offers his opinion, it is a competent one that has been logically thought out by an able and qualified individual.

Although authorities are accepted as good forms of proof, they cannot be considered final, since authorities often conflict and contradict each other. A lawyer who seeks to prove that his client's physical inability prevents resumption of employment will call upon a competent physician to substantiate his point, but the opposing attorney can rebut by introducing testimony of another medical authority who is prepared to contradict the first. Inasmuch as authorities conflict, they cannot be considered definitive tests of truth.

Correspondence.

Bertrand Russell, in his *An Inquiry into Meaning and Truth* (1941), defends the correspondence theory of truth. Correspondence as a theory of truth may be defined as the belief that when an idea agrees (corresponds) with its object, it is proof of its truth, or to put it differently, if an idea of an object and the object are in accord or conform with one another, then the idea is said to be true. For example, if I have the idea that there is a building called the 'White House,' occupied by the President of the United States, located on Pennsylvania Avenue in Washington, D. C., and the object of my idea (the actual White House) is a reality identically corresponding with it, then my idea has been verified.

No valid objection may be found with the correspondence theory of truth except that it is a definition of truth, not a criterion of it. How does a person tell whether or not his idea does in fact correspond with its object? Not by the criterion of correspondence – one must seek a further test to prove that his idea actually does correspond with its object, for although correspondence is an excellent definition of truth, it is erroneous to assume it to be a criterion of truth as well, despite the fact that many able persons use it this way.

Pragmatism.

As a criterion of truth in its simplest and unsophisticated form, Pragmatism may be defined as: 'If an idea works, then it is true.' Accordingly, it is the workability of an idea which validates it; in other words, the consequences which follow from an idea serve to verify it. On the other hand, if an idea is inconsequential, that is, if no results issue from it, then it is considered a meaningless one. Meaningless questions are those which are devoid of consequences. Ideas, as *William James* put it, should have 'cash value,' that is, they should produce effects, results, otherwise they are meaningless. "It is astonishing to see how many philosophical disputes collapse into insignificance the moment you subject them to this simple test of tracing a concrete consequence." [1] For example, if a research medic has the idea that a compound of his invention is a cure for cancer, then proof of it would be to test it for its workability – if it works, then it is proved true.

A critical evaluation of simple Pragmatism would indicate that certain ideas may appear to work but are not necessarily true; for example, a woman chronically troubled with headaches assumed her cure to be a cherry flavored medicine obtained on a physician's prescription. Because with each dose of medicine her headaches were relieved, she associated the medicine with the cure. However, when her physician died, the new doctor, to whom she was forced to go, discovered her ailment to be psychic, and proved this by omitting the active ingredient of the prescription, yet obtaining equally favorable results, thus demonstrating conclusively that although an idea might appear to be working, it is not necessarily true.

There is a phase of Pragmatism which is invariably correct, namely

[1] William James, *Pragmatism* (London: Longmans, Green and Co., 1907), lecture II.

that which William Ernest Hocking one time student of William James at Harvard University, termed 'negative Pragmatism.' It may be concisely stated thus: 'If an idea does not work, then it is not true.' This conclusion is premised on the thesis: 'The truth always works,' but its converse, 'What always works is true,' does not maintain. Its logic is comparable to converting the proposition, 'All Bostonians are Americans.' Although 'All Bostonians are Americans,' it does not follow that 'All Americans are Bostonians.' Accordingly, the proposition 'The truth always works' is not equivalent to 'What always works is true.' Consequently it does not follow that the workability of an idea guarantees its truth.

A further difficulty posed by the criterion of Pragmatism is its lack of an adequate definition of 'workability' or 'consequences.' If consequences lend credence to an idea, and if ideas are vertified by consequences, then a nonpragmatic criterion is required to evaluate the nature, worth, adequacy, and workability of consequences. Who or what is to say (certainly not consequences) whether consequences are working adequately or are worthwhile? Is it not a man's system of values in the last resort? The religion of the savage and civilized are both working, but obviously not of equal value; the same holds true for the technique of the medicine man of the jungle and the competent surgeon of civilized America.

Consistency.

By 'loose or mere consistency' is meant the absence of any contradiction. Contrary to the doubts of the average layman, the following statements are consistent with one another because of the lack of any contradiction: 'John likes corn.' 'The sun is shining.' 'Today is Wednesday.' 'Automobiles are motor vehicles.' 'The United States of America is a powerful nation.' Although the foregoing statements are consistent, they, nevertheless, do not cohere, hence are of little value.

Since loose or mere consistency means simply the elimination of contradiction, it is hardly a very worthwhile criterion of truth except to inform one of falsehoods due to contradictions. Nevertheless, the detection of falsehood is an important facet in the discovery of truth: scientific, philosophical, and otherwise, but much more than mere elimination of contradiction is necessary in the pursuit of truth and its verification.

Another form of consistency is known as 'rigorous consistency' or as *Borden Parker Bowne* (a founder of the philosophy of Personalism) coined it, 'the method of vigor and rigor.' In rigorous consistency, statements or propositions must follow necessarily from one another. Essentially, it is the method of formal or symbolic logic, accordingly may be illustrated by one of Aristotle's classic syllogisms: "All men are mortal; Socrates is a man, therefore Socrates is mortal." The conclusion follows necessarily from the premises; Socrates must be mortal provided all men are mortal and he is a man.

In itself as a closed system, rigorous consistency is a most effective criterion of truth, but once the system is disrupted by the introduction of new and incompatible data, it breaks down. Consider the above example: True, it necessarily follows that Socrates is mortal, provided that all men are mortal and Socrates is a man, but the premise 'All men are mortal' must be assumed as true.

Many dogmatic religions use consistency as their basic criterion of truth, and do so effectively only by remaining within a closed system with fundamental premises assumed.

Coherence.

An acceptable definition of coherence is: 'a systematic consistent explanation of all the facts of experience.' Inasmuch as it considers all facts of experience, coherence includes the earlier criteria of truth whenever applicable and profitable. Whereas consistency remains within a closed system, coherence purports to explain not only the facts within its system, but stands prepared to explain any new fact brought to light. Coherence requires that facts be more than consistent; they must cohere together in an integrated whole, not only compatible within themselves, but with any other fact of the universe. The late *Edgar S. Brightman,* an ardent proponent of the coherence criterion of truth, writes: "Any judgment is true, if it is both self-consistent and coherently connected with our system of judgments as a whole."[1] *Hegel* is considered the originator of the coherence theory of truth.

Essentially, coherence is another, more technical, name for reason. Since this is the case, one is obligated to accept it as *the* criterion of truth, otherwise if he rebels against it, he will find himself in the logically embarrassing position of attacking reason with reason, thus tacitly consenting to it. The only alternative would be to employ an irrational criterion which, of course, is absurd. According to *Brand Blanshard,* coherence is the nature of truth as well as its criterion. "Assume coherence as the test, and you will be driven by the incoherence of your alternatives to the conclusion that it is also the nature of truth."[2]

In the final evaluation, despite the limitations of reason, it must nevertheless be accepted as the most adequate of all the criteria con-

[1] *Introduction to Philosophy* (New York: Henry Holt and Co., 1925), 61.
[2] *The Nature of Thought* (London: George Allen and Unwin, Ltd., 1941).

sidered; thus a person is logically obligated to accept as proof that which is most reasonable, that is, what is most coherent.

Having treated the criteria of truth, and having concluded that coherence (reason) is the most valid test, let us now direct our attention to the errors of reasoning.

II

THE FALLACIES OF REASONING

Material Fallacies.

The bulk of a college course in formal logic is derived from the efforts of Aristotle. It would be beyond the scope of this work to give an exhaustive account of formal logic or even that portion of logic which is exclusively Aristotle's, accordingly only a selected number of material fallacies will be treated, including some which are non-Aristotelian, in order to give the novice an appreciative understanding of the subtleties involved in fallacious reasoning.

By a 'material' fallacy is meant an error in content rather than in the structure or consistency of an argument. What has gone awry is inherent in the argument's factual content, such as faulty or defective evidence, abuse of language, or an appeal to feeling instead of logic. For example, one group of material fallacies, termed 'linguistic' errors, misuses language by a clever and subtle play on words; another class, called *ad populum* fallacies, is an appeal to the masses by playing on their feelings of sympathy, etc.; a third group of pitfalls, composed of a multiplicity of types, is unclassified or miscellaneous. However, all three groups are classified under the general heading 'material fallacies' and no serious or conscious attempt to classify them specifically has been made.

The first set of fallacies to be discussed are the linguistic, namely those dealing with a play on words or an abuse of language, such as: (1) accent, (2) amphibology, (3) equivocation, (4) emotive language and ambiguity, (5) figure of speech, (6) composition, (7) division.

Fallacy of Accent.

One commits the fallacy of accent by shifting emphasis or punctuation in a statement, thus altering its meaning as well. For example, the story is told of a Russian prisoner who sought his release from a Siberian prison by appealing to the czar for pardon. The czar returned the unpunctuated reply: 'Pardon impossible to be executed' with execution its intended meaning, but the jailer in charge read it with the following accent or emphasis: 'Pardon — impossible to be executed;' consequently the prisoner was released.

Other instances of this fallacy are: Traffic signs such as, 'Children — *Go Slow*,' may be read, '*Children* Go Slow;' in the case of the former the driver is directed to go slowly but in the case of the latter, the children. Another traffic sign reads: '*Slow* — Cattle Crossing,' but may be emphasized, '*Slow cattle* — crossing;' in the first instance, the driver is instructed to drive slowly but in the second, it appears that the cattle are slow in crossing the highway.

A conceited individual may by saying: 'Nothing is too good for me,' boast himself worthy of the best which this world affords, but by a shift in accent it can be inverted to the opposite meaning: 'Nothing is *too good* for me,' signifying that even nothing is more than he deserves.

An amusing instance of this fallacy is found in a verse of the English translation of the Old Testament which reads: "And he spake to his sons saying, saddle me the ass, and they *saddled* him." A shift in accent obviously alters the entire meaning: "And he spake to his sons saying, saddle me the ass; and *they* saddled *him*."

One of the Ten Commandments reads: "Thou shalt not bear false witness against thy neighbor," which can be altered by shifting the accent to read: "Thou shalt not bear false witness against *thy* neighbor," the implication being that it is permissible to lie about anyone else provided that he is not your neighbor.

Amphibology (Amphiboly).

A statement which lends itself to confusion by expressing more than a single meaning commits the fallacy of amphibology. It is not that the statement has been abused due to a misplaced accent, but that a dual or multiple interpretation is inherent in the argument, rendering it susceptible to more than one interpretation, consequently any argument from which two meanings can be derived commits this fallacy.

Illustrations of amphibology are prevalent everywhere, particularly in newspaper classified advertisements where, due to limited space, dangling or misplaced modifiers are frequently found such as: 'For sale: convertible car by a teacher with a damaged top,' or 'For sale: a carriage for a baby with a damaged bottom.' Another is a sign on a dance hall which reads: 'Clean and decent dancing every night except Sunday;' although its intended meaning is, no dancing is held on Sunday, the intimation is that on Sunday, a depraved type is found. The majority of amphibological fallacies strike one humorously because humor is inextricably related to logic; only human, that is *rational* beings, have a sense of humor.

Shakespeare committed an amphibology which has since become somewhat of a classic illustration. In his *Henry VI,* he writes: "The Duke yet lives that Henry shall depose." The question is begged: Who is to depose whom, Henry depose the Duke, or the Duke, Henry?

Equivocation.

The fallacy of equivocation is committed when one uses a word containing two different meanings, but gives the impression that the ambiguous term imparts a single connotation. Often, but not necessarily, an attempt to deceive is implied. The British philosopher *T. H. Green* said that logic is the ethics of thought; consequently if one commits an intentional fallacy, he is immoral. Using a word with two different meanings with intent to deceive is an example of this unethical practice.

Illustrations of equivocation appearing in this section, have purposely been made obvious and even extreme for pedagogical reasons. Often they can be very subtle when ingeniously employed by competent individuals. The following illustration exemplifies the fallacy of equivocation:

Feathers are light,
Light comes from the sun,
Therefore, feathers come from the sun.

The fallacy of equivocation is committed on the word 'light;' in the first premise it pertains to weight, but in the second, to illumination. Actually, not one, but two words have been used to effect this ludicrous conclusion.

A second illustration plays upon the word 'right:'

The right should be enforced by law,
Voting in this country is a right,
Therefore, voting in this country should be enforced by law.

Note the equivocal use of the word 'right;' in the first instance it has reference to moral right, but in the second it relates to privilege. Consequently the word 'right' stands, not for one, but two distinctly different terms; since the impression is given that it is but a single word, equivocation is committed.

Another example of it is found in the absolutely weird syllogism:

No cat has nine tails,
Any cat has one tail more than no cat,
Therefore, any cat has ten tails.

Although this syllogism commits, not one, but many logical errors, it is difficult for the novice to detect any fallacy whatever despite the obvious fact of their presence. The fallacy of equivocation is committed on the term 'no cat;' in the major premise the adjective 'no' is a term of quality used to deny the existence of cats with nine tails but in the minor premise, 'no cat' is employed as a type of species – a species of animal called 'no-cat,' hence the equivocal use of the term 'no cat.'

This particular syllogism contains not only a material, but a formal fallacy as well; according to the rules governing the syllogism, 'any syllogism which has a negative premise must have a negative conclusion as well.' Consequently, the conclusion should read: 'Therefore, no cat has ten tails.'

Emotive Language and Ambiguity.

The fallacy of ambiguity is committed when one uses terms which are ill-defined or carry no meaning whatever, except an emotive one, that is, the only apparent value which the term possesses is to incite or emotionally disturb one's opponent. Often a person hides behind a word, that is to say, although he, himself, is incapable of defining the term, he assumes that his audience is completely cognizant of its meaning. Usually, neither is capable of defining the word accurately as it is used, but both parties are subject to the term's emotive capability.

Many terms have little or no cognitive meaning, however, they are frequently used for their emotive value, for their ability to incite or excite an opponent or audience. These terms are commonly used, not so much for the logical content conveyed, but for their ability to evoke feelings. The word 'mother,' for example, is frequently used in this manner. To use it in its strict biological sense, as a female biological organism capable of producing offspring, is objectionable to the average person, due to its lack of warmth. The average person's conception of mother is closer to 'motherhood,' for he experiences warm feelings when the word is used, and, at least subconsciously, associates it with his own mother who, probably true to the concept of motherhood, often loved, sacrificed for, and unselfishly devoted her life to her children. Consequently, the term mother is saturated with emotional overtones which can obscure, if not completely distort, its true meaning.

James Michael Curley, former mayor of Boston and governor of Massachusetts, was one of the most able political orators of his time who used to maintain that he could take the most hostile audience and establish a strong and warm rapport with it by invoking three words: 'mother,' 'God,' 'flag.' Careful examination will reveal that these three words are richly emotive, for they represent three of man's greatest values: his family, his religion, and his country. As the term mother is capable of inciting warm familial feelings, the term God evokes deep religious ones, and the term flag elicits strong patriotic sentiments.

Other emotive words are: 'Democracy,' 'father,' 'country,' and on the adverse side for an American, 'Communism.' For example, to call a person a 'dirty Communist' is not to imply uncleanness, but contempt. Used in this sense, it is cognitively meaningless, and at best, is a term of opprobrium. Certainly it is not used as *Karl Marx* defined it: "the common ownership of the means of production," for if it were so understood, the average person would respond to it indifferently instead of emotionally.

Logically, one may use any term which appeals to him, provided he defines it explicitly and concisely; furthermore it is logically, and morally, incumbent upon him to use the word precisely as he has defined it without variation. A good example to follow regarding the precise use of terms is that of *Spinoza,* who before he employed an important or doubtful word, such as 'God,' would define it with preciseness and then use it consistently in the manner defined.

Figure of Speech Fallacy.

Words may be abused in still another manner, namely, by verbal inflection. Although this is not a common error in the English language because of the minimal use of inflection, it is, nevertheless, still possible, particularly by playing upon words which have similar suffixes – words which sound or seem alike, yet differ in meaning. For example, a man who writes is called a writer, one who fishes is termed a fisher, one who runs is a runner, one who flies is a flier, one who sings is a singer, but is one who typewrites, a typewriter?

The classic illustration of this error is one committed by the brilliant philosopher and logician *John Stuart Mill* in support of his ethical theory in his book *Utilitarianism.* He writes: "The only proof capable of being given that an object is visible, is that people actually see it. The only proof that a sound is audible, is that people hear it; and so of the other sources of our experience. In like manner, I apprehend, the sole evidence it is possible to produce that anything is desirable, is that people do actually desire it." The ambiguity or play on words is effected with the prefix *ble*; with 'audible' and 'visible' it signifies 'can be seen' whereas with desirable it connotes 'ought to be.' Visible means can be *in fact* seen; for example, while you are reading this book, you have no choice but to see what is before you. Audible also carries a similar meaning; for example, slam this book shut and the sound can in fact be heard, however, desirable does not signify can in fact be desired but rather, 'ought to be' desired. To illustrate, if you are told that the reading of this book is highly desirable, you may, however, experience no desire whatever to read it; actually, you may recognize the desirability of reading it, but still have to force yourself to undergo the strenuous effort. To put it another way, a competent surgeon may advise you: 'My friend, an appendectomy in your case is highly desirable.' Does this mean that you will relish the idea with enthusiasm and in fact desire it? No, it merely means that you ought to desire it, not that you actually will desire it.

Composition.

The fallacy of composition occurs when one reasons that what is true of each part taken separately is necessarily true of the composite whole. This fallacy results only when the whole is a composite and the parts are not independent but relative to the whole. For example, one does not necessarily construct the most beautiful girl in the world by combining in a composite whole selected features of various girls, such as the most beautiful legs, the most beautiful hands, the most beautiful arms, the most beautiful face, the most beautiful hair, and the most beautiful torso. As a composite, it would probably turn out to be grotesque rather than beautiful.

A second example is to reason that because giving one American a million dollars solved his financial problems, and it also held true in the case of a second, third, fourth, and fifth, giving every American a million dollars will necessarily solve his financial problems. The truth of the matter is that the situation will revert to its original status due to the ensuing inflation. Instead of a car selling for five thousand dollars, it will cost thirty thousand or more.

Division.

The fallacy of division is committed when one reasons that what is true of the composite whole is necessarily true of each part considered separately. Merely because the New York Yankees baseball team is the world's champion ball club for any given year, it does not necessarily follow that they have the world's champion first baseman or the best center fielder in the league. The fallacy of division is the converse of the fallacy of composition.

Certain material fallacies appeal to human susceptibility rather than to the point at issue *(argumentum ad rem).* These irrelevant appeals carry the following Latin names: (1) *argumentum ad populum,* (2) *argumentum ad misericordiam,* (3) *argumentum ad verecundiam,* (4) *argumentum ad hominem,* (5) *argumentum ad baculum,* (6) *argu-*

mentum ad ignorantiam, (7) *argumentum ad crumenam,* (8) *argumentum ad invidiam,* (9) *argumentum ad captandum.*

Ad Populum

The *ad populum* argument is one which shifts emphasis from the issue under discussion to an appeal to the populace, that is, to emotions, prejudices, feelings, and other factors capable of moving the masses to agreement. The speeches of Hitler were laden with an appeal to the populace; people are moved, he claimed, by feeling, not by logic; consequently he ruled them through fear and wishful thinking. The American politician who promised a chicken in every pot was employing the *ad populum* argument since he held out to them promises of hope and wish-fulfillment instead of logical motivation.

Ad Misericordiam

Ad Misericordiam, a variation of the *ad populum,* is the error of by-passing logic and the point under discussion by appealing to pity or sympathy. When one shifts from the point which is the real issue to an appeal to pity, he commits the *ad misericordiam* argument. Pity may be a worthy point of consideration, but in the last analysis only objective rational thought, namely, logic should be the decisive factor in any deliberation. Lawyers, fully cognizant of the weakness of man and his feeling of affinity for his fellow man, will often, in a court case when a client brings a suit against an impersonal insurance company, call for a jury trial in order to make an effective emotional appeal on behalf of a client, whereas such an irrelevant appeal would leave a seasoned jurist unmoved.

Ad Verecundiam.

When one fails to debate the logical point at issue, but appeals instead to prestige, awe, respect, reverence, etc., he commits the *ad verecundiam* error. Many salesmen, finding this mode of reasoning effective, have used it flagrantly as depicted in the following illustrations: 'Men of distinction drink Calvert's.' A real estate salesman, told by a prospective customer that the house he was selling for $30,000 was overpriced by $8,000, replied, 'But this is a *prestige* address!' To accept the arguments of one man over another merely because the first is a graduate of Harvard University and the second a graduate of Podunk Junction U. is to commit this error.

Ad Hominem.

When one shifts his argument from the thesis under discussion and directs it against the person of his opponent, he commits the *ad hominem* fallacy. This type of argument is perhaps the most vicious of all fallacies since it is a direct attack upon the personality of one's opponent, an attempt at assassination of reputation and personality. It involves 'mud-slinging' as well as other base tactics resulting in defamation of character.

An example of such would be as follows: 'My opponent, John Doe, is obviously wrong in his contention, and it is hardly necessary for me to bother to discredit the thesis of this Communist foreigner who has the audacity to challenge an American idea; I wager he is no more than a savage judging from the nation which he represents; his uncouth, ill-educated, and broken English are proof enough that his argument is not worthy of consideration.

Ad Baculum.

When one's argument rests, not upon the persuasiveness of logic, but on force, he commits the *ad baculum* fallacy; the force appealed to may be overt and obviously manifest or covert in the form of disguised coercion. The word *baculum* literally means club, rod. When one resorts to force in order to persuade his opponent, whether he employs blackmail and other forms of extortion, political influence, military force, etc., he makes use of the *ad baculum* argument.

An example of this fallacy is the reply of a father whose young son declared his disbelief in 'Santa:' 'If you don't believe in Santa, he will not bring you anything for Christmas.' Another is the attitude of a dictator who threatens those who disagree with his policies with imprisonment or death.

Ad Ignorantiam.

The English equivalent of the Latin *argumentum ad ignorantiam* is 'pleading ignorance,' and constitutes the fallacy of assuming that merely because one's opponent is incapable of disproving a thesis, it is by virtue of the fact deemed true. The burden of proof always falls on the person who advances the thesis, not on the individual who stands in opposition to it. One is not entitled to conclude that his position is valid simply on the basis that it cannot be disproved; a position must be supported by positive evidence, and is not proved by the absence of it.

For example, if I claim that there are living beings on the sun who can withstand its heat, it is my responsibility to substantiate my claim; merely because you cannot furnish evidence to disprove my contention does not allow me to assume that I have proved my case. In a philosophy club, a youthful novice presented what he believed to be a valid thesis, namely, that fifty million angels existed in heaven dressed in chantilly lace. When they realized that the boy was serious with no intention of being facetious or ludicrous, his fellow members objected strenuously to this illicit and unverifiable hypothesis. The reply given in defence was: 'Can you prove it is not so?' When his colleagues capitulated, admitting that they could not prove him false, he replied: 'Then I must be right.' Merely because a hypothesis cannot be proved false does not automatically render it true; the individual who advances a hypothesis is not entitled to claim proof of it unless he can furnish positive forms of evidence.

There are other ways in which this fallacy is committed, namely, by arguing from possibility to actuality. For example, one assumes that since it is possible for something to exist, it therefore follows that it actually does exist. To illustrate: One could argue that in ten years it is possible that the United States could become a communist country. Since anything is possible, one would have to concede the possibility of this as well. The argument then follows: 'It is possible that the United States could become a communist country, and if that should ever happen, the best thing to do is to enlist early in the Communist Party in order to be in a position of seniority for promotions to high level appointments, therefore it is wise to join that party early.' A student who lacks training in logic often argues in this manner.

A student debating with his professor found himself without factual evidence to support his claim. Defenceless, he inquired: 'Is it not true that it might be possible in subsequent years for some scientist to discover facts which could prove my case?' In response to the professor's answer, 'Anything is possible,' the student triumphantly retorted: 'If it is possible, then you have not proved me wrong, hence I must be right.' Note that it was only on the basis of 'pleading ignorance' that the student was able to present any defence whatever. One is not entitled to imagine a future, as if it were already factual, just to please his own fancy, merely on the ground that everyone is ignorant of what the future may bring.

Still another way in which the fallacy of pleading ignorance is committed deals with the individual who assumes that because he has been successful in destroying an accidental or minor portion of another's thesis, he has or can completely demolish his opponent's entire position. Unless one has destroyed the basic premises or foundation of another's argument, he is not entitled to assume that he has completely leveled his opponent's stand. To break a branch of a tree with one's bare hands does not prove that a person has the ability to destroy the entire tree.

Ad Crumenam.

The *argumentum ad crumenam,* literally means, an argument appealing to the purse; in practice it connotes an argument which appeals to a person's interests, particularly his vested interests. Ordinarily, Socialistic arguments lack cogency for a Capitalist, for he stands to lose considerably whenever Socialistic measures are enacted by the government. Conversely, arguments favoring Capitalism appear to possess a greater potency than they inherently contain, since they favor the financial outlook of the Capitalist.

Ad Invidiam.

The *argumentum ad invidiam* is an appeal to man's lower passions, his prejudices, his biases, etc. Human reason is vulnerable to passion and prejudice; consequently, an argument which preys upon a person's prejudices is one which is readily agreed to; the logically incredible often makes a person susceptible to credulity when his passions and prejudices are involved.

Ad Captandum.

The *argumentum ad captandum* or the *argumentum ad captandum vulgus* is an argument designed to please the masses, to attract the crowds; it is an argument whose basic attraction is that of pleasing, an argument directed to please the rabble. Its strength lies in the argument's ability to be winsome to the masses, rather than any appeal to a coherent set of facts or logical reasoning.

Instead of subdividing the remainder of the material fallacies further, the following fallacies are treated under the general heading, *miscellaneous:* (1) accident (*dicto simpliciter* or *secundum quid*), (2) irrelevance (*ignoratio elenchi*), (3) *non sequitur,* (4) false cause (*post hoc*), (5) compound questions (multiple questions), (6) false analogy, (7) special pleading, (8) genetic error, (9) misplaced authority, (10) vicious abstraction, (11) insufficient evidence, (12) contradictory premises, (13) contrary to fact conditional, (14) selected instances (hasty generalization), (15) *tu quoque,* (16) pathetic fallacy, (17) circular reasoning or begging the question (*petitio principii*).

The Fallacy of Accident.

Aristotle distinguishes between the fallacy of accident and *dicto simpliciter* or what is sometimes called *secundum quid* (its complete title is *a dicto simpliciter ad dictum secundum quid*), but the present treatment will follow those logicians, such as Jevons, who equate the two. The error lies in taking a qualified statement and interpreting it in an unqualified manner, forcing the statement to apply to its accidental features (exceptions). To take a general rule and apply it to its exceptional cases, while giving the impression that it is not being anomalously applied, is to commit the fallacy of accident. Philosophically speaking, accident means non-essential; it is a correlative term used in opposition to essential. Accidental qualities of an object are those which are not vital or necessary, hence they are unessential or merely incidental. For example, if a man loses a leg in war, is he still a man? Certainly! If he loses an arm in an industrial accident, is he still a man? Of course! Even if he loses all four of his limbs, he is, nevertheless, a man, for these are accidental to his nature, that is, to his being a man. But a man entirely devoid of reason is no longer considered a man since this is essential to his nature. (The mentally ill and sub-normal have some degree of reason, hence are still human beings).

Burglary, juvenile delinquency, crime, sickness, disease, war, are found in every civilized society, but they are only accidental or incidental to it for a society can not only survive without them, but would fare much better. Consequently an argument such as the following commits the fallacy of accident: 'Ignorance, disaster, destruction, crime, war, disease, death, wastefulness, etc. are actually economic blessings for the simple reason that architects and builders find the destruction of houses by disasters most lucrative; lawyers profit mainly due to marital quarrels, civil disagreements, criminal clients, etc.; pawnbrokers do well in cases of human poverty and need; physicians and dentists thrive on human illnesses; and undertakers' livelihoods depend on loss of human life.'

Another form of the fallacy of accident is to abuse a qualified rule by applying it in an unqualified manner, that is, to force a rule to apply to its exceptional cases for which it was never intended. For example: 'Inasmuch as theft is a crime (general rule of which a notable exception is found in the laws of Sparta), and since the Spartans encouraged stealing, therefore the Spartans encouraged crime.' Theft was not a criminal act in Sparta, consequently they did not encourage crime, and to infer that they did, is to commit the fallacy of accident.

Another illustration involves the rule: 'He who kills another person is a murderer.' Since Dr. John Doe's patient died while undergoing surgery, Dr. Doe is a murderer. Ordinarily, he who kills another commits murder but there are exceptional cases to which the rule was never intended to apply, such as the executioner, surgeon, soldier, etc.

Fallacy of Irrelevance (Ignoratio Elenchi).

One commits the fallacy of irrelevance by proving or disproving the wrong point. Instead of proving *A*, *B* is proved; or instead of disproving *C*, *D* is disproved, otherwise the argument may be quite intact, consistent, and cogent. To illustrate, instead of a big bully of a fellow proving that he had a right to exchange suits with a smaller boy, he proves that the exchange is advantageous to both by showing that the suit the little fellow received in the exchange is the better bargain, is in better condition, made of better material, costlier, fits better, and is much more becoming, when logically he should be proving that he had every right to force the exchange.

The fallacy of irrelevance is most evasive because on the surface it strikes one as an 'air-tight' and convincing argument, accordingly one must be on his guard to note whether or not an argument (pro or con) is pertinent to the thesis under discussion. This fallacy is essentially a mistake in identity whereby one misses the whole point under consideration, and proves (or disproves) the wrong conclusion.

In a court of law, when a witness commits the fallacy of irrelevance by not answering the question posed by a lawyer, but giving instead an evasive answer, he is instructed by the judge to be responsive.

Non Sequitur (Does Not Follow).

The *non sequitur* fallacy is committed when one's conclusion does not follow *logically* from his premises or when two consecutive ideas are incongruous or disconnected. For example:

Roses are red
Violets are blue
I love my teacher
My father has a horse.

Or, 'I enjoy basking in the sunshine, therefore I like fish.' Usually when confronted with a *non sequitur* fallacy, one senses a feeling of logical repugnance.

DeMorgan offers another example of this fallacy: "Episcopacy is of Scripture origin; the Church of England is the only Episcopal Church in England; ergo, the Church established is the Church that is to be supported."

False Cause (Post Hoc).

The full name of the *post hoc* fallacy is *post hoc ergo propter hoc* (after this and therefore in consequence of this). Although some logicians distinguish between it and a 'false cause' fallacy (Aristotle's *non causa pro causa*), the present treatment draws no distinction between them. To argue that merely because one thing precedes another in time, it is therefore the cause of it, is to commit the *post hoc* error. Simply because two events occur in sequence, a person is not entitled to claim that the second is a consequence of the first. Mere temporal sequence does not produce logical consequence or connection. Most superstitions illustrate this fallacy: For a man who has had a black cat cross his path earlier in the day, and later has been fired from his employment, to conclude that his dismissal was caused by the black cat solely on the grounds that the cat incident was temporally prior to his dismissal is to be guilty of the *post hoc* fallacy.

Another example is: "The seventh Durhams," said the Colonel, "were in the trenches when there came rolling towards them the dreaded poison gas. Men were in front of it and falling. I had with me twelve signallers, and I said to them, 'It is no use running; come up on the parapet and sing a hymn.' They stood up and sang *Abide With Me.* The cloud of death disappeared, and not a man was affected."[1] This incident implies that the singing of a hymn was the cause of the disappearance of the deadly gas. Even granting the intervention of God, the facts are insufficient to warrant the conclusion – at best, it is an act of faith. However, if one insists on concluding that the hymn actually did cause the gas to disappear, he succeeds only in committing a *post hoc* fallacy.

Although the last three fallacies discussed have certain resemblances which sometimes prove confusing to the novice, sharp distinctions exist among them: In a *post hoc* error, *B* does not follow *causally* from *A*; in a *non sequitur* fallacy, *B* does not follow *logically* from *A*; in the fallacy of irrelevance, *B* has been proved instead of *A*.

Compound Questions (Multiple Questions).

This particular fallacy is called by *Aristotle* 'many questions,' and by *Cardinal Newman,* 'poisoning the wells.' The error is committed when an individual poses a question which presupposes a prior question to have been raised and satisfactorily answered. What is taking place is that what appears to be a simple and single question is actually a composite of more than one. Usually, an opponent is expected to answer

[1] Adapted from A. Wolf, *Exercises in Logic.*

'yes' or 'no,' but the question does not permit a 'yes' or 'no' answer without self-incrimination. The manner in which the question is posed precludes all discussion. Aristotle's objection is: "Several questions put as one should be at once decomposed into their several parts. Only a single question admits of a single answer: so that neither several predicates of one subject, nor one predicate of several subjects, but only one predicate of one subject, ought to be affirmed or denied in a single answer."

A classic example of this fallacy is the compound question posed by a lawyer to a witness: 'Have you stopped beating your wife?' and requiring a 'yes' or 'no' answer. If the witness answers 'no,' then he will be admitting that he is guilty of the practice of beating his wife, and if he answers 'yes,' he will be admitting that he beat her in the past but has discontinued the practice.

Other examples are: 'Only a vicious person would oppose me.' 'Have you stopped passing bad checks?' How do you account for your stupidity?' 'Who made God?' Note that in each case a prior question is assumed to have been raised and satisfactorily answered, enabling one to proceed with a further question such as the ones posed above. 'Only a vicious person would oppose me' presupposes that one has substantiated the claim that opposition to him implies viciousness. 'Have you stopped passing bad checks?' assumes the fact has been established that bad checks have been passed, opening the way for further questioning, namely, 'Do you continue to pass them?' 'How do you account for your stupidity?' is not asking proof of whether or not a person is stupid; it presupposes the question of stupidity to have been properly answered and proceeds to the further question of the reason for it. The question, 'Who made God?' presupposes that satisfactory proof was furnished establishing as a fact that He was created which logically would lead to the further question, 'Who was His creator?' However, the fallacy lies in the assumption that God's creatureliness has been established. In each case, although a single question is implied, a prior question is assumed to have been raised and properly answered.

Other examples are: 'What time was it before time began?' 'What place is it where space ends?' 'What was God doing before He created anything?'

False Analogy.

The analogy *per se* is not necessarily considered a fallacy; it is so regarded only when the situation is not analogous. An analogy is an argument which runs along the same logical lines of a second argument whose truth has already been accepted; the theory being that if one line of reasoning is accepted as true then a second which parallels it logically must also be valid.

Some logicians discredit all analogies on the ground that they are nothing more than illustrations; others claim that it is impossible to obtain a perfect analogy since no analogy 'stands on all fours.' The simile is that of a table with four legs; it is impossible to construct a table in which all four are perfectly coordinated with each other.

An example of a false analogy is as follows: 'It is evident that women should be elected to political office since government is similar to national housekeeping; and in this respect it is obvious that women have much more experience than men.' This analogy is imperfect, breaking down in its supposition that affairs of state with all of their complexities constitute nothing more than attending ordinary household chores.

A number of alcoholics and heavy drinkers take refuge in the following false analogy to rebut critics who refuse to condone their heavy drinking, objecting to it on moral grounds. The incident is told of the famous boxer, John L. Sullivan, who was rebuked by close friends for indulging excessively in alcoholic beverages causing embarrassment to himself and others; he retorted that it was morally permissible since it was analogous to St. Paul advising Timothy to take a little wine for his stomach's sake. This analogy breaks down at several points, but particularly with regard to the excessive use of alcohol for purposes of intoxication as compared to a limited use of wine for medicinal purposes.

Special Pleading (Neglected Aspect).

It is said that there are two sides to every story, but when a person presents only one side of the story (as a lawyer would ordinarily do in a court case) to the complete neglect of any fact which might favor his opposition, he commits the fallacy known as 'special pleading' or 'neglected aspect.' To arrive at a logical conclusion properly, a person must include every pertinent fact, whether or not it favors his own position, and then allow the facts to determine which conclusion is permissible.

This fallacy is like 'stacking a deck of cards' so that no desirable cards are dealt to one's opponent, while all of the preferred cards are dealt to oneself. A person should always become suspicious of an argument which gives only one side of the story; the reason being that if one must ignore facts which favor the other side, the usual reason for doing so is that if they were brought to light, his own position would be devastatingly affected.

Consider the following example of special pleading which is attributed to the philosopher Voltaire: "Organized religion should be abolished on the grounds that it has incorporated masses of fables and superstitions; it has been believed in by the weak and the ignorant; it has been manipulated by the enlightened for selfish political objectives; it has been the tool of vested interests to oppose social reform and scientific progress; therefore, it should be repudiated."[1] Let us grant, for purposes of debate, that organized religion is guilty of the foregoing; but what should arouse our suspicion is the totally onesided account, as if organized religion were completely devoid of any merit whatever. Often, in a case of special pleading, a person is driven to giving only one side of a question because if facts on both sides were brought to light, his argument would seem trivial or puny. When a person is compelled to depend on special pleading to render his case cogent, he must present it before opposing facts of the case are offered. Consider the case for organized religion: In this country alone, organized religion has fostered world renowned universities, such as Harvard, Yale, Princeton, etc. for purposes of enlightenment. Many great hospitals were inspired by religious persons and religious organizations; a sizable number of charitable organizations for the poor, the homeless, the mentally and spiritually ill, were founded by religious institutions. Proceeding in this manner, a person can build a strong case for organized religion which would render the special pleading argument of Voltaire logically feeble.

Genetic Error.

To trace an argument to its source and thereby assume that one has either proved or disproved a point is to commit the fallacy known as the 'genetic error.' It may prove highly interesting and even enlightening to trace an argument to its source but to fancy that thereby a person has established his case is to fall prey to fallacious reasoning.

A number of psychologists appear to take great delight in showing how Schopenhauer's pessimistic philosophy was the direct result of his unhappy and unfortunate childhood, thereby implying that his philosophy must be false by virtue of this fact. Although it may be interesting to learn how Schopenhauer came to develop and believe in his philosophy, how he derived it is irrelevant to its truth or falsity. The same argument is sometimes launched against the religion which John Fox founded. The claim is that since John Fox was insane, the religion which

[1] Adapted from Alburey Castell, *A College Logic* (New York: Macmillan Co., 1935).

he founded must be false. It is totally irrelevant what a man is or how he came to believe in a thesis, the task of a logician is to prove or disprove the thesis under discussion, not its source. For example, if an insane person were to dash into your room shouting, 'H_2O is water!' could you contend that his statement is false because the person asserting it is abnormal?

Accordingly, the source of any argument is logically irrelevant; to trace an argument to its source neither proves nor disproves it. Certain Atheists are fond of trying to disprove or discredit religion on the basis that belief in God grew out of humble and unattractive beginnings, such as, fear, superstition, etc., consequently they feel entitled to conclude that God and other religious values have been proved false, but it matters little logically where or how the belief in God came into being, the question up for discussion is: 'Does God exist?' not *how* the belief came into existence. For that matter, science grew out of equally humble beginnings, magic, alchemy, etc., but one would hardly assume that he has discredited modern science as it is known today merely by tracing it to such undesirable beginnings.

Misplaced Authority.

In the section dealing with criteria of truth, it was noted that authorities are acceptable forms of proof or evidence, particularly in a court of law. Here, authority as proof is not challenged, but rather misplaced authority, that is, using an expert as an authority outside of his field of specialization. Usually it is not the authority who commits this fallacy, but another individual who cites the authority as proof in a field in which the authority is not competent. Actually, an authority may speak on any subject he wishes, whether or not it is in his field of specialization, since he is first and foremost a person, and as such, is entitled to express his opinion on whatever subject he pleases, but once he leaves his fields of *specilization,* he can no longer be regarded as an authority, nor is anyone entitled to cite him as such. Once an expert departs from his authoritative standing, he becomes a mere layman, accordingly, he must speak and be regarded as such; sometimes an authority outside of his field not only becomes a layman but not even a good or average one at that.

An individual, who argues that God exists on the premise that Albert Einstein believed in God, commits the fallacy of misplaced authority since Einstein is not a philosopher of religion. The argument assumes that since Einstein is an eminent and venerated authority in physics that his opinion outside of his field of specialization is equally competent. The fact of the matter is that once Einstein departs from his field, he becomes a layman and no more, as is evidenced by the fact that if one were to require heart surgery, he would not secure the services of Einstein as his surgeon. An average or poor surgeon is preferable to an Einstein outside of his field. Who would want Einstein to be his defending attorney if he were charged with murder? It would be preferable to accept the services of a mediocre lawyer than to obtain the legal services of an Einstein. Once an expert speaks outside of his field of specialty or is quoted outside of his field, he is divested of his status as an authority; to assume otherwise results in committing the fallacy of misplaced authority.

Vicious Abstraction.

To remove or isolate a text from its context, thereby altering the logic or meaning of a statement is to commit the fallacy of 'vicious abstraction.' Some persons will quote certain portions of the Bible displaced from their context, resulting in a distortion of meaning; for example, there are individuals who erroneously assert that St. Paul said: "Money is the root of all evil," whereas he said: "The *love* of money is the root of all evil." A number of times, Ralph Waldo Emerson has been quoted as saying: "Consistency is the hobgobblin of little minds," as if to sanction illogical and incoherent thinking, but Emerson said: "*Foolish* consistency is the hobgobblin of little minds;" which certainly differs considerably.

Advertisers often seize upon this fallacy to promote their interests. For example, a Broadway show whose unsuccessful run appears imminent may insert the following advertisement in newspapers and billboard posters: " 'Fabulous . . . finest show of the year,' N. Y. Times." However, should a person take the trouble to read the critic's complete article, he would discover a totally adverse report such as: 'The worst show to appear on Broadway within the last four years; the scenery is poor, the acting is mediocre, the sequences are incoherent; however, the basic idea of the plot, if it were in the hands of an Oscar Hammerstein and a Richard Rodgers could turn out to be a *fabulous* musical, perhaps even the *finest show of the year.*' Once a text has been removed from its context and in so doing a person has distorted its logical meaning, the fallacy of vicious abstraction is said to have taken place.

Insufficient Evidence.

When due to insufficient facts, deficient either in quality or quantity, one is unable legitimately to arrive at a conclusion, but does so despite the lack of necessary evidence, he is guilty of committing the fallacy of 'insufficient evidence.' Unlike special pleading, an individual con siders facts representative of both sides of the case, but the difficulty is that the facts do not warrant the conclusion.

This fallacy may be illustrated in the following manner. If a district attorney were to seek a murder conviction against a man merely on the grounds that the gun used in the crime was registered to the defendant, and that the defendant could have been in the neighborhood at the approximate time of the murder, the judge would dismiss the case on the grounds of insufficient evidence. Weighty conclusions are unwarranted on the basis of feeble and petty facts.

Contradictory Premises (Self-Contradiction).

That which is self-contradictory is *ipso facto* false; hence two premises which are mutually contradictory, cancel each other out, thereby rendering any legitimate conclusion impossible.

A classic example of contradictory premises is: 'What would happen if an irresistible force met an immovable object?' Since the universe does not permit contradictions, one of the two of these premises cannot be true. If a thing such as an irresistible force exists, then there cannot be an immovable object, but on the other hand, if an immovable object exists, then an irresistible force is a nonentity. Both cannot coexist simultaneously.

Other examples are: 'Can God make a thirty year old tree in three seconds?' 'How would you interpret the dream of a man who believed in dreams, but had a dream that dreams were not to be trusted?'

Contrary to Fact Conditional.

To alter a fact and then draw a conclusion from such premises is to commit the 'contrary to fact conditional error.' One is not entitled to arrive at any conclusion once he has changed the facts; such an alteration is tantamount to soaring into the realm of fantasy from fact; consequently one's conclusion from unrealistic premises can be no better or any more than the 'make-believe' of which the premises consist. Once a fact of the universe has been altered, no licit conclusion is permissible; actually, the outcome of such a situation is pure conjecture and equivalent to a guess at best.

It is fallacious for someone to argue after meeting with an automobile accident: 'I met with an accident because I took a short cut this morning on my way to work. If I had taken my regular route then I would not have had an accident.' Logically, a person cannot predict that if the regular route were taken, an accident would have been avoided, for it may have been the case that a much more serious accident would have resulted.

If it is logically permissible to draw conclusions on the basis of altered facts (which is equivalent to falsified or pretended truths) then grotesque and absurd results can follow. It could be argued that if Napoleon had not been defeated at the Battle of Waterloo, then America would be a French colony and the people of the United States would be speaking French instead of English. No one, simply from pure conjecture stemming from supposition of Napoleon's victory at Waterloo, is entitled to conclude what the state of the present world would be *in fact.* Facts are facts, and cannot be altered without doing violence to logic. However, the preceding does not hold true for principles, since they are based upon necessary premises, whereas facts must be predicated upon actual data.

Selected Instances (Hasty Generalization).

When one arrives at a generalization, that is, a law of science (law of nature), on the basis of insufficient or an unrepresentative number of instances, then he is said to commit the fallacy of 'hasty generalization.' Proper generalizations (laws of science) are derived from gathering large and representative numbers of instances from any source from which they can be derived without bias or favor. When a person fancies that he has arrived at a law of nature on the basis of a few selected cases, then he commits the 'selected instances error.' Examples of the point under discussion are: 'Gentlemen prefer blonds,' 'Charity begins at home,' 'Diplomats wear ascot ties.'

The error is committed in the following manner: A person may find himself at a gathering where diplomats are present in sizable numbers; on being introduced to the first diplomat, he may discover that he is wearing an ascot tie. The second diplomat encountered is also wearing an ascot tie; the third, fourth, fifth, and each successive one up to a dozen; consequently he concludes, but only by way of the hasty generalization fallacy, 'All diplomats wear ascot ties.'

Tu Quoque (Thou Also).

When an individual attempts a logical justification of his position or behavior on the grounds that another person is doing the same, he is said to commit a '*tu quoque*' fallacy or argument. It is an argument whose sole foundation appears to be that of charging one's opponent with committing an act which one would like to do himself; in other words, privileges enjoyed by another are claimed for oneself. For example, a child may take issue with his father when ordered to go to bed, by arguing that he also should be permitted to stay up late since his father is not retiring early. The child does not realize that his situation is not equivalent to his father's, one difference being that a child's sleep requirements are greater.

Pathetic Fallacy.

When one becomes anthropomorphic in his thinking, that is, when he ascribes human or personal qualities to nonhuman objects, he is said to commit the 'pathetic fallacy.' Some speakers and writers will at times be carried away emotionally and speak of the 'cruel sea' or the 'pitiless and raging fire' as if these natural phenomena had human characteristics and feelings.

A woman once remarked, when she had returned from a vacation and found to her chagrin that her husband had neglected to water her favorite plant: 'Look at her drooping leaves, she must be in excruciating agony and in dire thirst from lack of water.' A person is not allowed logically to indulge in anthropomorphism to prove his thesis. In the field of philosophy of religion, this fallacy is occasionally committed when a person ascribes human qualities to God.

Circular Reasoning or Begging the Question (Petitio Principii).

One is said to commit the fallacy of 'circular reasoning' when offering the original thesis which was to be proved as final proof; in other words, that which requires proof is assumed as its own proof. For example, a person may attempt to prove *A* by evidence *B*, but since *B* is not self-supporting or ultimate, therefore stands in need of proof, then *B* is supported by *C*, but *C* is inconclusive and must be substantiated, whereupon *A* is used in support of *C*. The circle is now complete; *A* is ultimately used to prove itself.

An example of this is that of three 'gate crashers' (Smith, Jones, Doe) seeking entry to a formal party:

DOORMAN: 'May I see your invitations?'
SMITH: 'I am very sorry, I mislaid mine; but Mr. Jones, who is standing beside me will vouch for me.'
JONES: 'I shall be very happy to vouch for Mr. Smith.'
DOORMAN: 'Very well. May I see your invitation, Mr. Jones?'
JONES: 'I'm terribly sorry, but I don't seem to have brought mine along with me, but Mr. Doe, who is particularly well known in these circles, will testify on my behalf.'
DOE: 'I shall be more than happy to speak on behalf of my good friend, Mr. Jones.'
DOORMAN: 'May I then see your invitation?'
DOE: 'I don't seem to have it with me, but I assure you that I do have one. Mr. Smith, you saw it the other day, won't

you be good enough to confirm my statements to the doorman?'

SMITH: 'Indeed I will. I give you my word, Mr. Doorman.'

Another example is: 'Lincoln's speeches are better oratory than Churchill's speeches. How can it be proved that Lincoln's speeches are better forms of oratory than Churchill's speeches? That is quite simple, the opinion of experts will verify that fact. How can one determine who the experts in this matter are? That poses no problem, you can tell them for they are the ones who prefer Lincoln's speeches to Churchill's.' Note that in the final analysis, the thesis which required proof was used in support of itself.

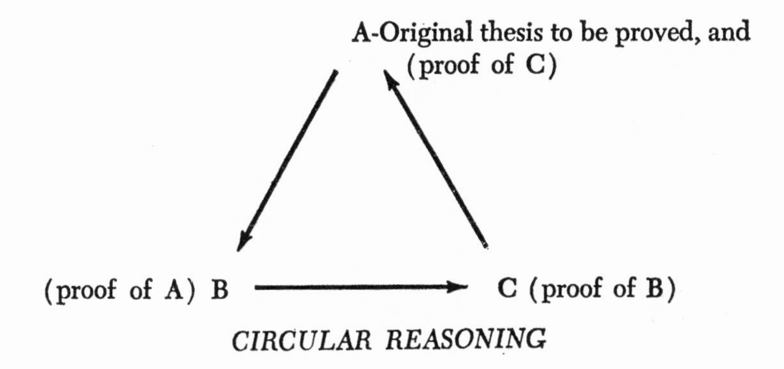

CIRCULAR REASONING

III

TRUTH: ITS RELATIVITY, OBJECTIVITY, AND ABSOLUTENESS

Sophists and Sophistry.

The Sophists, brilliant philosophers of the Socratic era, were literally the first professional philosophers, that is, the first teachers to exact fees for instruction. The practice of accepting a fee for instruction was regarded by Socrates as a questionable moral practice, if not a reprehensible one. Many Sophistic practices and tactics were definitely of doubtful morality, eventuating in such disrepute that the term sophistry acquired opprobrious connotations.

Protagoras, the most illustrious of these sages, boasted that he was the wisest man in the world and was prepared to defend his claim against any challengers. In fact, boastfulness of his superior ability to impart his knowledge to others went so far that he claimed that anyone who came under his tutelege would be able to emulate him. Sophists bragged about their many victories and numerous successful court cases. Protagoras advertised the claim that any protege of his would win his very first court case. So proficient did he fancy himself that he permitted any pupil to pay only half of the tuition bill at the start of the course, and the balance when, and if, he won his first case in court. Protagoras guaranteed success; the agreement was that should the initial court case be lost, the bill would be cancelled.

Euathlus, a clever young student, seized the opportunity which Protagoras offered, and undertook the entire course of instruction, paying only the required initial fee of fifty per cent. On the conclusion of the course, Euathlus evaded payment by deferring the practice of law, consequently the balance of the bill went unpaid according to the terms of the contract. Protagoras, furious that an impudent young upstart could outwit him at his own game, forced the issue by suing Euathlus, thereby bringing him into court where his first case would be tried. The confident Protagoras boasted that he could not lose inasmuch as: 'If Euathlus loses this case, then he must pay me by the judgment of the court; and if he wins it, then he must pay me in accordance with the terms of his contract. But he must either lose or win it; therefore he must pay me in either case.'

The young Euathlus, apparently well tutored if not brilliant in his own right, cared little about Protagoras' plot and rebutted his master's argument with a counter dilemma: 'If I win the case, I ought not to pay by the judgment of the court; and if I lose it, I ought not to pay by the terms of the contract. But either I must win or lose it; therefore I ought not to pay.'

The preceding *Litigiosus,* as it is called, gives one an insight into the nature of disputations which generated the term sophistry. In a *Litigiosus,* no attempt is made to define terms, often resulting in a conflict of rival standards by which it seems possible for two antithetical positions to co-exist. The above dilemma is not a logical matter, but one which must be resolved by a court of equity in which case the judge's decision is final.

Another famous sophism, called the *Liar,* is one in which *Epimenides,* the Cretan, asserted that all Cretans were liars. The question is begged: Was he lying or telling the truth? The nature of this statement is also basically dilemmatic in form: 'If Epimenides' statement is true, then he is a liar (since he is a Cretan also); and if his statement is false then he is a liar (owing to the false assertion which he made). But it must be either true or false; therefore in either case, he is a liar.'

If all Cretans are liars, then a non-Cretan would have to make the assertion for it to be true; otherwise it would be false that all Cretans are liars, since one who invariably lies made the statement, hence its opposite must be true.

A pre-Socratic philosopher, named *Zeno,* posed a similar type of argument to defend monistic philosophy (the belief that the universe is ultimately composed of one basic substance; by inference therefore, motion is not a genuine reality since it implies many substances moving from place to place). His dilemma assumed the following form: 'If a thing moves, then it must move either in the place where it is or in a place where it is not. But it cannot move where it is, nor can it move where it is not; therefore it cannot move.'

Aristotle quotes him as saying: "If space *is,* it will be in something; for everything that *is* is in something; and to be in something is to be in space. Space then will be in space, and so on *ad infinitum.* Therefore space does not exist." Essentially, Zeno is saying that motion is not genuinely real, but only apparent (phenomenal), and proves it by asserting that an object must move either in the position it presently occupies (which is an impossibility) or it must proceed to a position which it does not occupy at the present moment, which is (according to Zeno) also an impossibility since it cannot move to a point where it is not, for it is not there, and if it is not there, how then can it reach that point? What Zeno refuses to take into account is motion, consequently an object cannot move to a place where it is not at the moment, but motion is an empirical fact and must be considered; furthermore, an object can move in the place where it is, by moving on its axis.

Zeno had a number of puzzles supporting his contention that motion was not ultimately real. He hypothesizes that an arrow at any given moment of its flight will be found to be at rest. It is analogous to a high speed still picture camera snapping a picture of an arrow as it soars through the air; it matters little how often pictures of the arrow are snapped, each time the arrow will be found to be at rest. As the arrow flies through the air, a person at any moment saying 'now' will find the arrow to be at rest; since the mere enumeration of any group of 'nows' will never add up to motion, therefore motion cannot exist. For Zeno, motion in nature ultimately is reducible to pseudo action similar to animated cartoons.

The unwarranted assumption of Zeno is that time is composed of a series of *nows* or indivisible instants, units, or basic components of time.

The Protagorean Doctrine of Relativity.

Protagoras believed that truth is relative, that is, it is merely a matter of opinion. 'What is true for you, is true for you, and what is true for me, is true for me.' Each person is not only entitled to his own particular opinion but each person's particular opinion is true regardless of whether or not it contradicts the opinions of others, since truth is not absolute, but only relative.

The basis for this conclusion is his assertion that "man is the measure of all things," that is, reality is relative to man; in a sense, man creates reality, at least his sensations are personal reflections of the external world. No two persons' images of the external world are identical, therefore no two individual views of reality can be exactly alike. Furthermore, the various life experiences of one person cannot be exactly the same set which another person acquires, hence each person's conclusions as to the nature of reality must differ.

The above conclusions are predicated on the premise that knowledge is attained through sense experience. Since no person's sense perceptions are perfect, no one can claim to possess absolute truth; truth is relative to each person's experience. Each individual's facts of experience from which his opinions are derived are as good as any other person's, consequently one individual's personal opinion is equally valid to any other's. In the final analysis, truth is reducible to opinion, hence lacks all objectivity; the world as it is known by an individual is merely his own subjective viewpoint of it.

PLATO: THE OBJECTIVITY OF TRUTH

Plato early recognized the self-defeating position in which the Relativist is caught. In the *Theaetetus,* he ironically notes: "The best of the joke is, that Protagoras acknowledges the truth of their opinion who believe his opinion to be false; for in admitting that the opinions of all men are true, in effect he grants that the opinion of his opponents is true." In other words, Protagoras and Plato could conceivably be engaged in the following debate:

PROTAGORAS: 'Plato, what is true for you, is true for you, and what is true for me, is true for me.'

PLATO: 'Do you mean to say that my personal opinion is true?'

PROTAGORAS: 'Indeed, that is precisely what I mean.'

PLATO: 'But, my dear Protagoras, my opinion is that truth is not relative; truth is not a matter of opinion, but objective and absolute. Furthermore, my opinion is that your belief in the relativity of truth is absolutely false and should be abandoned. Do you still hold that my opinion is true?'

PROTAGORAS: 'Yes, you are quite correct.'

A person who believes that truth is subjective, solely a matter of opinion, must capitulate to his opponent who believes in the objectivity or absoluteness of truth.

Some Sophists went still further, as did *Gorgias,* a notable Skeptic who taught that no knowledge is possible, that is, nothing can be known. He asserted: "First, nothing exists; second, if anything did exist we could never know it; third, if perchance a man should come to know it, it would remain a secret, he would be unable to describe it to his fellow-men." However, the Skeptic's stand is less secure than even that of the Subjectivist's – if nothing can be known then the question is begged: 'How did the Skeptic come to *know* that?' By the same token, one can come to know other things as well.

Plato, in his *Theaetetus,* records Socrates' opposition to the Protagorean Doctrine of Relativity; the discussion occurs between Socrates and Theaetetus: [1]

SOCRATES: Well, you have delivered yourself of a very important doctrine about knowledge; it is indeed the opinion of Protagoras, who has another way of expressing it. Man, he says, is the measure of all things, of things that are, and of the non-existence of things that are not: – You have read him?
THEAETETUS: Oh, yes, again and again.
SOCRATES: Does he not say that things are to you such as they appear to you, and to me such as they appear to me, and that you and I are men?
THEAETETUS: Yes, he says so.
SOCRATES: A wise man is not likely to talk nonsense. Let us try to understand him: the same wind is blowing, and yet one of us may be cold and the other not, or one may be slightly and the other very cold?
THEAETETUS: Quite true.
SOCRATES: Now is the wind, regarded not in relation to us, but absolutely, cold or not; or are we to say, with Protagoras, that the wind is cold to him who is cold, and not to him who is not?
THEAETETUS: I suppose the last.
SOCRATES: And 'appears to him' means the same as 'he perceives.'
THEAETETUS: True.
SOCRATES: Then, appearing and perceiving coincide in the case of hot and cold, and in similar instances; for things appear, or may be supposed to be, to each one such as he perceives them?
THEAETETUS: Yes.
SOCRATES: Then perception is always of existence, and being the same as knowledge is unerring?
THEAETETUS: Clearly.
SOCRATES: In the name of the Graces, what an almighty wise man Protagoras must have been! He spoke these things in a parable to the common herd, like you and me, but told the truth, 'his Truth,' in secret to his own disciples.
THEAETETUS: What do you mean, Socrates?
SOCRATES: I am about to speak of a high argument, in which all things are said to be relative; you cannot rightly call anything by any name, such as great or small, heavy or light, for the great will be small and the heavy light – there is no single thing or quality, but out of motion and change and admixture all things are becoming relatively to one another, which 'becoming' is by us incorrectly called being, but is really becoming, for nothing ever is, but all things are becoming . . . All things are the offspring of flux and motion? Then now apply his doctrine to perception, my good friend, and first of all to vision; that which you call white color is not in your eyes, and is not a distinct thing which exists

[1] Plato, *Theaetetus,* tr. by B. Jowett.

out of them. And you must not assign any place to it: for if it had position it would be, and be at rest, and there would be no process of becoming.
THEAETETUS: Then what is color?
SOCRATES: Let us carry out the principle which has just been affirmed, that nothing is self-existent, and then we shall see that white, black, and every other color, arises out of the eye meeting the appropriate motion, and that what we call a color is in each case neither the active nor the passive element, but something that passes between them, and is peculiar to each percipient; are you quite certain that the several colors appear to a dog or to any animal whatever as they appear to you?
THEAETETUS: Far from it.
SOCRATES: Or that anything appears the same to you as to another man? Are you so profoundly convinced of this? Rather would it not be true that it never appears exactly the same to you, because you are never exactly the same?
THEAETETUS: The latter.
SOCRATES: And if that with which I compare myself in size, or which I apprehend by touch, were great or white or hot, it could not become different by mere contact with another unless it actually changed; nor again, if the comparing or apprehending subject were great or white or hot, could this, when unchanged from within, become changed by any approximation or affection of any other thing. The fact is that in our ordinary way of speaking we allow ourselves to be driven into most ridiculous and wonderful contradictions, as Protagoras and all who take his line of argument would remark . . . I am charmed with his doctrine, that what appears is to each one, but I wonder that he did not begin his book on Truth with a declaration that a pig or a dogfaced baboon, or some other yet stranger monster which has sensation, is the measure of all things, then he might have shown a magnificent contempt for our opinion of him by informing us at the outset that while we were reverencing him like a God for his wisdom he was no better than a tadpole not to speak of his fellow-men — would not this have produced an overpowering effect? For if truth is only sensation, and no man can discern another's feelings better than he, or has any superior right to determine his opinion is true or false, but each, as we have several times repeated, is to himself the sole judge, and everything that he judges is true and right, why, my friend, should Protagoras be preferred to the place of wisdom and instruction, and deserve to be well paid and we poor ignoramuses have to go to him, if each one is the measure of his own wisdom . . . The attempt to supervise or refute the notions or opinions of others would be a tedious and enormous piece of folly, if to each man his own are right; and this must be the case if Protagoras's truth is the *real* truth.

As Socrates proved above, one must begin on a positive footing in matters pertaining to the nature or objectivity of truth; to assert that truth cannot be known or that truth is relative leads to absurd conclusions which prove self-defeating. It is necessary to begin with the philosophical stand: At least some things can be known; and that truth is not merely a matter of subjective opinion.

The mere assertion that truth is a matter of opinion does not make it so; for example, if a child, or adult for that matter, sincerely and completely believes that a drink containing arsenic is wholesome and nourishing, the mere belief that he holds it to be true will not make it so. Should he chance to drink it, then he will be as dead as if he believed it to be lethal.

Error is subjective and relative to the person whose mind entertains the erroneous notion, not truth. Error does not exist in outer reality, but only in the mind of the individual who fancies it. In the above illustration of the individual who fancied arsenic to be harmless, that false belief existed *only in the mind* of the person who held to the erroneous belief, not in fact, that is, not in the outside world of objective reality.

SOCRATES: THE SOCRATIC DIALECTIC

The Socratic dialectic is essentially a method of conversation, one in which an issue is discussed concerning an object with every possible point of view represented. Socrates regarded reasoning as inner conversation. Truth concerning an object is attained by viewing it and discussing it from every conceivable angle thereby deriving the nature of an object, its law, its essence; this technique is essentially the *dialectical method.* Its objective is to determine what one object in particular has in common with those similar to it; for example, whatever quality water has in common with other bodies of water constitutes its true nature or its law. Socrates "observed that the expression *dialegesthai,* 'to reason,' had its origin in people's practice of meeting together to reason on matters, and distinguishing them according to their several kinds." [1]

The truth or nature of an object is essentially its definition; consequently if one is capable of adequately defining an object, he has, in effect, discovered its truth. One method of effecting this goal was through the use of *Socratic irony,* that is, pretending complete ignorance of a subject, thereby forcing one's opponent to forego all presuppositions and biases so as to begin from scratch.

One reason for beginning on such an elementary level was due to the constant misuse or abuse of words, such as the employment of

[1] Xenophon, *Memorabilia,* IV, 5, 12; tr. by John Selby Watson.

ambiguous and vague language which although basically meaningless, functions at times as an effective shield when logical defenses are inadequate and weak. The Socratic method of irony would 'smoke out' all such offenders by pretending ignorance of the meaning of such terms and humbly requesting that his opponent, who seemingly uses them authoritatively and ably, confident of understanding their full meaning, define them. Definition is a most difficult and exasperating requirement; occasionally, even the most able find themselves groping for proper definitions of terms. This being the case, meaningless and vague terms are bandied about, particularly by individuals who deliberately take refuge in ambiguous terminology to support their inherently indefensible positions, despite the fact that to do so is intellectually dishonest.

An indispensable requisite to the successful utilization of the Socratic method and its element of irony, besides feigning ignorance, is the almost invariable employment of questions. Socrates rarely made declarative statements; even when confronted with a question, he would answer with another question. The Socratic method is basically one of interrogation; not merely interrogating an opponent regarding the logical consistency of his reasoning, and the definition ascribed to various words, but a thorough interrogation of the topic under discussion from every possible relationship. By weighing the pros and cons of a particular subject, one may derive its truth or nature, that is, he may establish a law or thesis regarding it.

In the following excerpt from Xenophon's *Memorabilia of Socrates,*[1] note carefully the masterful technique of Socrates as he beautifully executes his dialectical method with most of its phases apparent: (1) exploring a topic from every conceivable point of view, (2) restricting oneself to asking questions only, even when confronted with a question, (3) arriving eventually at a definition or principle regarding a discussed issue, (4) the pretence of ignorance and the assumption that his opponent in debate is the learned one on the presently discussed matter, (5) the eventual persuasion of an opponent to his own position. The following discussion entails a moral issue which is of typical Socratic interest. Socrates was indifferent to cosmological issues, the results of which proved sterile, that is, they lacked pertinency to life situations, whereas moral and psychological matters issued in results which were conducive to a good and happy life.

"Are you willing then," said Socrates, "that we should made a *delta* on this side, and an *alpha* on that, and then that we should put whatever

[1] Xenophon, *Memorabilia,* IV, 2, 13–19; tr. by John Selby Watson.

seems to us to be a work of justice under the *delta*, and whatever seems to be a work of injustice under the *alpha*?" "If you think that we need those letters," said Euthydemus, "make them." Socrates, having made the letters as he proposed, asked, "Does falsehood then exist among mankind?" "It does assuredly," replied he. "Under which head shall we place it?" "Under injustice, certainly." "Does deceit also exist?" "Unquestionably." "Under which head shall we place that?" "Evidentally under injustice." "Does mischievousness exist?" "Undoubtedly." "And the enslaving of men?" "That, too, prevails." "And shall neither of these things be placed by us under justice, Euthydemus?" "It would be strange if they should be," said he. "But," said Socrates, "if a man, being chosen to lead an army, should reduce to slavery an unjust and hostile people, should we say that he committed injustice?" "No, certainly," replied he. "Should we not rather say that he acted justly?" "Indisputably." "And if, in the course of the war with them, he should practise deceit?" "That also would be just," said he. "And if he should steal and carry off their property, would he not do what was just?" "Certainly," said Euthydemus; "but I thought at first that you asked these questions only with reference to our friends." "Then," said Socrates, "all that we have placed under the head of injustice, we must also place under that of justice?" "It seems so," replied Euthydemus. "Do you agree, then," continued Socrates, "that, having so placed them, we should make a new distinction, that it is just to do such things with regard to enemies, but unjust to do them with regard to friends, and that towards his friends our general should be as guileless as possible?" "By all means," replied Euthydemus. "Well, then," said Socrates, "If a general, seeing his army dispirited, should tell them, inventing a falsehood, that auxiliaries were coming, and should, by that invention, check the despondency of his troops, under which head should we place such an act of deceit?" "It appears to me," said Euthydemus, "that we must place it under justice." "And if a father, when his son requires medicine, and refuses to take it, should deceive him, and give him the medicine as ordinary food, and, by adopting such deception, should restore him to health, under which head must we place such an act of deceit?" "It appears to me that we must put it under the same head." "And if a person, when his friend was in despondency, should, through fear that he might kill himself, steal or take away his sword, or any other weapon, under which head must we place that act?" "That, assuredly, we must place under justice." "You say, then," said Socrates, "that not even towards our friends must we act on all occasions without deceit?" "We must not indeed," said he, "for I retract what I said before, if I may be permitted to do so." "It is indeed much better that you should be permitted," said Socrates, "than that you should not place actions on the right side. But of those who deceive their friends in order to injure them (that we may not leave even this point unconsidered), which of the two is the more unjust, he who does so intentionally or he who does so involuntarily?" "Indeed, Socrates," said Euthydemus, "I no longer put confidence in the answers which I give; for all that I said before appears to me now to be quite different from what I then thought; however, let me venture to say that he who deceives intentionally is more unjust than he who deceives involuntarily."

Socrates bound virtue inextricably with knowledge, equating the two, for 'knowledge is virtue' and 'virtue is knowledge.' Sinful actions are reducible to ignorance as also are servile ones. Socrates interrogates Euthydemus: [1] "'Do you know any persons called slave-like?' 'I do.' 'Whether for their knowledge or their ignorance?' 'For their ignorance, certainly . . .' 'It therefore becomes us to exert ourselves in every way to avoid being like slaves.'" Socrates pursues the discussion of ignorance still further by delving into self-knowledge, an area in which few persons are adept, but most fancy themselves to be quite expert. Self-knowledge is of particular value, not only in gaining psychological self-control but in acquiring control over one's overt or moral behavior, in other words, gaining moral excellence. The average person assumes that he possesses control and knowledge of self since he is closer and more familiar with his own person than is anyone else; but this is not strictly the case, often a psychologist or a person of insight knows more about an individual than he does himself. In the vein of the present discussion, Socrates continues engaging in conversation with Euthydemus with the query: [2]

"Tell me, Euthydemus, have you ever gone to Delphi?" "Yes, twice," replied he. "And did you observe what is written somewhere on the temple wall, KNOW THYSELF?" "I did." "And did you take no thought of that inscription, or did you attend to it, and try to examine yourself, to ascertain what sort of character you are?" "I did not indeed try, for I thought that I knew very well already, since I should hardly know anything else if I did not know myself." "But whether does he seem to you to know himself, who knows his own name merely, or he who (like people buying horses, who do not think that they know the horse that they want to know, until they have ascertained whether he is tractable or unruly, whether he is strong or weak, swift or slow, and how he is as to other points which are serviceable or disadvantageous in the use of a horse, so he), having ascertained with regard to himself how he is adapted for the service of mankind, knows his own abilities?" "It appears to me, I must confess, that he who does not know his own abilities, does not know himself." "But is it not evident," said Socrates, "that men enjoy a great number of blessings in consequence of knowing themselves, and incur a great number of evils, through being deceived in themselves? For they who know themselves know what is suitable for them, and distinguish between what they can do and what they cannot; and, by doing what they know how to do, procure for themselves

[1] *Ibid.*, 24–29.
[2] *Ibid.*, excerpts from 22–23.

what they need, and are prosperous, and, by abstaining from what they do not know, live blamelessly, and avoid being unfortunate. By this knowledge of themselves, too, they can form an opinion of other men, and, by their experience of the rest of mankind, obtain for themselves what is good, and guard against what is evil. But they who do not know themselves, but are deceived in their own powers, are in similar case with regard to other men, and other human affairs, and neither understand what they require, nor what they are doing, nor the characters of those with whom they connect themselves, but, being in error as to all these particulars they fail to obtain what is good, and fall into evil. They, on the other hand, who understand what they take in hand, succeed in what they attempt, and become esteemed and honored; those who resemble them in character willingly form connexions with them; those who are unsuccessful in life desire to be assisted with their advice, and to prefer them to themselves; they place in them their hopes of good, and love them, on all these accounts, beyond all other men. But those, again, who do not know what they are doing, who make an unhappy choice in life, and are unsuccessful in what they attempt, not only incur losses and suffering in their own affairs, but become, in consequence, disreputable and ridiculous, and drag out their lives in contempt, and dishonour. Among states, too, you see that such as, from ignorance of their own strength, go to war with others that are more powerful, are, some of them, utterly overthrown, and others reduced from freedom to slavery."

The Socratic injunction, 'Know thyself' together with the Socratic dictum, 'Virtue is knowledge' have far reaching psychological and ethical implications. The man who is cognizant of his limitations and remains within the bounds of discretion can accomplish more and be more content, if not happier, than he could possibly be otherwise. Often an individual's major worries stem from his inability to conquer self or resolve mental conflicts, whereas the problem can be greatly alleviated by learning to live with himself and remaining within the restrictions of his handicaps and other limitations resulting from individual differences.

HEGEL: THE HEGELIAN DIALECTIC

When dealing with either the Socratic dialectic or the Hegelian dialectic, it is necessary to retain the idea in mind that each is a system of logic or reasoning. The average person unwarrantedly assumes that principles of traditional logic (Aristotelian logic), since they are ideal immutable objects, are applicable to dynamic processes of life such as its swift and ever-changing tempo, nature, history, and individual life; but Aristotelian logic, the traditional logic of the syllogism, deals with static class relationships only, and is incapable of application to the ever-changing events which continually alter with time or with facts which never remain identical even from one instant to the next. The most that the syllogism is capable of accomplishing is to relate one class of objects to another by placing one set in another or denying that one class or a portion of it is included in another. It merely states that if all of the members of the class 'men' are included in the class 'mortal,' and if 'Socrates' is a 'man' then the class 'Socrates' is found to be in the class 'mortal' for such is the meaning of the classic syllogism:

All men are mortal
Socrates is a man
Therefore, Socrates is mortal.

It is a static logic which does no more than merely classify three different sets, two at a time in three different propositions:

All men are (in the class) mortal,

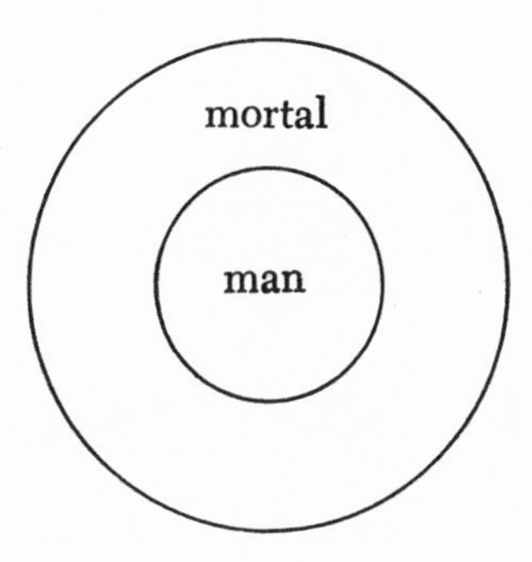

Socrates is (in the class) man,

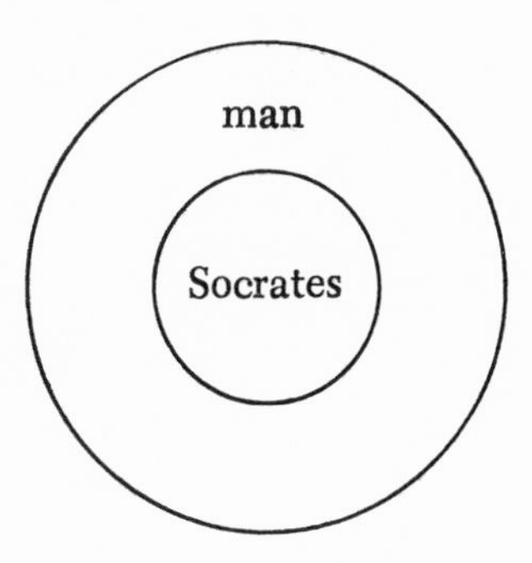

Hence, if he is in the class man then he is, by virtue of that fact, in the class of mortals.

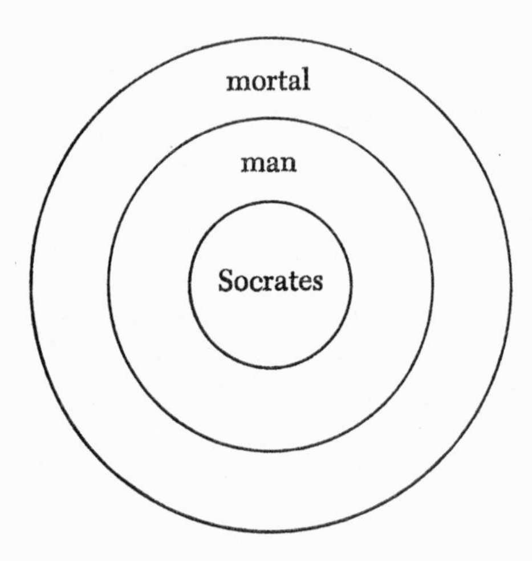

According to Hegel, the universe is basically an organic whole which grows and develops from age to age; this fact holds true for the physical and natural world as well as for individuals and society, including the history of the human race. This being the case, a dynamic logic which is capable of breaking through or transcending the barrier of 'class logic' (syllogism) is a vital necessity. The Hegelian dialectic rises to the occasion.

Hegel's dialectic is essentially a method based on the presupposition that all reality is ultimately related; the dialectic is a device which connects facts or points out their various relationships with each other, and ultimately with the whole of reality. Isolated relationships such as are found in Aristotle's syllogistic logic are abstractions, and owing to that fact do not constitute truth since "the truth is the whole."

Hegel would probably laugh himself to scorn at the American court system of requiring oaths by swearing to the formula: "tell the truth, the *whole* truth, and nothing but the truth." The whole truth is the Absolute, and requires an absolute mind to comprehend, hence only God knows the whole truth. The court room situation deteriorates further when the individual occupying the witness stand is asked a multiple question (fallacy) such as 'Where did you hide the murder weapon?' and is expected to be responsive to the question when he had nothing to do with the crime.

Such isolated statements are in Hegel's estimation abstractions, therefore are false. A correct statement cannot be regarded as truth unless it is the whole truth, that is, unless it is related to every object which is in any manner connected with it. A true statement is one which is concrete, one which is related to every pertinent fact associated with it. It is a relatively simple matter to lie by telling the truth, and in such cases Hegel would insist that a correct statement may have been uttered, but not the truth, unless the whole truth is brought to light. Consider the following example in which falsehood is conveyed through correct statements and which the average person would regard as truth: Mr. Milksop, a timid individual, is the only person at his place of employment who has not received a raise in salary. His wife, aware of a pattern that only persons who request an increase in pay receive it, demands that unless her husband goes to his superior the following day and requests a raise, she will divorce him. Mr. Milksop, deeply disturbed at the thought of either prospect, spends the following day attempting to rally enough courage to approach his employer. Unable to bring himself to confront his boss, he procrastinates until ten minutes before closing time, at which time he forces himself to go to his employer's office where he finds only the secretary present. She informs him that only a moment ago the boss left for the day and should he hurry, he might be able to overtake him. Mr. Milksop looks down the corridor in time to catch a glimpse of his superior rounding the corner and disappearing out of sight. Unable and unwilling to pursue the matter any further, he returns home where his wife, reading his forlorn countenance as a sign of defeat, asks in a stern voice: 'Did you see your boss today?' Actually, he did, hence he responds, 'Yes.' She inquires further, 'Did you get your raise in pay?' His reply is, 'No.' Most people would probably say that he told the truth in this situation, but Hegel would contend that only accurate statements were made, however, the truth was withheld since the 'truth is the whole,' and unless the whole truth is given, then abstract statements would have to be regarded as false.

The Hegelian dialectic is predicated on the *organic theory of truth and reality,* or as it is now coming more to be called, the *coherence theory of truth.* This theory implies that the universe is ultimately an organic whole whose parts compose a unified systematized interrelated network of facts. The network of facts of which the universe is composed is rationally ordered and constructed, accordingly it can be rationally deduced since the nature of the world is basically rational. In his *Philosophy of History,* Hegel writes: "Anaxagoras was the first to enunciate the doctrine that *nous,* Understanding generally, or Reason, governs the world. It is not intelligence as self-conscious Reason, – not a Spirit as such that is meant; and we must clearly distinguish these from each other. The movement of the solar system takes place according to unchangeable laws. These laws are Reason, implicit in the phenomena in question. But neither the sun nor the planets, which revolve around it according to these laws, can be said to have any consciousness of them . . . Nature is the embodiment of Reason . . . it is unchangeably subordinate to universal laws."[1] In the same work, he says: "Reason is the *substance* of the universe . . . the design of the world is absolutely rational." Again: "Reason is the *True,* the *Eternal,* the absolutely *powerful* essence . . . it reveals itself in the World, and that in that World nothing else is revealed but this."

Hegel's dictum: 'The real is the rational' and 'The rational is the real' is effectively illustrated in the light of modern scientific advancements; for example, consider the fact of infra-red or ultra-violet which are imperceptible as colors to the naked eye, yet have been discovered as genuine facts despite human inability to sense them at all. The explanation is that they are rational facts which behave according to rational principles and have been discovered by the use of human intelligence and reason. Although the range of human sense perception pertaining to color is limited approximately from 700 millimicrons to 400 millimicrons (infra-red and ultra-violet fall above and below this range), man transcends the limits of sense by the use of intelligence, gaining knowledge of extra-sensory reality such as infra-red, x-ray, etc., not because man has x-ray vision, but because the universe is ultimately and fundamentally rational, and consequently can be known by the use of rational techniques where sense knowledge is deficient.

The world, being fundamentally a *uni*verse, one huge integrated and related system, is an interconnected one in which a single fact is eventually linked with every other fact of the universe like a chain reaction, or like a fuse set off at any point which will eventually touch off every other point. Isolated facts do not exist; each is an integral part of an organic whole, and it is precisely for this reason that 'the truth is the

[1] Translated by J. Sibree.

whole,' whereas isolated parts are abstractions severed from the concrete whole, hence never constitute truth. Any abstraction whatever, such as the fallacy of vicious abstraction indicates, is a distortion of the facts of reality, and accordingly must be considered fallacious. Consider the example of a man who is branded a killer on the premise that he killed an innocent human being. However, when the complete facts of the case are brought to light and the total situation is considered as an organic whole, it is revealed that the murderer in question is a surgeon who was hastily summoned to a hospital and begged to do whatever possible to save the life of an automobile accident victim. The surgeon's findings indicate that the victim is a hopeless case who has only hours to live, but a remote possibility exists wherein emergency surgery may possibly prove successful. The victim's relatives plead with the surgeon to proceed immediately with the operation, but when he does the patient's weakened condition, unable to withstand the shock of surgery, succumbs to death as the incision is made by the surgeon. With enough facts in hand to see the truth which the organic whole reveals, it becomes obvious that the abstract fact of branding the surgeon a killer, although a correct statement, is not the truth.

The closer one arrives at the whole, the nearer he approaches the truth, whereas the less concrete or the more abstract his statements, that is, the more isolated they are, the more erroneous they are despite their correctness. Correct statements are not necessarily true unless they are bound integratively in a relationship with the organic whole. Since all truth coheres in one complete whole, it follows that the person who has the most complete or coherent explanation of all the facts of a situation must be regarded as possessing the truth, and of having best proved his case. For example, the more pieces a person has constructed in the formation of a jig-saw puzzle, the more meaningful the picture becomes until the entire picture is evident, whereas abstract pieces lack significance unless related to the rest which compose the whole. Note the close, if not identical, resemblance of this concept to the coherence criterion of truth which is predicated on the Hegelian dictum: 'the truth is the whole.'

One reason, perhaps *the* reason, why abstract statements, although correct are not true, is that the whole is an organic whole, consequently the parts do not add up mathematically to it since the organic whole *(Gestalt)* is always greater than the mathematical sum of its individual parts. For example, water usually possesses the characteristic of wetness but neither of its component parts, hydrogen nor oxygen, has the quality of wetness.

This is an excellent position from which to catapult to our next point, the triad of which the dialectic is chiefly composed: thesis, antithesis, and synthesis.

Thesis, Antithesis, and Synthesis.

"Dialectic is nothing more than a subjective seesaw of arguments *pro* and *con,* where the absence of sterling thought is disguised by the subtlety which gives birth to such arguments. But in its true and proper character, Dialectic is the very nature and essence of everything predicated by mere understanding, – the law of things and of the finite as a whole . . . By Dialectic is meant the in-dwelling tendency outwards by which the one-sidedness and limitation of the predicates of understanding is seen in its true light, and shown to be the negation of them." [1]

The principle parts of the Hegelian dialectic are: *thesis, antithesis, synthesis, principle of negativity, position, reconciliation* or *sublation.* Logical reasoning must begin with some fact, any fact; it does not matter where one's starting point is since the dialectical process will eventually relate every fact to every other due to the inherent reciprocal relation of each fact to every other in the universe.

One's *position* is his 'thesis,' the initial fact to come under the activation of the dialectical principle. Consider the concept 'man;' as an abstract concept it is meaningless; to define it or give it any meaning entails the *principle of negativity,* relating it to that which it is not, namely, its 'antithesis.' To define man as a rational animal is to ascribe to the abstract notion man a characteristic which in itself is not man but a quality other than man, *per se,* yet which man possesses. An antithesis is necessary for the thesis to be meaningful since the concept man in the abstract is meaningless. In this light, Hegel refers to pure abstract being as nothing. "Mere being, as it is mere abstraction, is therefore the absolutely negative: which, in a similarly immediate aspect, is just NOTHING." [2]

However, 'being,' that initial abstract concept 'man,' "yields to dialectic and sinks into its opposite," a procedure effected by the *principle of negativity.* In other words, every thesis contains within itself its own antithesis and when activated by the principle of negativity, a severe conflict ensues, following which clash the thesis and antithesis are 'reconciled' or 'sublated' *(aufgehoben)* in a higher synthesis. The synthesis, in turn, becomes a new thesis which encounters its antithesis producing, as a result of its conflict, a synthesis. The process is practically an endless

[1] *Idem.*
[2] *The Logic of Hegel,* tr. by William Wallace.

one which eventually entails relating the original thesis to every fact in the universe. Not only is the dialectic a system of logic, it constitutes the logic of a growing universe, history, and personality. In Hegel's estimation, there is no progress without conflict (of thesis and antithesis); the greater the intensity of conflict, the more accelerated the growth or progress. The severest form of conflict is war which would indicate that war is the greatest cause of progress, hence good. War is capable of bringing out man's finest qualities: heroism, sacrifice, loyalty to country, love of freedom, etc.

The dialectic, the only proper means of gaining a thorough or accurate understanding of personality, is applicable to individual life. An isolated act committed by a person is insufficient to judge his personality; such acts must be understood in the light of the history of an individual – a complete case study from infancy, and even before, including heredity, is relevant and necessary. Just as it is impossible to explain a person's phobia of flying in an airplane by the fear he exhibits on entering a plane, because the explanation lies hidden in some previous experiences which are responsible for the phobic symptoms, any other isolated action taken by itself is logically inexplicable unless related to other experiences in the light of the individual's history.

The nature of the dialectic is such that swings occur from thesis to antithesis by the principle of negativity; the more extreme the thesis, the wider the swing to its opposite, the antithesis. Occasionally, an extreme and militant Atheist in youth turns out to be a person whose childhood was very religious, such as one who served regularly as an altar boy. If the spirit of the dialectic continues, wholesome growth and development results, swinging the pendulum of the dialectic once more to the religious side, except that on its return, it ascends to a more moderate and elevated position.

What holds true of the dialectic in individual life is valid for society or history – the pendulum of the dialectic swings (by the principle of negativity) from one extreme (thesis) to the opposite extreme (antithesis), the clash of both issues in a reconciliation (sublation) from which a new synthesis emerges. The synthesis is a new creation of higher calibre than either thesis or antithesis, yet possesses characteristics of both. This synthesis, in turn, becomes a new thesis which finds its eventual conflict in its antithesis terminating by sublation or reconciliation in another synthesis which once more becomes a new thesis to continue the dialectical process anew. The dialectic is a continuing process which strives to attain the absolute.

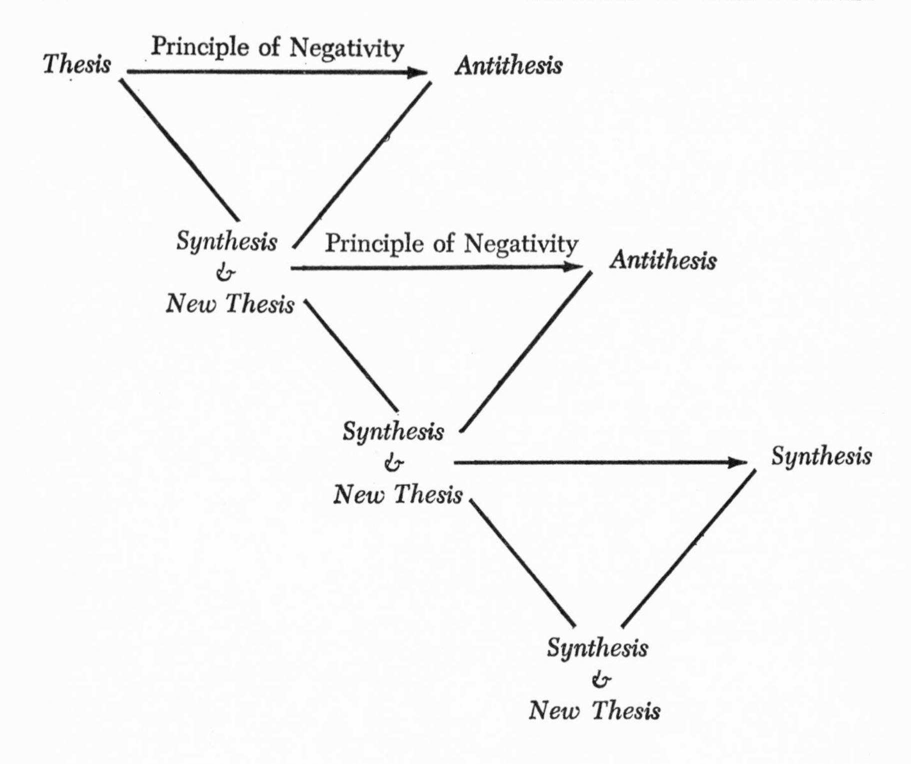

THE HEGELIAN DIALECTIC

The dialectic is active through the efforts of the 'World Spirit' *(Welt-Geist)* in human history, both intellectual and social. In the intellectual history of man, namely, the history of philosophy, the dialetic develops new ideas (synthesis) by the clash of one idea (thesis) with another (antithesis), proving that new ideas are generated out of a conflict of older antithetical ones. In early Greek philosophy, the Monistic school of thought clashed with the Pluralistic school of thought to stimulate the growth of philosophical ideas. Later, Plato's Idealism found its antithesis in Aristotelianism in the antithetical concepts of 'universals' and 'particulars.' The Middle Ages also underwent its dialectical process of Platonism in the first period as the thesis, and Aristotelianism in the second period as its antithesis. In the modern period of the history of philosophy, the dialectic found the *Welt-Geist* oscillating from the thesis which took the form of Continental Rationalism in Europe colliding with its antithesis, British Empiricism and eventuating in the synthesis of German Idealism, which subsequently became a new thesis finding its antithesis in the philosophies of the recent past such as Marx's Dialectical Materialism, Kierkegaard's Existentialism, etc.

The dialectical course of the *Welt-Geist* is manifest also in the social history of man from the beginning of time. Tracing it from Greco-Roman times to the present, we find the thesis, Greco-Roman culture, encountering its antithesis, Judeo-Christian culture. The sexually loose Roman mores drove Christians into monastic life resulting in the synthesis of the Dark Ages. The Dark Ages, as synthesis, becomes the new thesis which encounters its antithesis, the Renaissance, a period of return to an elevated level of a rebirth of Greco-Roman culture with its concomitant sexual excess and laxity, even to the extent of widespread homosexuality, such as was prevalent in the times of early Greece. The Renaissance, now the new thesis, finds the pendulum swinging once more to the other side, and on a higher level than ever before in the nature of the Reformation Period. When the Reformation Period, with its Puritanical way of life, becomes the new thesis, it confronts, as its antithesis, the present culture which is gradually becoming dominated by anti-Puritanical modes of life, as is evidenced by an emphasis on the irrational unconscious with its animal cravings of the 'id', such as taught by Freudian Psychoanalysis, and the bipolar nature of man as both good and evil, such as taught by Existentialists.

History does not move in cycles, but in ascending spirals whose swings gradually converge to a moderate position as they elevate toward the apex as the figure below indicates.

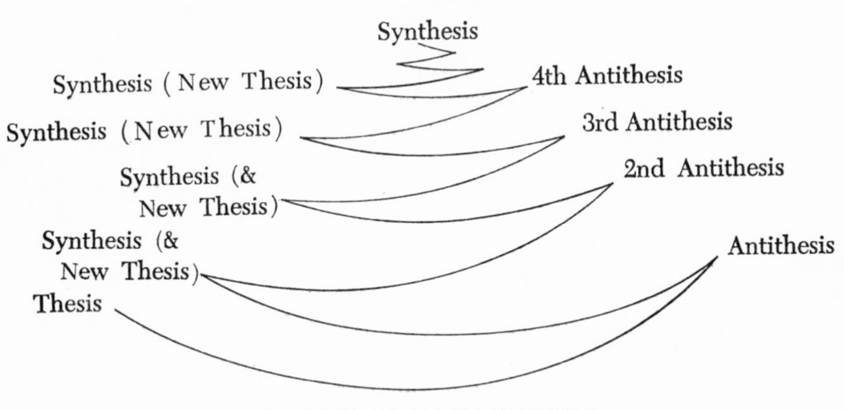

THE HEGELIAN DIALECTIC

All dialectical progress is of this same nature, and indeed it must be, for the dialectic is a principle inherent in all reality; furthermore the great World Spirit (*Welt-Geist*) determines the course of all human history, not great leaders who merely embody the 'spirit of the times' (*Zeit-Geist*). When Napoleon marched on Germany, which Hegel regarded as the inevitable outcome of the dialectic, he philosophically remarked that there goes the *Welt-Geist.*

However, at best, man merely is the embodiment of the *Welt-Geist,* "the higher judge is the universal and absolute Spirit alone — the World-Spirit . . . Out of this dialectic rises the universal Spirit, the unlimited World-Spirit, pronouncing its judgment — and its judgment is the highest — upon the finite nations of the world's history; for the history of the world is the world's court of justice." [1]

A. J. AYER: SKEPTICISM

The greatest Skeptic of ancient times was the philosopher *Gorgias,* a Sophist who contended that nothing can be known and if perchance anyone did by some strange circumstance come to know it, he could not impart his information to another. An interval of approximately two thousand years elapsed before another particularly outstanding Skeptic, under the name of *David Hume,* made an appearance on the philosophical scene. Hume's claim was that knowledge, if it were to be considered valid, had to be the object of sense perception; philosophically, this is termed *Empiricism.* The fundamental premise of the Empiricist, particularly Hume, is that sense impressions furnish the individual with the truth of the world around him.

David Hume

The Empiricist of Hume's type would deny the existence of God, unless a sense impression could be gained of Him; the same holds true of 'life eternal,' the human soul, and all things spiritual; however, in the case of Hume, he denies the existence not only of the aforementioned, but of matter, scientific laws (such as the law of gravity), and the laws of causation (such as heat is the cause of friction). His contention is that a law or cause is imperceptible, hence nonexistent. If one objects to this, he need only observe with meticulous care the repeated dropping of a pencil to determine whether or not he is capable of seeing the law of gravity. Obviously, the law of gravity is nonobservable, for if it were, a person could draw a picture of it, but this is impossible since the only

[1] Hegel, *The Philosophy of Law,* tr. by J. Loewenberg (New York: Charles Scribner's Sons, 1929).

thing observable is a *sequence* of events from the pencil at rest in one's hand through its descent to the floor — no more. He does not observe a *consequence* such as the law of gravity would necessarily be; a consequence is a logical inference, a principle, and as such cannot be perceived but conceived.

By the same line of reasoning, Hume denies the existence of an objective universe around us which is materially substantial; he asserts that material substance cannot be proved because we are unable to obtain impressions of it. To hold an orange in one's hand and say, 'I have a sense impression of a material orange,' is a mistaken notion, since a visual image of an orange is not orange itself, but only a psychological image of it. Inasmuch as the most that one can possibly have as evidence or proof of the orange is a mental perception, he has no right to claim that the mental image has any objective existence whatever, that is to say, what right has anyone to jump from the fact of a sense impression to claiming it is a sense impression *of* something, since the most that one has empirically, is an impression *per se,* not an impression *of* matter?

On the basis of the foregoing line of reasoning, Hume believes that he has disproved the existence of metaphysical (ultimate) reality. In his *An Enquiry Concerning Human Understanding,* he brazenly declares: "When we run over libraries, persuaded of these principles, what havoc must we make? If we take in our hand any volume; of divinity or school metaphysics, for instance; let us ask, *Does it contain any abstract reasoning concerning quantity or number?* No. *Does it contain any experimental reasoning concerning matter of fact and existence?* No. Commit it then to the flames; for it can contain nothing but sophistry and illusion."

Hume here has overlooked a serious and crucial point; when he confidently asserts that *all knowledge comes by impressions only,* he neglects to rule out the basic premise of his entire epistemological philosophy, namely, the *princip*le (and principles are invalid forms of knowledge since they are not impressions nor does one ever obtain an impression of them), 'all knowledge comes from sense experience.' In the last analysis, Hume assumes this principle as valid knowledge, despite the fact that it is not subject to sense impression. If Hume is entitled to claim validity for his principles then whatever grants him this right, entitles all others to the same privilege.

A. J. Ayer

A. J. Ayer's skepticism stems from a philosophy of Logical Positivism with its basic tenet or criterion of truth being: "A statement is directly verifiable if it is either itself an observation-statement, or . . . entails at least one observation-statement."[1] As we shall eventually discover, this fundamental and indispensable statement is a principle and as such is unverifiable by observation, consequently Ayer built his entire philosophy on a self-contradiction, namely, a principle rejected by itself.

At any rate, let us proceed and see what magnificent philosophical mansions are built upon this untenable foundation. Actually, Logical Positivists, aware of this serious and catastrophic weakness in their philosophy, feel justified in continuing to build the superstructure of their philosophy upon it despite its indefensible foundations, since it 'yields such fine productive results.' *Wittgenstein,* generally regarded as the father of Logical Positivism, aware of the inherent self-contradiction in the premise of this school of thought, in his classic work *Tractatus Logico-Philosophicus,* says that the Logical Positivist must discard the allegorical ladder which was used as the instrument to ascend, as if never used or needed at all. "My propositions serve as elucidations in the following way: anyone who understands me eventually recognizes them as *nonsensical,* when he has used them — as steps — to climb up beyond them. (He must, so to speak, throw away the ladder after he has climbed up it.)"[2] As is evidenced by the foregoing, it is most difficult, and some philosophers consider it impossible, to maintain a skeptical position without encountering self-contradictions; they appear to be inherent in the basic system itself.

Assuming the premise of the Logical Positivist to be true, namely that only observable statements are verifiable, then by simple inference, all metaphysical realities (ultimately real substances, not merely apparent objects) are, *ipso facto,* false. For example, God, who has no phenomenal manifestation (hence is imperceptible by sense observation) cannot be said to exist; and, if perchance He did have some appearance, then only the phenomenal manifestation would be real, not the Spirit which is the essence of God. Ayer writes: "If 'god' is a metaphysical term, then it cannot be even probable that a god exists. For to say that 'God exists' is to make a metaphysical utterance which cannot be either true or false. And by the same criterion no sentence which purports to describe the nature of a transcendent god can possess any literal significance."[3] The same maintains regarding the soul of any object; man's soul is not

[1] A. J. Ayer, *Language, Truth and Logic* (London: Victor Gollancz Ltd., 1946, and New York: Dover Publications, Inc.), 13.

[2] Ludwig Wittgenstein, *Tractatus Logico-Philosophicus* (London: Routledge & Kegan Paul Ltd., 1933), Proposition 6.54.

[3] *Ibid.,* 115.

real since it fails to meet the requirements of the above criterion of truth, only his outward manifestations are verifiable facts.

If, to the novitiate in philosophy, this appears unpalatable or difficult to accept, then he faces an even greater perplexity when scientific realities are subjected to the Logical Positivist's empirical test. For example, electricity *per se* is nonobservable although its phenomenal manifestations such as illumination, shock, heat, etc. are physically apparent; accordingly only the so-called effects of electricity are verifiable facts, not electricity itself. The 'soul' of artificial light, heat, electrical shock, etc. must be ruled out as genuinely real, only its observable manifestations, that is, only what is often referred to as the effects of electricity, are genuine facts, since these alone yield to the scrutiny of sense observation. What was just predicated of electricity and its effects maintains for all other 'scientific' realities such as light waves, sound waves, horsepower, x-rays, and even the atom itself. Since the atom is not subject to common inspection by the senses, it is at best a useful 'notion' by which scientists deal with physical facts. To be sure, the effects of the atom are quite perceptible, but this being the case, only the effects can be countenanced as existing.

The entire matter is complicated still further when an individual questions the status of effects as genuine facts of experience. Effects themselves are not observable facts, they are logical inferences, and as such are nonobservable, hence unreal. For example, although illumination from a lamp is observable, electricity as its cause is not, nor is illumination as *effect* (not as a phenomenal manifestation) observable either; in other words, an individual may experience illumination but he does not experience effect, since effect is a logical inference, not an observable fact.

Real electricity does not exist, only phenomenal illumination; electricity as nonobservable does not exist, only the manifestation of light. "Consequently, anyone who condemns the sensible world as a world of mere appearance, as opposed to reality, is saying something which, according to our criterion of significance, is literally nonsensical." [1]

Occasionally, an individual asks why Logical Positivists go to such extreme lengths in philosophy with such emphatic denials of ultimate reality. The answer is probably twofold: First of all, they are eager to keep science pure and unadulterated from pseudo and occult influences which can deteriorate it as well as hamper its progress, admittedly a noble endeavor. In a sense they are unofficial or self-appointed guardians of science, but secondly, a number of them may have gravitated to this position

[1] *Ibid.*, 39.

because the acceptance of the tenets of this philosophy would preclude belief in religious values such as God, soul, immortality, etc. In other words, it is an excellent philosophical foundation upon which to build an Atheistic philosophy despite Ayer's assertion that "It is important not to confuse this view of religious assertions with the view that is adopted by atheists or agnostics. For it is characteristic of an agnostic to hold that the existence of a god is a possibility in which there is no good reason either to believe or disbelieve; and it is characteristic of an atheist to hold that it is at least probable that no god exists. And our view that all utterances about the nature of God are nonsensical, so far from being identical with, or even lending any support to, either of these familiar contentions, is actually incompatible with them."[1] Nevertheless, an Atheistic spirit gravitates to this philosophy.

ROYCE: TRUTH AS ABSOLUTE

Josiah Royce, one of the most eloquent voices in defence of Idealism and Absolutism, was a professor of philosophy at Harvard University over the turn of the century. Few philosophers achieved the literary competence of Royce, who was in demand as a speaker by women's societies in the vicinity of Boston; although they may not have understood his profound philosophical ideas, they admired immensely the literary manner in which he phrased them.

Royce was an adherent of Scientific Agnosticism, the belief that scientific facts are not ultimate nor can reality be derived from science. Science is limited to facts of description, in other words, sense data; another technique is necessary to determine the nature of ultimate reality. "What we know is that events happen to us, and happen in a certain fixed order. We do not know the ultimate causes of these events. If we lived on some other planet, doubtless causes of a very novel sort would become manifest to us, and our whole view of nature would change. It is self-contradictory, it is absurd, to make our knowledge the measure of all that is! The real world that causes our experience is a great *x*, wholly unknown to us except in a few select phenomena, which happen to fall within our ken. How wild to guess about the mysteries of the infinite!"[2]

Scientific Agnosticism does not imply *Metaphysical Agnosticism,* namely the belief of Ayer and other Logical Positivists who purport the non-

[1] *Ibid.*, 115.

[2] Unless otherwise stated, the quotations cited in this section are from: Josiah Royce, *The Spirit of Modern Philosophy* (Boston: Houghton Mifflin Co., 1892), Lecture XI.

existence of ultimate reality, nor is Royce a Metaphysical Agnostic. On the contrary, he is a staunch defender not only of ultimate reality, but of absolute truth, maintaining that no foe can even possibly debate with him against his stand that *truth is absolute* unless first agreeing with him; should his foe accept these terms of agreement, then debate is unnecessary. The rationale of the argument rests on the contention that when the Relativist asserts 'Truth is relative' or 'Truth is a matter of opinion,' he is in effect making an absolute statement, which is tantamount to saying: 'The absolute truth is, truth is relative, not absolute.' In other words, if the Relativist is to take an absolute stand on the matter, he has in effect abandoned Relativism; accordingly, an attempt to deny or even doubt the existence of absolute truth is an affirmation of it. For example, the utterance, 'There is no absolute truth' is an absolute assertion, if not an absolute claim. "The agnostic, I say, already asserts this existence — unconsciously, of course, as a rule, but none the less inevitably . . . There is no escape from the infinite Self [Absolute] except by self-contradiction. Ignorant as I am about first causes, I am at least clear, therefore, about the Self. If you deny him, you already in denying affirm him. You reckon ill when you leave him out. 'Him when you fly, he is the wings.' He is the doubter and the doubt. You in vain flee from his presence . . . This truth is, I assure you, simply a product of dry logic."

The Validity of the Metaphysically Real.

As determined as Ayer was in his contention that ultimate reality (metaphysics) is nonexistent, equally adamant is Royce's stand on behalf of the validity of metaphysically real substances; nevertheless, all ultimate substances must be ideally real, that is, composed of the nature of mind or spirit, not matter.

Whereas, Ayer would deny the existence of electricity as being ultimately real, Royce would not; Royce admitted the reality of both the phenomenal appearances of objects as well as their metaphysical substance, but he would insist, however, on the nature or essence of their reality being ideal, spirit, or mind. This form of Idealism is known as *Panpsychism.* "But now, at this point, the Berkeleyan idealist goes one step further. The real outside world that is still left unexplained and unanalyzed after its beauty, its warmth, its odors, its tastes, and its colors, and its tones, have been relegated to the realm of ideal truths, what do you now *mean* by calling it real? No doubt it *is* known as somehow real, but *what* is this reality *known as* being? If you know that this world is still there and outer, as by hypothesis you know, you are bound to say *what* this outer character implies for your thought. And here you have trouble. Is the outer world, as it exists outside of your ideas, or of anybody's ideas, something having shape, filling space, possessing solidity, full of moving things? That would in the first place seem evident. The sound isn't outside of me, but the sound-waves, you say, are. The colors are ideal facts; but the ether-waves don't need a mind to know them. Warmth is ideal, but the physical fact called heat, this playing to and fro of molecules, is real, and is there apart from any mind. But once more, *is* this so evident? What do I *mean* by the shape of anything, or by the size of anything? Don't I mean just the idea of shape or of size I am obliged to get under certain circumstances? What is the meaning of any property that I give to the real outer world? How can I express that property except in case I think it in terms of my ideas? . . . Doubtless these ideas have a validity. They have *this* validity . . . All the reality that *we* attribute to our world, in so far as *we* know and can tell what we mean thereby, becomes ideal . . . Nothing whatever can I say about my world yonder that I do not express in terms of mind. *What* things are, extended, moving, colored, tuneful, majestic, beautiful, holy, *what* they are in any aspect of their nature, mathematical, logical, physical, sensuously pleasing, spiritually valuable, all this must mean for me only something that I have to express in the fashion of ideas. The more I am to know my world, the more of a mind I must have for the purpose. The closer I come to the truth about the things, the more ideas I get. Isn't it plain, then, that *if* my world yonder is anything knowable at all, it must be in and for itself essentially a mental world? . . . To what can things that go on in my mind conform unless it be to another mind? If the more my mind grows in mental clearness, the nearer it gets to the nature of reality, then surely the reality that my mind thus resembles must be in itself mental."

When Royce asserts that the world is mind or mental, he definitely does not mean my mind or any other human's mind; it is more than a mere subjective idea or mental notion, it is an outer real world of substance which is more than a dead inert substance such as the Materialists envision it. At this point, the Idealist is at a loss for an acceptable term to describe outer reality which is an object other than dead matter; although 'nonmaterial' is inappropriate, yet terms which are nonmaterial must be used, such as mind, ideal, spiritual, to express the nature of the ultimately real world without, which is laden with energy, vitality, mind, life, experience, etc., any substance but dead inert matter — unless, of course, a person is willing to redefine the concept matter to signify nonmaterial substance, such as mind, life, activity, energy, vitality, etc., instead of an inert substance.

Ayer purported that the ultimately real electricity did not exist, only the phenomenal manifestations of electricity (light, heat, etc.), but not electricity as a metaphysically real substance. Royce's position is diametrically opposed, for he asserts that electricity is a metaphysically real substance despite the fact that it cannot be sensed; nevertheless, it is knowable, yet not as matter, but as a substance which in nature or kind is objective or absolute mind. In the last analysis, all matter is ultimately mind. "Even matter you know just as a mass of coherent ideas that you cannot help having . . . The real world beyond you must in itself be a system of somebody's ideas . . . If it is, then you can comprehend what its existence means. If it isn't, then since all you can know of it is ideal, the real world must be utterly unknowable, a bare *x*. Minds I can understand because I myself am a mind. An existence that has no mental attribute is wholly opaque to me." In other words, human beings do not have the apparatus, the necessary sense organs to experience material substance, consequently if matter did exist, man would never know it, God or another type of being other than man might. A human being is equipped by his senses to obtain psychological experiences, mental knowledge, reasoning with ideas, logical and mathematical principles, but never material substance.

"Note the point we have reached. *Either,* as you see, your real world yonder is through and through a world of ideas, an outer mind that you are more or less comprehending through your experience, or *else,* in so far as it is real and outer it is unknowable, an inscrutable *x*, an absolute mystery. The dilemma is perfect. There is no third alternative. Either a mind yonder or else the unknowable; that is your choice . . . Well, try the darker choice that the dilemma gives you. The world yonder shall be an *x*, an unknowable something, outer, problematic, foreign, opaque. And you, — you shall look upon it and believe in it. Yes, you shall for argument's sake first put on an air of resigned confidence, and say, 'I do not only fancy it to be an extra-mental and unknowable something there, an impenetrable *x*, but I know it to be such. I can't help it. I didn't make it unknowable. I regret the fact. But there it is. I have to admit its existence. But I know that I shall never solve the problem of its nature.' Ah, its nature is a problem, then. But what do you mean by this '*problem*'? Problems are, after a fashion, rather familiar things, — that is, in the world of ideas . . .

"Any fair question could be answered by one who knew enough. No fair question has an unknowable answer. But now, *if* your unknowable world out there is a thing of wholly, of absolutely problematic and inscrutable nature, is it so because you don't *yet* know enough about it, or because in its very nature and essence it is an absurd thing, an x that *would* answer a question, which actually it is nonsense to ask? Surely one must choose the former alternative. The real world may be unknown; it can't be essentially unknowable."

Concentrate on what Royce is attempting to convey. Unknown and unknowable are quite dissimilar concepts; the former signifies lack of factual knowledge at the moment; for example, 'The Swedish language is not known to me,' but this does not imply that I cannot possibly come to know it for I can, by learning it. On the other hand, the latter, 'unknowable,' intimates the existence of facts or knowledge which are beyond knowing, not necessarily my knowledge, but all knowledge, even that of an omniscient mind. Such contends Royce is a contradiction of terms, and so it is.

Royce continues his monological debate: "Only ideas are knowable. And nothing absolutely unknowable can exist. For the absolutely unknowable, the x pure and simple, the Kantian thing in itself, simply cannot be admitted. The notion of it is nonsense. The assertion of it a contradiction. Round-squares, and sugar-salt-lumps, and Snarks, and Boojums, and Jabberwocks, and Abracadabras; such, I insist, are the only unknowables there are. The unknown, that which our human and finite selfhood hasn't grasped, exists spread out before us in a boundless world of truth; but the unknowable is essentially, confessedly *ipso facto* a fiction . . .

"To return, however, to our dilemma. *Either* idealism, we said *or* the unknowable. What we have now said is that the absolutely unknowable is essentially an absurdity, a nonexistent. For any fair and stable problem admits of an answer. *If* the world exists yonder, its essence is then already capable of being known by some mind. If capable of being known by a mind, this essence is then already essentially ideal and mental . . . In brief, then, the world as known would be found to be a world that had all the while been ideal and mental, even before it became known to the particular mind that we are to conceive as coming into connection with it. Thus, then, we are driven to the second alternative. The real world must be a mind."

Again, it must be noted that by a mind, Royce does not mean mine or yours, but a substance which is mind-like in nature or in quality, in other words, immaterial substance.

The essential difficulty with Idealism, especially the Roycean type, is that it fails to distinguish sharply and clearly between two different types of mind, such as real electricity which is composed of atoms, and a human being's psychological sense experience which is devoid of atomic structure; or the sense of sight which is definitely related to a physiological organism, and the self or reason which appears free from such physical[1] entanglements; or a biological living cell structure, and a rock composed of chemicals. Although each of these items mentioned is a component or aspect of spiritual substance, that is a substance of the same nature as mind, there is, nevertheless, a difference in their several qualitative characteristics, a difference in *kind.*

[1] *N.B.* 'Physical' and 'material' are not synonymous terms for Royce; whereas matter is understood to be an ultimately real object imperceptible to the senses, physical objects are directly experienced.

Part Two: ETHICS — The Life Worth Living

ETHICS:

The Study of Right Conduct and The Good Life

The study of ethics has two major phases: one is concerned with the study of *right conduct, i.e.*, the resolution of perplexing questions such as those raised in discussion regarding the morality of euthanasia (mercy killing), capital punishment, etc. The second phase concerns itself with the nature of the good life, *i.e.*, the deliberation of questions such as: Is life worth living? What in life is worth living for – or dying for? What is the most important thing in the world?

One can readily see that ethics is the study of "things that matter most" in life, as one philosopher entitled a book in ethics. This being the case, in a sense, ethics should be regarded as the most important study a college or university has to offer; the brilliant Socrates arrived at this conclusion. Kant, considered by some the greatest philosopher of modern times, also concurs, for he maintained that everything accomplished in science is for an ethical objective. He termed this concept "the primacy of practical reason," *i.e.*, the practical application of reason, viz., conduct; consequently, ethics is the end which motivates scientific endeavor.

The claims or implications of such a concept are far-reaching: it intimates that everything accomplished at a scientific institution such as the Massachusetts Institute of Technology subserves an ethical goal, *e.g.*, is concerned for the good of humanity and the enhancement of its individuals. (Note that this constitutes the second phase of the study of ethics, viz., the good life.) One can readily appreciate that the research efforts expended in an institution such as Harvard Medical School serve in the best interests of humanity, particularly when these efforts prove successful in discovering cures of dreaded diseases. One can understand the beneficial value to mankind of schools such as M.I.T., despite the objection from some quarters that atomic research, particularly that which leads to atomic weapons, is deleterious. Even conceding that the atomic bomb's objective is destruction of human life, Americans (or for that matter Russians) believe that it discourages aggression and promotes peace; thus proving that science in all its phases serves an ethical end, viz., the good of man.

The foregoing is but a single and minor aspect of the study of the good life, *i.e.*, the life worth living; the major aspect deals with life's most prized possessions: Aristotle concluded that the greatest good was happiness; Vincent Van Gogh, by maintaining that man is not here merely to be happy, but to realize great things, repudiates the finding of Aristotle. Many Christians, such as Henry Drummond, are persuaded that the greatest thing in the world is love. Some persons think that it is human life, hence will do anything possible to preserve and enhance it; Albert Schweitzer, contended "reverence for life" is the all-important issue, but Patrick Henry felt that life without liberty was not worth having, for this is the inference of his statement: "Give me liberty or give me death." The Hedonistic philosophers, *i.e.*, pleasure-seekers who devote their lives to the pursuit of pleasure, believe that pleasure is the world's greatest and only good. The case in support of the respective foregoing positions will be examined later.

The matter of right conduct is an equally difficult question to resolve: consider a hypothetical situation, yet a realistic one, of a transport airplane which has developed engine trouble high over the rough waters of the Atlantic Ocean on its way to Europe with its passengers and crew of twenty-two persons. The captain apprises the passengers of the plight of the ship and orders all excess weight and luggage to be thrown overboard in the expectation that the crippled plane will be capable of limping its way safely to the nearest airport. Although the captain's order is meticulously carried out, the ship's weight is still excessive; accordingly, the captain issues an order to the effect that everything except human life be cast overboard including seats, heavy amplifiers, etc., the only exception being those parts necessary to the ship's being kept aloft. This new action ameliorates the situation, but does not solve it.

Only one course of action remains: four persons are to be sacrificed, if eighteen are to be saved. The problem is: Who goes overboard? Since there are no volunteers, the decision which rests with the captain is: Should all perish or should four lives be sacrificed for the sake of the remaining eighteen?

The question which confronts us as philosophers is a moral one, namely, What is the right thing to do under the circumstances? We are not concerned with the legal, but with the moral problem; nor are we concerned with the action the passengers might in fact take, *e.g.*, they may panic and destroy each other, hence dispose of the matter in that beastial manner. As philosophers, we seek to deliberate which is the moral course of action.

Assuming that the persons aboard this plane have decided in favor of saving the maximum number of lives possible, what is the just criterion or rule by which the four are to be selected? One possibility is on the basis of weight, *e.g.*, by picking the heaviest passengers, one is relatively assured that no more than four lives will need to be sacrificed; but this seems hardly fair since the obese passengers did nothing which warrants the relinquishment of their lives. Suppose that on this plane it is discovered that two of the passengers are escaped convicts who have been sentenced to death, would it be just to execute them aboard this plane for reasons of expediency? The criterion which would be employed in this case is 'moral character.' To determine the other two to be sacrificed, one is required to seek out the two most immoral persons aboard; but if the remainder are of relatively equal moral standing, this criterion would prove ineffective. One of the passengers may have only a few months to live due to a malignant disease; perhaps he ought to be required to go overboard, hence suggesting another criterion, viz., 'age.' The case in support of age as a criterion rests on the notion that older persons, who would normally be those who are closest to dying, should be sacrificed on behalf of the others since they have had their opportunity of living; justice would require that the younger ones be spared and given a chance to live as long.

Perhaps aboard this plane they have decided that the only fair course of action is to resolve the matter democratically by drawing lots. Of the four men who draw the short ends, the first prepares to jump from the ship; the door is opened and as he is about to leap, the dreadful sight before him has a paralyzing effect on him and he shouts: "Push me! Push me!" Does anyone have the moral right to push him overboard to his death? The question is not: *Will* they do it? The question is: Do they have a *moral right* to do it?

When the second of the unfortunate four is expected to jump, he announces his unwillingness. Indifferent to their vituperations, he confesses that he did not expect to be one of the four since the odds were highly favorable. He declares that anyone who attempts to eject him from the plane by force will go over with him. The perplexing problem before us is: Although he cheated in the lottery by lying, does one have the moral right to push him overboard?

If one has not been aware of it, he should by now be quite convinced that ethical deliberations are both difficult and complicated; single answers will not suffice. Some persons would attempt to resolve the above dilemma by contending that everyone should go down together in the hope of a miraculous survival. Others would insist on saving the maximum possible number under existing conditions on the most equitable basis open to them. Subsequent sections of this chapter are devoted to prescriptions offered by classical moralists for issues such as this.

IV

ETHICAL TERMINOLOGY

It should prove helpful to have an understanding of the terms employed by ethical philosophers; although some of them are used in common parlance, their technical connotations may differ markedly. Terms used most commonly are: ethics, morals, unethical, immoral, unmoral, nonmoral, amoral, right, obligation.

Ethics is defined as the study of the right and the good, *i.e.*, right conduct in the affairs of human life, and the pursuit of the good life. Ethics is essentially a *study;* it is a course of study which one may elect to take in the curriculum of a college in contradistinction to morals which is the practice or application of ethical principles in daily living. *E.g.*, one may take a course in the theory and practice of plumbing or applied plumbing, but when one leaves the theory of ethics for the practice of ethics he enters the domain of morals, he becomes a moralist, a reformer, *i.e.*, he is practicing his religion. Ethics applied becomes morals, whereas the theory of morals is a duly constituted course in ethics. A further implication may be noted: An ethicist (a philosopher) need not be a highly moral person although he usually is, and a moralist (reformer, clergyman, etc.) need not be an expert in ethics (in fact he may not even be able to pass an ordinary college examination in ethics) though usually he is quite proficient.

The term *moral* carries a dual meaning and its intended significance must be determined from the context of the sentence in which it is used. The term's common meaning pertains to a person whose behavior conforms to a standard of right or good, but it carries a second connotation, viz., a being capable of right and wrong action, *i.e.*, a moral agent. In this sense, only human beings are moral; animals and vegetables cannot be so considered, nor are they, for when a tree struck by lightning falls upon a person, crushing him to death, one does not hold the tree morally responsible.

The trio: *amoral, unmoral, nonmoral* are equivalent in meaning; each connotes extra-moral, *i.e.*, outside the domain of morality. They are terms diametrically opposed to the latter meaning of the word moral. *Immoral* is the term used in contradistinction to the former connotation of 'moral;' it signifies a person who may be held responsible for his misbehavior.

Unethical is a dubious term which in common parlance is synonymous with immoral, but technically should convey the meaning: one devoid of a code of ethics. This term is commonly used in reference to persons in specific professions, such as physicians, lawyers, newspapermen, politicians, etc. who fail to live up to or recognize the moral standards or norms set for their respective professions. The implication is: if one lacks a code of ethics, then he must be immoral.

Rights and *obligations* are correlative terms: My rights toward you become your obligations, and your obligations toward me become my rights, and vice versa, e.g., if I am the rightful owner of a piece of real estate, then it becomes your obligation to respect my right to it by refraining from trespassing, etc. If a son has the obligation to respect his parents, then the parents are entitled to certain rights from that son, namely, respect.

We are now prepared to embark on the deliberations of the world's most eminent philosophers of ethical theory.

V

ARISTOTLE:

Self-Realizationism

The Ethics of Self-Realizationism.

Some persons consider Aristotle the greatest philosopher of them all; it is difficult and even impossible to ascribe the superlative to any single philosopher, but unquestionably he is one of the world's greatest philosophers. In fact, Aristotle comes from a royal line of the world's foremost philosophical thinkers: his illustrious teacher was Plato, who in turn was taught by that philosopher of philosophers, Socrates. Aristotle, too, had a notable student in Alexander the Great who furnished his respected teacher with an aggregation of biological species gathered on his military expeditions throughout the Hellenic world. The philosophical impact of Aristotle was so great that throughout the medieval period whenever the term 'the philosopher' was used, it signified Aristotle.

Aristotle founded a university which was named the Lyceum, but his scholars were referred to as 'Peripatetics' (to walk about) because they would promenade about the grounds while the professor delivered his lecture on some phase of philosophy. The school of ethical thought which Aristotle propounded is termed *Self-Realizationism,* implying that the goal of the ethical life is the actualization or the fulfillment of one's potentialities, one's true nature, or one's gifted talents. The philosophical treatise from which the ethics of Aristotle is derived almost exclusively is *Nicomachean Ethics,* named after his son Nicomachus to whom the book was dedicated.

Aristotle opens his treatise on ethics with a definition of *good*: "Every art and every inquiry, and similarly every action and pursuit, is thought to aim at some good; and for this reason the good has rightly been declared to be that at which all things aim."[1] Whatever one seeks and pursues as worthwhile is by virtue of that fact good. The next question Aristotle seeks to resolve is: Precisely what is that good? What is it

[1] Unless otherwise specified, quotations are from the *Nicomachean Ethics,* translated by W. D. Ross (Oxford: The Clarendon Press 1924).

that all mankind seeks as an end in itself; in other words, what is intrinsically and ultimately good, and not merely instrumental to some other good? For example, one would readily grant (unless a miser) that money is an instrumental good, *i.e.*, no one, except the miser, derives uninterrupted pleasure in gazing at money; the normal individual reviewing his financial earnings, may derive satisfaction from the fact that he is capable of earning the money, or the sense of security which it affords, or the many and varied things which he can buy with it, but money, *per se,* is not what holds his fascination. Consequently, money is of instrumental value only.

Aristotle's concern is for an intrinsic value, *i.e.*, some final value which is good in and of itself alone, and not as a means to some other good. Does any such object exist in life? His answer is, yes; there is one thing and one thing only which we seek for its 'dear sweet sake' alone and not for any other purpose, whereas everything else in the universe which enters the life of man is sought for as an instrument, *i.e.*, as a stepping stone to this one greatest of all goods. That such a *summum bonum* (greatest good) exists is of paramount importance because of its implications, *e.g.*, if there is a chief good, then moral action has been defined for us: it is that act which helps to materialize the *summum bonum;* on the other hand, evil would be whatever action impedes or is detrimental to the realization of the greatest good of man. Aristotle queries: "If, then, there is some end of the things we do, which we desire for its own sake (everything else being desired for the sake of this), and if we do not choose everything for the sake of something else (for at that rate the process would go on to infinity, so that our desire would be empty and vain), clearly this must be the good and the chief good. Will not the knowledge of it, then, have a great influence on life? Shall we not, like archers, who have a mark to aim at, be more likely to hit upon what is right?"

Morality is not merely a matter of doing what is good or right; it consists of knowing what is right, otherwise one will be at a loss to act intelligently. Anyone can commit any action, or live in the sense of merely existing; the task of life is to live *well.* Aristotle learned this from Socrates who taught: "The unexamined life is not worth living." Accordingly, a life of ignorance is fit only for animals and is quite unbecoming to man; in fact, it implies more than ignorance, it implies moral degeneration. It is morally incumbent upon one to be enlightened, a unique privilege extended to mankind, but conspicuously absent in the animal kingdom.

Mere knowledge will avail one little unless it is accompanied with self-control "for to such persons, as to the incontinent, knowledge brings no profit; but to those who desire and act in accordance with a rational principle knowledge about such matters will be of great benefit."

Let us return to the discussion of the *summum bonum*. What is the greatest of all goods? What is it that will end man's search and lead to no other end for it needs none? What is the end of all man's striving? "Let us return to the good we are seeking, and ask what it can be . . . So the argument has by a different course reached the same point; but we must try to state this even more clearly. Since there is evidently more than one end, and we choose some of these (*e.g.*, wealth, flutes, and in general instruments) for the sake of something else, clearly not all ends are final ends; but the chief good is evidently something final. Therefore if there is only one final end, this will be what we are seeking, and if there is more than one, the most final of these will be what we are seeking. Now we call that which is in itself worthy of pursuit more final than that which is worthy of pursuit for the sake of something else . . . therefore we call final without qualification that which is always desirable in itself and never for the sake of something else. Now such a thing *happiness*, above all else, is held to be; for this we choose always for itself and never for the sake of something else." We have now hit upon the *summum bonum*, viz., happiness, that intrinsically valuable object which excells all others in value, nor does it require any other for its own existence; on the other hand, all other objects are valuable, if they possess any value at all, by virtue of their contribution to happiness. Happiness is chosen for its dear sweet self alone, and not that it subserves another goal, "but honour, pleasure, reason, and every virtue we choose indeed for themselves . . . but we choose them also for the sake of happiness, judging that by means of them we shall be happy. Happiness, on the other hand, no one chooses for the sake of these, nor, in general, for anything other than itself . . . Happiness, then, is something final and self-sufficient, and is the end of action."

Although it is possible to challenge Aristotle's contention that mankind prizes happiness above all of life's values, it is a formidable position when one judges the matter from the standpoint of the actions and attitudes of average persons. There are many persons who stand ready to sacrifice many values, such as truth, religion, family, friends, honesty, integrity, etc. for the sake of happiness. For example, some individuals have sacrificed their own religion to embrace the religion of their fiancés, not because they believe their own to be false and their suitor's true, but primarily for the reason that in so doing their betrothed will consent to proceed with the marriage. In other words, the reason for abandoning one's religious values is the belief that marriage to the particular person in question will issue in happiness.

A similar situation holds true in the ethical realm: the reason why many persons behave morally is that they think they will be happier if they do, whereas if they break the moral code, *e.g.*, commit murder, they fear either public censure or hell's punishment. In fact, if heaven were merely a moral place devoid of happiness (solely a place of holiness) very few persons would (if they had to go alone) choose to go there. Persons are so terrified of loneliness that they would prefer to go to hell in a crowd than to heaven alone. The motivating factor behind it all is happiness.

Ironically, most persons seek happiness, but few ever find it, and for good reason, the *hedonistic paradox,* a principle which states that if anyone goes in direct pursuit of happiness, he will never succeed in finding it, since happiness is a by-product and issues as a concomitant of that which cannot be technically designated 'happiness.' What is happiness and where does it reside so that one may pursue it? Apparently, it is a state of mind. To be governor of a state would result in a fair measure of happiness for a certain type of individual, but by no stretch of the imagination can one call the governor's position happiness since it would make some persons miserable and ill to assume the task. There are individuals who derive considerable happiness in riding a roller coaster at the amusement park, but for others it would prove terrifying or even boring. Certainly no thoughtful person could look at a roller coaster and designate it happiness – even one who obtains pleasure from riding in it.

Happiness eludes the person who pursues it. How then does one find happiness? Aristotle answers: By fulfilling, realizing, actualizing, developing one's true nature with all of its talents and potentialities. Conversely, if one defies his own basic nature and attempts to go contrary to it, then he encounters frustration; the unhappy person is essentially frustrated, *i.e.*, he has personality needs which have gone unfulfilled. Persons who are misfits in life or in their place of employment can never find permanent happiness for the simple reason that they are forcing their constitutions to do what is unnatural for them. It is similar to forcing a tree to be a corn stock, or a boy to be a girl and vice versa. To make a boy behave as an adult will make him miserable; all perversion ends in unhappiness. Most persons are maladjusted and unhappy, as many psychologists and psychiatrists will readily testify, because they are doing jobs which are ill-suited to their personalities; it is tantamount to twisting, turning, or warping one's psychological constitution. Such a course of action inevitably terminates in a life of discomfort, dissatisfaction, misery, or even mental illness.

A young lawyer, a fine Harvard Law School graduate, confessed that he detested the practice of law and could think of nothing that would give him more satisfaction than to be a high school teacher of political science. He said that he could not make the move because he had too much invested in his career and law practice, and as a consequence he would have to force himself to fumble through life. He probably never cared to study law in the first place, but was carrying out the wish of his father who was a judge.

A physician friend, in a conversation, inquired about a mutual acquaintance who was a student. When told that the young student decided to devote his life to medicine, the physician cynically retorted: "He ought to have his head examined." Obviously the physician was in a profession for which he was not suited by natural constitution or personality; he was forcing his nature to behave in a manner which was totally illsuited to him.

When one finds his rightful place in life, and everyone has some suitable place according to Aristotle for nature (God) has deemed it so, happiness results. Animals are content when free to live like animals; humans can be happy only when they live normal lives harmonious with their natural constitution and abilities.

Let Aristotle speak for himself: "Presumably, however, to say that happiness is the chief good seems a platitude, and a clearer account of what it is is still desired. This might perhaps be given, if we could first ascertain the function of man. For just as for a flute-player, a sculptor, or any artist, and in general, for all things that have a function or activity, the good and the 'well' is thought to reside in the function, so would it seem to be for man, if he has a function. Have the carpenter, then, and the tanner certain functions or activities, and has man none? Is he born without a function? Or as eye, hand, foot, and in general each of the parts evidently has a function, may one lay it down that man similarly has a function apart from these? What then can this be? Life seems to be common even to plants, but we are seeking what is peculiar to man. Let us exclude, therefore, the life of nutrition and growth. Next there would be a life of perception, but *it* also seems to be common even to the horse, the ox, and every animal. There remains, then, an active life of the element that has a rational principle; of this, one part has such a principle in the sense of being obedient to one, the other in the sense of possessing one and exercising thought . . . Now the function of man is an activity of soul which follows or implies a rational principle . . . human activity turns out to be activity of soul in accordance with virtue, and if there is more than one virtue, in accordance with the best and most complete. But we must add 'in a complete life' . . . the happy man lives well and does well; for we have practically defined happiness as a sort of good life and action." Since happiness issues as the result of a life well lived, that is, a moral life in which one has fulfilled the obligation of actualizing his true self, it follows then that the happy person is good (moral) also. "Happiness then is the best, noblest, and most pleasant thing in the world."

Aristotle's Concept of Virtue.

The virtuous life is one in which a person's true nature has been cultivated and fulfilled; it is a life of self-actualization or self-realization, hence a life which fructifies into happiness. Virtue issues as a result of practicing the right act; it is the product of a habit. The term 'moral virtue' and the word 'habit' come from the same root; in the Greek, the word virtue is formed by a slight variation of the word habit. This striking resemblance is of particular interest to Aristotle because it is analogous to the manner in which virtues are cultivated in the personality.

Among philosophers, virtue is defined differently; little agreement exists; Aristotle's definition is *habitual moderation.* Although virtue resembles moral action, it is not identical with it since moral action is to do the right thing, to the right person, at the right time, in the right manner, to the right extent, and for the right purpose, whereas virtue demands that the right act flow effortlessly from the personality as its characteristic trait. The preceding prescription of a right act should make a person pause to think whether he has ever committed a right act inasmuch as it involves the timing of the deed as well as the mode of its performance, the intention, the other person involved, the degree, etc.

Although the assiduous practice of a right act blossoms into a virtue, the ability to discern and perform virtuous deeds is not within the intellectual grasp of everyone; consequently, not everyone can achieve the heights of virtue equally – that prerogative belongs exclusively to the enlightened. The right course of action is invariably the moderate; the closer one is to the middle of the road, the safer he is; similarly, moral extremes are to be eschewed. A definition of a grossly immoderate act would be to do the wrong thing, to the wrong person, in the wrong manner, to the wrong degree, and with the wrong intent. "Moral virtue is a mean, then, and in what sense is it so, and that it is a mean between two vices, the one involving excess, the other deficiency, and that it is such because its character is to aim at what is intermediate in passions and actions, has been sufficiently stated. Hence also it is no easy task to be good. For in everything it is no easy task to find the middle, e.g. to find the middle of a circle is not for every one but for him who knows; so, too, any one can get angry – that is easy – or give or spend money; but to do this to the right person, to the right extent, at the right time, with the right motive, and in the right way, *that* is not for every one, nor is it easy; wherefore goodness is both rare and laudable and noble."

Merely because it is difficult, and even at times impossible, to locate the middle course does not grant one license to abandon all moral principle and commit any pernicious deed. If one cannot navigate his life on dead center of the moral road, he can at least keep as close to it as possible for this is his moral obligation. Furthermore, although both extremes of any act are evil, one extreme is not necessarily as heinous as the other; consequently, when this is the case, it is advisable to lean or sin on the side of the lesser evil. "Hence he who aims at the intermediate must first depart from what is the more contrary to it, as Calypso advises – 'Hold the ship out beyond that surf and spray.' For of the extremes one is more erroneous, one less so; therefore, since to hit the mean is hard in the extreme, we must as a second best, as people say, take the least of the evils; and this will be done best in the way we describe."

Moral evil will always be found to be an extreme measure whether the physical, mental, or moral life is under consideration. This maintains whether the extreme falls on the side of deficiency or excess, *e.g.*, extreme behavior regarding the proper consumption of food is deleterious whether one overeats or consumes an insufficient quantity; the same holds true of exercise, its baneful effects result from overexercise or its abstinence. "It is the nature of . . . things to be destroyed by defect and excess, as we see in the case of strength and health . . . both excessive and defective exercise destroys the strength, and similarly drink and food which is above or below a certain amount destroys the health, while that which is proportionate both produces and increases and preserves it. So too it is in the case of temperance and courage and the other virtues. For the man who flies from and fears everything and does not stand his ground against anything becomes a coward, and the man who fears nothing at all but goes to meet every danger becomes rash; and similarly the man who indulges in every pleasure and abstains from none becomes self-indulgent, while the man who shuns every pleasure, as boors do, becomes in a way insensible; temperance and courage, then, are destroyed by excess and defect, and preserved by the mean."

We are now in a position to determine virtues (means) and vices (extremes): If courage is a virtue then the extreme on the side of deficiency must be cowardice and the extreme on the side of excess, foolhardiness. There is a saying which corroborates this principle: "Fools rush in where angels fear to tread." Often the insane are misconstrued as courageous, *e.g.*, homicidal maniacs who eagerly go 'over the top' in front lines of battle are often erroneously fancied heroic by laymen, whereas psychologists label them psychotic and rash. Although the coward, on the other hand, is not one to be envied either, his behavior is, nevertheless, preferable to the two since of these two extremes, cowardice is the lesser of the evils.

Practically any activity can be tested for its moral value by Aristotelian methods; take, for example, the consumption of alcoholic beverages: When and how much ought one to drink? A prima facie conclusion would call for moderate drinking, *i.e.*, the avoidance of intoxication. Although this is in a sense true, the crux of the matter depends upon the interpretation of the meaning of moderation. The average person thinks of moderate drinking as drinking for 'good fellowship' without becoming inebriated; on the other hand, the Women's Christian Temperance Union would define it in terms of 'temperance,' (which incidentally, in the Aristotelian vocabulary, is another word for moderation). The W. T. C. U. would be closer to the Aristotelian rendering than would others, for Aristotle would say that unless drinking is done at the right time, in the right way, for the right purpose, to the right extent, then it is not done in moderation, hence is immoral. The question is begged: Precisely when is drinking moderate? The answer is, for health or medicinal purposes; in all other cases, it is excessive. When then does deficiency occur? When one refuses to accept it even as a medical prescription. For this is one of the few times when one can drink at the right time, for the right purpose, to the right extent. If this explanation is objectionable because one feels justified in drinking for reasons of 'good fellowship' since drinking is uplifting to the spirit, then he must stand ready to defend the promiscuous use of strong narcotics such as opium on the same rational (or irrational) basis. By virtue of the fact that one declines an offer to consume opium for purposes of 'good fellowship' or 'kicks,' viz., because any use except that which is prescribed by a physician is excessive, so alcohol's moderate use should be similarly determined.

A rather interesting and peculiar relationship maintains between what is a fully developed virtue in an individual, and what is merely a right act. Virtues are internally located; they are human characteristics, whereas a right act is an external physical exercise, that is, an overt act; consequently, a person may commit a right act without necessarily being virtuous and a virtuous person may succumb to an immoral deed without forfeiting his virtuous nature. To fall from a virtuous state is to practice a vice until it becomes imbedded in one as a characteristic quality; in the same manner, to acquire a virtue, one must exercise the right act invariably until it becomes a virtue deeply rooted in the personality.

Accordingly, a man who steals is not necessarily a thief; he stole, to be sure, and committed a misdeed, but a thief steals because it is in his nature to do so. If an honest man steals, it is usually out of dire necessity, such as the avoidance of starvation, because everything that is in him rebels against stealing. The same holds true of a good man who kills; he is not a murderer unless he murders by nature, that is, becomes a killer, but the person who by nature is not a killer may commit an isolated act of homicide purely in self-defence. Similarly, a faithful spouse who indulges in an act of adultery is not necessarily an adulterer, since the adulterer is one by natural disposition; conversely, an individual predisposed to adultery by nature, but refraining from overt activity is doing the right act, yet is still an adulterer until the time comes when his practice of total abstinence fructifies into a characteristic of his nature. "Virtue, then, is a state of character."

The Twelve Aristotelian Virtues.

Aristotle lists twelve specific virtues, each with its accompanying vices; one on the side of defect (deficiency) and the other at the opposite extreme, excess. The following constitute the entire table of thirty-six; twelve virtues and twenty-four vices (twelve of defect and twelve of excess).

VICE OF DEFICIENCY.	VIRTUE OR MEAN STATE.	VICE OF EXCESS.
1. Cowardice	Courage	Foolhardiness
2. Insensibility	Temperance	Licentiousness
3. Illiberality	Liberality	Prodigality
4. Meanness	Magnificence	Vulgarity
5. Humility	Magnanimity	Vanity
6. Lack of Ambition	Unnamed	Ambitiousness (overdone)
7. Unirascibility	Gentleness	Irascibility
8. Self-depreciation	Truthfulness	Boastfulness
9. Boorishness	Wittiness	Buffoonery
10. Contentiousness	Friendliness	Obsequiousness, Flattery
11. Shamelessness	Modesty	Bashfulness
12. Maliciousness	Righteous Indignation	Envy

The various virtues and vices are self-explanatory; few of them require any commentary. The unnamed mean of ambition is a form of ambition: there are times when ambitiousness is considered a vice, *e.g.*, Marc Anthony's funeral oration derogatorily depicts Caesar as ambitious. When ambitiousness is not identified with the evils of aggression, then it is considered a virtue; consequently, those persons sufficiently fortunate to possess the trait are credited with a virtue. The total lack of ambition has always been considered a vice in western civilization.

Wittiness also is worth singling out for comment, since it is rarely found among the lofty list of virtues in major systems of ethics. Very few persons are blessed with a clever wit – many have not even a good sense of humor. Much of American humor depends upon sex to elicit laughter; Freud claims that the reason for this is sex repression, *i.e.*, vulgar jokes are one of the insidious ways for repressed sex to find release. It must be admitted that very few sex jokes are truly humorous; most of them depend on lewdness to excite laughter as is evidenced by the writings on the walls of public toilets.

Another form of the vice of excess pertaining to humor is 'slapstick' comedy which Aristotle terms buffoonery or as is sometimes called 'clowning around.' Much of American humor is of this type and too many Americans laugh loudest at this brand of comedy; actually it is tragedy, *e.g.*, on the stage or in a motion picture an individual will be portrayed as innocently promenading about without paying much attention to the pavement beneath, when suddenly he steps upon a banana peel, somersaults, then falls, almost breaking his neck – with this, the audience roars with laughter.

The distinction between magnificence and liberality is intriguing since magnificent persons are capable of being liberal, but the converse does not follow. Only the wealthy are capable of being magnificent inasmuch as its performance necessitates huge financial expenditures, such as the donation of a million dollar building to a hospital, church, college, etc. Consequently, a man of limited financial means will always fall short of this particular trait, but by virtue of the same fact the members of the middle class society cannot commit its vices either, *e.g.*, it takes a man of financial means to be mean or vulgar. For instance, a distasteful display of wealth is vulgar, and to be cheap when one has more than enough is to be mean. The former is illustrated by the case of a wealthy American actress who, when visiting Paris shortly after World War II during that nation's post-war recession, insulted the French people by adorning her costly mink coat with francs which were considerably depreciated compared to the American dollar.

The twelfth virtue, righteous indignation, with its excess of envy, causes misunderstanding in the minds of many. To be righteously indignant means to be angry for a just cause, *e.g.*, becoming angry when another person is denied his right of free speech, religion, etc., but when one feigns righteous indignation as a guise for envy, such as being envious of a rival, then he has exceeded the bounds of propriety, and righteous indignation degenerates into envy. On the other hand, a person who has not even reached the point of becoming righteously indignant is malicious in his anger; accordingly, anger stemming from maliciousness is a defective form of righteous anger, and that which emanates from envy is excessive, hence vicious.

The virtue of friendliness is not difficult to comprehend nor is its deficiency, contentiousness; the 'trouble maker' obviously is grossly deficient in friendliness. Obsequiousness and flattery call for some explanation; when an individual is a fawning character, *i.e.*, one who is compliant, servile, or the 'yes-man' type, then he has exceeded the bounds of friendship and has deteriorated into obsequiousness. Then, too, there is a second type of excess relative to this virtue, namely flattery, depicted by the insincere person who showers praise or attentions upon an individual to ingratiate himself.

Concerning friendship, three forms exist: (1) friendships of pleasure, (2) friendships of utility, (3) the good and perfect friendship. The friendship of pleasure maintains when two persons take delight in each other's company, such as a couple deeply in love; the friendship of utility grows out of a situation in which one person is in need of the services that another is capable of rendering, *e.g.*, making friends with the local grocer merely because of daily contact with him in the usual course of shopping for groceries – otherwise the friendship would never have arisen. The first two types of friendship can be cultivated by good and evil persons alike, *e.g.*, even a gangster has need of friends he can use in his criminal pursuits; moreover, his 'gun moll' is a friend often solely for the sake of pleasure or material gain. The third and supernal form of friendship is possible only among the virtuous; to be a good and perfect friend one must be altruistic and often concerned solely for a friend's welfare even at the cost of sacrifice. Concerning the three types, Aristotle writes: "For the sake of pleasure or utility, then, even bad men may be friends of each other . . . bad men do not delight in each other unless some advantage come of the relation. . . Friendship being divided into three kinds, bad men will be friends for the sake of pleasure or of utility, being in this respect like each other, but good men will be friends for their own sake, *i.e.*, in virtue of their goodness. These, then, are friends without qualification; the others are friends incidentally and through a resemblance to these."

The Threefold Nature of Man.

According to Aristotle, man has not a single nature, but a threefold nature: *animal, vegetable, rational;* the Aristotelian definition of man encompasses all three: Man is a (vegetative) rational animal. Since the moral task of man is to actualize or realize his nature, and inasmuch as his nature is threefold, all three must be cultivated. The physical body represents the vegetative aspect; for example, human hair grows as does any form of vegetation. Man's emotional, sensual, and sensuous nature is shared with the animal kingdom, however his rational nature is not only supernal, but exclusively and singularly his alone. Man cultivates his vegetative nature by wholesome food and proper exercise; he refines his animal nature by appropriate sex activity within the marriage vow; and he develops his rational nature in the pursuit of scientific knowledge, philosophical truth, political activity, religious and creative artistic endeavor. If one seeks true happiness, or at least his full complement and full measure, then he must actualize to the fullest extent, all three natures.

Nevertheless, all three sources of happiness do not issue in the same quality of happiness; its highest, richest, and supernal form stems from the cultivation of man's highest nature, viz., the rational. When the rational nature of man, his most God-like, is actualized and fully realized, then he is blessed with a sense of sheer joy, euphoria, happiness, a well-being which man alone is capable of experiencing. Aristotle speaks for himself: "If happiness is activity in accordance with virtue, it is reasonable that it should be in accordance with virtue; and this will be that of the best thing in us . . . whether it be itself also divine or only the most divine element in us, the activity of this in accordance with its proper virtue in us will be perfect happiness. That this activity is contemplative we have already said . . . If reason is divine, then, in comparison with man, the life according to it is divine in comparison with human life . . . For man, therefore, the life according to reason is best and pleasantest, since reason more than anything else *is* man. This life therefore is also the happiest . . . Therefore the activity of God, which surpasses all others in blessedness, must be contemplative; and of human activities, therefore, that which is most akin to this must be most of the nature of happiness . . . Happiness extends, then, just so far as contemplation does, and those to whom contemplation more fully belongs are more truly happy, not as mere concomitant but in virtue of the contemplation; for this is in itself precious. Happiness, therefore, must be some form of contemplation."

Hence we discover that although happiness in any form is the highest good for Aristotle, the *summum bonum* is happiness in its highest form, viz., *contemplation.* It is virtually *reason,* man's highest nature, cultivated, activated, realized until its productivity multiplies and fructifies into a well ordered life; it is essentially this which issues in happiness. Man's lower nature must be harnessed and held in reins by reason so that a well ordered life can result and the blessedness of happiness be completely realized.

VI

IMMANUEL KANT:

Intuitionism

The Ethics of Intuitionism.

If Aristotle was the foremost figure in ancient philosophy and if his thinking was the ruling force of the middle ages, then in the modern world that role may be ascribed to Kant. It may be safely said that without an understanding of the Kantian philosophy, one is seriously handicapped in understanding modern and contemporary philosophical thought. Although the contemporary American scene, as far as American morality is concerned, is a heterogeneous conglomeration of many diverse systems of ethics, its most dominant emphasis is Kantian. Consequently, the Kantian ethical theory should prove of particular interest.

Two rich sources from which Kantian ethical philosophy stems are: *The Metaphysic of Morality* and *The Critique of Practical Reason.* Note the use of the term 'practical reason' for ethics in Kantian terminology; the explanation is: what one acts on or puts into practice is in effect his conduct or behavior, *i.e.*, ethic. "Everything in nature acts in conformity with law. Only a rational being has the faculty of acting in conformity with the *idea* of law, or from principles; only a rational being, in other words, has a will. And as without reason actions cannot proceed from laws, will is simply practical reason."[1]

Kant is designated an Intuitionist in ethical philosophy, *i.e.*, one who believes that morality is exclusively within the human personality. Moral right or wrong is solely a matter of intent, motive, will and can never be predicated of overt actions; external actions lie outside the domain of morality and are foreign to what may be termed moral or immoral. An Intuitionist in ethics claims that consequences of one's actions cannot be properly designated right or wrong since they are morally irrelevant. Note the distinction in meaning of the word 'intuition' as it is used herein and in common parlance where it signifies 'hunch,' 'womanly intuition,' etc.

[1] Unless otherwise indicated, quotations in this section are taken from Immanuel Kant, *The Metaphysic of Morality,* tr. John Watson (1901).

The logical and practical ramifications of ethical Intuitionism can reach serious proportions with devastating results, *e.g.*, Kantian ethical philosophy directs that under no conditions may a promise be broken irrespective of its consequences, even if they prove injurious to all concerned. As far as consequences are concerned, the Intuitionist holds: "Let the chips fall where they may;" right is right and must be pursued regardless of the outcome. One is bound by a moral imperative to will the right by keeping his promises even though the heavens fall. "This imperative is *categorical.* It has to do, not with the matter of an action and the result expected to follow from it, but simply with the form and principle from which the action itself proceeds. The action is essentially good if the motive of the agent is good, let the consequences be what they may. This imperative may be called the imperative of *morality.*"

It is easier to understand and appreciate the stand of the Intuitionist by contrasting him to the Ideal Utilitarian in ethics since the two are diametrically opposed positions. An Ideal Utilitarian supports the belief that consequences which issue from actions committed by an individual are the essential moral factor in determining moral conduct, *e.g.*, if the consequences are good then the act is right, but on the other hand, if the consequences are deleterious then the act is ajudged immoral. He further points out that a man's morality is to be decided on the basis of the long chain of results which proceeds from actions, whereas the Intuitionist maintains that a man's will or good intentions alone constitute moral data. Although the Ideal Utilitarian criticizes the Intuitionist for this stand with the maxim 'Hell is paved with good intentions,' the Intuitionist believes the converse to be true, *e.g.*, the Ideal Utilitarian's claim that murder is wrong is based on the nature of its detrimental consequences resulting from such actions, but the Intuitionist would counteract with: unless there is intent to kill, it cannot be designated murder.

The Intuitionist is capable of defending his position in a number of ways. Suppose, for instance, you have an apartment on the fifth floor of a building with a window overlooking the sidewalk pavement. A man you detest walks by regularly from work at precisely five o'clock in the afternoon. Since the tenants in this apartment building seem to have a hobby of window sill plants, you too, along with them have taken to the same interest, but by a strange coincidence through no fault of your own, a strong wind suddenly blows your plant from the sill so that it falls and strikes your enemy on the head and kills him. Could it be designated an immoral act? The Intuitionist would give a negative answer, designating it a tragedy, since there was no intent to kill, and provided proper care was exercised in the placement of the plant.

The Intuitionist would designate it murder if instead of nature providing the gust of wind, a huge fan is purchased and set in motion intentionally, at the crucial moment, causing the plant to fall and resulting in the man's death. The essential differences in these two incidents is the absence of intent in the former; in law, this distinction is also taken into consideration since murder in the first degree (premeditated intent) is not on a par with murder in the third degree or manslaughter (the absence of premeditation).

To ignore intent carries serious complications: consider again the second instance (the one in which intent to murder was present), but with one difference, viz., instead of the flower pot striking its victim, it falls on the street a few steps in front of him at the moment he is about to cross. The startled would-be victim leaps back to the curb to discover that his life was saved by the action, for a truck out of control was about to overrun him. This anomaly would have to be designated as a good act by the Ideal Utilitarian but the Intuitionist would condemn it on the basis of the instigator's ill intent.

The foregoing raises some pertinent questions. Are there particular sins or merely sinners? *i.e.,* can one speak of an immoral act? For the Intuitionist, there probably exist only sinners, not sins since they are acts and as such mere natural occurrences. Note, that it was not the flower pot which was held morally responsible in the act discussed above, but the person who initiated the action; hence, human beings are moral or immoral, not natural objects.

The preceeding discussion is an argument favoring the position taken by the ethical Intuitionist; if overt actions are void of moral content then morality must be inner — within the personality as is claimed by Kant and other Intuitionists. All goodness is within a personality because only a person is capable of good will. "Nothing in the whole world, or even outside of the world, can possibly be regarded as good without limitation except a *good will.*"

What Is Right for One Is Right for All.

An interesting question stimulated by Kantian premises is: Is it moral for the U. S. government to practice deceit, that is, lie, cheat, etc. in order to apprehend criminals? *E.g.,* the story is told of a treasury agent who went as an undercover agent into the mountains of Virginia to win the confidence of some mountaineers who were conducting a thriving business in illegal liquor. It was this agent's assignment to discover and report on the whereabouts of the still and the participants. Through the employment of deception, the mountaineers' confidence was won and they accepted the undercover agent as a collaborator with themselves in the illegal liquor traffic. Once gaining the necessary information, the agent exposed the entire operation with the result that the participants were apprehended and sentenced to prison. The moral problem is: Did the government officer have the moral right to lie and cheat this way in his business life to gain his desired end? This entire discussion prompts still another question. Does the government have the moral right to destroy human life (capital punishment)?

Kant's answer would be: What is right for one person is right for all persons, and what is immoral for one is immoral for all. This conclusion is due to the fact that moral principles are categorical, *i.e.*, they are unconditional, they hold true under any and all circumstances; consequently, if it is immoral for an individual to lie, then it is immoral for a group of individuals, including the government, to lie.

The Kantian ethics is a most democratic one in its insistence that what is right for one is right for all, but its universality does not end here. Consider the question of the problem of keeping promises and the morality or immorality involved in breaking them. Postulate, for purposes of discussion, the hypothetical case of a situation in which it would prove most beneficial to all concerned if a promise were broken, but devastating if the promise were exercised. The perplexing moral question is: Is it ethical to break a promise under such extenuating circumstances? Most persons presumably would answer in the affirmative, contending that not only would it be moral, but to do otherwise would be morally unjustifiable.

Take the following example: A boy promises on a solemn oath never to lie to his father, but after a period of several years, he is confronted with the following situation. His father falls ill of a serious heart seizure and cannot at this time afford even the slightest emotional shock. Although the boy is assessed of the father's condition, he is held to strictest secrecy, and under these circumstances is asked pointedly by his father: What did the doctor say about my condition? The youth, aware that his father has not been apprised of the nature of his ailment, is dubious about keeping his promise.

Although a majority of people would condone breaking this promise, Kant would not, since he contends that the moral law maintains under any and all circumstances, *e.g.*, what is wrong under one set of conditions is immoral under all, and what is moral under one set of circumstances is right under all. Let Kant defend his own position: "May I, for instance, under the pressure of circumstances, make a promise which I have no intention of keeping? The question is not, whether it is prudent to make a false promise, but whether it is morally right. To enable me to answer this question shortly and conclusively, the best way is for me to ask myself whether it would satisfy me that the maxim to extricate myself from embarrassment by giving a false promise should have the force of a universal law, applying to others as well as to myself. And I see at once, that, while I can certainly will the lie, I cannot will that lying should be a universal law. If lying were universal, there would, properly speaking, be no promises whatever. I might say that I intended to do a certain thing at some future time, but nobody would believe me, or if he did at the moment trust to my promise, he would afterwards pay me back in my own coin. My maxim thus proves itself to be self-destructive, so soon as it is taken as a universal law.

"Duty, then, consists in the obligation to act from *pure* reverence for the moral law. To this motive all others must give way, for it is the condition of a will which is good *in itself,* and which has a value with which nothing else is comparable."

The Categorical Imperative.

Kant is saying: If one is allowed to break moral laws at his own pleasure or arbitrary discretion, then there may as well be no universal laws of morality. If one maintains that cheating is wrong, but makes allowances for his own cheating when it is to his advantage to do so or when it is beneficial to others, then moral law regarding cheating breaks down, resulting in moral anarchy. Either moral laws must be respected or there can be no moral laws at all; half way measures cannot exist. Moral law is binding on all persons alike, at all times, and in all circumstances; this is the meaning of what Kant has designated the *categorical imperative* – perhaps the most popularly known principle or criterion of morality in the philosophical community.

The 'categorical imperative' is the answer to the perennial question: How can I tell whether or not the act I am about to commit is moral? Accordingly, the categorical imperative is a test of moral right, a moral criterion, a calculus, a rule of conduct. The categorical imperative stated is: "*Act in conformity with that maxim, and that maxim only, which you can at the same time will to be a universal law,*" or, "*Act as if the maxim from which you act were to become through your will a universal law of nature.*"

To exercise the categorical imperative, one must detect the underlying principle of the deed he is about to commit; if the principle of the impending action is stealing, then he interrogates himself: Can I will that stealing become a universal law, hence permitting everyone to steal? The question is not: May I steal under conditions when I deem it advisable, such as stealing to feed hungry children or stealing from the rich to give to the poor as did Robin Hood? The question is *cate-*

gorically stated: Can I will that stealing become a universal law permitting everyone to steal as he so chooses? When one contemplates this question, he soon realizes his inability to will that stealing become a universal law binding on all mankind; although I may will to steal something for my own pleasurable enjoyment, I certainly cannot will that everyone be entitled to steal, for in that case others will rob me of my prized possessions – that I could never permit. Since I cannot will that stealing become a universal law to which everyone is entitled, then I personally cannot steal either. Note the similarity of this principle to the Golden Rule ("Do unto others as you would that they should do to you"); Kant believed that his categorical imperative was the philosophical expression of the Golden Rule.

The moral dictate of the categorical imperative forbids lying, breaking of promises, stealing, etc. under any and all circumstances. By simply invoking the categorical imperative, one can readily determine the morality of his actions; evil acts produce contradictory or repugnant results, *e.g.*, "a man reduced to despair by a series of misfortunes feels wearied of life, but is still so far in possession of his reason that he can ask himself whether it would not be contrary to his duty to himself to take his own life. Now he inquires whether the maxim of his action could become a universal law of nature. His maxim is: From self-love, I adopt it as a principle to shorten my life when its longer duration is likely to bring more evil than satisfaction. It is asked then simply whether this principle founded on self-love can become a universal law of nature? Now we see at once that a system of nature of which it should be a law to destroy life by means of the very feeling whose special nature it is to impel to the maintenance of life, would contradict itself, and therefore could not exist as a system of nature; hence that maxim cannot possibly exist as a universal law of nature, and consequently would be wholly inconsistent with the supreme principle of all duty."[1] In other words, if suicide became a universal law of nature, then all life would perish, hence it is a self-defeating or contradictory law.

On the other hand, moral actions do not result in repugnant and self-contradictory consequences as do immoral ones, *e.g.*, when the maxim of justice is subjected to the categorical imperative, the results prove coherent and feasible: Can I will that everyone be just? The answer is definitely and emphatically, *yes;* but this is never the case regarding immorality. For example: "When I think myself in want of money, I will borrow money and promise to repay it, although I know that I never can do so. Now this principle of self-love or of one's

[1] Unless otherwise noted, quotations in the remainder of this section are from Thomas Kingsmill Abbott's translation of *Metaphysics of Morals* (1883).

own advantage may perhaps be consistent with my whole future welfare; but the question now is, Is it right? I change then the suggestion of self-love into a universal law, and state the question thus: How would it be if my maxim were a universal law? Then I see at once that it could never hold as a universal law of nature, but would necessarily contradict itself. For supposing it to be a universal law that everyone when he thinks himself in a difficulty should be able to promise whatever he pleases, with the purpose of not keeping his promise, the promise itself would become impossible, as well as the end that one might have in view in it, since no one would consider that anything was promised to him, but would ridicule all such statements as vain pretences." Note that immoral actions also prove selfish, but this does not hold true of moral ones.

Actually, the Kantian ethic is not as austere as one would normally suppose, as is evidenced by the following illustration: If a man's children were hungry and starving, would it be permissible to steal food if that were the only possible way in which it could be obtained; for example, would it be moral to break into a huge apple orchard and steal some apples for one's hungry children? The categorical imperative would render an unequivocal, *No;* but assume that the father did take the apples to prevent his children from starving, would he have committed an immoral act? Kant's answer would be negative, because this man was not acting out of a *free* will, but was coerced to do so out of fear. It is analogous to the manner in which society regards the behavior of people on a sinking ship, who through panic and frenzy crush and kill each other while madly seeking to save their own lives. Their behavior would be classified as temporary insanity; consequently they would not be held responsible for their actions, but treated in similar manner as our society regards the insane. To be sure, the insane person is institutionalized, but if panic were not a temporary form of behavior in a person, he too, would be placed in an institution where he could not injure others.

The explanation given above holds true for all related instances, such as the example of the youth cited earlier; he probably would break his promise to his father and lie about the truth and gravity of his father's physical condition to prevent shock and its fatal consequences, yet his behavior would not be adjudged immoral, nor would it be judged moral, but *a*moral on the grounds that the youth was coerced into lying. Technically, he had no choice; his will was not free; coercive acts, whether prompted out of fear or any other emotion, lie outside the domain of morality, hence are morally neutral, that is, they are not questions of morality but questions of animal, instinctive, or some other form of nonmoral behavior.

Autonomy of Will.

Moral and immoral actions must stem from an 'autonomous will,' otherwise they are nonmoral and must be regarded as any other nonmoral act, *e.g.*, if one is faced with the choice of picking up a New York *Times* or a *Herald Tribune* from a library newsrack to read, his action could hardly be designated as having any moral consequence; it is simply not a moral issue regardless of the choice made. Many actions are of a nonmoral nature; actually very few have any moral significance, but, in any case, only those which are autonomous have any claim whatever to be considered a moral issue.

An autonomous will is one which is free, self-ruled, self-governed, self-legislated; obviously a will which is coerced by another, such as a desperado who commands one to do his bidding at the point of a gun, is not autonomous, nor is one free when forced by fear or any other factor extraneous to the will, as was true in the above instances of the youth and his ill father, also the father who was driven to steal for the sake of his family's welfare. These constitute cases of *non*morality, *a*morality, or *un*morality, but not *im*morality; cases of nonmorality are heteronomous, not autonomous; they involve forces extraneous to the will. "Now so long as man is thought to be merely subject to law, no matter what the law may be, he must be regarded as stimulated or constrained to obey the law from interest of some kind; for as the law does not proceed from *his own* will, there must be *something external* to his will which compels him to act in conformity with it. This perfectly necessary conclusion frustrated every attempt to find a supreme principle of duty. Duty was never established, but merely the necessity of acting from some form of interest, private or public. The imperative was therefore necessarily always conditioned, and could not possibly have the force of a moral command. The supreme principle of morality I shall therefore call the principle of the *autonomy* of the will, to distinguish it from all other principles, which I call principles of *heteronomy*." [1]

A person's summons to be moral does not imply that he will necessarily find any personal material gain for himself; in other words, it is morally irrelevant to inquire: What good will it do me to be moral? What will I gain out of it? The answer is: One is moral for the sake of morality. One is not moral for external reasons such as, 'I

[1] Translation by John Watson.

will be rewarded with a life of eternal bliss in heaven.' Anyone motivated to do what he deems moral out of fear that if he refrains, then he will be met with eternal damnation in hell fire (and if moral then God will reward him handsomely) is not an autonomous being, *i.e.*, he is not a moral agent; accordingly, no moral credit can accrue to him. In other words, when he is so motivated, then he cannot be held morally responsible, but must be classified with the insane, those motivated out of panic or other coercive impulses; such a person's actions are not prompted from a free will, but heteronomously determined.

Every person by virtue of his being human is autonomous, that is, has a free will, and no power on earth or in heaven can force one to will other than he chooses for himself, *e.g.*, a father may be able to force his young child to eat his spinach by holding a stick over him as a threat that if the child does not, then he will be severely punished, but the father cannot make the child *will* to eat — this must be done of the child's own accord. Rational persuasion is the only possible technique whereby another will choose to do one's bidding willingly, but rational persuasion is, after all, a person seeing for himself what is good and willing it for himself autonomously.

Human Dignity.

Since human beings are endowed with an autonomous will and are evaluators, they possess dignity, *i.e.*, infinite intrinsic value; consequently, persons are members of a kingdom of ends. "In the kingdom of ends everything has either Value or Dignity. Whatever has a value can be replaced by something else which is *equivalent;* whatever, on the other hand, is above all value, and therefore admits of no equivalent, has a dignity. Whatever has reference to the general inclinations and wants of mankind has a *market value;* whatever, without presupposing a want, corresponds to a certain taste, that is to a satisfaction in the mere purposeless play of our faculties, has a *fancy value;* but that which constitutes the condition under which alone anything can be an end in itself, this has not merely a relative worth, *i.e.*, value, but an intrinsic worth, that is, *dignity. . . . Autonomy* then is the basis of the dignity of human and of every rational nature."

The Kingdom of Ends.

Since persons possess dignity, that is, are of infinite intrinsic worth, they must be treated as an end in themselves, and never as means only, to serve the selfish ends of another individual. As members of a kingdom of ends, a person possesses more than mere utilitarian value; he is endowed with value intrinsically, regardless of whether he can be put to any practical use. "The moral law is *holy* (inviolable). Man is indeed unholy enough, but he must regard *humanity* in his own person as holy. In all creation everything one chooses, and over which one has any power, may be used *merely as means;* man alone, and with him every rational creature, is an *end in himself.*"[1] Man, as autonomous, as evaluator, and as formulator of the moral law, gains access to the Kingdom of Ends. "A rational being belongs as a *member* to the kingdom of ends when although giving universal laws in it he is also himself subject to these laws. He belongs to it *as sovereign,* when while giving laws he is not subject to the will of any other . . . The practical necessity of acting on this principle, *i.e.*, duty does not rest at all on feelings, impulses, or inclinations, but solely on the relation of rational beings to one another, a relation in which the will of a rational being must always be regarded as *legislative,* since otherwise it would not be conceived as *an end in itself.* Reason then refers every maxim of the will, regarding it as legislating universally, to every other will and also to every action towards oneself; and this not on account of any other practical motive or any future advantage, but from the idea of the *dignity* of a rational being, obeying no law but that which he himself also gives."

Reverence for Duty.

The essence of Kantian ethical theory is reverence for the moral law, respect for the categorical imperative. "*Morality* then is the relation of actions to the autonomy of the will, that is, to the potential universal legislation by its maxims. An action that is consistent with the autonomy of the will is *permitted;* one that does not agree therewith is *forbidden.* A will whose maxims necessarily coincide with the laws of autonomy is a *holy* will, good absolutely. The dependence of a will not absolutely good on the principle of autonomy (moral necessitation) is obligation. This then cannot be applied to a holy being. The objective necessity of actions from obligation is called *duty . . . Duty is the necessity of acting from respect for the law.*" Respect for the moral law is to will it even though one's actual behavior should be contrary to it, *e.g.*, even if one should succumb to lying, he nevertheless ought not *will* to do so.

I Ought Implies I Can.

It is worth noting that in Kantian theory a person never obligates himself to do that which is not within his own power; consequently, when a person says: 'I will,' the implication is 'I can.' For example, a

[1] Immanuel Kant, *Critique of Practical Reason* (1788), tr. Thomas Kingsmill Abbott (1898).

person never becomes self-indebted to shake hands daily with every person in the world for the simple reason that it is an impossibility, but a person may indebt himself by saying, 'I ought to improve myself.' "We ought to become better men resounds with undiminished force in our soul; consequently, we must be able to do so."[1] "The moral 'ought' then is one's own necessary 'I will.'"

Conclusion.

Only a perfectionist would adhere to the ethics of Kant, yet every rational being cannot help but feel in a certain sense that he is obliged or morally implicated to a certain extent to the principles laid down by Kant. One may criticize and even rebel against the enormous demands of this code, yet a person may never feel completely relieved of this Kantian moral imperative. It is therefore not surprising that this ethical system has so deeply penetrated into Western, and particularly American, civilization.

[1] Kant, *Philosophical Theory of Religion.*

VII

JEREMY BENTHAM:

Utilitarianism

Utilitarianism.

Not long after the philosophy of Bentham made its appearance, it acquired the unenviable appellation, 'the pig philosophy,' because of its sole emphasis on the physical or sensual pleasures while completely ignoring the higher pleasures and joys, such as those of the mind or spirit. Bentham's ethical theory, termed *Utilitarianism,* was defined as that philosophy which advocates the pursuit of pleasure as the chief good and the avoidance of pain as the only evil. He discusses this philosophy and its definition succinctly in his *Introduction to the Principles of Morals and Legislation:* [1] "By the principle of utility is meant that principle which approves or disapproves of every action whatsoever, according to the tendency which it appears to have to augment or diminish the happiness of the party whose interest is in question; or, what is the same thing, to promote or to oppose that happiness . . . By utility is meant that property in any object, whereby it tends to produce benefit, advantage, pleasure, good, or happiness . . . to prevent the happening of mischief, pain, evil, or unhappiness to the party whose interest is considered."

Bentham is what is termed a *Psychological Hedonist,* viz., one who holds that man, by human nature, is constructed in such a manner that he is incapable of doing other than to seek pleasure and avoid pain. One's constitution makes it unnatural for a man to do otherwise, either consciously or unconsciously. "Nature has placed mankind under the governance of two sovereign masters, *pain* and *pleasure.* It is for them alone to point out what we *ought to do, as well as* to determine what we shall do . . . They govern us in all we do, in all we say, in all we think; every effort we can make to throw off our subjection, will serve but to demonstrate and confirm it. In words a man may pretend to abjure their empire: but in reality he will remain subject to it all the while." The

[1] Quotations in this section are from Bentham's *Introduction to the Principles of Morals and Legislation.*

Psychological Hedonist reduces every motive in every man to pleasure; altruistic motives do not and cannot exist. To argue that a mother sacrifices out of love for her children would be explained by the Psychological Hedonist as selfishness, for he would claim that if the mother did not undergo her sacrificial actions, then she would be miserable; consequently, in the interests of happiness or pleasure, she subjects herself to sacrifices. The story is told of Abraham Lincoln which puts him in the light or camp of the Psychological Hedonist: Once he ordered his carriage stopped because he saw a pig caught in the roadside mire struggling to free itself from suffocation. Lincoln, in all of his finery, soiled his clothes in the mud while attempting to free the young animal. When he returned to his carriage, the driver's flattering commendation of this action moved Lincoln to reply that he was not altruistically motivated, but selfishly, since if he abandoned the pig and left it stranded, the thought of it would give him no peace of mind. Hence a noble action turns out to be ignobly motivated.

Those whose philosophy is not sympathetic with Psychological Hedonism take isue with the foregoing Hedonistic explanation, contending that it is invalid on the basis that a mother and Lincoln could, if they so desired, alter their personalities enabling them to disregard the plight of others (particularly animals) and go their selfish ways. A psychologist, for example, could, through psychotherapy, alter the personality of Lincoln to enable him to pass by the pig in its plight and gaze upon its misery with laughter instead of pity as some persons do: they enjoy boxing matches and are thrilled, particularly when one of the contenders is bruised, bleeding, or hurt. One would have to evaluate Lincoln's situation as a noble and moral one motivated not out of selfishness, but out of an understanding that what he did was the right act; consequently, he saw to it that his personality development was constructed along lines which would make him sensitive to another's needs, even though the creature was that of a lowly animal. A person may, by intelligent choice, decide what is morally praiseworthy and bend his efforts to achieving that end so that his personality responds to what he deems right and proper: Aristotle claimed that this could be done through the use of intelligence in deciding the right and through the instrument of habit in effectually imbedding it deep into the personality.

Bentham's ethical philosophy is also regarded as a form of *Egoistic Hedonism, i.e.,* the belief that one ought to be primarily or solely concerned about his own pleasures to the deprivation of others; in fact, one is entitled to enjoy pleasures at the expense of pain to others. This philosophy would permit the sadist to hurt and torture others because in so doing he is able to derive a measure of pleasure for himself.

Bentham argues that pleasure, providing it is physical or sensual, is good regardless of its form or consequences. He maintains that it is the only good which is indisputable, whereas any other so-called good is subject to question, *i.e.,* debate and argument. However, when one is enjoying a physical or sensual pleasure, whether it consists of dining at a sumptuous dinner or indulging in sex with his (married or unmarried) beloved, he must admit that it is good, *i.e.,* he likes it. To be sure, one may dispute whether or not he is morally entitled to the food or sex, but he cannot state that he does not like it, that is, it is not good. In any other ethical theory this axiomatic proof does not maintain, *e.g.,* to claim that stealing is wrong is at times, and in certain cultures, debatable: If someone were to steal ten dollars from your purse, do you have a right, if opportunity presents itself, to steal it back? This is a debatable issue; some persons would argue on the *contra* side while others would take the *pro* position. Although one may say it is immoral to indulge in a given pleasure, he can never experience the pleasure as bad.

Bentham further pursues his defence of Hedonism, *i.e.,* the philosophy of an individual whose prime goal is the enjoyment of pleasure, by charging that God would want his creatures to enjoy pleasure on the grounds that God is good and created pleasure for mankind's enjoyment. Since God created man a pleasure seeking being, it follows that *"there is no such thing as any sort of motive that is in itself a bad one"* since all motivation is the pusuit of pleasure (Psychological Hedonism).

It should be apparent why this school of thought is termed 'the pig philosophy' and why it drifted into the figurative mire. When a person emphasizes sensual pleasure as the only good to the complete exclusion of all other values, it is not too long before his life is reduced to the point of brute existence without proper (or for that matter, any) appreciation for the finer and cultural values of life, such as music, art, religion, science, etc. This was precisely the outcome of the Benthamites; they were reduced to such a low level of human existence that the word 'Benthamite' became a term of opprobrium — a philosophy fit only for pigs.

The Four Sanctions.

Bentham debated that one need not become alarmed concerning the possibility of pleasures getting out of hand and being exercised to excess since there exist four sanctions which are capable of keeping an individual within circumspect bounds of propriety wherever pleasures are concerned. The four sanctions are: (1) the physical, (2) the political, (3) the moral or popular, (4) the religious.

The *physical sanction* immediately and automatically comes into operation whenever an individual attempts to overindulge himself in pleasure beyond what is fitting. If one fails to keep his portion of pleasure temperate, the physical sanction reduces the pleasure into a displeasure or even a painful experience. *E.g.*, many persons have experienced outdoor enjoyment such as swimming or some other physical sport which is capable of stimulating the appetite to such an extent that one hungers for any food whatever, with zest and relish. Perhaps you have had the experience on such an occasion of purchasing a frankfurter on a roll at a nearby lunch stand with the positive conviction that it is the tastiest frankfurter that you ever ate, and wondering why they don't appear to taste as good when made at home. You will also recall that the second frankfurter never has quite the succulence or zestfulness as the first, but what is even more revealing is the fact that the third and fourth leave much to be desired; in fact, by then one finds himself discarding some of the roll, if not all of it. What is transpiring is that satisfaction is setting in the body and should one exceed these bounds and ignore the warning by eating more, he encounters an uncomfortable and unpleasant sense of satiation. Should one press the matter still further by gourging himself with more frankfurters, he can exceed the bounds of satiation and experience a disgusting sense of nausea or illness.

In this manner, the physical sanction is capable of restricting an individual's pleasures by keeping them within limit. What has been said of the experience of foods holds true of other sensual pleasures, whether they be sex, sleep, drink, etc. The psychologist claims that adaptation sets in as one's sensitivities subside.

The second or *political sanction* consists of the laws of the state which prohibit a person from carrying his pursuit of pleasure to excess, *e.g.*, if one seizes a pleasure to which he is not entitled, then he will find that he has transgressed one of the state's statutes and will have to pay the penalty for his misbehavior; in other words, the community enacts laws restricting the excessive or undesirable indulgence in pleasure. However, it must be quite evident to the reader that this is not a legitimate sanction since if pleasures are good, *i.e.*, moral, then any community which believed in Hedonism would enact laws conducive to the pursuit and enhancement of pleasure, not laws prohibiting its free access and expression.

The third sanction, which is called the *moral* or *popular*, is nearer to what in contemporary American society would be designated 'public opinion.' This sanction restricts a person within proper hedonic bounds by strictures created by the fear of what other people will say or think. It must be admitted that public opinion has a tenacious hold on a person, much more so than he realizes or is willing to concede. For example, there are some persons who would commit murder but refrain for one decisive inhibition, not because they fear the punishment meted for this crime including the death penalty, but because they fear what people will think and say of them. They cannot face their friends, relatives, associates, neighbors, etc. under such conditions, consequently they refrain from such acts. To illustrate the firm hold which public opinion has on an individual, consider the many persons who would prefer breaking some less weightier matter of the law than going contrary to public opinion; perhaps the majority of people would elect to break a law, such as overtime parking which is listed as a criminal offence, rather than wear a swim suit to their place of employment, to a downtown department store, or to school, even if this is not illegal or immoral, though it does create adverse public opinion. People are constantly concerned with what others think of them as is evidenced by a person who must make a public address; at home, during the rehearsal period in the privacy of his room, he may deliver an outstanding speech, but in a public hall filled with people, his thoughts of what his audience thinks of him prove most distracting and unnerving.

Nevertheless, as any critic of Bentham's philosophy will readily detect, this is not a valid sanction, since any community which embraced the principles of this Utilitarian ethic would unquestionably promote public opinion to encourage this brand of Hedonism.

The fourth and final sanction, termed the *religious,* comprises restrictions imposed by God regarding the improper exercise of pleasure, which if transgressed, issue in some form of retribution either in this life or the next. In other words, a person will remain within the confines of propriety regarding pleasure because he fears that if he sins in this respect, then he will suffer for it at the hands of God, either by some form of earthly punishment or that which is found in hell's perdition.

Once again, the critic finds this issue debatable as well by declaring that if pleasure is good, then why does God not condone it? Apparently pleasure *per se* is not moral, only that to which one is rightfully entitled.

Bentham illustrates all four sanctions in operation through a single example: "A man's goods, or his person, are consumed by fire. If this happened to him by what is called an accident, it was a calamity; if by reason of his own imprudence, (for instance, from his neglecting to put his candle out) it may be styled a punishment of the physical sanction; if it happened to him by the sentence of the political magistrate, a punishment belonging to the political sanction; that is, what is commonly called a punishment, if for want of any assistance which his *neighbor* withheld from him out of some dislike to his *moral* character, a punishment of the *moral* sanction; if by an immediate act of *God's* displeasure, manifested on account of some sin committed by him or through any distraction of mind, occasioned by the dread of such displeasure, a punishment of the *religious* sanction."

The Hedonistic Calculus.

Everyone needs some criterion of morality, *i.e.,* some rule which enables him to determine whether or not the act which he is about to commit is moral. The Kantian moral criterion is the 'categorical imperative;' for Aristotle it is moderation, viz., to do the right thing, to the right person, at the right time, to the right extent, and for the right purpose. Bentham's rule for right action is his 'hedonisic calculus,' a pleasure measuring device which determines which act out of two or more is the most pleasurable. The calculus is made up of seven units, each of which determines in some degree the quantitative value of a pleasure; they are: *intensity, duration, certainty, propinquity, fecundity, purity, extent.* Unless a pleasure measures up to the calculus' demands, it is defective.

1. *Intensity.* Whenever one is faced with two pleasures, each of which is equal to the other in every respect except one, viz., intensity; then one is obliged to pursue the pleasure which is higher in intensity. *E.g.,* if going to a cocktail party is more exciting than attending a barn dance, then one is morally obligated to forego the dance, provided being at both is out of the question.

2. *Duration. Ceteris paribus* (other factors being equal), if one is faced with the choice of only one of two pleasures, differing only in respect to duration, *i.e.,* one lasts longer than the other, then it is incumbent upon the individual to select the pleasure which does not terminate as early. To illustrate: if one enjoys a banquet and ballroom dancing equally well, then it would be preferable for him to select dancing inasmuch as dancing consumes a greater portion of time.

3. *Certainty.* This point of the calculus urges that one elect that course of action which he is certain will issue in pleasure in preference to one which is doubtful. Again, as is true for every point of the calculus, the assumption is that both pleasures cannot be had, and the choice of one eliminates the possibility of partaking the other. This point of the calculus is exemplified by the popular saying: "A bird in the hand is worth two in the bush." This rule can be exercised by the person who hopes to be invited to two parties which will be held in different places concurrently; although the invitation received first is not to the preferred party, it is wiser to accept than take the chance of not being able to attend either (assuming, of course, that he must accept or decline before knowing whether the second invitation will be forthcoming).

4. *Propinquity.* The propinquity or remoteness rule of the calculus determines the immediacy of the pleasure; those which have the promise of being enjoyed immediately or in the near future are preferable to those which are remote in time and place. For example, if one's employer allows a vacation to be taken at any time during the calendar year, then the appropriate choice to make is to enjoy the vacation forthwith in preference to one of a future date; the reason being that later, one may not be alive to enjoy it, or may be employed elsewhere.

5. *Fecundity.* The fruitfulness or fecundity of the pleasure, *i.e.*, its potential of providing or fructifying into still further pleasures is a consideration of the calculus. Some pleasures terminate with a single instance, while others recur regularly or intermittently; the preferable pleasure is the one which has possibilities of repetition. All things being equal, it is better to go to the country-club dinner with a neighbor than to dine with an out-of-town acquaintance, provided one cannot attend both and runs the risk of offending the individual whose invitation was declined. The prospects of subsequent invitations are much better from the person living in the vicinity.

6. *Purity.* "Its *purity,* or the chance it has of *not* being followed by sensations of the opposite kind: that is, pains, if it be a pleasure: pleasures, if it be a pain." Not all pleasures are equally pure; some are adulterated with pain, boredom, etc. while others eventuate in pain. Fried clams and roast chicken may be enjoyed equally well, but if the fried clams terminate in indigestion then it is wiser to select the chicken dinner.

7. *Extent.* "Its *extent;* that is, the number of persons to whom it extends; or (in other words) who are affected by it." This rule requires one to share his pleasures provided his own are not thereby diminished. One may enjoy the sport of fishing alone, but a friend or neighbor of his may enjoy it only in the company of others; this rule obliges one to permit his friend to accompany him to share in this pleasure, but if the intrusion of his friend detracts from his enjoyment then he would not be required to extend the invitation.

This final point of the calculus is hardly compatible with the prior six which are distinctly egoistic and completely inconsiderate of any person except oneself. It apparently appeared incongruous to Bentham as well, since he isolates it from the other six by adding it in the form of an appendix. Could the calculus have troubled Bentham's conscience to the extent that he was compelled to add this final one as an addendum?

Bentham, or perhaps a devotee of his, devised some mnemonic lines, that is, a verse to aid the memory in retaining the entire moral philosophy of Utiltarianism in a 'nutshell.' Bentham included it in the revised version of his *Introduction to the Principles of Morals and Legislation* so as to diminish the chances of his philosophy being forgotten:

> *Intense, long, certain, speedy, fruitful, pure* –
> Such marks in *pleasures* and in *pains* endure.
> Such pleasures seek, if *private* be thy end:
> If it be *public,* wide let them *extend.*
> Such *pains* avoid, whichever be thy view:
> If pains *must* come, let them *extend* to few.

VIII

JOHN STUART MILL:

Utilitarianism

Qualitative Hedonism.

John Stuart Mill sought to champion the cause of Bentham's Utilitarianism and defend it against the onslaught of its opponents. He attempted to prove that Kant was in error regarding his ethics of the categorical imperative, but that Bentham, promoting the cause of pleasure, had uncovered the only defensible truth pertaining to morality.

In Mill, Bentham found a formidable and staunch defender, owing to his keen intellect which has been estimated by some psychologists at approximately two hundred. He was taught Greek at the age of three and not long thereafter was reading Plato in the original language. The book in which his ethical ideas are developed is *Utilitarianism.* [1]

Mill's brilliant analytical mind saw with accurate and penetrating perception the fundamental problem which lay at the basis of Bentham's Hedonism, namely, Is it better to be a human being miserable than a pig satisfied? If the moral issue is predominantly and exclusively one of quantitative Hedonism, *i.e.*, if all pleasure is exclusively physical or sensual, then it is inconsequential who the being is which is experiencing the sensation of pleasure; it matters not whether it be an animal, such as a pig, or a person. If the *summum bonum* is pleasure and solely pleasure of the sensual or physical kind, then it nevertheless remains good, and the greatest good, regardless of whether it is experienced by man or beast.

Consequently, to raise the question: "Is it better to be a pig satisfied or a Socrates dissatisfied?" would unquestionably call for only one answer. The creature whose pleasures are satisfied, since it matters little who enjoys the pleasures, provided he or it is in a state of having his pleasures felt or sensed.

Mill, fully cognizant and satisfied that this question lay at the root of the matter, raised it and proceeded to give it an affirmative answer, that is, he was prepared to confess that he would rather be a pig

[1] Quotations in this section are exclusively from this book.

satisfied than Socrates (a human being) dissatisfied; accordingly, he set out to write a book in defence of Bentham's position, only to encounter disarming complications.

Note was made of Mill's brilliance, but to it should be coupled the fact that he was one of the most honest minds in history, possessing an intellectual integrity which was incorruptible. He underwent a peculiar and singular experience part way through his classic treatise: when the time arrived for him to cast his decision in favor of choosing the pleasures of the pig and exchanging places with it, he found himself incapable of jotting it down on his manuscript for the pen, as it were, would not write the words: "I would rather be a pig."

This experience raised a serious question: Why could he not bring himself to state that he would rather be a pig satisfied than a man dissatisfied, if physical or quantitative pleasure were the sole and reigning greatest good? Unquestionably, it meant that physical pleasure is not the sole good nor the greatest good, but there are other goods possessing far greater value than these, viz., the fact of merely being human. In other words, there is a value in just being human which far exceeds any physical pleasure which the body affords; so valuable is it to be accounted a human being that it is preferable to man, even though miserable, so wretched that he could wish for death, than to be a brute animal.

This conclusion opened a new area of goods or values, viz., *qualitative* ones, in contradistinction to quantitative (sensual) ones. It signified that there existed goods so tremendous in value, differing in kind, and capable of rendering even the highest magnitudinal quantities of sensual pleasure of little or negligible account. "If I am asked what I mean by a difference of quality in pleasures, or what makes one pleasure more valuable than another, merely as a pleasure, except its being greater in amount, there is but one possible answer. Of two pleasures, if there be one which all or almost all who have experience of both give a decided preference, irrespective of any feeling of moral obligation to prefer it, that is the more desirable pleasure. If one of the two is, by those who are competently acquainted with both, placed so far above the other that they prefer it, even though knowing it to be attended with a greater amount of discontent, and would not resign it for any quantity of the other pleasure which their nature is capable of, we are justified in ascribing to the preferred enjoyment a superiority in quality, so far outweighing quantity as to render it, in comparison, of small account."

One may in reference to this point raise the question: Why should this be so? Perhaps the happy pig would not care to exchange places with a miserable human being, distressed by his unfortunate lot. The answer is: It may be true that the pig would not exchange places with a man, but the pig is in no position to render an intelligent judgment concerning the relative values of the matter, whereas the human being is. The human being knows what it is like to have the sensual appetites of the pig, whether it be the enjoyment of eating food, the basking in the sun free from anxiety, or the sexual cravings conveniently satisfied, but the pig will never comprehend the values of being human (it will never know what it is like), hence is not in a position to pass judgment. The same holds true between the intelligent being and the moron or idiot: The subnormal human being may fancy that he is happier and better off with his lot than a member of the intelligentsia is with his, *i.e.*, the moron may think that he is happier, and accordingly would not *choose* to exchange places with the intelligent or enlightened person. One may even add that the moron, although happier than the intelligent individual, is nevertheless, in the less enviable position in the estimation of the intelligent person. Which of the two is correct? The enlightened person, because he knows what it is like to be a would not choose to exchange places with the intelligent or enlightened Consider the matter for yourself: A medical scientist knows what it is like to be ignorant – he once was – or probably is presently experiencing areas of his knowledge which are defective due to ignorance, but the moron will never be able to appreciate fully the values of being an enlightened person as the medical scientist is. There are times, for example, when a person is ill, that he begins to realize to a significant extent, any modicum of which will do, what the values are of being an intelligent or medically enlightened person, and such a person can understand that his own ignorant lot is deficient and not preferable to that of the enlightened person.

Listen to Mill debate the issue for himself: "Now it is an unquestionable fact that those who are equally acquainted with, and equally capable of appreciating and enjoying both, do give a most marked preference to the manner of existence which employs their higher faculties. Few human creatures would consent to be changed into any of the lower animals, for a promise of the fullest allowance of a beast's pleasures; no intelligent human being would consent to be a fool, no instructed person would be an ignoramus, no person of feeling and conscience would be selfish and base, even though they should be persuaded that the fool, the dunce, or the rascal is better satisfied with his lot than they are with theirs. If they fancy that they would, it is only in cases of unhappiness so extreme, that to escape from it they would exchange their lot for almost any other, however undesirable in their own eyes. A being of higher faculties requires more to make him happy, is capable of more acute suffering, and is certainly accessible to it at more points, than one of an inferior type; but in spite of these liabilities, he can never really wish to sink into what he feels to be a lower grade of existence."

The issue is reducible to this: It is true that animals and vegetables do not experience human misery, *e.g.*, the cabbage does not worry, have problems, frettings, anxieties, doubts, etc., it merely basks in the sun all day long, but the pertinent and searching question is: "Who wants to be a cabbage?" The cost of being human is at times incredibly expensive, almost too dear to afford, but the steadfast fact remains: It is better (more valuable) to be a human being (even though miserably unhappy) than to be an animal with its full complement of physical pleasures. To object to this is to object to one's birthright, one's humanity, or as Mill put it, human DIGNITY.

"It is indisputable that the being whose capacities of enjoyment are low, has the greatest chance of having them fully satisfied; and a highly endowed being will always feel that any happiness which he can look for as the world is constituted, is imperfect. But he can learn to bear its imperfections, if they are at all bearable; and they will not make him envy the being who is indeed unconscious of the imperfections, but only because he feels not at all the good which those imperfections qualify. It is better to be a human being dissatisfied than a pig satisfied; better to be a Socrates dissatisfied than a fool satisfied. And if the fool, or the pig, is of a different opinion, it is because they only know their own side of the question. The other party to the comparison knows both sides."

Mill speaks advisedly when he maintains that it is better to be a miserable wretch of humanity than the happiest pig alive, for he experienced in youth a nervous breakdown and came close to committing suicide, but fortunately he came through safely and lived to be 67 years of age. It is better to be a man so wretched that one wishes that he would live no longer (and even take his life) than to be a pig euphorically content.

"Everybody to Count for One, Nobody for More than One."

Mill terms this statement Bentham's dictum, but it remains more peculiarly Mill's than Bentham's. The dictum is the basis of a democracy: Each person is as important as any other; whether he be prince or pauper, the president of the United States or an unfortunate individual in the bread line. Each person's life is as dear to himself as anyone else's is to that individual; each person's happiness is just as important to that person, as any other person's is to himself. American criminal law also recognizes this fact by requiring that a life be paid for a life taken. If a person murders another individual, then he must stand trial and pay for it with his own life, even if the murdered victim is a lowly moron or an infant.

Mill contends that this principle is the very quintescence of Utilitarianism: "It is involved in the very meaning of utility, or the greatest happiness principle. That principle is a mere form of words without rational signification, unless one person's happiness, supposed equal in degree (with the proper allowance made for kind), is counted for exactly as much as another's. Those conditions being supplied, Bentham's dictum, 'everybody to count for one, nobody for more than one,' might be written under the principle of utility as an explanatory commentary. The equal claim of everybody to happiness in the estimation of the moralist and of the legislator, involves an equal claim to all the means of happiness."

"The Greatest Good for the Greatest Number."

This is a second principle, inherent in Democracies, which is prominent in the philosophy of Mill. He maintained that one should be concerned with the greatest good possible, and to him it was obvious that the greatest good lay with the greatest number. One interpretation of this principle is: If I can make another three times as happy, then it is my duty to do so despite the self-sacrifice it entails, that is, provided all factors are equal, and the happiness of other individuals is sufficiently great to warrant the sacrifice.

The greatest happiness of the greatest number could prove a devastatingly dangerous principle, depending upon its interpretation; if it is taken at face value, then it would be valid for a scientist to inflict cancer upon an individual (without the person's consent) in the hope of deriving a cure which will save the majority from this painful disease; furthermore, the cruelties which Hitler's scientists inflicted upon the minority Jews and others would be morally justifiable since they allegedly benefited the majority.

Jean Jacques Rousseau noted that this principle could prove selfish and base in actual practice in a Democracy; he spoke of a 'general will' which he distinguished from the 'will of all.' The 'will of all' is selfish and should not prevail in a Democracy; it consists merely of tallying votes of selfish individuals who cast votes which favored their own private interests without consideration for the rights or needs of the minority, whereas the 'general will,' which ought to dominate in a democratic State, is concerned with the good of the people in general, the needs of humanity—not necessarily what pleases the majority.

IX

ARTHUR SCHOPENHAUER:

Pessimism

Schopenhauer's Background.

Arthur Schopenhauer is the world's foremost systematic Pessimist; he condemns life as a sin: "For the greatest crime of man is that he ever was born," and "life must be some kind of mistake." The history of philosophy has seen relatively few Pessimists, in fact, there have been conspicuously few pessimistic thinkers anywhere, but none has been as systematic and as cogent as Schopenhauer. Some psychologists explain his Pessimism as a consequence of having a timid father who is reported to have committed suicide, but primarily it is because of his mother who consistently expressed ruthlessness in her relationship with him. The story is told of her casting Arthur down a flight of stairs because he intruded when a lover paid a call on her; another is that of his being forced to resign his instructorship at the University of Heidelberg because he scheduled his classes at the same hour the outstanding and popular Hegel, whom he detested out of a spirit of professional jealously, had scheduled his own; Schopenhauer did this in the belief that any student who was sufficiently fortunate to be able to study under him would never consider giving Hegel a second thought, but as it happened, Hegel's popularity won out, and Schopenhauer, without a single student registered for his classes, was forced to resign. His monumental work: *The World as Will and Idea* never sold well, leading Schopenhauer to believe that it was entirely due to a conspiracy led by Hegel and the other 'philosophers by trade' as he derogatorily designated philosophers who were university professors, but the lack of sales was attributable to the era of famine in which he and his generation were caught. People who are hungry and looking for food cannot afford the luxury of books and the things which pertain to the spirit, much less books promoting Pessimism, since they are overburdened with their own dismal life, but approximately two years before his death (he lived to be seventy-two), his books became best-sellers and Schopenhauer became a joyful creature. One could facetiously add, perhaps it is just as well that he did die, otherwise he may have, under such circumstances, become an Optimist and ruined his established philosophical position as the world's leading Pessimist. Schopenhauer harbored a very low opinion of women, and writes most disparagingly about them, which is obviously due to the fact that unlike most, he had an unloving, unsympathetic, and unkindly mother. Consequently his philosophical attitude toward women and life in general has been excessively dampened by his childhood experiences in the home.

The Ethics of Pessimism.

"All *willing* arises from want, therefore from deficiency, and therefore from suffering. The satisfaction of a wish ends it; yet for one wish that is satisfied there remain at least ten which are denied. Further, the desire lasts long, the demands are infinite; the satisfaction is short and scantily measured out. But even the final satisfaction is itself only apparent; every satisfied wish at once makes room for a new one; both are illusions; the one is known to be so, the other not yet. No attained object of desire can give lasting satisfaction, but merely a fleeting gratification; it is like the alms thrown to a beggar, that keeps him alive today that his misery may be prolonged till the morrow. Therefore, so long as our consciousness is filled by our will, so long as we are given up to the throng of desires with their constant hopes and fears, so long as we are the subject of willing, we can never have lasting happiness nor peace. It is essentially all the same whether we pursue or flee, fear injury or seek enjoyment; the care for the constant demands of the will, in whatever form it may be, continually occupies and sways the consciousness; but without peace no true well-being is possible." [1]

Man is a victim of a relentless *will* which makes living intolerable and dying an equally repugnant prospect; although man has the wish to end it all, he is driven to endure it with all of its concomitant suffering in abject slavery. Desire, passion, want, will, etc. keep man enslaved to a fate from which there is no escape or relief; the driving force of instinct is at bottom responsible for it all. Man wants life, craves it, fears death and cringes from it so immensely, because of his desire for living, that he becomes a spiritual paralytic incapable of living. The irony of life is that his needs, his wishes, his desires can never be fulfilled; a scant satisfaction of a single desire leaves but many unfulfilled cravings in its wake. Man is like a beggar to whom a pittance is thrown just to insure the prolongation of his existence to the following day that he may survive in

[1] Quotations in the section on Schopenhauer are taken from: *The World as Will and Idea* tr. by R. B. Haldane and J. Kemp (1883).

order to continue his abject misery. "Whoever is oppressed with the burden of life, whoever desires life and affirms it, but abhors its torments, and especially can no longer endure the hard lot that has fallen to himself, such a man has no deliverance to hope from death and cannot right himself by suicide . . . Suicide appears to us as a vain and therefore a foolish action" because there is an after life in which man must face the same driving forces which have made his lot wretched in this life. Death is an everpresent evil reminding one of life's miseries: "Life itself is a sea, full of rocks and whirlpools, which man avoids with the greatest care and solicitude, although he knows that even if he succeeds in getting through with all his efforts and skill, he yet by doing so comes nearer at every step to the greatest, the total, inevitable, and irremediable shipwreck, death; nay, even steers right upon it: this is the final goal of the laborious voyage, and worse for him than all the rocks from which he has escaped . . . The striving after existence is what occupies all living things and maintains them in motion." If it were not for this drive, humanity would commit universal suicide.

Nature is most careless of a single life, individual lives count for little; nature is concerned with the species only, and accordingly takes every precaution to insure its survival by potent forces such as the sex drive; in consequence thereof, man continues to procreate his kind, willy nilly, he has no choice, he is driven. "For it is not the individual, but only the species that Nature cares for, and for the preservation of which she so earnestly strives, providing for it with the utmost prodigality through the vast surplus of the seed and the great strength of the fructifying impulse. The individual, on the contrary, neither has nor can have any value for Nature, for her kingdom is infinite time and space, and in these infinite multiplicity of possible individuals."

The Philosophy of Sex and Love.

Life confronts us with a dilemma: either want or boredom, never a lasting sense of satisfaction and contentment. No wish can be conquered through an attempt to satisfy it for it leads merely to a greater desire the next time it appears, *e.g.*, one can never find sex satisfaction because its indulgence merely results in a stronger resurgence at the next appearance of the sex cycle.

The strongest driving force (will) within man is his sex drive; "man is at once impetuous and blind striving of will whose pole or focus lies in the genital organs." For sex satisfaction, a man will risk life, death, and reputation; since the sex drive is a tremendously potent force. "Certainly, however, it is also confirmed by experience . . . that that which as a rule only appears as a strong yet still controllable inclination may rise under certain circumstances to a passion which exceeds all others in vehemance, and which then sets aside all consideration, overcomes all obstacles with incredible strength and perserverence, so that for its satisfaction life is risked without hesitation, nay, if that satisfaction is still withheld, is given as the price of it . . . Still greater, however, is the number of those whom the same passion brings to the madhouse. Finally, every year can show cases of the double suicide of a pair of lovers who are opposed by outward circumstances. In such cases, however, it is inexplicable to me how those who, certain of mutual love, expect to find the supreme bliss in the enjoyment of this, do not withdraw themselves from all connections by taking the extremest steps and endure all hardships rather than give up with life a pleasure which is greater than any other they can conceive . . . All love, however ethereally it may bear itself, is rooted in the sexual impules alone."

Sex is irrational, a madness which engulfs any person sufficiently unfortunate to be caught in its folly; like a directionless tornado, it carries its victims on its tumultuous way. Read the following quotation from Schopenhauer which is but a *single* sentence regarding its unrelenting powers of destruction: "If now, keeping this in view, one considers the important part which the sexual impulse in all its degrees and nuances plays not only on the stage and in novels, but also in the real world, where, next to the love of life, it shows itself the strongest and most powerful of motives, constantly lays claim to half the powers and thoughts of the younger portion of mankind, is the ultimate goal of almost all human effort, exerts an adverse influence on the most important events, interrupts the most serious occupations every hour, sometimes embarrasses for a while even the greatest minds, does not hesitate to intrude with its trash interfering with the negotiations of statesmen and the investigations of men of learning, knows how to slip its love letters and locks of hair even into ministerial portfolios and philosophical manuscripts, and no less devises daily the most entangled and the worse actions, destroys the most valuable relationships, breaks the firmest bonds, demands the sacrifice sometimes of life or health, sometimes of wealth, rank, and happiness, nay, robs those who are otherwise honest of all conscience, makes those who have been hitherto faithful, traitors; accordingly, on the whole, appears as a malevolent demon that strives to pervert, confuse, and overthrow everything; — then one will be forced to cry, Wherefore all this noise? Wherefore the straining and storming, the anxiety and want? It is merely a question of every Hans finding his Grethe. Why should such a trifle play so important a part, and constantly introduce disturbance and confusion into the well-regulated life of man?" Schopenhauer has omitted the many neuroses and psychoses attributable to sex — the many sex assaults, sex murders, extortions due to sex, etc.

Nature is so intent on the species being reproduced, and at any cost, that she bends every effort and device toward this end; a sex drive is sufficiently potent to induce rape, to injure familial relationships, to disregard culture and propriety, even pain, punishment, disease, and death. "This is proved by forced marriages, and also by the frequent purchase of the favour of a woman, in spite of her dislike, by large presents or other sacrifices, nay, even by cases of rape. That this particular child shall be begotten is, although unknown to the parties concerned, the true end of the whole love story; the manner in which it is attained is a secondary consideration." The important factor is the reproduction of the race.

Man fancies himself to be rational, but little does he realize the many potent irrational forces in his nature which bind the reason in man and either paralyze it or force it to subserve the ends dictated by the irrational driving will as its handmaiden. For the sake of irrational impulses, man will cease to heed the dictates of reason; similar forces can also be detected in the animal. "For clearly the pains with which an insect seeks out a particular flower, or fruit, or dung, or flesh, or as in the case of the ichneumonidae, the larva of another insect, in order to deposit its eggs there only, and to attain this end shrinks neither from trouble nor danger, is thoroughly analogous to the pains with which for his sexual satisfaction a man carefully chooses a woman with definite qualities which appeal to him individually, and strives so eagerly after her that in order to attain this end he often sacrifices his own happiness in life, contrary to all reason, by foolish marriage, by love affairs which cost him wealth, honour, and life, even by crimes such as adultery or rape, all merely in order to serve the species in the most efficient way, although at the cost of the individual, in accordance with the will of nature which is everywhere sovereign."

The American society praises romance, but it is worthy of condemnation since it drives a person to love another who may be unlovable, a criminal, a degenerate — in this sense love is blind and irrational. Love is blind in still other respects; Shakespeare wrote: "I love and hate her." "Sexual love is compatible even with the extremest hatred towards its object . . . It is really no hyperbole if a lover describes the coldness of his beloved and the delight of her vanity, which feeds on his sufferings, as cruelty; for he is under the influence of an impulse which, akin to the instinct of insects, compels him, in spite of all grounds of reason, to pursue his end unconditionally, and to undervalue everything else; he cannot give it up."

It is vain to instruct an individual in the principles which are conducive to the selection of a proper mate and the cultivation of a happy marriage, for such good and rational principles are cast to the winds when the personality is overtaken by the potent and irrational sex drive. The individual seeks to marry the first person with whom he falls *madly* (this term is used advisedly) in love, and the principles which should have been used in the selection of a mate best suited to one's genes in order to effect the best possible production of offspring, and a marriage which is of lasting value and happiness, are painfully ignored.

The Philosophy of Suffering.

Schopenhauer asserts that all life is suffering; accordingly, if anyone had any choice he would not elect to be born; furthermore, if anyone had the choice, then he would not wish for any other person to be born either — offspring issue from the insurmountable forces of the sex drive which a person finds himself incapable of harnessing. Although physical misery taxes one almost beyond the point of human endurance, mental torture is capable of exceeding it even to the point of suicide; often a person's physical pains are self-inflicted in order to free the mind (or rather distract it) from being focused on mental tortures. "The causes of our pain, as of our pleasure, lie for the most part, not in the real present, but merely in abstract thoughts. It is these which are often unbearable to us — inflict torments in comparison with which all the sufferings of the animal world are very small; for even our own physical pain is not felt at all when they are present. Indeed, in the case of keen mental suffering, we even inflict physical suffering on ourselves merely to distract our attention from the former to the latter. This is why, in great mental anguish, men tear their hair, beat their breasts, lacerate their faces, or roll on the floor, for all these are in reality only violent means of diverting the mind from an unbearable thought. Just because mental pain, being much greater, makes us insensible to physical pain, suicide is very easy to the person who is in despair, or who is consumed by morbid depression, even though formerly, in comfortable circumstances, he recoiled at the thought of it. In the same way care and passion (thus the play of thought) wear out the body oftener and more than physical hardships."

There are those whose mental turmoil is compounded by the interference of the pangs of conscience complicating the distraught condition of the mind. Some psychologists believe that there exists no greater form of pain than the tyrannical squeeze and agony of conscience; knowledge of this matter stems back to the days of Biblical antiquity when people sought a balm in Gilead to heal the sin-sick soul. "In a healthy mind . . . only deeds oppress the conscience, not wishes and thoughts; for it is our deeds that hold up to us the mirror of our will. The deed referred to above, that is entirely unconsidered and is really committed in blind passion, is to a certain extent an intermediate thing between the mere wish and the resolve . . . I can never repent of what I have willed, though I can repent of what I have done."

The great majority of persons never live a positive life; their lives are negative, *i.e.*, they spend a lifetime attempting to escape misery and pain. Most persons live a life of boredom and rest relatively content in the thought that they have escaped life's torments — it is analogous to the individual who hit himself over the head with a hammer because he claimed that it felt 'so good' when he stopped. "It is really incredible how meaningless and void of significance when looked at from without, how dull and unenlightened by intellect when felt from within, is the course of the life of the great majority of men. It is a weary longing and complaining, a dreamlike staggering through the four stages of life to death accompanied by a series of trivial thoughts. Such men are like clockwork, which is wound up, and goes it knows not why; and every time a man is begotten and born, the clock of human life is wound up anew, to repeat the same old piece it has played innumerable times before, passage after passage, measure after measure, with insignificant variations. Every individual, every human being and his course of life, is but another short dream of the endless spirit of nature, of the persistent will to live."

The ceaseless sufferings which plague man are at times partially ameliorated by escaping into fantasy, *i.e.*, by taking refuge in day-dreams, where the abhorrent world vanishes and is transformed into a pleasant and palatable existence; here, the homely and ugly find themselves desirable and beautiful; the failure and the weak find themselves successful and strong; desires of the poor, the hungry, and the romantically starved are pleasantly fulfilled. However, "according to the true nature of things, everyone has all the suffering of the world as his own, and indeed has to regard all merely possible suffering as for him actual, so long as he has the fixed will to live, *i.e.*, asserts life with all his power. For the knowledge that sees through the principle of individuation, a happy life in time, the gift of chance or won by prudence amid the sorrows of innumerable others, is only the dream of a beggar in which he is a king, but from which he must awake and learn from experience that only a fleeting illusion had separated him from the suffering of his life."

Life is further complicated when injustices emerge triumphant, and give sway to the reign of evil; this is the rub – eternal justice withdrawing itself from this world. "It sees the bad, after misdeeds and cruelties of every kind, live in happiness and leave the world unpunished. It sees the oppressed drag out a life full of suffering to the end without an avenger, a requiter appearing."

Life's ultimate outcome is never one of success, but of misery, unsolved problems, boredom, and discontent; life is one extended chain of dissatisfactions, sparcely interspersed with scanty satisfactions. There is no basic romantic element in life; it is composed fundamentally of tragedy. Happiness is essentially negative, *i.e,* it appears only when misery is absent. "That all happiness is only of a negative not a positive nature, that just on this account it cannot be lasting satisfaction and gratification, but merely delivers us from some pain or want which must be followed either by a new pain, or by languor, empty longing and ennui . . . Every epic and dramatic poem can only represent a struggle, an effort, and a fight for happiness, never enduring and complete happiness itself. It conducts its heroes through a thousand difficulties and dangers to the goal; as soon as this is reached, it hastens to let the curtain fall; for now there would remain nothing for it to do but to show that the glittering goal in which the hero expected to find happiness had only dissappointed him, and that after its attainment he was no better off than before. Because a genuine enduring happiness is not possible, it cannot be the subject of art."

The Philosophy of Death and Suicide.

"Man alone carries about with him, in abstract conceptions, the certainty of his death;" the animal is spared the grueling thoughts of his own impending death. Man's unwillingness to relinquish his hold on life is basically responsible for his dread of death; "whoever is oppressed with the burden of life, whoever desires life and affirms it, but abhors its torments, and especially can no longer endure the hard lot that has fallen to himself, such a man has no deliverance to hope for from death, and cannot right himself by suicide . . . suicide appears to us as a vain and therefore a foolish action." Death does not end all, for there exists a future life in which the driving forces of will, insatiable desire, misery continue to thrive on there as well as here.

Fear of death has proved a perplexing problem for many persons, for they are bewildered as to precisely what it is they fear in respect to death; it cannot be pain for only the living are capable of experiencing that, hence it must be personal annihilation. "For what we fear in death is by no means the pain, for it lies clearly on this side of death, and, moreover we often take refuge in death from pain, just as, on the contrary, we sometimes endure the most fearful suffering merely to escape death for a while, although it would be quick and easy. Thus we distinguish pain and death as two entirely different evils. What we fear in death is the end of the individual . . . and since the individual is a particular objectification of the will to live itself, its whole nature struggles against death."

Life and death are both aspects of one and the same thing, viz., the invincible *will* in nature which assumes many forms and modes; "for life is inseparable from the will to live, and the only form of life is the present. Death is like the setting of the sun, which is only apparently swallowed up by the night, but in reality, itself the source of all light, burns without intermission, brings new days to new worlds, is always rising and always setting . . . Outside time lies only the will . . . Therefore suicide affords no escape; what every one in his most consciousness *wills,* that must *be;* and what every one *is,* that he *wills.*"

Ethical Salvation.

Man's salvation is achieved through shunning joys, not sorrows; repudiating the will to live, not death. "A man who had thoroughly assimilated the truths we have already advanced, but had not come to know, either from his own experience or from deeper insight, that constant suffering is essential to life, who found satisfaction and all that he wished in life, and could calmly and deliberately desire that his life, as he had hitherto known it, should endure for ever or repeat itself ever anew, and whose love of life was so great that he willingly and gladly accepted all the hardships and miseries to which it is exposed for the sake of its pleasures, — such a man would stand 'with firm-knit bones on the well-rounded, enduring earth,' and would have nothing to fear. Armed with the knowledge we have given him, he would await with indifference the death that hastens towards him on the wings of time."

Ethical salvation consists in a complete escape from the will, viz., its annihilation, a state of Nirvana which renders one oblivious to its vain strivings. The *summum bonum* is "a final satisfaction of the will, after which no new desire could arise, — a last motive, the attainment of which would afford enduring satisfaction of the will." However, inasmuch as this constitutes an impossibility, since there exists no such thing as a permanent or final fulfillment capable of completely satisfying the insatiable cravings of the will, there is therefore no highest good, no absolute good, but merely a temporary good. Accordingly, absolute good is a contradiction in terms. "If however, we wish to give an honorary position, as it were emeritus, to an old expression, which from custom we do not like to discard altogether, we may, metaphorically and figuratively, call the complete self-effacement and denial of the will, the true absence of will, which alone for ever stills and silences its struggle, alone gives that contentment which can never again be disturbed, alone redeems the world, and which we shall now soon consider at the close of our whole investigation – the absolute good, the summum bonum – and regard it as the only radical cure of the disease of which all other means are only palliations or anodynes." Since all suffering is simply unfulfilled volition, then good is its fulfillment, but inasmuch as the perfect satisfaction of the will can never be realized, then evil is the ever prevailing victor over good. Accordingly, to beseech that one be delivered from evil is to beg that he be relieved or rather freed from desire.

The royal road to salvation is effected when man "attains to the state of voluntary renunciation, resignation, true indifference, and perfect will-lessness." However, many great individuals have testified concerning the almost insurmountable task it is to will salvation, *e.g.*, Jesus claims it is easier for a camel to go through the eye of a needle than to relinquish the desire of wealth; the Hindu sacred scriptures, the Upanishads, teach: "The sharp edge of a razor is difficult to pass over: thus the wise say the path to salvation is hard." In sympathy with the foregoing stated positions, Schopenhauer writes: "If at times, in the hard experience of our own suffering, or in the vivid recognition of that of others, the knowledge of the vanity and bitterness of life draws nigh to us also who are still wrapt in the veil of Maya (illusion), and we would like to destroy the sting of the desires, close the entrance against all suffering, and purify and sanctify ourselves by complete and final renunciation; yet the illusion of the phenomenon soon entangles us again, and its motives influence the will anew; we cannot tear ourselves free. The allurement of hope, the flattery of the present, the sweetness of pleasure, the well-being which falls to our lot, amid the lamentations of a suffering world governed by chance and error, draws us back to it and rivets our bonds anew."

It is not life itself which one must shun but the desire to live; the denial or the renunciation of the will to live, thereby annihilating all striving, gives one the release he seeks. When a person mortifies the will's strivings then he has cut the nerve which seeks satisfaction of the wishes so that the will can never again be aroused. Such a man, who after many bitter struggles with his new won nature, has emerged the definitive victor, continues to exist only as a pure, knowing being, the undimmed mirror of the world. "Nothing can trouble him more, nothing can move him, for he has cut all the thousand cords of will which hold us bound to the world, and as desire, fear, envy, anger, drag us hither and thither in constant pain."

The Ethics of Pity.

Man's predicament calls for only one type of ethics, viz., an ethics of pity and sympathy. After all, 'we are in the same boat,' suffering and miserable; there is no need to make each other's lot worse; consequently, the only intelligent course of action is to pity the other fellow – be kind to him for he has enough trouble and misery. The person who can rise above his earthly existence by facing a wretched individual suffering in his intense misery and say: "This thou art," has attained ethical salvation. "Others have set up moral principles which they give out as prescriptions for virtue, and laws which it was necessary to follow . . . I do not know how to express better than by the formula of the Vedas already quoted: 'Tat twam asi!' (This thou art!) whoever is able to say this to himself, with regard to every being with whom he comes in contact with clear knowledge and firm inward conviction, is certain of all virtue and blessedness, and, as the conclusion of my exposition, show how love, the origin and nature of which we recognized as the penetration of the principle of individuation, leads to salvation, to the entire surrender of the will to live, *i.e.*, of all volition, and also how another path, less soft but more frequented, leads men to the same goal, a paradoxical proposition must first be stated and explained; not because it is paradoxical, but because it is true, and is necessary to the completeness of the thought I have present. It is this: 'All love (*agape, caritas*) is sympathy.'"

Evaluation of the Philosophy of Schopenhauer.

Schopenhauer is apparently an extremist both in attitude and in conclusions arrived at in philosophy. His major error lies in neglecting to furnish facts which would counterbalance his onesided position, consequently, his entire viewpoint is out of perspective, *e.g.*, sex is a real fact of life, and an important one, it is granted as true, but there is more to human existence than sex. When one views sex in its proper perspective, viz., as the means whereby one acquires a family, community, society, and the reproduction of the human race, then one realizes that it is at most, an *instrumental value, not* a final value, in human existence.

Furthermore, Schopenhauer regards the drive for superiority and other instinctual urges as the sole motivation of mankind; granted that they are forms of motivation, and strong ones, he does not prove that they are the strongest forms of motivation, nor does he prove that they are the only ones. Even Freud recognizes that 'mother love' is one of the most potent of all human forces, unaccountable in terms of mere sex or other instincts of the selfish mode. The psychiatrist Carl Jung proved that man has within him a nature equally powerful in its desire to do good as any which is selfish – man possesses a genuine spiritual nature and a true soul.

Schopenhauer's philosophy suggests a sick man's outlook on life, *i.e.*, a neurotic, with overwhelming neurotic needs, substituting for a complete and balanced life one which is wholly onesided. Like a true neurotic, he fears and is suspicious of his drives, wishes, and desires; yet wishes and desires are not only enjoyable in themselves much of the time, but without them, an individual or mankind itself would make little or no progress. Often a desire is much more pleasant than its realization; this is indicated in 'anticipation,' *e.g.*, often the anticipation of a happy vacation is much more exciting than the actual fact, which frequently as a result of anticipation is a 'let-down.'

Schopenhauer's philosophy pertaining to the extinction of desires was borrowed from the Buddhists whose belief in Nirvana compelled them to find happiness via the extinction of all desire; according to Schopenhauer this was the only potent and effective method of combatting desire. There are two inherent objections to such a philosophy: First, one can never extinguish all desire since *one* always remains, viz., the *desire* to extinguish all desire. Second, to rid oneself of all desire does not bring happiness, but misery and death as is evidenced by the mendicants of India who consciously practice this philosophy by desiring nothing, neither food, sleep, health, shelter, progress, nor life itself; accordingly, they would drift along the streets in beggardly fashion and literally collapse and die by the wayside. Desires, provided they are good, noble, rational, progressive, etc., are highly valuable for human enhancement, since by their impetus man is capable of building a better world for tomorrow.

The Stoics, similar to the Schopenhauerians and Buddhists, were suspicious of desire, pleasure, and enjoyment; consequently, they avoided the pleasurable things of life because when once taken away, they left misery in their wake, *i.e.*, once being accustomed to that which gives pleasure, whether it be an object or a person, the time will come when it will be no longer in one's possession due to death, loss, destruction, etc., terminating in the sad state of misery when one must endure the experience of relinquishing the desired object. The Hedonists, on the one hand, were eager for pleasure and would seize it wherever and whenever they could find it in spite of the fact that it would often lead to misery and death. They were committed to the philosophy: "Eat, drink, and be merry, for tomorrow we die," but the practice of this philosophy issued in an obstacle: What happens if we do not die tomorrow, but live to suffer for what we committed today? Perhaps in this regard, the best *Weltanschauung* is offered by thinkers such as

Aristotle who advocates moderation in all things, and St. Paul who chooses the course of enjoying this world's pleasures when provided and learning to be content when the time comes that he is deprived of them. He writes: "Not that I speak in respect of want: for I have learned, in whatsoever state I am, therewith, to be content. I know both how to be abased, and I know how to abound: everywhere and in all things I am instructed both to be full and to be hungry, both to abound and to suffer need." This, one must concede, would be a most desirable state in which to find oneself; the task is to achieve it.

X

EPICTETUS:

Stoicism

Stoicism.

Epictetus (pronounced ep ik · te tus) was the foremost proponent of classical Stoicism although not its founder, that honor remaining for Zeno, a fourth century B.C. figure. The Stoic mind prized a number of values such as: (1) the innate goodness of the universe which (ultimately) is devoid of all evil, (2) moral virtue as the highest good, (3) the virtue of endurance which together with indifference is capable of furnishing its possessor a mental state of tranquility, *i.e.*, peace of mind, (4) the doctrine of resignation.

Tranquility of Mind.

The Stoic's treasured aim is 'tranquility of mind,' *i.e.*, a state of mind in which a person is at peace with himself and the world, "for it is better to die of hunger, so that you be free from pain and free from fear, than to live in plenty and be troubled in mind." [1] One must not infer from this statement that blessedness is necessarily a fortunate fate or state of affairs in which he has escaped the hazards and pestilences of life, but rather a state of mind which renders one immune to the sting of life's evils. Actually, life's tumults should be regarded as excellent opportunities for grooming one's character for a life of peace; they should be regarded as exercises which harden and purify the spirit, or at least prepare it for life's exigencies; accordingly, they should be embraced with a grateful attitude. "Difficulties are what show men's character. Therefore when a difficult crisis meets you, remember that you are the raw youth with whom God the trainer is wrestling."

Technically, peace of mind comes to the person who is in harmony with nature and does not inject unnatural tendencies into his life. Quoting Chrysippus, Epictetus writes: "That you may know that these

[1] Unless otherwise indicated, quotations from Epicurus are from his *Discourses* translated by P. E. Matheson (Oxford: The Clarendon Press, 1916).

truths from which tranquility and peace of mind come to men are not false – take my books and you shall find that what gives me peace of mind is true and in harmony with nature."

The fundamental cause of mental anguish is not the external world without but the *will* within an individual which capitulates to trying circumstances and permits the spirit within to become disturbed: "What is it then which disturbs and confounds the multitude? Is it the tyrant and his guards? Nay, God forbid! It is impossible for that which is free by nature to be disturbed or hindered by anything but itself. It is a man's own judgments which disturb him. For when the tyrant says to a man, 'I will chain your leg,' he that values his leg says, 'Nay, have mercy,' but he that values his will says, 'If it seems more profitable to you, chain it.' 'Do you pay no heed?' 'No, I pay no heed. I will show you that I am master.'" Accordingly, it is the will which is the supreme factor within man capable of screening out all external anxiety-producing elements from disturbing the personality. It is an accomplishment achieved by valuing the will above all exterior objects; this devaluation of everything extraneous to personality is the sole effective means of barricading one's inner spirit from the tumultuous world without, hence fortifying the mind against the onslaught of outside disturbances.

The Invincible Will.

Whatever the will attaches value to, *ipso facto,* becomes important to the personality; as a consequence it is capable of issuing pleasure, but by virtue of the same fact it possesses the power to torment as well. "The essence of good and of evil lies in an attitude of the will," or to put it dialectically: "Where lies the good? In a man's will. Where lies evil? In the will. Where is the neutral sphere? In the region outside the will's control."

Fate is impotent unless empowered by the individual, *i.e.*, unless one capitulates to fate, thereby permitting it to rend the will, *e.g.*, death, *per se,* has no affect on a man, but the fear or shame of it, if such there be, has. "For it is not death or pain which is a fearful thing, but the fear of pain or death. Therefore men praise him who said: '*Not death, but shameful death, is to be feared.*'"

One's tranquility is threatened by those objects which a person treasures; withdraw your desire from a given object and its power or hold over you diminishes proportionately. As overt objects become endeared, their powers of vulnerability increase, *e.g.*, it is not disturbing to have a thief steal a worthless watch or one which was to be discarded anyway, but to have him take a valued new one can prove most provoking. "Why then are we angry? Because we admire the material things of which they rob us. For cease to admire your clothes, and you are not angry with him who steals them: cease to admire your wife's beauty, and you cease to be angry with the adulterer. Know that the thief and the adulterer have no place among things that are your own, but only among things that are another's and beyond your power. If you let them alone and count them as nothing you have no one to be angry with any more. But as long as you admire these things you must be angry with yourself rather than with them."

A man cannot be said to be free unless his life is in complete subjection to his will. "What else is freedom but power to pass our life as we will?" A few lofty souls have successfully scaled the summit of Stoicism but these men are rare indeed; one such blessed individual was Socrates. When his enemies won political power, they contrived a diabolical scheme, which although it eventuated in his death, was powerless over the invincible will of Socrates who had *conquered* death itself by becoming unaffected and unafraid even in the face of it. Epictetus cites Socrates as saying of his two enemies who were responsible for his execution: "Anytus and Meletus have the power to kill me, but not to harm me." A will yielded and broken is the only corridor to a beaten spirit. "Accept all things in a spirit of content. What punishment is there, you ask, for those who do not accept things in this spirit? Their punishment is to be as they are. Is one discontented with being alone? Let him be deserted . . . 'Cast him in prison.' What do you mean by prison? He is in prison already; for a man's prison is the place that he is in against his will, just as, conversely, Socrates was not in prison, for he chose to be there."

The wisdom of the preceding is clear: a person cannot break your will unless you allow it; enemies cannot hurt your spirit without your permission. To be physically hurt and to feel hurt are not equivalent, much less, identical facts; someone may do all in his power to make you feel badly but will meet with little or no success unless you allow your spirit to be broken by succumbing to sorrow. The Stoical philosophy of life is designed to cope with life's tragedies and exigencies: "What then must a man have ready to help him in such emergencies? Surely this: he must ask himself, 'What is mine, and what is not mine? What may I do, what may I not do?' I must die, but must I die groaning? I must be imprisoned. But must I whine as well? I must suffer exile. Can any one then hinder me from going with a smile, and a good courage, and at peace? 'Tell the secret!' I refuse to tell, for this is my power. 'But I will chain you.' What say you, fellow? Chain me? My leg you will chain – yes, but my will – no, not even Zeus can conquer that. 'I will imprison you.' My bit of a body, you mean. 'I will behead you.' Why? When did I ever tell you that I was the only man in the world that could not be beheaded? . . . It is yours to kill, mine to die without quailing."

Like Socrates, Agrippinus also succeeded in self-mastery; his tranquil spirit never lost its serenity even during life's coarsest buffetings. Faced with expulsion and possible death, he remained calm while his collected spirit enjoyed whatever offerings of life remained. Listen to Epictetus tell the beautiful story: " 'Will you study to be content with what is given you?' It was in this spirit that Agrippinus used to say – do you know what? 'I will not stand in my own way!' News was brought to him, 'Your trial is on in the Senate!' 'Good luck to it, but the fifth hour is come' – this was the hour when he used to take his exercise and have a cold bath – 'let us go and take exercise.' When he had taken his exercise they came and told him, 'you are condemned.' 'Exile or death?' he asked. 'Exile.' 'And my property?' 'It is not confiscated.' 'Well then, let us go to Aricia and dine.' Here you see the result of training as training should be, of the will to get and the will to avoid, so disciplined that nothing can hinder or frustrate them. I must die, must I? If at once, then I am dying: if soon, I dine now, as it is time for dinner, and afterwards when the time comes I will die. And die how? As befits one who gives back what is not his own."

The person who is miserable is the one who has compromised his spirit to such an extent that he is incapable of relinquishing the goods of this life, including the body itself, but the person who is happy is the one who is free, free in spirit and in complete control of his will. "Of one thing beware, O man; see what is the price at which you will sell your will. If you do nothing else do not sell your will cheap."

Some persons have sold their wills and have submitted to spiritual slavery by placing their emotions at the disposal of others, including complete strangers. To grant others the extravagant license of holding power over one's mental equilibrium is unthinkable, yet this is precisely what transpires when a person allows another to disturb his state of composure. "If any one trusted your body to the first man he met, you would be indignant, but you trust your mind to the chance comer, and allow it to be disturbed and confounded if he revile you; are you not ashamed to do so?" [1]

Once an individual possesses the object of your desire, he has control over your spirit and you becomed enslaved to him; consequently, to avoid vulnerability, one should prevent this situation from ever coming

[1] Epictetus, *Manuel,* 28.

to pass by becoming independent, not only of impersonal things but people as well. "Exercise yourself then in what lies in your power. Each man's master is the man who has authority over what he wishes or does not wish, to secure the one or to take away the other. Let him then who wishes to be free not wish for anything or avoid anything that depends on others; or else he is bound to be a slave."

Some persons enslave themselves to beguiling emotions such as sex, as Menander notes: "A worthless girl made a slave of me, whom never foe subdued." Sex practices can reach tyrannical heights, and when they do few, if any, can escape unscathed. Epictetus queries, "When the pretty girl was too much for you, did you get away unpunished?"

One must keep eternal vigilance to escape seduction by sex; it is accomplished through the cultivation of wholesome practices which develop into firm and protective habits. Epictetus demonstrates its technique: "If, then, you wish not to be choleric, do not feed the angry habit, so as not to add fuel to the fire. To begin with, keep quiet, and count the days when you were not angry. I used to be angry every day, then every other day, then every three days, then every four. But if you miss thirty days, then sacrifice to God: for the habit is first weakened and then wholly destroyed. I kept free from distress today, and again next day, and for two or three months after; and when occasions arose to provoke it, I took pains to check it. Know that you are doing well. Today when I saw a handsome woman I did not say to myself, 'Would that she were mine!' and 'Blessed is her husband!' For he who says that will say, 'Blessed is the adulterer!' Nor do I picture the next scene: the woman present and disrobing and reclining by my side. I pat myself on the head and say, 'Bravo, Epictetus, you have refuted a pretty fallacy, a much prettier one than the so-called 'Master'.' And if, though the woman herself, poor thing, is willing and beckons and sends to me, and even touches me and comes close to me, I still hold aloof and conquer . . . This is a thing to be really proud of . . . How, then, is this to be done? Make up your mind at last to please your true self, make up your mind to appear noble to God; set your desires on becoming pure in the presence of your pure self and God."

Resignation.

One must make peace with himself by coming to terms with the world. He must never lose sight of the fact that he is a mere mortal surrounded by perishable objects regardless of their respective natures, human, animal, vegetable, etc. If one remains constantly cognizant of this basic and simple truth, then his soul will be able to contain itself when others lose their composure.

Among the many things capable of rendering a man vulnerable is love, *e.g.*, a man who dearly loves his wife is subject to dire distress in the case of her death. Life can become unbearable when loved ones have been separated; consequently, to steel himself in the face of such circumstances, a man must incessantly remind himself of the perishable nature of human life and affairs. "When anything, from the meanest thing upwards, is attractive or serviceable or an object of affection, remember always to say to yourself, 'What is its nature?' If you are fond of a jug, say you are fond of a jug, then you will not be disturbed if it be broken. If you kiss your child or your wife, say to yourself that you are kissing a human being, for then if death strikes it you will not be disturbed." [1] In other words, if one remains in complete realization of the fact that nothing in life is permanent or immutable then he can more easily become resigned to whatever fate has in store. Nevertheless, this attitude is assumed only when objects and circumstances are beyond one's power to alter.

One may, however, assume another attitude than the foregoing which is equally effective in coping with tragedy: "Never say of anything, 'I lost it,' but say, 'I gave it back.' Has your child died? It was given back. Has your wife died? She was given back. Has your estate been taken from you? Was not this also given back? But you say, 'He who took it from me is wicked.' What does it matter to you through whom the Giver asked it back? As long as He gives it you, take care of it, but not as your own; treat it as passers-by treat an inn." [2]

Cynicism.

Originally the Cynic was an individual worthy of high praise and admiration for his outstanding moral and spiritual achievements (two such exemplary individuals were Socrates and Diogenes), but with the passing of time the Cynic fell into such complete disrepute that the word became a term of opprobrium. Homer depicted Cynics as, "Dogs of the table, guardians of the gate." A Cynic fancied himself superior to his contemporaries and loathed the society in which he was forced to live; consequently, he depicted the people and culture of his day with scornful criticism.

Epictetus, however, portrays the Cynic in glowing terms and employs Cynic in that finest sense of the term exemplified by himself, Diogenes, and Socrates. As a true Cynic, "you must show a complete change in your conduct, and you must cease to accuse God or man: you must utterly put away the will to get, and you must will to avoid only what lies

[1] *Manuel* 3.
[2] *Ibid.*, 11.

within the sphere of your will; you must harbour no anger, wrath, envy, pity: a fair maid, a fair name, favourites, or sweet cakes, must mean nothing to you. For you must know that other men, when they indulge in such things, have the protection of their walls and houses and darkness. There are many things to hide them: one, may be, has closed the door, or has set someone to guard his chamber: If anyone comes, say, 'He is out' or 'He is busy.' But the Cynic, instead of all these, should have self-respect for his shelter: if he has not that, he will be naked and exposed and put to shame. This is his house, his door, his chamberguards, this his darkness: for he must not wish to conceal anything that is his: if he does, he disappears; he loses the true Cynic, the free openair spirit, he has begun to fear outward things, he has begun to have need of concealment, and when he would hide himself he cannot; for he has no place or means to hide himself . . . First then you must make your Governing Principle pure, and hold fast this rule of life, 'Henceforth my mind is the material I have to work on, as the carpenter has his timber and the shoemaker his leather: my business is to deal with my impressions aright. My wretched body is nothing to me, its parts are nothing to me. Death? Let it come when it will, whether to my whole body or to a part of it. Exile? Can one be sent into exile beyond the Universe? One cannot. Wherever I go, there is the sun, there is the moon, there are the stars, dreams, auguries, conversation with the gods.' The true Cynic when he has ordered himself thus cannot be satisfied with this: he must know that he is sent as a messenger from God to men concerning things good and evil, to show them that they have gone astray and are seeking the true nature of good and evil where it is not to be found."

XI

EPICURUS:

Hedonism

Epicureanism.

Epicureanism is one of the most misconstrued philosophies in the understanding of the layman who views it as a complete abandonment to voluptuous appetite. This is an erroneous conception for at least two reasons: The first is that Epicurus emphasizes primarily the avoidance of pain, and secondly, he stresses the embracement of spiritual pleasures in preference to those which are physical. Sensual pleasure which fails to fructify into physical and mental well-being should be eschewed. Those who propagate the false doctrine: "Eat, drink, and be merry, for tomorrow we die," beg the question: What if we do not die tomorrow, but live to regret the actions of today? Unbridled carnal appetite satisfaction may easily lead its victim into a regrettable pit of pain and sorrow; one ought to be cautious of and shun dangerous pleasures which are in reality 'booby traps' in disguise. "We must then meditate on the things that make our happiness, seeing that when that is with us we have all, but when it is absent we do all to win it."[1]

God.

Epicurus lists a number of elements which are vitally necessary if one is to have a wholesome, healthy, and happy outlook on life; the first is a belief in God, since such a belief is most effective in maintaining a pleasant and optimistic disposition, inasmuch as it is conducive to happiness. Epicurus admonishes the youth, Menoeceus: "The things which I used unceasingly to commend to you, these do and practise, considering them to be the first principles of the good life. First of all believe that God is engraved on men's minds, and do not assign to him anything alien to his immortality or ill-suited to his blessedness: but

[1] Unless otherwise indicated, quotations are from *Epicurus To Menoeceus.* Translations in this entire section are by Cyril Bailey (Oxford: The Clarendon Press, 1926).

believe about him everything that can uphold his blessedness and immortality."

The Philosophy of Death.

As was mentioned earlier Epicurus' foremost concern is alleviation or total escape from pain, the essence of which is evil, and its chief form death. Epicurus wrestles with the problem of the fear of death and removes its sting by exposing the entire question to philosophical scrutiny. He poses the problem in the form of a dilemma: Either one is alive or he is dead: if he is alive then he need not fear death (since he is not in its clutches), and if he is dead either he has discovered a life after death or he is a nonentity. If immortal then he is no longer troubled with death, but if death ends all then he will be in no position to experience fear or harm. Epicurus debates the issue: "Become accustomed to the belief that death is nothing to us. For all good and evil consists in sensation, but death is deprivation of sensation. And therefore a right understanding that death is nothing to us makes the mortality of life enjoyable, not because it adds to it an infinite span of time, but because it takes away the craving for immortality. For there is nothing terrible in life for the man who has truly comprehended that there is nothing terrible in not living. So that the man speaks but idly who says that he fears death not because it will be painful when it comes, but because it is painful in anticipation. For that which gives no trouble when it comes, is but an empty pain in anticipation. So death, the most terrifying of ills, is nothing to us, since so long as we exist death is not with us; but when death comes, then we do not exist. It does not then concern either the living or the dead, since for the former it is not, and the latter are no more."

The wise man does not allow the fear of death to cripple or paralyze his zest for living; he makes no attempt to escape life nor does he shun death nor allow morbid thoughts of death to overwhelm him, but maintains an outlook on each that is wholesome and balanced. In contrast to this attitude, the masses "at one moment shun death as the greatest of evils, at another yearn for it as a respite from the evils in life. But the wise man neither seeks to escape life nor fears the cessation of life, for neither does life offend him nor does the absence of life seem to be any evil. And just as with food he does not seek simply the larger share and nothing else, but rather the most pleasant, so he seeks to enjoy not the longest period of time, but the most pleasant." Accordingly, life's values are not to be measured in terms of quantity, viz., longevity, but in terms of qualitative expenditures, *i.e.*, did you gain anything out of life or did you squander and waste its opportunities?

A similar attitude must be assumed regarding life's future prospects: "We must bear in mind that the future is neither ours, nor yet wholly not ours, so that we may not altogether expect it as sure to come nor abandon hope of it as if it will certainly not come."

Hedonism (The Philosophy of Pleasure).

In essence, the philosophy of Epicurus is Hedonistic, *i.e.*, pleasure is life's prime good and supreme blessing. Pleasure is the *sine qua non* of goodness; when pleasure is lacking then goodness is absent, but indiscriminate pleasures or the promiscuous gratification of appetite is unequivocally repudiated since all pleasures are not on a par as to their productivity of happiness. "We must consider that of desires some are natural, others vain, and of the natural some are necessary and others merely natural; and of the necessary some are necessary for happiness, others for the repose of the body, and others for very life. The right understanding of these facts enables us to refer all choice and avoidance to the health of the body and the soul's freedom from disturbance, since this is the aim of the life of blessedness. For it is to obtain this end that we always act, namely, to avoid pain and fear. And when this is once secured for us, all the tempest of the soul is dispersed, since the living creature has not to wander as though in search of something that is missing, and to look for some other thing by which he can fulfill the good of the soul and the good of the body. For it is then that we have need of pleasure; but when we do not feel pain, we no longer need pleasure. And for this cause we call pleasure the beginning and end of the blessed life. For we recognize pleasure as the first good innate in us, and from pleasure we begin every act of choice and avoidance, and to pleasure we return again, using the feeling as the standard by which we judge every good.

"And since pleasure is the first good and natural to us, for this very reason we do not choose every pleasure, but sometimes we pass over many pleasures, when greater discomfort accrues to us as the result of them: and similarly we think many pains better than pleasures, since a greater pleasure comes to us when we have endured pains for a long time. Every pleasure then because of its natural kinship to us is good, yet not every pleasure is to be chosen: even as every pain also is an evil, yet not all are always of a nature to be avoided. Yet by a scale of comparison and by the consideration of advantages and disadvantages we must form our judgment on all these matters. For the good on certain occasions we treat as bad, and conversely the bad as good."

An element of Stoicism creeps into the Hedonism of Epicurus when he advocates that one keep aloof from desires by becoming free and independent from them. A simple life in which basic physical needs are moderately satisfied is preferable to a life abandoned to the overgratification of sensual appetite. Overgratification is neither pleasurable nor desirable but is an excessive practice to be eschewed since it leads to satiation, nausea, and illness. One may even detect a principle in nature which rations pleasures quantitatively, and restricts an individual to his allotted quota. Should one consume his full complement of pleasure, then desire wanes and perishes; consequently, many rich persons who have consumed their allotment of pleasure, be they pleasures of sex, drink, food, etc. must go to extreme limits in order to experience any sensitivity or responsiveness to pleasure, and when that too has been exhausted then they become hedonic beggars and paupers. *E.g.*, desire diminishes with the overindulgence of sex activity and to pursue the matter further is to dullen one's sensitivity to sex even to the point of numbness, nausea, or disgust, depending on the extent to which the matter was pressed. When normal sex pleasure has been consumed, one may deviate into sexual aberrations for the promise of additional pleasure. The same holds true for the individual whose wealth allows him to overindulge his appetite in food; for instance, a steady diet of a banquet for each daily meal and inbetween snacks results in a distaste and even abhorrence of food. Accordingly, the man who lives the simple and continent life is the one who is in the most advantageous and enviable position for enjoying physical pleasures, since he is the one whose body will be most sensitive and responsive to them. A man who fasts for a period of time is the one who can most enjoy a sumptuous meal, not the individual who banquets morning, noon, and night. To experience the richest pleasure possible, one is admonished to live the simple life.

"And again independence of desire we think a great good – not that we may at all times enjoy but a few things, but that, if we do not possess many, we may enjoy the few in the genuine persuasion that those have the sweetest pleasure in luxury who least need it, and that all that is natural is easy to be obtained, but that which is superfluous is hard. And so plain savours bring us a pleasure equal to a luxurious diet, when all the pain due to want is removed; and bread and water produce the highest pleasure, when one who needs them puts them to his lips. To grow accustomed therefore to simple and not luxurious diet gives us health to the full, and makes a man alert for the needful employments of life, and when after long intervals we approach luxuries, disposes us better towards them, and fits us to be fearless of fortune. When therefore we maintain that pleasure is the end, we do not mean the pleasures of profligates and those that consist in sensuality, as is supposed by some who are either ignorant or disagree with us or do not understand, but freedom from pain in the body and from trouble in the mind. For it is not continuous drinkings and revellings, nor the satisfaction of lusts, nor the enjoyment of fish and other luxuries of the wealthy table, which produce a pleasant life, but sober reasoning, searching out the motives for all choice and avoidance, and banishing mere opinions, to which are due the greatest disturbance of the spirit."

The Summum Bonum — Prudence.

Much to the surprise and even astonishment of many individuals, the *summum bonum* in the estimation of Epicurus is not pleasure, *per se*, but pleasure interpreted in the light of, or in the form of prudence. Since the Epicurean does not advocate the pleasure of profligates, viz., carnality, alcoholic orgies, lascivious revellings, etc., then his pleasures must be discreetly delineated, *i.e.*, restricted to the dictates of prudence and a well-ordered life, inasmuch as this is wholesome and natural.

"Of all this the beginning and the greatest good is prudence. Wherefore prudence is a more precious thing even than philosophy: for from prudence are sprung all the other virtues, and it teaches us that it is not possible to live pleasantly without living prudently and honourably and justly, nor, again, to live a life of prudence, honour, and justice without living pleasantly. For the virtues are by nature bound up with the pleasant life, and the pleasant life is inseparable from them."

The prudent or well-ordered life is to be prized above all else since genuine and lasting happiness is unquestionably its concomitant. One must be guided by intelligence and not permit his life to be left to mere chance or fate which characteristically results in disorder. With respect to chance, the prudent individual "does not regard it as a god as most men do (for in a god's acts there is no disorder), nor as an uncertain cause of all things; for he does not believe that good and evil are given by chance to man for the framing of a blessed life, but that opportunities for great good and great evil are afforded by it. He therefore thinks it better to be unfortunate in reasonable action than to prosper in unreason. For it is better in a man's actions that what is well chosen should fail, rather than that what is ill chosen should be successful owing to chance.

"Meditate therefore on these things and things akin to them night and day by yourself, and with a companion like yourself, and never shall you be disturbed eating or asleep, but you shall live like a god among men. For a man who lives among immortal blessings is not like to a mortal being."

Part Three: SOCIAL AND POLITICAL PHILOSOPHY — The Ideal Community

In the philosophical community, social or political philosophy is referred to as social ethics, and rightly so, since political or social philosophy is ethics, not of an individual person, but of the group. Human beings are both individual and social; as individuals, they practice a personal code of ethics, but as social beings living collectively in a society, they practice collective or social ethics. The social ethics of a given people can be found codified in their laws, religious scriptures, or in the more or less generalized mores which are guarded by public opinion or other modes of social sanction.

Many philosophers are not content with allowing their philosophies to remain merely a personal ethic; they follow their ethical lines of reasoning through to its ultimate and logical climax – a social ethic. This is particularly true of Aristotle whose political philosophy must be read as the natural sequel and conclusion of his personal system of ethics, and even more so of Bentham, who combines both personal and social (political) ethics in a single treatise: *An Introduction to the Principles of Morals and Legislation.* In the case of Plato, his personal ethic is found in the body of the text, *Republic*, which contains his political philosophy, and when he discusses the virtue, 'justice,' although he recognizes it as a personal characteristic, nevertheless, for him it must be practiced socially, that is, only in a society.

At the present time, social and political philosophy are grouped as one and the same study, but it would be a fair prognostication to venture into the not too distant future and envision the time when the two are treated as distinct and separate disciplines.

IIX

PLATO'S *REPUBLIC*:

An Aristocracy

Plato's political philosophy originates with his triune concept of the biological nature of man: head, heart, stomach or liver, which find their correlates in the psychological nature of man: intellect (thinking), spirit (conation), appetite (physiological nature). In turn, the three psychological components of mind produce a corresponding virtue when an individual is sufficiently fortunate to possess any one in abundance so as to excel in it. *Excellence* is the Plantonic definition of virtue; to excel in intellect blessed with a high I.Q. issues in the virtue, *wisdom;* to excel in spirit with a strong will and determination produces *courage* as its concomitant virtue; to excel in control of appetite so as to possess the trait of moderation yields *temperance* as its accompanying virtue. When the possessors of these virtues exercise each in a suitable occupation in society issuing in a harmonious State, a resultant virtue appears, *justice.* Hence the appearance of the four cardinal virtues as they are called: temperance, courage, wisdom, justice.

Justice prevails only in the presence of harmony, a harmony which is possible only when individuals who make up any given society apply themselves to a career corresponding to the particular virtue with which they are endowed. That is to say, a person who is courageous should pursue an occupation in accord with his virtue, namely, a military career, police duty, or any task which calls for expressions of courage. Accordingly, the wise are expected to contribute their talents to the enhancement of society as wise leaders and teachers, while the temperate apply themselves to jobs for which they too, are suited. Such harmonious activity, with everyone doing that to which he is naturally disposed and innately talented, blossoms in justice, the glory which crowns the good State.

Since rulers of the State are to be selected from among the few virtuous in wisdom, Plato's Republic is an 'Aristocracy,' or 'Monarchy,'

SCHEMATIC OUTLINE OF PLATO'S *REPUBLIC*

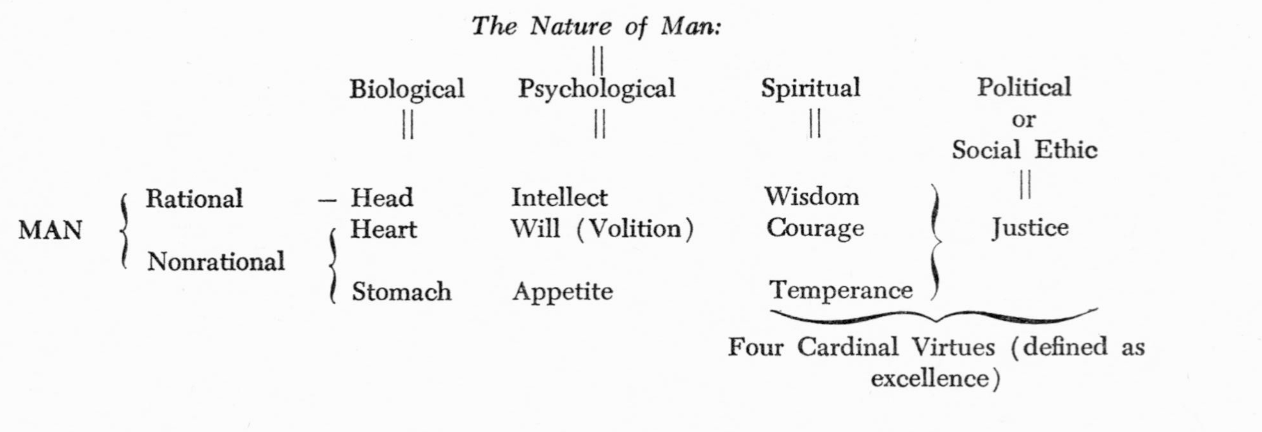

Virtues: — Profession:

1. Wisdom — Guardians — Aristocrats-or-Monarch, viz., Philosopher King
   - Communism prevails at this level.
2. Courage — Warriors, Police (Protectors of the State)
3. Temperance — Artisans
4. Justice (The essential ingredient of a good State)

when only one person is selected from among the sages, owing to his extraordinary ability to excel the rest, so that he is without peer as was true in the case of Socrates. This virtuous monarch becomes the Republic's 'philosopher king.' Plato was convinced: "*Until philosophers are kings, or the kings and princes of this world have the spirit and power of philosophy, and political greatness and wisdom meet in one, and those commoner natures who pursue either to the exclusion of the other are compelled to stand aside, cities will never have rest from their evils,* — no, nor the human race, as I believe, — and then only will this our State have a possibility of life and behold the light of day." [1]

With the foregoing synopsis of Plato's *Republic* before us as a guide, we can penetrate deeper and broader into his thoughts by way of amplification.

Justice.

The *Republic* confronts and seeks to resolve a major problem, namely, injustice; on the surface its solution seems obviously simple — justice. The difficulty arises as to an adequate definition, nature, elaboration, and implementation of justice in the State. The *Republic* supplies all of the necessary particulars.

Plato is teleologically oriented; nature has its various objectives, its specific functions or purposes for any given thing, "and that to which an end is appointed has also an excellence." Virtue is excellence, the more one excels, the more virtuous he is said to be. In the light of this definition of virtue, vice would be defect since "things which fulfill their ends fulfill them by their own proper excellence, and fail of fulfilling them by their own defect."

Justice prevails when, and only when, the soul fulfills its purpose which is "to superintend and command and deliberate and the like."

> An evil soul must necessarily be an evil ruler and superintendent, and the good soul a good ruler? [2]
>
> Yes, necessarily.
>
> And we have admitted that justice is the excellence of the soul, and injustice the defect of the soul?
>
> That has been admitted.
>
> Then the just soul and the just man will live well, and the unjust man will live ill?
>
> That is what your argument proves.

[1] Quotations from Plato in this section are from the *Republic,* tr. Benjamin Jowett, (3rd ed., 1888).

[2] The *Republic* of Plato is written in the form of a dialogue, a play, and must be read and understood in that form as is true of the following quotation and others taken from the *Republic.*

And he who lives well is blessed and happy, and he who lives ill the reverse of happy?

Certainly.

Then the just is happy, and the unjust miserable?

So be it.

Although justice is the soul's fulfillment of its life's purpose which results in the reward of happiness, we are not told specifically as yet, the precise nature of happiness, except that "justice is the greatest good, and injustice the greatest evil." At this point, however, we can surmise that without just persons there cannot be a just State, since justice issues from the just soul which excels in its prescribed nature, and does what a good soul ought to do. But, excellence comes only to "the soul of him who is rightly educated . . . And when a beautiful soul harmonizes with a beautiful form, and the two are cast in one mould, that will be the fairest of sights to him who has an eye to see it."

Not only is the just man happy, but his justice is imputed to the State as a whole, consequently when just persons predominate in a society, then that nation too, becomes just. As will shortly become apparent, the rulers or guardians of the State must be just if that State is to be so; guardians who are just are happy as well, and their happiness carries over to the rest of the State. "Our guardians may very likely be the happiest of men; but that our aim in founding the State was not the disproportionate happiness of any one class, but the greatest happiness of the whole; we thought that in a State which is ordered with a view to the good of the whole we should be most likely to find justice, and in the ill-ordered State injustice." Happiness does not fall to all persons equally; of the three different classes of society, of which the highest consists of guardians, happiness comes greatest to the upper echelons and proportionately to those of the lesser two classes. In a well ordered State, "the several classes will receive the proportion of happiness which nature assigns to them."

Owing to their personalities, each of the three groups is attracted by one of three different kinds of pleasure indicative of their respective natures: guardians are lovers of wisdom (philosophers), warriors are lovers of honor, while artisans are lovers of gain. A society ruled by any one of these three types of individuals will be characterized by the peculiar biases of each.

Justice cannot prevail in a State whose class structure is dominated by two primary sources of evil: wealth and poverty. Wealth destroys industry and creates indolence, while poverty paralyzes creative activity and causes evil or discontent.

> There seem to be two causes of the deterioration of the arts.
> What are they?
> Wealth, I said, and poverty.
> How do they act?
> The process is as follows: When a potter becomes rich, will he, think you, any longer take the same pains with his art?
> Certainly not.
> He will grow more and more indolent and careless?
> Very true.
> And the result will be that he becomes a worse potter?
> Yes; he greatly deteriorates.
> But, on the other hand, if he has no money, and cannot provide himself with tools or instruments, he will not work equally well himself, nor will he teach his sons or apprentices to work equally well.
> Certainly not.
> Then, under the influence of poverty or of wealth, workmen and their work are equally liable to degenerate?
> That is evident.
> Here, then, is a discovery of new evils, I said, against which the guardians will have to watch, or they will creep into the city unobserved.
> What evils?
> Wealth, I said, and poverty; the one is the parent of luxury and indolence, and the other of meanness and viciousness, and both of discontent.

Justice is found only in the presence of another virtue, moderation; moderation in reference to wealth, gratification of appetite, geographical size and population of a State, etc.

Justice is the fruit which appears in consequence of each man's doing that job for which he is best suited, thereby contributing to the good of the State those talents with which he is gifted by nature. In this way, unity or harmony, a chief characteristic of justice, makes its appearance. "Each individual should be put to the use for which nature intended him, one to one work, and then every man would do his own business, and be one and not many; and so the whole city would be one and not many."

The foregoing concept of justice, namely, every one in his right place doing his rightful task as his nature deems fit, sets the stage for a proper understanding of Plato's political theory.

> You remember the original principle which we were always laying down at the foundation of the State, that one man should practice one thing only, the thing to which his nature was best adapted; now justice is this principle or a part of it.
> Yes, we often said that one man should do one thing only.
> Further we affirmed that justice was doing one's own business, and not being a busybody; we said so again and again, and many others have said the same to us.

Yes, we said so.
Then to do one's own business in a certain way may be assumed to be justice.

The Four Cardinal Virtues: Temperance, Courage, Wisdom, Justice.

The topic 'justice,' having been sufficiently treated, opens the way for inquiry into the remaining three Platonic virtues: temperance, courage, wisdom. The perfect State consists of one which is rightly ordered, one which is wise, valiant, temperate, and just, because the individuals of whom it is composed possess these virtues.

Temperance, the mastery of self, consists in "the ordering or controlling of certain pleasures and desires; this is curiously enough implied in the saying of 'a man being his own master' . . . The meaning is, I believe, that in the human soul there is a better and also a worse principle; and when the better has the worse under control, then a man is said to be master of himself; and this is a term of praise; but when, owing to evil education or association, the better principle, which is also the smaller, is overwhelmed by the greater mass of the worse—in this case he is blamed and is called the slave of self and unprincipled . . . Look at our newly-created State, and there you will find one of these two conditions realized; for the State, as you will acknowledge, may be justly called master of itself, if the words 'temperance' and 'self-mastery' truly express the rule of the better part over the worse."

Temperance, or its equivalent, moderation, is the subjugation of pleasures and desires to reason, an achievement most readily attained by the 'best born' and 'best educated.' In like manner, a city also acquires temperance by becoming "master of its own pleasures and desires, and master of itself." Although the virtue of courage should predominate in the State's warrior class, and wisdom in its leaders, temperance is a necessary virtue in all three classes for from it a type of harmony results. "Temperance is unlike courage and wisdom, each of which resides in a part only, the one making the State wise and the other valiant; not so temperance, which extends the whole, and runs through all the notes of the scale, and produces a harmony of the weaker and the stronger and the middle class, whether you suppose them to be stronger or weaker in wisdom or power or numbers or wealth, or anything else. Most truly then may we deem temperance to be the agreement of the naturally superior and inferior, as to the right to rule of either, both in states and individuals."

Courage, one of the four cardinal virtues, is not a necessary quality for every member of the State to possess, but only those in whose care falls the responsibility of protecting its citizens from enemies foreign and domestic, namely, the class of soldiers, police, etc. "One who calls any State courageous or cowardly, will be thinking of the part which fights and goes out to war on the State's behalf... The city will be courageous in virtue of a portion of herself which preserves under all circumstances that opinion about the nature of things to be feared and not to be feared in which our legislator educated them; and this is what you term courage."

Courage, if it is to be of the virtuous type, must be qualified or moderated in order to prevent its becoming beastial on the one extreme or cowardly deficient on the other. Music appreciation and physical gymnastics are two effective methods of cultivating courage, yet preventing this virtue from deteriorating into either effeminate defect or bestial excess. "You will understand what our object was in selecting our soldiers, and educating them in music and gymnastic; we were contriving influences which would prepare them to take the dye of the laws in perfection, and the colour of their opinion about dangers and of every other opinion was to be indelibly fixed by their nurture and training, not to be washed away by such lyes as pleasure — mightier agent far in washing the soul than any soda or lye; or by sorrow, fear, and desire, the mightiest of all other solvents. And this sort of universal saving power of true opinion in conformity with law about real and false dangers I call and maintain to be courage. But I agree, he replied; for I suppose that you mean to exclude mere uninstructed courage, such as that of a wild beast or of a slave."

Wisdom, a virtue of vital necessity to the ruling class, is the dominant feature of the guardian group, the State's smallest class by a considerable margin. "And so by reason of the smallest part or class, and of the knowledge which resides in this presiding and ruling part of itself, the whole State, being thus constituted according to nature, will be wise; and this, which has the only knowledge worthy to be called wisdom, has been ordained by nature to be of all classes the least."

Class Stratification.

Three sharp distinctions in class structure are clearly noted in Plato's utopia: (1) artisans, (2) warriors, (3) legislators or guardians. Each with its own prescribed task, making its peculiar contribution to the good of the whole, contributes to the materialization of justice. Justice is "having and doing what is a man's own, and belongs to him... But when the cobbler or any other man whom nature designed to be a trader, having his heart lifted up by wealth or strength or number of his followers, or any like advantage, attempts to force his way into the class of warriors, or a warrior into that of legislators and guardians, for which he is unfitted, and either to take the implements or the duties of the other; or when one man is trader, legislator, and warrior all in one, then I think you will agree with me in saying that this interchange and this meddling of one with another is the ruin of the State ... There are three distinct classes, any meddling of one with another, or the change of one into another, is the greatest harm to the State, and may be most justly termed evil-doing ... This then is injustice; and on the other hand when the trader, the auxiliary, and the guardian each do their own business, that is justice, and will make the city just."

Class membership stems originally from human nature or psychological constitution. When a person has been classified as a given type, he is given training and education suitable to his native abilities since only in this way can an individual perform his best and be placed in the occupation for which he is best suited. "A State was thought by us to be just when the three classes in the State severally did their own business; and also thought to be temperate and valiant and wise by reason of certain other affections and qualities of these same classes ... And so of the individual; we may assume that he has the same three principles in his own soul which are found in the State; and he may be rightly described in the same terms, because he is affected in the same manner."

Human nature is composed of three principal parts: (1) the *rational*, whose excellence fructifies into the virtue of wisdom and the possessors of which become guardians or legislators of the State owing to their talents; (2) the *spirited*, whose constitution is predisposed to the virtue of courage due to the fact of their excelling in this characteristic; (3) the concupiscent-controlled, composed of those who possess excellent self-control or moderation of appetite, accordingly they acquire the virtue of temperance. Plato places the following query in the mouth of Socrates:

> Is passion different from reason also, or only a kind of reason; in which latter case instead of three principles in the soul, there will only be two, the rational and the concupiscent; or rather, as the State was composed of three classes, traders, auxiliaries, counsellors, so may there be in the individual soul a third element which is passion or spirit, and when not corrupted by bad education is the natural auxiliary of reason?
>
> Yes, he said, there must be a third ... We may observe even in young children that they are full of spirit almost as soon as they are born, whereas some of them never seem to attain to the use of reason and most of them late enough ...
>
> We have reached land, and are fairly agreed that the same principles which exist in the State exist also in the individual, and that they are three in number ... The same quality which constitutes courage in the State

> constitutes courage in the individual, and that both State and the individual bear the same relation to all the other virtues . . . and the individual will be acknowledged by us to be just in the same way in which the State is just . . . We cannot but remember that the justice of the State consisted in each of the three classes doing the work of its own class . . . And ought not the rational principle, which is wise, and has the care of the whole soul, to rule, and the passionate or spirited principle to be the subject and ally?

As indicated in the preceding discussion, the rational nature of man is his supernal, to which the rest of his nature must conform if order and justice are to prevail within an individual and throughout the State at large, hence the one ruling principle in man and State is reason.

Keep in mind that every human individual possesses by virtue of his humanity all three traits: temperance, courage, wisdom, but some persons naturally excel in one of the three, and consequently are said to be virtuous in relation to that particular characteristic. Accordingly, one's virtue determines a person's classification within society. Justice is the harmonious interplay of all three virtues, both within an individual and within the group, whereas disunity or disharmony contribute to vice and disorder within a particular person and the State as well. Socrates rhetorically inquires: "Must not injustice be a strife which arises among the three principles – a meddlesomeness, and interference, and rising up of a part of the soul against the whole, an assertion of unlawful authority, which is made by a rebellious subject against a true prince, of whom he is the natural vassal, – what is all this confusion and delusion but injustice, and intemperance and cowardice and ignorance, and every form of vice?" Note that vice stands in direct antinomy to the cardinal virtues: temperance, courage, wisdom, justice.

The State or individual which is well integrated experiences justice or is said to be just. In reference to the State, this consists of a proper distribution of labor without one individual's usurping the prerogatives of any other for "the division of labour which required the carpenter and the shoemaker and the rest of the citizens to be doing each his own business, and not another's, was a shadow of justice." Within the individual, a similar set of circumstances maintains; injustice is the disruption of various functions of the soul producing chaotic consequences, whereas their harmonious or just activity issues in integrity, peace of soul, or psychological adjustment. "The just man does not permit the several elements within him to interfere with one another, or any of them to do the work of others, – he sets in order his own inner life, and is his own master and his own law, and at peace with himself; and when he has bound together the three principles within him, which may be compared to the higher, lower, and middle notes of the scale, and the intermediate intervals — when he has bound all these together, and is no longer many, but has become one entirely temperate and perfectly adjusted nature, then he proceeds to act, if he has to act, whether in a matter of property, or in the treatment of the body, or in some affair of politics or private business; always thinking and calling that which presides over it, wisdom, and that which at any time impairs this condition, he will call unjust action, and the opinion which presides over it ignorance." Note that the executive of the personality which deliberates and gives it direction is wisdom, and that which holds it in perfect proportion and balance is justice. Note also the definite intimation that virtues are placed in an ascending order, temperance and courage being relegated to a lower position than wisdom and justice.

For Plato, virtue is more than merely 'Virtue for virtue's sake;' it fructifies in happiness and health, whereas vice consumes both State and individual in disease. "Virtue is the health and beauty and well-being of the soul, and vice the disease and weakness and deformity of the same . . ."

Education and the Philosopher King.

Education in the State is of major import since "the direction in which education starts a man, will determine his future life." Furthermore, a talented man accelerates the progress of his natural endowments through education "for good nurture and education implant good constitutions." Finally, education facilitates the determination of the particular class into which an individual is to be placed: artisan, warrior, or guardian.

The principle purpose of education consists in training each of the three classes for assuming the proper function of their respective duties: the artisans to become builders, mechanics, tradesmen, etc.; warriors to become effective defenders of the State from foreign enemies, and the maintenance of domestic tranquility; guardians to protect and uphold the laws and administrative functions of the State.

The Republic, although an Aristocracy, is founded on a democratic basis; every citizen has an equal right to prove himself and strive for the nation's position of the highest honor. Education serves as a segregation process as well, for by it, members of various classes are determined, or technically, a person's natural endowment or talent is disclosed. If his natural constitution excels in temperance, then that individual is relegated to the class of artisans; if courage, then he is classified a warrior; and if wisdom, a guardian.

The core curriculum of studies beginning at the age of ten, consists of gymnastics, music, and elementary academic studies; but gymnastics alone may be given on a compulsory basis without ill effects, whereas knowledge cannot be imparted under compulsion for it 'obtains no hold on the mind.' Athletics precedes serious academic studies and terminates when academic subjects are assumed "for sleep and exercise are unpropitious to learning," though competitive sports possess considerable value.

On completion of gymnastics and a rudimentary academic education in youth, "those who are selected from the class of twenty years old will be promoted to higher honour, and the sciences which they learned without any order in their early education will now be brought together, and they will be able to see the natural relationship of them to one another." The test, which determines those who possess ability to achieve further and are to continue their academic studies to advanced levels, discloses a native talent for debate, argument, aptitude for logic, reflective insight, High I.Q., sagacity for the significant, etc., "and the capacity for such knowledge is the great criterion of the dialectical talent: the comprehensive mind is always the dialectical" (logical).

At an age when academic disciplines of the curriculum are intensified, artisans are screened out, and owing to their lack of logical talent, accordingly are excused from further study and released to assume their respective occupations in the 'work a day' world, whereas those possessing dialectical talent (scholastic aptitude) continue their academic disciplines until the age of thirty, when the most promising students are selected as an elite body, due to their penetrating rational abilities, and placed in a special class, thereby 'elevated to higher honour.' "Our citizens who are now thirty years of age, every care must be taken in introducing them to dialectic . . . There is a danger lest they should taste the dear delight too early; for youngsters, as you may have observed, when they first get the taste in their mouths, argue for amusement, and are always contradicting and refuting others in imitation of those who refute them; like puppy-dogs, they rejoice in pulling and tearing at all who come near them."

From the age of thirty to thirty-five, these scholarly aristocrats are to be thoroughly trained in philosophy, not so much for the sake of acquiring knowledge thereof, but for becoming a philosopher and dialectician "who is seeking for truth and not eristic who is contradicting for the sake of amusement; and the greater moderation of his character will increase instead of diminishing the honour of the pursuit." At thirty-five, our freshmen philosophers are required to obtain first hand experience of life to determine whether or not they are properly fit to assume high office or whether under the strain of life's temptations, military obligations, or public office appointments, they yield and prove failures.

From age thirty-five to fifty, this elite class of aristocrats, called guardians, thoroughly trained philosophers and dialecticians, are required to hold high political positions, where every care has been exercised to insure their successful tenure of office. These guardians of the law are 'true philosopher kings,' "despising the honours of this present world which they deem mean and worthless, esteeming above all things right and the honour that springs from right, and regarding justice as the greatest and most necessary of all things, whose ministers they are, and whose principles will be exalted by them when they set in order their own city." They are philosophers, naturally gifted with virtues of courage, magnificence, apprehension, memory; such noble and gracious persons favor truth, justice, courage, temperance. Regarding such persons, even the 'god of jealousy' himself could find no fault.

As an insulation against yielding to any possible form of corruption, these aristocrat rulers are required to live on a communistic plane without right of private ownership of property of any kind, although provided with all things needful. Denied right of personal property, corrupting influences such as graft, using one's office for self-gain or family-gain, indifference to public good, etc. will diminish and be held to a minimum, if not entirely abolished. Guardians of the State live in houses 'common to all,' possess 'nothing private or individual,' receive 'in lieu of annual payment, only their maintenance,' are without families for they have both 'wives and children in common.' So that the offspring of the guardians will be the finest breed possible, the women with whom they unite will be carefully screened from among those of the highest magnitude, physically and intellectually.

Twenty to forty years of age is a woman's prime of life, whereas a man's is from twenty-five to fifty-five. Children of the guardians do not necessarily become members of the guardian class themselves, unless they possess the natural propensities and talents, moreover, members of the upper classes are subject to being degraded to one of lower rank if behavior unbecoming to their station warrants it. However, aristocracy is principally a matter of birth, of natural talent, and innate intelligence; training alone is ineffectual. "There will be discovered to be in some, natures who ought to study philosophy and to be leaders in the State; and others who are not born to be philosophers, and are meant to be followers rather than leaders."

Polity.

Although five basic forms of government exist, only one may be considered good and just, Aristocracy, or Aristocracy consisting of a single man, *Monarchy;* the remaining four: *Timocracy, Oligarchy, Democracy, Tyranny,* are degenerate and unjust forms. Plato favored a Monarchy, provided that within the state there could be found a 'philosopher king' who was so outstanding that he was without peer, in other words, a Socrates, but if such could not be found, and a number of distinguished guardians of equal calibre prevailed, then they were to sit together as a unit and rule as a senate, namely, an Aristocracy.

Plato's Aristocracy is composed of 'those who love the truth in each thing,' lovers of wisdom (philosophers) who because they 'guard the laws and institutions of our State' are called guardians. Their clear vision of 'absolute truth' enables them to fashion laws according to 'beauty, goodness, justice.' "He whose desires are drawn towards knowledge in every form will be absorbed in the pleasures of the soul, and will hardly feel bodily pleasure – I mean if he is a true philosopher and not a sham one." Obviously such a person is temperate, free from vices of illiberality, meanness, cowardice, covetousness, boastfulness; contrariwise he will be just, truthful, courageous, temperate, magnificent, gentle, so that he may be a 'true pilot' of his 'ship of state.' "The perfect guardian must be a philosopher," a 'lover of knowledge' engaged in "philosophy, the noblest pursuit of all." The philosopher king is interested in knowledge of the highest magnitude, even that which surpasses justice, namely, 'the good,' "and if we only have a guardian who has this knowledge our State will be perfectly ordered."

Government of States may run the entire gamut from 'pure justice' to 'pure injustice,' each form issuing from the character of its individuals of which the State is composed. "States are as the men are; they grow out of human characters. Then if the constitutions of States are five, the dispositions of individual minds will also be five." The five are: *Aristocracy,* the rule of the best, just, good; *Timocracy* (or Timarchy), rule by those which our State seeks to honor – usually military leaders; *Oligarchy,* rule by a few selfish wealthy opportunists for private gain; *Democracy,* rule by many (poor, lower classes for selfish gain); *Tyranny,* rule by a despot without regard for law.

Timocracy is a rule by men who are by natural constitution fitted for war rather than peace since they value "military strategems and contrivances, and the waging of everlasting wars." The Timocrat is contentious, covetous, ambitious, rough with slaves, uncultured, yet fond of culture, "courteous to freemen, and remarkably obedient to authority; he is a lover of power and a lover of honour; claiming to be a ruler, not because he is eloquent, or on any ground of that sort, but because he is a soldier and has performed feats of arms; he is also a lover of gymnastic exercise and of the chase."

Timocracy degenerates into *Oligarchy* when its rulers devise illegal modes of expenditure of public funds for private gain. Oligarchal disregard of virtue makes them "lovers of trade and money; they honour and look up to the rich man, and make a ruler of him, and dishonour the poor man . . . They next proceed to make a law which fixes a sum of money as the qualification of citizenship . . . Changes in the constitution they effect by force of arms."

A sharp and penetrating cleavage exists in Oligarchies, a dichotomous division of two extreme classes, one of immense wealth and the other of utter poverty. Oligarchs cannot cope with war since they are "few to fight as they are few to rule." The Oligarch is a penurious and "shabby fellow, who saves something out of everything and makes a purse for himself; and this is the sort whom the vulgar applaud." Both his philosophy and that of his State rests on the high valuation of money. The Oligarch is 'two-faced,' his virtue being merely a forced external veneer which breaks down when the opportunity to cheat presents itself. "The man, then, will be at war with himself; he will be two men, and not one; but, in general, his better desires will be found to prevail over his inferior ones . . . The miser and the moneymaker answers to the oligarchical State."

Democracies spawn out of Oligarchies; poverty and indebtedness create a class 'eager for revolution' so that all things may be free. The poor conquer their oligarchal leaders and institute their own magistrates elected by lot. Democracies are not composed of a single type of personality because democratic freedom fosters the greatest variety of character and constitutions. "Because of the liberty which reigns there – they have a complete assortment of constitutions; and he who has a mind to establish a State, as we have been doing, must go to a democracy as he would to a bazaar at which they sell them, and pick out the one that suits him; then, when he has made his choice, he may found his State . . . These and other kindred characteristics are proper to democracy, which is a charming form of government, full of variety and disorder, and dispensing a sort of equality to equals and unequals alike." The chief characteristics of a Democracy are liberty, equality, and multiformity.

Democracies may degenerate into *Tyranny* when "modesty, which they call silliness, is ignominiously thrust into exile by them, and temperance, which they nickname unmanliness, is trampled in the mire and cast forth; they persuade men that moderation and orderly expenditure are vulgarity and meanness, and so, by the help of a rabble of evil appetites, they drive them beyond the border . . . Insolence they term breeding, and anarchy liberty, and waste magnificence, and impudence courage. And so the young man passes out of his original nature, which was trained in the school of necessity, into the freedom and libertinism of useless and unnecessary pleasures." A degenerate, 'disordered in his wits,' 'indulging in the appetite of the hour,' without regard for law or order, living in the 'heydey of passion' a life that is "motley and manifold and an epitome of the lives of many . . . answers to the State which we described as fair and spangled," namely a Democracy.

The principle cause of a Democracy's deteriorating into a Tyranny is its insatiable desire and obsession for freedom which enslaves it to the complete neglect of all else. Complete freedom signifies Anarchy, such as children becoming equals with parents without respect or reverence for either parent. The same disease which reduced Oligarchy to a Democracy, 'magnified and intensified by liberty,' destroys Democracy — "the truth being that the excessive increase of anything often causes a reaction in the opposite direction . . . The excess of liberty, whether in States or individuals, seems only to pass into excess of slavery . . . and so tyranny naturally arises out of democracy, and the most aggravated form of tyranny and slavery out of the most extreme form of liberty."

Originally, tyrants were usually protectors of the common people who once 'tasting blood' degenerate to Tyranny with wolfish characteristics. The embryonic tyrant "having a mob entirely at his disposal . . . is not restrained from shedding the blood of kinsmen; by the favourite method of false accusation he brings them into court and murders them, making the life of man disappear, and with unholy tongue and lips tasting the blood of his fellow citizens; some he kills and others he banishes, at the same time hinting at the abolition of debts and partition of lands . . . standing up in the chariot of State with the reins in his hand, no longer protector, but tyrant absolute . . . And this is real tyranny, . . . the people who would escape the smoke which is the slavery of freemen, have fallen into the fire which is the tyranny of slaves. Thus liberty, getting out of all order and reason, passes into the harshest and bitterest form of slavery . . . from democracy to tyranny."

Conclusion.

Although this concludes the social philosophy found in the *Republic,* Plato modifies some of his thoughts given herein in two of his other works: *Politicus* and *Laws,* but neither of these compares with his crowning literary effort, the *Republic.* The chief modification is prompted by a skeptical attitude on the part of Plato, who originally regarded laws as infallible, but now notes their dependence upon the integrity of officials. Well aware that a corrupt person may always find devious ways of circumventing the law if he so desires, Plato admonishes the enactment of one unchangeable rule administered by a just and wise person, namely, to rule every situation intelligently.

The main point of the *Politicus* is reasonable voluntary persuasion on the part of the ruler in governing his people. Although Plato enumerates and discusses three main forms of government, he selects a Monarchy as the superior one. The chief modification in the *Laws* is the abandonment of Communism.

XIII

ARISTOTLE'S *POLITICS:*

A Monarchy

Definition of the State.

It may be fairly stated of *Aristotle* that he is 'panteleological,' that is to say, he believes that everything has a purpose for being, some goal for its existence, some aim in life which may be regarded as its good. The reason is: "Nature makes nothing in vain;" whatever nature does, it does with a purpose.

Inasmuch as this is the case, it would follow logically that society and the State also have a purpose for their existence. "Every State is a community of some kind, and every community is established with a view to some good; for mankind always act in order to obtain that which they think good. But, if all communities aim at some good, the state or political community, which is the highest of all, and which embraces all the rest, aims at good in a greater degree than any other, and at the highest good."[1] Accordingly, the objective of every society is the pursuit of the *summum bonum,* life's highest good.

Although man forms a government, the State is nature's creation stemming from the natural constitution of man. Man is created a social animal; the State is the necessary fulfillment and realization of this basic nature – otherwise man would lapse into some form of perverted existence, such as the hermit, an anomaly of society. The miserable and wretched existence of the hermit is evidence enough that man's wholesome and normal habitat is society, and it is among people that he finds happiness and self-fulfillment. "Hence it is evident that the State is a creation of nature, and that *man is by nature a political animal.* And he who by nature and not by mere accident is without a State is either a bad man or above humanity."

[1] Quotations from Aristotle in this section are from *Politica,* tr. Benjamin Jowett, (1885).

The State — A Moral Idea.

The State is a moral idea, not merely a formation upon which men choose to agree; without society, neither the good life nor morality is possible. For example, how is it possible to steal, murder, commit adultery, bear false witness, etc., in isolation, without any other person involved? How is it possible to do deeds of kindness, to express brotherly love, to be friendly or helpful in a situation in which you are the only member? "And it is characteristic of man that he alone has any sense of good and evil, of just and unjust, and the like, and the association of living beings who have this sense makes a family and a State."

The State is not only a reality in its own right, but it is of greater import than the individual for without it, the individual loses his significance. "Further, the State is by nature clearly prior to the family and to the individual, since the whole is of necessity prior to the part," the reason being that if the whole of society is destroyed then no individual survives, but if an individual or a number of individuals perish, society nevertheless survives. The broader the social unit, the wider the range of human needs which are satisfied. The family unit being small satisfies but a relatively small number of man's needs; the community being larger satisfies more of his needs, but the State, society's largest segment, satisfies most of his needs.

The State has two basic functions: the satisfaction of man's social instinct, and fitting him for the good life. Nature created man a gregarious being, accordingly even if man were able to live alone successfully, he would not choose to, in preference to living together. "Man is by nature a political animal. And, therefore, men, even when they do not require one another's help, desire to live together; not but that they are also brought together by their common interests in proportion as they severally attain to any measure of well-being. This is certainly the chief end, both of the individuals and of States."

Citizenship.

Not every person in a State may be regarded as a citizen; certainly citizenship does not extend to slaves. Contrary to Platonic theory, a good citizen need not be a good man. A good citizen is regarded as such by rendering valuable service to the State as well as discharging duties of office and submitting obediently to law. A good man exceeds the good citizen by becoming sufficiently competent to rule, but he learns by obeying.

Citizenship training is tantamount to moral training. "One citizen differs from another, but the salvation of the community is the common business of them all. This community is the constitution; the virtue of the citizen must therefore be relative to the constitution of which he is a member. If, then, there are many forms of government, it is evident that there is not one single virtue of the good citizen which is perfect virtue. But we say that the good man is he who has one single virtue which is perfect virtue. Hence it is evident that the good citizen need not of necessity possess the virtue which makes a good man . . . But will there then be no case in which the virtue of the good citizen and the virtue of the good man coincide? To this we answer that the good *ruler* is a good and wise man, and that he who would be a statesman must be a wise man."

Types of Government.

Unlike Plato, Aristotle concludes that not one, but three forms of good government are possible: (1) Monarchy, (2) Aristocracy, (3) Polity. A government may be designated good if it is just, that is, if public good is its prime consideration, not selfish gain of its leaders. "Governments which have a regard to the common interest are constituted in accordance with strict principles of justice, and are therefore true forms; but those which regard only the interest of the rulers are all defective and perverted forms, for they are despotic, whereas a State is a community of freemen."

The three possible forms of good States are those in which one man rules in the interests of its citizens, namely, a *Monarchy* or one man rule; an *Aristocracy,* or a government of a few motivated by public concern; a *Polity,* a nation governed by law with a view to common interest. Each, however, may degenerate through perversion, by its rulers displacing interest in public concern with private gain. "The true forms of government, therefore, are those in which the one, or the few, or the many, govern with a view to the common interest; but governments which rule with a view to the private interest, whether of the one, or of the few, or of the many, are perversions . . . Of the forms of government in which one rules, we call that which regards the common interests, kingship or royalty; that in which more than one, but not many, rule, aristocracy; and it is so called, either because the rulers are the best men, or because they have at heart the best interests of the State and of the citizens. But when the citizens at large administer the State for the common interest, the government is called by the generic name — a constitution . . . Of the above-mentioned forms, the perversions are as follows: — of royalty, tyranny; of aristocracy, oligarchy; of constitutional government, democracy. For tyranny is a kind of monarchy which has in view the interest of the monarch only; oligarchy has in view the interest of the wealthy; democracy, of the needy: none of them the common good of all."

The following diagram serves to clarify the foregoing account of the three good forms of government and their corresponding degenerate forms owing to the rulers in each case shifting concern from public interest to private gain:

GOOD FORMS OF GOVERNMENT		BAD FORMS OF GOVERNMENT
(Rulers concerned for the common good)	Good forms of government in the left column may degenerate into perverted corresponding forms on the right.	(Rulers interested primarily in private gain)
1. *Monarchy:* (one good and wise leader)		1. *Tyranny:* (selfish rule by a despot without regard for law)
2. *Aristocracy:* (few leaders – good and wise)		2. *Oligarchy:* (rule of the selfish wealthy few)
3. *Polity* or *Constitutional Form of Government:* (Many good and wise leaders governing according to law)		3. *Democracy:* (extreme form – rule by the poor without regard for law or others)

Polity or constitutional form of government is not unlike a Monarchy or Aristocracy; essentially all three are alike since each is equally interested in the common good and ruling in its favor, differing only in reference to the number of persons engaged in the administration of government. When but a single man assumes the task of government as sole administrator, that State is termed a Monarchy; when a few share the responsibilities of rule, sitting as a senate in its undertaking, then such government is termed an Aristocracy, but when a sizable number of persons or the entire community sits as a body in the determination and administration of the laws of the city or State, it is termed a Democracy.

On the other hand, perverse forms of government are also similar, differing only as to the number of persons sitting as a governing body, 'one' would constitute a Tyranny, 'few' would be termed an Oligarchy, whereas 'many' would compose a Democracy. 'Democracy' literally means lower class rule, the rule of the poor with liberty and equality as its cardinal principle. Aristotle noted that in democratic States of his time, Democracies were governments 'of the poor, by the poor, and for the poor' with utter disregard for the rights of the middle or upper classes – in fact, even hostility for them. It was a corrupt Democracy which was in power in Athens that executed Socrates and later came into power once again and sought to put Aristotle to death as well. Aristotle fled the city with the attitude that he had no intention of allowing Athens a second opportunity to sin against philosophy. Democracies as Aristotle depicted them were not of the American type (representative republics), but more of the New England town type in which the entire citizenry convenes in its town hall to deliberate and enact the laws, unrestricted by a constitution, often carried on in the heat of emotion, leaving much regret, and even injustice, in their wake.

A Democracy, in the finest sense of the word, is a polity or constitutional form of government in which rule is by law, not by majority decision. Citizens are protected by a constitution which majority decision cannot override or suspend with every whim of fancy. The essence of a Democracy is majority rule without regard for law or constitution. This type of Democracy is "what tyranny is to other forms of monarchy. The spirit of both is the same, and they alike exercise despotic rule over the better citizens. The decrees of the demos correspond to the edicts of the tyrant; and the demagogue is to one what the flatterer is to the other ... The law ought to be supreme over all, and the magistrates should judge of particulars, and only this should be considered a constitution."

The criterion of defective or corrupt forms of government is the rulers' lack of concern for public good, or more accurately their interest in private gain. Each good form of government has its corresponding defective form and degenerates to the level of the corrupt form when its primary interest deteriorates from the good of the people governed to selfish advantage of the individual or individuals governing.

Tyranny, the lawless rule of one man, may assume one of three forms: (1) Barbarian Despotism, in which a despot assumes reign through heredity, (2) Elective Dictatorship, which may limit term of office, (3) Tyranny (in its strict sense), a lawless rule of one man over his unwilling subjects. "The monarch rules according to law over willing subjects; but they are tyrannical in so far as he is despotic and rules according to his own fancy ... Tyranny is just that arbitrary power of an individual which is responsible to no one, and governs all alike, whether equals or better, with a view to its own advantage, not to that of its subjects, and therefore against their will." Of the three perverse forms of government, Tyranny is regarded as the worst, and Democracy the most tolerable of the three. In Plato's estimation of these defective forms of government,

Democracy was considered best when each person was under the protection of a constitution, but worst in the absence of any constitution.

In a Democracy, the rule of the many, the many are also poor; in an Oligarchy, the rule of the few, the few are also the wealthy. "Democrats say that justice is that to which the majority agree, oligarchs that to which the wealthier class; in their opinion the decision should be given according to the amount of property. In both principles there is some inequality and injustice. For if justice is the will of the few, any one person who has more wealth than all the rest of the rich put together, ought, upon the oligarchal principle, to have the sole power — but this would be tyranny; or if justice is the will of the majority . . . they will unjustly confiscate the property of the wealthy minority." In the last analysis, the best form of government is a Monarchy, the rule of a single man who is good and wise.

In All Things, Moderation.

The State in all of its various aspects should be as much as possible a mean, the middle road between two extremes, mean in size, mean in middle class rule, middle class dominance, mean in respect to the number of soldiers, number of slaves, number of tradesmen, etc. "Now in all States there are three elements: one class is very rich, another very poor, and a third is a mean. It is admitted that moderation and the mean are best, and therefore it will clearly be best to possess the gifts of fortune in moderation; for in that condition of life men are most ready to follow rational principle . . . The middle class is least likely to shrink from rule, or to be over-ambitious for it; both of which are injurious to the State . . . A city ought to be composed, as far as possible, of equals and similars; and these are generally the middle classes. Wherefore the city which is composed of middle-class citizens is necessarily best constituted in respect of the elements of which we say the fabric of the State naturally consists. And this is the class of citizens which is most secure in a State, for they do not, like the poor, covet their neighbors' goods; nor do others covet theirs, as the poor covet the goods of the rich; and as they neither plot against others, nor are themselves plotted against, they pass through life safely."

A constitution is unable to be upheld without support from its ruling class. Since States of Greece rarely have the middle as their strongest class, but upper or lower, most Grecian governments are oligarchal (rule of the wealthy class) or democratic (government controlled by the poor). However, even in governments of extremes, States of either upper or lower class rule, the middle has an important role to play in keeping balance between the classes as arbitrator. Feuds between rich and poor must be mediated by the middle class, "the arbiter is always the one trusted, and he who is in the middle is arbiter." In middle class governments there is less chance of disruption or internal chaos, nor is their much possibility that the extremes of rich and poor will unite in a coalescent government pitted against the middle class rule. "Thus it is manifest that the best political community is formed by citizens of the middle class, and that those States are likely to be well-administered, in which the middle class is large, and stronger if possible than both the other classes, at any rate than either singly; for the addition of the middle class turns the scale, and prevents either of the extremes from being dominent." Accordingly, the State is fortunate indeed which has an abundance of persons from the middle class with moderate means and of sufficient property, for it is from either extreme that a Tyranny emerges.

The ideal State should also be moderate in size, large enough to supply the necessities of a liberal and temperate life, but not too large so that it becomes unmanageable and unwieldy. Moreover, its city, the center of activity, rule, communication, etc. should be centrally located. "It is not difficult to determine the general character of the territory which is required . . . it should be difficult of access to the enemy, and easy of egress to the inhabitants . . . for a country which is easily seen can be easily protected. As to the position of the city, if we could have what we wish, it should be well situated in regard both to sea and land. This then is the one principle, that it should be a convenient centre for the protection of the whole country: the other is, that it should be suitable for receiving the fruits of the soil, and also for the bringing in of timber and any other products that are easily transported."

Moderation, or a balanced personality should characterize the nature of the citizens of the State as a whole. Ideally, a blend of northern Europeans, who are spirited and courageous, with Asiatics, who are intelligent with inventive genious, should be sought and inculcated, but, individually, either of these two groups have deficiencies which ushers in their downfall: the Asiatics lacking courage, fall prey to enemies who would enslave them for their talents, and northern Europeans, although enjoying comparative freedom owing to their courageous spirit, lack political acumen. "Those who live in a cold climate and in Europe are full of spirit, but wanting in intelligence and skill; and therefore retain comparative freedom, but have no political organization, and are incapable of ruling over others. Whereas the natives of Asia are intelligent and inventive, but they are wanting in spirit, and therefore they are always in a state of subjection and slavery. But the Hellenic race, which is situated between them, is likewise intermediate in character, being high-spirited and also intelligent. Hence it continues free, and is the best governed of any nation, and, if it could be formed into one State, would be able to rule the world."

Education in the Ideal State.

The philosophy of the State is essentially a social morality whose ethical goal is the good life of its inhabitants, namely a life of happiness. A happy nation is one in which its citizens are virtuous, and a perfect State has perfect happiness because its people exercise virtue perfectly. "No one will dispute the propriety of that partition of goods which separates them into three classes, viz. external goods, goods of the body, and goods of the soul, or deny that the happy man must have all three. For no one would maintain that he is happy who has not in him a particle of courage or temperance or justice or prudence, who is afraid of every insect which flutters past him, and will commit any crime, however great, in order to gratify his lust of meat or drink, who will sacrifice his dearest friend for the sake of half-a-farthing, and is as feeble and false in mind as a child or a madman."

The happiness of a State is inextricably intertwined with the happiness of its individuals; without one the other is impossible. The happy State implies the happiness of its individuals; when its individuals are disorderly, disorganized, immoral, then the State also will be so inclined. The happiness of the State is to be identified with that of an individual; of this "there can be no doubt – no one denies that they are the same."

The goal of education is the realization of the good State by training the young to obey during their youthful years, and to become good rulers in adulthood. Accordingly, rule is the prime objective of education; moreover, it becomes the ultimate and highest function, but the good ruler must also be a good man for the two are one. Hence, the goal of education is essentially that of producing good men.

The natural state of man is peace, not war, therefore a military education of all its citizens is unwarranted. The military should be moderate in size, adequate for defence, but not of a magnitude which would cripple the State. The Spartans exemplify this point of excess well by their military State which could cope only with wartime conditions, consequently in times of peace 'rusted as a sword in a scabbard.' "For most of these military States are safe only while they are at war, but fall when they have acquired their empire; like unused iron they lose their temper in time of peace. And for this the legislator is to blame, he never having taught them how to lead the life of peace." Military States contain their own self-destructive forces; their inevitable collapse is from within, not from foreign enemies.

Military States, if they are to survive, must educate their people for a life of peace for, paradoxically, this is the end result of all wars; moreover, man's natural constitution craves a peaceful existence. "Since the end of individuals and of States is the same, the end of the best man and of the best constitution must also be the same; it is therefore evident that there ought to exist in both of them the virtues of leisure; for peace, as had been often repeated, is the end of war, and leisure of toil."

The curriculum of infants and very young children consists of physical and moral education which is in the hands of overseers. Intellectual training follows when a period of preparation from five to seven years of age has been completed. "The directors of education should have an eye to their bringing up . . . For until they are seven years old they must live at home; and therefore, even at this early age, it is to be expected that they should acquire a taint of meanness from what they hear and see. Indeed, there is nothing which the legislator would be more careful to drive away than indecency of speech; for the light utterance of shameful words leads soon to shameful actions." An individual's life is divided into periods of seven years each for purposes of convenience, but natural divisions also exist. "There are two periods of life with reference to which education has to be divided, from seven to the age of puberty, and onwards to the age of one and twenty."

Since the goal of the State is one and the same for all individuals, education should be alike and public, for the character of people in a given State determines the nature of its government; democratic personalities create Democracies, oligarchal types institute Oligarchies, and tyrants, Tyrannies. "Since the whole city has one end, it is manifest that education should be one and the same for all, and that it should be public, and not private – not as present, when every one looks after his own children separately, and gives them separate instruction of the sort which he thinks best; the training in things which are of common interest should be the same for all." These ideas are based on the premise that citizens belong to the State as integral and inseparable parts of it owing, among other things, to the fact that a life in solitude is not conducive to survival, whereas the life of richest fulfillment is always in a society. Accordingly, a State is a moral concept, a place where a person finds self-realization, happiness, and the fulfillment of moral values.

Life, moral life of the highest magnitude, is reserved for the leisure class exclusively, for man's highest goal is the noble employment of leisure which should be spent on music, art, science, philosophy, etc. A slave is prevented from moral achievement since his life is completely occupied with menial pursuits, but the same holds true for any laborer whose day from the rising of the sun to its setting must be spent on toil for daily bread. Men of leisure can afford time for the fine and liberal arts, scientific research, religious activity, political endeavor, cultural values, and the rest of those things which compose the virtuous, or what is the same, leisure life. "I must repeat once again, the first principle of all action is leisure . . . Leisure is better than occupation and its end . . . Leisure of itself gives pleasure and happiness and enjoyment of life, which are experienced, not by the busy man, but by those who have leisure . . . Happiness is an end, since all men deem it to be accompanied with pleasure and not with pain. This pleasure, however, is regarded differently by different persons . . . the pleasure of the best man is best, and springs from the noblest sources. It is clear then that there are branches of learning and education which we must study merely with a view to leisure spent in intellectual activity, and these are to be valued for their own sake."

Slavery.

The ancient world accepted slavery as a way of life; little was its morality questioned either in the Greco-Roman or the Judeo-Christian world. It should not come as too great a surprise, therefore, to find it condoned by Aristotle. Aristotle finds sanction for the practice on the grounds that it is natural; nature foreordained that some persons should be slaves and others masters. A slave is not he who is one by unfortunate circumstances such as a victim of war, he is one by natural constitution, created that way by nature. Furthermore, unless he resigns himself to the fact and accepts a life of slavery, he will become a miserable unhappy creature, because happiness comes only when he lives the life which his nature intends. Aristotle queries and provides his own answer: "Is there any one thus intended by nature to be a slave for whom such a condition is expedient and right, or rather is not all slavery a violation of nature? . . . That some should rule and others be ruled is a thing not only necessary, but expedient; from the hour of their birth, some are marked out for subjection, others for rule . . . The male is by nature superior, and the female inferior; and the one rules, and the other is ruled; this principle, of necessity, extends to all mankind. Where then there is such a difference as that between soul and body, or between men and animals (as in the case of those whose business is to use their body, and who can do nothing better), the lower sort are by nature slaves, and it is better for them as for all inferiors that they should be under the rule of a master. For he who can be, and therefore is, another's, and he who participates in rational principle enough to apprehend, but not to have, such a principle, is a slave by nature . . . It is clear, then, that some men are by nature free, and others slaves, and that for these latter slavery is both expedient and right."

Despite the arguments of Aristotle for the legitimacy of slavery, it is obviously neither morally right nor natural, but there is a point to what he says, namely, that some persons have made slaves of themselves, perhaps not by nature, but by second nature. Some individuals, owing to a retiring psychological personality, shrink from making decisions; not only do they avoid them, they refuse to make them. Others make their decisions for them; such persons are content and often faithful in carrying out decisions made by others. The masses of mankind seldom think independently, whether in important matters such as religion, politics, or lesser matters; others deliberate on their behalf. How many persons belong to a religious group or political party of their own independent and deliberate choice, rather than one to which their parents belonged?

Communism.

In contrast to and in sharp criticism of Plato, Aristotle repudiates the communistic ideas found in the *Republic*. Withholding from the statesman class both family and private property creates dissension and destroys natural affection normally found in familial circles. Private property contributes to the individual's happiness, moreover, it inculcates virtues, such as generosity. "That which is common to the greatest number has the least care bestowed upon it. Every one thinks chiefly of his own, hardly at all of the common interest; and only when he is himself concerned as an individual. For besides other considerations, everybody is more inclined to neglect the duty which he expects another to fulfill . . . Each citizen will have a thousand sons who will not be his sons individually, but anybody will be equally the son of anybody, and will therefore be neglected by all alike."

In the last analysis, the advantages which are claimed for Communism, particularly the common ownership of property, are even better secured on the basis of private property in the hands of a liberal owner of private property whose generous spirit sees to the alleviation of the wants of others.

XIV

MACHIAVELLI'S *PRINCE:*

A Tyranny

Machiavellianism.

Niccolo Machiavelli's *The Prince* ushered in a new era of political philosophy by sanctioning unscrupulous and devious tactics on the part of political heads of State. So emphatic and unequivocal is his stand in this respect that the word 'Machiavellian' has been coined as a term of opprobrium, signifying a person characterized by political cunning or bad faith. Webster defines Machiavellianism as "the doctrine that any means, however unscrupulous, may be justifiably employed by a ruler in order to maintain a strong central government." In Shakespeare's *Merry Wives of Windsor*, the insinuative query is made: "Am I subtle? Am I a Machiavel?" "A damned Machiavellian holds candle to the devil for a while," writes Marston in *Pygmalion.* Consensus unquestionably indicates a reprobative status in which a Machiavellian is held and the attitude of critics regarding Machiavellianism.

The Prince.

By 'the prince' is meant any totalitarian head of State, but in the book *The Prince* it refers to Cesare Borgia, Italian cardinal, military leader, and Duke of Milan. Of him, Machiavelli writes: "I know of no better precepts for a new prince to follow than the example of his actions." [1]

The Problem and Its Solution.

The fundamental problem raised in *The Prince* is: 'How princes should keep the faith,' that is, faith with their subjects, and the solution offered is: 'By laws and force,' but since the former is often ineffectual, and despite the fact that the latter is fit only for the rule of beasts, it must nevertheless be resorted to for maximum efficiency and results. It is

[1] Quotations in this section are from Niccolo Machiavelli, *The Prince,* tr. Luigi Ricci (Oxford University Press, 1903).

imperative that the prince possess both the qualities of a lion and a fox (force and fraud), a lion for power and a fox for wisdom. Since some subjects are dishonest, the prince is excused from keeping faith with his people, but it is necessary that he assume a virtuous air when in the presence of his subjects. For their sakes he must assume a virtuous image, which requires little effort, since the masses are extremely gullible; however, it is not necessary to actually be virtuous, but only to appear so. Let Machiavelli, who writes so eloquently, speak for himself:

> How laudable it is for a prince to keep good faith and live with integrity, and not with astuteness, every one knows. Still the experience of our times shows those princes to have done great things who have had little regard for good faith, and have been able by astuteness to confuse men's brains, and who have ultimately overcome those who have made loyalty their foundation. You must know, then, that there are two methods of fighting, the one by law, the other by force: the first method is that of men, the second of beasts; but as the first method is often insufficient, *one must have recourse to the second.* It is therefore necessary to know well how to use both the beast and the man . . . This system of having for teacher one who was half beast and half man is meant to indicate that a prince must know how to use both natures, and that the one without the other is not durable. A prince being thus obliged to know well how to act as a beast must imitate the fox and the lion, for the lion cannot protect himself from snares, and the fox cannot defend himself from wolves. *One must therefore be a fox to recognise snares, and a lion to frighten wolves.* Those that wish to be only lions do not understand this. Therefore, a prudent ruler ought not to keep faith when by so doing it *would be against his interest,* and when the reasons which made him bind himself no longer exist. If men were all good this precept would not be a good one; but as they are bad, and would not observe their faith with you, so you are not bound to keep faith with them. Nor are legitimate grounds ever wanting to a prince to give colour to the non-fulfilment of his promise. Of this one would furnish an infinite number of modern examples, and show how many times peace has been broken, and how many promises rendered worthless, by the faithlessness of princes, and those that have been best able to imitate the fox have succeeded best. But it is necessary to be able to disguise this character well, and to be a great feigner and dissembler; and men are so simple and so ready to obey present necessities, that *one who deceives will always find those who allow themselves to be deceived* . . . Alexander VI did nothing else but deceive men, he thought of nothing else, and found the way to do it; no man was ever more able to give assurances, or affirmed things with stronger oaths, and no man observed them less; however, he always succeeded in his deceptions, as he knew well this side of the world. It is not, therefore, necessary for a prince to have all the above-mentioned qualities, but *it is very necessary to seem to have them.* I would even be bold to say that *to possess them is dangerous,* but to appear to possess them is useful. Thus it is well to seem pious, faithful, humane, religious, sincere, and also to be so; but you must have the mind so watchful that when it is needful to be otherwise you may be able to

change to the opposite qualities. And it must be understood that a prince, and especially *a new prince, cannot observe all those things which are considered good in men,* being often obliged, in order to maintain the State, to act against faith, against charity, against humanity, and against religion. And, therefore, he must have a mind disposed to adapt itself according to the wind, and as the variations of fortune dictate, and, as I said before, not deviate from what is good, if possible, but *be able to do evil if necessitated.* A prince must take care that nothing goes out of his mouth which is not full of the above-named five qualities, and, to see and hear him, he should *seem* to be all faith, all integrity, all humanity, and all religion. And nothing is more necessary than to seem to have this last quality, for men in general judge more by the eyes than by the hands, for every one can see, but very few have to feel. Everybody sees what you appear to be, few feel what you are, and those few will not dare to oppose themselves to the many, who have the majesty of the State to defend them; and in the actions of men, and especially of princes, from which there is no appeal, *the end justifies the means.*[1]

Let a prince therefore aim at living and maintaining the State, *the means will always be judged honourable* and praised by every one, for *the vulgar is always taken by appearances* and the result of things; and *the world consists only of the vulgar,* and the few find a place when the many have nothing to rest upon. A certain prince of the present time, whom it is well not to name, never does anything but preach peace and good faith, but he is really a great *enemy to both,* and either of them, had he observed them, would have lost him both State and reputation on many occasions.

Obviously, this is a 'tongue in cheek' philosophy written to please the 'powers that be' in order to find favor with them, but it failed to achieve its purpose because the political and philosophical atmosphere of Italy underwent a rapid change to the detriment of both Machiavelli and Machiavellianism. The fundamental ethic, if there be any morality whatever in this system, rests in the dictum: "The end justifies the means." It is noteworthy that according to Machiavelli, moral, intellectual, respectable persons, and their attitude regarding this matter may be totally ignored and summarily dismissed for they constitute only an insignificant and harmless minority who need not be feared but readily submit without a struggle.

The Character of a Successful Prince.

It is imperative that the prince exercise all diligence to avoid being despised and hated, otherwise his career is subject to collapse; success in this respect compensates for all other vices combined since none produce the disastrous effects of these two. The chief of State is principally hated for rapacious activities such as usurpation of property and

[1] E.R.P. Vincent's rendition.

women, for they rightfully belong to his subjects. He may rest content when he respects his subjects rights and holds them inviolate. Provided he adheres to this line of strategy, the only adversaries remaining are an ambitious few who can be held in check with ease.

Objectionable qualities must be eliminated from the prince's personality. "He is rendered despicable by being thought changeable, frivolous, effeminate, timid, and irresolute; which a prince must guard against as a rock of danger, and manage so that his actions show grandeur, high courage, seriousness, and strength; and as to the government of his subjects, let his sentence be irrevocable, and let him adhere to his decisions so that no one may think of deceiving him or making him change."

The prince's public image stands him in good stead in maintaining control over his subjects; furthermore, it discourages potential pretenders to his throne. "The prince who creates such an opinion of himself gets a great reputation, and it is very difficult to conspire against one who has a great reputation, and he will not easily be attacked, so long as it is known that he is esteemed and reverenced by his subjects. For a prince must have two kinds of fear: one internal as regards his subjects, one external as regards foreign powers." Overthrowing the established power is no easy task since it requires a formidable force composed of sizable numbers. Groups sufficiently large to attempt successful revolutions are usually composed of disgruntled cobelligerents, (not faithful and loyal allies), who conspire to seize power for their own factions, or at least engage in the common purpose of dethroning a common enemy. "Experience shows that there have been many conspiracies, but few have turned out well, for whoever conspires cannot act alone, and cannot find companions except among those who are discontent... he must either be a rare friend to you or else a very bitter enemy to the prince if he keeps faith with you . . . On the side of the conspirator there is nothing but fear, jealousy, suspicion, and dread of punishment which frightens him; and on the side of the prince there is the majesty of government, the laws, the protection of friends and of the State which guards him. When to these things are added the goodwill of the people, it is impossible that any one should have the temerity to conspire."

The prince must exercise an important rule, namely, to delegate unpopular duties to others, but to be completely successful in this regard, he must complement this act by reserving for himself the privilege of bestowing favors. "I conclude, therefore, that a prince need trouble little about conspiracies when the people are well disposed, but when they are hostile and hold him in hatred, then he must fear everything and everybody. Well-ordered States and wise princes have studied diligently not to drive the nobles to desperation, and to satisfy the populace and keep it contented, for this is one of the most important matters that a prince has to deal with . . . Princes should let the carrying out of unpopular duties devolve on others, and bestow favours themselves. I conclude again by saying that a prince must esteem his nobles, but not make himself hated by the populace."

Other qualities or characteristics of the prince which make for success are the manifestation of a militant spirit before the militia and a peaceful one before the masses. "People love tranquility, and therefore like princes who are pacific, but the soldiers prefer a prince of military spirit, who is insolent, cruel and rapacious. They wish him to exercise these qualities on the people so that they may get double pay and give vent to their avarice and cruelty . . . *Hatred is gained as much by good works as by evil,* for when that party, whether populace, soldiery, or nobles, whichever it be that you consider necessary to you for keeping your position, is corrupt, you must follow its humour and satisfy it, and in that case good works will be inimical to you."

The true character of the prince is of little consequence for he may be as despicable, vile, or vicious as his nature pleases, but his princely image before his subjects must be incorruptible, distinct, and unambiguously clear as indicated previously, "and above all a prince must endeavour in every action to obtain fame for being great and excellent." Irresolute princes usually adhere to neutrality which proves ruinous. The prince must shun flatterers for they are untruthful counselors who offer untrustworthy advice. The prudent prince chooses wise men for his counsel and grants them full authority to speak the truth with frankness and candor, free from intimidation, the only restriction being that the privilege is limited to questions he himself raises. "A prince must show himself a lover of merit, and honour those who excel in every art. Moreover he must encourage his citizens to follow their callings quietly . . . he should offer rewards to whoever does these things, and to whoever seeks in any way to improve his city or State. Besides this, he ought, at convenient seasons of the year, to keep the people occupied with festivals and spectacles; and as every city is divided either into trades or into classes, he ought to pay attention to all these things, mingle with them from time to time, and give them an example of his humanity and magnificence, always holding firm, however, the majesty of his dignity, which must never be allowed to fail in anything whatever."

Two Methods of Becoming a Prince.

Two chief avenues open the way to princedoms: (1) ability and (2) good fortune; either one suffices. Some princes achieve their positions through ability while others do so by fortunate circumstances.

A person who is the chief instrument of a prince's rise to success assumes a serious risk and places himself in a highly vulnerable position by placing his own life in jeopardy. One may depend on the following "general rule, which never or very rarely fails, that whoever is the cause of another becoming powerful, is ruined himself; for that power is produced by him either through *craft* or *force*; and both of these are suspected by the one that has become powerful."

Two Varieties of Government.

According to Machiavelli, existing or former States have been only of two basic types: Republics or Monarchies. Republics, the superior of the two, are free States, but are successful only in those lands where the citizens are virtuous, otherwise a Princedom is preferable.

Assessment of Machiavellianism.

Scanning the vast field of the history of philosophy from antiquity to the contemporary scene, one finds almost every major philosopher, almost without exception, devoted to his theories with utmost sincerity. Among the notable few, who have become conspicuous owing to their paucity in numbers, are Hobbes in the expression of his philosophy contained in the *Leviathan*, and Machiavelli's philosophy found in *The Prince*. Both were 'tongue in cheek' or 'hypocritical' philosophies apparently written to please the 'powers that be,' to find favor and status with reigning political magistrates of their times.

In a sense, this explanation may be accepted as an apology for the boldly hypocritical philosophy expounded in *The Prince*, whereas the true spirit of Machiavelli's mind is found in his *Discourses* in which he favors a Republic as opposed to the philosophy of State advocated in *The Prince*.

Although Machiavellianism would be found repugnant to the average person in the United States, there are times when almost anyone can detect, in not a few American politicians, definite indications of Machiavellian characteristics. At times, one almost has the uncomfortable feeling that certain politicians have not only read *The Prince*, but have, in the practice of political life, rendered devoted service to it. Outside of the United States, indications of Machiavellianism are easily perceptible in the methods of dictators of the not too distant past, particularly in Europe, and especially in the actions of Hitler.

XV

HOBBES' *LEVIATHAN*:

A Social Contract

Thomas Hobbes' political philosophy is found mainly in his *Leviathan* (1651), but also in *De Corpore Politico* (1651), and *De Cive* (1642). The essence of his political theory is a 'social contract,' a democratic organization in which participants are considered equal, excepting the sovereign, who enjoys a privileged status, unbound by the social contract and entirely above the law, free to do what he will, provided he guarantees that his subjects live up to the terms of the compact; and further, that no power superior to his own displace his sovereign position.

Hobbes is a philosophical Materialist who adheres to a 'double truth' theory, namely, the belief that two contradictory ideas may both be true simultaneously; for example, he sought to maintain a belief in God and Atheism; truth concerning God is derived from theological grounds, but Atheism, which is equally true is derived from science, or so Hobbes fancied it. Like Machiavelli who preceded him, this too, is probably a 'tongue in cheek' philosophy designed to please the 'powers that be' in order to win their favor, but Hobbes failed to please either ecclesiastical or political powers and fled to France to escape danger, since, as he fancied, "fear and I were born together."

The Roman Catholic Church was particularly displeased with his *Leviathan,* the latter chapters of which consist of a violent attack on the abuses of that church under the striking title: "The Kingdom of Darkness." The king's displeasure was incurred by his doctrine: 'might makes right,' that is, whatever government has the power, by virtue of that fact, also has the right to rule. Any power, stronger than the established one, has every right to acquire the ruling position of the existing one; in other words, *de facto* governments alone have the right of rule, never *de jure* ones merely.

Hobbes, due to his being branded an Atheist, created a clamor that almost resulted in his being burned at the stake. His philosophy of metaphysical Materialism precludes the possibility of any existent spiritual reality including God, that is, what appears spiritual is ultimately only a material body, or at most, body in motion. A body in motion (physiological activity) gives the epiphenomenon (resulting appearance or manifestation) of mind or spirit. Since mind or soul does not exist, neither do other spiritual realities such as 'freedom of the will,' only Determinism remains.

Man's Corrupt and Belligerent Nature.

Hobbes based his political theory on his concept of the nature of man whom he depicts as a corrupt and untrustworthy being by natural constitution. People are in tacit agreement with Hobbes, he claims, because they too consider man untrustworthy as is evidenced by locking the doors of their houses; even within the family circle, one is found locking his private chest because of his mistrust of family. "It may seem strange to some man, that has not well weighed these things; that nature should thus dissociate, and render men apt to invade, and destroy one another: and he may therefore, not trusting to this inference, made from the passions, desire perhaps to have the same confirmed by experience. Let him therefore consider with himself, when taking a journey, he arms himself, and seeks to go well accompanied; when going to sleep, he locks his doors; when even in his house he locks his chests; and this when he knows there are laws, and public officers, armed to revenge all injuries done him; what opinion he has of his fellow subjects, when he rides armed; of his fellow citizens, when he locks his chests. Does he not there as much accuse mankind by his actions, as I do by my words?" [1] Although this is a plausible argument, it can hardly be taken as conclusive since man locks his door not against his neighbor, as Hobbes points out, but against a thief, who percentagewise, represents only a tiny portion of mankind. If you were to leave your door unlocked, perhaps only one in a thousand, if that, would enter and steal; in fact, even if the door were left completely ajar, the average person who called and found no one at home would perhaps close it; the rare exception would raid the house.

Not only is man corrupt and untrustworthy by nature, but by nature he has the perfect right, provided he has the necessary power, to take whatever he pleases from whomever he pleases. Nature's law is that which prevails in the jungle, namely the law of 'tooth and claw;' whoever possesses power possesses also the right to acquire whatever he can take since 'might makes right.' An examination of nature 'in the raw'

[1] Quotations in this section are from Hobbes, *Leviathan;* his archaic English has been modernized wherever deemed advisable.

proves that right belongs to the stronger, consequently the lion has the right to the 'lion's share,' and whatever he leaves behind is for the rest to take, in turn, according to their respective levels of power. The lion, king of the jungle, has the right to kill and to plunder; since he acquires this from nature, it is just.

Man, a corrupt and belligerent creature by nature, is entitled to the same laws enjoyed by brute animals; "every man has a right to every thing: even to another's body." The most important law is to keep from being destroyed, and the second is to keep alive by using whatever means is at one's disposal.

Man's natural state is one of war, owing to his inherent bellicose psychological constitution. His state of war may be overt or covert "for *war* consists not in battle only, or in the act of fighting; but in . . . the will to contend by battle . . . For as the nature of foul weather, lies not in a shower or two of rain; but in an inclination thereto of many days together; so the nature of war consists not in actual fighting; but in the known disposition thereto, during all the time there is no assurance to the contrary. All other time is *peace*."

Within man's psychological constitution exists three characteristics which account for his belligerent tendency: (1) competition, (2) diffidence, (3) glory. Competition creates within him an insatiable hunger for gain; diffidence drives him to seek security or safety; and glory, the lust for superiority, causes him to build a reputation. "The first use violence to make themselves masters of other men's persons, wives, children, and cattle; the second, to defend them; the third, for trifles, as a word, a smile, a different opinion, and any other sign of undervalue either direct in their persons, or by reflection in their kindred, their friends, their nation, their profession, or their name."

As long as man makes no agreements with his fellow men, he is not under any moral obligation whatever – he cannot sin. "Desires, and other passions of man, are in themselves no sin. No more are the actions, that proceed from those passions, till they know a law that forbids them: which till laws are made they cannot know: nor can any law be made, till they have agreed upon the person that shall make it." In man's natural state, nothing can be said to be unjust; furthermore, in such a state, force and fraud are the reigning virtues. "To this war of every man against every man, this also is consequent; that nothing can be unjust. The notions of right and wrong, justice and injustice have there no place. Where there is no common power, there is no law: where no law, no injustice. *Force and fraud are in war the two cardinal virtues.* Justice and injustice are none of the faculties neither of the body, nor mind. If they were, they might be in a man that is alone in the world, as well as his senses and passions. They are qualities that relate to men in society, not in solitude."

Natural Rights of Man.

"The *right of nature,* which writers commonly call *jus naturale,* is the liberty each man has to use his own power as he will himself for the preservation of his own nature; that is to say, of his own life; and consequently, of doing anything which in his own judgment and reason he shall conceive to be the aptest means thereto." Man has this right because he is in an inherent state of war, "and because the condition of man is a condition of war of every one against every one: in which case every one is governed by his own reason and there is nothing he can make use of, that may not be a help to him in preserving his life against his enemies."

In addition to a 'natural right' there exists a natural law as well, the first law of man, namely, the law of self-preservation. Man is forbidden to do anything destructive to his life since there is nothing in this world for which it is worth risking one's life. It is imperative that a man preserve his life at all costs. "*A law of nature (Lex Naturalis),* is a precept, or general rule, found out by reason, by which a man is forbidden to do that which is destructive of his life or take away the means of preserving the same; and to omit that by which he thinks it may be best preserved." The law of self-preservation leads to or has as its concomitant a 'rule of reason,' namely, "*that every man ought to endeavour peace, as far as he has hope of attaining it; and when he cannot obtain it, that he may seek and use all helps and advantages of war.*"

Man would not be civilized and peaceful if it were not for his dread of death for "the passions that incline men to peace are fear of death." Societies, or more particularly governments are built due solely to the "fundamental law of nature; which is *to seek peace and follow it,*" and "the second the sum of the right of nature; which is, *By all means we can, to defend ourselves.*" These two principles are responsible for men engaging in a social contract with one another.

Although man is entitled by nature to whatever he can seize by power, it would prove a futile and vain effort since men in numbers are equal. For a strong man to attack a weak brother would cause the weak to unite with others who share his predicament to ward off the attacks of the strong, or possibly even to attack the strong by invoking the principle: 'United we stand, divided we fall.'

Moreover, with the use of weapons and in numbers, it is meaningless to speak of strong and weak since the weakest person with a gun in his hand is stronger than any man of whatever physical might. "Nature has made men so equal, in the faculties of body and mind; as that though there be found one man sometimes manifestly stronger in body, or of quicker mind than another; yet when all is reckoned together, the difference between man and man is not so considerable as that one man can thereupon claim to himself any benefit to which another may not pretend as well as he. For as to the strength of body, the weakest has strength enough to kill the strongest, either by machination, or by confederacy with others that are in the same danger with himself."

Eventually, man must sue for peace since war is vain and obsolete. For example, if a strong group attacks another, the second will devise weapons to repell the first; the strong in turn, may obtain better ones, causing the weak to improve upon theirs until the time comes when weapons prove futile, hence obsolete. To illustrate: cave men fought with brute strength, such as hands and fists, driving their weaker enemies to devise weapons, such as clubs. Should the stronger then acquire clubs to gain the advantage over the weak, the weak may then, by the use of intelligence, in time construct knives. When the strong equip themselves with knives, then the weak construct longer knives called swords, and with the next round of battle, knives that can be thrown, namely, spears. In the next evolution of battle, bows and arrows are developed which is equivalent to tossing spears to great distances. Later, when the strong group is likewise equipped, guns are developed, then cannons, followed by tanks, aircraft, submarines, and finally terminating in missiles equipped with atomic bombs. At this point, war becomes obsolete, since an all-out atomic war is capable of destroying the entire human populace. Men, now compelled to sue for peace, insist on talking the matter over around a conference table since this recourse remains the only alternative to total destruction and death. Men are driven to agree upon a 'social contract.'

The right of the stronger is no longer exercisable when sizable numbers are taken into consideration, for men in groups are equal. Contemporary sociologists corroborate the testimony of this fact. Technologically speaking, men of whatever nation or race, can be trained to do whatever any other nation or race has been doing. The I.Q. of single individuals may vary widely, but collectively, the I.Q. of one group is comparable to another. In modern times, the average man never credited the Russians, Chinese, Japanese, etc. with the intellectual potential currently exhibited; sociologists are convinced that the same holds true for others, including the savages of the African jungle.

The Social Contract.

Hobbes is right, "nature has made men so equal, in faculties of body and mind" that if a person is to survive in society, his only recourse is to enter into a social compact. The principle or impetus for engaging in a social contract stems form a second law derived from the first law of nature (the law of self-preservation), namely, *"That a man be willing when others are so too, as far as for peace and defence of himself he shall think it necessary, to lay down this right to all things: and be content with so much liberty against other men, as he would allow other men against himself."* Note that the right of nature must also be relinquished: 'the right to defend oneself by whatever means' – since the end justifies the means, and since "man is forbidden to do that which is destructive of his life."

The social contract consists essentially in exchanging one's rights granted by nature for moral or legal rights provided by a compact. Its basic principle is the surrender of whatever liberties are presently enjoyed by nature, provided others are so inclined, for the guarantee or sake of survival. In a sense, the social contract is the 'Golden Rule' negatively formulated. *"This is that law of the Gospel; Whatever you require others should do to you, that do ye to them* . . . To *lay down* a man's *right* to anything is to divest himself of liberty, of hindering another of the benefit of his own right to the same . . . Right is laid aside, either by simply renouncing it, or by transferring it to another. By *simply renouncing,* when he cares not to whom the benefit thereof redoundeth. By *transferring,* when he intends the benefit thereof to some certain person, or persons. And when a man has in either manner abandoned, or granted away his right, then he is said to be *obliged,* or *bound,* not to hinder those to whom such right is granted, or abandoned, from the benefit of it: and that he *ought,* and it is his *duty,* not to make void that voluntary act of his own: and that hindrance is *injustice* and *injury,* as being *Sine Jure;* the right being before renounced or transferred." Until a social contract is entered into, morality does not exist; natural 'might makes right' since morality is merely civil law resulting from a compact participated in by men who are to live in a common community. Essentially, it consists in the transference or reciproccal exchange of rights. "The mutual transferring of right is that which men call contract."

Although the social contract rescinds or suspends an individual's right of nature (to attack another by might), it does not relinquish the fundamental law of nature, the law of self-preservation. "A covenant not to defend myself from force, by force, is always void. For no man can transfer or lay down his right to save himself from death, wounds, and imprisonment, the avoiding whereof is the only end of laying down any right, and therefore the promise of not resisting force, in no covenant transfers any right, nor in obliging. For though a man may covenant thus, *Unless I do so or so, kill me;* he cannot covenant thus, *Unless I do so or so, I will not resist you when you come to kill me* ... A covenant to accuse oneself without assurance of pardon is likewise invalid." These two exceptions are intimations, if not precursors, of American law; the former is 'killing in self-defence' and the latter 'self-incrimination.'

Laws of Nature.

The success of the social contract form of government is due to the operation within society of a number of natural laws which are in essence immutable and eternal. *Justice* is adherence to these laws, injustice their violation.

The laws of nature are as follows: (1) "*Seek peace and follow it*" (law of self-preservation).

(2) "*That a man be willing when others are so too, as far as for peace and defence of himself he shall think it necessary, to lay down this right to all things: and be content with so much liberty against other men as he would allow other men against himself*" (Golden Rule).

(3) "*That men perform their covenants made.*" If a man does not live up to his promises, conditions revert to a belligerent state of affairs. Adherence to this law is the essence of justice, "without which covenants are in vain, and but empty words; and the right of all men to all things remaining, we are still in the condition of war." Without this law, "no action can be unjust. But when a covenant is made, then to break it is *unjust:* And the definition of *injustice* is no other than *the nonperformance of covenant.* And whatever is not unjust is *just.*"

(4) Fourth law of nature: "*That a man which receives benefit from another of mere grace, endeavor that he which gives it has no reasonable cause to repent of his good will.*" Injustice is the outcome when one violates the third law of nature; ingratitude results as the breach of this law.

(5) Fifth law of nature – 'compleasance' (complaisance): "*That every man strive to accommodate himself to the rest.*" This law obliges one to be sociable or affable in a community rather than stubborn, unsociable, or intractable.

(6) Sixth law of nature: "*That upon caution of future time, a man ought to pardon the offenses past of them that repenting desire it.*" Pardon is necessary in the maintenance of peace, unforgiven actions are deterrents to peace. "Pardon is nothing but granting of peace;" fail-

ing to do so is "an aversion to peace; and therefore contrary to the law of nature."

(7) Seventh law of nature: *"That in revenges* (that is, retribution of evil for evil), *men look not at the greatness of the evil past, but the greatness of the good to follow."* Cruelty is the transgression of this law, "and to hurt without reason tends to the introduction of war."

(8) Eighth law of nature: *"That no man by deed, word, countenance, or gesture, declare hatred or contempt of another."* A breach of this law is contumely, insult, contempt, arrogance, scorn. Inasmuch as men are equal, there is no call for violating this rule.

(9) Ninth law of nature: *"That every man acknowledge other for his equal by nature."* Abuse of this law is termed 'pride.'

(10) Tenth law of nature: *"That at the entrance into conditions of peace, no man require to reserve to himself any right which he is not content should be reserved to every one of the rest."* Unless a person relinquishes certain rights of nature, peace is impossible; this rule requires that a man so yield. Those who observe this rule are said to be 'modest' and those who violate it, 'arrogant,' that is, they are desirous of more than their fair share.

(11) Eleventh law of nature: *"If a man be trusted to judge between man and man,* it is a precept of the law of nature *that he deal equally between them."* Without this law, controversies ensue, resulting in war.

(12) Twelfth law of nature: *"That such things as cannot be divided, be enjoyed in common, if it can be; and if the quantity of the thing permit, without stint; otherwise proportionably to the number of them that have right."* This law is necessary if equity is to be maintained, otherwise unfair distribution and discriminatory practices will result, causing inequities.

(13) Thirteenth law of nature – the law of equity:*"That the entire right; or else, (making the use alternate), the first possession be determined by lot."* Equal distribution is distributive justice, and the lack of it unimaginable in a just society. A lot may be 'arbitrary' or 'natural:' Arbitrary lots are based upon mutual agreement among those concerned; a natural lot falls to one by primogeniture or 'first seisure,' that is, whatever cannot be enjoyed in common by right belongs to the original or initial possessor.

(14) Fourteenth law of nature: *"That all men that mediate peace, be allowed safe conduct."* If peace is ever to be achieved as the end of man, then intercession is necessary as the means, "and to intercession the means is safe conduct."

(15) Fifteenth law of nature: *"That they that are at controversy, submit their right to the judgement of an arbitrator."* Men in controversy

cannot be fair arbitrators of their own disagreements, consequently it is necessary to accept the decision of an impartial judge.

The above mentioned fifteen laws of nature are reducible to one, namely, the 'Golden Rule:' *"Do not that to another, which thou wouldst not have done to thyself."* These laws may be considered immutable because their abuse or violation: injustice, ingratitude, arrogance, pride, iniquity, etc. are vices and can never be considered lawful; whereas their fulfillment results in moral virtues: justice, gratitude, modesty, equity, mercy, etc.

The Leviathan.

Leviathan, the title of Hobbes' treatise, is literally a huge aquatic monster, but its use in this work is figurative, representing the sovereign head of State, a monarch, who sees to it that subjects of the social compact live up to the contract entered. The leviathan is more than a monarch, he is a 'mortal god' who is above the law and its restraints, a man to whom all citizens are subject and to whom their right of nature and right of self-government is surrendered. The sovereign, leviathan, is a man's guarantee that others will fulfill their end of the contract; accordingly, the monarch must be sufficiently powerful to force his subjects to fulfill their promise made in respect to the compact, or undergo suitable punishment if they refuse or fail.

"The only way to erect such a common power as may be able to defend them from . . . injuries of one another . . . is to confer all their power and strength upon one man, or upon one assembly of men, that may reduce all their will by plurality of voices to one will: which is as much as to say, to appoint one man, or assembly of men, to bear their person; and every one to own, and acknowledge himself to be author of whatever he that so bears their person shall act, or cause to be acted, in those things which concern the common peace and safety; and therein to submit their wills, every one to his will, and their judgements, to his judgement. This is more than consent or concord; it is a real unity of them all, in one and the same person, made by covenant of every man with every man, in such manner, as if every man should say to every man, *I authorize and give up my right of governing myself to this man or to this assembly of men on this condition, that you give up your right to him, and authorize all his actions in like manner.* This done, the multitude so united in one person, is called a COMMONWEALTH, in Latin *civitas.* This is the generation of that great *LEVIATHAN,* or rather (to speak reverently) of the *mortal god,* to which we owe under the *immortal God,* our peace and defence. For by this authority given him by every particular man in the commonwealth, he has the use of so much power and strength conferred on him that by terror thereof, he is enabled to form the will of them all, to peace at home and mutual aid against their enemies abroad. And in him consists the essence of the commonwealth; which (to define it) is *one person of whose acts a great multitude, by mutual covenants one with another, have made themselves every one the author to the end he may use the strength and means of them all as he shall think expedient for their peace and common defence.*

"And he that carries this person is called *sovereign,* and said to have *sovereign power;* and every one besides, his *subject.*

"The attaining to this sovereign power is by two ways. One, by natural force; as when a man makes his children to submit themselves, and their children to his government, as being able to destroy them if they refuse; or by war subdue his enemies to his will, giving them their lives on that condition. The other is when men agree amongst themselves to submit to some man, or assembly of men, voluntarily, on the confidence to be protected by him against all others. This latter may be called a political Commonwealth or Commonwealth by *Institution,* and the former, a Commonwealth by *Acquisition.*"

Concluding Comments.

Whether to designate Hobbes' *Leviathan* a social contract, a Democracy, a Monarchy, or a Dictatorship is difficult to say inasmuch as there are obvious rival or contradictory doctrines, such as totalitarian power in a single monarch, rivalling the doctrine of a social contract of free and equal people democratically organized. The American Democracy owes the *Leviathan* its philosophical foundation along with other social philosophies such as Rousseau's *Social Contract.*

Hobbes regards man as an unsocial being, yet his entire philosophy is based upon man's social relations with his fellow man. How such an unsocial being can eventuate into a highly social matrix called a society is incredible. If man is so completely unsocial, it is amazing that society ever survived, or even came into existence at all. He identifies man's instincts with that of the wild animal's of the jungle, but such beasts are not social beings – if man is likewise unsocial with kindred instincts, why is it that he too does not share a similar existence to theirs? In other words, on the basis of the Hobbesian philosophy, man should prefer and live the life of hermitage – Hobbes does not explain adequately why man does not.

The place and right of the sovereign is doubtful – do people grant might or does he possess it in his own right by nature? *Spinoza* noted that his power is maintained because he administers the State in a manner satisfactory to his subjects; should he rule as to incur their displeasure, rebellion and the overthrow of his reign would result.

Hobbes does not reconcile the conflict which may ensue among two or more sovereigns except to say that should a greater power overthrow the existing monarch, (which he has a right to do by nature), he may reign in his stead. But this would indicate that war is an inevitable and ever present condition among powers or sovereigns since they do not enter into social compacts among themselves, but are free to overthrow each other at will.

Hobbes argued that sovereignty is indivisible, hence is not shared with other powers such as that of the church, etc.; all other authorities are subordinate to one totalitarian sovereign, yet no adequate reason exists to substantiate this contention except that Hobbes is attempting to placate the king of his time.

Perhaps a more acceptable explanation than Hobbes provided as to why men ought to, and do enter into social contract with each other on a democratic basis, is: man's mutual understanding, social concern, and mutual enhancement of each other's condition, despite the fact that there are many persons who are principally motivated out of self-interest.

XVI

ROUSSEAU'S *SOCIAL CONTRACT:*

A Democracy

Unlike his predecessors in political philosophy, *Jean Jacques Rousseau* does not seek merely a revision of government, he desires to revamp civilization from its very roots. Governments are defective because modern civilization has drifted from its pure and unadulterated natural state into a corrupt form of existence called 'civilization' which has barely, if any, semblance of its original characteristics. Since nature's edicts are good and civilization its evil perversion, only one recourse remains if social salvation is to be effected: *'Back to nature.'*

A cursory glance at surrounding civilization is sufficient to warrant the conclusion that it is nature corrupted. "*Man is born free, and everywhere he is in chains.* Many a one believes himself the master of others, and yet he is a greater slave than they . . . If I considered only force and the results that proceed from it, I should say that so long as a people is compelled to obey and does obey, it does well; but that, so soon as it can shake off the yoke and does shake it off, it does better; for, if men recover their freedom by virtue of the same right by which it was taken away, either they are justified in resuming it, or there was no justification for depriving them of it." [1] *Diderot,* a French philosopher of considerable influence during the period of the French Enlightenment and editor of the French *Encyclopaedia,* contended in his article, "Authority," that power usurped by force may be justifiably displaced by force, hence giving sanction to conditional revolution.

Rousseau himself was not French, but a citizen of a free State; his birthplace was Geneva (1712), an aristocratic government of which he was proud to be a citizen, enjoying full political rights as a member of a sovereign body.

The *Social Contract's* chief doctrines are: (1) Man's inalienable right

[1] Quotations in this section are from Jean Jacques Rousseau, *The Social Contract,* tr. Henry J. Tozer (London: Swan Sonnenschein and Co. Ltd., 3rd ed., 1902).

of freedom, (2) Man's inalienable right of equality, (3) Sovereignty of the people, (4) Civil society as a social contract, (5) The 'General Will,' (6) The constitution of a government, (7) Civil religion.

Freedom and Equality as Inalienable Rights.

Modern societies should take as their prototype the only natural one, the 'family.' The chief characteristics of a family are freedom and equality, rights which accrue to man by birth. States, essentially extended families, must likewise be organized and administrated.

Certain definite implications, such as the preclusion of slavery, follow from the above premises. "Since no man has any natural authority over his fellow-men, and since force is not the source of right, convention remains as the basis of all lawful authority among men." Will, freedom, equality are inalienable rights. Alienation implies giving or selling, but inalienable rights are irrevocable, hence cannot be given away. "To say that a man gives himself for nothing is to say what is absurd and inconceivable; such an act is illegitimate and invalid, for the simple reason that he who performs it is not in his right mind. To say the same thing of a whole nation is to suppose a nation of fools; and madness does not confer rights . . . They are born free men . . . To renounce one's liberty is to renounce one's quality as a man, the rights and also the duties of humanity . . . Such a renunciation is incompatible with man's nature, for to take away all freedom from his will is to take away all morality from his actions."

A person's rights cannot be abrogated by force for 'might does not make right,' and "if it is necessary to obey by compulsion, there is no need to obey from duty; and if men are no longer forced to obey, obligation is at an end. We see, then, that this word *right* adds nothing to force; it here means nothing at all. Obey the powers that be. If that means, yield to force, the precept is good but superfluous; I reply it will never be violated. All power comes from God, I admit; but every disease comes from him too; does it follow that we are prohibited from calling a physician?"

Slavery is abhorrent for it proposes that a man buy his life at the cost of his liberty; "it is, therefore, an iniquitous bargain to make him purchase his life, over which the victor has no right, at the cost of his liberty." It is imperative that people guard their liberty jealously; true, they may rescue it from barbarous tyrants, but not when it has been abused at their own hands such as when its civic vitality has been exhausted for *"liberty may be acquired but never recovered."*

The *summum bonum* which any State can possibly pursue is *liberty* and *equality,* – "liberty, because any individual dependence is so much force withdrawn from the body of the State; equality, because liberty cannot subsist without it . . . With regard to equality, we must not understand by this word that the degrees of power and wealth should be absolutely the same; but that, as to power, it should fall short of all violence, and never be exercised except by virtue of station and of the laws; while, as to wealth, *no citizen should be rich enough to be able to buy another, and none poor enough to be forced to sell himself.*" The implication here is more than the mere repudiation of slavery, it suggests that a State should be moderate, avoiding extremes of wealth and poverty; the existence of wealth and poverty breeds slavery, and from the same two extreme classes spring tyrants and tyranny. Even excessive or dangerous liberty is preferable to servitude.

The General Will and Social Contract.

One of the most important doctrines in Rousseau's *Social Contract* is the 'general will,' an idea which must be sharply distinguished from the 'will of all.' The 'general will' converts a town into a city (houses make a town, citizens compose a city); an individual, a citizen; a group, a body politic. "If, then, we set aside what is not of the essence of the social compact, we shall find that it is reducible to the following terms: '*Each of us puts in common his person and his whole power under the supreme direction of the general will; and in return we receive every member as an indivisible part of the whole.*'"

People alone compose a State; they constitute the 'body politic,' hence possess sovereignty. The State apart from persons does not exist; it is a compact into which they enter; monarchs and other leaders do not rule from above, but derive power from below as public servants. The 'social contract' is the essence of every true and natural State, for only the social contract form of government is decreed by nature, and comes into being as follows: "Instead of the individual personalities of all the contracting parties, this act of association produces a moral and collective body, which is composed of as many members as the assembly has voices, and which receives from this same act its unity, its common self (*moi*), its life, and its will. This public person, which is thus formed by the union of all the individual members, formerly took the name of *city,* and now takes that of *republic* or *body politic,* which is called by its members *State* when it is passive, *sovereign* when it is active, *power* when it is compared to similar bodies. With regard to the associates, they take collectively the name of *people,* and are called individually *citizens,* as participating in the sovereign power, and *subjects,* as subjected to the laws of the State."

Contrary to the thinking of Aristotle, Hegel, and others who fancy the State to be an organ in its own right, independent of the people and greater as well, Rousseau contends that the State is a creation which came into existence exclusively for the sake of the common good, and therefore must be at the disposal of the general will) the citizenry's inalienable right, and the basis upon which all sovereignty rests. "The body politic or sovereign, deriving its existence only from the sanctity of the contract, can never bind itself, even to others, in anything that derogates from the original act, such as alienation of some portion of itself, or submission to another sovereign. To violate the act by which it exists would be to annihilate itself."

The State is a unity which depends for support on its citizenry assuming their respective responsibilities; should anyone neglect his duty or offend in any way, the entire body is affected. "So soon as the multitude is thus united in one body, *it is impossible to injure one of the members without attacking the body,* still less to injure the body without the members feeling the effects." Members of a social contract share common interests; what is injurious to one proves detrimental to all, what benefits one is conducive to the good of all, accordingly to hurt another is harmful to oneself. "Now, the sovereign, being formed only of the individuals that compose it, neither has nor can have any interest contrary to theirs; consequently the sovereign power needs no guarantee towards its subjects, because it is impossible that the body should wish to injure all its members; and . . . it can injure no one as an individual." Private wills incompatible with the general will must be suppressed; this is necessary not only for the sake of the State as a whole but for the individual himself since private wills ultimately injure self as well as the body politic, hence "whoever refuses to obey the general will shall be constrained to do so by the whole body; which means nothing else than that he shall be forced to be free; for such is the condition which, uniting every citizen to his native land . . . which without it, would be absurd and tyrannical, and subject to the most enormous abuses."

An important factor of the social contract principle is its guarantee of legal equality, endorsing that endued by nature to men; furthermore the compact compensates for any deficiency and discrepancy in physical or intellectual inequality owing to individual differences. "Instead of destroying natural equality, the fundamental pact, on the contrary, substitutes a moral and lawful equality for the physical inequality which nature imposed upon men, so that, although unequal in strength or intellect, *they all become equal by convention and legal right.*" Equality is not genuinely experienced, but only illusory or merely apparent in corrupt forms of government despite their democratic or social compact nature. Corrupt States serve as a device to keep the poor in poverty and the wealthy in a position of exploitation. This is indicated by the fact that laws useful to property owners are threatening to those who lack property, accordingly corrupt States are advantageous only to the monied class.

Sovereign power, stemming from the general will, rests with the people as a natural birthright. Although persons may relegate power to another, *will* cannot be transferred, much less, alienated. The common good rests in the general will which is the State's reason for being. "The general will alone can direct the forces of the State according to the object of its institution, which is the common good . . . I say, then, that sovereignty, being nothing but the exercise of the general will, can never be alienated, and that the sovereign power, which is only a collective being, can be represented by itself alone; *power indeed can be transmitted, but not will.*"

'Masters' are a foreign concept to a body politic philosophy based on the social contract principle; their appearance destroys the body politic. No single individual may claim sovereignty inasmuch as it is indivisible and belongs to the body politic; furthermore, although an individual will is subject to error, the general will cannot err. "The general will is always right and always tends to the public advantage; but it does not follow that the resolutions of the people have always the same rectitude. Men always desire their own good, but do not always discern it; *the people are never corrupted,* though often deceived and it is only then that they seem to will what is evil."

A distinction must be drawn between the 'will of all' and the general will: the former is merely the enumeration or sum total of individual wills which may possibly be, and usually is, selfish, base, and erroneous, but the latter is for the common good, the good of the State. The will of all, composed solely of tallying votes of selfish persons concerned with private or vested interests is indicative of a corrupt Democracy, however, in a good State, people do not vote for selfish benefits merely, but for that which is beneficial to the nation or body politic as a whole. What is good for the nation as a whole will, in the long run, prove beneficial to private citizens as individuals; conversely, what is detrimental to the body politic as a whole will eventually prove harmful to single individuals. "There is often a great deal of difference between the will of all and the general will; the latter regards only the common interest while the former has regard to private interests, and is merely a sum of particular wills; but take away from these same wills the pluses and minuses which cancel one another, and the general will remains as the sum of the differences. If the people came to a resolution when adequately informed and without any communication among the citizens, the general will would always result from the great number of slight differences, and the resolution would always be good. But when factions, partial associations, are formed to the detriment of the whole society, the will of each of these associations becomes general with reference to its members, and particular with reference to the State; it may then be said that there are no longer as many voters as there are men, but only as many voters as there are associations . . . There is then no longer a general will, and the opinion which prevails is only a particular opinion."

Theoretically, in a State predominantly composed of good people, the general will manifests itself in the decisions of the majority to which the minority must yield, but a majority decision arrived at genuinely should benefit the body politic as a whole, not merely favor the majority faction.

Due to its vital importance, the acceptance of the social contract itself must be by a unanimous majority; such unanimous consent is tacitly given when a person moves within the political environs of the State. "There is but one law which by its nature requires unanimous consent, that is, the social compact; for civil association is the most voluntary act in the world . . . When a State is established, consent lies in residence; to dwell in the territory is to submit to the sovereignty. Excepting this original contract, the vote of the majority always binds all the rest, this being a result of the contract itself." A citizen is morally and legally obligated to consent and accept every law which his nation passes, including those passed despite any opposition which he may have registered against them. "*The unvarying will of all the members of the State is the general will; it is through that that they are citizens and free.* When a law is proposed in the assembly of the people, what is asked of them is not exactly whether they approve the proposition or reject it, but whether it is conformable or not with the general will, which is their own; each one in giving his vote expressed his opinion thereupon; and from the counting of the votes is obtained the declaration of the general will. When, therefore, the opinion opposed to my own prevails, that simply shows that I was mistaken, and that what I considered to be the general will was not so." In such a case, it is well that my private will was defeated, otherwise something other than my best interests would have prevailed, and I would not have been free; in other words, the minority, in contrast to the unerring majority, is always in error.

The foregoing opinion of Rousseau's has been severely critized, even by adherents of political Democracies, for it is at times obvious that the majority is wrong and the minority clearly in the right; realization of this fact by the majority has, at times, resulted in its decisions being rescinded.

Rousseau makes the basic assumption that the general will is found invariable in the infallible majority. The implication is that in a nation of one million persons, 500,001 votes on any given issue is invariably and infallibly right while 499,999 is invariably wrong – an incredible idea. In a close vote, for all practical purposes, the majority is equally weighted. However, when these conditions maintain, "two general principles may serve to regulate these proportions: the one, that the more important and weighty the resolutions, the nearer should the opinion which prevails approach unanimity; the other, that the greater the despatch requisite in the matter under discussion, the more should we restrict the prescribed difference in the division of opinions; in resolutions which must be come to immediately, the majority of a single vote should suffice." In other words, important matters, such as the enactment of laws, should be carried on the basis of a decisive majority, but in matters of general business of the State, a simple majority will suffice.

Three separate wills are detectable in the State, the first is that of the 'private citizen,' namely the *individual will;* the second is that of the 'governing or administrative body' called a *corporate will*; the third is that of the 'people' and is the *sovereign will.* "We can distinguish in the person of the magistrate three wills essentially different: first, the will peculiar to the individual, which tends only to his personal advantage; secondly, the common will of the magistrates, which has reference solely to the advantage of the Prince, and which may be called the corporate will, being general in relation to the government, and particular in relation to the State of which the government forms part; in the third place, the will of the people, or the sovereign will, which is general both in relation to the State considered as the whole, and in relation to the government considered as part of the whole."

The Constitution of a Government.

Ultimately, there is only one form of State proper for free and equal men, a social contract, and "there is only one contract in the State, the contract of association, and that in itself precludes all others." People, free and equal, possess sovereign power, and accordingly have the right to enter into a social contract.

The form of government which sovereign people institute may be varied: If the exercise of government is entrusted in the hands of the people as a whole, it is termed a 'Democracy;' if the administration of government is entrusted in the hands of a few, it is called an 'Aristocracy;' if the reins of government is concentrated in the hands of a single magistrate, it is designated a 'Monarchy' or 'Royal Government.' The particular form of government depends upon the number of people within a given State: "the number of supreme magistrates should be in inverse ratio to that of the citizens . . . in general, democratic government is suitable to small States, aristocracy to those of moderate size, and monarchy to large ones."

When governments are subjected to abuse they degenerate; complete deterioration is generally known as 'Anarchy.' Corrupt Democracies degenerate into Ochlocracies (mob rule), Aristocracies into Oligarchies, and Monarchies into Tyrannies.

The government *per se* is not sovereign nor is it to be identified with sovereignty; it is the agent of sovereign people and subservient to them. "The public force, then, requires a suitable agent to concentrate it and put it in action according to the directions of the general will, to serve as a means of communication between the State and the sovereign, to effect in some manner in the public person what the union of soul and body effect in a man. That is, in the State, the function of the government, is improperly confounded with the sovereign of which it is only the minister."

Governments are established by sovereign decree; people appoint rulers who are entrusted with the duties of government. People can appoint or remove government officials at pleasure. Regarding government officials, their status is not a matter of contract, but of obedience to the power which placed them in their respective positions. When sovereign people elect or appoint officials, they have not relinquished power, but relegated it, nor do government officials have the right to usurp the will of the people since it is inalienable. "Sovereignty cannot be represented, for the same reason that it cannot be alienated; it consists essentially in the general will and the will cannot be represented . . . The deputies of the people, then, are not and cannot be its representatives; they are only its commissioners and can conclude nothing definitely. Every law which the people in person have not ratified is invalid; it is not a law."

The State may be illustrated in the simile of an organism; the vital force of political life being the sovereign authority, the people. The heart of the State is its legislative power, and the brain its executive power. Oddly enough, the brain may become paralyzed and the organism remain alive except that it will suffer an imbecilic existence, but when the heart ceases to function, death results.

Concluding Remarks.

Although Rousseau designates his political theory a 'social contract,' it is what would be termed today, a 'Democracy.' Rousseau, however, reserves the term 'Democracy' for a type of governmental organization, the manner in which a government is administrated, not a form of State. His *Social Contract* has been indirectly the foundation stone of our American Democracy, an instrument our forefathers used to shape our nation's political structure and documents.

His thinking also had a definite influence on the fashioning of other political philosophies, particularly that of Kant. With the possible exception of Hobbes, from whom he derived a fair portion of his political ideas, Rousseau deserves the credit for engineering the democratic concept of life in modern times.

XVII

KANT'S *ETERNAL PEACE:*

A World State

Immanuel Kant was attracted to a philosophical consideration of the possibility of eternal peace among men and nations by a sign which caught his attention with the satirical inscription over a representation of a graveyard scene reading: "Eternal Peace." Is eternal peace to be found only when one is buried in a cemetery? queried Kant. Certainly it must be possible for men to live among each other in peace. Consequently, he set out to delineate the principles which would make it possible for men to live in peace without the fear or threat of war, and prior to being laid to rest in a grave. His philosophical conclusions pertaining to the present discussion are principally found in the book: *Eternal Peace.*

The political program laid down in *Eternal Peace* is a Republic, a federation of States of the world in which a person becomes a cosmopolitical citizen with appropriate rights and privileges. Kant admired greatly the United States which he termed 'the New England of America' and envisioned the entire humanity of the earth as one world or a 'universal cosmopolitical institution' functioning similarly to America or, still better, to the European Common Market Nations. The United Nations of the contemporary scene perhaps approaches most closely to what the philosopher had in mind. The designation 'World State' is perhaps the most appropriate title of this political philosophy.

Eternal Peace is divided into two sections followed by two supplements and an appendix of two parts; its outline is as follows:[1]

1. *Eternal Peace:*
   A. Section One:
      a. *Preliminary Articles* of an Eternal Peace between States:

[1] Unless otherwise noted, quotations in this section are from Immanuel Kant, *Eternal Peace,* tr. W. Hastie (Boston: World Peace Foundation, 1914).

1. No conclusion of peace shall be held to be valid as such when it has been made with the secret reservation of the material for a future war.
2. No State having an existence by itself – whether it be small or large – shall be acquirable by another State through inheritance, exchange, purchase or donation.
3. Standing armies shall be entirely abolished in the course of time.
4. No national debts shall be contracted in connection with external affairs of the State.
5. No State shall intermeddle by force with the constitution or government of another State.
6. No State at war with another shall adopt such modes of hostility as would necessarily render mutual confidence impossible in a future peace; such as the employment of assassins (percussores) or poisoners (*venefici*), the violation of a capitulation, the instigation of treason and such like.

B. Section Two:
a. Three *Definitive Articles* of an Eternal Peace between States:
1. The civil constitution in every State shall be republican.
2. The law of nations shall be founded on a federation of free States.
3. The rights of men as citizens of the world in a cosmopolitical system shall be restricted to conditions of universal hospitality.

C. First Supplement of the *Guaranty of Eternal Peace.*
a. The guaranty of eternal peace is nature. The mechanical course of nature visibly exhibits a design to bring forth concord out of the discord of men, even against their will.
b. The provisory arrangements of nature consist mainly in these three things:
1. She has provided so that men shall be able to live in all parts of the earth.
2. She has scattered them everywhere by means of war so that they might populate even the most inhospitable regions.
3. By the same means she has compelled them to enter into relations more or less legal with one another.
c. Nature's design for perpetual peace by three phases of *public law:* (1) civil law, (2) international law, (3) cosmopolitical law (law of world citizenship).
1. *Civil law:*
(a) Even if a people were not compelled by internal discord to submit to the coercion of public laws, war as an external influence would effect this.
(b) A multitude of rational beings all requiring laws in common for their own preservation, and yet of such a nature that each of them is inclined secretly to except himself from their sway, have to be put under order, and a constitution has to be established among them so that, although they may be antagonistic to one another in their private sentiments, they have yet to be so organized that, in their public relations, their conduct will have the same result as if they had no such bad sentiments.

(c) Nature irresistibly wills that right shall at last obtain the supremacy.

2. *International law:*

(a) The idea of international law presupposes the separation of several neighboring States that are independent of each other.

(b) Peace is developed and secured among powers by an equilibrium which is brought forth and guaranteed through their competition with each other.

3. *Cosmopolitical law:*

(a) Nature unites nations because of mutual interests. This is effected by the commercial spirit, which cannot exist along with war and which sooner or later controls every people. Hence, wherever war threatens to break out in the world, the States have an interest to avert it by mediations, just as if they stood in a constant league with each other for this purpose.

(b) Nature guarantees the conditions of perpetual peace by the mechanism involved in our human inclinations themselves.

(c) Thus it becomes a duty to labor for the realization of this purpose as not at all chimerical in itself.

D. Second Supplement – *Secret Article* Relating to Eternal Peace:

a. The *maxims* (opinions) of the philosophers regarding the conditions of the possibility of a public peace shall be taken into consideration by the States that are armed for war.

b. That "kings will philosophize or philosophers become kings" is not to be expected. Nor, indeed, is it to be desired, because the possession of power inevitably corrupts free judgment of reason.

E. Appendix One: Discord between Morals and Politics in Reference to Eternal Peace.

a. Maxims of *political sophistry:*

1. Seize the favorable opportunity for taking into your own possession what is either a right of the State over the people or over a neighboring State; and the justification of the act will be much more easily and gracefully presented after the fact and will palliate its violence.

2. What you may have wrongfully done yourself, such as may even bring the people to despair and to rebellion, should be denied as being any fault of yours.

3. There are certain privileged heads among the people who have chosen you merely for their sovereign. See, then, that you embroil them with each other and put them at variance with the people.

b. Maxims of the *political moralist:*

1. "Act so that you can will that your maxim shall become a universal law, whatever may be its end."

2. "Seek ye first the kingdom of pure practical reason and its righteousness, and then will your object, the benefit of perpetual peace, be added unto you."

3. *Fiat justitia, pereat mundus.* (Let righteousness prevail though all the knaves in the world should perish for it).

c. There is, objectively in theory, no antagnoism at all between morals and politics.

d. Rights of men must be regarded as holy, however great may be the sacrifice which the maintenance of them lays upon the ruling power.
e. All politics must bow the knee before the principle of right.

F. Appendix Two: Of the Agreement of Politics with Morals According to the Transcendental Conception of Public Law.

a. Principles of public right:
1. "All actions relating to the rights of other men are unjust if the maxims on which they are based are not compatible with publicity."
2. "All maxims which require publicity in order that they may not fail of their end are in accordance with both right and politics."

Philosophy of Law.[1]

The preceding extensive outline summary of Kant's *Eternal Peace* is self-explanatory, and, unlike other works of Kant, it is particularly readable as the novitiate will happily discover. The work does not, however, exhaust Kantian ideas in the field of political theory, nor does the present undertaking presume to give a complete account of Kant's social ethics, for such would lie beyond its scope, but it is deemed advisable to round out the Kantian political philosophy by treating his philosophy of law as contained in his *Metaphysics of Morals.*

In a natural state, two types of law maintain: public and private. Public law is expressed by the postulate: "In the relation of unavoidable coexistence with others, thou shalt pass from the state of nature into a juridical union constituted under the condition of a distributive justice." Man, in an uncivilized state of nature, may pursue the law of the jungle, but in a rational state of civilization, right is to be differentiated from mere might as violence.

Public law offers certain guarantees, particularly the right of restraining others from interfering with one's possessions by guaranteeing property rights. Unless a person consents to such guarantees, the law of the jungle prevails, granting anyone the right to lawless freedom. Under such conditions, justice or wrong are inapplicable; should a state of war break out, all activity incurred would be considered fair. "For what seems good for the one is equally valid for the other, as if it were so by mutual agreement." However, existence under such conditions is categorically wrong, and is beneath the dignity of man; rational man should be unwilling to rest content in a lawless state.

"The State, as constituted by the common interest of all to live in a juridical union, is called, in view of its form, the commonwealth or

[1] Quotations in the remainder of this section are from Kant: *The Metaphysics of Morals,* tr. W. Hastie (Boston: The World Peace Foundation, 1914).

the republic in the wider sense of the term." The 'State,' a body of people, is a power, and constitutes a nation with a law of its own and one regarding other 'States,' namely, *international law.* 'National law' and 'international law,' eventuate in 'cosmopolitical law,' (*jus cosmopoliticum*), "and national, international and cosmopolitical law are so interconnected that, if any one of these three possible forms of the juridical relation fails to embody the essential principles that ought to regulate external freedom by law, the structure of legislation reared by the others will also be undermined, and the whole system would at last fall to pieces."

A primary obligation binds man, namely that of entering into relations of a civil State governed by law; persons refusing to accept this obligation may be constrained to do so by force. "Men thus enter into a civil union in which every one has it determined by law what shall be recognized as his; and this is secured to him by a competent external power distinct from his own individuality."

By definition, "a State (*civitas*) is the union of a number of men under juridical laws," that is, laws which are necessary, not mere statutes which may be dissolved without concomitant damage to the State. The State, which is essentially the universal united will of the people, contains three powers (political dignities) by virtue of its citizens: *legislative power, executive power, judicial power,* in the person of the lawgiver, the ruler, the judge. Citizens enjoy certain permanent rights: constitutional freedom, civil equality, political independence. "The act by which a people is represented as constituting itself into a State is termed the original contract . . . The commonwealth is the people viewed as united all together into a State," in which wild, lawless freedom is abandoned and a new civil freedom gained. "Every true republic is and can only be constituted by a representative system of the people . . . The best constitution is that in which laws, not men, exercise power."

By power of the united will of the people, the State may assume one of three forms: Autocracy, Aristocracy, Democracy. "The relation of the supreme power to the people is conceivable in three different forms: either one in the State rules over all; or some, united in a relation of equality with each other, rule over all the others; or all together rule over each and all individually, including themselves." The simplest form of administration of law in the State is best, and of the three, the first, Autocracy, is the simplest, progressing to the third, Democracy, the most complex.

International Law.

Law among nations, international law, is divisible into three aspects: (1) law, prior to war; (2) law, during war; (3) law, during peace or after the cessation of hostilities. Prior to international law, nations assume a position similar to persons before engaging in civil law – they are like savages in a nonjuridical state.

A condition prior to law, namely a lawless one, is in effect a state of war granting right to the stronger. In the same manner that persons engage in an original social contract, nations must enter into an alliance to protect themselves from external aggression. An alliance of nations is a federation of States, not individuals; accordingly it must dispense with any particular sovereign power – no State may emerge sovereign over any other. The alliance "can only take the form of a federation, which as such may be revoked on any occasion and must consequently be removed from time to time. This is therefore a right accessory of another original right, to prevent the nations from falling away and lapsing into the state of actual war with each other."

A nation has the right to declare war as the result of any overt act of injury, including arbitrary retaliation or act of reprisal. However, during war, something analogous to a contract must be assumed, otherwise no law at all can exist during a state of war between nations.

Wars for the sake of punishment are unjustifiable since relations between nations are not that of superior to subject, but equals. Although defensive measures are permissible by a nation forced to declare war, certain measures, such as spies, assassins, poisoners, agents who spread lies, are forbidden for the use of "any such malignant and perfidious means . . . would destroy the confidence which would be requisite to establish a lasting peace thereafter."

The right of nations after war commences with the signing of the treaty of peace which must not contain punitive articles, for this would be tantamount to the infliction of injury and the prolongation of war. "In the same category belongs also the exchange of prisoners, which is to be carried out without regard to equality of numbers. Neither the conquered State nor its subjects lose their political liberty by conquest of the country to the extent that the former should be degraded to a colony or the latter to slaves; for otherwise it would have been a penal war, which is contradictory to itself." Slavery also is not a legitimate conquest of people engaged in war, and still more unjust is the use of war for hereditary slavery; one reason being that "guilt cannot be inherited from the criminality of another. Further, that an amnesty is involved in the conclusion of a treaty of peace is already implied in the very idea of a peace."

Kant lists the rights of peace as:

> 1. The right to be in peace when war is in the neighborhood, or the right of neutrality.
> 2. The right to have peace secured so that it may continue when it has been concluded, that is, the right of guaranty.
> 3. The right of the several States to enter into a mutual alliance so as to defend themselves in common against all external or even internal attacks. This right of federation, however, does not extend to the formation of any league for external aggression or internal aggrandizement.

The cause of peace among States is further promoted by a permanent 'congress of nations' whose duty it is to decide on matters among States, including those which have been acquired by war. Acquisitions through war, being merely provisional, are subject to ratification by a congress of nations, whose ultimate objective is perpetual peace by a law of nations. The union of States acts at times as a world court to which even the smallest Republics may sue against larger, registering their complaints regarding hostilities suffered. The union of nations appears as a single federated State and functions as an umpire when any of the several nations encounter public differences. "By a congress is here meant only a voluntary combination of different States dissoluble at any time, and not such a union as is embodied in the United States of America, which is founded upon a political constitution and therefore is indissoluble. It is only by a congress of this kind that the idea of a public law of nations can be established and that the settlement of their differences by the mode of a civil process rather than by the barbarous means of war, can be realized . . . If the idea is carried forward by gradual reform and in accordance with fixed principles, it may lead by a continuous approximation to the highest political good, and to perpetual peace."

XVIII

MARX'S *MANIFESTO:*

A Communism

Two principal sources of Marx's social philosophy come from a three volume verbose, relatively unread, and painfully uninteresting *Capital* (1867); and the fascinating, stimulating, brief pamphleteer type work written in collaboration with Friedrich Engels, *Manifesto of the Communist Party* (1848).

The chief doctrines contained in the Communism of *Karl Marx* are: (1) Economic Determinism, (2) Historical Materialism, (3) Inherent class struggle, (4) Violent revolution, (5) Withering away of the State, (6) Labor Theory of Value, (7) Profiteering and the exploitation of labor, (8) Religion as a police force and the opium of the masses, (9) Dialectical Materialism, (10) Ten measures for social reform, (11) Abolition of private property, (12) Communism (a Marxian definition), (13) The doctrine of Surplus Value, (14) The doctrine of Evolving Matter, (15) Dictatorship of the Proletariat.

Synopsis of Marxism.

The constituent components of Marxism comprise a *philosophy, political economy,* and *socialism.* Its doctrine of *Scientific Socialism* purports to trace the struggle of oppressed classes, and the ushering in of a new concept of social thought, namely the *dictatorship of the proletariat,* the working class, 'toiling humanity.' The proletariat have been accorded a historic mission, namely "the emancipation of mankind from all oppression and exploitation," and the inauguration of a new social system, *Communism.*

The Communist's basic program is found in the classic document: *Manifesto of the Communist Party* which proposes to present the basic ideas of 'scientific socialism.' Of it, Nikolai Lenin (1870–1924), a leading exponent of the doctrines of Marx and Engels for the Communist Party, comments: "This work outlines the new world conception, consistent materialism, which also embraces the realm of social life, dialectics, as the most comprehensive and profound doctrine of development, the theory of the class struggle and of the world-historic revolutionary role of the proletariat – the creator of the new, communist society." The *Manifesto's* objective is the conquest of political power by the proletariat through class struggles and violent revolutions, after which a classless society will emerge.

Marxism rests heavily upon the following tenets: Freuerbach's philosophy of Materialism, the Dialectic of Hegel, Historic Materialism, the doctrine of Evolving Matter, the Labor Theory of Value, the Common Ownership of the Means of Production, the doctrine of Surplus Value, the doctrine of Class Struggle, Institutional Foundations as Economically Determined. The Theory of Class Struggle is regarded by Engels as the most fundamental doctrine of the *Manifesto.*

Marx, in his *A Contribution to the Critique of Political Economy,* develops the doctrine of Historical Materialism, the application of the propositions of Dialectical Materialism to social life, a materialistic and economic interpretation of social history. In what is regarded as Marx's masterpiece, *Capital,* he develops his doctrine of Economic Determinism, the Labor Theory of Value, and the doctrine of Surplus Value, which Lenin regards as "the keystone of the economic theory of Marx."[1] The Institute of Marxism-Leninism (Russian Communists) claims that *Capital* is "a classic analysis of the economic law of motion of capitalist society, an investigation of this society and of its rise, development and decline . . . Marx reveals the historical tendency of capitalist accumulation, the inevitable intensification of the contradictions between the working class and the bourgeoisie, the inevitability of the proletarian revolution and of the 'expropriation of the expropriators.'"

Economic Determinism.

The doctrine of Economic Determinism is fundamental in Marxist social philosophy, and ultimately serves as the explanation of all social phenomena. Economic Determinism may be defined as follows: "*It is not the consciousness of men that determines their existence, but rather it is their social existence that determines their consciousness,*" which is to say that man's ideological, social, political, religious, philosophical life and ideas are derived from his actual social existence, not the other way round as is commonly supposed. "In effect, this means that the prevailing intellectual ideas and ethical ideals, the artistic tastes

[1] V. I. Lenin, *The Three Sources and Three Constituent Parts of Marxism,* (1913).

and political institutions, and everything else that comprises the culture and civilization of the period are consistent with and reflect the interests of the dominant class, the class in control of the means of production." [1] The *Manifesto* states: "The ruling ideas of each age have ever been the ideas of its ruling class."

Economic determinism implies, among other things, that morals are economically determined, which is evidenced by the fact that sociologists and others speak of a middle class morality, or an upper or lower class morality. The Capitalist has not only immorally driven women and children into labor exploitatively, but "our bourgeois [capitalist], not content with having the wives and daughters of their proletarians at their disposal, not to speak of common prostitutes, take the greatest pleasure in seducing each others' wives. Bourgeois marriage is in reality a system of wives in common, and thus, at the most, what the Communists might possibly be reproached with, is that they desire to introduce, in substitution for a hypocritically concealed, an openly legalized community of women. For the rest, it is self-evident that the abolition of the present system of production must bring with it the abolition of the community of women springing from that system, *i.e.*, of prostitution both public and private." [2]

Jobs, careers, professions, are all economically determined and selected; a man does what pays well financially, not that for which he is best suited by nature. "The bourgeoisie has stripped of its halo every occupation hitherto honored and looked up to with reverent awe. It has converted the physician, the lawyer, the priest, the poet, the man of science, into its paid wage laborers." Even familial relations have been reduced to bare economics; a person marries when he is economically able, not when physically or naturally prepared for it. "The bourgeoisie has torn away from the family its sentimental veil, and has reduced the family relation to a mere money relation." Not only is economic life explicable in economic terms, but all phases of social life — the social sciences are intelligible only when reduced to economic terms. "The bourgeoisie, whenever it has got the upper hand, has put an end to all feudal, patriarchal, idyllic relations. It has pitilessly torn asunder the motly feudal ties that bound man to his 'natural superiors,' and has left no other nexus between man and man than naked self-interest, than callous 'cash payment.' It has drowned the most heavenly ecstasies of religious

[1] Arthur P. Mendel, *Essential Works of Marxism* (New York: Bantam Books, Inc., 1961), 5.

[2] Unless otherwise indicated, quotations in the remainder of this section are from Marx and Engels, *Manifesto of the Communist Party* (1848), tr. Samuel Moore in 1888.

fervor, of chivalrous enthusiasm, of Philistine sentimentalism, in the icy water of egotistical calculation. It has resolved personal worth into exchange value, and in place of the numberless indefeasibly chartered freedoms, has set up that single, unconscionable freedom – Free Trade. In one word, for exploitation, veiled by religious and political illusions, it has substituted naked, shameless, direct, brutal exploitation."

Labor Theory of Value.

Unlike capitalistic societies which are principally motivated by the 'profit motive,' in Marxian Communism, a person is socially motivated to offer his utmost in talent and receive only that which is necessary: "*From each according to his abilities, to each according to his needs.*"[1] People are not allowed to engage in 'profiteering,' the practice of making money with money. The only honest way of making money is to earn it, either by the 'sweat of the brow' as professionals and intellectuals do, or by the 'sweat of the hand,' as laborers do, but to obtain money by clipping stock or bond coupons, as some old dowagers do, without knowing anything about the firm or expending any effort or work for the company issuing the dividend, is an immoral appropriation of funds. A merchant purchasing books at a cost of ten dollars each and selling them for eleven in his shop is not said to be making a profit in the sense of profiteering; he has earned his money through laborious effort, whereas profiteering is 'making money with money without labor.' On the other hand, the shopkeeper's landlord, the property owner, is the profiteer.

Commodities acquire their monetary value according to the proportionate amount of labor expended in producing the object. "*We see then that that which determines the magnitude of the value of any article is the amount of labour socially necessary, or the labour-time socially necessary for its production* . . . 'As values, all commodities are only definite masses of congealed labour-time.' The value of a commodity would therefore remain constant . . . In general, the greater the productiveness of labour, the less is the labour-time required for the production of an article, the less is the amount of labour crystallised in that article, and the less is its value; and *vice versa*, the less the productiveness of labour, the greater is the labour-time required for the production of an article, and the greater its value. The value of a commodity, therefore, varies directly as the quantity, and inversely as the productiveness, of the labour incorporated in it."[2]

At this point, Marx, faithful to the Utilitarianism of *Bentham*, insists

[1] *The Criticism of the Gotha Program.*
[2] Marx, *Capital.*

that labor *per se* is devoid of value if the commodity produced is useless. On the other hand, an object may have some use, and good use at that, but is without economic value, that is without cost, if no labor was employed in its construction. "A thing can be a use-value, without having value. This is the soil, natural meadows, etc. A thing can be useful, and the product of human labour, without being a commodity. Whoever directly satisfies his wants with the produce of his own labour creates, indeed, use-values, but not commodities . . . Lastly, nothing can have value, without being an object of utility. If the thing is useless, so is the labour contained in it; the labour does not count as labour, and therefore creates no value."[1]

Laborers must not be bought and sold like any other commodity on the market, for they possess intrinsic value and impute value to objects of their laborious efforts. Commodities may fluctuate in price, but the laborer must not be similarly placed on the auction market, selling himself at the lowest bid to the Capitalist for his disposition; laborers must not be so treated, for they do not possess exchange value, only commodities do. "In proportion as the bourgeoisie, *i.e.*, capital, is developed, in the same proportion is the proletariat, the modern working-class, developed, a class of laborers who live only so long as they find work, and who find work only so long as their labor increases capital. These laborers, who must sell themselves piecemeal, are a commodity, like every other article of commerce, and are consequently exposed to all the vicissitudes of competition, to all the fluctuations of the market." The results of their efforts acquire value in proportion to labor expended to manufacture the article.

The capitalistic system of paying minimum wages, instead of wages earned, is unfair and must be abolished. "The average price of wage labor is the minimum wage, *i.e.*, that quantum of the means of subsistence which is absolutely requisite to keep the laborer in bare existence as a laborer. What, therefore, the wage laborer appropriates by means of his labor, merely suffices to prolong and reproduce a bare existence. We by no means intend to abolish this personal appropriation of the products of labor . . . All we want to do away with is the miserable character of this appropriation, under which the laborer lives merely to increase capital and is allowed to live only in so far as the interests of the ruling class require it."

Inherent Class Struggle.

"*The history of all hitherto existing society is the history of class struggles.* Freeman and slave, patrician and plebeian, lord and serf,

[1] *Idem.*

guild-master and journeyman, in a word, oppressor and oppressed, stood in constant opposition to one another, carried on uninterrupted, now hidden, now open fight, a fight that each time ended, either in a revolutionary re-constitution of society at large, or in the common ruin of the contending classes."

According to Engels, the essential thesis underlying the entire *Manifesto* is: the whole of the history of mankind, social, political, intellectual, has been a history of class struggles, irreparable and unavoidable conflicts between the exploiting and exploited, the ruling and ruled, the aggressor and oppressed. The history of class war assumes an evolutionary turn; it forms a series of stages until it reaches a point where the exploited and oppressed class, called the proletariat, cannot become emancipated from the exploiters, the bourgeoisie, without an across the board revolution sufficiently encompassing to include all phases and segments of society; in other words, "emancipating society at large from all exploitation, oppression, class-distinction and class-struggles." Engels believed that the doctrine of the 'history of class struggle's' is doing for society or sociology what Darwin's Theory of Evolution accomplished for biology.

The *Manifesto* defines 'bourgeoisie' as "the class of modern Capitalists, owners of the means of social production and employers of wage-labor. By proletariat, the class of modern wage laborers who, having no means of production of their own, are reduced to selling their labor-power in order to live." An inherent class struggle maintains between these two groups which is totally irreconcilable in a capitalistic economic system for the simple reason that out of profits earned by any given company a share goes to the employer and the remainder to laborers. If laborers need and demand more wages, it must come out of the common profit shared by these two classes, consequently the employer is obliged to relinquish a share of his profits; since this is repugnant to him, or at least is not in his best financial interest, it causes these two discordant groups to remain in an ever enduring and irresolute conflict.

Violent Revolution.

One of the most, if not the most objectionable feature of Marxian Communism, is the tenet which advocates the violent overthrow of existing governments in order to establish a Communistic one. This is particularly offensive to American Democracy which, although accepting revolutionary change, does not countenance *violent* revolution, but that which is accomplished through due process of law. A 'revolution' is a sudden or abrupt change; in a Democracy, such as maintains in America, this may be accomplished by a complete and instantaneous change of government via the voting polls, for example, citizens voting out the predominant party and replacing it with another. According to Communistic doctrine, a sudden change in government may be accomplished through violence; furthermore, in a Communistic regime, rival parties are dissolved once the Communist Party is elected into power, eliminating permanently all competition and terminating the democratic process – these Communistic practices are repugnant to Western Democracies.

Communists regard violent revolutions merely as civil wars, internal national struggles; proletariat and bourgeoisie settling their private internal affairs. Class struggle, although it has not reached the stage of overt war, is nevertheless, a 'cold war.' "In depicting the most general phases of the development of the proletariat, we traced the more or less veiled civil war, raging within existing society, up to the point where that war breaks out into open revolution, and where the violent overthrow of the bourgeoisie, lays the foundations for the sway of the proletariat."

Some Socialists, particularly American Socialists, attempt to claim that Marx's doctrine of violent revolution must not be regarded as an integral part of his philosophy for it is incompatible with his other doctrines of social reform. Others insist that he did not advocate a violent revolution in democratic countries, since in a Democracy education is all that is required, inasmuch as laborers necessarily outnumber their employers, and once enlightened as to their best interests, will vote their oppressors out of government and wealthy class existence. Despite attempts to palliate Marxism, it categorically promotes violent revolution as the concluding sentences of the *Manifesto* unequivocally testify: "In short, the Communists everywhere support every revolutionary movement against the existing social and political order of things . . . The Communists disdain to conceal their views and aims. They openly declare that *their ends can be attained only by the forcible overthrow of all existing social conditions.* Let the ruling classes tremble at a Communistic revolution. The proletarians have nothing to lose but their chains. They have a world to win. Working men of all countries, unite!"

Communism and its Doctrine of Private Property.

The average person when asked to define Communism finds himself at a loss; to most persons it is a term which incites emotion rather than intellectual content. Marx defines it as *"the common ownership of the means of production"* which is tantamount to saying it is the *"abolition of private property."* In Marx's estimation, this constitutes the essence of Communism, not private property *per se,* but that which is necessary as the means of production. "The distinguishing feature of Communism is not the abolition of private property generally, but the abolition of bourgeois property. But the modern bourgeois private property is the final and most complete expression of the system of producing and appropriating products, that is based on class antagonism, on the exploitation of the many by the few. In this sense, the theory of the Communists may be summed up in the single sentence: Abolition of private property."

One major objection to the capitalistic ownership of property is that it is not a personal matter merely, but 'social power,' hence all property must be regarded as social. Under existing conditions in a capitalistic State, property represents 'class character' only. "And the abolition of this state of things is called by the bourgeois abolition of individuality and freedom! And rightly so . . . By freedom is meant, under the present bourgeois conditions of production, free trade, free selling and buying . . . In one word, you reproach us with intending to do away with your property. Precisely so: that is just what we intend. From the moment when labor can no longer be converted into capital, money, or rent, into a social power capable of being monopolized, *i.e.*, from the moment when individual property can no longer be transformed into bourgeois property, into capital, from that moment, you say, individuality vanishes. You must, therefore, confess that by 'individual' you mean no other person than the bourgeois."

Ten Measures of Social Reform.

The *Manifesto* opens with the striking and ominous: "A SPECTRE is haunting Europe—the spectre of Communism. All the Powers of old Europe have entered into a holy alliance to exorcise this spectre; Pope and Czar, Metternich and Guizot, French Radicals and German police-spies." But when one considers what precisely are the pressing ten points of reform demanded by this spectre, it subsides to but a mild threat. Of the ten Marxian measures of social reform demanding immediate attention, one finds that most of them have been, to a more or less extent, incorporated into the social and political life of America. They are as follows:

1. Abolition of property in land and application of all rents of land to public purposes.
2. A heavy progressive or graduated income tax.
3. Abolition of all right of inheritance.
4. Confiscation of the property of all emigrants and rebels.
5. Centralization of credit in the hands of the State, by means of a nation-

al bank with State capital and an exclusive monopoly.
6. Centralization of the means of communication and transport in the hands of the State.
7. Extension of factories and instruments of production owned by the State; the bringing into cultivation of waste lands, and the improvement of the soil generally in accordance with a common plan.
8. Equal liability of all to labor. Establishment of industrial armies, especially for agriculture.
9. Combination of agriculture with manufacturing industries; gradual abolition of the distinction between town and country by a more equable distribution of the population over the country.
10. Free education for all children in public schools. Abolition of children's factory labor in its present form. Combination of education with industrial production, etc., etc.

A careful perusal of these ten Marxian measures of social reform quickly reveals how many of them, and to what extent, have already been implemented into the laws of the United States. Free education in public schools obviously is, but how few Americans recognize it as a form of Communistic Socialism; the same holds true for a heavy graduated income tax. The U. S. Federal Reserve System is the American version of the centralization of credit by means of a national bank; the same pertains to F.C.C. and I.C.C. regarding number six. Measure number seven has been accomplished by means of T.V.A., Hoover Dam, etc. Number nine appears to be transpiring currently. Note that in number four, the confiscation of property refers to emigrants and rebels, not immigrants – this measure prevents emigrants from draining a nation of its wealth.

Critique of Marxian Communism.

Major objectionable features of Marxian Communism are: (1) Suspension of the democratic process once the Communist Party assumes power by eliminating all rival political parties, thus operating the government on a one party system.

(2) The loss of individual freedom and initiative by the centralization of all power and enterprize in the hands of the State. Inherent in every social measure is a concomitant loss of individual freedom. For example, socialized religion, a State religion removes all right of individual choice or freedom of religious thought – that is, provided any religion at all is allowed. Socialization of any matter whatever curbs individual freedom in that area.

(3) Removal of the 'profit motive,' thereby killing the nerve of individual initiative. Greater and varied progress is made more readily by a profit incentive than by social concern.

(4) The doctrine of violent revolution through the use of force of arms is particularly objectionable to a nation democratically oriented and whose ideal it is to live in peace, providing for change in the social order only through due process of law.

(5) Fundamental realities of man are ignored or abruptly dismissed or discarded, as evidenced by the rejection of man's cherished religious values.

(6) Marx has no clear cut plan of reform and is vague on many issues. For example, he speaks of the "withering away of the State," an inconceivable doctrine, totally unsubstantiated by evidence. When the bourgeoisie is stripped of its power and only a classless society of laborers remains, a government will prove superfluous. How is this conceivable?

Part Four: PHILOSOPHY OF RELIGION— God, the Soul, and Immortality

XIX

The Study of Religious Values

1. ***The Nature of Philosophy of Religion.*** The study of philosophy of religion is often confused with that of *theology,* perhaps because *natural theology* is identical with philosophy of religion, but by theology, unless 'natural' is prefixed to it, is meant *dogmatic theology* or *revealed theology;* philosophy of religion, although a similar study, in that like topics are treated, differs radically in its approach. Theology approaches the study of God, immortality, etc. from the standpoint of *revelation,* authorities deemed divinely inspired, whereas philosophy of religion treats these topics in the light of reason, scientific data, facts of nature, etc.

Theologians speak of special revelation and general revelation, signifying by the former revealed theology, revelation of truth by God to a specific person, whereas by the latter is meant philosophy of religion, detection of God's existence (and will) in natural phenomena. As an artist who paints a picture leaves traces of his personality, genius, style, etc., in like manner, God, the creator or architect of the universe has left his imprint upon it. Divine revelation is accepted upon the basis of faith, while reason, proof, evidence, etc. must be offered before a person is expected to accept the conclusions of philosophy. For example, in theology the doctrine of the Trinity is not to be debated on rational grounds, it precludes scientific findings; proof, scientific or philosophical, is unnecessary since its acceptance is on faith. The same attitude of faith holds true for the doctrine entailing the existence of God, but in philosophy of religion, nothing is granted without rational justification; acceptance is forthcoming only when warranted on the basis of proof, evidence beyond mere faith or revelation.

2. ***The Scope of Philosophy of Religion.*** The realm encompassed by the study of philosophy of religion is principally: (a) the existence and nature of God, (b) the existence and nature of the human spirit (soul), (c) the problem of immortality, (d) the problem of natural evil; closely related to these are: (e) the question of miracles, and (f) the question as to the validity or efficaciousness of prayer. The study of theology

spans much more, including among those subjects listed, others, such as: (a) Christology, the study of Jesus as the Christ; (b) soteriology, the study of the soul's salvation; (c) eschatology, the study of the end of the world; etc.

Various areas of philosophy of religion are referred to as *problems,* yet not necessarily with the connotation that these are inscrutable, problems without solution, such as a murder mystery which remains unsolved, but problem in the strict sense of the word, signifying a question which is proposed for solution. In the light of this definition, philosophy of religion is confronted with six major problems: (1) The Problem of God, (2) The Problem of Immortality, (3) The Problem of the Soul (Human Spirit), (4) The Problem of Evil, (5) The Problem of Miracles, (6) The Problem of Prayer. Although other legitimate areas covered within the scope of philosophy of religion exist, these six predominate; and among the six, the Problem of God, Soul, and Immortality are of paramount importance.

3. *Conceptions of God.* Perhaps the chief issue confronting philosophy of religion at the present time is the nature, concept, or definition of God; at present, the problem is not so much: Does God exist? as, What do you mean when you use the term *God?*

Currently, a number of concepts have been accumulated regarding the nature of God, some of which date back to the dawn of human thought. Among them are: (1) *Polytheism,* the belief in many gods (and goddesses); according to this concept, God has been personified into a specific particular value, such as, the god of fertility, love, etc. (2) *Henotheism,* from the Greek, meaning *one-God,* but in practice it need not exclude belief in other gods, though usually adherents of Henotheism distinguish one God from among the rest as supreme, such as the Hebrew God, Jahwe, and the Greek God, Zeus. (3) *Monotheism* is the belief in a supreme personal creator, a divine spirit, who is the source of all value. Monotheism and (4) *Theism* are terms used synonymously, Monotheism being employed when emphasis on the *oneness* of God is desired, such as in differentiating this concept from Polytheism. Theism, a special form of Monotheism, defines God as spirit, or conscious mind, with particular stress on the personal nature of God; God, the supreme person, is immanent both in physical nature and in values; he is both the source of all value (*axiogenesis*) and the conserver of value (*axiosoteria*).

(5) *Pantheism* is the belief that God is the whole of reality, all which exists is God and God is all that exists, including vegetation such as trees, minerals such as rocks, and persons. Found among outstanding Pantheists are Hegel, Spinoza, Royce, Parmenides, Plotinus, and adher-

ents of Hinduism in their acceptance of the Pantheistic teachings of the *Upanishads.*

(6) *Agnostic Realism,* the belief that God is the unknowable source of all Being, finds its adherent in *Herbert Spencer* (1820-1903), who in his *First Principles* (1862), speaks of God as *The Unknowable,* meaning by it that although some form of God exists, the particulars regarding his nature are not within the range of human knowledge. He writes: "Very likely there will ever remain a need to give shape to that indefinite sense of an Ultimate Existence, which forms the basis of our intelligence. We shall always be under the necessity of contemplating it as *some* form of thought, however vague. And we shall not err in doing this so long as we treat every notion we thus frame as merely a symbol. Perhaps the constant formation of such symbols and constant rejection of them as inadequate, may be hereafter, as it has hitherto been, a means of discipline. Perpetually to construct ideas requiring the utmost stretch of our faculties, and perpetually to find that such ideas must be abandoned as futile imaginations, may realize to us more fully than any other course, the greatness of that which we vainly strive to grasp. By continually seeking to know and being continually thrown back with a deepened conviction of the impossibility of knowing, we may keep alive the consciousness that it is alike our highest wisdom and our highest duty to regard that through which all things exist as *The Unknowable.*" [1]

(7) *Humanism,* the belief that God is human aspiration for ideals and values, stems from *Auguste Comte* (1759-1857), the Father of Positivism, who repudiated belief in all forms of ultimate force, both personal in the form of God or gods, and impersonal ones in the form of scientific forces or realities such as gravity, energy, etc. God, *le grande être* (the grand being), is humanity; man's highest aspirations, the best in man, becomes God. Prominent among modern Humanists are: John Dewey, Max C. Otto, Roy Wood Sellars, and Corliss Lamont.

(8) *Impersonal Idealism,* a concept which identifies God with ideal values, resembles some of the views previously expressed, especially Humanism, but differs from them by emphasizing the belief that values are more than man's highest aspirations, they possess an objective existence of their own, *sui generis.* For this group, ideal principles, both universally valid and objective, constitute God.

(9) *Deism,* the belief that a transcendent God has divorced himself from the universe which he has created, was common during the period of the Enlightenment, and was popular with many of the forefathers of our country, such as, Jefferson, Paine, etc., but supporters of this view rapidly dwindled in number with the appearance of Twentieth Century

[1] Chapter V, Section 31.

science, particularly with the devastating blow dealt it by the Theory of Evolution which regards the world as yet in the making. Deists propound an "absentee God" who, after having created the world like a machine, which once begun is capable of running on its own mechanism, withdraws himself from his creation, never to interfere with it again. Whatever God intended to do, he did, and it is up to man to acquaint himself with the laws of God which are the laws of the universe, thereby enhancing his own existence; in this sense, 'God helps those who help themselves.'

(10) *Deistic Supernaturalism,* the belief that God is the supernatural revealer of values, differs markedly from Deism in maintaining that although God transcends the universe, at times he enters it to grant a revelation or suspend the laws of nature to perform a miracle, but God is totally other and distinct from the world which is his creation. This view is shared by contemporary Protestant Fundamentalists, and finds its roots in Martin Luther (1483-1546), John Calvin (1509-1564), Sören Kierkegaard (1813-1855), and Contemporary Neo-Orthordoxists such as, Karl Barth (1886-).

(11) *Religious Naturalism,* the belief that God is the tendency found in nature which supports or produces values, nature's tendency to strive toward perfection, is principally found among adherents of Evolutionary Naturalism, such as, C. Lloyd Morgan's (1852-1936) *emergent evolution,* Samuel Alexander's (1859-1938) *nisus toward Deity,* and Henry Nelson Wieman (1884–) who terms God "the growth of meaning and value in the world."

(12) *Panentheism,* the belief that God interpenetrates all that exists without necessarily being the object in which God is immanent, differs from Pantheism which identifies God with the entire world of reality. The former regards God as immanent in the world, while the latter makes God all that exists, one and the same entity. Among contemporary Panentheists are to be found: Alfred North Whitehead (1861-1947), Albert Schweitzer (1875-), Edgar Sheffield Brightman (1884-1953).

As the above enumeration of concepts testifies, a dichotomous division of belief pertaining to God's existence into either the class of Theism or Atheism is insufficient; today's question is not primarily whether or not a person believes in the existence of God, rather it is a question of defining one's term as to the nature of God.

XX

THE PROBLEM OF GOD

Of the three principal religious values, God is undoubtedly one, and if not the paramount one, it is because he is rivalled by the values, immortality and soul. Proof of this fact is easily determined merely by inquiring of a person which of the three he most prizes, prefers to be true over all others, if one and only one were to be true. The majority of individuals would probably select immortality of human personality, since the mere existence of God does not in itself guarantee that the soul will survive to immortality, though it would follow predicated on the premise of a good God. St. Paul, aware of this matter, registered his preference for the immortality of the human personality; he argued: "If Christ be not risen, then is our preaching vain, and your faith is also vain . . . If in this life only we have hope in Christ, we are of all men most miserable."[1] Without immortality it appears that the lustre of many concomitant values diminish, if they do not completely perish, and for some persons, the value of morality and God fall into this category. Some persons question the value of being moral if there is no future life in the offing; they query: Why be moral, if there is no life beyond the grave?

Later, it will be learned that one of the strongest arguments for immortality is the existence of a good God; some philosophers are of the opinion that in order to prove immortality, it is necessary merely to prove the existence of a good God, and the rest logically follows from such premises, thus is found the added necessity or importance of proving the existence of God, and the further fact of the logical cohering of religious values.

A Synopsis of Proofs for God's Existence.

Among arguments advanced in behalf of the existence of God will generally be found: (1) the *Ontological Argument* which seeks to prove

[1] I Corinthians 15:14,19.

God's existence by the fact that the concept, God, is universally inbedded in the mind of man; (2) the *Aetiological Argument* which attempts to prove God's existence by the necessity of our contingent world requiring a First Cause; (3) the *Cosmological Argument* which relies upon design inherent in the world as indicating the necessity of a designer; (4) the *Teleological Argument* which predicates the existence of God on the presence of purpose in the world; up to and including the period of Enlightenment, this argument sought to prove purpose in the universe by design, the utility of objects in the world; but since the introduction of the Theory of Evolution, purpose is based upon the inherent pattern which the course of evolution appears to be assuming from lower forms of existence to higher, as poetically depicted in Alfred, Lord Tennyson's (1850-1892) *In Memoriam:*

> That God, which ever lives and loves,
> One God, one law, one element,
> And one far-off divine event,
> To which the whole creation moves.

Others are: (5) the *Axiological Argument* which bases the proof of God's existence on the presence of values in a world of facts, goodness in a naturalistic universe, ideals in a world of things, the existence of morality in a nonmoral nature; (6) the *Anthropological Argument,* an argument which seeks to postulate God's existence on facts of human nature, such as moral agency, intelligence, goodness, self-consciousness, will, etc.; (7) the *Epistemological Argument* which finds evidence for God's existence in a meaningful universe, a world which can be understood, scientifically interpreted, which responds to the reason of man because it is itself rational, made rational by a Supreme Mind; (8) the *Religio-Empirical Argument* which finds God active in the life of man, not only in the life of the mystic, but all mankind, for man in every age and in every society practices some form of religion.

A. THE ATHEISTIC POSITION

Before discussing arguments for the existence of God in detail, it may be well to consider the negative side of the issue, the Atheistic stand. A little later in these deliberations, classical arguments propounded by certain outstanding Atheists, will be treated, but for the time being, attention will be concentrated on specific types of arguments for Atheism. By argument is not meant heated discussion, emotive diatribe, but proof advanced in behalf of a given position, either pro or con, dispassionately offered and with the support of evidence logically grounded.

1. A Chaotic Universe (Not Cosmos, but Chaos)

The strongest argument for Atheism is one entertained by some persons that the world instead of being a cosmos, an orderly universe, is a chaos, void of meaning and significance. Curiously, this argument is *not* often advanced in support of the Atheist's cause, perhaps the reason being that in the process of eliminating the significance of life and the world, a person would be concomitantly attacking science. Science, such as the discovery of a new law as well as its other findings, is a reaffirmation of the fact of order inherent in the world; consequently, an offensive attack launched by an Atheist using this avenue of approach would at the same time be an attack on science. Atheists in academic circles seldom, if ever, attack science, for they prefer to fancy themselves scientifically inclined, or even defenders of science against religion which some of them view as hostile to scientific enterprise; but it is erroneous to suppose that scientists are at enmity with, or indifferent to, religion, and that religious persons reciprocally retaliate.

This argument for Atheism, the contention that the world is a meaningless chaos, is shared, among others, by a number of Atheistic Existentialists, but it would be grossly inaccurate to conclude that all Existentialists are Atheists, or even that the majority of them are; for many of them, and if Neo-orthodoxists were included among them, it would be safe to say that the majority of them, are not Atheists.

Surprisingly, the man chosen to represent this argument, the one who best formulated it, William Shakespeare (1564-1616), was not an Existentialist, though he has been called that occasionally. Not that William Shakespeare believed in this argument, nor even that he was an Atheist, but that he formulated the argument, and appropriately enough in the estimation of many, placed it in the mouth of a fool:

> To-morrow, and to-morrow, and to-morrow,
> Creeps in this petty pace from day to day,
> To the last syllable of recorded time;
> And all our yesterdays have lighted fools
> The way to dusty death. Out, out, brief candle!
> Life's but a walking shadow; a poor player,
> That struts and frets his hour upon the stage,
> And then is heard no more: *it is a tale*
> *Told by an idiot, full of sound and fury,*
> *Signifying nothing.*[1]

If you believe that the world in which we live is so completely devoid of all intelligence and meaning that it appears to be the handiwork of

[1] *Macbeth,* Act V, Scene V.

an *idiot,* that life is sheer madness not worth the trouble of living out one's existence, then your feelings are sympathetic to and your thoughts allied with this point of view; accordingly, Atheism is the only conclusion at which you can logically arrive. On the other hand, if you believe that life is worth living, that it does possess meaning, thus has value, then you are convinced without the necessity of our going through the logical steps of the Teleological Argument (and as it will be developed herein, the Cosmological Argument) for God's existence.

Criticism of the Argument from Chaos.

The chief weakness of the foregoing argument for Atheism based on the chaotic nature of the universe is that it repudiates the significance of science as well as the belief in God. If the world is meaningless, then how is it possible for scientists to extract any meaning from it as they consistently, and with unfailing regularity, do, for such is the meaning of *laws* of science. Daily, new scientific discoveries and laws are brought to light, because the scientist has faith that his efforts expended daily, without any guaranteed promise of results, will nevertheless prove rewarding, that is to say, he believes that one day he will discover or conquer that which he set out to do because the world is pregnant with meaning. For example, a scientist such as Dr. Salk was not given any promise (except that the universe is meaningful) that man could find a vaccine which would control polio, yet he was of the conviction that one day he, or some other scientist, would discover the rationale which would give him the control. Actually, as Alfred North Whitehead has asserted, men of science exercise more faith than others, including men of religion, because they never know, except on faith, that they will succeed, and by virtue of this faith they are confident that the particular scientific law of which they are in search is available; the only remaining task is to seek it out. It is as if these scientists were assured of the providence of God, that is, they are confident that God has provided that which they need, such as, laws of causation, elements necessary to effect cures, etc., and consequently they go in search of them. If the world were not orderly, science would be impossible; in such a chaotic world H_2O would make water at one time and acid or arsenic at another; it would prove healthful to man at one time and poisonous at another.

To prove that the world is chaotic would not only disprove the existence of God, but would prove the existence of a supernatural devil who experiences diabolic delight in his madness; however, he would not be an idiot, as Shakespeare proposed, but a 'mad scientist,' provided that expression is meaningful.

2. "Foxhole Religion"

'There are no Atheists in foxholes' has become a fairly common expression, one growing out of World War II, particularly from the South Pacific Theatre of activity where often it was necessary to dig little holes into the ground which resembled foxholes into which a service man could leap for safety during surprise enemy aircraft attacks. Sometimes these men in foxholes found themselves in the unhappy predicament either of sharing the hole with snakes, rats, etc. which were there, or of leaving to face the strafing of bullets or bombings by enemy airplanes. Under such agonizing and terrifying situations, some of these men in desperation would turn to prayer to God; occasionally for the first time in their lives they found themselves in intense prayer. Some of the prayers were in the form of propositions, wherein it was promised that if God spared the life of the individual in question, in return he would repay the deed in some manner, such as, a life in service to his fellow man or in service to God directly by entering the clergy. In a number of cases, these war veterans returned successfully, assured that God was with them and directly responsible for their safety; consequently, they fulfilled their promises to God in the way they deemed most suitable.

The Atheistic argument is that all religion is generated similarly, through fear. If man did not sense fear, he would not be religious; in his fear, he creates his God or gods. It is fundamentally the view that religion grew out of humble beginnings of fear, superstition, magic, etc., therefore belief in the existence of God must be false. This argument against religion is one which is favored by Soviet Communists.

Criticism of the Argument from Fear.

The error of the foregoing argument lies in assuming that merely by tracing an argument to its humble beginnings is valid proof of its falsehood, in other words, this argument commits the *genetic fallacy*. Logically, it is irrelevant how a person comes to believe in God, the relevant question is: Does God exist? not the causes of belief. Of interest particularly to the psychologist are the various steps involved in a person's becoming religious, or coming to the specific belief in God, but the thesis which remains before us for consideration is, Does God exist? not, How do we come to believe in this concept? In like manner, to show how a person falls away from believing in God, that is, the steps involved in how one lapses into Atheism, does not disprove Atheism either. Logically, an individual must prove the thesis under discussion, not create a substitute, a toy soldier at which to shoot, then assume he has destroyed the argument presented for consideration.

In conclusion, it may be added that it is a pity that some persons come to believe in God through fear, and that it would be much more satisfactory to be prompted by love; but the particular road which a person has travelled to a given belief is logically irrelevant, and is not admissable as proof.

3. "Up From the Apes"

(The Argument Based on the Theory of Evolution)

An argument which has waned in popularity, one stemming from the findings of Darwinian Evolution, is that man descended from one of the primates, such as the ape. This argument has fallen into disrepute owing to several factors, such as, modifications which have taken place within the Theory of Evolution. Since scientists have been unable to substantiate or corroborate as facts, gradual changes from lower species to higher, substitute theories have been offered by a number of Evolutionary philosophers subsequent to Darwin, among whom are found: *C. Lloyd Morgan* (1852-1936) whose theory of *Emergent Evolution* (1922-1923) indicated that, not gradual, but emergent, new and unpredictable qualities make their appearance by virtue of a power operating in the universe; *Samuel Alexander* (1859-1938) whose *Space, Time, and Diety* (1920) argues that a *nisus* towards Deity is operative in the evolutionary process moving upwards to more complex and higher forms of life in an inseparable *space-time* world; *Henri Bergson* (1859–1941) who contended that a *Creative Evolution* (1907) is transpiring. The Darwinian Theory of Evolution begs the question as to *why* there should be any evolution whatever, the *survival of the fit* is inexplicable divorced from the doctrine of the *arrival of the fit*. These three men: Morgan, Alexander, and Bergson, fully cognizant of this deficiency in Darwinianism, offered their supplementary and vital explanations: Morgan, in his Emergent Evolution; Alexander, in his *nisus* towards Deity; and Bergson explains the matter by postulating a vital impulse *(Élan Vital)*, whose role is the direction of the evolutionary process, the work of God. [1] Without the necessary impetus, postulated by the above men, the evolutionary process would have been rendered inoperative.

The Argument for God Based on the Theory of Evolution.

The Theory of Evolution, which at its inception was prematurely concluded by many to be an argument for Atheism, turned out to be

[1] For an additional and extended discussion on this topic, see "Vitalism" in Part VI.

an argument favoring the existence of God. Evolution, *per se*, explains nothing as it stands; it necessitates an interpretation, an explanation for its process, and still more for its upward *progress;* this explanation has been furnished by the above three mentioned men in terms of a principle; the activity of Deity is intimated. The Theory of Evolution merely records the process, the path which evolution assumes, the operation or activity of God; thus *to show how God does a thing does not prove that he is not doing it;* on the contrary, his existence is actually being proved. For example, to describe how an architect-builder constructs a building, step by step, does not prove that he did not build it, or that it was constructed on its own, but contrariwise, it proves the existence of an architect-builder.

William Carruth poetically illustrates the point under discussion in his "Each in His Own Tongue:"

A fire mist and a planet, –
A crystal and a cell, –
A jelly-fish and a saurian,
And caves where the cave-men dwell;
Then a sense of law and beauty,
And a face turned from the clod, –
Some call it Evolution,
And others call it God.

4. God, the Product of Anthropomorphic Thinking

Sigmund Freud (1856-1939), among others, offers the argument that God is the product of man's thinking; man's need of God caused him to construct a superhuman Being, a great father God, the transference of a father-image. It is not as the Bible asserts: "God made man in his own image;" but rather that man made God in man's own image, and the passage of time inverted the statement. Anthropomorphism means to conceive of God with human qualities, ascribing human characteristics to God, a Being who is other than merely human. Anthropomorphism, strictly speaking, signifies the ascription of human traits to anything nonhuman, not merely God. Ruskin defined anthropomorphic thinking as committing the *pathetic fallacy,* referring to the ocean as the 'angry sea,' whereas persons become angry, not seas.

Criticism of the Anthropomorphic Argument.

Anthropomorphism is not committed by alluding to qualities shared both by men and nonhuman beings, but only when a person ascribes what is a peculiarly human trait to nonhumans. For example, humans are sexual beings, but to ascribe sex feelings to certain animals does not entail the pathetic fallacy. Actually, man can conceive of nothing which is completely divorced from all human characteristics, for he cannot escape human experiences: he sees, hears, reasons, understands, etc. as a human being. We are creatures caught inescapably in Ralph Barton Perry's "Ego Centric Predicament;" [1] furthermore, it appears that Charles Sanders Peirce was right in his assertion that we must either plead Skepticism, reality as unknowable, or else escape by finding reasonable anthropomorphisms. John Fiske is correct in his contention "that the total elimination of anthropomorphism from the idea of God abolishes the idea itself." [2] All human reason to some degree has anthropomorphic aspects regarding it, hence to use it against Theism would open the argument to using it against all reasoning, scientific or otherwise. Moreover, if God's nature is personal, as Theists believe, then to predicate it of God would be to assert a truth, and it would then become irrelevant to raise anthropomorphism as an objection.

5. Who Made God?

Occasionally, a person will query, 'If God created all things, then: Who made God?' This question as phrased commits the fallacy of *compound questions* (poisoning the wells), and in its logical structure is related to questions, such as, 'Have you stopped passing bad checks?' 'What have you done with my unicorn horses?' These questions, both meaningless and based on unwarranted premises, assume the logical explanation of prior questions; for example, the one referring to checks assumes a person known to have been passing bad checks, while the other assumes the existence of unicorn horses without warrant. *Who made God?* assumes a prior question has been raised and satisfactorily answered, the question being: 'Is God made?' and the answer found to be in the affirmative, thus entitling us to proceed further with the appropriate question: 'Who made him?'

To analyze this question, 'Who made God?' yields results which show it to be a meaningless question ridden with contradiction. *Who* implies an antecedent, the antecedent being either God or that which is other than God (let us term it Non-God). If it is God, then what we have asserted is: 'God made God,' which is tantamount to saying that God is self-created, which accords with the view of many that God is a self-existent Being. On the other hand, if we hypothesize: 'Non-God made God,' this would imply that the Being we called Non-God is really the ultimate and genuine God who made the creature we supposed to be God.

Later, this matter will be dealt with once again in an argument

[1] See the discussion of the "Ego Centric Predicament" in Part VI.

[2] John Fiske, *The Idea of God* (Boston: Houghton Mifflin Co., 1885), 135.

advanced by William Paley who maintains that God is necessary as a First Cause, and to postulate the world as ultimate is unsatisfactory because it would be like a chain of links, to regard the chain as infinite is to commit the fallacy of begging the question, since as a chain of ten links cannot be suspended in air unsupported, neither can one with an infinite number of links. However, what is predicated of contingent objects, such as links of a chain, does not hold true of the noncontingent, spiritual, God.

6. Naive Realism — Seeing Is Believing (Show Me God)

There are those who appeal to *Naive Realism* as their criterion of truth, thus taking the attitude, 'I'm from Missouri, I must be shown before I believe.' The argument is: 'If God exists, then let me see him, otherwise I refuse to believe in his existence.' Little do many of the adherents of this argument realize that the proof which they require for God's existence is not the same which they require in order to believe in other matters, such as the realities of science. These same Naive Realists are not shown: 'horse power,' 'atoms,' 'x-ray,' etc., yet they accept them without requiring the test of Naive Realism, 'seeing is believing.'

Criticism of the Argument based on Naive Realism.

The argument: 'God does not exist because he cannot be observed' is the most feeble of those heretofore encountered, for it rests on the weak foundation that the test of truth is sense observation, and that things are in reality precisely as they are sensed, things are as they appear to the senses. Yet, we know very well that this is not the case: A white spot painted on a wheel appears as a circle when the wheel is spinning, but we know the circle to be merely illusory.

Knowledge in science is based on thought, not merely that which is sensed, as is evidenced by the fact that animals have every sense which man possesses, yet science is conspicuously absent in the animal kingdom, indicating the fact that science is more than mere sense observation, sense verification, and that a human quality other than sense is required for scientific knowledge. The human quality in question, man's intelligence, logical reasoning, should likewise be appealed to in proving the existence of God.

7. The Psychological Atheist

By the *psychological Atheist* is meant a person who for psychological factors, reasons other than logical ones, rejects belief in the existence of God. There are a wide variety of types of psychological Atheists, but they share in common the fact that emotive factors, subconscious feelings, constitute the motivation for their disavowal of God's existence. For example, there are a number of persons who argue that God cannot possibly exist because an individual of their acquaintance, an evil, sinister, vicious person, attends church regularly, and if persons of that type believe in God, then they will have nothing to do with religion, reasoning: 'How could God, if he existed, permit such persons to go unpunished?'

Criticism of Psychological Atheism.

An argument, such as that presented above, is hardly worth refuting, but it must be acknowledged that many persons, and it would not be surprising if a statistic were uncovered to prove that the majority of Atheists, particularly those of the militant and aggressive type, were from the ranks of 'psychological' Atheism. Philosophically, and by that term is particularly meant logical objectivity, all that can be said in respect to the psychological Atheist is that he needs a psychiatrist, rather than someone with whom he can debate the issue philosophically. However, in order to avoid being accused of committing the *genetic* or *ad hominem* fallacy in this regard, it need merely be mentioned that evil persons may believe in God as well as good ones; who is to judge which of us is good or evil, and on what relative scale we as individuals may be standing? Furthermore, the alleged evil person may not be going unpunished by God, and even if he were not punished, he, more than a good person, needs the environment of a church which encourages morality.

8. Karl Marx — Religion as the Opium of the Masses

Marxism repudiates religious values including belief in the existence of God on various grounds, but particularly based on the argument that religion serves as a *police force* or the *opium of the people*. "*Religious* distress is at the same time the *expression* of real distress and the *protest* against real distress. Religion is the sigh of the oppressed creature, the heart of a heartless world, just as it is the spirit of a spiritless situation. It is the *opium of the people.* The abolition of religion as the *illusory* happiness of the people is required for their *real* happiness. The demand to give up the illusions about its condition is the *demand to give up a condition which needs illusions.* The criticism of religion is therefore *in embryo the criticism of the vale of woe*, the *halo* of which is religion."[1] Marx regards religion as merely the tool of the

[1] Karl Marx, *Contribution to the Critique of Hegel's Philosophy of Right* (Moscow: Foreign Languages Publishing House).

Capitalist who, having vested interests which may be affected by any new change, must make every effort to maintain the status quo, and does so by supporting institutions which do likewise; among these institutions is the Church whose eye to progress and change is not only too slow, but looks to her own vested interests, and to the interests of the Bourgeoisie from whom her richest source of revenue emanates.

Consequently, the Church, in order to protect her own vested interests, must ally herself with the Capitalist on the side of preserving the status quo, thus placing herself at odds with the Proletariat, who in working for the Capitalist, is his enemy by circumstance. That is to say, an *inherent class war,* both cold and hot, continuously rages between worker and employer, whose interests are always and inevitably at variance. Inasmuch as the Church sides with the Capitalist against the Proletariat, the worker's natural enemy becomes organized religion; therefore, the best attack against this enemy is to destroy her value, her cherished beliefs, which is her power. How is that to be effected? By exposing her; by pointing out that the Church is functioning merely as a *police force,* a tool of the Bourgeoisie to keep the people in check, to keep them from uprising against their employers, to argue that religious values, cherished beliefs such as God, soul, immortality, etc. are fictions, illusions, fancies, to maintain a hold on the masses, as the Communist lyrics of one song depicts:

You will get your pie
In the sky,
Bye and bye,
It's a lie.

Marx argues that religion is a fiction created by man. "*Man makes religion,* religion does not make the man . . . Man is *the world of man,* the state, society. This state, this society, produce religion, *a reversed world-consciousness,* because they are a *reversed world.*" [1] Thus runs Marx's objections to religion.

Criticism of Marxian Objections to Religious Values.

In evaluating objections to religious values by Marx, it is noteworthy that if religion did at one time affiliate itself with the Capitalist against the interests of the Proletariat, it need not have been the case, for it is not the case today; in fact, organized religion in this country favors the worker's cause and supports his welfare. Marx, with sufficient insight or foresight could have won the support of the Church for the cause of labor without engaging in extreme and desperate measures of

[1] *Idem.*

denying the existence of religious values on such feeble grounds. To reject religion as false because it functions as a *police force,* because it encourages people to obey the law rather than rise up in violent revolt, is not to the detriment of organized religion, but to its credit; organized religion should be praised for its beneficial influence of encouraging citizens to obey the laws of their respective communities.

The objection of Marx to the effect that religious beliefs are the *opium of the people* is an assertion too sweeping to be factually supported by the data of religious experience. Many social reformers, whose major impetus is religiously oriented, certainly must be finding religion a 'thorn in the flesh,' rather than the pleasant insensuous effect of opium. For many persons, religion is an effort, a sacrifice which although willingly accepted, is nonetheless, remote from pleasantries which are akin to the effects of opium.

In conclusion, it may be added that to assert religion to be the opium of the people or a police force is irrelevant, for by so doing, Marx has neither proved nor disproved the existence of God nor of any other religious value; he has not as yet treated the thesis.

9. Sigmund Freud — Religion as an Illusion, a Father Complex, and an Obsessional Neurosis

Sigmund Freud (1856–1939) dismisses religion as an illusion, ideas spawned to alleviate man's intolerable condition and helpless existence. Religious ideas are generated in the childhood of the race of man as well as in the life of each individual man. "Culture creates these religious ideas," creates them to humanize a seemingly hostile nature, and to bring her under man's command.

In *Totem and Tabu* (1913), Freud develops the idea that religion is a son-father relationship in which God is the exalted father, thus bringing us to the root of religion, namely, religion as the longing for a father, a father who will compensate for human weaknesses, a father to whom a person may transfer helplessness. Religion is, therefore, a *father complex,* the projection or objectification of the father need or desire which is in us. It is not difficult to understand that to a young child his father appears to have all of the valuable characteristics which religious persons ascribe to God: to a child, his father can do anything (comparable to the omnipotence of God), to a child, his father is always present when needed (the omnipresence of God). Accordingly, as a child grows to adolescence and manhood, he discovers that he has been disillusioned regarding the true nature of his father; the faith which was initially bestowed on his father is withdrawn from him, then either left floating as an uncomfortable floating faith or in time is grounded in a Being capable and worthy of his high confidence; thus such a person creates an illusion, a God, in which he can place this faith. Such is the explanation of God as a *father complex.*

Freud discusses the father complex at length in *Totem and Tabu,* but summarizes it concisely in *The Future of an Illusion* (1927): "Now when a child grows up and finds that he is destined to remain a child forever, and that he can never do without protection against unknown and mighty powers, he invests these with the traits of the father-figure; he creates for himself the gods, of whom he is afraid, whom he seeks to propitiate, and to whom he nevertheless entrusts the task of protecting him. Thus the longing-for-the-father explanation is identical with the other, the need for protection against the consequences of human weakness; the child's defensive reaction to his helplessness gives the characteristic features to the adult's reaction to his own sense of helplessness, *i.e.* the formation of religion."[1] The father complex is found to be at the root of the need for religion.

The illusions of religion must be rationalizations, doctrines which are claimed to be above reason, beyond its jurisdiction, yet inwardly known and felt, though not necessarily comprehended. Religion is a philosophy of 'as if,' a make-believe, a fiction, a religious fairy tale. Religious beliefs "are illusions, fulfillments of the oldest, strongest and most insistent wishes of mankind; the secret of their strength is the strength of these wishes. We know already that the terrifying effect of infantile helplessness aroused the need for protection — protection through love — which the father relieved, and that the discovery that this helplessness would continue through the whole of life made it necessary to cling to the existence of a father — but this time a more powerful one. Thus the benevolent rule of divine providence allays our anxiety in face of life's dangers, the establishment of a moral world order ensures the fulfillment of the demands of justice, which within human culture have so often remained unfulfilled, and the prolongation of earthly existence by a future life provides in addition the local and temporal settings for these wish-fulfilments." These wish fulfillments stem from the father complex arising out of childhood, and are illusions, but an illusion is not necessarily false, unreal. Beliefs are defined as illusions when their wish-fulfillment factor dominates a person's motivation, while at the same time ignoring its connection, or lack of it, with reality. "Thus we call a belief an illusion when wish-fulfilment is a prominent factor in its motivation, while disregarding its relations

[1] Unless otherwise noted, quotations in this section on Freud are from his *The Future of an Illusion,* tr. W.D. Robson-Scott (New York: Liveright Publishing Corporation, 1953).

to reality, just as the illusion itself does... Of the reality value of most of them we cannot judge; just as they cannot be proved, neither can they be refuted." Religious values are illusions which cannot be proved, wish-fulfillments which would be pleasant if true; a good God responsible for creation, a benevolent providence such as a moral world order, and a future life is something anyone would wish for himself, accordingly these are wish-fulfillments and illusions.

Freud has also postulated in "Obsessive Actions and Religious Practices" (1907), that religion is a *universal obsessional neurosis,* but later he assesses religion to be more than merely that, yet as men must be freed from a neurosis, they must also be saved from religion. Characteristic symptoms of an obsessional neurosis[1] (those pertinent to the present discussion) are: atoning for one's sins, performing rituals, although rationally meaningless, but done nevertheless for the sake of peace of mind. Freud believes that the mind of a child has been psychologically poisoned so that as an adult he is unable to cope with reality without psychological intoxicants such as religious illusions.

A person "not suffering from neurosis, will need no intoxicant to deaden it." Freud grants that life's vicissitudes can make a person feel utterly helpless, but he must not remain a child forever, and must face up to the hostile world properly weaned from childhood, weaned from a warm and comfortable home. Freud asserts that the entire purpose of *The Future of an Illusion* is to portray the nature and possibility of proper education, "education to reality" as he terms it, to train a person to face life and its harsh realities without the 'crutch' of religion's illusions. "Religion is a childhood neurosis," a phase in the life of mankind which will eventually be overcome in the same manner that children overcome theirs; religion is an infantile stage in the life of the human race.

Freud concedes that everyone has illusions to some extent, but the religious person's illusions are depended upon to such an extent that once discredited, his whole world collapses, while the rest of us who keep our illusions limited can afford to be disillusioned without serious damage. Freud argues: "Note the difference between your attitude to illusions and mine. You have to defend the religious illusion with all your might; if it were discredited – and to be sure it is sufficiently

[1] As used here, the obsessional neurosis includes the compulsive neurosis, and the characteristics listed here are typical, not of the obsessional, but of the compulsive neurosis, when the two are treated as separate maladies. Many psychologists, following Freud, consider the two to be one and the same ailment, and identify their diagnosis by the prevailing symptoms, as to whether the neurosis is to be designated obsessional or compulsive.

menaced – then your world would collapse, there would be nothing left for you but to despair of everything, of culture and of the future of mankind. From this bondage I am, we are, free. Since we are prepared to renounce a good part of our infantile wishes, we can bear it if some of our expectations prove to be illusions." Perhaps the moral Freud seeks to propound is: 'Keep your God little and your disappointments will also be little.'

Assessment of Freudian Objections to Religion.

Directing our attention to a criticism of the Freudian repudiation of religion, it may be said, without proceeding further, that Freud commits a glaring genetic fallacy. Logically, it makes no difference how a person, or for that matter mankind, comes to believe in religious values, of God, soul, immortality; provided the belief is true. The confronting task is to prove or disprove the thesis: God exists, the soul exists, or that there is an eternal life; not where do these ideas come from, but whether they are true is of primary interest. It may be of major interest to the psychologist how beliefs are generated, and it may even engage the curiosity of others, including the philosopher, but the issue which stands squarely before us, and which cannot be dismissed with merely furnishing the source of ideas, is the validity of ideas.

The following is offered as an illustration of the foregoing objection: Logically, nothing necessarily exempts the mad man from uttering truth; we cannot say that the statement of a lunatic or of any other psychotic who enters the room shouting, "H_2O is water, and $2 + 2 = 4$," is false, simply because a psychotic uttered it. Logically, the source of ideas is irrelevant, despite our interest in the mode of their emergence; the logical issue is: Does God exist? not *where* did the idea originate.

To designate religious values as illusions, father complexes, wish-fulfillments, neuroses, etc., is to evade the issue, since they conceivably can be true, despite the presence of Freudian symptoms; for example, God in my particular circumstances may be both a father complex and a wish-fulfillment, but the fact that God exists is independent of the presence of these symptoms.

B. AN INTERMEDIARY POSITION: AGNOSTICS AND OTHERS

Should you inquire of the average person, unacquainted with philosophy, as to the number of various positions an individual may assume in regard to a stand pertaining to the existence of God, he would probably reply, two: Theism and Atheism; some would be sufficiently enlightened to offer three as an answer, adding as the third, Agnosticism, a noncommital position, a state of suspended judgment. *Agnosticism,* a term introduced by *Thomas Henry Huxley* (1825–1895), is a stand assumed by a person who does not pretend to know whether or not God exists, either because he personally does not have enough facts to warrant a considered judgment, or he believes that facts are unavailable, not only to himself but others, and those who do take a stand are either pretentious, presumptuous, or dogmatic. Some Agnostics, as innocent bystanders, observe the debate between Theist and Atheist without committing themselves to either position, while others dogmatically insist that God is unknowable but that Atheism is equally unknowable; neither will ever become a topic of genuine knowledge now or ever.

There remains yet another group, a nondescript miscellaneous number of persons who are neither Theists in the strict sense of the word, nor are they Atheists, nor even Agnostics, but a *tertium quid* that escapes classification. Some of them take a very Pragmatic attitude toward the matter of religious values, treating them *as if* true, others accept them as of practical value, while some find in them poetic or symbolic value. Since logically such arguments cannot be classified as pro or con, it was deemed best to establish a new category designated "An Intermediary Position," and to include within it the Agnostic's position as well.

1. Bertrand Russell — Agnosticism

Bertrand Russell (1872–   ), an Agnostic from his youth, has been vitally active in philosophical discussion involving religious values. This fact is fairly common to many individuals, philosophers and laymen alike; whether or not a person believes in the existence of God, he often has an active interest in matters pertaining to Deity's existence, and to the question of immortality. Russell has been an outspoken adherent of Agnosticism, one who readily and regularly voices his opinions respecting religious values, and regarding which he has assumed the Agnostic's position, viz., that God's existence is not subject to proof.

Russell adheres to *Scientism,* the belief that only the scientifically verifiable can be validly proved, and it is often accompanied with the implication that what is not scientifically verifiable does not exist. Therefore, belief in God or any other religious value is unacceptable from the standpoint of valid knowledge. "God and immortality, the central dogmas of the Christian religion, find no support in science,"[1] but from this statement one is not entitled to conclude the opposite, for Russell adds,

[1] Bertrand Russell, *What I Believe* (New York: E.P. Dutton & Co., 1925).

"I do not pretend to prove that there is no God. I equally cannot prove that Satan is a fiction. The Christian God may exist; so may the Gods of Olympus, or of ancient Egypt, or of Babylon. But no one of these hypotheses is more probable than any other: they lie outside the region of even probable knowledge, and therefore there is no reason to consider any of them." [1] But Russell, however, continues to consider them; he cannot avoid them for they possess an irresistible fascination, as he confesses in his *My Philosophical Development*: "My brother-in-law, Logan Pearsall Smith, had a set of questions that he used to ask people. One of them was, 'What do you particularly like?' I replied. 'Mathematics and the sea, theology and heraldry, the two former because they are inhuman, the two latter because they are absurd.'" [2] Absurd or not, the keen attention Russell devoted to the topic of religious values is worthy of that accorded science by a dedicated scientist.

Russell defines an Agnostic as one who "thinks it impossible to know the truth in matters such as God and the future life with which Christianity and other religions are concerned. Or, if not impossible, at least impossible at the present time." [3] He denies that Agnostics are Atheists, because an Atheist claims, as does the Theist, that knowledge regarding God is available, while the Agnostic suspends judgment, although for all practical purposes usually, the Agnostic is one with the Atheist. "An atheist, like a Christian, holds that we *can* know whether there is a God. The Christian holds that we can know there is a God; the atheist, that we can know there is not. The Agnostic suspends judgment, saying that there are not sufficient grounds either for affirmation or for denial. At the same time, an Agnostic may hold that the existence of God, though not impossible, is very improbable; he may hold it so improbable that it is not worth considering in practice. In that case, he is not far removed from atheism . . . An Agnostic may think the Christian God as improbable as the Olympians; in that case, he is, for practical purposes, at one with the atheists." [4] Some Agnostics regard the philosopher's God in the same category of Zeus and other gods of the Polytheistic ancient Greeks, hence Agnosticism is practically tantamount to Atheism; as for Russell, he concedes, "I do not know of any conclusive argument against the existence of God." [5]

[1] *Ibid.*

[2] Bertrand Russell, *My Philosophical Development* (New York: Simon and Schuster, 1959).

[3] Bertrand Russell, *Look* Magazine, (Cowles Magazine, Inc. 1953). Reprinted in *The Religions of America,* ed. Leo Rosten, (London: Heinemann).

[4] *Idem.*

[5] Bertrand Russell, "Reply to Criticisms," in *The Philosophy of Bertrand Russell,* ed. Paul Arthur Schilpp (Evanston: The Library of Living Philosophers, 1944), Vol. II, 727.

As to religious values other than God, the Agnostic may assume a variety of positions; for example, regarding the question of the meaning of life, the Agnostic does not believe that life has any purpose in general; things 'just happened' as we find them.

Russell believes that religion is spawned in fear, 'terror of the unknown,' the wish or need for support similar to that forthcoming from an elder brother upon whom a younger may rely. "Fear is the basis of the whole thing – fear of the mysterious, fear of defeat, fear of death. Fear is the parent of cruelty, and therefore it is no wonder if cruelty and religion have gone hand in hand. It is because fear is at the basis of those two things."[1] The road to liberation and enlightenment is science, thus the reason science stands in opposition to religion; science is our salvation, for it will free us from our craven fears which have paralyzed mankind over numerous generations.

Evaluation of Russell's Argument.

In criticism of Russell's Agnostic beliefs, it may be said that ascribing religion to fear and thereby assuming to have disproved the existence of religious values, such as, God, soul, immortality, is to commit the *genetic error*. The manner in which religion grew, the source from which it sprang is irrelevant; to say it grew out of fear and therefore is false, is grossly erroneous, for the reason that, if for no other reason, science also grew out of fear, but this fact does not discredit contemporary science. It is fear that drives us in search of a cure of cancer, fear that drives us to explore space so as to prevent our enemies from gaining the upper hand, but because fear is our scientific motivation, does that imply that science is false? By the same line of reasoning, to trace religion to fear does not rule out its conclusions as valid, and brand them false.

2. George Santayana — Religion as Symbolism and Escape from Reality (Practical Theism)

George Santayana (1863–1952), was a brilliant man of letters as well as philosopher, whose exceptional singular mastery of English, a language not his native tongue, summons praise of the highest magnitude; from his childhood days he shared the attitude which his parents assumed regarding "all religion as a work of human imagination." This low esteem which he adopted in childhood remained permanently, but he rejected the view of his parents and others who leaped to the conclusion that since religion is false, it is therefore bad. He maintained

[1] Bertrand Russell, *Why I Am Not a Christian*, ed. Paul Edwards (London: Allen & Unwin; New York: Simon & Schuster, 1957).

that the work of human imagination, including that stemming from religious imagination may indeed be, and unquestionably is, good.

He relates an interesting episode in early life: "Thus, although I learned my prayers and catechism by rote, as was then inevitable in Spain, I knew that my parents regarded all religion as a work of human imagination: and I agreed, and still agree, with them there. But this carried an implication in their minds against which every instinct in me rebelled, namely that the works of human imagination are bad. No, said I to myself even as a boy: they are good, they alone are good; and the rest – the whole real world – is ashes in the mouth."[1] The falsity of religion does not imply its lack of value; on the contrary, religion is of utmost value.

Here we have a very peculiar position of a person who is intellectually an Atheist, yet pragmatically very religious. Santayana is religious because he maintains religion possesses value; he enjoys it, despite its fictitious nature. Perhaps, this view can be defended on the basis that the ordinary person who reads novels or attends the theatre fully cognizant that the story is fictitious, nevertheless, does not refrain from theatre attendance or reading novels. Why? Because he enjoys them, they possess value, they are good, they serve as a respite, an escape. In the same manner, religion can be defended on the basis that it possesses value, is enjoyable, an escape, and worthwhile.

It is curious that a person can intellectually repudiate belief in religious values, yet embrace them devotedly and vigorously in practice. Read the talent, the expression, the brilliance, the words, which flow from the pen of a religious spirit, though an Atheist:

O WORLD, thou choosest not the better part!
It is not wisdom to be only wise,
And on the inward vision close the eyes,
But it is wisdom to believe the heart.
Columbus found a world, and had no chart,
Save one that faith deciphered in the skies;
To trust the soul's invincible surmise
Was all his science and his only art.
Our knowledge is a torch of smoky pine
That lights the pathway but one step ahead
Across a void of mystery and dread.
Bid, then, the tender light of faith to shine
By which alone the mortal heart is led
Unto the thinking of the thought divine.[2]

[1] George Santayana, "Brief History of My Opinions," in *Contemporary American Philosophy* (New York: Macmillan Co., 1930).

[2] George Santayana, *Sonnets and Other Verses* (New York: Stone and Kimball, 1894, 1896), 5.

What could be more religious, or a greater expression of the soul's devotion to religious values? Yet, Santayana would sigh, 'Alas, if only it were true.' Santayana is a metaphysical Materialist, regarding matter only as ultimately real. To him, those things which seem most real, the realm of the spiritual, the poetic, the religious, etc. are ultimately false, because the opposite, matter, which is known by 'animal instinct' is ultimately real. "Religion has the same original relation to life that poetry has; only poetry, which never pretends to literal validity, adds a pure value to existence, the value of a liberal imaginative exercise. The poetic value of religion would initially be greater than that of poetry itself, because religion deals with higher and more practical themes." [1]

The value of religion is *escape*, to carry us to halcyon lands. "Every living and healthy religion has a marked idiosyncrasy. Its power consists in its special and surprising message and in the bias which that revelation gives to life. The vistas it opens and the mysteries it propounds are another world to live in; and another world to live in – whether we expect ever to pass wholly into it or no – is what we mean by having a religion." [2] Religion is mythical philosophy, sheer poetry, symbolism; and interpreted in this light, it cannot be said to be either true or false.

Assessment of Santayana's Philosophy of Religion.

Critically viewing Santayana's philosophical position regarding religious values primarily as symbolism, poetry, and as an escape from reality, it may be said that it suffers from contradiction. To attempt to maintain religious values as good and at the same time to assert they are false is not that which a rational individual will accept, yet Santayana claims that theoretical religion is false while practical religion is good.

To postulate that religious values are sheer poetry, symbolism, hence an escape from reality is unjustified, for the reason that all escapes are not necessarily escapes from reality, and for the additional reason that not all persons use religion as an escape, but on the contrary, for many persons religion becomes their greatest and harshest fact of reality. Many social reformers and moralists are driven relentlessly to accomplish what they deem right and just, prompted by religion; such men would find respite in being released from demands of religion which constitute their severest pressure in life.

Considering those persons who use religion as an escape as some do, including Santayana, it does not follow that escape is bad or that it is

[1] George Santayana, *The Life of Reason: Reason in Religion* (New York: Charles Scribner's Sons, 1905), 11.

[2] *Ibid.*, 6.

an escape from reality. Not all escapes are necessarily flights from reality, flights into unreality. Every vacation is an escape, an escape from the regular duties which confront a person, but a vacation escape from one's regular activities to the mountains or seashore is not a flight into unreality, but an exchange of one set of *real* circumstances for another. The value of it is that one returns to his daily tasks refreshed to meet his responsibilities with better perspective, rejuvenated. Religion can rejuvenate, and for some persons does, and should as one of its values, just as any other form of *re*-creation which rebuilds the spirit. It is not to the detriment of religious values, nor a criticism of them that they possess the virtue of providing desirable escapes. An undesirable escape, one which may be designated false, is a flight into unreality, one which is incapable of returning us to our confronting tasks, renewed in strength. Alcoholism is an example of an unreal escape, for it does not equip an individual to return with greater strength to face reality, but hinders that which he seeks to achieve, compounding his problems, and operating in the form of a vicious circle, but religion used as an escape does aid the person who seeks refuge in it by fortifying him, and returning him to cope with the severest facts of reality; something of which few things in life are capable. This valuable pragmatic element of religion is, to a certain extent, evidence of its objective validity.

3. Hans Vaihinger — Religious Values 'As If' Experiences (Practical Theism)

Hans Vaihinger (1852–1933) presents a philosophy of *Fictionalism* in his classic work: *The Philosophy of 'As If,'* in which he treats religious beliefs as useful or practical fictions. His philosophy approaches closely to that of Pragmatism, the philosophy of practical consequences, the philosophy which seeks to maintain that if an idea works then it is true; but Vaihinger insists that his Fictionalism is not Pragmatism, and defines it: "An idea whose theoretical untruth or incorrectness, and therewith its falsity, is admitted, is not for that reason practically valueless and useless; for such an idea, in spite of its theoretical nullity may have great practical importance." [1] Although Fictionalism and Pragmatism differ in principle, Vaihinger admits that in practice they share much in common, such as, acknowledging the value of metaphysical ideas, yet each of these philosophies does so for different reasons and with different results.

[1] Quotations in this section are from: Hans Vaihinger, *The Philosophy of 'As If'* (London: Routledge and Kegan Paul Ltd; also New York: Barnes and Noble, Inc., 2nd ed., 1935).

Although Vaihinger initiated this philosophy independently, it actually originated with *Jeremy Bentham's* (1748–1832) Theory of Fictions. Vaihinger's philosophy is based on the fictional nature of general or theoretical ideas, that is, although certain ideas cannot be proved to exist in theory, they are of vital practical necessity. Such is the case with religious values: God, soul, immortality, etc.; for example, we pray '*as if*' God listens and heeds our pleas and petitions, we behave morally '*as if*' we will be accountable for our actions to God, we live and think '*as if*' an Absolute or God existed, we act '*as if*' we had freedom of will, etc. We must be religious for the sake of expediency, we are left with no other choice. According to this philosophy, *truth* is 'the most expedient error,' the most useful error, the one which enables us to cope best with confronting circumstances, the one which enables us to act best in life's vicissitudes, the one which reduces to a minimum, irrationality. "Truth is merely the most expedient degree of error, and error the least expedient degree of ideation, of fiction. We call our conceptual world true when it permits us best to gauge objectivity and to act therein." The foregoing is the only acceptable criterion of truth, not correspondence, the theory generally accepted, viz., that if an idea agrees with its object then truth maintains.

Viewed from the practical standpoint, God, soul, immortality, are self-made ideas, purely fictive, practical expedient fictions. Although theoretically the existence of God cannot either be proved or disproved, an individual must nevertheless act *as if* God existed, furthermore, it is imperative that he do so. "'I believe in God,' means simply that 'I act *as if* a God really existed.'" The same holds true for *good,* a person must live *as if* a 'moral world-order' existed, independent of theoretical considerations to the contrary. "To act morally means, in contradistinction to the empirical conditions, to act *as if* the good had an unconditioned value, *as if* it had the power to extend into a super-empirical world in which a supreme ruler provided for the harmonizing of good and evil. In this sense good action is identical with a belief in God and immortality. In this sense the atheist who acts morally also believes *practically* in God and immortality, since he acts *as if* God and immortality existed. All ethical conduct, therefore, involves the fiction of God and immortality – this is the meaning of the practical rational belief in God and immortality... The morally-good can say to himself and to his kind: 'Your acts are good and, for that reason, you are, in your way, a believer, for you act as though a God existed: in short, your actions are good and therefore you believe.'" Religion and religious values are in essence practical, not theoretical, and a person's actions postulate the existence of God, not his rational theories.

"The whole As-if philosophy that we have been discussing has Him in view 'as the Supreme Idea.' 'God' is an expedient, a necessary idea, and ideas are 'heuristic fictions,' As-if modes of approach. Kant and others like him act *as if* such a God were judging them; that constitutes their belief in God, their 'practical belief' in a God" which presupposes the theoretical; we act *as if* our theories were true. To be human, we must act *as if* our ideas regarding important religious values: God, soul, immorality, freedom, etc. were true.

Evaluation of Vaihinger's Fictionalism.

According to Vaihinger's philosophy of *As-if,* only 'useful' religion is recognized, and even this statement is not strictly correct, only those actions or practices on a person's part which imply certain religious beliefs are recognized as significant and valuable. A person's actions reveal his beliefs, but whether these beliefs are therefore true, Vaihinger does not explicitly say, whereas the Pragmatist would assent to them under such circumstances. In the light of this conclusion, we would have to classify Vaihinger as a theoretical Agnostic, despite his denial of Agnosticism and his belief that only the useful or practical aspect of ideas are significant. For Vaihinger, God practically exists, but theoretically we must remain silent regarding his existence.

The most serious objection to the philosophy under consideration is that theory determines practice, much more so than vice versa; whatever a person conscientiously believes, he will eventually do; deep convictions convert to commitments in practice. However, Vaihinger appears to have the entire matter in reverse. Theory fructifies into practice; practice does not give a person his theory, although each has an influential bearing on the other, but as to the temporal order in which each occurs, it would be easier to support a case which postulates that theory influences practice.

4. Immanuel Kant — God, Freedom, and Immortality as Postulates of Practical Reason (Practical Theism)

In respect to speculative or theoretical reason, *Immanuel Kant* (1724–1804) is an Agnostic regarding proof of the existence of God, attempting to maintain the thesis that God is impossible of proof or disproof. The Theist cannot, nor will he ever be in a position to prove the existence of God, because evidence in this area is beyond human experience, but at the same time, and by the same token, he claims that the Atheist cannot now nor will he ever be able to prove the non-existence of God, and again, the reason being that such beliefs are not within the scope of reason's jurisdiction, hence must be accepted on faith, or else proved as postulates of practical reason (morality), not theoretical or scientific reasoning. Kant, in this matter, concludes that although he has closed the door to speculative reason, he has opened the door to faith.

Kantian Agnosticism.

Kant believes that the three traditional arguments for God's existence: (1) Ontological, (2) Cosmological, and (3) Teleological (Physico-Theological) are inadequate proofs because they transcend the bounds of experience to obtain proof necessary to establish God's existence, and this is an impossibility. He defines these three arguments: "There are only three kinds of proofs of the existence of God from speculative reason. All the paths that can be followed to this end begin either from definite experience and the peculiar nature of the world of sense, known to us through experience, and ascend from it, according to the laws of causality, to the highest cause, existing outside the world; or they rest on indefinite experience only, that is, on any existence which is empirically given; or lastly, they leave all experience out of account, and conclude, entirely *a priori* from mere concepts, the existence of a supreme cause. The first proof is the *physico-theological,* the second the *cosmological,* the third the *ontological* proof. There are no more, and there can be no more." [1]

Kant's dogmatic Agnosticism is a necessary implication stemming from his theory of epistemology which regards genuine knowledge as a synthesis of sense experience combined to, and modified by, the 'machinery' of the understanding. Only a combination of the two: *percepts* and *concepts,* results in legitimate knowledge, all else is illicit, hence erroneous, false. Kant objects to the *Ontological* Argument, God exists because we can conceive of him, on the grounds that it proves nothing more than a conception. "The concept of a Supreme Being is, in many respects, a very useful idea, but, being an idea only, it is quite incapable of increasing, by itself alone, our knowledge with regard to what exists... Time and labour therefore are lost on the famous ontological (Cartesian) proof of the existence of a Supreme Being from mere concepts; and a man might as well imagine that he could become richer in knowledge by mere ideas, as a merchant in capital, if, in order to improve his position, he were to add a few thoughts to his cash account."

[1] Except where indicated, quotations in this section are from Immanuel Kant, *Critique of Pure Reason,* tr. F. Max Muller (London: Macmillan & Co., Ltd., 1881).

The *Cosmological* Argument, the argument from a necessary First Cause, is also defective. Kant formulates the Cosmological Argument: "If there exists anything, there must exist an absolutely necessary Being also. Now I, at least, exist; therefore there exists an absolutely necessary Being." Kant notes a number of difficulties in this argument, such as, "the transcendental principle of inferring a cause from the accidental," that is, reasoning from contingency, the accidental, to necessity, from a contingent fact to a necessary principle. "This principle, that everything contingent must have a cause, is valid in the world of sense only, and has not even a meaning outside it. For the purely intellectual concept of the contingent cannot produce a synthetical proposition like that of causality, and the principle of causality has no meaning and no criterion of its use, except in the world of sense, while here it is meant to help us beyond the world of sense." At the risk of oversimplifying this rejoinder of Kant's, it may be said that he is claiming that *thoughts cannot cause facts.*

The third of the traditional arguments for the existence of God, the *Physico-Theological* or the *Teleological* Argument, is based on design or order in the universe. Kant acknowledges a limited or partial proof in the Teleological Argument; although it does not prove the existence of a creator of the universe, it does prove the existence of an Architect of the universe. Kant formulates and assesses this argument: "The principal points of the physico-theological proof are the following. 1st. There are everywhere in the world clear indications of an intentional arrangement carried out with great wisdom, and forming a whole indescribably varied in its contents and infinite in extent. 2dly. The fitness of this arrangement is entirely foreign to the things existing in the world, and belongs to them contingently only; that is, the nature of different things could never spontaneously, by the combination of so many means, co-operate towards definite aims, if these means had not been selected and arranged on purpose by a rational disposing principle, according to certain fundamental ideas. 3dly. There exists, therefore, a sublime and wise cause . . . 4thly. The unity of that cause may be inferred with certainty from the unity of the reciprocal relation of the parts of the world, as portions of a skillful edifice; so far as our experience reaches, and beyond it, with plausibility, according to the principles of analogy." Having stated the argument, Kant later evaluates it, extracting from it the cogent features and the extent of its proof, indicating its limitations. "According to this argument, the fitness and harmony existing in so many works of nature might prove the contingency of the form, but not of the matter, that is, the substance in the world, because, for the latter purpose, it would be necessary to prove in addition, that the things of the world were in themselves incapable of such order and harmony, according to general laws, unless there existed, even in their *substance,* the product of a supreme wisdom. For this purpose, very different arguments would be required from those derived from the analogy of human art. The utmost, therefore, that could be established by such a proof would be an *architect of the world,* always very much hampered by the quality of the material with which he has to work, not a *creator,* to whose idea everything is subject. This would by no means suffice for the purposed aim of proving an all-sufficient original Being." To prove the existence of a creator, it is necessary to prove the contingency of matter, to show that matter is not eternal in nature or essence, hence requires a cause; but in order to effect this, Kant claims, it necessitates having recourse to a transcendental argument, one which exceeds the limits of experience, and this is impossible since conclusions derived from such modes of reasoning issue in illegitimate knowledge, that which is not universally valid. For knowledge to meet the qualifications of validity, it must be grounded in sense experience, not based purely on abstract reasoning, but rooted in factual experiences, sense phenomena. Nevertheless, it must be firmly born in mind that despite the weakness in the traditional arguments for proving the existence of God because he is supersensible, no form of reasoning, scientific or otherwise, will ever be able to prove his non-existence, since it is impossible for man to obtain scientific data (sense data) which can disprove his existence.

C. THE CASE FOR THEISM

1. Immanuel Kant — The Moral Argument for God's Existence

The Proof of God's Existence as a Postulate of Practical Reason.

Although by pure speculative reason it was not possible to prove the existence of God definitively, we were able to prove that it was the most reasonable position to hold, that is, reason is more favorable in supporting God's existence than Atheism. Kant, with the Teleological Argument for God's existence in mind, reasons: "Thus I see before me order and design in nature, and need not resort to speculation to assure myself of their *reality,* but to *explain* them I have *to pre-suppose a Deity* as their cause; and then since the inference from an effect to a definite cause is always uncertain and doubtful, especially to a cause so precise and so perfectly defined as we have to conceive in God, hence the highest degree of certainty to which this pre-supposition can be brought is, that it is the most rational opinion for us men."[1] Thus we find that arguments supporting God's existence are superior, yield greater probability, than those favoring Atheism.

Although we can argue for the existence of God by pure speculative reason, we are not justified in *postulating* his existence, but we can maintain it as an *hypothesis;* in order to be able to establish God's existence as a postulate, we must resort to pure *practical reason* (ethics) for support. Kant's moral argument for Theism is based on man being a moral agent; since man is a moral agent, there must be sufficient cause to bring about this effect, and the only adequate cause is God, hence it is necessary to postulate the existence of God in order to give any meaning to the appearance or presence of morality in a world of facts. The existence of man as a moral agent, possessing a free will, necessitates "a cause adequate to this effect; in other words, it must postulate the *existence of God,* as the necessary condition of the possibility of the *summum bonum* (an object of the will which is necessarily connected with the moral legislation of pure reason)." Furthermore, justice demands that there be a God, a good God who apportions happiness according to each person's moral stature, if not meting it out in this world, at least he, being moral, would provide for it in another, in a life to come, immortality.

Kant formulated his argument for Theism as a postulate of pure practical reason: "The existence of a cause of all nature, distinct from nature itself, and containing the principle of this connexion, namely, of the exact harmony of happiness with morality, is also *postulated.* Now, this supreme cause must contain the principle of the harmony of nature, not merely with a law of the will of rational beings, but with the conception of the *law,* in so far as they make it the *supreme determining principle of the will,* and consequently not merely with the form of morals, but with their morality as their motive, that is, with their moral character. Therefore, the *summum bonum* is possible in the world only on the supposition of a supreme Being having a causality corresponding to moral character. Now a being that is capable of acting on the conception of laws is an *intelligence* (a rational being), and the causality of such a being according to the conception of laws is his *will;* therefore the supreme cause of nature by *intelligence* and *will,* consequently its author, that is God. It follows that the postulate of the possibility of the *highest derived good* (the best world) is likewise the postulate of the reality of a *highest original good,* that is to say, of

[1] Except where indicated, the quotations in this section are from: Immanuel Kant, *Critique of Pratical Reason,* tr. Thomas Kingsmill Abbott, 5th ed. (London: Longmans, Green & Co., 1898).

the existence of God. Now it was seen to be a duty for us to promote the *summum bonum;* consequently it is not merely allowable, but it is a necessity connected with duty as a requisite, that we should presuppose the possibility of this *summum bonum;* and as this is possible only on condition of the existence of God, it inseparably connects the supposition of this with duty; that is, it is morally necessary to assume the existence of God." Thus runs the Kantian Moral Argument for Theism; if man is a moral being, then this fact must of necessity be predicated on the basis of a wise, benevolent, 'Author of the world.'

2. Blaise Pascal — The Religious Wager

One of the most unique arguments presented on behalf of the existence of God is *Blaise Pascal's* (1623–1662) *Religious Wager,* or simply *Pascal's Wager* as it has been traditionally termed. William James was enamored with it to the extent that he based his *The Will to Believe* on its logical foundations. Essentially, its logic assumes the form of a dilemma in which one is confronted with a forced choice, an option consisting of two alternatives, one of which *must* be elected; refusal to make a selection in itself constitutes a choice, for such is the meaning of a forced option.

William James summarily translates it freely: "You must either believe or not believe that God is — which will you do? Your human reason cannot say. A game is going on between you and the nature of things which at the day of judgment will bring out either heads or tails. Weigh what your gains and your losses would be if you should stake all you have on heads, or God's existence: if you win in such case, you gain eternal beatitude; if you lose, you lose nothing at all. If there were an infinity of chances, and only one for God in this wager, still you ought to stake your all on God; for though you surely risk a finite loss by this procedure, any finite loss is reasonable, even a certain one is reasonable, if there is but the possibility of infinite gain. . . At bottom, what have you to lose?"[1] If nothing else is said, it must be admitted that this is a novel approach. It may be of further interest to know that Pascal was a mathematician, scientist, philosopher, and logician whose logic, based on mathematics, enabled him to travel over Europe attending gambling houses, and occasionally breaking the bank.

Later, Pascal enlisted his gambling talents in the service of philosophy of religion in the form of the famous Wager. For the reader's clarification, the salient features of Pascal's Wager, extracted from his *Pensées,* are as follows: "'God is, or He is not.' But to which side shall we

[1] William James, *The Will to Believe* (1897).

incline? Reason can decide nothing here. There is an infinite chaos which separated us. A game is being played at the extremity of this infinite distance where heads or tails will turn up. What will you wager? According to reason, you can do neither the one thing nor the other; according to reason, you can defend neither of the propositions. Do not then reprove for error those who have made a choice; for you know nothing about it. 'No, but I blame them for having made, not this choice, but a choice; for again both he who chooses heads and he who chooses tails are equally at fault, they are both in the wrong. The true course is not to wager at all.' Yes; but you must wager. It is not optional. You are embarked. Which will you choose then? Let us see. Since you must choose, let us see which interests you least. You have two things to lose, the true and the good; and two things to stake, your reason and your will, your knowledge and your happiness; and your nature has two things to shun, error and misery. Your reason is no more shocked in choosing one rather than the other, since you must of necessity choose. This is one point settled. But your happiness? Let us weigh the gain and the loss in wagering that God is. Let us estimate these two chances. If you gain, you gain all; if you lose, you lose nothing. Wager, then, without hesitation that He is. – 'That is very fine. Yes, I must wager; but I may perhaps wager too much.' – Let us see. Since there is an equal risk of gain and of loss, if you had only to gain two lives, instead of one, you might still wager. But if there were three lives to gain, you would have to play (since you are under the necessity of playing), and you would be imprudent, when you are forced to play, not to chance your life to gain three at a game where there is an equal risk of loss and gain. But there is an eternity of life and happiness. And this being so, if there were an infinity of chances, of which one only would be for you, you would still be right in wagering one to win two, and you would act stupidly, being obliged to play, by refusing to stake one life against three at a game in which out of an infinity of chances there is one for you, if there were an infinity of an infinitely happy life to gain. But there is here an infinity of an infinitely happy life to gain, a chance of gain against a finite number of chances of loss, and what you stake is finite. It is all divided; wherever the infinite is and there is not an infinity of chances of loss against that of gain, there is no time to hesitate, you must give all. And thus, when one is forced to play, he must renounce reason to preserve his life rather than risk it for infinite gain, as likely to happen as the loss of nothingness."[1] Thus runs the logical course

[1] Blaise Pascal, *Pensées,* tr. William Finlayson Troter (1904) from the edition of Léon Brunschvicg (1897).

of Pascal's *Religious Wager,* nothing to lose if you cast your coin for God, since a life of devotion and belief in God can be and is a rewardingly pleasant one, he contends; but if you select the alternative option, the losses which you stand to suffer could be immense, not only the pleasure, happiness, or blessedness which religion affords in this life, but should there be a life to come, you stand to lose for an eternity – the stakes are overwhelming.

Evaluation of Pascal's Religious Wager.

How anyone can fail to be charmed by the argument of this *Wager* is difficult to comprehend, but the logic of it in its theoretical aspects, not its practical application, appears to overlook an important characteristic of the nature of God which most Theists accept, viz., his lofty and majestic *goodness.* Even the Agnostic Bertrand Russell was aware of this fact and sought to capitalize on it, if not to take refuge in it almost to the extent of betraying what could possibly be his true belief, namely, the belief in a good God, at least, if any God exists, he is sure to be a good one. To the question: Are you never afraid of God's judgment in denying him? Russell answered: "Most certainly not... And if there were a God, I think it very unlikely that He would have such an uneasy vanity as to be offended by those who doubt His existence." [1] Nevertheless, we have not escaped, nor can we escape the practical aspects of Pascal's Wager, since the forced option remains permanently before us; we must choose, and the refusal to make a choice is in itself one.

3. William James — The Pragmatic Argument for God

William James' (1842–1910) classic essay, *The Will to Believe* (1897), offers a Pragmatist's approach to belief in the existence of Deity based upon the practical benefits which are gained from such a belief, and upon the fact that a *forced option,* an inescapable choice, confronts everyone, a choice which is laden with immense value and serious consequences. Originally, the essay was an address delivered to the Philosophical Clubs of Yale and Brown Universities, and later published in the *New World,* 1896; the following year it was included in a volume dedicated to Charles Sanders Peirce, entitled: *The Will to Believe and Other Essays In Popular Philosophy.*

According to James, beliefs are hypotheses similar to dead and live electrical wires; "a live hypothesis is one which appeals as a real possi-

[1] Bertrand Russell, *Look* Magazine, *op. cit.*

bility to him to whom it is proposed."[1] A dead hypothesis holds neither interest nor does it prompt a person to action; for example, to say that Cleopatra's maid preferred the color yellow to red is a dead hypothesis because it lacks sufficient interest to create in us any motivating power. A live hypothesis is measured by an *individual's willingness to act* on it.

Decisions between hypotheses are termed *options*. "Options may be of several kinds. They may be – 1, *living* or *dead*; 2, *forced* or *avoidable*; 3, *momentous* or *trivial*; and for our purposes we may call an option a *genuine* option when it is of the forced, living, and momentous kind." Living options are live ones, as discussed above in reference to live wires; forced options are choices which must be made whether or not a person actively wills to or not, avoidance of choice is tantamount to electing one of two options; forced options confront the individual as two horns of a dilemma, one of the two disjunctions is necessarily chosen. Momentous options are one-time opportunities, a 'chance of a lifetime,' opportunities which knock but once, choices which alter our future, our lives.

A still further consideration in this matter pertains to the psychology of human opinions, that is, whether our passional or volitional nature "lay at the root of all our convictions." Deliberations which cannot be decided on the basis of the intellect alone are subject to passional tendencies and volitions, occurring either before or after our beliefs. "The thesis I defend is, briefly stated, this: *Our passional nature not only lawfully may, but must, decide an option between propositions, whenever it is a genuine option that cannot by its nature be decided on intellectual grounds; for to say, under such circumstances, 'Do not decide, but leave the question open,' is itself a passional decision, – just like deciding yes or no, – and is attended with the same risk of losing the truth.*" For example, moral questions are not decided on sense proof, but are decisions resting on our will.

Our will can in certain circumstances determine the facts, that is, our faith and will can actually create facts, *e.g.*, "a whole train of passengers (individually brave enough) will be looted by a few highwaymen, simply because the latter can count on one another, while each passenger fears that if he makes a movement of resistance, he will be shot before any one else backs him up. If we believed that the whole car-full would rise at once with us, we should each severally rise, and train-robbing would never even be attempted. There are, then, cases

[1] Quotations in this section are from: William James, *The Will to Believe and Other Essays in Popular Philosophy* (1897).

where a fact cannot come at all unless a preliminary faith exists in its coming. *And where faith in a fact can help create the fact,* that would be an insane logic which should say that faith running ahead of scientific evidence is the 'lowest kind of immorality' into which a thinking being can fall. Yet such is the logic by which our scientific absolutists pretend to regulate our lives!" Science merely states facts, morality evaluates some as better than others, while religion asserts that the best things are the eternal, and "that we are better off even now if we believe her first affirmation to be true." We are now in a position to apply these findings to religious values.

First of all, religious beliefs must be live wires; if they have no 'living possibility' of being true, they may be discarded, but if religion offers us a *momentous option,* if by our belief we gain a vital good, and by its repudiation we stand to lose, then such religious beliefs become *forced options* which cannot be evaded or ignored. "We cannot escape the issue by remaining sceptical and waiting for more light, because, although we do avoid error in that way *if religion be untrue,* we lose the good, *if it be true,* just as certainly as if we positively chose to disbelieve. It is as if a man should hesitate indefinitely to ask a certain woman to marry him because he was not perfectly sure that she would prove an angel after he brought her home. Would he not cut himself off from that particular angel-possibility as decisively as if he went and married some one else? Scepticism, then, is not avoidance of option; it is option of a certain particular kind of risk. *Better risk loss of truth than chance of error,* — that is your faith-vetoer's exact position. He is actively playing his stake as much as the believer is; he is backing the field against the religious hypothesis, just as the believer is backing the religious hypothesis against the field. To preach scepticism to us as a duty until 'sufficient evidence' for religion be found, is tantamount therefore to telling us, when in presence of the religious hypothesis, that to yield to our fear of its being error is wiser and better than to yield to our hope that it may be true." The choice is comparable to Pascal's Religious Wager. "If religion be true and the evidence for it be still insufficient, I do not wish, by putting your extinguisher upon my nature (which feels to me as if it had after all some business in this matter), to forfeit my sole chance depending, of course, on my willingness to run the risk of acting as if my passional need of taking the world religiously might be prophetic and right." Religion is vital, it is a live hypothesis and may be true.

From a very practical standpoint, the Skeptic alienates himself from much that is valuable in religion, despite whatever deficiency it may have by way of proof. "To take a trivial illustration: just as a man who in a company of gentlemen made no advances, asked a warrant for every concession, and believed no one's word without proof, would cut himself off by such churlishness from all the social rewards that a more trusting spirit would earn, — so here, one who should shut himself up in snarling logicality and try to make the gods extort his recognition willy-nilly, or not get it at all, might cut himself off forever from his only opportunity of making the gods' acquaintance. . . I, therefore, for one, cannot see my way to accepting the agnostic rules for truth-seeking, or wilfully agree to keep my willing nature out of the game. I cannot do so for this plain reason, that *a rule of thinking which would absolutely prevent me from acknowledging certain kinds of truth if those kinds of truth were really there, would be an irrational rule.*" This rule pertains only to living options, those which the intellect cannot resolve; live hypotheses have the power to tempt our wills.

Beliefs are commensurate with action, and are measured by action; for anyone to deny you the right of religious belief is concomitantly to deny you the right to perform certain actions. "The whole defence of religious faith hinges upon action. I myself believe, of course, that the religious hypothesis gives to the world an expression which specifically determines our reactions, and makes them in a large part unlike what they might be on a purely naturalistic scheme of belief." Religious beliefs, unlike many other beliefs, are living, forced options beyond the intellect's capacity to settle, "and living options never seem absurdities to him who has them to consider. When I look at the religious question as it really puts itself to concrete men, and when I think of all the possibilities which both practically and theoretically it involves, then this command that we shall put a stopper on our heart, instincts, and courage, and *wait* — acting of course meanwhile more or less as if religion were *not* true — till doomsday, or till such time as our intellect and senses working together may have raked in evidence enough, — this command, I say, seems to me the queerest idol ever manufactured in the philosophic cave." This is the only reasonable course of action for a person to take because he is neither infallible nor does he possess absolute truth; other alternatives would be justifiable if we had infallible intellects or possessed objective certitude. "But if we are empiricists, if we believe that no bell in us tolls to let us know for certain when truth is in our grasp, then it seems a piece of idle fantasticality to preach so solemnly our duty of waiting for the bell. Indeed we *may* wait if we will, — I hope you do not think that I am denying that, — but if we do so, we do so at our peril as much as if we believed. In either case we *act*, taking our life in our hands." At any rate, we should respect each other's intellectual freedom, and declare an intellectual republic, where the spirit of tolerance prevails, so that we 'live and let live' in speculative issues as well as in practical matters.

James brings his argument to a close with an appropriate quotation from Fitz James Stephen's *Liberty, Equality, Fraternity:* "In all important transactions of life we have to take a leap in the dark... *If we decide to leave the riddles unanswered, that is a choice; if we waver in our answer, that, too, is a choice: but whatever choice we make, we make it at our peril.* If a man chooses to turn his back altogether on God and the future, no one can prevent him; no one can show beyond reasonable doubt that *he* is mistaken. Each must act as he thinks best; and if he is wrong, so much the worse for him. We stand on a mountain pass in the midst of whirling snow and blinding mist, through which we get glimpses now and then of paths which may be deceptive. If we stand still we shall be frozen to death. If we take the wrong road we shall be dashed to pieces."

Thus runs the Pragmatist's forced option; religious values are more than a matter of mere belief, they constitute a course of action which we have chosen and followed whether we consciously realize it or not. Our actions reveal our basic philosophical beliefs in the area of religious values, and whether we are aware of it or not, we have chosen sides.

Evaluation of the Pragmatic Argument.

Despite the very important fact which James calls to our attention, viz., religious values are more than passive beliefs, they constitute courses of action, which action determines a person's true philosophical beliefs; the fact still remains that man's intellect seeks, desires, requires, rational satisfaction also, and remains mentally disquieted until the problem is solved from the point of speculative or intellectual satisfaction as well.

4. William Paley — The Classic Watch Argument (Teleological Argument)

The Argument from Adaptation.

The argument for God's existence based upon adaptation is teleological in structure, arguing from the standpoint that design is present in the universe. Prior to the Darwinian Evolutionary Period, this argument's most classic expression is found presented in its most cogent form by *William Paley* (1743–1805) who illustrates the entire argument by the simile of a watch. To avoid depreciating Paley's brilliant presentation, the argument is presented verbatim almost in its entirety.

Paley's Classic Watch Argument: [1]

In crossing a heath, suppose I pitched my foot against a *stone,* and were asked how the stone came to be there, I might possibly answer, that for anything I knew to the contrary, it had lain there forever; nor would it perhaps be very easy to show the absurdity of this answer. But suppose I had found a *watch* upon the ground, and it should be inquired how the watch happened to be in that place: I should hardly think of the answer which I had before given, – that, for anything I knew, the watch might have always been there. Yet, why should not this answer serve for the watch, as well as for the stone? For this reason, and for no other, viz., that, when we come to inspect the watch, we perceive (what we could not discover in the stone) that its several parts are framed and put together for a purpose, e.g. that they are so formed and adjusted as to produce motion, and that motion so regulated as to point out the hour of the day; that, if the several parts had been differently shaped from what they are, of a different size from what they are, or placed after any other manner, or in any other order, than that in which they are placed, either no motion at all would have been carried on in the machine, or none which would have answered the use that is now served by it. To reckon up a few of the plainest of these parts, and of their offices, all tending to one result: – We see a cylindrical box, containing a coiled elastic spring, which, by its endeavour to relax itself, turns round the box. . . We take notice that the wheels are made of brass, in order to keep them from rust; the springs of steel, no other metal being so elastic; that over the face of the watch there is placed a glass, a material employed in no other part of the work, but in the room of which, if there had been any other than a transparent substance, the hour could not be seen without opening the case. This mechanism being observed . . . the inference, we think, is inevitable; that the watch must have had a maker; that there must have existed, at some time, and at some place or other, an artificer or artificers who formed it for the purpose which we find it actually to answer; who comprehended its construction, and designed its use.

I. Nor would it, I apprehend, weaken the conclusion, that we had never seen a watch made; that we had never known an artist capable of making one; that we were altogether incapable of executing such a piece of workmanship ourselves . . .

II. Neither, secondly, would it invalidate our conclusion, that the watch sometimes went wrong, or that it seldom went exactly right . . . It is not necessary that a machine be perfect, in order to show with what design it was made: still less necessary, where the only question is, whether it were made with any design at all.

III. Nor, thirdly, would it bring any uncertainty unto the argument, if there were few parts of the watch, concerning which we could not discover, or had not yet discovered, in what manner they conduced to the general effect; or even some parts, concerning which we could not ascertain, whether they conducted to that effect in any manner whatever . . .

IV. Nor, fourthly, would any man in his senses think the existence of

[1] William Paley, *Natural Theology; or, Evidences of the Existence and Attributes of the Deity,* (1802).

the watch, with its various machinery, accounted for, by being told that it was one out of possible combinations of material forms; that whatever he had found in the place where he found the watch, must have contained some internal configuration or other; and that this configuration might be the structure more exhibited, viz. of the works of the watch, as well as a different structure.

V. Nor, fifthly, would it yield his inquiry more satisfaction, to be answered, that there existed in things a principle of order, which had disposed the parts of the watch into their present form and situation. He never knew a watch made by the principle of order; nor can he even form to himself an idea of what is meant by a principle of order, distinct from the intelligence of the watch maker.

VI. Sixthly, he would be surprised to hear, that the mechanism of the watch was no proof of contrivance, only a motive to induce the mind to think so:

VII. And not less surprised to be informed, that the watch in his hand was nothing more than the result of the laws of *metallic* nature. It is a perversion of language to assign any law, as the efficient, operative cause of anything. A law presupposes an agent; for it is only the mode, according to which an agent proceeds: it implies a power; for it is the order, according to which that power acts. Without this agent, without this power, which are both distinct from itself, the *law* does nothing; is nothing. . .

VIII. Neither, lastly, would our observer be driven out of his conclusion, or from his confidence in its truth, by being told that he knew nothing at all about the matter. He knows enough for his argument: he knows the utility of the end: he knows the subserviency and adaptation of the means to the end. These points being known, his ignorance of other points, his doubts concerning other points, affect not the certainty of his reasoning. The consciousness of knowing little, need not beget a distrust of that which he does know.

State of the Argument Continued:

Suppose, in the next place, that the person who found the watch, should, after some time, discover, that, in addition to all the properties which he had hitherto observed in it, it possessed the unexpected property of producing, in the course of its movement, another watch like itself . . . what effect ought such a discovery to have upon his former conclusion?

I. The first effect would be to increase his admiration of the contrivance, and his conviction of the consummate skill of the contriver . . .

II. He would reflect, that though the watch before him were, *in some sense,* the maker of the watch, which was fabricated in the course of its movements, yet it was in a very different sense from that, in which a carpenter, for instance, is the maker of a chair; the author of its contrivance, the cause of the relation of its parts to their use. With respect to this, the first watch was no cause at all to the second: in no such sense as this was it the author of the constitution and order, either of the parts which the new watch contained, or of the parts by the aid and instrumentality of which it was produced . . .

III. Though it be now no longer probable, that the individual watch, which our observer had found, was made immediately by the hand of an artificer, yet doth not this alteration in any wise affect the inference, that an artificer had been originally employed and concerned in the production. The argument from design remains as it was. Marks of design and contrivance are no more accounted for now than they were before . . . We are now asking for the cause of that subserviency to a use, that relation to an end, which we have remarked in the watch before us. No answer is given to this question by telling us that a preceding watch produced it. *There cannot be a design, without a designer; contrivance, without a contriver; order, without choice; arrangement, without anything capable of arranging; subserviency and relation to a purpose, without that which could intend a purpose; means suitable to an end, and executing their officer in accomplishing that end, without the end ever having been contemplated, or the means accommodated to it. Arrangement, disposition of parts, subserviency of means to an end, relation of instruments to a use, imply the presence of intelligence and mind.* No one, therefore, can rationally believe, that the insensible, inanimate watch, from which the watch before us issued, was the proper cause of the mechanism we so much admire in it; — could be truly said to have constructed the instrument, disposed its parts, assigned their office, determined their order, action, and mutual dependence, combined their several motions into one result . . .

IV. Nor is anything gained by running the difficulty further back, *i.e.* by supposing the watch before us to have been produced by another watch, that from a former, and so on indefinitely. Our going back ever so far brings us no nearer to the least degree of satisfaction upon the subject. Contrivance is still unaccounted for. We still want a contriver. A designing mind is neither supplied by this supposition, nor dispensed with. If the difficulty were diminished the further we went back, by going back indefinitely we might exhaust it . . . There is no difference as to the point in question . . . between one series and another; between a series which is finite, and a series which is infinite. *A chain composed of an infinite number of links can no more support itself, than a chain composed of a finite number of links.* . . By increasing the number of links, from ten for instance to a hundred, from a hundred to a thousand, etc. we make not the smallest approach, we observe not the smallest tendency, towards self-support. . . This very much resembles the case before us. The machine, which we are inspecting, demonstrates, by its construction, contrivance and design. *Contrivance must have had a contriver; design, a designer; whether the machine immediately proceeded from another machine, or not.* That circumstance alters not the case. . . A contriver is still necessary. No tendency perceived, no approach towards a diminution of the necessity. It is the same with any and every succession of these machines; a succession of ten, of a hundred, of a thousand; with one series as with another; a series which is finite as with a series which is infinite. . . In all equally, contrivance and design are unaccounted for.

The question is not simply, How came the first watch into existence? . . . To suppose it to be so, is to suppose that it made no difference whether we had found a watch or a stone. As it is, the metaphysics of that question have no place; for, in the watch which we are examining, are seen contrivance, design; an end, a purpose; means for the end, adaptation to the purpose. And the question which irresistibly presses upon our thoughts, is, whence this contrivance and design? The thing required is the intending mind, the adapting hand, the intelligence by which that hand was directed. This question, this demand, is not shaken off by increasing a number or succession of substances . . . It is vain, therefore, to assign a series of such causes, or to allege that a series may be carried back to infinity . . .

V. . . . The conclusion which the first examination of the watch, of its works, construction, and movement, suggested, was, that it must have had, for the cause and author of that construction, an artificer, who understood its mechanism, and designed its use. This conclusion is invincible. A *second* examination presents us with a new discovery. The watch is found, in the course of its movements, to produce another watch similar to itself: and not only so, but we perceive in it a system or organization, separately calculated for that purpose. What effect would this discovery have, or ought to have upon our former inference? What, as hath already been said, but to increase, beyond measure, our admiration of the skill, which had been employed in the formation of such a machine?

Or shall it, instead of this, all at once turn us round to an opposite conclusion, viz. that no art or skill whatever has been concerned in the business . . . Can this be maintained without absurdity? Yet this is atheism.

Evaluation of Paley's Argument by Design.

Paley's argument is critized on the basis that it was predicated on a mechanistic type of universe of Eighteenth Century science, and is displaced with the Darwinian concept of the world, which postulates an organic, developing, growing universe, not a static machine subject to the laws of mechanics. Darwinian Evolution explains Paley's artificer in terms of "Natural Selection," thereby purporting to eliminate the function of Paley's God, but what Darwinian "Natural Selection" does not do, and has not as yet explained, is the adaptation of human reason to the cosmic order. Natural Selection restricts itself to explaining life-preservation. As William Sorley claims: "If we still hold to the theory of evolution and reject ordinary teleology, we must nevertheless admit that there is an adaptation (not accounted for by natural selection) between our reason and the actual cosmic order — a design greater than any Paley ever dreamed of. And it is not of intellect alone, but also of morality and the whole world of intrinsic values, that we may have to assert adaptation between our minds and the universal order."[1] Of what these values consist, and how they prove the existence of God, we shall discover subsequently when our attention is directed to Sorley's Axiological Argument.

[1] W. R. Sorley, *Moral Values and the Idea of God* (Cambridge: Cambridge University Press, 2nd ed. 1921), 326.

5. Charles Darwin and John Fiske — The Evolutionary Argument for God (Teleological Argument)

When *Charles Darwin* (1809–1882) first presented the Theory of Evolution, some persons hastily concluded that it displaced Theism, hence assumed it to be an argument supporting Atheism, but almost immediately, certain philosophers with insight were quick to realize that the theory merely describes the manner, process, by which God conducts creative activity; accordingly they argued that to show how God operates, (does a thing), does not prove that he is not doing it; on the contrary, it proves the reverse.

Charles Darwin's Theory of Natural Selection, the Theory of the Survival of the Fittest, was offered to replace Paley's explanation of design. Paley argued that design is preconceived in the mind of God, and deliberately executed by God; otherwise there can be no design whatever, for design implies a designer. Darwin sought to explain design on the basis of Natural Selection, namely, the fit survive while the unfit are left to perish; at least, that which is most fitting is retained, while the undesirable are not replaced or retained. Darwin frames it: "We may be sure that any variation in the least degree injurious would be rigidly destroyed. This preservation of favorable individual differences and variations, and the destruction of those which are injurious, I have called Natural Selection, or the Survival of the Fittest. Variations neither useful nor injurious would not be affected by natural selection... Natural selection is daily and hourly scrutinizing, throughout the world, the slightest variations; rejecting those that are bad, preserving and adding up all that are good; silently and insensibly working, *whenever and wherever opportunity offers,* at the improvement of each organic being in relation to its organic and inorganic conditions of life. . . Natural selections can act only through and for the good of each being. . . Can we wonder, then, that Nature's productions should be far 'truer' in character than man's productions; that they should be infinitely better adapted to the most complex conditions of life, and should plainly *bear the stamp of far higher workmanship?*" [1] Thus we see that the Darwinian explanation of design and adaptation in the world is on the basis of the Doctrine of Natural Selection, but as is implied in the above quotation from *The Origin of Species,* philosophers early noted the "survival of the fit" begs the question of the "arrival of the fit," namely, the Being whose "stamp of higher workmanship" this world of ours is. This activity of "hourly scrutinizing," "rejecting

[1] Charles Darwin, *The Origin of Species* (1859).

those that are bad," "serving . . . the good of each being," etc. intimates Theism. It is precisely upon this point and issue that philosophers arguing for the existence of God upon the premises of the Theory of Evolution plead their case.

John Fiske (1842–1901), an American philosopher and one-time librarian at Harvard University's Widener Library, dismissed Paley's argument for God on the basis of design, for a Teleological Argument for Theism grounded on the Theory of Evolution. Fiske repudiates Paley's position on the grounds that it 'proves too much;' "the very success of the argument in showing the world to have been the work of an intelligent Designer made it impossible to suppose that Creator to be at once omnipotent and absolutely benevolent. For nothing can be clearer than that Nature is full of cruelty and maladaptation. In every part of the animal world we find implements of torture surpassing in devilish ingenuity anything that was ever seen in the dungeons of the Inquisition."[1] Fiske does not deny the presence of design in the world on which Paley bases his argument, nor does he deny that such design implies a Designer (God), but he contends that the God which is proved is not necessarily infinite in wisdom, power, and goodness.

Owing to the presence of evil in the world, it cannot be said that God is both all-powerful and all-good; he is deficient in one of these qualities. "But indeed it is not necessary to refer to the problem of evil in order to show that the argument from design cannot prove the existence of an omnipotent and benevolent Designer. It is not omnipotence that contrives and plans and adapts means to ends. These are the methods of finite intelligence; they imply the overcoming of obstacles; and to ascribe them to omnipotence is to combine words that severally possess meanings into a phrase that has no meaning. 'God said, Let there be light: and there was light.' In this noble description of creative omnipotence one would search in vain for any hint of contrivance. The most the argument from design could legitimately hope to accomplish was to make it seem probable that the universe was wrought into its present shape by an intelligent and benevolent Being immeasurably superior to Man, but far from infinite in power and resources." Fiske's objection is not that Paley has failed to prove the existence of God, but that he has not proved 'true Theism,' a God who is absolute, infinite in power, goodness, intelligence, etc.

Eighteenth Century science viewed the world as a machine, hence it was to be expected that Paley should use the simile of the *watch* to explain the nature of the world, and consequently to conceive of the

[1] Except where indicated, quotations in this section are from: John Fiske, *The Idea of God* (Boston: Houghton Mifflin & Co., 1885).

nature of God mechanistically represented as an architect; but the world is more than a mere machine, and should be viewed in the simile of a *flower*, an organism, a growing developing universe, instead of a machine. Paley's watch-type world and its concomitant design suffers under the blows of the Darwinian Theory of Natural Selection. "It is not that the organism and its environment have been adapted to each other by an exercise of creative intelligence, but it is that the organism is necessarily fitted to the environment because in the perennial slaughter that has gone on from the beginning only the fittest have survived ... Paley's simile of the watch is no longer applicable to such a world as this. It must be replaced by the simile of the flower. The universe is not a machine, but an organism, with an indwelling principle of life. *It was not made, but it has grown.*" The world is full of most beautiful adaptations, design; but they have been propagated by Natural Selection, even the beautiful orderly laws of nature have evolved by the same process. "The all-pervading harmony of Nature is thus itself a natural product;" the only inference left to draw is that the world of nature did not come about through the efforts of a transcendent Creator who remains outside of the world as the Deists fancied, but by an immanent God who works within it constantly.

The Evolutionary Hypothesis allows us to predicate the existence of God on the basis of a tremendous purpose being worked out in the evolutionary process. "In the story of the evolution of life upon the surface of our earth, where alone we are able to compass the phenomena, we see all things working together, through countless ages of toil and trouble, toward one glorious consummation. . . The glorious consummation toward which organic evolution is tending is the production of the highest and most perfect psychical life. . . In the natural selection of such individual peculiarities as conduce to the survival of the species, and in the evolution by this process of higher and higher creatures endowed with capacities for a richer and more varied life, there might have been a well-marked dramatic tendency, toward the *dénouement* of which every one of the myriad little acts of life and death during the entire series of geologic aeons was assisting. *The whole scheme was teleological,* and *each single act of natural selection had a teleological meaning.* Herein lies the reason why the theory so quickly destroyed that of Paley. It did not merely refute it, but supplanted it with explanations which had the merit of being truly scientific, while at the same time they hit the mark at which natural theology had unsuccessfully aimed." Evolution is not a haphazard process, but a progressive, directive course aiming unswervingly and inevitably at a higher course of development. "The wondrous process of evolution" is "itself the working out of a mighty Teleology of which our finite understandings can fathom but the scantiest rudiments."[1] Man, too, is a part of this mighty teleology, a very important part of it, for in him evolutionary progress finds its 'unlimited psychical progress.'

In man, the course of evolution has reached its apex and its final stage in its process of development, "the last act in the great drama of creation; and that all the remaining work of evolution must consist in the perfecting of the creature thus marvelously produced. . . The action of natural selection upon Man is coming to an end, and his future development will be accomplished through the direct adaptation of his wonderfully plastic intelligence to the circumstances in which it is placed." Intelligence and goodness in man have replaced strife which no longer needs to discharge its normal function, hence will perish from disuse, thus leading man to a level of civilization in which human sympathy and peace will reign, and the spirit of Christ shall triumph and reign supreme throughout the entire earth.

God, who is responsible for the course, direction, and the entire process of evolution has established man, the universe's crowning glory, its 'chief object of divine care.' Man, although burdened with sin, will find his ultimate salvation eventually in the evolutionary process which shall be achieved slowly 'through ages of moral discipline.' "We see the chief agency which produced him – natural selection which always works through strife – ceasing to operate upon him, so that, until human strife shall be brought to an end, there goes on a struggle between his lower and his higher impulses, in which the higher must finally conquer." This desire and inevitable outcome of man – his conquering of lower impulses and the attaining of the higher – becomes his strongest imaginable incentive for righteousness. "The infinite and eternal Power which is manifested in every pulsation of the universe is none other than the living God. . . Humanity is not mere local incident in an endless and aimless series of cosmical changes. The events of the universe are not the work of chance, neither are they the outcome of blind necessity. Practically there is a purpose in the world whereof it is our highest duty to learn the lesson, however well or ill we may fare in rendering a scientific account of it. When from the dawn of life we see all things working together toward the evolution of the highest spiritual attributes of Man, we know, however the words may stumble in which we try to say it, that God is in the deepest sense a moral Being. The everlasting source of phenomena is none other than the infinite Power that makes

[1] John Fiske, *Outlines of Cosmic Philosophy* (1875), Vol. II, 406.

for righteousness." Thus we find, that by and through the process of evolution, Fiske has led us 'through nature to God.'

Religion and its God is a reality because in the long struggle upwards through countless ages from the "seaweed up to Man, the progress of life was achieved through adjustments to external realities," therefore in man it is inconceivable that the method employed by the evolutionary process so successfully throughout past ages will prove to be false in our own, in the life of man. Since throughout the vast province of evolution, each stage achieved its desired end through adjustments to external reality, man in this age makes his adjustment by adapting to his external reality, by the power which makes for righteousness, God. "To suppose that during countless ages, from the seaweed up to Man, the progress of life was achieved through adjustments to external realities, but that then the method was all at once changed and throughout a vast province of evolution the end was secured through adjustments to external non-realities, is to do sheer violence to logic and to common sense."[1] Accordingly, if one is to be reasonable, and not flout data of biological evolution, then the objective validity of religious values must be granted, and the fact of God's existence recognized.

Concluding Comments on the Evolutionary Argument.

As discovered from the preceding discussion, the argument for the existence of God based upon the Theory of Evolution is principally one grounded on the fact of adaptation or adaptability of organisms to their surrounding environment, and their higher development, suggesting both a grander, greater, and vastly higher teleology than Paley ever dreamed of, or could dream of in his day, owing to scientific limitations, particularly in the field of biology, and secondly suggests the existence of God on the basis of the necessity of the "arrival of the fittest." In other words, it is insufficient to assert that organisms in this world are capable of surviving, without explaining the reason of their *entering a world fit* to survive. It seems much more reasonable to conclude that the fact organisms are capable of survival is that they were created that way by a Supreme Mind, God, who is responsible for their initiation and execution; rather than attempting to defend the weaker hypothesis, viz., that the entire production of evolutionary development merely happened in the manner it did without offering any explanation whatever, except to regard the entire matter as due to accident. The *survival of the fit* implies the *arrival of the fit,* thus to have a competent explanation, one

[1] John Fiske, *Through Nature to God* (Boston: Houghton Mifflin and Co., 1899).

which adequately interprets the facts of evolution by its inclusiveness of the *arrival of the fit,* necessitates the postulation of God, a Supreme Being capable of being sufficient ground for such happenings. Otherwise, the question is eternally begged: Whence the arrival of the fit? Essentially, what we are saying here, is that the Theory of Evolution is not logically self-supporting; it requires a mind which organized, directed, executed, navigated, the entire process; consequently, without hypothesizing the existence of God, the Theory of Evolution is critically weakened since it is incapable of standing on its own, that is to say, it makes much more sense when predicted on the existence of God.

6. Sorley and Rashdall — The Axiological Argument

The Axiological Argument for God's existence, one based on the presence of values in the universe, is most ably framed by the combined efforts of *Hastings Rashdall* (1858-1924) and *William R. Sorley* (1855-1935):

> We say that the Moral Law has a real existence, that there is such a thing as an absolute Morality, that there is something absolutely true or false in ethical judgements, whether we or any number of human beings at any given time actually think so or not, such a belief is distinctly implied in what we mean by Morality. The idea of such an unconditional, objectively valid, Moral Law or ideal undoubtedly exists as a psychological fact. The question before us is whether it is capable of theoretical justification. We must then face the question *where* such an ideal exists, and what manner of existence we are to attribute to it. Certainly it is to be found, wholly and completely, in no individual human consciousness. Men actually think differently about moral questions, and there is no empirical reason for supposing that they will ever do otherwise. Where then and how does the moral ideal really exist? As regards matters of fact or physical law, we have no difficulty in satisfying ourselves that there is an objective reality which is what it is irrespectively of our beliefs or disbeliefs about it. For the man who supposes that objective reality resides in the things themselves, our ideas about them are objectively true or false so far as they correspond or fail to correspond with this real and independent archetype, though he might be puzzled to give a metaphysical account of the nature of this 'correspondence' between experience and a Reality whose *esse* is something other than to be experienced. In the physical region the existence of divergent ideas does not throw doubt upon the existence of a reality independent of our ideas. But in the case of moral ideals it is otherwise. On materialistic or naturalistic assumptions the moral ideal can hardly be regarded as a real thing. Nor could it well be regarded as a property of any real thing: it can be no more than an aspiration, a product of the imagination, which may be useful to stimulate effort in directions in which we happen to want to move, but which cannot compel respect when we feel no desire to act in conformity with it. An absolute Moral Law or moral ideal cannot exist *in* material things. And it does not

(we have seen) exist in the mind of this or that individual. Only if we believe in the existence of a Mind for which the true moral ideal is already in some sense real, a Mind which is the source of whatever is true in our own moral judgments, can we rationally think of the moral ideal as no less real than the world itself. Only so can we believe in an absolute standard of right and wrong, which is as independent of this or that man's actual ideas and actual desires as the facts of material nature. The belief in God, though not (like the belief in a real and an active self) a postulate of their being any such thing as Morality at all, is the logical presupposition of an 'objective' or absolute Morality. A moral ideal can exist nowhere and nohow but in a mind; an absolute moral ideal can exist only in a Mind from which all Reality is derived (or at least a mind by which all Reality is controlled). Our moral ideal can only claim objective validity in so far as it can rationally be regarded as the revelation of a moral ideal eternally existing in the mind of God.

Up to this point Rashdall [1] has been presenting the case; from here on, the argument is relayed to Sorley: [2]

The argument as thus put may be looked upon as a special and striking extension of the cosmological argument. In its first and most elementary form the cosmological argument seeks a cause for the bare existence of the world and man: to account for them there must be something able to bring them into being: God is the First Cause. Then the order of nature impresses us by its regularity, and we come by degrees to understand the principles of its working and the laws under which the material whole maintains its equilibrium and the ordered procession of its changes: these laws and this order call for explanation, and we conceive God as the Great Lawgiver. But beyond this material world, we understand relations and principles of a still more general kind; and the intellect of man recognises abstract truths so evident that, once understood, they cannot be questioned, while inferences are drawn from these which only the more expert minds can appreciate and yet which they recognise as eternally valid. To what order do these belong and what was their home when man as yet was unconscious of them? Surely if their validity is eternal they must have had existence somewhere, and we can only suppose them to have existed in the one eternal mind: God is therefore the God of Truth. Further, persons are conscious of values and of an ideal of goodness, which they recognise as having undoubted authority for the direction of their activity; the validity of these values or laws and of this ideal, however, does not depend upon their recognition: it is objective and eternal; and how could this eternal validity stand alone, not embodied in matter and neither seen nor realised by finite minds, unless there were an eternal mind whose thought and will were therein expressed? God must therefore exist and his nature be goodness . . .

[1] Hastings Rashdall, *The Theory of Good and Evil* (Oxford: Oxford University Press, 1907), Vol. II, 211-212.

[2] William R. Sorley, *Moral Values and the Idea of God* (Cambridge: Cambridge University Press; New York: G. P. Putnam's Sons, 1919), 351 ff. Reprinted by permission of Mr. Kenneth W. Sorley and Mrs. Geoffrey Bickersteth.

. . . We acknowledge that there are objective values, although men may not recognise them, that the moral law is not abrogated by being ignored, and that our consciousness is striving toward the apprehension of an ideal which no finite mind has clearly grasped, but which is none the less valid although it is not realised and is not even apprehended by us in its truth and fullness. Where then is this ideal? It cannot be valid at one time and not at another. It must be eternal as well as objective. As Dr. Rashdall urges, it is not in material things, and it is not in the mind of this or that individual; but "it can exist nowhere and nohow but in a mind"; it requires therefore the mind of God.

Against this argument, however, it may be contended that it disregards the distinction between validity and existence. Why is it assumed that the moral ideal must exist somehow and somewhere? Validity, it may be said, is a unique concept, as unique as existence, and different from it. And this is true. At the same time it is also true that the validity of the moral ideal, like all validity, is a validity for existents. Without this reference to existence there seems no meaning in asserting validity. At any rate it is clear that it is for existents – namely, for the realm of persons – that the moral ideal is valid. It is also true that the perfect moral ideal does not exist in the volitional, or even in the intellectual, consciousness of these persons: they have not achieved agreement with it in their lives, and even their understanding of it is incomplete. Seeing then that it is not manifested by finite existents, how are we to conceive its validity? Other truths are displayed in the order of the existing world; but it is not so with moral values. And yet the system of moral values has been acknowledged to an aspect of the real universe to which existing things belong. How are we to conceive its relation to them? A particular instance of goodness can exist only in the character of an individual person or group of persons; an idea of goodness such as we have is found only in minds such as ours. But the ideal of goodness does not exist in finite minds or in their material environment. What then is its status in the system of reality?

The question is answered if we regard the moral order as the order of Supreme Mind and the ideal of goodness as belonging to this Mind. The difficulty for this view is to show that the Mind which is the home of goodness may also be regarded as the ground of the existing world. That reality as a whole, both in its actual events and in its moral order, can be consistently regarded as the expression of a Supreme Mind has been the argument of the present lecture.

Concluding Comment of the Axiological Argument.

The Axiological Argument is predicated on the existence of moral values as being truly an integral aspect of our universe. To object to this argument on the grounds that values are merely relative, existing only as matters of subjective opinion in some person's mind, is insufficient to dismiss the argument because even relative truth implies an absolute, an absolute standard by which to judge. A system of values, one which embodies justice and goodness, implies a moral order, and the only adequate inference is to postulate God as its source. As we earlier learned from Vaihinger and James, whether or not it is theoretically proved to a person's satisfaction that values truly exist in the outer world, we, nevertheless, do behave *as if* they did, which for a Pragmatist would constitute proof of their existence, and for others ought to imply in some sense their existence.

The existence of values entails the existence of a Supreme Being, one who is also good, as the ground, the adequate or best explanation of values in a natural world of facts. Why? Because only the postulation of a Personal Being is sufficient ground for accounting for values, since they exist only in and for persons.

7. Anselm and Descartes — The Ontological Argument

St. Anselm (1033-1109), Archbishop of Canterbury, and *René Descartes* (1596-1650) are two of the most outstanding proponents of the classic Ontological Argument for God's existence. This particular argument has never enjoyed united support, either from Theistic philosophers or theologians; yet it possesses an intriguing logical quality about it which is responsible for its intermittent cycles of support, consequently the argument has never been discarded.

In its Anselmic form it may be reduced to its barest terms:

We have a conception of a Perfect Being.
Such a Perfect Being must exist.
Why?
If he did not exist, then he would not be perfect.

Anselm's basic premise is correct; man does have a concept of a perfect being, in the same sense that he has concepts of mathematical and logical principles. We have, for example, a concept of a perfect triangle; yet, in actual fact, constructed either by nature or by man, there never has been a perfect triangle. Accordingly, Anselm, in his *Proslogium* (between 1070-1078), argues: "Even the fool is convinced that something exists in the understanding . . . than which nothing greater can be conceived . . . Therefore, if that, than which nothing greater can be conceived, exists in the understanding alone, the very being, than which nothing greater can be conceived, is one, than which a greater can be conceived. But this is impossible. Hence, there is no doubt that there exists a being, than which nothing greater can be conceived, and it exists both in the understanding and in reality." [1]

[1] St. Anselm, *Proslogium*, tr. Sidney Norton Deane (La Salle, Illinois: The Open Court Publishing Co., 1903).

Evaluation of Anselm's Ontological Argument.

Before attacking this argument, note that Anselm does not say we have an idea of perfection merely, nor that we have an idea of Being merely, but that we entertain an idea of a *Perfect-Being.* An *attribute* of a Perfect-Being is *existence;* therefore the only Perfect-Being must be an existent one.

Anselm's argument is not properly refuted by saying: We have an idea of a perfect island, therefore it must exist, or it is not perfect; as *Gaunilo,* a monk of Marmoutier and Anselm's contemporary, argued; because the island is not a necessary Being, it is a contingent arbitrary fiction which entails contradiction.

The weakness of Anselm's argument lies chiefly in two areas: first, it *assumes* that existence is an attribute of perfection, while, for example, *subsistence* (a quality mathematical principles possess) may be a more appropriate characteristic of a Perfect Being; second, Anselm has presented an a priori argument, one which is independent of but also devoid of empirical facts, consequently giving little or no particulars or content to the nature of God.

The Cartesian Ontological Argument.

The Ontological Argument Descartes offers pursues the same logical lines as that of St. Anselm in concluding the existence of a most real or perfect Being is necessary, or that definition is accompanied by existence, that is, the concept of God is sufficient to prove his existence. The Cartesian position asserts that the concept of God is one of infinity, yet since man is only finite, an Infinite Being must have been responsible for inserting the idea of himself in man's mind.

Descartes reasons: "There only remains, therefore, the idea of God, in which I must consider whether there is anything that cannot be supposed to originate with myself. By the name God, I understand a substance infinite (eternal, immutable), independent, all-knowing, all-powerful, and by which I myself, and every other thing that exists, if any such there be, were created. But these properties are so great and excellent, that the more attentively I consider them the less I feel persuaded that the idea I have of them owes its origin to myself alone. And thus it is absolutely necessary to conclude, from all that I have before said, that God exists: for though the idea of substance be in my mind owing to this, that I myself am a substance, I should not, however, have the idea of an infinite substance, seeing I am a finite being, unless it were given me by some substance in reality infinite... The idea, I say, of a being supremely perfect, and infinite, is in the highest degree true; for although, perhaps, we may imagine that such a being does not exist, we cannot, nevertheless, suppose that his idea represents nothing real." [1]

Decartes felt justified in debating in this manner because his criterion of truth was reason, ideas imprinted upon the mind with clearness and distinctness, as mathematical and logical principles are distinctly perceived; the idea of God is likewise conceived, hence must equally exist.

8. St. Thomas Aquinas — Five Ways of Proving God's Existence

St. Thomas Aquinas (1225–1274), dissatisfied with the Anselmic Ontological Argument for God's existence, repudiated it, and supplanted it with his *Quinque Viae* (Five Ways): (1) The Way of Motion, (2) The Way of Efficient Causality, (3) The Way of Possibility and Necessity, (4) The Way of Degrees of Perfection, (5) The Way of Purposiveness.

The first of the five is the First Mover argument for God's existence; the universe requires a First Mover, this Prime Mover is God. This is essentially Aristotle's argument for God based on his classic *Prime Mover.* Aquinas presents it as follows: [2]

> The existence of God can be proved in five ways. The first and more manifest way is the argument from motion. It is certain, and evident to our senses, that in the world some things are in motion. Now whatever is moved is moved by another, for nothing can be moved except it is in potentiality to that towards which it is moved; whereas a thing moves inasmuch as it is in act. For motion is nothing else than the reduction of something from potentiality to actuality. But nothing can be reduced from potentiality to actuality, except by something in a state of actuality. Thus that which is actually hot, as fire, makes wood, which is potentially hot, to be actually hot, and thereby moves and changes it. Now it is not possible that the same thing should be at once in actuality and potentiality in the same respect, but only in different respects. For what is actually hot cannot simultaneously be potentially hot; but it is simultaneously potentially cold. It is therefore impossible that in the same respect and in the same way a thing should be both mover and moved, *i.e.*, that it should move itself. Therefore, whatever is moved must be moved by another. If that by which it is moved be itself moved, then this also must needs be moved by another, and that by another again. But this cannot go on to infinity, because then there would be no first mover, and, consequently,

[1] René Descartes, *Meditations on the First Philosophy*, tr. John Veitch (Edinburgh: Blackwood & Sons, Ltd., 1899).

[2] St. Thomas Aquinas, *Summa Theologica*, tr. Laurence Shapcote, revised by Anton Pegis (New York: Random House, 1945), Q2, Art. 3.

> no other mover, seeing that subsequent movers move only inasmuch as they are moved by the first mover; as the staff moves only because it is moved by the hand. Therefore it is necessary to arrive at a first mover, moved by no other; and this everyone understands to be God.

The difficulty of this argument is that for whatever type of God it may prove, it definitely does *not* prove the God of Theism, the God of the Judeo-Christian Scriptures.

The second argument, The Way of Efficient Cause, is the Aetiological aspect of the Cosmological, often termed the argument from First Cause.

> The second way is from the nature of efficient cause. In the world of sensible things we find there is an order of efficient causes. There is no case known (neither is it, indeed, possible) in which a thing is found to be the efficient cause of itself; for so it would be prior to itself, which is impossible. Now in efficient causes it is not possible to go on to infinity, because in all efficient causes following in order, the first is the cause of the intermediate cause, and the intermediate is the cause of the ultimate cause, whether the intermediate cause be several, or one only. Now to take away the cause is to take away the effect. Therefore, if there be no first cause among efficient causes, there will be no ultimate, nor any intermediate, cause. But if in efficient causes it is possible to go on to infinity, there will be no first efficient cause, neither will there be an ultimate effect, nor any intermediate efficient causes; all of which is plainly false. Therefore it is necessary to admit a first efficient cause to which everyone gives the name of God.

Like the one preceding it, this one does not prove the God of the Bible, Theism, but what may be termed, a *Trigger God,* one who merely starts things going, initiates the original action or motion, an impersonal God who would mean little to the religious needs of man.

The third argument, The Way of Possibility and Necessity, is based on the empirical fact that all things generate and later perish, which indicates that at one time nothing contingent existed. If nothing existed at some time in the past, then it is impossible for the world to have come into existence, unless a noncontingent eternal Being, God, exists. Hence the proof of God's existence by necessity. Aquinas formulates his argument:

> The third way is taken from possibility and necessity, and runs thus. We find in nature things that are possible to be and not to be, since they are found to be generated, and to be corrupted, and consequently, it is possible for them to be and not to be. But it is impossible for these always to exist, for that which can not-be at some time is not. Therefore, if everything can not-be, then at one time there was nothing in existence. Now if this were true, even now there would be nothing in existence, because that which does not exist begins to exist only through something already existing. Therefore, if at one time nothing was in existence, it

> would have been impossible for anything to have begun to exist; and thus even now nothing would be in existence – which is absurd. Therefore, not all beings are merely possible, but there must exist something the existence of which is necessary. But every necessary thing either has its necessity caused by another, or not. Now it is impossible to go on to infinity in necessary things which have their necessity caused by another, as has been already proved in regard to efficient causes. Therefore we cannot but admit the existence of some being having of itself its own necessity, and not receiving it from another, but rather causing in others their necessity. This all men speak of as God.

Again we have another approach to the Cosmological Argument, one which rests upon causation.

The fourth, The Way of Degrees of Perfection, is a mixture of the Cosmological and Teleological Arguments:

> The fourth way is taken from the gradation to be found in things. Among beings there are some more and some less good, true, noble, and the like. But *more* and *less* are predicated of different things according as they resemble in their different ways something which is the maximum, as a thing is said to be hotter according as it more nearly resembles that which is hottest; so that there is something which is truest, something best, something noblest, and, something which is most being, for those things that are greatest in truth are greatest in being . . . Now the maximum in any genus is the cause of all in that genus, as fire, which is the maximum of heat, is the cause of all hot things. . . Therefore there must also be something which is to all beings the cause of their being, goodness, and every other perfection; and this we call God.

This argument is by far the best of those thus far presented, for in it are the seeds of several modern cogent ones, including the Anthropological and Axiological Arguments.

The fifth, The Way of Purposiveness, is the Teleological Argument, one which bases its case on the presence of purpose in a meaningful world:

> The fifth way is taken from the governance of the world. We see that things which lack knowledge, such as natural bodies, act for an end, and this is evident from their acting always, or nearly always, in the same way, so as to obtain the best result. Hence it is plain that they achieve their end, not fortuitously, but designedly. Now whatever lacks knowledge cannot move towards an end, unless it be directed by some being endowed with knowledge and intelligence; as the arrow is directed by the archer. Therefore some intelligent being exists by whom all natural things are directed to their end; and this being we call God.

Aquinas' final argument, the Teleological, is also his finest; basically, it has an inherent cogency which cannot be easily dismissed. However, the Teleological Argument has been refined to much higher levels of cogency in the capable hands and work of Paley and Fiske.

D. CONCLUDING COMMENTS REGARDING THE PROBLEM OF GOD

The perceptive mind will have recognized that a person's philosophy of religion, his philosophical position regarding the existence of God, is based essentially upon two conditions: (1) his metaphysical position and beliefs, (2) his criterion or criteria of truth; it is not so much a matter of being able to prove the existence of God, as it is a matter of determining what proofs of his existence are acceptable to you personally.

For example, to allow only 'naive realism' as valid verification so that a person will insist that unless he can see God, he will withhold belief in him, subjects that person to criticism respecting the inconclusiveness of his criterion. No form of ultimate reality can be proved by naive realism, not even the accepted 'truths' of science, such as x-ray, light waves, horse power, or even the atom itself; thus is naive realism placed under serious criticism as a grossly inadequate test of truth.

Merely because an object cannot be proved by an individual's favored criterion of truth does not make it false, yet many persons seem to assume that it does. Even Immanuel Kant fell into this pitfall by assuming that what could not be proved by his critical philosophy was beyond knowing, and for this reason he rejected the validity of God's existence based on speculative reason, while Hegel, who would not be bound by the Kantian narrow epistemological restrictions, felt that proof of the existence of Deity could be advanced.

The matter perhaps may be best concluded by asserting that the most reasonable position is that which is proved, that is to say, the most coherent one, the one which provides the most conclusive explanation by its widest inclusiveness of data logically integrated. The chief defect of most arguments is their narrowness which accounts for merely a restricted area of facts.

XXI

THE PERSON: HIS SOUL, FREE WILL, AND IMMORTALITY

Man's greatest problem is himself, and he is also his greatest value, for 'what shall a man give in exchange for his soul?' Even the existence of God is not as important as his own soul and its survival. Actually, it is erroneous to speak of man's soul, since he *is* that very soul; man does not *have* a soul, he *is* a soul. We speak of man as a soul, and his survival beyond death as his greatest value, even greater than that of God's existence; the reason being that God's existence without man's soul being eternal is not as preferable as God's nonexistence and man's being eternal. However, as we shall soon learn in ensuing deliberations, the predication of a good God is one of the best possible arguments for the proof of immortality.

A. THE SOUL

Positions Held Regarding the Nature of the Soul.

There are many views regarding the soul and its relation to the human organism, but for present purposes we can reduce them to three categories: (1) those who believe in the existence of a body, but disallow belief in a soul or mind; (2) those who believe in the existence of a body and soul, but identify the soul with the mind, treating the two terms synonymously; (3) those who believe in the separate existence of all three: body, soul, and mind. Schematically, the three may be represented as follows:

Three Beliefs Regarding the Human Organism

I EPIPHENOMENALISM	II ORGANIC THEORY or SELF-PSYCHOLOGY	III SUBSTANTIALISM
1. Body exists, but 2. No mind, and 3. No soul. Mind and soul are epiphenomena of the body.	1. Body exists, and 2. Mind exists, and 3. Soul exists, but mind and soul are one and the same entity, immanent parts of the human organism.	1. Body exists, 2. Mind exists, 3. Soul exists; each represents separate entities. Doctrine of: Transcendent Soul Substance.
Behavioristic in Psychology.	Psychology of Interactionism.	Thomistic Psychology.

1. The Doctrine of Epiphenomenalism

The first position respecting the nature of the soul relies upon a psychology of Behaviorism which has its roots in the findings of the Russian psysiologist, *Ivan Pavlov* (1849-1936), and in this country its school's initial founder, *John Watson* (1878-1958); they revert to the doctrine of *Reductionism* in order to explain mental phenomena. The Behaviorist regards only the body as factually real, and whatever appears to be other than body is reduced to a state of functions of the body; for example, the spiritual nature of man is explained away as the workings of the body, its physiological activity. This view is based upon the assumption that whatever cannot be measured in physical terms does not exist; since the mind (or soul) cannot be observably measured, it does not exist as a reality.

To inquire as to what precisely is the experiential data every human being obviously is acquainted with in the mental realm, would result in the reply from the Behaviorist School of Psychology that it is merely appearances, phenomena; a Behaviorist would explain it as a curious manifestation which occurs at times when bodily functions are activated, such as, thinking is merely the activity of vocal cords at a subaudible level. Regarding the mental as a mere by-product of the physical is called the doctrine of *Epiphenomenalism,* a term coined by Thomas Henry Huxley (1820-1903).

2. Interactionism

A second position, termed *Interactionism,* is the belief that mind and body, although composing one and the same organism, are nevertheless two entities, one of which is capable of surviving should the other perish. This view is fairly widely held, and as it will be later discovered, William James based his argument for immortality on it. Interactionism, also referred to as the *Organic* theory or *Self-Psychology,* views the soul as immanent, not transcendent as the Substantialists posit.

Current psychology supports this view, particularly since the appearance of Depth Psychology which has brought to light many interesting facts substantiating Interactionism. Carl Jung (1875-1961), founder of Analytic Psychology, maintains that the soul, as an independent entity, affects the physical body, hence is a fact of reality. He writes: "We have been taught by all too many mistakes that organic medicine fails completely in the treatment of neuroses, while psychic methods cure them . . . It was by recognizing these facts that science discovered the psyche, and *we are honour bound to admit its reality.*"[1] *Sigmund Freud* (1856-1939) too, has brought to light corroborating evidence of the fact that the psyche can seriously affect the body as is evidenced by neurosis, hypnosis, and Psychoanalysis. It is obvious that the body affects the mind; we have constant evidence of this fact everywhere about us, such as that which results from imbibing alcoholic beverages; and, on the other hand, Freud proved with finality that the mind affects the body to the degree of causing physical ailments. Today, the field of psychosomatic medicine (illnesses brought on by the mind) has irrefutable evidence that the psychical affects the body to such an extent that not only can physical ulcers and heart disease come about from mental causes, but a sizeable and growing list of ailments, including a form of rheumatoid arthritis; the list of psychosomatic ailments increases with the expansion of our knowledge in this area.

A contemporary psychologist, Benjamin B. Wolman, exploring the mind-body problem in his *Contemporary Theories and Systems in Psychology* (1960), concludes that despite the acknowledged fact that mind-body interactions occur regularly many times a day, no one has ever been able to explain the locus of the entire matter; it is a fact that the two interact, but how and where, nobody knows.

3. Substantialism

The third stand regarding the soul, one shared primarily by Thomists and Neo-Scholastic philosophers, is the belief that man is triune, possessing not only a body and mind, but a soul which is distinguishable from the mind. The soul is understood to be a substance, a *soul substance,*

[1] Carl Jung, *Modern Man in Search of a Soul,* tr. W. S. Dell and Cary F. Bayes (New York: Harcourt, Brace and Co., 1933).

capable of surviving the death of both body and mind. The soul is an intellectual substance, and as such, is imperishable; its essence assumes a spiritual form, thus is an immaterial substance performing immaterial operations. The human soul is identified with the *intellective soul* and *intellective principle;* in man, each of these constitutes one and the same entity; accordingly, the soul is an incorporeal, subsistent, principle of intellectual operation. The nature of man as triadic is not restricted to Neo-Thomists; many non-Scholastics adhere to the belief that man possesses a soul which is not to be equated with either body or mind.

As to classic arguments proving the existence of the soul, the reader is referred to René Descartes' treatment of the matter in Part V immediately subsequent to the present one. The Kantian argument for the *autonomy of the will* may also be considered an argument for the soul's existence.

B. FREEDOM OF THE WILL

Among Theists will be found Determinists, those who assert that man is devoid of any freedom of will; and Indeterminists, those who contend that man's will is free to make choices. Religious Determinism rests upon the Doctrine of *Predestinarianism,* a theory emphasized particularly by *John Calvin* (1509-1564) in his *Institutes of the Christian Religion* (1536), accordingly the doctrine has been commonly referred to as *Calvinism;* in Islamic philosophy, the doctrine is termed *Kismet* (fate). In both religious bodies, the belief in Predestination rests upon the doctrine of the Absolute Sovereignty of God, who is the Determiner of Destiny.

1. Fatalism

The Predestinarian believes that God has foreordained all that will occur in a person's life; a man cannot do other than what God has predetermined; his destiny, including the appointed hour of his death has been decided beforehand; regardless of the extent of a man's exertions or efforts to alter his particular fortune or condition, they will prove completely vain and ineffectual.

Kismet implies that 'what will happen, will happen;' man cannot implement any force whatever which will change his future one iota, a future which God has determined from, and to all, eternity. Some Predestinarians believe that God knows even now what a man will do who is not to be born for a thousand years hence. The concept of Kismet or fate is both beautifully and vividly expressed in Edward Fitzgerald's translation of the Rubáiyát of Omar Khayyám:

The Moving Finger writes; and, having writ,
Moves on: nor all your Piety nor Wit
  Shall lure it back to cancel half a Line
Nor all your Tears wash out a Word of it.

Note the emphasis with which it is suggested that one's entire life, like a book that has already been written, is a foregone conclusion, and all that a person does, or can do, is to live his life out as an actor enacts the lines of a play which the author has determined. God, the author of our lives and destinies, has decided beforehand what we shall do, and the appointed hour of our death.

Fatalism has been a relatively popular belief among service men while in action; it tends to relieve the mind of unendurable strain. It is not difficult to imagine a soldier in the front lines of battle with bullets flying unpredictably about him, succumbing to the thought that there is no use in expending any effort attempting to escape them; for he may, in his escape attempt, inadvertently walk into a flying bullet. Discovering that he can relieve his tensions with the fatalistic thought: 'If my time is up, then it is up,' or 'If the next bullet has my number on it, then there is nothing I can do about it,' he takes refuge in Fatalism.

Evaluation of Fatalism.

Practical Fatalism, as experienced by the soldier in the foregoing example, is due to a person's inability to be furnished with sufficient data or to cope intellectually in understanding data supplied. If the soldier in question had all of the pertinent facts necessary, he could predict with satisfactory accuracy the disposition of the bullets, but since this is out of the question, our soldier takes refuge in ignorance, and like the proverbial ostrich hides his figurative head in the sand of Fatalism, thereby gaining pseudo peace of mind. This situation is analogous to a game of chance, where a wheel is spun, the winner being the holder of the number at which the indicator rests when the wheel stops. The loser is interpreted by many persons as being the victim of ill-fortune, bad luck, fate, whereas the matter should have been explained in terms of a lack of proper calculation owing to both ignorance and insufficient facts. If the velocity with which the wheel is spun, plus all of the other pertinent factors, such as the pressure which the number indicator bears upon the wheel, could be taken into account, the outcome could be predicted.

Fatalism is Pragmatically unsound as well; for example, no Fatalist would leap out of an upper story of a building to the cement ground beneath, reasoning on the Fatalistic premise that if his time is not as yet up, then he has nothing to be concerned about, he will not die, and if his time is up, then there is nothing he can do about the matter; nor will a

Fatalist cross the street before an oncoming rushing truck out of control, reasoning that if his time is not yet up, then all is well.

Determinism.

Before dismissing the discussion on Fatalism, let us direct a few remarks to what may be termed secular Fatalism, *Determinism*. The Determinist, like the Fatalist, believes man to be devoid of freedom, and that his every act has been externally controlled, but unlike the Predestinarian, he asserts that man's lack of choice is due to natural causes, which serve as motivation. Rather than God determining our destinies, the Determinist contends that natural laws do; not only are the destinies of individual persons determined, but all facts within the physical universe, including social as well as natural history. The term probably originated with the British philosopher, Sir *William Hamilton* (1788-1856), who used it to describe the Metaphysical Materialism of *Thomas Hobbes* (1588-1679); Hobbes attempted to defend the thesis that the sum total of the world consisted of 'bodies and bodies in motion,' repudiating all immaterial reality, including free will, as false.

2. Indeterminism

Based upon the Pragmatic criterion of truth, Indeterminism enjoys the stronger position; persons, as a group, expect people to be responsible for their actions, and do in fact hold them responsible; only in exceptional cases is responsibility voided, such as when an individual is designated incompetent or insane. For all practical purposes, in life in general, freedom of the will is, in practice, acknowledged.

The will of man, maintains *Immanuel Kant* (1724-1804), is free; he refers to it as *autonomous*, self-legislated, uncoerced by extraneous force, adhering only to the voice of reason. Kant's claim is a valid one, for it is impossible to force another person to will in accordance with your own wishes; true, you may force a person to do your bidding, but you cannot force him to *will* to do it, to do it willingly; you may prove successful in forcing a man to turn over his money to you should you point a gun at him, but you cannot make him will to do it regardless of whatever extent of forceful measures are employed. Rational persuasion is the method which must be employed to gain another to will according to you own decisions.

John McTaggart Ellis McTaggart (1866-1925) distinguishes four types of human freedom in his classic *Some Dogmas of Religion* (1906): (1) *Freedom of Self-Determinism*, that is, "man is free to do anything which nothing but his own nature prevents him from doing. In this sense I am not free to draw a triangle with two right angles, since this would be impossible whatever my nature might be. Nor am I, in this sense, free to save a man's life if I am tied at a distance from him by a chain which cannot break." (2) *Freedom of Self-Direction,* that is, "man is free to do anything which nothing but his own will prevents him from doing. So far as a man is free in this sense he can direct his life as he chooses." (3) *Freedom of Self-Realization,* that is, "man is said to act freely when he acts according to the ultimate ideal of his nature. The implication here seems to be that freedom is essentially the absence of such limitation as is felt to thwart and constrain the being who is limited, and that no person can be completely free from such constraint except by attaining the ultimate of his nature." (4) *Freedom of Indetermination,* or *Free Will,* that is, "a man is free in any action, if his choice of that action is not completely determined." This view allows for motivation, yet it does not consider motivation incompatiable with freedom. Despite the presence of motives, and it is well that there should be motives, a person may decide and choose as a free agent which of the surrounding motives will influence him. Of the four views mentioned, this one is the most preferable from the standpoint of coherency.

C. SPURIOUS FORMS OF IMMORTALITY

In present deliberations, reference when made to immortality will invariably mean immortality of the individual person, not *spurious* forms of immortality which have been at times offered as substitutes, such as:

(1) ***Biological Immortality,*** the belief that a man's progeny will survive him, thus satisfying any need he may have for immortality; this is accepted by some persons as a suitable substitute for immortality. The objections to this form of immortality include the fact the specific individual in question is not surviving, but another in his place; secondly, some persons, and a number of fine people included in the group, cannot issue offspring, yet are more deserving of immortality than many persons who do have children. A third objection is, in a sense, the severest, viz., the world will at one time in the future come to an end, at which time no one will have offspring surviving.

(2) ***Immortality of Influence, (Social Immortality),*** the belief that the influence left behind of a person's good deeds is sufficient immortality; for example, we speak of *immortal Shakespeare* in the sense that he can never die, owing to the heritage he has left to surviving humanity.

Although it is a highly desirable thing to be remembered and respected by posterity, it is hardly the person himself who is enjoying the appreciation of posterity; and the only Shakespeare remembered is the works of the man; as for the man himself personally, for all practical purposes, it may just as well be anyone else, such as, Francis Bacon or John Doe for all that it matters. Shakespeare, the real personality himself, is not enjoying the credit posthumously. Another objection to this form of immortality is that fine persons have existed on earth who are neither known nor remembered, while infamous characters, such as a Nero or a Hitler, are long remembered and immortalized in books and in the minds of men.

(3) ***Impersonal Immortality,*** is the view of Plato, Hindus, and others who believe that although individual personality ceases at bodily death, the universal person survives; as Brahmans assert, we become one with the over-soul. Impersonal immortality is a view common to Pantheists who believe that values and the impersonal consciousness of one-time individual persons become one with the Absolute.

D. ARGUMENTS AGAINST IMMORTALITY

A number of arguments have been used to discredit belief in immortality; while the gravity of some are serious, most of them are weak, if not completely feeble. Among them are:

(1) ***Disbelief of Scientists.***

This objection, immortality is false because the consenus among scientists opposes the belief, is invalid for several reasons. According to Leuba's findings released in his *Belief in God and Immortality,* only a third of the scientists covered in the poll registered disbelief, a third belief, while the remainder were noncommital. John Clover Monsma, interested in this subject as to whether scientists believed in religious values, published his *The Evidence of God in an Expanding Universe* (1958) to prove that not only were they vitally interested, but forty leading scientists throughout the country contributed evidence gained in their respective fields as proof of the validity of religious values.

Technically, to use scientists as authorities in the field of philosophy of religion is to commit the *fallacy of misplaced authority,* a fallacy of transferring an authority from one area of specialization to another which is not his field of specialty; his authoritative sanction is voided, he reverts to becoming a layman. To prove this point, one need merely query: Would you use a literary authority such as a Shakespeare to perform a surgical operation upon your body? For the same reason, voices of scientific authorities do not carry over to areas foreign to their fields of specialization, such as, philosophy of religion.

(2) *Its Humble Origin.*

Certain individuals seeks to repudiate belief in immortality on the basis that it originated in ignorance, superstitution, dreams, etc. This argument is faulty on two major counts: (a) dreams are not *ipso facto* false; many true things have been dreamed by mankind. Dreams must be regarded as neither true nor false until they have been subject to verification. (b) Science also originated in humble beginnings, in alchemy, magic, etc., yet does this fact discredit belief in science?

(3) *Wishful Thinking.*

Some persons, particularly psychologists, repudiate belief in immortality on the grounds that it is merely wishful thinking; man's intense wish for eternal life spawned the thought which crystalized into belief, they claim.

Like the argument preceding it, this one also is subject to two serious errors: (a) it commits a *genetic fallacy* by assuming that because it can be shown how an idea originated, it is by virtue of that fact false. (b) The second fallacy committed is irrelevence because it assumes that wishes are *ipso facto* false – I may wish that my brother who lives some distance from me continue in fine health, but merely possessing the wish does not nullify its being true.

(4) *Immortality Would Create Overcrowded Conditions.*

William James is credited with having sowed the seed of this thought, but consensus appears to be that he was probably not serious in offering it. The overcrowding of the universe with souls is a contradiction of terms, since souls, by definition, do not occupy space; and even if they did, God could provide a universe sufficiently large to accommodate them, infinite in magnitude, if necessary. There are those persons who regard the present universe as infinite.

(5) *That Which Exists Must Eventually Terminate.*

'What begins must at the some time come to an end' has been used as another argument against immortality, but there is no law which implies this conclusion. Moreover, it is possible to conceive of that which has beginning, but continues endlessly, such as enumerating arithmetically beginning with the number one and continuing infinitely; or drawing a line from a given point and continuing it indefinitely.

(6) *Immortality: A Selfish Desire.*

The argument that 'immortality must be false because it is a selfish desire' is hardly worth taking the time to refute. It is obvious that many of the selfish desires of persons have been realized as true.

(7) *Epiphenomenalism.*

Perhaps the strongest argument against immortality is based upon Behavioristic psychology, namely, that personality or soul is dependent upon the physiological organism, a bodily state, for its existence; consequently with the destruction of the body, the soul perishes. This argument rests upon the fundamental assumptions of the philosophy of Metaphysical Materialism, a philosophy predicated upon an unprovable inert substance. For the present, we shall refrain from delving into this argument any further because in the section immediately subsequent, William James and John McTaggart will be found to launch a crucial blow against it. Suffice it to say at this time, there is adequate proof in psychology that the mind or soul affects the body as effectively as the body affects the spirit, yet is it concluded that the body is the product of the mind?

E. THE REFUTATION OF MORTALITY

(1) *William James — The Transmission-Theory.*

William James' argument for immortality is effected by removing objections posed by the Physiological Argument. The Physiological Argument, as it is sometimes called, is predicated on the philosophy of Metaphysical Materialism, presenting its case in the form of the doctrine of *Epiphenomenalism,* the belief that spirit is an outgrowth or by-product of the physiological organism, and perishes with the destruction of the body.

James, in his *Human Immortality* (1898), contends that the physiological brain's relationship to the spirit of man is merely *transmissive,* not *productive;* the brain merely transmits the thoughts of the mind, it does not produce them. "My thesis now is this: that, when we think of the law that thought is a function of the brain, we are not required to think of productive function only; *we are entitled also to consider permissive or transmissive function.* And this the ordinary psycho-physiologist leaves out of his account."[1] James accepts the psycho-physiologist's theory, "Thought is a function of the brain," but he repudiates his unjustified

[1] Quotations in this section are from William James, *Human Immortality* (1898).

conclusion that when the body perishes, then the mind or soul, as its concomitant, must also perish; rather, he argues, "though our soul's life (as here below it is revealed to us) may be in literal strictness the function of a brain that perishes, yet it is not at all impossible, but on the contrary quite possible, that the life may still continue when the brain itself is dead." This maintains on the premise that bodily functions may be either of the transmissive type or of the productive mode.

James explains and illustrates the functional mode of each: "When the physiologist who thinks that his science cuts off all hope of immortality pronounces the phrase, 'Thought is a function of the brain,' he thinks of the matter just as he thinks when he says, 'Steam is a function of the tea-kettle,' 'Light is a function of the electric circuit,' 'Power is a function of the moving waterfall.' In these latter cases the several material objects have the function of inwardly creating or engendering their effects, and their functions must be called *productive* function... But in the world of physical nature productive function of this sort is not the only kind of function with which we are familiar. We have also releasing or permissive function; and we have transmissive function. The trigger of a crossbow has a releasing function: it removes the obstacle that holds the string, and lets the bow fly back to its natural shape. So when the hammer falls upon a detonating compound. By knocking out the inner molecular obstructions, it lets the constituent gases resume their normal bulk, and so permits the explosion to take place. In the case of a colored glass, a prism, or a refracting lens, we have transmissive function. The energy of light, no matter how produced, is by the glass sifted and limited in color, and by the lens or prism determined to a certain path and shape. Similarly, the keys of an organ have only transmissive function. They open successively the various pipes and let the wind in the air-chest escape in various ways. The voices of the various pipes are constituted by the columns of air engendered in the organ. The organ proper, as distinguished from its air-chest, is only an apparatus for letting portions of it loose upon the world in these peculiarly limited shapes." According to this line of argument, the entire world of phenomena as we know it to be could be merely a 'surface-veil' which cloaks the real world of genuine objects, viz., the spiritual world.

Respecting the relationship of brain and mind, a transmissive function maintains; when the brain expires, consciousness remains because it is an aspect of that "*mental world behind the veil,*" as James phrases it. The conclusion of the entire argument here is evident, namely, spirit does not require a physical brain in order to survive because it is not its product.

(2) ***John McTaggart — The Improbability of Morality.***

A British philosopher, John McTaggart Ellis McTaggart (1886-1925), assumed the extremely rare position of believing in immortality without accepting belief in the existence of God. McTaggart, an Idealist whose ideas are most poignantly and lucidly recorded in his classic *Some Dogmas of Religion* (1906), and later in *Human Immortality and Pre-Existence* (1915),[1] concluded what to many philosophers would be an incongruous position: a simultaneous belief in both Atheism and immortality. McTaggart's Idealistic, or his anti-Materialistic, stand prompts him to repudiate the belief that man is mortal.

His arguments against *mortality,* as they are found in *Some Dogmas of Religion* and *Human Immortality and Pre-Existence,* proceed as follows: In speaking of the immortality of the soul, McTaggart means by the term *soul* or man, not something that a man or self *has,* but something that he *is.* To say that a man possesses a soul suggests that something of himself is lost in immortality.

McTaggart assesses the major objections against immortality to consist of (1) *epiphenomenalism,* the belief that the soul is an ephemeral illusion produced by bodily functions; and (2) that nature characteristically leads us to believe that all objects are transitory, they come into existence and later pass out of it.

The first objection is eliminated on the basis of *interactionism,* the belief the mind affects the body as much as the body affects the mind as is evidenced by the fact that "grief, or fear, or anger, can produce bodily death."[2] This being the case, it appears much more reasonable to conclude that mind and body are separate realities, neither of which is the mere product of the other, despite the fact that each may be alterably affected by the other. Inasmuch as action between the mind and body is reciprocal, neither is in a subordinate position, but each independent of the other.

Although body is independent of the mind, body cannot be assumed to be material; physical objects possess psychological qualities which are lost to the object when not sensed, such as, soft, yellow, sweet, and odorous. In fact, these qualities are not in the object itself, but in us; yet the object does possess its own qualities independent of our experiencing them, such as, size, shape, position in space, motion, impenetrability. Belief in matter is ultimately an inference drawn from facts furnished by sensations; however, sensations are subject to serious doubt since we

[1] The latter work is composed merely of a few chapters of the former.

[2] Quotations in this section are from John McTaggart, *Some Dogmas of Religion* (London: Edward Arnold, 1906).

sense illusions we know to be false, and we sense (in dreams) objects which appear to be extended in space, yet are not. No one in a dream knows that he is dreaming until he awakens to realize that his dream state was merely illusory. In the light of such phenomena, what is to prevent the experience following death to give man greater reality so that he realizes that this life is the lesser reality? Furthermore, dreams prove that the mind does not require a body in order to have experiences, even experiences of objects extended in space; dreams indicate the possibility of possessing sensations which are real yet not grounded in material objects. "I may be wrong in believing that matter exists independently of me. But the suggestion that I am wrong in believing I have a sensation is absurd." Sensations are ultimate certainties since they cannot exist apart from the self which possesses the experience, but they do have external causes which incite them.

The body is not, as is commonly supposed, essential to the soul or self; although the self possesses a body, the body is not a necessity. "For example, no self can be conceived as conscious unless it has sufficient data for its mental activity. This material is only given, as far as our observations can go, in the form of sensations, and sensations again, as far as our observations can go, seem invariably connected with changes in a body. But it does not follow, because a self which has a body cannot get its data except in connexion with that body, that it would be impossible for a self without a body to get data in some other way. It may be just the existence of the body which makes these other ways impossible at present. If a man is shut up in a house, the transparence of the windows is an essential condition of his seeing the sky. But it would not be prudent to infer that, if he walked out of the house, he could not see the sky because there was no longer any glass through which he might see it. With regard to the connexion of the brain with thought, the chief evidence for it appears to be that diseases or mutilations of the brain affect the course of thought. But this does not prove that, even while a man has a brain, his thoughts are directly connected with it. Many things are capable of disturbing thought, which are not essential to its existence. For example, a sufficiently severe toothache may render all consecutive abstract thought impossible. But if the tooth was extracted, I should still be able to think. And, in the same way, the fact that an abnormal state of the brain may affect our thoughts does not prove that the normal states of the brain are necessary for thought. Even if the brain is essential to thought while we have bodies, it would not follow that when we ceased to have brains we could not think without them. . . It might be that the present inability of the self to think except in connexion with the body was a limitation which was imposed by the presence of the body, and which vanished with it." McTaggart's reasoning in this passage is cogent and forceful; to assume that the brain can affect the mind, does not allow us to conclude that the brain therefore is the cause of the mind; to do so would be to commit a *post hoc* fallacy. For example, oxygen can affect my thinking and my mind, so can the sun, but this does not entitle a person to draw the inference that the sun or oxygen is the cause of my thought or my mind. Even if someone were to prove that the body is the cause of the mind, this still would not prove that the mind could not survive the body, since *a chain of effects may and often does exist long after its cause has been destroyed.*

F. THE CASE IN SUPPORT OF IMMORTALITY

Among the arguments favoring belief in immortality are to be found the following:

1. The Weaker Arguments

(1) *The Universal Desire for Immortality.*

This argument assumes that inasmuch as immortality is universally desired by all mankind, it holds some credence for us. The objection earlier registered against *desire* as constituting proof holds true here as well. Everyone may desire to rid the world of disease, but the mere desire is impotent in effecting the desired goal. Furthermore, it is highly doubtful that every person desires to live on eternally.

(2) *Immortality as an Inspiring Belief.*

Inspiration may be a wholesome feeling under certain circumstances, but not when a person is inspired to indulge in evil or deleterious behavior. Granted that immortality is a wholesome thought, we would first be obliged to prove that *inspiration* is a criterion of truth before using it in such a capacity.

(3) *Psychic Phenomena or Psychic Experiences.*

Some persons accept as valid data contact with the dead via mediums, seances, etc., but such alleged evidence is empirically weak and unreliable at the present time.

(4) *Revelation.*

The declaration of immortality through Sacred Scriptures is sufficient proof for many individuals for accepting belief in immortality, but the question begged here is: Is revelation valid? What is the proof of a valid revelation? Until the validity of revelation as a suitable process of verification is established, we are not entitled to claim it as an adequate argument.

(5) *Consensus of Belief.*

Some persons seek to prove the existence of immortality on the basis that everyone entertains belief, or at least thought, in it. If *Consensus Gentium* were a good criterion of truth, then this argument would be acceptable, provided it could be proved that everyone believes in it, which is hardly the case.

(6) *The Argument from Analogy.*

Joseph Butler (1692-1752), a British philosopher, sought to prove the reality of immortality on the premise that a number of nature's actions indicate possibilities in that direction, such as the remarkable and completely new life of a butterfly which emerges from the life of a pre-existing caterpillar.

The most that this argument proves is the possibility of startling or remarkably different objects being produced from sources that pure reason, unaided by facts, least suspects. However, to prove this true of biological life still does not prove that the same can obtain between the physical and spiritual realm.

(7) *The Resurrection of Jesus.*

For many Christians, one of the strongest arguments for immortality is what they regard as the *fact* of the resurrection of Jesus. By the resurrection of Jesus, some Christians mean the resurrection of the physical body, while others accept it as a spiritual resurrection. The difficulty that confronts us with this argument is that it is not subject to philosophical scrutiny; it lies beyond current investigatory techniques, hence must be relegated to the province of faith. Although it cannot be proved that Jesus was resurrected, neither can anyone disprove his resurrection from the dead.

(8) *Right the Wrongs of This World.*

There are those individuals who argue for the existence of immortality on the basis that it is necessary to 'right the wrongs suffered in this world' in a place of atonement where suitable compensations are effected. An element of this argument is found in Immanuel Kant's *Critique of Practical Reason,* where he argues for happiness being apportioned commensurate with the morality of an individual, and for this reason it becomes a postulate for immortality since man's moral goal cannot be realized upon earth nor is he rewarded according to his moral achievement here either.

Another aspect of this argument concerns the intense suffering of many persons who in this earthly life were handicapped physically, mentally, socially, etc., due to no fault of their own and without opportunity of overcoming their miserable state; hence the necessity of a heaven to justify, to make up for, the many wrongs endured here unjustly.

(9) *The Soul by Nature Eternal.*

Some philosophers, St. Augustine and Descartes among them, argue for immortality on the grounds that the soul is by virtue of its nature, indestructible. Descartes contends that material objects are contingent, they are subject to laws of causation, accordingly are subject to destruction by some particular cause, while spirit, not being contingent, is immune to laws of material causation, hence nothing can cause the death of the soul.

Although a soul is eternal by nature, there is no guarantee that the spirit will survive the death of the body unless God so chooses, for he can annihilate the soul as well as body. Ultimately, survival of the soul beyond bodily death depends upon God's pleasure; if he sees fit and so chooses, man will survive, otherwise, a soul, even constructed of everlasting substance, is subject to being annihilated by God.

2. Arguments of Greater Cogency

(1) *The Character of God.*

One of the most conclusive arguments for immortality is grounded on the goodness of God. To be sure, this argument rests on the assumption of the existence of God, but if reasonableness allows us to predicate the existence of God, then it follows that he would provide immortality. A good God (not necessarily one of justice), one who created man a being of supreme worth, at least evolution's highest creation, would see to his survival beyond death. It is incongruous, even to the point of being grotesque, that a good God would create man aware of his impending death, allow him to entertain desirously the thought of immortality, then deceitfully and fiendishly extinguish him. Such behavior would be the work of a 'devil,' not the 'requiter of justice,' who himself would, *a fortiori,* be just. It is inconceivable for a good God to 'tease,' tantalize, man, as it were, with the thoughts of immortality, then diabolically destroy him.

This argument would collapse unless predicated upon a good God, a good God capable of effecting immortality. If he were not capable of effecting man's survival, he would not have held out the desire for it; otherwise, he would be either incapacitated or psychopathic. Accordingly, predicating our argument on the existence of a good God, logically insures immortality.

Edgar Sheffield Brightman (1884-1953) considers the argument from goodness crucial, reasoning: "If there is a God – a supreme, creative, cosmic person – then there is an infinitely good being committed to the eternal conservation of values. That being is the controlling and directing power in all natural processes and is engaged in a process of immanent cooperation with all other persons. Since all true values are experiences of the fulfillment of ideal purposes by persons, the existence of values depends on the existence of persons. Value is personality at its best. God, the conserver of values, must be God, the conserver of persons." [1] Thus, every argument for a good God serves concomitantly as an argument for immortality, for it binds God to the obligation of saving the creatures who are his embodiment of intrinsic value, accordingly, extinguishing persons constitutes the elimination of intrinsic values as well, resulting in the failure of God's *good* purpose, viz., the promotion and conservation of intrinsic value. "If all persons were to perish with their bodily death, God would be in an unenviable position. He would either continue forever to create new persons, or he would give up the enterprise of creation. If he continued to create new persons, then he would be conducting a cosmic bonfire, with each new generation warmed by the burning of the previous one . . ." [2] The result would be that man, an intrinsic value and the being in whom value is posited, would perish; intrinsic value would then be irretrievably lost except in the being of a 'disappointed and frustrated God' confronted with the consequences of centuries of effort without permanent results, and his highest creation, man, never reaching full development. Brightman concludes, "If there be a God, man's immortality is certain; if not, immortality would not be worth having." [3]

[1] Edgar S. Brightman, *A Philosophy of Religion*, © 1940, original material only by permission of Prentice-Hall, Inc., Englewood Cliffs, N. J.

[2] *Idem.*

[3] Edgar S. Brightman, *An Introduction to Philosophy* (New York: Henry Holt and Co., 1925), 349.

(2) ***The Conservation of Values.***

Closely related to the argument which predicates immortality on the goodness of God is that which argues from the vantage point of the conservation of values. God is not only *axiogenesis* (source of all value), he is *axiosoteria,* (conserver of value); only in personal immortality is the conservation of value guaranteed, thereby making persons worthy of survival. Annihilate all persons and the world's greatest values are concomitantly eliminated: truth, beauty, goodness, knowledge, love, happiness, friendship, etc., etc.; only by personal immortality in this devastating catastrophe avoided. For God to idly stand by permitting the erosion and dissipation of value is to diminish his majesty, goodness, and worth, until the time arrives when no persons whatever remain, except God, to view the final results of his vast efforts, which will total to *nothing of value,* except himself.

Douglas Clyde Macintosh (1877-1948), one of philosophy's most articulate spokesmen regarding the argument based on the conservation of value, argues in his *Reasonableness of Christianity* (1925) that if spiritual values are to be conserved from final loss, then it cannot be that personal existence perishes with the death of the body.

Love gives personality its true worth; and noble love, true love, gives infinite worth to the individual person; yet, if persons in whom these values reside cease to exist, then values would degenerate to a state of nothingness, consequently would no longer allow us to recognize God as the conserver of value. Without personal immortality, the time will eventually be as if all values had never existed, thus the necessity of personal survival, if God is to be the conserver of value.

Physiologically speaking, the human body may perish without the concomitant destruction of the person; "if mind is an agent and not a mere phenomenon, it may conceivably find or be furnished with another instrument when the one it is now using becomes no longer serviceable." [1] Although not proved with absolute certainty, the immortality of persons is proved with reasonableness on the basis that "after an appreciation of the worth of human personality, the chief factor in the belief has been the idea of God, that is, of a Power great enough and good enough to conserve the human individual in spite of bodily death. . . If we can be assured that the Supreme Being in the universe loves man with an everlasting love, we can be assured that man is intended for everlasting life." [2] *A fortiori,* it may be argued that if man values persons, and out of his

[1] Douglas Clyde Macintosh, *The Reasonableness of Christianity* (New York: Charles Scribner's Sons, 1925).
[2] *Ibid.*

human love for them would choose, if within his power, to grant them immortality, then God, love in its sublimest form, would unquestionably grant it. In this connection, it matters little whether or not the mind or soul is dependent upon the body, since God, who is sufficiently powerful to create, is with equal power to sustain and continue it beyond bodily death.

(3) ***The Goal of Evolution.***

That each of these arguments dovetails and overlaps is to be expected provided it is valid, since truth is a coherent whole, and each argument is a phase or aspect of that coherent explanation which ultimately is one integrated, systematic network of interrelated ideas. The argument from the Theory of Evolution is essentially that the logical culmination of a long process of evolution is immortality; otherwise, the only implication remaining is that the creation of the world from its inception to the present time, costing God millions of years to produce, results in the loss of the highest value which it now possesses for him, namely, man – the world's highest value as far as evolution is concerned, because with the destruction of man, God's goal, that "one far-off divine event to which the whole creation moves," is voided. If from the beginning God knew that his efforts would prove vain, he would not have proceeded with the abortive endeavor. It appears much more reasonable to assert that if God knew that all his efforts would prove vain, he would not have undertaken his extended evolutionary enterprise in the first place, but the fact that he did engage in this long process of building a world to the level of values which reside in man, indicates that he is in a position to conserve values worthy of saving. Therefore, if nature, as we observe her operating in the process of evolution, is to keep her promise of continuing toward her goal of eternal development of spiritual values, she must have provisions for the preservation of truth, beauty, goodness, and man in whom they dwell. This thought is beautifully worded for us in verse by Alfred, Lord Tennyson in his *In Memoriam:*

> That nothing walks with aimless feet;
> That not one life shall be destroy'd
> Or cast as rubbish to the void,
> When God hath made the pile complete.

John Fiske (1842-1901), an outstanding American philosopher deeply committed to the philosophy of Evolutionary Naturalism, presents a case for immortality based on evidence stemming from the Theory of Evolution. He regards man's belief in his own immortality as a supreme achievement, the outcome of evolutionary processes; belief in a life beyond death is attributable to an emergent factor in evolution. All religious ideas and values are the products of evolutionary development, so also is the case with immortality. "Man is not only the primate who possesses articulate speech and the power of abstract reasoning, who is characterized by a long period of plastic infancy and a corresponding capacity for progress, who is grouped in societies of which the primordial units were clans; he is not only all this, but he is the creature who expects to survive the event of physical death. This expectation was one of his acquisitions gained while attaining to the human plane of existence."[1] Fiske proceeds to argue that Materialists are mistaken regarding their doctrine of Epiphenomenalism. "Materialists sometimes declare that the relation of conscious intelligence to the brain is like that of music to the harp, and when the harp is broken there can be no more music. An opposite view, long familar to us, is that the conscious soul is an emanation from the Divine Intelligence that shapes and sustains the world, and during its temporary imprisonment in material forms the brain is its instrument of expression. Thus the soul is not the music, but the harper."[2] Fiske concludes that evolutionary process is "the dramatic tendency or divine purpose indicated in the long cosmic process which has manifestly from the outset aimed at the production and perfection of the higher spiritual attributes of humanity."[3] We learn from nature, a lesson taught by the evolutionary process, namely "that belief in an Unseen World, especially associated with the moral significance of life, was coeval with the genesis of Man, and had played a predominating part in his development ever since, and . . . that under such circumstances the belief must be based upon an eternal reality, since a contrary supposition is negatived by all that we know of the habits and methods of the cosmic process of Evolution."[4] In this way, the Theory of Evolution testifies to the reality of immortality and other religious values, since, as Brightman asserts, "it is unthinkable that the purpose of the universe should fail."[5] If the course of evolution is not frustrated, and if it is not to have spent these millions of years of production in vain, then the only coherent outcome is its aim toward immortality and divinity fulfilled.

[1] John Fiske, *Life Everlasting* (Boston: Houghton Mifflin and Co., 1901), 37-38.
[2] *Ibid.*, 80.
[3] *Ibid.*, 86.
[4] *Ibid.*, 87
[5] *An Introduction to Philosophy, op. cit.*, 351.

XXII

THE PROBLEM OF EVIL

In philosophy of religion, the problem of evil refers to natural, rather than human evil; not that human evil is beyond the quest of the philosopher; on the contrary, man's immorality is of major concern to which at least an entire field of philosophy is devoted, *ethics*. The Problem of evil concerns itself with natural evil, the ethics of God, as it were. It may appear strange to the layman to speak of God's behavior, but the problem of evil is precisely such an enquiry.

The Problem Stated.

The problem of evil is based on the presence of natural evils in the world which are not attributable to man. Much of the evil in this world is initiated by man, such as, wars, murders, tortures, etc., but there exist certain conditions in whose inception or continuance man has played no part whatever, such as, tornadoes, disease, floods, etc. Who then is responsible, if not God? The problem of evil may be stated in the form of a dilemma: Since evils exist in the world, then God apparently either permits them or he does not; if he permits them by choice, then he cannot be all-good, and if they occur despite his objection, then he cannot be all-powerful. Thus, either God's goodness or his omnipotence is at stake.

This limitation upon God of either goodness or power cannot be a self-limitation, but a force, extraneous to his will; a self-restriction is not recognized as a genuine limitation. For example, God gave man free will, and if man abuses his freedom, God will not interfere, not because he is impotent, but because he does not choose to, perhaps by eternal decree; otherwise, the interference of God implies that man is devoid of a genuine free will. Thus, the problem of evil does not question any self-imposed limitation, but a restriction which is inherent in the very nature of God, from which he cannot extricate himself. If God allows natural evils to exist, then he must be limited either in goodness or in power; he cannot be both all-good and omnipotent, a deficiency must maintain either in his goodness or omnipotence.

A. SOLUTIONS TO THE PROBLEM OF EVIL

(1) *Theistic Finitism.*

By Theistic Finitism is meant the belief that God is limited in some capacity or quality, usually *power* or *goodness;* either he lacks absolute power or absolute goodness. The majority of Finitists accept the absolute goodness of God, while relinquishing belief in his omnipotence.

The Theistic Finitest accepts the problem of evil at its face value, that is, he acknowledges the presence of evil in the world, and is persuaded that God did not will its existence; hence it exists despite God's objections, which is equivalent to asserting that God is impotent in annihilating completely the existence of all evil; he is limited in this capacity. The power of evil frustrates the efforts of God. The Finitist does not conclude that God is weak, far from it; for all practical purposes, God's power may be regarded as infinite, but for this exceptional instance where natural evils prevail.

Among Theistic Finitists are to be found Edgar Sheffield Brightman, Alfred North Whitehead, and Plato, just to mention a few of a fairly large number, but a relatively diminutive number when compared to the sizable group adhering to the majority belief, Theistic Absolutism.

Plato's position is fairly clear in giving us an appreciative insight into the complications of this matter and the reason why these men favor Finitism. As we well know, nothing in the physical world is perfect, neither that which is man-made nor that which is produced by nature; for example, we cannot find a perfect ball, one which is a perfect inch in diameter, perfectly round and smooth. Although it is an accepted fact that it is impossible to construct a perfect one inch ball, our approximations approach perfection depending upon the judicious choice of materials; for example, steel is preferable to cement owing to the coarseness of the latter, but even using steel will never enable us to make that *perfect* ball since it may be a billionth of an inch off in diameter due to a number of factors affecting size, such as temperature, just to mention one. As to the ball's smoothness, looking at it with the naked eye or feeling it would not be sufficiently critical from the standpoint of perfection; a microscope would provide a better vantage point, but not perfection (even microscopes are imperfect); an atomic microscope would reveal many defects, defects not necessarily resulting from human limitation as from the nature of the material with which one is working. For instance, a steel ball is theoretically composed of atoms in motion, and despite the atoms remaining within the circumscribed limits of the ball, because they are in motion, they will never be arranged in perfect roundness. It should now be clear that the reason a perfect ball cannot be made is that the materials used are imperfect by their nature; the best possible which can be expected is to manufacture a ball which most approximates perfection.

The above represents precisely Plato's contention; he maintains that God did not create this world out of nothing, rather he *fashioned* it by taking raw material, a *given,* and formed the existent world according to a plan. The plan itself is perfect, for its structure is *ideal,* and ideal substance permits of perfection since it is by its very nature perfect, while matter, by its nature cannot be molded into the structure which the perfect form of an ideal assumes. Thus we live in two worlds: a perfect world of ideals, and an imperfect world of matter or the stuff of which the object of sense (nature, phenomena) is made. God did not make raw matter; it was eternally present, provided for him in a *receptacle,* and using it, he fashioned the world the best he possibly could restricted by the limitations which are inherent in matter, the present world being the outcome of his hampered efforts. There is a saying: 'you cannot make a silk purse out of a sow's ear;' for the same reason, God cannot make a perfect world out of imperfect substance. The perfect world is the world to come, an *ideal world,* an eternal one.

Evil is caused by the very *nature* of things; matter's imperfection is the source of evil, its cause and nature. According to some Finitists, such as Brightman, God is laboring to perfect matter, or to put it more accurately, God, with man's cooperation, is striving to overcome and annihilate all evil by reaching for perfection. As *Rabindranath Tagore* (1861-1941) phrased it: "The question why there is evil in existence is the same as why there is imperfection, or, in other words, why there is creation at all. We must take it for granted that it could not be otherwise; that creation must be imperfect, must be gradual." [1] Since creation is gradual, it builds up to perfection, and is not originally made perfect.

Evaluation of Theistic Finitism.

The Theistic Absolutist criticizes the Finitist's position by claiming that the Finitist's God is a schizophrenic, a dual personality who is striving to overcome his shortcomings, his limitations, his fight with matter. The Absolutist repudiates Finitism; he asserts that God is whole, sane, integrated, and free from internal struggle involving different aspects of his nature. A further objection to Finitism is its predication on the belief

[1] Rabindranath Tagore, *Sadhana: The Realization of Life* (New York: The Macmillan Co,. 1930).

of *surd* or *dysteleological evil,* evil in and of itself, intrinsic evil, whereas, contends the Absolutist, all evil serves some worthwhile purpose in the world.

(2) ***Theistic Absolutism.***

The Theistic Absolutist supports the stand that God is perfect in all respects, lacking perfection neither in power nor goodness. This school of thought predicates its conclusions on the premise that surd or dysteleogical evil does not exist. All evil subserves some good as is evidenced by pain; for example, a pain in the abdomen suggests the malfunctioning of bodily activity in that region, summoning our attention. If we were incapable of experiencing pain when something had gone awry, such as appendicitis, we would be seriously handicapped. To be able to sense pain is not ultimately an evil, but desirable, a good.

The Absolutist repudiates the notion of any surd or dysteleological evil; according to the Absolutist, evil exists only as an *instrumental good;* all evil serves some use, is of some value, some worthwhile cause, as the example of pain depicts. God created evil, such as pain, because it serves a good purpose; all so-called evils are not in and of themselves evil, intrinsically evil, but aids to good ends.

Benedict Spinoza (1632-1677), a Continental Rationalist, offers one defence of this view; he maintains that evil does not exist, it is merely due to man's ignorance. If man could view the world through the eyes of God as an omniscient mind, he would readily see everything in the world in its proper place serving a necessary purpose; what man calls evil is man's imperfect perspective of the facts of reality properly arranged. A fact out of place appears distorted, as if it did not belong to the scheme of things, accordingly, it is designated evil by man's limited knowledge, or ignorance, but if man could see the complete picture, he would realize that every individual portion is necessary, and contributes to the perfect whole. Evil is analogous to the confused mind of a person, who, confronted with a partially constructed five thousand piece jig-saw picture puzzle, holds one small displaced piece in his hand which he feels does not belong to the picture puzzle, but on completion of the puzzle, it becomes obvious that the supposed misfit is a necessary part of the integral whole.

Thus, dysteleological or surd evil does not exist; what is called evil is error, owing to man's ignorance. According to Spinoza's basic premises, it may be argued that even illnesses are evils due to man's ignorance, since God has granted man sufficient intelligence to conquer his diseases; man's God-given intelligence is adequate to master any of his problems. God has provided man with intelligence, the necessities to conquer disease, the factors and elements necessary to effect cures; it remains for man to rise and accomplish the remaining task through scientific research or other modes of solving human problems. The Theistic Finitist's reply to the foregoing argument is that it commits the fallacy of pleading ignorance.

(3) *Frederick Robert Tennant — The Necessity of Evil.*

F. R. Tennant (1866-1961), in a two volume work which has become classic, *Philosophical Theology* (1928), presents a view which regards evil as necessary, a view comparable to that found in Leibniz' *Theodicy.*[1] Tennant argues that evils are necessary by-products of the uniformity of nature, a necessary precondition of man's moral and rational life. To argue that the omnipotence of God could eliminate natural evil involves absurdity, or to argue that it is decreed by divine providence is ethically untenable. Natural evil is the price man pays for his moral status, the cost of merely being human, the price of being more than mere animal.

Evil is the necessary outcome of a world whose ingredients are those such as ours, a world of moral beings, of scientific laws, of human intelligence. To create a world in which these valuable factors are desired, necessarily results in natural evils, such as, doubts, worries, problems, disease, etc., but to rebel against problems is to rebel against one's manhood, his superior being; for example, it is impossible to create a moral being free from temptation. Actually, all things work together for good, for the good of the whole, not necessarily for each particular part viewed in isolation from the rest. "In our developing world all things work together, as a whole, for the highest conceivable good. The possibility of moral evil and the actuality of its consequences are inevitable concomitants of the 'best possible' evolutionary world."[2] This statement must not be interpreted as meaning 'whatever is, is right,' or even that the existence of isolated partial evils is not detectable in the world, but that everything taken as a complex organic whole will prove to be good, will be found to be a universe coherently ordered.

Tennant does not endorse the argument that pain is prophylactic, a danger warning, or that it is punitive, or even purgatorial, thereby subserving good ends. Although each of these arguments is true and important, the only conclusive one is: that despite physical pain, life is, on the whole, happy. To plead the arguments listed as completely valid would

[1] Leibniz' discussion of the matter as contained in his *Theodicy* is reserved for Part V (Metaphysics); however, it is suggested that the reader acquaint himself with Leibniz' ideas on this subject before proceeding further on Tennant's position.

[2] Frederick Robert Tennant, *Philosophical Theology* (Cambridge: Cambridge University Press, 1928), Vol. II, 197.

be to beg the question: "The knife may be necessary to cure the disease, but why the necessity of the disease?" or "The escape from mortal danger may require the painful warning, but why the mortal danger?" Thus the only real solution is to show "that pain is either a necessary by-product of an order of things requisite for the emergence of the higher goods, or an essential instrument to organic evolution, or both." [1] The former alternative serves as the explanation of human suffering, while the latter adequately explains animal pain, physical pain as a necessary instrumental factor to organic progress.

Natural evil is part of the cost of having an evolutionary process; it is inherent in the nature of things owing to natural law. "That painful events occur in the causal chain is a fact; but, that there could be a determinate evolutionary world of unalloyed comfort, yet adapted by its law-abidingness to the development of rationality and morality, is a proposition the burden of which must be allotted to the opponent of theism. One can only add that, in so far as experience in this world enables us to judge, such proof seems impossible. To illustrate what is here meant; if water is to have the various properties in virtue of which it plays its beneficial part in the economy of the physical world and the life of mankind, it cannot at the same time lack its obnoxious capacity to drown us. The specific gravity of water is as much a necessary outcome of its ultimate constitution as its freezing-point, or its thirst-quenching and cleansing functions . . . Thus physical ills follow with the same necessity as physical goods from the determinate 'world-plan' which secures that the world be a suitable stage for intelligent and ethical life." [2] Laws are a necessity, not only for the coherent order of the universe, but for man to conduct an orderly, rational, and moral existence. These so-called evils are not absolute, because they subserve the highest good by providing opportunity for moral development; the world's ills are not superfluous, but the necessary resultant of order, law.

Hedonistically, evil may not be regarded as good, but it is 'good for good,' provided good is defined in a non-Hedonistic sense. "Physical evil, then, must necessarily be. And the goodness of God is vindicated if there be no reason to believe that the world-process involves more misery than Nature's uniformity entails." [3] Not every form of suffering is willed by God, but only that which is necessary to their being a universe of law and morality. Evil, though a necessity in the present physical life, must be absent in a future, in immortality where one is free from the hazards to which flesh is heir.

[1] *Ibid.*, 198
[2] *Ibid.*, 201.
[3] *Ibid.*, 202.

B. CONCLUSION AND TRANSITION

With the discussion of the problem of evil concluded, our deliberations in the area of philosophy of religion terminate, and prepare us for focusing our attention on the subject of metaphysics. The transition from philosophy of religion to metaphysics is a logically suitable one, for metaphysics forms the base of a person's philosophy of religion; to penetrate into the depths of philosophy of religion brings one to its lower regions, metaphysics.

The mastery of metaphysics, the most difficult of the realms of philosophy, is a necessity if a person seeks an appreciable understanding of the schools of philosophy dominating the contemporary scene, since metaphysics forms the core of contemporary philosophical schools.

Part Five: METAPHYSICS — The Study of Ultimate Reality

METAPHYSICS: *THE STUDY OF ULTIMATE REALITY*

Metaphysics, the study of ultimate reality, is a term of Greek origin, as is the case with much philosophical terminology; *ta meta* (beyond, after) prefixed to *ta physika* (nature or physics) yields metaphysics, the study which transcends or goes beyond the physical; namely, ontology and cosmology. Whereas science is restricted to the physical or phenomenal realm of nature, metaphysics concerns itself with the area beyond the physical, that is, the province of ultimate reality.

Some philosophers conjecture, following Andronikos of Rhodes, that the term metaphysics originated as the result of a coincidental arrangement of books in Aristotle's library. Books on philosophy were placed after those on physics; accordingly, whenever Aristotle requested his metaphysical treatises, he would refer to them as those books which came after the physics, hence *meta*physics. Be that as it may, today whenever metaphysics is used, reference is regularly made to the subject matter contained in those books, namely the study of ultimate reality, or as Aristotle thought of it, the First Philosophy.

The present chapter purports to trace metaphysical deliberations of the great philosophers from Descartes to Schopenhauer (plus an abbreviated section on Greek metaphysics), thereby providing a basis upon which to understand contemporary philosophy, for practically all philosophy of the present day finds its foundation on one or a combination of these philosophical giants.

As the history of metaphysics unfolds, one becomes aware that the existence of *matter* gradually disappears. Proof of this fact is readily had by scanning current philosophical schools of thought and discovering the paucity of contemporary schools which recognize the metaphysical presence of material substance. In this regard, *George Santayana,* a contemporary philosopher of note, was compelled to say that he was a materialist, but the last of the clan. According to present day philosophers, it appears that the world does not consist of matter, at least, not the old concept of it. Materialism seems to have died; it belongs to beliefs of the past. The contemporary European philosopher, I. M. Bochenski, probably with the thought before us in mind, was moved to remark[1] that the average man is one hundred years behind in philosophical thought. Not only is his conclusion worth endorsing, but it would not be far from the truth to say that 'the man on the street' is from three hundred to three hundred fifty years behind in philosophy.

Modern philosophy finds its chief and accelerated impetus during the period of the enlightenment in Europe mainly through the efforts of *Continental Rationalists* such as René Descartes (1596–1650), Benedict Spinoza (1632-1677), and Gottfried Wilhelm Leibniz (1646-1716). A reaction to the Rationalist's thesis generated in the British Isles; this antithesis, termed *British Empiricism,* was championed principally by John Locke (1632-1704), George Berkeley (pronounced Barkeley; 1685-1753), and David Hume (1711-1776). The squabble between these two antithetical philosophies was to be resolved in a synthesis in the form of *German Idealism,* initiated by Immanuel Kant (1724-1804) and later pursued by George Wilhelm Friedrich Hegel (pronounced Hā'gêl; 1770-1831) and Arthur Schopenhauer (1788-1860). The following chart is supplied in order to orient the reader as to the relative chronology of the men in question:

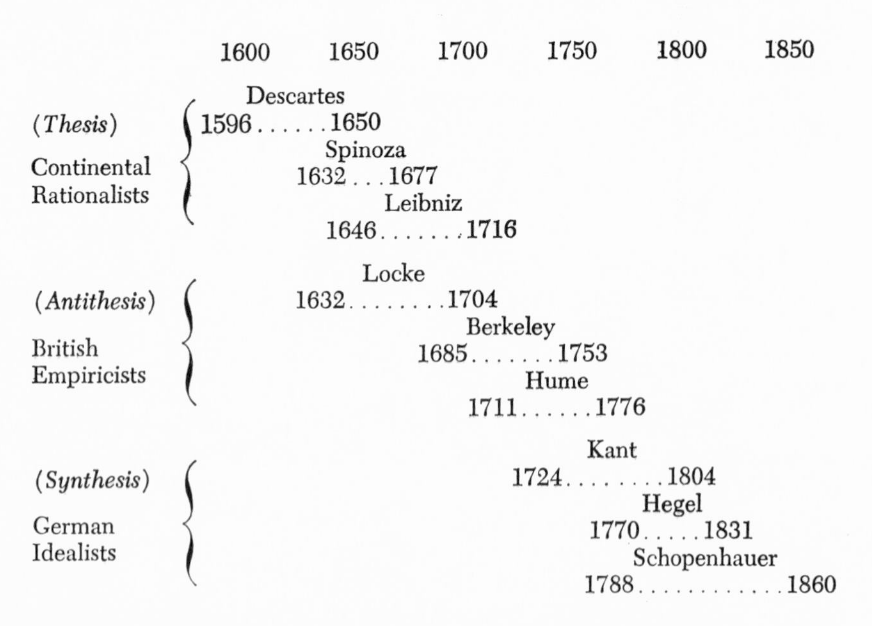

[1] See I. M. Bochenski, *Contemporary European Philosophy* (1956).

XXIII

PRE-CARTESIAN METAPHYSICS

The present treatment of pre-Cartesian metaphysics is limited to Hellenic philosophy, inasmuch as this is all that is necessary as an essential basis for understanding modern metaphysics. As far as Medieval philosophy is concerned, its first period is predominantly Platonic and its second, Aristotelian. No attempt at comprehensiveness is intended in this section; merely a brief sketch is deemed sufficient to provide the reader with a synoptic or 'bird's eye' view of the development of metaphysics as it unfolds in Western thought.

The Milesian School.

The first period of metaphysics, the pre-Socratic, opens with the Milesian School, consisting of three Ionian physicists: *Thales* (624-546), *Anaximander* (610-546), and *Anaximenes* (585-528). The problem confronting these cosmologists was the essential nature of cosmic matter, or 'world-stuff' which was the substratal ingredient of the ultimately real universe. The Milesians were in accord on the presupposition of the unity of the universe, but differed as to the component materials of which it was composed. Thales asserted it was *water;* Anaximenes, air; and Anaximander, infinity or 'the boundless' (*to apeiron*), as he termed it.

Anaximander regarded cosmic matter as infinite corporeal mass, and associated it with divinity. With this man, the world finds its first philosophical conception of God, a view free from mythical and religious biases.

These primitive philosophers, materialistic in outlook, hastily dismissed problems of motion, change, and other questions inexplicable on a purely materialistic basis, by resorting to the doctrine of *Hylozoism,* the belief that all matter is inherently animated or living.

The Pythagoreans.

Tradition has it that the Pythagoreans were the first to employ the term *philosophy*. The school is named after its foremost proponent, Pythagoras (580-497), who is also credited with the discovery of the theorem which is identified by his name, ($A^2 + B^2 = C^2$ or $3^2 + 4^2 = 5^2$).

The thinkers of this school claimed that ultimate Being, the object of search of every philosopher, is to be determined through numbers or mathematical conceptions. Since mathematical principles are eternal, immutable, indestructible substance; ultimate 'Being' must be of like consistency.

The Pythagorean number philosophy had wide reaching significance. They discovered many things responding to mathematical calculation, such as, music, science, etc.; consequently, they felt justified in concluding the world to be a harmony of numbers. The essence of physical objects is basically mathematical forms; laws of science are mathematically determined; the physical world abides by mathematical formula. Mathematics is lord of the universe, and independent of time and space; whereas all else is subject to temporal and spatial relations. Accordingly, the Pythagorean world is dualistic: (1) perfect and infinite mathematically; (2) limited and imperfect corporeally. Mathematical reality is permanent Being, whereas physical reality is mere process or becoming.

Matter, as brute stuff, takes form and shape according to mathematical formula; in a true sense, material things are copies or imitations of mathematical principles. In a manner of speaking, they have been shaped by being cast into mathematical forms. Empirical reality is a mere copy of these higher, more original and more truly real, mathematical forms. Plato will have more to say of this matter later.

The Eleatic School.

Metaphysics continued to develop; the philosophy of matter and God advanced another step in the thought of *Xenophanes* of Elea (c. 570-475) by his critical attack of anthropomorphic Polytheism, which he displaced with Monotheism, or more accurately, *Pantheism*. While Polytheism is predicated on the premise that multifarious nature is basically grounded in disunity, Xenophanes maintained the oneness of nature owing to the oneness of Supreme Being (Monotheism). He identified God with the world; accordingly his metaphysical 'world-stuff' is essentially a 'World-God'. His attack upon anthropomorphic Polytheism assumes the following interesting line of debate: [1] "If oxen and lions had hands, and could paint with their hands, and fashion images, as men do, they would make pictures and images of their gods in their own likeness; horses would make them like horses, oxen like oxen." Again, "Ethiopians make their

[1] Xenophanes, *Fragments;* in Charles M. Bakewell, *Source Book in Ancient Philosophy* (New York: Charles Scribner's Sons, 1907), 8.

gods black and snub-nosed; Thracians give theirs blue eyes and red hair;" but, he goes on to say, "There is one God, supreme among gods and men; resembling mortals neither in form nor in mind."

Accordingly, the world is made ultimately of a divine substance, homogeneous in its composite parts, yet immovable. The corporeal world is, at the same time, a thought world.

The problem of metaphysical Being or world-stuff was later scrutinized by *Parmenides* (540-470), father of Materialism, founder of the Eleatic School, and its most dominant thinker. Parmenides, who termed metaphysical world-stuff 'Being,' was so completely convinced of its reality that he did not consider it necessary to prove it. Not only did he regard the unthinkable as existentially impossible, but he assumed that what was thinkable, existed. The thought-world and the corporeal-world were identical.

His unempirical approach was purely logical, and based primarily on the notion that since 'non-Being' was unthinkable, Being must exist. Being is equivalent to that which occupies space; non-Being signifies incorporeality or empty space, which, in his estimation, was an impossibility. Since 'void' or empty space cannot exist, he concluded that both plurality and motion also cannot be real, for the reason that between any two objects, either another object or empty space must exist. If another object exists, it must be connected to the first; but if empty space intervenes between the two, then the existing void dividing the two is empty space or nothingness. Since nothingness cannot exist, *plurality* (many ultimate entities), which assumes the interposition of empty spaces between objects, cannot be. *Motion* cannot be said to exist either, the reason being that in order for an object to move, it must move into an occupied area; but unoccupied areas cannot exist since to say they do, is to admit the existence of nothingness. The Parmenidean concept of ultimate Being is categorized *Metaphysical Monism* that is, ultimate reality consists of a *single* entity, which Parmenides regarded as *The One.*

Heraclitus, the Obscure **(544–484).**

The antithesis of the Eleatic doctrine of absence of motion was found in the philosophy of Heraclitus who emphasized perpetual change or evolution as inherent in all things. For him, deity was not a particular object, but a cosmic process which he termed *Becoming* or *Change.* Change and Movement are Lord of the universe. "All things flow; nothing abides. One cannot step twice into the same river." Just as a river is never the same any two moments since new waters enter it while the old flow into the sea, so is all reality similarly constituted with like transiency. Heraclitus postulated fire as the universe's ultimately real substance, inasmuch as fire epitomizes in a vivid manner his view of an ever altering world completely devoid of anything static.

Nevertheless, he noted that nature is not permitted to run wild in any chaotic direction, but follows a prescribed path, or at least, remains within circumscribed limits. In other words, nature is under law, the only permanent element in the universe. This common element inherent in diversity, governing and regulating objects, this order or natural law, he termed the *Reason* (*Logos*) of the world. "This Word (*Logos*) is everlasting . . . Although the Word *(Logos)* is common to all, yet most men live as if each had a private wisdom of his own."[1] Reason (natural law) orders what otherwise would be a meaningless, disorderly, and unpredictable world of capricious facts wandering aimlessly in a directionless course.

The Pluralists.

The synthesis, reconciling the antithetical positions of Eleatics, who maintained that *changeless* Being alone exists, with that of Heraclitus, who declared that *becoming* is the sole nature of things, was proposed by the Pluralists: *Empedocles* (495-435), *Anaxagoras* (499-428), *Leucippus* (5th century), *Democritus* (460-370). The latter two are also Atomists.

One mediating system, that of *Anaxagoras,* reasoning on the Eleatic premise that if nothing can arise or pass away, concluded that the world must be composed of a countless number of elements (differing in color, shape, and form) capable of a variety of arrangements, and present in all objects. These primary elements, eternal and immutable, are capable of *motion* owing to an extraneous force, termed *Nous* (Reason). If it were not for *Nous,* the world would be a chaos rather than a meaningful, orderly, beautiful, purposeful cosmos in which its innumerable elements of mass harmonize in a unitary coherent system. *Nous,* not only directs the orderliness of the world, but governs its purposeful course. In Anaxagoras' *Nous,* we find for the first time, a teleological explanation of nature.

The Atomists.

Two outstanding Greek Atomists, Leucippus and Democritus, explained the world-stuff out of which the universe is composed, in terms of a countless number and variety of *atoms* (uncuttables). *Leucippus* envisioned atoms as tiny particules of diverse gradations, smoothness, and

[1] *Ibid.,* Heraclitus, *Fragments,* 1-2.

liveliness darting about irregularly, but when functioning in aggregate groups, behaving according to mathematical necessity; consequently forming the integrated world as we know it. "Nothing comes into being without a reason, but everything arises from a specific ground and is driven by necessity."[1] The Atomists conceived the sun and moon as independent worlds which in time drew together into a single universe with the earth as its center.

Democritus maintained a dual conception of the world: The first, based on his *doctrine of images* (a theory which had a marked influence on the British Empiricists) predicated the existence of a sense-world. The second, derived from reason, indicated the existence of an orderly, rational, and ultimately real world. The world, the one which is known to us by our senses, he called *phenomena* (appearances); it was neither an ultimate world, nor one from which valid knowledge issues. However, the second world, both ultimate and real, had true essence or substance, could be known validly, and possessed permanency as well as rationality. Knowledge of the world of phenomena is inadequate or invalid because it is acquired by sense perception, a form of cognition which is subjective, variable, and untrustworthy; whereas knowledge of the world of reality is by the understanding, a form of cognition which employs thought or logic, hence is reliable, accurate, and universally valid.

Ultimate reality or world-stuff, for Democritus, consisted of atoms (atom-forms), or as he termed them *ideai* (ideas) or *schemata* (forms). In this respect, the philosophy of Democritus approaches closely to the thought of Plato. True Knowledge (knowledge of reality) was understood by Democritus to be an *idea* of ultimate *Being*, whose essence is eternally abiding and unchanging. Ultimate Being is known rationally by the understanding or through a coherent explanation of sense phenomena.

He conceived ultimate reality as comprised of numberless atoms, varying in size and description, and beyond the reach of the senses, but within the range of human reason to fathom. Atoms, which constitute the true nature of reality, are in constant motion soaring about empty space; it is they which produce the visual corporeal world as it is manifested to us phenomenally. The postulating of atoms as the ultimate substance of the world classifies this philosophy as *Materialism*.

Protagoras and the Sophists.

Protagoras (481-411), whose *perception theory* ("Man is the measure of all things"), allowed for facts of sense only, and not for ultimate (imperceptible) reality, limited the nature of the world to what Democritus

[1] *Ibid.*, Leucippus, *Fragments*, 2.

designated as imperfect knowledge. For Protagoras, reality was relative because knowledge was relative; knowledge is dependent upon limited and inaccurate sense perception. This being the case, Protagoras felt justified in denying ultimate reality or world-stuff altogether, thereby restricting reality to objects of sense exclusively. If reality did exist, it was, at most, relative and transient.

Gorgias (483-375), the most extreme of the Sophists, pressed Protagoras' Relativism to the point of Nihilism, by declaring that Being or world-stuff did not exist. He argued: "Nothing exists; second, if anything did exist, we could never know it." Consequently, Being or ultimate reality of the pre-Sophists, is now being challenged at its very roots.

We now look to the men of the systematic period of philosophy, Plato and Aristotle, to provide a more acceptable explanation of the metaphysical world of reality.

Platonic Idealism.

Plato (427-347), an Athenian and founder of his school, the Academy, constructed his own philosophy upon foundations laid by his predecessors in metaphysical thought, especially upon the premises of Parmenides, Pythagoras, Protagoras, and Democritus, also to an indeterminate but major degree, upon the teachings of Socrates. From Protagoras, he accepted the relativity of perception and the mere appearance of phenomenal objects; but unlike Protagoras, he accepted *ontos* (true Being) and *ousia* (real essence), perhaps from Parmenides and Pythagoras. From Democritus, he obtained the concept of phenomena, the concept that perception offers a transient reality, an actuality, a semblance of reality, or the manner in which reality is revealed to us through our senses. From Parmenides, he learned that thought or reason penetrates phenomena or appearance to reach and disclose reality itself (true Being). From Pythagoras, he gained insight into (what was to be termed) Platonic Ideals; principles ideal in nature, mathematically precise, eternal, immutable, and independent of temporal or spatial limitations.

Plato recognizes *two levels and types of reality:* (1) The *lower,* acquired through sense perception, is transient, imperfect, and, at best, a copy or approximation of the higher. (2) The *higher,* the ultimately real, is ideal, possesses true Being, perfection, and is grasped by the intellect. Thus Plato is a Rationalist; and, because he believes in Ideal Being, is also a Realist and an Idealist as well. Platonic Idealism and Platonic Realism are identical; the former emphasizes the view that ultimate reality is idea, the latter stresses the idea as being objectively real. *Ideals are real* is the simplest formulation of Platonic Idealism, or for that matter, Platonic Realism.

Sense knowledge is relative, owing to a diversity of sense perceptions, and complicated still further by differing sense organs. Only when the mind has abstracted from multifarious sense data does it derive knowledge of the actual, truly real, and genuine nature; only through such a process is essence (pure form) revealed or known; furthermore, it is disclosed and known as ideal, immaterial conceptions corresponding to the logical or rational quality of the perceived object. The truly existent is composed of *ideai* or *eide* (forms); forms of a mathematical nature and quality are found to be the essence of things. Knowledge of mathematical principles and knowledge of true Being (world-stuff) are alike, ideally real.

The ultimate nature of world-stuff is ideal (immaterial). The ideal does not have mere phenomenal existence, nor is it manifested to the senses at all; it consists of *ousia* (substance, being, essence), true reality. Ideal substance is neither relative nor actual, but real and absolute – a metaphysically absolute substance. The ultimately real world is ideal, incorporeal, immaterial, insensuous; Plato identified it as *Idea,* hence Platonic Idealism. The actual world, the phenomenal, is a semblance of the real world, the manner in which the real world appears via our senses; at best it is an outward manifestation of the world, a manifestation which deceives the mind. Plato's distinction between the actual and real is discussed in every major philosophical period: the Medieval, in terms of *universals* and *particulars;* the Renaissance, in terms of *primary* and *secondary qualities* in things; the Contemporary, in current philosophies such as that of Alfred North Whitehead, Karl Jaspers (the Existentialist), and others.

Immaterial reality, consisting of incorporeal substance, is known, not through sense perception, but by the soul. Actually, all knowledge, for Plato, is recollection; the soul's recollection of a pre-existent state in a previous life. Plato believes in both a post-existence, a life after death; and a pre-existence, a life prior to the present. The soul once dwelt in the real world now hidden from the senses. Knowledge of ultimate reality, the ideal world, was gained from a pre-existent life of the soul; accordingly, the inner recesses of the soul are the repository of all truth. To gain new truth is merely to remember that which lies forgotten in the unconscious; truth is that which is hidden deep in the distant regions of the soul, and surfaces to consciousness and assumes the form of knowledge. Plato places the following words into the mouth of Socrates: "The soul of man is immortal, and at one time has an end, which is termed dying, and at another time is born again, but is never destroyed . . . The soul, then, as being immortal, and having been born again many times, and having seen all things that there are, whether in this world or in the world below, has knowledge of them all; and it is no wonder that she should be able to call to remembrance all that she ever knew about virtue, and about everything; for as all nature is akin, and the soul has learned all things, there is no difficulty in eliciting, or as men say learning, all out of a single recollection, if a man is strenuous and does not faint; for all inquiry and all learning is but recollection." [1] At this point, Socrates proceeds to prove his claim by approaching a young man who never knew the Pythagorean theorem, and merely by asking questions (never offering any information), is able to elicit from the boy the Pythagorean theorem as if the lad himself had made an original discovery of that mathematical principle. Mathematical, logical, ethical, and all a priori principles may be discovered independently of facts; consequently, if a person has sufficient intellectual acumen, it is possible to elicit such truths from him; but truths entailing empirical data require sense perception.

In the *Timaeus,* Plato discusses the manner in which the world was constituted, the process by which the sense world comes into being according to a pattern prescribed by the Ideas. The entire process necessitates a 'world-forming' God, or as he termed it, Demiurge (*Demiourgos*), literally, a 'hand-worker,' who fashions or forms the cosmos (orderly world) out of chaos, or rather, unformed matter; "out of disorder he brought order." [2] God, the artisan, using this raw material drawn from the *'receptacle,'* (the repository of unformed matter), constructs the physical world according to the pattern of Ideas which is used as a master by which to make a copy. Accordingly, God shaped the phenomenal world around us out of indefinite plasticity of raw matter, a world of Not-Being, residing in empty space. God, the artificer, does not create, he merely designs or copies the physical world in the light of the original world, namely, eternal Ideas. Consequently, Plato's two worlds, phenomena and reality (Ideas), become three with the addition of the receptacle, the repository of unformed, uncreated, raw matter. Of it, Plato writes: "This new beginning of our discussion of the universe requires a fuller division than the former; for then we made two classes, now a third must be revealed. The two sufficed for the former discussion; one, which we assumed, was a pattern intelligible and always the same; and the second was only the imitation of the pattern, generated and visible. There is also a third kind which we did not distinguish at the time, conceiving that the two be enough. But now the argument seems to require that we

[1] Plato, *Meno,* tr. Benjamin Jowett.
[2] Plato, *Timaeus,* tr. Benjamin Jowett.

should set forth in words another kind which is difficult of explanation and dimly seen. What nature are we to attribute to this new kind of being? We reply, that it is the receptacle, and in a manner the nurse, of all generation." [1] In the light of the above, Plato's ultimates are reducible to God, Ideas, and the Receptacle.

Although Aristotle gained much from Platonic theory, and incorporated a number of its concepts into his own philosophical system, he was, nevertheless, dissatisfied with a number of Plato's theories, including the 'theory of ideas,' and supplanted it with his own brand of *Realism.* Let us direct our attention to Aristotelian metaphysics.

Aristotelian Realism.

In Aristotle, the line of great teachers continues; Plato's illustrious master was Socrates, but Aristotle too had a teacher of no mean repute in Plato, and also a brilliant student in Alexander the Great. Aristotle's university was named the Lyceum, and the philosophers of his school, *Peripatetics,* because the class promenaded about as the instructor deliberated on philosophy.

The crucial problem confronting Hellenic philosophers was essentially twofold: (1) the nature of ultimate reality, (2) the problem of motion or changing multiplicity in physical objects. Democritus resolved the problem by regarding atoms, the ultimate element of which phenomenal nature was comprised in his system, as being in motion. Plato dealt with the question by establishing eternal immaterial Ideas as ultimately real; they teleologically motivated or moved phenomena.

Aristotle introduced the concept of *entelechy,* the potential power in objects, by which they gradually unfold according to the process indicative of their respective natures. Entelechy is the object's essence or nature by which it realizes or actualizes itself. The function of entelechy is assumed by Ideals in Plato's philosophy. All ultimate Being (world-stuff or matter) possesses an essence, a nature, laws, by which it behaves or is directed; consequently, all phenomenal manifestation is reducible to the realization of an object's essence by the force or power of entelechy.

Along with Democritus and Plato, Aristotle also wrestles with what appears to be a duality in nature, a duality of appearance and reality. Although the two exist in Aristotle's estimation, form, which is in a sense comparable to Plato's Idea, holds the ascendency, for Aristotle's highest Being, God, consists completely of Pure Form. Pure matter, if such there could be, would be the lowest level of existence; but Aristotle claims that all matter, of whatever gradation, is infused with some measure of form

[1] *Idem.*

(entelechy) which is the innate power or potentiality to develop, actualize, or realize one's being or nature. Accordingly, Plato's universal Ideas are regarded as real in the Aristotelian system, when, and only when, they are actualized in particular nature, phenomena. On the other hand, particular objects of sense exist owing to the *universal* nature within, the force by which they are striving to be realized. The Aristotelian explanation of cosmic processes is reducible to entelechy, or the realization of the essence contained within each phenomenal object.

The process governing self-actualization proceeds along four principles, or laws of causation. Aristotle does not restrict the concept of cause to a single one, the mere material object which happens to precede an effect. *Four causes* are detectable: (1) the immanent *material cause* which provides the physical substance comprising the effect; (2) the *formal cause* or pattern which functions as the 'blue-print,' plan, or design which the effect will assume; (3) the *efficient cause,* energy, or effort required to bring about the necessary change from cause to effect; (4) the *teleological* or *final cause,* the end or purpose to which the effect is to be put; in other words, its reason for coming into being originally. Each cause may be found illustrated in the following example of a sculptor's statuary creation. In making a statue out of marble, the sculptor requires physical marble (the material cause); he probably has some idea in mind which serves as his plan or pattern (the formal cause); his action or energy spent in working on raw material constitutes the efficient cause; while the final cause is the purpose, objective, goal he has in mind for the work of art. The four principles constitute the manner by which objects realize or actualize themselves. Individual phenomena are self-realizing forms. In addition to causation, other modes govern the behavior of phenomena, termed categories, such as, quantity, quality, relation, position, condition, substance, passion or passivity. All told, the categories number ten.

Many philosophers include some form of the Theory of Evolution in their philosophical systems, though only a few of the ancients conceive of it as a *process* resembling the Darwinian mode. Aristotle also offers a Theory of Evolution, but it is a static one in which all things are created in 'one fell swoop' arranged in a graded series from lower to higher forms of existence or metaphysical value. The lower represent predominantly material objects, whereas the higher contain more of spirit, mind, or as he termed it, form. The highest form, completely free of matter, is the Prime Mover (*Proton Kinoun*) of all matter, namely God. Pure Form or the First Mover is telic motion, cause which is itself unmoved. By virtue of its own self-contained activity, the Prime Mover is capable of exciting matter to the point of actuality, the realization of its essential nature.

Plato's Idea, particularly his Idea of the Good, is comparable to Aristotle's Prime Mover, inasmuch as each of these is composed of Pure Form and assumes like activity. For both men, each concept constitutes deity; each is perfect Being; each is the highest and finest reality; and for Aristotle, all potentiality within the Prime Mover is, at the same time, actuality. In Aristotle's God, the Prime Mover, the highest Being and Essence, pure act (*actus purus*) becomes pure thought; the actualization of pure thought (Pure Form) is thought of thought (*noesis noeseos*), self-consciousness.

Aristotle's Monotheism, God as absolute mind, predicates God as self-sufficient and eternally blessed since he has no other goal to realize, or nature to actualize, except self-contemplation, self-consciousness; whereas, for the remainder of the world, both human and nonhuman, there exists a longing of matter after God in an effort towards self-realization. Matter, restricted to the realm of possibility or potentiality, incapable of moving itself or anything else toward realization, requires an external power to move it toward self-actualization, a function effected solely through God, the completely actual, and the only power capable of motion. Man and the various gradations of nature, each found on its respective level of the evolutionary scale, by virtue of the Prime Mover, strive toward higher development and realization, or which is the same thing, toward Pure Form, God.

Conclusion.

Hellenic metaphysics, although not indispensable to the understanding of modern philosophy, certainly is advantageous in furnishing the necessary background for a penetrating understanding of many of the great masters. Some philosophers have gone so far as to say that every person is born either a Platonist or an Aristotelian, and may be so classified. The statement is probably an exaggeration, but it is indicative of the importance of the philosophy of ancient Greece. The sketchy outline offered in this section is hardly sufficient for understanding in depth the mind of Greece, yet it does attempt to trace, and it is hoped with a fair measure of success, philosophical thinking as it unfolds from the time of the earliest of the great thinkers to Aristotle, whose philosophy dominated the intellectual community for over a thousand years. The next section picks up where Aristotelian thinking no longer holds sway — with Descartes, the father of modern metaphysics.

XXIV

RENÉ DESCARTES:

A Metaphysical Dualist

Metaphysical Dualism is the philosophy of one who believes that ultimate reality is composed exclusively of two entities; in the case of the dualist *René Descartes,* the two basic substances are *mind* and *matter*. That is to say, everything in the universe is eventually reducible to (1) mind (*mens, esprit*), thoughts, spiritual realities, etc.; or (2) matter, things; whatever else seems to exist is mere appearance — not reality.

Cogito, ergo sum (I think, therefore I am): An Innate Idea.

Although every object in the world is reducible to one of two basic substances: mind or material things; in the last analysis, matter's existence must be assumed, for it cannot be proved with finality; whereas the existence of spiritual substance (mind) can be proved with certainty. By certainty, not psychological but logical certainty, is meant proof beyond any possible doubt. A curious logical predicament confronts the person who attempts to doubt the existence of his own soul; during the very act of doubting, he is in effect proving it.

For me to say: 'I doubt that I exist' begs the question: Who is doing the doubting? Obviously the doubter must exist to do any doubting whatever. At least, the doubting doubter must exist; since I am the doubter, then it follows that I must exist. Doubting is an aspect of thinking, and thinking is a phase of existence; therefore, to doubt is to think, and to think is to be.

The Cartesian *Cogito* appears to be most formidable; an opponent cannot even refute it with the argument: 'Perhaps I am being deceived;' since to this the resounding answer may be given: 'I cannot be deceived without first existing.' "Am I so dependent upon the body and the senses that without these I cannot exist? But I had the persuasion that there was no sky and no earth, neither minds nor bodies; was I not, therefore, at the same time, persuaded that I did not exist? Far from it; I assuredly existed, since I was persuaded. But there is I know not what being, who is possessed at once of the highest power and the deepest cunning, who is constantly employing all his ingenuity in deceiving me. Doubtless, then, I exist, since I am deceived; and, let him deceive me as he may, he can never bring it about that I am nothing, so long as I shall be conscious that I am something. So that it must, in fine, be maintained, all things being maturely and carefully considered, that this proposition (*pronunciatum*) I am, I exist, is necessarily true each time it is expressed by me, or conceived in my mind." [1]

Although a person can prove the existence of his own soul beyond all doubt, he cannot prove indubitably the existence of any other person's, nor can he prove with certainty the existence of anything else including the very room in which he presently finds himself. The inability to prove material objects with certainty, including one's own body, did not escape Descartes' attention; he made a determined attempt to prove (with certainty) the existence of his very body, but the attempt proved futile. The reason for a person's inability to prove the existence of a table which may be in front of him is that he can never completely eliminate the possibility (not probability) that it may be a hallucination or a dream. Realistic dreams are never verified as unreality until the sleeper awakens — even then, doubt is never completely removed. A war veteran, who has lost a leg in battle, is known at times to dream that his leg is intact, and some have even suffered hallucinations in which they fancy the leg never to have been severed. It should be emphasized that Descartes does not contend that he has proved the nonexistence of the table or leg, but that a person cannot prove with logical certainty its existence.

"Accordingly, seeing that our senses sometimes deceive us, I was willing to suppose that there existed nothing really such as they presented to us; and because some men err in reasoning. . . When I considered that the very same thoughts (presentations) which we experience when awake may also be experienced when we are asleep, while there is at that time not one of them true, I supposed that all the objects (presentations) that had ever entered into my mind when awake, had in them no more truth than the illusions of my dreams. But immediately upon this I observed that, whilst I thus wished to think that all was false, it was absolutely necessary that I, who thus thought, should be somewhat; and as I observed that this truth, *I*

[1] Unless otherwise noted, quotations in this section are from René Descartes, *Meditations on the First Philosophy*, tr. John Veitch (1902).

think hence I am, was so certain and of such evidence, that no ground of doubt, however extravagant, could be alleged by the skeptics capable of shaking it, I concluded that I might, without scruple, accept it as the first principle of the philosophy of which I was in search. . . And as I observed that in the words *I think, hence I am,* there is nothing at all which gives me assurance of their truth beyond this, that I see very clearly that in order to think it is necessary to exist."[1]

The Cartesian argument for the existence of the soul, and parenthetically it should be inserted here that for Descartes the soul and mind are synonymous terms, may be syllogistically formulated:

To doubt is to think
To think is to exist
Therefore, to doubt is to exist.

In other words, doubting is an aspect of thinking, and it is impossible not to exist while thinking.

The Cartesian *Cogito* has stimulated much discussion in philosophical circles, particularly in the immediate post-Cartesian era, and in the contemporary era among Phenomenalists and Existentialists who rest a considerable portion of their philosophy on this Cartesian premise.

Rationalism.

Note, in the above deliberations, how heavily dependent Descartes is on reason in preference to sense experience. In fact, a keen distrust of sense knowledge is most apparent; senses deceive, and are unreliable in reporting factual data accurately. "The philosophers of the schools accept as a maxim that there is nothing in the understanding which was not previously in the senses, in which however it is certain that the ideas of God and of the soul have never been; and it appears to me that they who make use of their imagination to comprehend these ideas do exactly the same thing as if, in order to hear sounds or smell odours, they strove to avail themselves of their eyes; unless indeed that there is this difference, that the sense of sight does not afford us an inferior assurance to those of smell or hearing; in place of which, neither our imagination nor our senses can give us assurance of anything unless our understanding intervene."[2] Without reason, sense knowledge is impossible; reason gives to sense its meaning.

Uncritical sense data is conflicting and requires reason to order it coherently; otherwise it remains an incoordinate meaningless jumble of facts, scientifically useless. "In fine, whether awake or asleep, we

[1] Descartes, *Discourse on Method,* tr. John Veitch (1902).
[2] *Discourse on Method.*

ought never to allow ourselves to be persuaded of the truth of anything unless on the evidence of our reason. And it must be noted that I say of our *reason,* and not of our imagination or of our senses: thus, for example, although we very clearly see the sun, we ought not therefore to determine that it is only of the size which our sense of sight presents; and we may very distinctly imagine the head of a lion joined to the body of a goat, without being therefore shut up to the conclusion that a chimera exists; for it is not a dictate of reason that what we thus see or imagine is in reality existent; but it plainly tells us that all our ideas of notions contain in them some truth." [1] Raw sense data devoid of reason issues in scientifically sterile results, a world akin to what brute animals experience.

For sense data to be reliable, it must be assimilated, ordered, classified, etc., that is, it must come under the scrutiny of reason; otherwise, dreams will be indistinguishable from reality, and mere appearances indistinguishable from true facts of reality. For example, "I am a man, and that, consequently, I am in the habit of sleeping, and representing to myself in dreams those same things, or even sometimes others less probable, which the insane think are presented to them in their waking moments. How often have I dreamt that I was in these familiar circumstances—that I was dressed, and occupied this place by the fire, when I was lying undressed in bed? At the present moment, however, I certainly look upon this paper with eyes wide awake; the head which I now move is not asleep; I extend this hand consciously and with express purpose, and I perceive it; the occurrences in sleep are not so distinct as all this. But I cannot forget that, at other times, I have been deceived in sleep by similar illusions; and, attentively considering those cases, I perceive so clearly that there exist no certain marks by which the state of waking can ever be distinguished from sleep, that I feel greatly astonished; and in amazement I almost persuade myself that I am now dreaming." Sensation *per se* is disqualified as reliable knowledge, independent of reason. Reason is the criterion of truth, and the sole criterion.

Descartes guided his life by four rules; it is interesting to note that the one which assumed a position of primacy was reason, his test of truth. Of the four rules, "the first was never to accept anything for true which I did not clearly know to be such; that is to say, carefully to avoid precipitancy and prejudice, and to comprise nothing more in my judgment than what was presented to my mind so clearly and distinctly as to exclude all ground of doubt." [2] Often, this, along with

[1] *Idem.*
[2] *Discourse on Method.*

what has been previously discussed, has been referred to as the Cartesian method of doubt, or Cartesian Skepticism.

Metaphysical Dualism of Mind and Matter.

Descartes envisioned reality as comprised of two distinct and independent substances: the world of mind and the world of matter. The mind or "soul is of a nature wholly independent of the body, and that consequently it is not liable to die with the latter; and, finally, because no other causes are observed capable of destroying it, we are naturally led thence to judge that it is immortal."[1] On the other hand, matter and body are mechanisms which function as any machine, and, as such, are subject to corruption and deterioration. Although these two worlds are mutually disparate, they nevertheless coexist in one universe. "The substance in which thought immediately resides is here called *mind* (*mens, esprit*). . . The substance which is the immediate subject of local extension, and of the accidents that presuppose this extension, as a figure, situation, local motion, etc., is called *body*. . . Two substances are said to be really distinct, when each of them may exist without the other. . . The mind and body are really distinct;"[2] each is substantially real.

Despite the fact that our senses without reason give us inadequate knowledge, objects of sense may be taken as reliable facts which truly exist, provided they are aided by reason, and given the premise that a good God exists. "Since God cannot deceive us, for this is repugnant to his nature . . . we must unhesitatingly conclude that there exists a certain object extended in length, breadth, and thickness, and possessing all those properties which we clearly apprehend to belong to what is extended. And this extended substance is what we call body or matter."[3]

From the principle: 'I think, therefore I am,' it was established with logical certainty that mind or soul exists, but an equivalent certitude is lacking in the realm of matter. Belief in matter is predicated on assumed premises. If matter exists, it is, at best, an assumption; "I cannot obtain a certain proof of the existence of corporeal objects. . . If it is true that there are bodies, and because I find no other obvious mode of explaining it, I thence, with probability, conjecture that they exist, but only with probability; and although I carefully examine all things, nevertheless I do not find that, from the distinct idea of corporeal

[1] *Discourse on Method.*

[2] Descartes, *Reasons which Establish the Existence of God, and the Distinction between the Mind and Body of Man, Disposed in Geometrical Order,* tr. John Veitch.

[3] Descartes, *The Principles of Philosophy,* tr. John Veitch.

nature I have in my imagination, I can necessarily infer the existence of any body."

The reason that matter or corporeal substance is incapable of logical certainty lies in its inscrutable nature, that is, other than knowing it possesses three dimensions or, as Descartes refers to it, extension, there is actually nothing permanent which may be predicated of matter. Spiritual substance, mind, is nondimensional, or unextended, but space is a form of matter. "Space or internal place, and the corporeal substance which is comprised in it, are not different in reality but merely in the mode in which they are wont to be conceived by us. Nothing remains in the idea of body, except that it is something extended in length, breadth, and depth; and this something is comprised in our idea of space, not only of that which is full of body, but even of what is called void space." Since time, unlike space, lacks customary spatial extension, it poses a serious problem; its reality is inexplicable. Time, if it is to be regarded as real duration, and not merely an illusion, must be postulated on the basis of God's existence; in other words, it must be explained as a miraculous act of God.

Descartes' wrestling with the problem of the existence and nature of matter is beautifully portrayed in his analysis of a particular piece of wax. Read the fascinating explication in his own words:

> Take, for example, this piece of wax; it is quite fresh, having been but recently taken from the beehive; it has not yet lost the sweetness of the honey it contained; it still retains somewhat of the odour of the flowers from which it was gathered; its colour, figure, size, are apparent (to the sight); it is hard, cold, easily handled; and sounds when struck upon with the finger. In fine, all that contributes to make a body as distinctly known as possible, is found in the one before us. But, while I am speaking, let it be placed near the fire – what remained of the taste exhales, the smell evaporates, the colour changes, its figure is destroyed, its size increases, it becomes liquid, it grows hot, it can hardly be handled, and, although struck upon, it emits no sound. Does the same wax still remain after this change? It must be admitted that it does remain; no one doubts it, or judges otherwise. What, then, was it I knew with so much distinctness in the piece of wax? Assuredly, it could be nothing of all that I observed by means of the senses, since all the things that fell under taste, smell, sight, touch, and hearing are changed, and yet the same wax remains. It was perhaps what I now think, viz., that this wax was neither the sweetness of honey, the pleasant odour of flowers, the whiteness, the figure, nor the sound, but only a body that a little before appeared to me conspicuous under these forms, and which is now perceived under others. But, to speak precisely, what is it that I imagine when I think of it in this way? Let it be attentively considered, and, retrenching all that does not belong to the wax, let us see what remains. There certainly

remains nothing, except something extended, flexible, and moveable. But what is meant by flexible and moveable? Is it not that I imagine that the piece of wax, being round, is capable of becoming square, or of passing from a square into a triangular figure? Assuredly such is not the case, because I conceive that it admits of an infinity of similar changes; and I am, moreover, unable to compass this infinity by imagination, and consequently this conception which I have of the wax is not the product of the faculty of imagination. But what is this extension? Is it not also unknown? for it becomes greater when the wax is melted, greater when it is boiled, and greater still when the heat increases; and I should not conceive [clearly and] according to truth, the wax as it is, if I did not suppose that the piece we are considering admitted even of a wider variety of extension than I ever imagined. I must, therefore, admit that I cannot even comprehend by imagination what the piece of wax is, and that it is the mind alone (*mens*, Lat., *entendement*, F.) which perceives it. I speak of one piece in particular; for, as to wax in general, this is still more evident. But what is this piece of wax that can be perceived only by the [understanding of] mind? It is certainly the same which, from the beginning, I believed it to be. But (and this it is of moment to observe) the perception of it is neither an act of sight, of touch, nor of imagination, and never was either of these, though it might formerly seem so, but is simply an intuition (*inspectio*) of the mind, which may be imperfect and confused, as it formerly was, or very clear and distinct, as it is at present, according as the attention is more or less directed to the elements which it contains, and of which it is composed.

Note the Cartesian claim that, ultimately, all that may be said of the material piece of wax is that it is extended, not that it has a particular essence which is depictable. Furthermore, the wax's material essence is the same as that found in any other material object, sensuously unknowable. Note also, that the matter of which one object is composed, such as a living flower, is the same material substance found in any other object, such as nonliving stone.

The Mind-Body Problem.

Two serious questions emerge as a result of the Cartesian analysis of wax which philosophers have never been able to resolve even to the present day: What is the nature of matter—if such there be? If matter and mind, corporeal substance and spiritual substance, are ultimately distinct and disparate entities, made wholly of different substances, how is it possible that they interact at all? The fact that they do interact is undeniable, for instances of interaction of a person's mind and body take place many times daily, but no philosopher or scientist, dead or alive, has been able to explain wherein, or at what point in the human being, the interaction occurs. One need merely look about him to observe first hand the interaction of mind with body:

alcoholic intoxication obviously affects the mental state of a person; on the other hand, worry causes physical damage to the body, such as, ulcers, high blood pressure, etc.

Precisely where the two connect, no one knows. Descartes postulated the nexus to be localized in the pineal gland, a region of the brain; he made a fair guess, since a number of psychologists speculate that the area of interaction possibly may be found in the endocrine gland system. Some contemporary medics do not consider the pineal even to be a gland. The pineal is found in all craniate vertebrates, and, in ancestral forms, has served as a sense organ; for example, in certain reptiles it assumes the structure of an eye.

The followers of Descartes, *Arnold Geulincx* (1625–1669) and *Nicole Malebranche* (1638–1715), called *Occasionalists,* believed the interaction of body and mind to be a miracle, and fancied that each specific 'occasion' of interaction required a special act of God, hence the appellation, *Occasionalism.*

One school of thought, particularly Metaphysical Materialists, subscribes to *Epiphenomenalism,* the doctrine that body alone is ultimately real, mind being merely its by-product, dependent upon and perishing with the destruction of the body. A second school of thought, including the Cartesian, maintains that mind is independent of the body, eternal and indestructible; consequently survives to immortality at the death of the body. Later, we shall encounter still another school of thought, the Berkeleyan, which contends that matter does not exist, only mind or spirit does; matter being the gross assumption of a Naive Realist. A fourth school of thought, in order to escape the problem of interaction, postulates that mind-body are identical substances, a single organism, not two distinct entities. Descartes is to be followed by a member of this fourth school, Spinoza, a Metaphysical Monist, who will contend that a substance which is neither mind not matter, but possesses attributes of both, ultimately exists.

XXV

SPINOZA:

A Metaphysical Monist

Descartes' passion for absolute certainty resulted in the development of a method which would produce definitive conclusions; this hopeful achievement he sought to realize through the only instrument he knew capable of yielding certitude, namely, mathematics. But the task of implementing the geometric method remained for Benedict Spinoza, his contemporary Rationalist, who admired the ingenious method, and applied it to philosophy to a degree excelling that of any other philosopher, including Descartes himself. For example, Spinoza's classic treatise, *The Ethics,* reads almost like a mathematical work, opening with precise definitions, followed by axioms, propositions, corollaries, and leading to proofs terminating with Q. E. D. He writes: "I will, therefore, write about human beings, as though I were concerned with lines, and planes, and solids."

Spinoza, a controversial figure and a Jew by birth, was called by a variety of epithets which ran the entire gamut from a 'God intoxicated man' (*ein Gottbetrunkener Mensch*) by Novalis, to an 'Atheist' whose books were placed on the index of the Roman Catholic Church. His devout religious phrases resound as those of a devoted Christian; for example, he regards Christ as 'the mouthpiece of God.' "Christ was sent to teach the whole human race," he writes; and speaks of the Bible as 'the Word of God.' Renan, at the dedication of Spinoza's statue at the Hague, said: "The truest vision ever had of God came, perhaps, here." Despite these lofty eulogies, he was excommunicated from the Synagogue, and an assassination attempt made on his life. Subsequent to his excommunication from the Jewish community, he changed his name from Baruch (the Hebrew word for blessed) to Benedictus de Spinoza, its Latin equivalent, feeling that he could be equally blessed in Latin as in Hebrew.

Metaphysical Monism.

Spinoza's philosophy is an integrated system which fuses philosophy of religion, ethics, and metaphysics into an organic whole; for example, his concept of God is so inextricably woven into his theory of ultimate reality that it becomes impossible not only to sever the two, but to attempt to understand one without the other. Ultimate reality is composed of a single substance, namely, God; the remainder of reality consists merely of the attributes and modifications of Substance (God); hence, reality is God, and God is reality, a doctrine philosophers designate *Pantheism*. He defines each: "By Substance, I mean that which is in itself, and is conceived through itself: in other words, that of which a conception can be formed independently of any other conception . . . By God, I mean a being absolutely infinite — that is, a Substance consisting in infinite attributes, of which each expresses eternal and infinite essentiality."[1]

Substance, God, has an infinite number of attributes, though we are cognizant of only two; mind and matter, thought and extension. Note that Spinoza considers mind and matter, not independent ultimate reality, which belongs to Substance alone, but attributes of Substance. "Substance thinking and Substance extended are one and the same Substance." For Descartes, a Metaphysical Dualist, mind and matter constitute two independent ultimate realities. Since Spinoza designates Substance, or which is the same thing, God, as the sole ultimate reality, he therefore is classified a Metaphysical Monist, one who believes that ultimate reality consists of a single entity. "There is but one Substance in the universe, and . . . it is absolutely infinite." Because Spinoza claims that we know only two of the infinite number of attributes which Substance possesses, he becomes a Skeptic to the degree of 'infinity minus two.' Beyond thought and extension, the infinite number of other attributes remains an eternal mystery.

Inasmuch as Spinoza is a Pantheist, one who believes all that exists is God and God is all that exists, he encounters little or no difficulty proving the existence of God with finality. He merely raises the question: Does anything exist? and expects an affirmative reply to which he may respond: That is God. God exists by definition. "The existence of God and his essence are one and the same . . . God is Substance, which necessarily exists, that is, existence appertains to its nature, or follows from its definition." Furthermore, he writes: "God, or Substance, consisting of infinite attributes, of which each expresses eternal and infinite

[1] Quotations which follow, in this section, are from Spinoza, *The Ethics*, tr. R. H. M. Elwes (1883).

essentiality, necessarily exists . . . If this be denied, conceive, if possible, that God does not exist: then his essence does not involve existence. But this is absurd. Therefore God necessarily exists." Only if you can conceive of substance, ultimate reality, not existing, can you deny the existence of God.

Psychophysical Parallelism.

The doctrine that for every mental change there is a corresponding physical one, and vice versa, is termed 'psychophysical parallelism.' Since Spinoza maintains that body and mind, thought and extension, are but attributes of a single substance, whatever change occurs in Substance is accompanied by a corresponding variation in both mind and matter. The analogy of a sheet of paper may be used to explain this concept by designating one side *mind,* and the other, *matter;* whatever happens to the sheet itself concomitantly affects each side. Changes occurring in Substance have concomitant effects on thought and extension; accordingly, whatever change occurs in mind has its corresponding modification in body, and vice versa, because "the order and connection of ideas is the same as the order and connection of things . . . A mode of extension and the idea of that mode are one and the same thing, though expressed in two ways . . . Whether we conceive nature under the attribute of extension, or under the attribute of thought, or under any other attribute, we shall find the same order, or one and the same chain of causes – that is, the same things following in either case."

It will be recalled that Descartes' attempted solution of the mind-body problem was by a principle of interaction, the nexus of which was the pineal gland. Extreme as this explanation is, it was better than none whatever; perhaps he was driven to it by the fact that the human mind appears to eschew dualistic concepts. Spinoza's resolution of the problem was effected through his 'doctrine of psychophysical parallelism.' Subsequently, the opportunity of considering Leibniz' contribution to the solution of this persistent philosophical problem, namely, the 'doctrine of pre-established harmony,' will be discussed.

Sub Specie Aeternitatis (Under the Aspect of the Eternal).

Inasmuch as truth, by definition, is a relationship to the eternal, it must be viewed in this aspect. Since all reality ultimately is Substance, then all truth ultimately must relate or correspond to Substance. Reality is an integrated whole; accordingly truth must be a coherent whole corresponding to reality. To obtain the meaning, import, or truth of an idea, it is necessary to pinpoint its relationship to the absolute whole, God or

Substance. "It is in the nature of reason to perceive things under a certain form of eternity (*sub quâdam aeternitatis specie*). . . It is in the nature of reason to regard things, not as contingent, but as necessary. Reason perceives the necessity of things truly — that is, of a thing as it is in itself. But this necessity of things is the very necessity of the eternal nature of God; therefore, it is in the nature of reason to regard things under this form of eternity. We may add that the bases of reason are the notions which answer to things common to all, and which do not answer to the essence of any particular thing: which must therefore be conceived without any relation to time, under a certain form of eternity."

One application of this principle pertains to distinguishing the relative importance of matters by querying as to whether a matter which seems important at the moment will be equally important ten years hence. If the answer is in the affirmative, then an important issue is definitely under consideration, otherwise the question is relatively minor. For example, a person distressed by an insulting remark should simply ask, What significance will this incident have in a dozen years or so? If little or none, then the matter cannot be regarded as of major import. The closer an idea is to the eternal, the greater its truth and importance. The task is merely to locate its relative position of importance. "Every idea of everybody, or of every particular thing actually existing, necessarily involves the eternal and infinite essence of God."

The Problem of Evil and Free Will.

An implication of Metaphysical Monism, at least that form predicating a good God as its ultimate Substance, is the absence of evil. If all that exists is God, then to postulate the presence of evil is to designate God as evil; consequently, evil is nonexistent, except as ignorance, in the Spinozistic philosophical system. Ultimately, the world being good, evil is that ignorance which hampers an individual from viewing the objective world in its proper perspective. Evil is misunderstanding, a distortion of reality, the viewing of a fact out of its proper relationship to the eternal. It is analogous to a piece of a large 'jig-saw' picture puzzle which is out of place, and whose position in the whole remains an indeterminate mystery, and subjectively appears not as belonging to the picture puzzle at all. Accordingly, evil is perplexity, confusion, ignorance, misunderstanding, etc., since it is a concept repugnant to and discordant with that of a good and perfect God. "Each particular thing perseveres in existing follows from the eternal necessity of God's nature. . . The knowledge of the eternal and infinite essence of God which every idea involves is adequate and perfect. . . Wherefore, that, which gives knowledge of the eternal and infinite essence of God is common to all, and is equally in the part and in the whole. Falsity consists in the privation of knowledge, which inadequate, fragmentary, or confused ideas involve." If it were possible to understand the world with an omniscient mind such as God's, with every fact in its proper relationship to the whole, then evil would be nonexistent.

The absence of evil, or at least its reduction to a state of ignorance, removes the necessity of *free will.* Spinoza repudiates the 'doctrine of the freedom of the will;' in this regard, he assumes a Socratic position, namely, if anyone knows what is right then he will automatically do it. Will is synonymous with understanding; to understand the right is to choose it. "In the mind there is no absolute or free will; but the mind is determined to wish this or that by a cause, which has also been determined by another cause, and this last by another cause, and so on to infinity." If one had enough facts in hand, he could predict what a person would do even ten years hence. "Will and understanding are nothing beyond the individual volitions and ideas. . . A particular volition and a particular idea are one and the same; therefore, will and understanding are one and the same."

Under the Spinozistic ethical system, moral salvation is achieved through 'the intellectual love of God,' understanding and embracing the will of God, or which amounts to the same thing, understanding the laws of your nature and obeying them. "The mind's highest good is the knowledge of God, and the mind's highest virtue is to know God... The mind's highest virtue is therefore to understand. . . The highest that the mind can understand is God; therefore the highest virtue of the mind is to understand or to know God. Q.E.D."

Contrary to Aristotle and others who conclude that happiness is the culmination or reward for virtue, Spinoza maintains a position not too distant from the belief that 'virtue is its own reward.' He asserts: "Blessedness is not the reward of virtue, but virtue itself; neither do we rejoice therein, because we control our lusts, but contrariwise, because we rejoice therein, we are able to control our lusts. . . Blessedness consists in love toward God. . . In proportion as the mind rejoices more in this divine love or blessedness, so does it the more understand; that is, so much the more power has it over the emotions, and so much the less is it subject to those emotions which are evil; therefore, in proportion as the mind rejoices in this divine love or blessedness, so has it the power of controlling lusts. And, since human power in controlling the emotions consists solely in the understanding, it follows that no one rejoices in blessedness, because he has controlled his lusts, but, contrariwise, his power of controlling his lusts arises from this blessedness itself. Q.E.D."

Thus Spinoza concludes his monumental and posthumous publication, *The Ethics,* a treatise which this pietistic, saintly, misunderstood, and abused mystic left without a motto, but if he had penned one, it would probably have read similarly to the one which his *Tractatus Theologico-Politicus* bore: "Hereby know we that we dwell in him and he in us because he hath given us of his spirit." (I John 4:13).

XXVI

LEIBNIZ:

A Metaphysical Pluralist

Gottfried Wilhelm Freiherr von Leibniz, the third member of this majestic triad of Rationalists, appeared on the scene when Descartes was fifty years of age, and Spinoza but a youth of fourteen. Interesting comparisons may be drawn regarding these three: the first, Descartes, a French Roman Catholic; the second, Spinoza, a Dutch Jew; and the third, Leibniz, a German Protestant; each with a strong bent toward Rationalism, mathematics, and logic. Descartes discovered analytic geometry; Leibniz, symbolic or mathematical logic, and with Newton, the differential calculus. A deep interest in theology led Spinoza to a discovery of a new method of understanding the Bible and historical documents called 'higher criticism.' None of them were, what Schopenhauer disparagingly termed, 'philosophers by trade,' that is, professors of philosophy. Leibniz, a man of varied interests, wrote in more fields than any other up to his time, with the possible exception of Aristotle; to the chagrin of many philosophers, much of his manuscript material to date has not been published.

Metaphysical Pluralism (Monads).

Spinoza's Monism stemmed from his position of Substance as the sole ultimate reality, Cartesian Dualism from the belief that substance was comprised of two distinct and independent entities, while Leibnizian Pluralism was grounded in the belief that ultimate reality is a substance consisting of a multiplicity of *Monads,* a precursory concept to the modern atom. Each Monad is individually distinct, with no two identical; they are simple, hence indivisible; and eternal in the sense that once created they remain forever, unless annihilated. The Monad "is merely a simple substance entering into those which are compound; simple, that is to say, without parts. . . Where there are no parts, neither extension nor figure, nor divisibility is possible; and these

Monads are the veritable atoms of nature and, in a word, the elements of things. There is thus no danger of dissolution, and there is no conceivable way in which a simple substance can begin naturally, since it could not be formed by composition. Therefore we may say that the Monads can neither begin nor end in any way other than all at once; that is to say, they cannot begin except by creation, nor end except by annihilation; whereas that which is compounded, begins and ends by parts. There is no intelligible way in which a Monad can be altered or changed in its interior by any other created thing." [1]

These ultimately real entities, termed Monads, possess individual, conscious, active, alive, inner natures; although lacking spatial shape, each contains a thought life. They are ordered in a graded series from the lower, which constitute matter, to the higher, mind, soul, or spiritual substance. The Monads are said to have no windows, yet each mirrors the rest; "each, accordingly, is a living and perpetual mirror of the universe." Their inner reality is actiivitiy; for them, *esse* is *agere* (to be is to act); in other words, matter is essentially force or activity. "Moreover, each Monad must differ from every other, for there are never two beings in nature perfectly alike, and in which it is impossible to find an internal difference. . . I assume, therefore, that every created being, and consequently the created Monad, is subject to change; and likewise that this change is continual in each. It follows from what we have now said, that the natural changes of Monads proceed from an internal principle, since no external cause can influence their interior." The Leibnizian Monad is comparatively closer to contemporary ideas of the atom than is the traditional Hellenic concept.

The Mind-Body Problem and the Doctrine of Preëstablished Harmony.

Leibniz' unique approach to the problem of interaction between mind and body entails his 'principle of preëstablished harmony,' a doctrine which seeks to explain interaction as an apparent phenomenon, rather than a genuine reality. Although each Monad is blind to what every other Monad is doing, by perfect obedience to its internal nature, by functioning according to the laws of its own prescribed nature, a seeming, but not real, interaction occurs.

In the case of a human being, the soul behaves as a mind should, and a body is true to its principles or nature, with the concomitant effect that the two harmonize in their independent activities as if each knew the behavior of the other, or were connected to the other. "The soul follows its proper laws, and the body likewise follows those which

[1] Except where indicated, quotations in the section on Leibniz are from his *Monadology*, tr. Frederic Henry Hedge (1884).

are proper to it, and they meet in virtue of the preëstablished harmony which exists between all substances, as representations of one and the same universe. Souls act according to the laws of final causes, by appetitions, means and ends; bodies act according to the laws of efficient causes, or the laws of motion. And the two kingdoms, that of efficient causes and that of final causes, are in harmony with one another. . . According to this system, bodies act as if there were no souls, and souls act as if there were no bodies; and yet both act as though the one influenced the other." Hence, interaction is merely a phenomenal manifestation, not a reality.

Leibniz illustrates this principle by the figure of two perfectly constructed clocks which are synchronized and set in motion simultaneously. The two mark time as if one clock were conscious of the behavior of the second, and guiding its actions accordingly; but in truth, neither is cognizant of the activity of the other, and as each behaves according to its own pre-arranged mechanism, it appears as if they conspired in a cooperative activity. "Now substitute the *soul* and *body* for these two time-pieces . . . From the beginning God has made each of these two Substances of such a nature that each by following its own laws, given to it with its being, still agrees with the other, just as though there were a mutual influence or as though God always took a hand in it beyond his general supervision of things."[1] To believe in interaction is to read into nature that which is absent.

Leibniz is satisfied that no one has better established the mutual independence of mind and body than he. "Descartes recognized that souls communicate no force to bodies, because the quantity of force in matter is always the same. Nevertheless, he believed that souls might change the direction of bodies. But this was because the world was at that time ignorant of the law of nature, which requires the conservation of the same total direction in matter. Had he known this, he would have hit upon my system of preëstablished harmony." Of the three Rationalists, only Descartes believed in a genuine interaction of mind and body.

The Best of All Possible Worlds.

The optimistic Leibniz maintained that the world in which we live, inasmuch as it was created by God who has the power, choice, and goodness to create, was created the best of all possible worlds. Since God is in control, then all must be right with the world. "In the ideas

[1] Leibniz, "Second Explanation of the System of the Communication of Substances, in Philip P. Weiner, Ed. *Leibniz Selections* (New York: Charles Scribner's Sons, 1951), 119.

of God there is an infinity of possible worlds, and as only one can exist, there must be sufficient reason for the choice of God, which determines Him to decide upon one rather than another. And this reason can be no other than *fitness,* derived from the different degrees of perfection which these worlds contain, since each possible world has a claim to exist according to the measure of perfection which it enfolds. And this is the cause of the existence of that Best, which the wisdom of God discerns, his goodness chooses, and his power effects. . . And this is the way to obtain the greatest possible variety, along with the greatest possible order; that is to say, it is the way to obtain the greatest possible perfection." A God, perfect in goodness and wisdom, is our guarantee that this is the best of all possible worlds.

Leibniz is cognizant of the objection of those persons who argue that since the world contains evil, its creator must be lacking perfection in either power, knowledge, or goodness. Although Leibniz grants the fact of the presence of evil in this world of God's construction, he notes that it was possible for God to create a world in which evil is entirely absent, or for that matter, he could have chosen not to create any world whatever, but the fact that his wisdom designed this one, his will selected it, and his power decreed it, indicates that it is the best of all possible worlds.

Perhaps a better or more accurate word than 'possible' is 'compossible,' for what Leibniz had in mind is: the present world is the best possible considering all of the 'ingredients' which must necessarily be used in the making of it. For example, God could have withheld freedom of will from man, thereby preventing his committing evil, but the result would be a universe of an inferior grade to that of the present; or God could have created man devoid of intelligence enabling man to be free from worry, doubts, problems, etc., but the consequence would be a world grossly inferior in value to the one in which we now live. The world, as it stands, testifies to the greater glory of God than one lacking intelligence, will, morality, etc., but the inherent cost of it is suffering, wickedness, etc., which are usually designated evil. To desire the lesser world, the one without evil, thereby tolerating its concomitants: the absence of intelligence, free will, moral stature, etc., is to rebel against being a man. "The best plan is not always that which seeks to avoid evil, since it may happen that *the evil is accompanied by a greater good.* . . An imperfection in the whole. . . God has permitted evil in order to bring about good, that is, a greater good."[1] Leibniz illustrates this point by an army general who, in preference to no victory

[1] Leibniz, *The Theodicy,* in *Leibniz Selections, op. cit.,* 510.

and no casualties, would choose a great victory at minimal cost. Leibniz concludes his defence with: "This universe must be in reality better than every other possible universe."

The City of God.

Taking his cue from St. Augustine, Leibniz speaks of a 'City of God' comprising two worlds within one, and of which every human being is a member, with God its supreme head. The first world is a kingdom of minds (persons), the second a kingdom of nature (things); of the first God is monarch, of the second, its architect. "The assembly of spirits must constitute the City of God, that is to say, the most perfect state that is possible, under the most perfect of monarchs. This City of God, this truly universal monarchy, is a moral world within the natural; and it is the most exalted and the most divine among the works of God. It is in this that the glory of God most truly consists, for it would be wanting if his greatness and his goodness were not recognized and admired by spirits. It is in relation to this Divine City that he possesses, properly speaking, the attribute of goodness, whereas his wisdom and his power are everywhere manifest. As we have above established a perfect harmony between the two natural kingdoms, – the one of efficient, the other of final causes, – it behooves us to notice here also still another harmony between the physical kingdom of nature and the moral kingdom of grace, that is to say, between God considered as the architect of the mechanism (*machine*) of the universe, and God considered as monarch of the divine City of Spirits." God's functions are dual: that of creator, and designer, on the one hand; and the duty of governing, on the other.

In such a world, natural laws subserve moral ends; for example, by natural methods "there will be no good deed without its recompense, and no evil without its punishment. . . Sins must carry their punishment with them in the order of nature . . . and that good deeds in like manner will bring their recompense, through their connection with bodies, although this cannot, and ought not always to happen immediately." Through moral excellence, which should be the aim of every person, the blessed life is found.

Necessary Truths and Innate Ideas.

Immanuel Kant, through the great systematizer of Leibniz, *Christian Wolff* (1679–1754), came under considerable influence of the Leibnizian philosophy, particularly the ideas found in the *New Essays* which attacked the Empiricism of Locke and defended the Rationalism of Descartes. Leibniz argued that innate ideas must exist in some a priori form, otherwise, animals, which have the same organs of sense as man does, would have some semblance of science, but scientific knowledge is conspicuously absent in the animal kingdom. On the basis of Leibnizian 'necessary truths' (universals), Kant constructed his 'transcendental method.' Leibniz contended the existence of "two kinds of *truth,* – those of reasoning and those of fact. Truths of reasoning are necessary, and their opposite is impossible; those of fact are contingent, and their opposite is possible. When a truth is necessary, we may discover the reason of it by analysis, resolving it into simpler ideas and truths, until we arrive at those which are primitive (*primitifs*). It is thus that mathematicians by analysis reduce speculative *theorems* and practical *canons* to *definitions, axioms,* and *postulates.*" The Cartesian 'innate ideas' or innate knowledge essentially were necessary logical principles utterly devoid in the animal kingdom. If a person is predisposed to challenge this contention, then let him attempt to instruct an animal in the principles of logic or algebra, and discover the impossibility for himself. Aristotle, Locke, and others who fancy minds or souls to be "blank tablets prepared for writings," and that "nothing is in the understanding which does not come through the senses," have omitted an important factor relating to knowledge, namely the *mind* itself. The dictum should be altered to read: "There is nothing in the understanding which was not previously in the senses, except the understanding itself" (*Nihil est in intellectu quod non fuerit in sensu, excipe, nisi ipse intellectus*).

Concluding Comments.

Leibnizian philosophy has unquestionably made its impact upon contemporary science, logic, and philosophy: From the groundwork laid in symbolic logic, mathematical logic grew; the modern concept of the atom, as distinguished from that of the Greek philosophers, Democritus and Leucippus who originated the term, found its precursor in the Leibnizian Monad.

Scientific presuppositions, such as, *natura non facit saltum* (nature makes no leap), there are no gaps in nature, there are no big or sudden changes in nature, emanate or are emphasized by him. The significance of this principle is penetrating; for example, a car does not gain full speed abruptly nor does it stop suddenly, even if it were to smash into a steel or cement wall. The fact that it is demolished testifies to the truth of the principle under consideration; for if it did stop suddenly, no impact or damage would be experienced. The Leibnizian *principle of sufficient reason* removes all mystery from the universe for it claims that whatever exists or occurs in the world must possess adequate ground or reason for its nature or behavior. Since God had good and sufficient reason for whatever he created, nature cannot possess inscrutable mysteries.

Among contemporary philosophers, Leibnizian ideas have inspired Bertrand Russell in his efforts in the area of symbolic logic which culminated in *Principia Mathematica,* the now classical work accomplished in collaboration with Alfred North Whitehead. Whitehead also was inspired by Leibniz as were all of the adherents of the *Panpsychist* school of philosophy.

The difficulty regarding Leibniz's *Theodicy* (which incidentally means the justification of the ways of God to man, a vindication of God's justice in permitting the existence of evil) is that it reduces much of the contents of the universe to necessary evils. Although this may be 'the best of all possible worlds,' "everything in it is a necessary evil" remarked *Francis Herbert Bradley* (1846–1924), the British philosopher. Be that as it may, the *Theodicy* is a fine piece of apologetics which has earned its place among the classics.

XXVII

LOCKE:

A Metaphysical Agnostic

John Locke, the first of the great British Empiricists, with the possible exception of *Francis Bacon* (1561-1620) and *Thomas Hobbes* (1588-1679), leads the antithethical attack against the philosophical giants on the continent of Europe, the Rationalists. What the British philosophers had to say was in direct antithesis to the thinking of the philosophers across the British Channel, namely, that no ideas are innate, all knowledge is derived from experience.

The Mind — A Tabula Rasa (Blank Tablet).

The attack against the Cartesian *innate ideas,* knowledge at birth, was led by Locke, who went to great length to amass considerable data in support of his stand. Locke's thesis, the mind at birth is a *tabula rasa,* a blank tablet which records facts as they are experienced, is predicated on the dictum: 'There is nothing in the mind which was not previously in the senses.'

Locke was adamant in his stand that the mind was a blank tablet, a *white paper,* that permanently records data which are fed to it through the senses. Of the four books comprising his *Essay Concerning the Human Understanding,* one is entirely devoted to attacking innate ideas. Although he uses the figure of a 'white paper' to illustrate the nature of the mind, perhaps a better metaphor, one which was unavailable to him in his day, is that of light-sensitive photographic film which records by the instrument of the camera (representing the organ of sight) the world within its range of view. Consequently, the principles which Decartes claimed were innate in children, Locke contended were indoctrinations during early childhood. "How really it may come to pass, that doctrines that have been derived from no better original than the superstitions of a nurse, or the authority of an old woman, may, by length of time and consent of neighbours, grow up to the dignity of *principles* in religion or morality. For such, who are careful (as they call it) to principle children well, (and few there be who have not a set of those principles for them, which they believe in,) instil into the unwary, and as yet unprejudiced, understanding, (for white paper receives any characters,) those doctrines they would have them retain and profess. These being taught them as soon as they have any apprehension." [1] Hence, Locke reduces principles, innate ideas, to the ignorance, gullibility, and indoctrination of childhood.

The Cartesian "primary notions, *koinai ennoiai,*[2] characters, as it were, stamped upon the mind of man, which the soul receives in its very first being, and brings into the world with it," do not exist, argues Locke, for the following reasons:

1. Universal consent proves nothing innate.
2. Principles of faith and justice are not universally agreed upon.
3. Moral rules need a proof, *ergo* not innate.
4. They are not naturally imprinted on the mind because they are not known to children, idiots, etc.
5. It is false that reason discovers them. Even if reason discovered them, that would not prove them innate.
6. Those who maintain innate principles fail to tell us what they are.

Having disproved innate knowledge to his own satisfaction, Locke proceeds to explain the presence of principles in the human mind in terms of sensation, reflection, and experience. "Let us suppose the mind to be, as we say, white paper, void of all characters, without any ideas: How comes it to be furnished? Whence comes it by that store, which the busy and boundless fancy of man has painted on it with an almost endless variety? Whence has it all the materials of reason and knowledge? To this I answer, in a word, from *experience.* In that all our knowledge is founded; and from that it ultimately derives itself. Our observation employed either about external objects or about the internal operations of our minds perceived and reflected on by ourselves is that which supplies our understandings with all the *materials* of thinking. These two are the fountains of knowledge, from whence all the ideas we have, or can have, do spring." Without experience, knowledge is impossible.

The term 'experience' as employed by Locke suffers from ambiguity; actually 'innateness' and 'experience' are not necessarily contradictory, provided experience is not rendered merely as 'sense.' It was not until the concept of experience is examined in the treatment of Kant that the two are identified as compatible ideas.

[1] Quotations in this section are from John Locke, *Essay Concerning the Human Understanding* (1690).

[2] Locke used the Greek alphabetical characters; they have been transliterated for the benefit of English readers.

The 'doctrine of the *tabula rasa*' had wide reaching implications, and was met with ready acceptance in Locke's community. Its implications, that a man's personality is nothing more than the collection and association of ideas which were gathered from a lifetime of experience, meant that society could construct any type of personality it desired, simply by regulating the experiential environment to which a person is to be exposed. This optimistic doctrine was enthusiastically received by church, civic, and school authorities in the belief that they could establish a society free from immorality and crime, merely by guiding childhood experience. If the doctrine did not eventually fall into complete disrepute, it was proved invalid as is evidenced by the fact that two persons in the same envirnoment, even in the same family, develop different, if not opposite personalties. These Lockean conclusions have been implemented into Association Psychology, a school of thought which is yet in existence.

Metaphysical Agnosticism.

Experience, the source of all knowledge, entails two mental operations: (1) sensations and (2) reflections. "First, our senses, conversant about particular sensible objects, do convey into the mind several distinct perceptions of things, according to those various ways wherein those objects do affect them. And thus we come by those *ideas* we have of *yellow, white, heat, cold, soft, hard, bitter, sweet,* and all those which we call sensible qualities; which when I say the senses convey into the mind, I mean, they from external objects convey into the mind what produces there those perceptions. This great source of most of the ideas we have, depending wholly upon our senses, and derived by them to the understanding, I call *sensation.*" The foregoing use of 'perception' and 'idea' are practically synonymous; 'external object' and 'sensible quality' are correlative terms, the former pertains to the nonpsychological, whereas the latter refers to psychological sensations, purely mental in nature.

"Secondly, the other fountain from which experience furnishes the understanding with ideas is, – the perception of the operations of our own mind within us, as it is employed about the ideas it has got; – which operations, when the soul comes to reflect on and consider, do furnish the understanding with another set of ideas, which could not be had from things without. And such are *perception, thinking, doubting, believing, reasoning, knowing, willing,* and all the different actings of our own mind. The source of ideas every man has wholly in himself; and though it be not sense, as having nothing to do with external objects, yet it is very like it, and might properly enough be called *internal sense.*" This 'internal sense' is what is often referred to by some persons, including philosophers, as 'common sense' or reason, the only sense which we, as human beings, have in common. All other sensation is private; accordingly it does not permit of an exchange of experiences. Knowledge of the 'material world' is gained by sensations through the appropriate sense organ; knowledge of the 'internal world' is derived from thought; beyond these two avenues of knowledge, no other remains. "*External objects* furnish the mind with the ideas of sensible qualities, which are all those different perceptions they produce in us; and *the mind* furnishes the understanding with ideas of its own operations. . . We have nothing in our minds which did not come in one of these two ways." By implication, a person handicapped in one or more organs of sense, is limited in both knowledge and personality development.

Contrary to the opinion of a number of persons, Locke maintains that souls, as well as bodies, exist. Just as the chief characteristic of the body is 'extension,' the distinctive quality of the soul is 'its ideas;' consequently, the soul remains a blank tablet until it receives perceptions. "To ask at what *time* a man has ideas, is to ask, when he begins to perceive; — *having ideas*, and *perception*, being the same thing." The soul does not always think, the soul of a child cannot think until it has acquired a sufficient number of ideas to think about, relate, associate; furthermore, ideas emanate from sensations. "For, by this account, soul and its ideas, as body and its extension, will begin to exist at the same time. . . If a child were kept in a place where he never saw any other but black and white till he were a man, he would have no more ideas of scarlet or green than he that from his childhood never tasted an oyster or a pineapple has of those particular relishes." Ideas are not conveyed by reason, but are the objects of experience.

Two varieties of *ideas* are distinguishable: (1) simple and (2) complex. *Simple ideas* are perceptions which are unanalyzable; they do not 'hang in the air alone,' but are related to specific actual experiences, and as such are concrete; whereas *complex ideas* are abstractions and are 'made by us' with the use of imagination and thought. For example, God is a complex idea constructed from simple ideas of reflection. "Having, from what we experiment in ourselves, got the ideas of existence and duration; of knowledge and power; of pleasure and happiness; and of several other qualities and powers, which it is better to have than to be without; when we would frame an idea the most suitable we can to the Supreme Being, we enlarge every one of these with our idea of infinity; and so putting them together, make our complex idea of God. For the mind has such a power of enlarging some of its ideas, received from sensation and reflection." Not only the concept of God, but all intangible things, abstract qualities, are manufactured by the mind's manipulation of simple ideas into complex ones.

Moreover, two *qualities* of bodies are distinguishable: (1) *primary* and (2) *secondary.* 'Ideas' should not be confused with 'qualities;' the former are exclusively in the mind, whereas the latter are in the bodies, in the outside world of things which occupy space. Qualities in physical objects produce ideas in the mind. "Whatsoever the mind perceives in itself, or is the immediate object of perception, thought, or understanding, that I call *idea;* and the power to produce any idea in our mind, I call *quality* of the subject wherein that power is. Thus a snowball having the power to produce in us the ideas of white, cold, round, — the power to produce those ideas in us, as they are in the snowball, I call qualities; and as they are sensations or perceptions in our understandings, I call them ideas; which *ideas,* if I speak of sometimes as in things themselves, I would be understood to mean those qualities in the objects which produce them in us." Qualities are the sensuous and insensuous nature of external objects, whereas ideas are restricted to the subject's mind alone.

Primary qualities are absolutely inseparable from the physical body of the object under consideration; they are constant qualities independent of the transient changes which the object may undergo. For example, "take a grain of wheat, divide it into two parts, each part has still solidity, extension, figure, and mobility; divide it again, and it retains still the same qualities: and so divide it on till the parts become insensible, they must retain still each of them all those qualities. For division (which is all that a mill or pestle or any other body does upon another, in reducing it to insensible parts) can never take away either solidity, extension, figure, or mobility from any body, but only makes two or more distinct separate masses of matter of that which was but one before; all which distinct masses, reckoned as so many distinct bodies, after division, make a certain number. These I call *original* or *primary qualities* of body, which I think we may observe to produce simple ideas in us, viz. solidity, extension, figure, motion or rest, and number." Primary qualities constitute the subject matter of the science of physics, whereas secondary qualities furnish the data of psychological science.

Secondary qualities, distinguishable by their psychological characteristics rather than by any physical nature which they may possess, constitute those "qualities which in truth are nothing in the objects themselves but powers to produce various sensations in us by their primary qualities, i.e. by the bulk, figure, texture, colours, sounds, tastes, etc." We shall find that in the chapter immediately subsequent to this one, Berkeley will reduce all quality to the secondary, eliminating the primary completely.

Metaphysical Reality — A Je-ne-sais-quoi (I-know-not-what).

Locke, at this juncture in his philosophy, faces a serious philosophical question: How do bodies produce ideas in us, and how do primary qualities produce the secondary? How is it possible for the nonpsychological to generate that which is mental in nature? To extricate himself from this delicate position, Locke introduces the concept of *powers,* causation, which he tacitly regards as a third sort of quality. But what Locke neglects to explain is how powers, which exist in bodies, can somehow leave them to enter into our sensations to create ideas, as if a power were a spirit which leaped from an external material object into our inner mental consciousness. Does the physical body turn into a psychological sensation? How is that possible, since, for example, the sensation of sight never leaves the body, but receives, at most, a mental image? Locke's partial answer is: "*Ideas of primary qualities are resemblances; of secondary, not.* —From whence I think it is easy to draw this observation, that the ideas of primary qualities of bodies are resemblances of them, and their patterns do really exist in the bodies themselves; but the ideas produced in us by these secondary qualities have no resemblance of them at all. There is nothing like our ideas existing in the bodies themselves. They are, in the bodies we denominate from them, only a power to produce those sensations in us; and what is sweet, blue, or warm in idea, is but the certain bulk, figure, and motion of the insensible parts of the bodies themselves, which call so. . . The particular bulk, number, figure, and motion of the parts of fire or snow are really in them, whether anyone's senses perceive them or no; and therefore they may be called *real* qualities, because they really exist in those bodies. But light, heat, whiteness, or coldness, are no more really in them than sickness or pain is in manna. Take away the sensation of them; let not the eyes see light or colours, nor the ears hear sounds; let the palate not taste, nor the nose smell; and all colours, tastes, odours, and sounds, as they are such particular ideas, vanish and cease, and are reduced to their causes, i.e., bulk, figure, and motion of parts." Consequently, qualities of sense, secondary qualities, are apparent or illusory in nature, lacking metaphysical substance or reality.

Since Locke has proved that ultimately real objects are devoid of sense qualities, then what is the nature of ultimate substance? Locke, of the opinion that sensible qualities cannot subsist by themselves and therefore must have some *substratum* to support and produce them, calls their metaphysical foundation or basis, *substance.* But at this point, a serious problem presents itself: If *substance* is composed neither of primary nor secondary qualities, what then can possibly be its nature? Of what does it consist, what is its Being? Primary and secondary qualities, rather than being substance, are results of substance. Locke writes: "If anyone will examine himself concerning his notion of pure substance in general, he will find he has no other idea of it at all, but only a supposition of *he knows not what support* of such qualities which are capable of producing simple ideas in us; which qualities are commonly called accidents. If anyone should be asked, what is the subject wherein colour or weight inheres, he would have nothing to say, but the solid extended parts; and if he were demanded, what is it that solidity and extension adhere in, he would not be in much better case than the Indian . . . who, saying that the world was supported by a great elephant, was asked what the elephant rested on; to which his answer was – a great tortoise: but being again pressed to know what gave support to the broad-backed tortoise, replied – something, *he knew not what.* And thus here, as in all other cases where we use words without having clear and distinct ideas, we talk like children: who, being questioned what such a thing is, which they know not, readily give this satisfactory answer, that is something: which in truth signifies no more, when so used, either by children or men, but that *they know not what;* and that the thing they pretend to know, and talk of, is what they have no distinct idea of at all, and so are perfectly ignorant to it, and in the dark. The idea then we have, to which we give the *general* name substance, being nothing but the supposed, but unknown, support of these qualities we find existing, which we imagine cannot subsist *sine re substante,* without something to support them, we call that support *subsantia;* which, according to the true import of the word, is, in plain English, standing under or upholding." Accordingly, the most we know of ultimate reality is that it consists of an *I-know-not-what,* and supports or holds up the world as it is known to us through our senses.

Unless we are able to determine the exact nature of this ultimate substance, we shall have to plead ignorance, and remain content with being *Metaphysical Agnostics.* Locke continues his quest of the internal constitution or unknown essence of substance. Note that he does not designate it matter, since he has no grounds for concluding that substance is material. "When we speak of any sort of substance, we say it is a thing having such or such qualities; as, body is a thing that is extended, figured, and capable of motion; spirit, a thing capable of thinking; and so hardness, friability, and power to draw iron, we say, are qualities to be found in a loadstone. These and the like fashions of speaking, intimate that the substance is supposed always *something besides* the extension, figure, solidity, motion, thinking, or other observable ideas, though *we know not what it is.*" In other words, what we are in search of is the hidden ingredient of which substance is composed, or its integrant nature. We seek more than the phenomenal or apparent nature of substance, we desire to know its real nature, or internal Being.

Souls or spirits we say possess a *spiritual substance,* and physical objects have a *corporeal substance,* but we find ourselves at a complete loss in determining the nature of this underlying quality of both, called *substance.* "Every one, upon inquiry into his own thoughts, will find, that he has no other idea of any substance, v.g. let it be gold, horse, iron, man, vitriol, bread, but what he has barely of those sensible qualities which he supposes to inhere with a supposition of such a *substratum* as gives, as it were, a support to those qualities, or simple ideas, which he has observed to exist united together. Thus, the idea of the sun, — what is it but an aggregate of those several simple ideas — bright, hot, roundish, having a constant regular motion, at a certain distance from us, and perhaps some other: as he who thinks and discourses of the sun has been more or less accurate in observing those sensible qualities, ideas, or properties which are in that thing which he calls the sun. . . Our Specific ideas of substances are nothing else but a collection of *a certain number of simple ideas, considered as united in one thing.* . . For our idea of substance is . . . but a supposed *I-know-not-what,* to support those ideas we call accidents. . . By the complex idea of extended, figured, coloured, and all other sensible qualities, which is all that we know of it, *we are as far from the idea of substance of body, as if we knew nothing at all.*"

In the last analysis, we must remain *Metaphysical Agnostics,* for we find ourselves at a complete loss in determining the precise nature of substance. That it exists, we know only by logical inference, but *what* it is remains a mystery. Berkeley, Locke's successor in the British school of Empiricism, continues his philosophical investigations where Locke concluded, in an attempt to disclose the mysterious nature of substance.

XXVIII

BERKELEY:

A Metaphysical Idealist

George Berkeley began his philosophical inquiry by accepting the Lockean conclusions regarding the empirical nature of knowledge. Among the important philosophical questions which Berkeley sought to resolve, the chief was concerned with the meaning of *material substance;* other problems up for serious consideration were: the significance of *power* or *cause,* the immateriality of substance or ultimate reality, the existence of God and spirit.

Berkeley's prime impetus, responsible for his stimulating philosophical interest, was religion. By profession, he was an Anglican Bishop; by nationality, an Irishman; by philosophical disposition, an Empiricist. It is interesting to note that member nations of the British Isles are well represented among the three British Empiricists whose philosophies are up for consideration; as mentioned, Berkeley is Irish; Locke, English; and Hume, a Scot.

Of the many pregnant thoughts sired by Berkeley, the most devastating, one which incurred widespread vehement objections from every quarter, yet never adequately refuted, was his contention that the outer world which surrounds us is spiritual in nature, essence, substance, or Being. A second noteworthy, and to many persons a startling observation, was the nonexistence of cause; at least cause, understood as power, did not exist for Berkeley.

Esse Is Percipi (To Be Is to Be Perceived).

The fundamental premise of Berkeleyan Idealism, "*esse* is *percipi,*" signifies that for an object to be real, it must be perceived; the perceivability of a thing is verification of its reality. "Some truths are so near and obvious to the mind that a man need only open his eyes to see them. Such I take this important one to be, viz., that all the choir of heaven and furniture of the earth, in a word all those bodies which compose the mighty frame of the world, have not any subsistence without a mind, that *their being is to be perceived* or known; that consequently so long as they are not actually perceived by me, or do not exist in my mind or that of any other created spirit, they must either have no existence at all, or else subsist in the mind of some Eternal Spirit — it being perfectly unintelligible, and involving all the absurdity of abstraction, to attribute to any single part of them *an existence independent of a spirit*. To be convinced of which, the reader need only reflect, and try to separate in his own thoughts the *being* of a sensible thing from its *being perceived*." [1] Accordingly, nothing can possibly exist without a spiritual being, such as man or God, experiencing the object.

In desperation, John Locke termed the essence or substance of objects an *I-know-not-what*, but Berkeley contended that its essence is known; it is known to possess the nature of perceptibility, mind. As far as Berkeley is concerned, the mystery of the *substratum* of substance is solved. "That neither our thoughts, nor passions, nor ideas formed by the imagination, exist without the mind, is what everybody will allow. And to me it is no less evident that the various sensations, or ideas imprinted on the sense, however, blended or combined together (that is, whatever objects they compose), cannot exist otherwise than in a mind perceiving them. — I think an intuitive knowledge may be obtained of this by any one that shall attend to what is meant by the term *exist*, when applied to sensible things. The table I write on I say exists, that is, I see and feel it; and if I were out of my study I might perceive it, or that some spirit actually does perceive it. There was an odour, that is, it was smelt; there was a sound, that is, it was heard; a colour or figure, and it was perceived by sight or touch. This is all that I can understand by these and the like expressions. For as to what is said of the absolute existence of unthinking things without any relation to their being perceived, that is to me perfectly unintelligible. Their *esse* is *percipi*, nor is it possible they should have any existence out of the minds or thinking things which perceive them." Without perception, there can be no substance, no reality.

The ultimate world consists exclusively of objects capable of being perceived and the souls which perceive them, nothing more. Matter cannot exist because it consists of insensible substance; even assuming the possibility of matter's existence, we could never know it since we lack the necessary organ capable of knowing matter. In Berkeleyan Idealism, there is no room for material existence; objects subject to sense experience solely exist, together with the minds, souls, spirits, or whatever

[1] Except where indicated, quotations in this section are from George Berkeley, *A Treatise Concerning the Principles of Human Knowledge* (1710, 1734) The first edition of this classic was published when Berkeley was only twenty-five years of age.

you choose to call the being which does the experiencing. "This perceiving, active being is what I call *mind, spirit, soul,* or *myself.* By which words I do not denote any one of my ideas, but a thing entirely distinct from them, wherein they exist, or, which is the same thing, whereby they are perceived—for the existence of an idea consists in being perceived." Only a mind possesses ideas; they do not float about without a mind to which they belong.

Locke spoke of primary and secondary qualities, as if only the secondary were psychological, but this was a mistake, for primary qualities devoid of any sense quality cannot exist. For example, I can possess no knowledge of the desk before me except its sensible qualities: color, shape, size, along with its tactual, visual, olfactory, auditory, and taste characteristics, but I cannot establish any contact whatever with an underlying substance, called matter. I lack the sense organ capable of receiving matter, or any substance which is not of the nature of mind. Consequently, I am faced with the following dilemma: Either material substance does not exist or the sense necessary to perceive matter is lacking in the human being. I cannot take the second horn of the dilemma by saying that matter exists despite the fact man is deficient in the necessary organ to sense it without committing the *ad ignorantiam* (pleading ignorance) fallacy; consequently, I have no alternative except to recognize the validity of Berkeley's position in admitting the nonexistence of material substance. "But, say you, though the ideas themselves do not exist without the mind, yet there may be things like them, whereof they are copies or resemblances, which things exist without the mind in an unthinking substance. I answer, an idea can be like nothing but an idea; a colour or figure can be like nothing but another colour or figure. If we look . . . into our own thoughts, we shall find it impossible for us to conceive a likeness except only between our ideas . . . They will have our ideas of the primary qualities to be patterns or images of things which exist without a mind, in an unthinking substance which they call *Matter.* By Matter, therefore, we are to understand an inert senseless substance, in which extension, figure, and motion do actually subsist . . . Extension, figure, motion are only ideas existing in the mind, and that an idea can be like nothing but another idea, and that consequently neither they nor their archetypes can exist in an unperceiving substance. Hence it is plain that the very notion of what is called *Matter* or *corporeal substance,* involves a contradiction in it . . . For my own part, I see evidently that it is not in my power to frame an idea of a body extended and moving, but I must withal give it some colour or other sensible quality which is acknowledged to exist only in the mind. In short, extension, figure, motion, abstracted from all other qualities, are inconceivable. Where therefore the other sensible qualities are, there must these be also, to wit, in the mind and nowhere else." Matter, defined as inert insensitive substance, remaining ever opaque to human sense experience, cannot possibly exist. Furthermore, a material substance, devoid of sense qualities, as well as other characteristics, is impossible even to conceive.

Solipsism.

A person's initial encounter with Berkeleyan Idealism usually elicits a negative response, the sensation that his mind has been put through a psychological somersault resulting from the world's reality evaporating into nothingness, and feelings of insecurity in the wake of it all. Dr. Johnson's reply, as penned by Boswell, is typical of the average layman's response: "After we came out of church, we stood talking for some time together of Bishop Berkeley's ingenious sophistry to prove the non-existence of matter, and that everything in the universe is merely ideal. I observed, that though we are satisfied his doctrine is not true, it is impossible to refute it. I never shall forget the alacrity with which Johnson answered, striking his foot with mighty force against a large stone, till he rebounded from it, 'I refute it *thus!*' " Dr. Johnson did not realize that rather than disproving Berkeley's philosophy, he was actually substantiating it since the only stone with which he made any contact whatever was a sensible one, one which gave him psychological sensations of pain, not an insensitive underlying substance. "From what has been said it is evident there is not any other Substance than *Spirit,* or that which perceives . . . For an idea to exist in an unperceiving thing is a manifest contradiction, for to have an idea is all one as to perceive . . . hence it is clear there can be no unthinking substance or *substratum* of those ideas." If reality, or substance, exists, and Berkeley believes it does, then it must be of the nature of mind; and insensitive matter is not of the nature of mind, but spiritual substance is.

A question occasionally raised is: If a tree falls in the forest with no one around to hear, does it make sound? Obviously not, if by sound is meant the actual sense experience. Even if a tape recorder were left operating in the absence of all organs of auditory sense, it could not be designated sound until the tape is played before organisms capable of hearing, but the recording is not identical with the original sound, since neither tape nor frequencies constitute auditory sensations called sound. If sound is real, a mind must experience it. "Ideas imprinted on the senses are real things, or do really exist; this we do not deny, but we deny they can subsist without the minds which perceive them, or that they are resemblances of any archetypes existing with the mind; since the very being of a sensation or idea consists in being perceived, and an idea can be like nothing but an idea. Again, the things perceived by sense may be termed *external,* with regard to their origin, in that they are not generated from within by the mind itself, but imprinted by a Spirit distinct from that which perceives them. Sensible objects may likewise be said to be 'without the mind' in another sense, namely when they exist in some other mind; thus, when I shut my eyes, the things I saw may still exist, but it must be in another mind." If this other mind is not the mind of a human being, then it must be the mind of God. For example, no one has seen the other side of the moon; does it exist? Yes, because God perceives it, as the following limerick depicts:

There was a young man who said, "God
Must think it exceedingly odd
    If he finds that this tree
    Continues to be
When there's no one about in the Quad."

Dear Sir: Your astonishment's odd:
I am always about in the Quad.
    And that's why the tree
    Will continue to be,
Since observed by, Yours faithfully, God.

Berkeley has been accused of *Solipsism,* the belief that I alone exist, and the world is a figment of my subjective imagination. But Berkeley is far removed from any solipsistic doctrine, for he insists that there is a real world out yonder; however, it is spiritual in nature, not insensitive matter. One argument he uses to prove the existence of an objectively real world is to show that the facts of reality are hard and genuine facts which do not obey our wills, our whims and fancies, but rather, they obey the will of another, namely God. If the world were composed merely of subjective ideas, the machinations of our own minds, then they would do our bidding in the same manner that our daydreams and reveries obey us; for example, when we desire to be sunning in a boat on the high seas, our daydreams carry us there instantly, but if we desire to eat real food, our minds are incapable of providing such even by way of hallucination. Therefore, the object of our ideas must really be out there in an objective universe. "Whatever power I may have over my own thoughts, I find the ideas actually perceived by Sense have not a like dependence on my will. When in broad daylight I open my eyes, it is not in my power to choose whether I shall see or no, or to determine what particular objects shall present themselves to my view; and so likewise as to the hearing and other senses; the ideas imprinted on them are not creatures of my will. There is therefore some *other* Will or Spirit that produces them." A number of philosophers have designated Berkeley a Solipsist, but his foregoing statement unequivocally and conclusively repudiates the charge.

It is manifestly false that Berkeleyan Idealism is a rejection of reality; and those philosophers, particularly Materialists and Realists, err in so believing. Berkeley categorically states: "The question between the materialists and me is not, whether things have a real existence out of the mind of this or that person, but whether they have an absolute existence distinct from being perceived by God, and to all minds."[1] In this sense, Berkeley is a Realist, believing in objective reality; but a total disrespect for reason and facts prompts the audacity which poses 'matter' as real. If matter is real, it must be redefined in terms of mind, in spiritual terms. "Let us examine a little the description that is here given us as *matter.* It neither acts, nor perceives, nor is perceived; for this is all that is meant by saying it is an *inert, senseless, unknown* substance; which is a definition entirely made up of negatives, excepting only the relative notion of its standing under or supporting: but then it must be observed, that it *supports* nothing at all; and how nearly this comes to the description of a *nonentity,* I desire may be considered." Matter does not exist, for the simple reason that it cannot be known; and if it ever did come to be known, it would be known as spirit, since the mind, being mental, can receive ideas of sense, not matter. The world in which we live is essentially spiritual, and the persons in it also are spiritual beings.

The Doctrine of Divine Arbitrariness.

Hume is generally credited with detecting the fact that causes are nonobservable; a person may stare at a cause and effect sequence of two successive events, as long and as often as he desires, but he will never observe a cause in action. If cause, in the sense of a power or force, were observable, then a person would be able to detect the cause of cancer with a single and initial observation of it, that is, merely by looking, as all of the factors of the causes of cancer transpire, he could put his finger, as it were, on the true causes; but causes are discovered only after many repeated observations, and the implementation of logical techniques. If causes do exist as genuine realities, they must, in nature, be principles, not observable facts. Since they cannot be experienced, they must be logically deduced. Take as an example, 'friction is the cause of heat;'

[1] Berkeley, *Dialogues Between Hylas and Philonous* (1713).

you may observe friction and heat indefinitely without ever having the cause come before the view of the senses. Berkeley illustrates: "It is certain by experience, that when we look at a near object with both eyes, according as it approaches or recedes from us, we alter the disposition of our eyes, by lessening or widening the interval between the pupils. This disposition or turn of the eyes is attended with a sensation, which seems to me to be that which in this case brings the idea of greater or lesser distance into the mind. Not that there is any natural or necessary connexion between the sensation we perceive by the turn of the eyes and greater or lesser distance. But – because the mind has, by constant experience, found the different sensations corresponding to the different dispositions of the eyes to be attended each with a different degree of distance in the object – there has grown an habitual or customary connexion between those two sorts of ideas; so that the mind no sooner perceives the sensation arising from the different turn it gives the eyes, in order to bring the pupils nearer or farther asunder, but it withal perceives the different idea of distance which was wont to be connected with that sensation. Just as, upon hearing a certain sound, the idea is immediately suggested to the understanding which custom had united with it." [1]

Another way of expressing this new found fact is to note that causes are not necessary factors, they are accidental, that is, things just *happen* to behave in a given manner, they do not have to *necessarily*; such is the meaning of Berkeley's 'doctrine of *divine arbitrariness*.' God arbitrarily chose that certain objects would be the specific causes of others, necessity did not play a factor. For example, God arbitrarily decided (although reason was a factor, logical necessity was not) that water would cause certain things to become wet, there was nothing in water which necessitated it; if God so chose, he could have had heat perform wetness instead. To put it another way, the laws of nature and the laws of causation are merely the *habitual* ways in which God performs actions. God does not necessarily have to create a person with two hands; it is possible for God to create humans with four (two protruding from his sides), but it is his custom or habit to make people two handed. If God apodictically constructed persons in a logically necessary manner, experimentation would no longer be requisite in the detection of causes; logical contemplation alone would suffice, as is done in those fields of study which deal with the a priori given, such as, formal logic and mathematics. To express it still another way, no absolute or a priori necessity maintains between any two facts of nature, hence cause is not a necessary determ-

[1] Berkeley, *A New Theory of Vision* (1709).

inant, nor produced by necessary connections between a set of facts. Our only recourse in the determination of a cause is to uncover its regular uniformity of behavior, to discover the habitual way in which God acts regarding the behavior of nature. Hume will have more to say concerning this discussion.

Concluding Remarks.

The Idealism of Berkeley opened a new era in the history of philosophy; owing largely to his influence today there is scarcely a contemporary school of philosophy which believes in Metaphysical Materialism. The section of this book devoted to contemporary schools of philosophy will testify to this fact.

When the average layman thinks of the philosophy of Idealism, he usually has in mind a person who pursues high ideals, or is devoted to lofty principles, but all Idealism is not of this nature. That mode of Idealism is particularly true of American Transcendentalism, whose chief exponent was *Ralph Waldo Emerson,* (1803-1882), but the Idealism of Berkeley is a Metaphysical Idealism which regards all ultimate reality as mind or spirit, whereas the Idealism of Emerson emphasizes the metaphysical reality of high ideals, such as, justice.

XXIX

HUME:

A Metaphysical Skeptic

David Hume's skeptical philosophy brought about, as he put it, a 'revolution in philosophy,' not so much by its denial of the existence of God, soul, or even matter, but by denying the validity of scientific principles and the real world, substance. Philosophers, heretofore, assumed ultimate reality to be a substance of a kind; Hume challenges the existence of any ultimate substance whatever. This denial of all reality is more than mere Skepticism, it is Metaphysical Nihilism, the belief that no reality whatever exists.

Hume, the Empiricist, argues from the premise: experience constitutes verification; but he restricts experience to *impressions,* and impressions cannot be gained of God, soul, matter, substance, scientific principles and realities, or any ultimate reality whatever. All that remains are impressions, the *appearances* of reality, called phenomena; since impressions alone exist, Hume's philosophy is labeled *Phenomenalism.*

As Berkeley constructed his philosophy on Locke's foundation, Hume built upon the Berkeleyan, as epitomized by Hendel:

> Berkeley had set himself to shatter one of the firmest beliefs of man, in order to give cogent demonstration of the truth of religion. The physical world of matter was not to be regarded as real – in the same sense of reality as that we appreciate in our own existence. For mind alone can act and cause things to happen; matter is without any power or energy, being unable even to affect our minds and to make us take notice of it. In fact, matter is as good as nothing, since it does nothing. Thus the common-sense view that we are living in an external world of substantial existence beyond ourselves is a sheer illusion. Were we discerning enough, we should perceive that we are actually in the presence of none other than the Divine Being Himself. God alone is known to exist besides ourselves and other persons.[1]

[1] Charles W. Hendel, Jr., *Hume Selections* (New York: Charles Scribner's Sons, 1927), vii-viii.

Hume carried the Berkeleyan metaphysical position one step further by repudiating the necessity of substance in any of its multifarious forms: mind, matter, God, reality, soul, scientific and moral principles. He reduced his system to Atheism by eliminating the need for God; not only are we incapable of obtaining an impression of God, his function as the First Cause of the world is no longer a necessity by considering nature eternal.

Hume's Epistemology.

Since the metaphysics of Hume is rooted and woven into his epistemology, without a comprehension of what Hume believes the nature of knowledge to be, it is difficult to appreciate, much less understand, his metaphysical conclusions.

Hume follows in the tradition of the British Empiricists who assert that all knowledge originates from *impressions,* experience; as far as he is concerned, impression is the only fact confronting the mind; or *idea,* the mental state after the impression has become a past experience. "We may divide all perceptions of the mind into two classes or species, which are distinguished by their different degrees of force and vivacity. The less forcible and lively are commonly denominated *Thoughts* and *Ideas.* The other species want a name in our language, and in most others; I suppose, because it was not requisite for any but philosophical purposes, to rank them under a general term or appellation. Let us, therefore, use a little freedom, and call them *Impressions;* employing that word in a sense somewhat different from the usual. By the term *impression,* then, I mean all our more lively perceptions, when we hear, or see, or feel, or love, or hate, or desire, or will. And the impressions are distinguished from ideas, which are the less lively perceptions, of which we are conscious, when we reflect on any of those sensations or movements above mentioned."[1] Note that impressions are more than mere sensations, they include emotions, such as, love, hate, desire, and even the experience of willing. Ideas do not possess the force or validity of impressions; at best, they are reproductions, "or, to express myself in philosophical language, all our ideas or more feeble perceptions are copies of our impressions or more lively ones."

The association of ideas functions on the basis of three principles: (1) *resemblance,* (2) *contiguity,* (3) *cause* and *effect.* Hume illustrates these three principles in operation: "That these principles serve to connect ideas will not, I believe, be much doubted. A picture naturally

[1] Except where indicated, quotations in this section are from David Hume, *An Enquiry Concerning Human Understanding* (1748).

leads our thoughts to the original, (resemblance):[1] the mention of one apartment in a building naturally introduces an enquiry or discourse concerning the others, (contiguity): and if we think of a wound, we can scarcely forbear reflecting on the pain which follows it, (cause and effect)." Except for these three types of association of ideas, no other exists.

The *operations of the human understanding* fall into two categories: (1) *relations of ideas,* (2) *matters of fact.* Relations of the first type are those employed in logical and mathematical reasoning, and may be regarded as intuitively or demonstratively certain; for example, two plus two equals four is both intuitive, and known with certainty. "Matters of fact, which are the second objects of human reason, are not ascertained in the same manner; nor is our evidence of their truth, however great, of a like nature with the foregoing. The contrary of every matter of fact is still possible; because it can never imply a contradiction, and is conceived by the mind with the same facility and distinctness, as if ever so conformable to reality. *That the sun will not rise to-morrow* is no less intelligible a proposition, and implies no more contradiction that the affirmation, *that it will rise.* We should in vain, therefore, attempt to demonstrate its falsehood. Were it demonstratively false, it would imply a contradiction, and could never be distinctly conceived by the mind." All scientific knowledge and principles, such as cause and effect relationships, relate to matters of fact solely.

Cause and Effect Relationships.

Hume argues that cause and effect relationships do not exist by *necessity.* For example, although friction happens to be the cause of heat, it need not of necessity be the case; consequently the *principle* of cause and effect does not exist, which is tantamount to saying that the principles of science do not exist, or simply, science does not exist. Because Hume reduced scientific principles to an unreal entity, Kant was disturbed, saying that Hume awoke him from his dogmatic slumber. Kant was mentally shaken, not because of Hume's Atheism, or his disclaim of the existence of mind and matter; but because of Hume's denial of the fundamental principles of science. Kant, who esteemed the physics of Newton highly, was ill at ease thinking that Newtonian science rested on false foundations. For this reason, we shall find Kant restoring the broken pieces left by Hume's Skepticism in order to preserve the basic structure of science.

Since we cannot obtain an impression of cause, it cannot be said to

[1] The parenthetical inclusions are the author's.

exist. To illustrate this point, let us take the law of gravity as an example; the pencil which I have in my hand, I may drop repeatedly, but regardless of how often it is dropped, I never can observe gravity. The most obtainable from observation is a series of sequences transpiring before me: (1) The first is the pencil in my hand, (2) the second, the pencil falling through the air, (3) and the third is the pencil at rest on the floor; but never do I experience any sort of sensation of the law of gravity; the feeling of air circulating perhaps, as the pencil passes close to me in its flight, but never gravity. The fact that the pencil's nature has a tendency toward falling is known only by repeated experience, not by any principle which it is *compelled to follow necessarily.* Its nature adheres to mere arbitrary *habit* or custom (Berkeley's doctrine of divine arbitrariness), not to any principle *necessitating* its behavior. It *need* not behave in that manner, it merely *happens* to respond that way. It could have, just as well, gone sideways or upwards, judging from our *first* experience, but its habitual behavior, reasoning from repeated experiences, just happens to be that it tends to fall toward the earth. On this basis, to invent a principle which caused it, termed the law of gravity, is not justifiable experientially.

Hume illustrates this point by using as an example, a billiard ball, whose course of behavior, when struck for the first time in any person's experience is unpredictable; its line of direction is logically indetectable. No one really knows the first time what course the ball will take; only after several repeated similar occurrences can a reliable forecast be made. "But to convince us that all the laws of nature, and all the operations of bodies without exception, are known only by experience, the following reflections may, perhaps, suffice. Were any object presented to us, and were we required to pronounce concerning the effect, which will result from it, without consulting past observation; after what manner, I beseech you, must the mind proceed in this operation? It must invent or imagine some event, which it ascribes to the object as its effect; and it is plain that this invention must be entirely *arbitrary.* The mind can never possibly find the effect in the supposed cause, by the most accurate scrutiny and examination. For the effect is totally different from the cause, and consequently can never be discovered in it. Motion in the second billiard-ball is a quite distinct event from the motion of the first; nor is there anything in the one to suggest the smallest hint of the other. A stone or piece of metal raised into the air, and left without any support, immediately falls: but to consider the matter *a priori,* is there anything we discover in this situation which can beget the idea of a downward, or any other motion, in the stone or metal?" If there existed *necessary* connections between causes and their effects, then causes could be detected without requiring experiments or experience; they could be deduced formally by sheer logic or mathematics in the same manner that one discovers mathematical and logical principles without necessitating the facts of experience.

Cause and effect relationships are therefore merely *arbitrary* ones, not necessary connections. A thousand sequences can never add up to a relationship of consequence. "And as the first imagination or invention of a particular effect in all natural operations, is *arbitrary,* where we consult not experience; so must we also esteem the supposed tie or connexion between the cause and effect, which binds them together, and renders it impossible that any other effect could result from the operation of that cause. When I see, for instance, a billiard-ball moving in a straight line towards another; even suppose motion in the second ball should by accident be suggested to me, as the result of their contact or impulse; may I not conceive that a hundred different events might as well follow from that cause? May not both these balls remain at absolute rest? May not the first ball return in a straight line, or leap off from the second in any line or direction? All these suppositions are consistent and conceivable. Why then should we give the preference to one, which is no more consistent or conceivable than the rest? All our reasonings *a priori* will never be able to show us any foundation for this preference." The reason that it cannot be done through the use of pure logic is that no two effects are precisely alike; each effect has its own causal relationship.

"In a word, then, every effect is a distinct event from its cause. It could not therefore, be discovered in the cause, and the first invention or conception of it, *a priori,* must be entirely arbitrary. And even after it is suggested, the conjunction of it with the cause must appear equally arbitrary; since there are always many other effects, which, to reason, must seem fully as consistent and natural. In vain, therefore, should we pretend to determine any single event, or infer any cause or effect, without the assistance of observation and experience." To ascribe causation to nature, such as, elasticity, gravity, cohesion of parts, communication of motion by impulse, force, electricity, etc., merely "staves off our ignorance a little longer," since these powers are empirically unverifiable.

Metaphysical Skepticism.

Just as it was proven that necessary connections do not exist on the grounds that impressions cannot be gained of them, the same verdict holds true for all forms of ultimate reality, such as, material substance, power, force, energy, etc. Locke fancied that a 'force' or 'power' existed by which causes were connected necessarily to their effects, but Hume categorically denied the existence of power, matter, and all metaphysical ultimates.

Since "all of our ideas are nothing but copies of our impressions," and since we do not receive an impression of material substance, or of any substance whatever, then substance of any kind cannot be said to exist. For example, when I view the typewriter before me, the most I receive of it is an impression; the typewriter does not leave the table to enter into my consciousness. The most I obtain of it is an image, and so of the rest of the world; the only world I receive is one composed of my own images, my own psychological sensations of it. Since the only world which enters my mind is one of images or impressions, then I have no grounds to say that I have an image *of* something objective, something external to me or beyond my images; I have nothing more than images. To say that I have an impression *of* something beyond conscious experience, is to say that there exists an underlying substance which produces my sensations, such as material or spiritual substance. Since I never make contact with substance of any nature, but only with my personal impressions, I must remain to be content that the world is composed of impressions, not metaphysical substances, such as, matter and mind. Consequently, only phenomena exist, hence the appellation of this school, *Phenomenalism*.

The same conclusions hold true for power, force, energy, necessary connections, etc. "When we look about us towards eternal objects, and consider the operation of causes, we are never able, in a single instance, to discover any power or necessary connexion; any quality, which binds the effect to the cause, and renders the one an infallible consequence of the other. We only find, that the one does actually, in fact, follow the other. The impulse of one billiard-ball is attended with motion in the second. This is the whole that appears to the *outward* senses. The mind feels no sentiment or *inward* impression from this succession of objects: consequently there is not, in any single, particular instance of cause and effect, any thing which can suggest the idea of power or necessary connexion." Beyond phenomena, the object of impressions, nothing can be said to exist, neither the forces of nature, nor their underlying substances.

No person has the capacity to experience ultimate reality, accordingly ultimates, such as, matter, force, power, causal connections, mind, spirit, laws of nature, do not exist. "From the first appearance of an object, we never can conjecture what effect will result from it. But were the power or energy of any cause discoverable by the mind, we could foresee the effect, even without experience; and might, at first, pronounce with certainty concerning it, by mere dint of thought and reasoning."

Man, devoid of an organ of sense capable of receiving a stimulus of ultimate reality, must be satisfied to resign himself to the fact that none exists. Ultimates are beyond experience; they lack sensitive qualities; consequently, we must deny that they are real. "In reality, there is no part of matter, that does ever, by its sensible qualities, discover any power or energy, or give us ground to imagine, that it could produce anything, or be followed by any other object, which we could denominate its effect. Solidity, extension, motion; these qualities are all complete in themselves, and never point out any other event which may result from them. The scenes of the universe are continually shifting and one object follows another in an uninterrupted succession; but the power of force, which actuates the whole machine, is entirely concealed from us, and never discovers itself in any of the sensible qualities of body. We know, that, in fact, heat is a constant attendant of flame; but what is the connexion between them, we have no room so much as to conjecture or imagine. . . Therefore, external objects as they appear to the senses, give us no idea of power or necessary connexion." Confirmation of scientific laws, laws of nature, substance, matter, soul, are by impressions; otherwise they are merely man's inventions or conventions.

The Mind-Body Problem.

Hume, dissatisfied with solutions heretofore advanced by his predecessors regarding the mind-body problem, owing to their incompatibility with his own metaphysical stand, advances his own novel explanation. He dismisses as ludicrous the Occasionalist theory of Malebranche and other disciples of Descartes who asserted that God was active on occasions when mind-body interactions occurred. Locke's solution, that matter possesses a genuinely real power capable of penetrating the mind, proved equally unacceptable. Hume, consistent with his philosophical Skepticism, carries his Agnosticism into this area. He asserts: "We are ignorant, it is true, of the manner in which bodies operate on each other: their force or energy is entirely incomprehensible; but are we not equally ignorant of the manner of force by which a mind, even the supreme mind, operates either on itself or on body? Whence I beseech you, do we acquire any idea of it? We have no sentiment or consciousness of this power in ourselves. . . We surely comprehend as little the operations of one as of the other. Is it more difficult to conceive that motion may arise from impulse than that it may arise from volition? All we know is our profound ignorance in both cases." Again, verification in this matter is the same as in any other, impression; and direct experience in this matter is lacking.

Since man has no sense experience of power, he likewise lacks any impression of *will power,* that is, the power of the mind to direct the body. "The motion of the body follows upon the command of our will. Of this we are every moment conscious. But the means, by which this is effected; the energy, by which the will performs so extraordinary an operation; of this we are so far from being immediately conscious, that it must forever escape our most diligent enquiry. . . Is there any principle in all nature more mysterious than the union of soul with body. . . ?" Although Hume is at a loss to explain the particulars of precisely how the mind interacts with body, he is persuaded that it is not through metaphysical force or energy.

We should not be too severe with Hume regarding his vain attempt at resolving the mind-body problem, and his final retreat into Agnosticism and Skepticism, because to the present day this problem has persisted without an adequate solution. The *fact* of interaction is well known and attested to a thousand times a day, such as, when a person wishes to be seated, he merely directs his body to obey; when physical alcohol is introduced into the bloodstream, it has its concomitant effects on the mind, but no philosopher or scientist has been able to detect *how.*

Concluding Remarks.

Although Humean philosophy wielded minor or negligible influence in his lifetime, some members of the Logical Positivist school of philosophy trace their beginnings to ideas he formulated. Hume writes of his first, and according to a number of philosophers, his major effort: "Never literary attempt was more unfortunate than my *Treatise of Human Nature.*[1] It fell *dead-born from the press,* without reaching such distinction, as even to excite a murmur among the zealots."[2] The work, *An Enquiry Concerning Human Understanding* (1748), from which most of the quotations in this section were derived, was the fruit of his efforts to revive the ill-fated *Treatise* by rewriting it in a simpler and more satisfactory form.

The last portion of the *Treatise* was devoted to ethics, and appeared in rewritten form under the title: *An Enquiry Concerning the Principles of Morals* (1751). In moral theory, Hume is a *Subjectivist,* the belief of one who regards moral principles as merely a matter of personal or social opinion. Hume, a Social Subjectivist, reduces morality to social

[1] Published in 1738.
[2] David Hume, *The Life of David Hume,* Esq. (1777).

conventions, customs, matters of social opinion; *social approbation,* public opinion, determines the moral code.

Hume's Phenomenalism, his denial of substance of any kind, and his assertion that phenomena only exist, proved most disturbing, particularly for Kant, who, eventually developed a Phenomenalism of his own – a debt he owes, at least indirectly, to Hume. The Humean conclusions regarding causation have permanently altered the attitude of philosophers and scientists toward the philosophy of science.

Kant, awakened from his dogmatic slumbers by Humean Phenomenalism, set himself to the task of reconstructing the shattered pieces left strewn behind, by assembling a Synthetic Philosophy which harmonized the antithetical positions of the British Empiricists and the Continental Rationalists. Kant noted that his philosophical predecessors merely traced knowledge to its source, and this he concluded was the cause of the confusion and conflict of the time; consequently, he undertook to assume the task of constructing a *critique of knowledge* and of the understanding. Let us direct our attention to the German Idealists, and in particular, to the Kantian Synthesis.

XXX

KANT:

A Metaphysical Idealist

Immanuel Kant is considered by some to be the greatest of all philosophers, and if not paramount, at least peer of the world's foremost philosophical thinkers. Kant, the man who brought philosophical splendor to Germany, was from a poor family of Scotch descent and religious piety; he was born, taught, and died in the city of Königsberg, East Prussia, without once leaving that province.

The oft quoted passage by Heine shares with us some of Kant's personal life and characteristics: "The life of Immanuel Kant is hard to describe; he had indeed neither life nor history in the proper sense of the words. He lived an abstract, mechanical, old-bachelor existence, in a quiet, remote street of Königsberg, an old city at the northeastern boundary of Germany. I do not believe that the great cathedral-clock of that city accomplished its day's work in a less passionate and more regular way than its countryman, Immanuel Kant. Rising from bed, coffee-drinking, writing, lecturing, eating, walking, everything had its fixed time; and the neighbors knew that it must be exactly half past four when they saw Professor Kant, in his gray coat, with his cane in his hand, step out of his house-door, and move towards the little lime-tree avenue, which is named, after him, the Philosopher's Walk. Eight times he walked up and down that walk at every season of the year, and when the weather was bad, or the gray clouds threatened rain, his servant, old Lampe, was seen anxiously following him with a large umbrella under his arm, like an image of Providence. Strange contrast between the outer life of the man and his world-destroying thought. Of a truth, if the citizens of Königsberg had had any inkling of the meaning of that thought, they would have shuddered before him as before an executioner. But the good people saw nothing in him but a professor of philosophy, and when he passed at the appointed hour, they gave him friendly greetings — and set their watches."[1] To say more of the life of Kant would be anticlimactic.

The Kantian Synthesis.

Kant, before constructing his own Synthetic Philosophy, made a serious attempt to refine Rationalism, but met with dismal failure; furthermore, he sought to develop a philosophy along the empirical lines of the British, but with equal lack of success. Finally, he concluded that neither alone was adequate; both must be utilized coincidentally.

"There can be no doubt whatever that all our knowledge begins with experience,"[2] but knowledge, mature and genuine, requires more than a mere start; it needs to be properly processed. "Although all our knowledge begins *with* experience, it by no means follows that it all originates *from* experience." The reason being that knowledge is composed of more than mere sense impressions; the faculty of knowledge is indispensably necessary as the machinery which manufactures the raw materials of sense into scientific or genuine knowledge.

Sense impressions, devoid of understanding, do not constitute knowledge; on the other hand, pure understanding, isolated from the facts of sense experience, likewise, lacks a necessary ingredient of which genuine knowledge is composed. That is to say, the pure reason of the Rationalists is equally inadequate as the pure facts of the Empiricists when each is considered separately, but a combination of rational *conceptions* with empirical *perceptions* is vital in the establishment of genuine knowledge. "Perception and conception, therefore, are the two elements that enter into all our knowledge. To every conception some form of perception corresponds, and no perception yields knowledge without conception . . . Without sensibility no object would be given to us, without understanding none would be thought. *Thoughts without content are empty, perceptions without conceptions are blind . . . Understanding can perceive nothing, the senses can think nothing.* Knowledge arises only from their united action." These lessons Kant learned from antithetical deliberations carried on between Rationalists and Empiricists.

Although empirical facts are necessary in any complete system of knowledge, a *tabula rasa* type of mind as indicated by Locke in his attack on Descartes, is hardly adequate as Leibniz ably pointed out.

[1] Also quoted by Edward Caird, *Philosophy of Immanuel Kant*, Vol. 1, 63; Josiah Royce, *The Spirit of Modern Philosophy*, 108-109; Arthur Kenyon Rogers, *A Student's History of Philosophy*, 376-377.

[2] Unless otherwise noted, quotations in this section are from Immanuel Kant, *The Critique of Pure Reason*, tr. John Watson (1901). The A edition of Kant's *Critique* appeared in 1781, and the B in 1787.

The Leibnizian argument was: If knowledge comes purely from experience, why is it that animals who have senses akin to human beings lack even rudimentary and inchoate scientific knowledge? Apparently, much more than a *tabula rasa* thesis based on Empiricism is required.

Time and Space.

One of the philosophical revolutions attributed to Kant was his radically different views regarding the concepts of *time* and *space*. To him, discussion concerning each inevitably terminates in antinomies, that is, rival conclusions, irreconcilably contradictory; diametrically opposed assertions, yet each logically true.

The antinomous nature of time and space led Kant to conclude that they must be phenomena stemming from the mind, an inner condition of consciousness; space and time are our ideas, not objectively real properties in things. They constitute the forms of experience; we cannot experience objects except in terms of time and space; they constitute the categories of experience. Space and time are given a priori, prior to all experience – without space and time, a person would not be able to have any experiences whatever. "We cannot be conscious of time as external, any more than we can be conscious of space as something within us . . . Space and time have no meaning except as forms of perception, belonging to the subjective constitution of our own mind, apart from which they cannot be predicated of anything whatever . . . Space is not an empirical conception, which has been derived from external experiences . . . The consciousness of space is, therefore, necessarily presupposed in external perception. No experience of the external relations of sensible things could yield the idea of space because without the consciousness of space there would be no external experience whatever. . . . Space is a necessary *a priori* idea, which is presupposed in all external perceptions . . . Space is not a discursive or general conception of the relation of things, but a pure perception. For we can be conscious only of a single space . . . From this it follows, that an *a priori* perception, and not an empirical perception, underlies all conceptions of pure space . . . Hence the original consciousness of space is an *a priori* perception, not a conception." We do not see space out there; it is within us; it is the manner in which we perceive all objects as being external to us; it is the mind which spaces objects. But, space must not be construed as a thought, an idea; it is *how* the mind perceives objects of the outside world.

Kant lists the qualities of space: "(a) Space is in no sense a property of things in themselves, nor is it a relation of things in themselves to one another . . . (b) Space is nothing but the form of all the phenomena of outer sense. It is the subjective condition without which no external perception is possible for us . . . Our exposition, therefore, establishes the *reality,* or objective truth of space, as a determination of every object that can possibly come before us as external; but, at the same time, it proves the *ideality* of space, when space is considered by reason relatively to things in themselves, that is, without regard to the constitution of our sensibility. We, therefore, affirm the *empirical reality* of space, as regards all possible external experience; but we also maintain its *transcendental ideality,* or, in other words, we hold that space is nothing at all, if its limitation to possible experience is ignored, and it is treated as a necessary condition of things in themselves." Space is not in the object as its property, such as, color, taste, and the other sense qualities are; we, as experiential beings, place objects in mental space.

Most of the properties of time are akin to those of space: "(1) Time is not an empirical conception, which has been derived from any experience . . . (2) Time is a necessary idea, which is presupposed in all perceptions. We cannot be conscious of phenomena if time is taken away, although we can quite readily suppose phenomena to be absent from time. Time is, therefore, given *a priori* . . . (3) Time is not a discursive, or general conception, but a pure form of sensible perception. Different times are but parts of the very same time . . . (4) The infinity of time simply means, that every definite quantity of time is possible only as a limitation of one single time. There must, therefore, be originally a consciousness of time as unlimited."

Again, "time is nothing but the form of inner sense, that is, of the perception of ourselves and our own inner state . . . Time has but one dimension . . . Time is not an independent substance . . . Time is the formal *a priori* condition of all phenomena without exception. Space, as the pure form of all external phenomena, is the *a priori* condition only of external phenomena. But all perceptions, external as well as internal, are determinations of the mind, and, from that point of view, belong to our inner state . . . Time is an *a priori* condition of all phenomena: it is the immediate condition of inner phenomena, and so the mediate condition of outer phenomena." Time is an empirical reality, it is a true experience; the mind will not accept any experience presented to it which does not conform to the conditions of time, that is, which is not chronologically ordered. But as a metaphysically objective substance, time does not exist, it does not exist in, or as a *thing-in-itself.* "From this we infer the *transcendental ideality* of time; by which we mean that, in abstraction from the subjective conditions of sensible perception, time is simply nothing, and cannot be said either to subsist by itself, or to inhere in things that do so subsist." On the other hand, things which cannot be spatial or temporal remain unknowable.

Time and space are the first step or order of synthesis whereby the rational and empirical combine to manufacture knowledge. Temporal and spatial relations are activities of the understanding as it receives data from the senses; it orders or classifies all sense data temporally and spatially. The understanding stamps a dateline upon perceptions, as it were, dating them and designating their location; it orders perceptions chronologically as well as according to their respective spatial relationships, where and when certain objects occur in relation to others. For example, when I see an automobile, my mind instantly classifies it as being seen in a specific time order, such as, January 1, 1964; and categorizes it in a specific spatial relationship, such as, Boston, Massachusetts, (and may continue identifying it still further, such as Boston, Mass., U.S.A., North America, Western Hemisphere, Planet Earth, Solar System of the Sun, the Universe). Space, however, is not something out there by which my classifications are made, it is something within me, my understanding, which accomplishes this.

Let us consider another illustration of the a priori nature of time and space. As I listen to the ticking of a clock, I do not hear 'tick, tick, tick,' discursively, isolated from each other in a 'one, one, one' relationship; my mind orders them temporally as 'one, two, three,' that is, the second tick is connected to the first, and the third related temporally to the second and the first. This is a synthetic process of the understanding, ordering sensations which are presented to the mind. If the mind were not able to do this, we would have no basis whatever for constructing a science, consequently there would be no such thing as scientific knowledge.

How can I distinguish a real dollar from an imaginary dollar? Or, How can I tell whether a dollar I had two weeks ago, was in reality spent, or that I imagined or dreamt was spent? The Kantian resolution to such problems, in the light of the mind's synthetic processes, renders them quite simple. If the money were really spent, then it would have been restricted or bound to spatial and temporal order, you could trace your actions step by step back to the time of having the dollar, and if it were really spent, it would be locked in the space-time order of events to which all real events are subject. On the other hand, if you merely dreamt or imagined you spent it, then tracing the matter in the same manner would give it no location whatever in time or space. This is precisely the same procedure detectives use to prove whether or not a murder suspect is guilty of the crime in question; if guilty, then the orderly reconstruction of facts would inevitably point to him, he would be placed at the scene of the murder at the time it had taken place.

Kantian Epistemology.

Kant introduces two fundamental types of judgments which are basic in the resolution of the Rationalist-Empiricist debate: (1) *analytic judgments,* and (2) *synthetic judgments;* the two may be referred to as *explicative* and *ampliative* respectively. Analytic judgments predicate nothing new of their subjects; whatever is found in the predicate may, by analysis, be detected in the subject. Principles, a priori or axiomatic statements, etc. are of this nature since only ideas detectable in the subject are found in the predicate; $2 + 2 = 4$ is an example of an analytic judgment since the predicate four adds nothing new to the subject, $2 + 2$.

Synthetic judgments contribute new data to the statement which are absent in the subject; a thorough analysis of the subject can never reveal the factual addition which the predicate contributes to the proposition. An example of such would be: 'John's auto is red,' since a mere analysis of the subject, 'John's auto,' is incapable of determining the fact that it is red. The predicate adds something new to its subject.

Kant offers the following summary explanation: "There are two ways in which the predicate of an affirmative judgment may be related to the subject. Either the predicate B is already tacitly contained in the subject A, or B lies entirely outside of A, although it is in some way connected with it. In the one case I call the judgment *analytic,* in the other case *synthetic.* Analytic judgments are those in which the predicate is related to the subject in the way of identity, while in synthetic judgments the predicate is not thought as identical with the subject. The formed class might also be called *expliative,* because the predicate adds nothing to the subject, but merely breaks it up into its logical elements, and brings to clear consciousness what was already obscurely thought in it. The latter class we may call *ampliative,* as adding in the predicate something that was in no sense thought in the subject, and that no amount of analysis could possibly extract from it. 'Body is extended,' for instance, is an analytic judgment. For, to be conscious that extension is involved in the conception signified by the term body, it is not necessary to go outside that conception, but merely to analyze it into the various logical elements that are always thought in it. But the proposition 'Body has weight,' the predicate is not implied in the very conception of body, but is a perfectly new idea. The addition of such a predicate, therefore yields a synthetic judgment." In other words, it is impossible to think of any 'body' which is not extended, which does not take up space of some amount, but the mere thought or concept 'body' is insufficient to furnish us with the information as to whether or not it is weightless.

Kant considers his most classic work, *The Critique of Pure Reason,* not a doctrine, but a 'criticism' of pure speculative reason because it contributes no new facts to the body of scientific knowledge, but keeps it free from error. It is *transcendental* knowledge, and by it "I mean all knowledge that is occupied, not with objects, but with the way in which a knowledge of objects may be gained, so far as that is possible *a priori.*" Transcendental knowledge is comprised of: (1) *Transcendental Aesthetic,* which is concerned with the principles which govern sense, and (2) *Transcendental Logic* which includes the *Transcendental Analytic,* the science of the principles of pure thought. "A science, as setting forth the origin, the limit, and the objective validity of pure conceptions, we must call *Transcendental Logic* . . . Just as in Transcendental Aesthetic we isolated the sensibility, so in Transcendental Logic we shall isolate the understanding . . . That part of Transcendental Logic which sets forth the pure element in knowledge that belongs to understanding, and the principles without which no object whatever can be thought, is Transcendental Analytic." Transcendentals are the categories of all experience; they are a priori given, no experience is possible without them. They are the bare essentials necessary to there being a universe; they are necessary to the existence of any universe whatever. The creation of any universe whatever without them is impossible. Transcendental is to be distinguished from 'transcendent' or 'transcendence' which means to go beyond the bounds or limits of all possible experience, that is, the realm of ultimate reality.

The Transcendental Aesthetic pertains to the operations of experiencing the sense world, phenomena. "Sensation is the actual affection of our sensibility, or of receiving impressions, by an object. The perception which refers itself to an object through sensation, is *empirical perception.* The undetermined object of such a perception is a *phenomenon* (*Erscheinung*). That element in the phenomenon which corresponds to sensation I call *matter,* while that element which makes it possible that the various determinations of the phenomenon should be arranged in certain ways relatively to one another is its *form.* Now, that without which sensations can have no order or form, cannot itself be sensation. The matter of a phenomenon is given to us entirely *a posteriori,* but its form must lie *a priori* in the mind, and hence it must be capable of being considered by itself apart from sensation. This pure form of sensibility is also called *pure perception.*" Sense experience alone is insufficient to be acceptable as genuine knowledge until it becomes classified, or still better, categorized by the 'understanding,'[1] the faculty of judgment, which is the 'non-sensuous faculty of knowledge.' Judgment, the knowledge of knowledge, is the function which produces conceptions. "All perceptions, as sensuous, rest upon affections, whereas conceptions rest upon functions . . . Conceptions are based on the spontaneity of thought, sensuous perceptions on the receptivity of impressions." Consciousness which is prior to all thought, conscious experience, is *perception.* Perceptions, accompanied by sensations, constitute *empirical knowledge,* or what is the same, *experience.* Genuine knowledge is a synthesis of both: (1) conception or category, and (2) perception, the channel by which sensation is fed to the understanding.

Categories, the pure conceptions of understanding, are neither knowledge nor experience, they are the principles which make experience possible. "Categories, as proceeding from understanding, contain the grounds of the possibility of any experience whatever." Categories are the manner in which we understand our world; if it were not for categories, scientific knowledge would be impossible. Categories formulate the body of empirical data out of which emerge our scientific laws and causation. They connect facts of experience in such a manner as to create laws of nature, hence the understanding is responsible for creating laws of phenomenal nature. Laws, causality, necessity, etc. are categories of the understanding which man projects to phenomenal nature and the world about him.

Metaphysical Idealism.

Ultimate reality, for Kant, abides in the realm of the transcendent; it lies beyond all possible experience, consequently metaphysical substance is unknowable according to the Kantian definition of genuine knowledge. Any conclusions pertaining to ultimate reality, whether it be of God, soul, immortality, material substance, spiritual substance, is unknowable since it transcends the bounds of experience, therefore claims of knowledge in this area must be deemed illegitimate.[2]

The only world man experiences is the sense world, the phenomenal world produced by substance, for this is the only world with which he

[1] The 'understanding' and the 'faculty of judgment' are not quite the same; "The understanding is explained as the faculty of rules, the faculty of judgment consists in performing the subsumption under these rules, that is, in determining whether anything falls under a given rule *(casus datae legis)* or not."

[2] Although Kant regards the proof of God by pure reason impossible, Atheism is equally impossible to prove, that is, no one can now, nor will any one in the future ever be able to prove Atheism. However, Kant does prove the existence of God as a postulate of practical reason.

can establish any empirical contact. The phenomenal world is a world of appearance, a 'show world' which somehow has as its base an ultimate reality, a metaphysical substance which must remain forever unknowable since man does not have the capability of establishing sense contact with it. These ultimately real substances, *things-in-themselves,* produce the phenomena that our senses perceive, but they themselves remain forever hidden, and out of cognitive reach.

Phenomena are not things-in-themselves, for if they were, man could not come into touch with them. Perhaps the best way of introducing a novitiate to Kantian philosophy is to break it down into three worlds: (1) the world of mind and understanding pure conception; (2) the sense-world of phenomena; (3) the ultimately real world of substance, noumena. The following 'Nebbish-type' schematic diagram may help to elucidate:

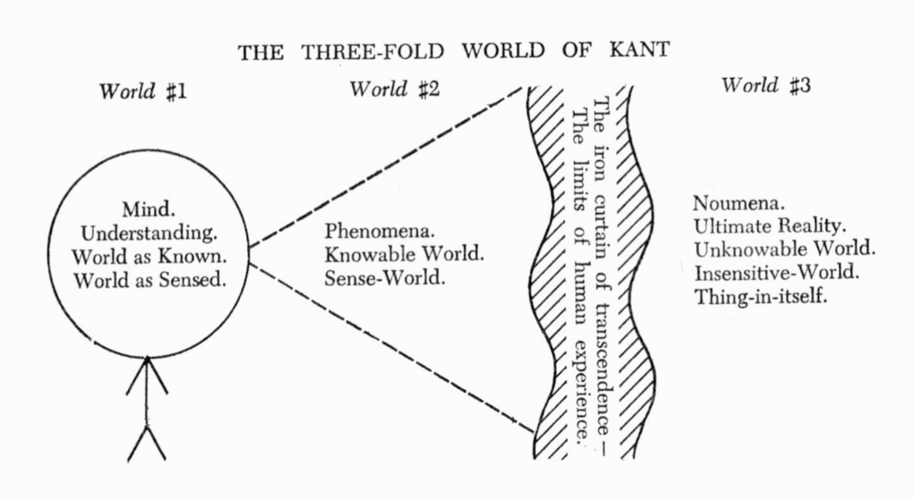

Since human experience is limited to the sense world of phenomena, and the world of reality forever barred from human sensitivity, man must reconstruct reality mentally by the use of his understanding and whatever data of experience is obtainable from the phenomenal world. Consequently, reality is a reconstruction in mind, a model, as it were, of the real world; it is similar to having an excellent model of the Empire State building in its minute details (such as elevators, air conditioners, windows, stairs, heating system, etc.) but never being able to have a first-hand experience of the real building itself. By virtue of the understanding's ability to organize, order, and interpret sense phenomena, the mind reconstructs the real world, but never participates empirically in it. *Substance,* which to Locke was an 'I-know-not-what,' and to Hume was nonexistent, becomes in the Kantian system, a reconstruction in mind, an *ideal world.*

The world of ultimate reality, of substance (*substrata*), of the thing-in-itself, is composed of *noumena,* the objects of a 'nonsensuous intuition,' an unknowable 'x.' Noumena, objects which exceed the bounds of all experience, are transcendent; whereas phenomena are immanent. "All principles the application of which is entirely confined within the limits of possible experience, we shall call *immanent;* those, on the contrary, which tend to transgress those limits, *transcendent* . . . As nothing can be an object of experience except the phenomenon, it follows that the understanding can never go beyond the limits of sensibility, within which alone objects are given to us. Its principles are principles for the exhibition of phenomena only . . . Now the concept of noumenon, that is of a thing which can never be thought of as an object of the senses, but only as a thing by itself (by the pure understanding), is not self-contradictory, because we cannot maintain that sensibility is the only form of intuition. That concept is also necessary, to prevent sensuous intuition from extending to things by themselves; that is, in order to limit the objective validity of sensuous knowledge (for all the rest to which sensuous intuition does not extend is called noumenon, for the very purpose of showing that sensuous knowledge cannot extend its domain over everything that can be thought by the understanding). But, after all, we cannot understand the possibility of such noumena, and whatever lies beyond the sphere of phenomena is (to us) empty."[1]

The world is thus divided into (a) phenomena, or the sensible world, and (b) noumena, or the intelligible world. The first is that in which we live and move and have our being, that in which we walk about daily and see, whereas the second is the real world which is contacted solely by the understanding. Perhaps it may be illustrated thus: An example of the first world is our actual experience of the color green; if you have not or cannot experience green because of colorblindness, no one can possibly give the experience to you, or even explain it to you; but the second world, the real world which is not sensed, but understood, known in scientific terms, or terms of intelligence only, such as green being 550 millimicrons on the spectrum, and its relative position on the color solid, etc., can be explained. These objects of the real world constitute our world of understanding as well; accordingly, the real world is a recon-

[1] Kant, *Critique of Pure Reason,* tr. F. Max Müller (London: Macmillan and Co. Ltd., 1881).

struction in the human mind, fashioned by the laws of the understanding, an ideal world, hence *Kantian Idealism.*

Concluding Remarks.

Kant has been thus far the most difficult thinker we have had to understand, but the importance of the man's philosophy continues into contemporary times. Without an appreciation of Kantian philosophy, not only will an unnecessary barrier be constructed inhibiting one's understanding of Kant's immediate legatees of his German Idealism, Hegel and Schopenhauer, but many contemporary philosophers frequently refer to his ideas in explaining their own, and an adequate grounding in Kantian Idealism will definitely give a person a margin of advantage in understanding contemporary philosophical thought.

Kant had the audacity to write a book entitled, *Prolegomena to any Future Metaphysic* (1783), which is tantamount to saying: If you intend to write a book in metaphysics, then you had better not begin without having read mine. Whether this is an act of temerity or not, it is nevertheless true. The *Prolegomena* sheds helpful light on the understanding of Kant's masterpiece, the *Critique of Pure Reason* (1781), which antedates the *Prolegomena* by two years.

XXXI

HEGEL:

An Absolute Idealist

Schopenhauer's scathing remark directed against Hegel, that there have been no great philosophers since the time of Kant except himself, would have been correct were it not for the imposing figure of a philosophical giant who stood between him and Kant, namely *Georg Wilhelm Friedrich Hegel,* Kant's intellectual successor. Hegel, 'the philosopher' [1] of modern times, perhaps did more for the study of philosophy than any other single man by way of founding or establishing courses in philosophy.

Of Hegel's many important works, *Phenomenology of the Spirit* and *Science of Logic* emerged to positions of highest honor. His philosophy is one of the most difficult to understand since he uses a new language in which even familiar words acquire new meaning. A legend is told of him: "Only one man has understood me, and even he has not." Hegelian philosophy was not written for the beginner, and cannot be approached in gradual steps; it begins on the apex established by other philosophers, and ascends still higher.

Hegel continues in the great tradition of German Idealism inaugurated by Kant, but differs from him in at least a few major respects: (1) He refused to accept the Kantian doctrine regarding substance (things-in-themselves) as unknowable and beyond the scope of reason; reality is knowable, it is known as *Absolute Spirit.* (2) Reason, for Hegel, is not only the instrument by which all reality is known, but *reality is rational, and the rational is real.* In this respect, he returns to, or at least favors, Rationalism.

Absolute Idealism.

Hegel, whose system is Absolute Idealism, regards reality as Idea (*Idee*), Reason, an all inclusive Absolute Spirit, a unified comprehensive

[1] Hegel is referred to as *the philosopher* by a number of influential thinkers, among whom are Sören Kierkegaard, the father of Existentialism, and Karl Marx, the founder of Dialectical Materialism; in ancient or medieval times, Aristotle enjoyed this title.

system which is an *organic unity* or *whole* encompassing every fact, thought, statement, etc. in a related, coherent, and systematic universe. The Absolute, for the Pantheistic Hegel, is God. The objective of philosophy is "Truth, in that supreme sense in which God and God only is the Truth . . . God, who is the truth, is known by us in his truth, that is, as absolute spirit." [1]

Hegel, a first rank German Idealist, understands the world of reality to be *Idea;* thought and reality are identical, for Idea is thought, and thought is *Being.* "The Idea is truth in itself and for itself, – the absolute unity of the notion and objectivity . . . The definition, which declares the Absolute to be the Idea, is itself absolute . . . The Idea is the Truth: for Truth is the correspondence of objectivity with the notion . . . Everything actual, in so far as it is true, is the Idea, and has its truth by and in virtue of the Idea alone . . . When we hear the Idea spoken of, we need not imagine something far away beyond this mortal sphere. The Idea is rather what is completely present: and it is found, however confused and degenerated, in every consciousness . . . The purpose of philosophy is the truth . . . The Idea may be described in many ways. It may be called reason." Hence Idea, Reason, Reality, God, may all be regarded as aspects of one and the same Absolute Truth, a whole which is an organic unity, that is, everything in its concrete relationship to everything else in the universe.

Although the Absolute is itself unchanging, the world within it is in a process of historical and evolutionary development, and philosophy must view it as such. The world evolutionary process and man's historical development are manifestations of the Absolute, God's activity. The Absolute remains eternally present in the background as a self-unfolding world transpires according to dialectical principles, the laws of dialectical logic. Only through philosophy can God be detected as revealing himself in the ideal organism of thought.

Idea, conformable to God, and Spirit to humanity, permeate every phase of the cosmos, and are responsible for the activity and progress of our dialectical world. "History in general is . . . the development of Spirit in *Time,* as Nature is the development of the Idea in Space." [2] These two, Spirit and Idea, comprise one organic unity, a single whole; Idea as ultimate substance of nature, and Spirit as the activity of human progress both individual and social, fairly well explain, in the light of dialectical logic, the nature and development of the world as Reason. "The principles of successive phases of Spirit that animate

[1] Except where indicated, quotations in the section on Hegel are from his *Logic,* tr. by William Wallace (1892), and extracted from his *Encyclopaedie* (1817).

[2] Hegel, *Philosophy of History,* tr. J. Sibree.

the Nations in a necessitated gradation, are themselves only steps in the development of the one universal Spirit, which through them elevates and completes itself to a self-comprehending *totality*. While we are thus concerned exclusively with the Idea of Spirit, and in the History of the World regard everything as only its manifestation, we have, in traversing the past, — however extensive its periods, — only to do with what is *present*; for philosophy, as occupying itself with the True, has to do with the *eternally present*. Nothing in the past is lost for it, for the Idea is ever present; Spirit is immortal; with it there is no past, no future, but an essential *now*. This implies that the present form of Spirit comprehends within it all earlier steps. These have indeed unfolded themselves in succession independently; but what Spirit is it has always been essentially; distinctions are only the development of this essential nature. The life of the ever present Spirit is a circle of progressive embodiments, which looked at in one respect still exist beside each other, and only as looked at from another point of view appear as past. The grades which Spirit seems to have left behind it, it still possesses in the depths of its present."[1] Spirit, not individual, but the World-Spirit, directs the course of history, and forces it to assume a rational and deliberate course. "Reason directs the world . . . the world is not abandoned to chance and external contingent causes, but that a Providence controls it."[2] Not physical or psychological causes ultimately control the world and its progress, but dialectical Reason, World-Spirit.

The world's great leaders, although selfishly motivated, have nevertheless been directed by the impulse of the World-Spirit. The history of the world is merely 'the theatre' in which the World-Spirit unfolds its drama, its development, its striving to realize itself. In regard to the motivation of any great world leader, "it was not, then, his private gain merely, but an unconscious impulse that occasioned the accomplishment of that for which the time was ripe. Such are all great historical men, — whose own particular aims involve those large issues which are the will of the World-Spirit . . . World-Historical persons, whose vocation it was to be agents of the World-Spirit . . . History is the exhibition of the divine, absolute development of Spirit in its highest forms, — that gradation by which it attains its truth and consciousness of itself . . . The only consistent and worthy method which philosophical investigation can adopt, is to take up History where Rationality begins to manifest itself in the actual conduct of the World's affairs, — where a condition of things is present in which it realises itself in consciousness,

[1] *Idem.*
[2] *Idem.*

will and action."[1] Man, even when he is carrying out what may appear to be the basest of selfish acts, is nevertheless serving the purposes of the World-Spirit, that is, when his actions are motivated from natural passions, predispositions, innate interests, etc., which have social consequences as well. "We may affirm absolutely that *nothing great in the World* has been accomplished without *passion.* Two elements, therefore, enter into the object of our investigation; the first the Idea, the second the complex of human passions; the one the warp, the other the woof of the vast arras-web of Universal History . . . I shall, therefore, use the term 'passion;' understanding thereby the particular bent of character, as far as the peculiarities of volition are not limited to private interest, but supply the impelling and actuating force for accomplishing deeds shared in by the community at large."[2] Fundamentally, all nature, human, physical, social, functions harmoniously, consciously and unconsciously, under the direction of Universal Reason, the World-Spirit.

There are three stages in the logical development of Spirit: (1) *Subjective Mind,* (2) *Objective Mind,* (3) *Absolute Spirit.* Subjective Mind is concerned with the individual person, and its subject matter is discussed in the fields of psychology and anthropology; here, man is treated as segmental, an abstraction, a portion of nature possessing consciousness. Objective Mind is essentially composed of society, social man, man in his fullness, rather than man as mere abstraction. For example, man without a mate, a woman, is only partially man; the same holds true for man isolated from society; as mere individual, he is not a person, for he lacks 'freedom' which is found only in a relationship to other men. "Freedom is nothing but the recognition and adoption of such universal substantial objects as Right and Law, and the production of a reality that is accordant with them — the State."[3] Areas of study dealing with Objective Mind are: philosophy of law, ethics, sociology.

The embodiment of Objective Mind is the State; without it, individual reality fades along with human values. The State is exemplified in the form of an individual, who as a Monarch, or even more so, as a Dictator, expresses the spirit of the people, which is actually, not the spirit of the nation, but of the times, the World-Spirit (*Welt-Geist*), the destiny of all. The State, although greater than the individual, and without which an individual cannot find his full reality, is not ultimate, for beyond it stands Absolute Mind, its fulfillment and reality. Subject

[1] *Idem.*
[2] *Idem.*
[3] *Idem.*

matter in this realm is found in art, religion, philosophy. Absolute Mind is the totality of reality, God, pantheistically understood; and within this reality, this Absolute, all progress, history, and activity unfolds evolutionally, according to the logic of the Hegelian dialectic.

The Real Is the Rational, and the Rational Is the Real.

Hegelian philosophy identifies thought with reality; thinking and Being are synonymous. Reality is a coherent rational whole which is to be understood, rather than experienced; for example, scientific progress regarding outer space is not, and cannot, be experienced prior to the first spacecraft launching; logical and mathematical formula of the behavior of outer space was necessary, but it was determined logically and mathematically, not experientially. Why was it possible to detect the nature of outer space? Because reality, such as outer space, assumes a rational pattern which is subject to the laws of logic and mathematics; in other words, reality is rational.

The same holds true for all reality; x-ray cannot be sensed, it has to be logically understood, and success was obtained only because its reality was rational; x-ray, and all reality for that matter, behaves according to the rules or dictates of reason, because it is Reason. Reality responds to mathematical and rational calculations because it is rational. "Reason governs the world, and has consequently governed its history." [1]

Reason is not a mere subjective exercise, it is objective, it resides in things as their reality; man observes experience unfold itself, and as it so unfolds, the laws involved therein come to light because the entirety is Reason. Reality cannot be severed into parts without critical loss and damage both to itself and to man's understanding of it. "Reason is the Sovereign of the World; that the history of the world, therefore, presents us with a rational process . . . Reason is the *substance* of the Universe: viz. that by which and in which all reality has its being and subsistence. On the other hand, it is the *Infinite Energy* of the Universe; since Reason is not so powerless as to be incapable of producing anything but a mere ideal, a mere intention — having its place outside reality, nobody knows where; something separate and abstract, in the heads of certain human beings. It is the *infinite complex of things*, their entire Essence and Truth. It is its own material which it commits to its own Active Energy to work up; not needing, as finite action does, the conditions of an external activity. It supplies its own nourishment, and is the object of its own operations. While it is exclusively its own basis of existence, and absolute final aim, it is also the energising

[1] *Idem.*

power realising this aim; developing it not only in the phenomena of the Natural, but also of the Spiritual Universe – the History of the World. That this 'Idea' or 'Reason' is the *True*, the *Eternal*, the absolutely *powerful* essence; that it reveals itself in the World, and that in that World nothing else is revealed but this and its honour and glory – is the thesis which . . . has been proved in Philosophy, and is here regarded as demonstrated,"[1] namely, the real is the rational, and the rational is the real.

Concluding Remarks.

Hegelian Idealism basically is an optimistic system which regards God as in control of all progress, human and natural; nature behaves and follows her course under the direction and guidance of God, but to add to this optimistic note, so is the course of man in history. Cosmic optimism is undergirded by a supporting rationalism; since 'what is real is rational' and 'what is rational is real,' all irrationality is removed from the world; life and nature become richly pregnant with meaning.

Accordingly, the universe is not only good, it is meaningful; and this situation is augmented with the pleasant thought that the order which maintains within the State is also good, in the sense that it is right; for, according to Hegel, whatever is, is right. He has, as Santayana put it, "a hearty adoration of things as they are."

Hegel's philosophy is one of the most difficult to understand and follow, for its understanding requires a dialectical grasp and orientation; one is directed through a myriad of triads to the Absolute. A philosopher, closer to Hegelian thinking than most, J. Loewenberg, comments that the "Secret of Hegel" (a title of one of Hegel's books) "is still a secret." It is possible, but highly doubtful, that Hegel, as has been attributed to him, "created the darkness in which all cows appear grey." Doubtful, because his dialectical philosophy has sired a number of contemporary philosophies.

Hegel, the antithesis of those philosophers who preceded him, predicted that his philosophy, in becoming a new thesis, would create and clash with rival antitheses. This prediction has become true to such a degree that without a knowledge of Hegel, unnecessary difficulty is created in understanding a number of contemporary philosophies which sprang up as the predicted antitheses to Hegelianism, such as, the Existentialism of Kierkegaard, the Instrumentalism of John Dewey, the Dialectical Materialism of Karl Marx, to name a few. In the dialectical phase of his philosophy alone, Hegel has given us such penetrating insights, and new ways of viewing and proving things, that it becomes

[1] *Idem.*

well worth the laborious effort necessary to understand the hidden gems of truth his system offers, such as, 'dialectical logic,' 'the coherence theory of truth,' 'the real is the rational,' 'the truth is the whole,' 'the organic theory of truth,' etc. Perhaps Spinoza was right when he observed, "All things excellent are as difficult as they are rare."

XXXII

SCHOPENHAUER:

A Metaphysical Voluntaristic Idealist

The full title of *Arthur Schopenhauer's* philosophical school of thought is *Pessimistic Voluntaristic Idealism,* a term suggesting three ideas of primary importance inherent in his philosophy as contained in his classic work: *The World as Will and Idea.* As well as being a Pessimist, Voluntarist, and Idealist, as indicated above, Schopenhauer is an Irrationalist, in the sense of antirationalist, and one of those rare Atheists who believes in immortality.

Schopenhaeur, who completes the triad of the great German Idealists, was strongly influenced in his thinking by Kant, Plato, Leibniz, Berkeley, and Hume; he built his philosophical superstructure upon the foundation provided by these men. From Leibniz, he borrowed the 'principle of sufficient reason,' and not only implemented it as an integral part of his philosophical system, but devoted his first book to it, *On the Fourfold Root of the Principle of Sufficient Reason.* He may have borrowed much from others, but he bequeathed still more to his successors, philosophical and scientific, such as the following who are deeply indebted to him: Bergson, for his *Élan Vital;* Freud, for his 'libido' concept, the concept of 'sublimation,' and the mechanism of defence which is termed 'rationalization;' Nietzche, for his 'will to power' 'philosophy of Pessimism,' and 'philosophy of Irrationalism;' the Existentialists, for their philosophy of Irrationalism;' Pragmatists and others.

Metaphysical Idealism.

Schopenhauer opens his monumental work, *The World as Will and Idea,* with the words: "The world is my idea: – this is a truth which holds good for everything that lives and knows, though man alone can bring it into reflective and abstract consciousness. If he really does this, he has attained to philosophical wisdom. It then becomes clear and certain to him that what he knows is not a sun and an earth, but only an eye that sees a sun, a hand that feels an earth; that the world which surrounds him is there only as *idea, i.e.,* only in relation to something else, the consciousness, which is himself . . . No truth therefore is more certain, more independent than all others, and less in need of proof than this, that all that exists for knowledge, and therefore this whole world, is only object in relation to subject, perception of a perceiver, in a word, idea . . . . All that in any way belongs or can belong to the world is inevitably thus conditioned through the subject and exists only for the subject. *The world is idea.*"[1] Thus, Schopenhauer's Idealism, but only the phenomenal aspect of it, is idea, for we will soon discover that ultimate reality for him is *Will.*

'Subject' signifies 'the thinking being,' 'I, myself,' who thinks about all other things which, in turn, are 'objects' to me, the 'subject.' By 'object' is meant 'that which is thought about,' anything which comes into the consciousness of the thinking subject, that which is external to me, the thinking being. According to this definition, even my body becomes my object, not part of my subjective being. It is interesting to note that the philosophical concept, which has been the traditional concept of 'subject' and 'object,' has become completely reversed today in common parlance, so that when the word 'subject' is used, such as the subject of a thesis or book, object is meant, in the sense of objective, goal, purpose, etc. The terms 'subject' and 'object' will be used in their strict philosophical sense throughout our philosophical discussions, the same meaning Schopenhauer gives them.

Schopenhauer's Idealism consists of the Phenomenalism of Hume joined to Berkeleyan Idealism; the world which is known to us by our experiences is the only world we know, consequently my world is my idea; "all that exists, exists only for the subject." True, there is an objective world, but it is known only through ideas, and in my particular case, by my particular ideas which my particular experiences furnish me. Although my subjective world is my idea, the objective world is *will* (force, drive, instinct, impulse, etc.). "We must, without reserve, regard all presented objects, even our bodies, . . . merely as ideas, and call them merely ideas. By so doing we always abstract from will . . . which by itself constitutes the other aspect of the world. For as the world is in one aspect *idea,* so in another it is entirely *will* . . . The world is my will." The ultimate world, metaphysical reality, is more than my will, it is an objective will of which my own is a participating aspect.

[1] Quotations throughout this section are from Arthur Schopenhauer, *The World as Will and Idea* (1819), tr. R. B. Haldane and J. Kemp (1883).

Accordingly, the world is reducible to *will* and *idea;* in turn, the world as idea is dichotomized into: (1) *subject,* that which is every percipient being, that part of him which is present, entire, and undivided, but not in space or time; (2) *object,* those phenomenal manifestations occurring in space and time. The single percipient being (the subject) with the object, his conscious ideational content, constitutes the whole world as idea. To assert that the world is idea does not mean it is mere illusion or appearance solely, for it possesses transcendental ideality, that is, it truly exists out there beyond us.

In another sense, however, reality is not independent from the subject, as some dogmatically assert, for other than idea, nothing can be known. "The real world in space and time which makes itself known as causation alone, is entirely real, and is throughout simply what it appears to be, and it appears wholly and without reserve as idea, bound together according to the law of causality. This is empirical reality. On the other hand, all causality is in the understanding alone, and for the understanding. The whole actual, that is, active world is determined as such through the understanding, and apart from it is nothing . . . No object apart from subject can be conceived without contradiction. The whole world of objects is and remains idea, and therefore wholly and forever determined by the subject; that is to say, it has transcendental ideality. But it is not therefore illusion or mere appearance; it presents itself as that which it is, idea, and indeed as a series of ideas of which the common bond is the principle of sufficient reason." Schopenhauer's point of emphasis here is that the real world, although ideational, has an objective basis in reason; ideas don't occur haphazardly, they behave rationally.

Ideational *substance,* that which supports ideas, which otherwise would be mere floating ideas, figments of human imagination, is reason. In this respect, note how close this system of metaphysics approaches Hegel's; its major point of departure is that reason serves as the ground of knowing ideas, whereas for Hegel, reason constitutes their very Being.

Metaphysical Voluntarism.

Schopenhauer has led us to understand that the world is *will* and *idea;* the phenomenal world around us, the world as it manifests itself to us is idea, but its inner nature, its essence, its Being, its reality, is will. "Besides will and idea nothing is known to us or thinkable. If we wish to attribute the greatest known reality to the material world which exists immediately only in our idea, we give it the reality which our own body has for each of us; for that is the most real thing for every one. But if we now analyse the reality of this body and its actions, beyond the fact that it is idea, we find nothing in it except the will; with this its reality is exhausted." Will is reality; its phenomenal manifestation is idea.

As for the existence of a material world, there is none; it is the prejudice of a dogmatic mind which cannot keep abreast with modern philosophy, a mind which vainly strives to become philosophical. The real nature of the material world, the world which surrounds us, if it is something more than idea, must be *will.* "Will alone is; it is the thing-in-itself, and the source of all these phenomena." Will is not only the essence of a person's world, "his will is the real inner nature of his phenomenal being, which manifests itself to him as idea, both in his actions and in their permanent substratum, his body, and his will is that which is most immediate in his consciousness, though it has not as such completely passed into the form of idea." Schopenhauer believes that in the foregoing statement consists the secret of knowledge; with it, a person is provided the key to unlocking reality; without it, he wanders vainly.

Kant maintained, on the basis of the Lockean conclusion, that reality is an unknowable substance (*substratum*), an *I-know-not-what (Je-ne-sais-quoi)*; that reality, the substance which is the *thing-in-itself* is unknowable; but Schopenhauer differs, claiming that the thing-in-itself is knowable, it is known to us as *will.* "He alone will recognise this will of which we are speaking not only in those phenomenal existences which exactly resemble his own, in men and animals as their inmost nature, but the course of reflection will lead him to recognise the force which germinates and vegetates in the plant, and indeed the force through which the crystal is formed, that by which the magnet turns to the North Pole, the force whose shock he experiences from contact of two different kinds of metals, the force which appears in the elective affinities of matter as repulsion and attraction, decomposition and combination, and lastly, even gravitation, which acts so powerfully throughout matter, draws the stone to the earth and the earth to the sun, – all these, I say, he will recognise as different only in their phenomenal existence, but in their inner nature as identical, as that which is directly known to him so intimately and so much better than anything else, and which in its most distinct manifestation is called *will.* It is this application of reflection alone that prevents us from remaining any longer at the phenomenon, and leads us to the *thing-in-itself.* Phenomenal existence is idea and nothing more. All idea, of whatever kind it may be, all *object,* is *phenomenal* existence, but the *will* alone is a *thing-in-itself.*" Although there are many individuals, owing to our phenomenal existence, there are not many individual wills, but only one and the same will which permeates all phenomenal existence, whether it be my particular will, yours, or the will in nature assuming the form of gravitational force.

Will, as reality, is outside both time and space, and is completely free from their limitation or interference. When the will assumes its many multifarious appearances, it is called phenomena (idea), but as ultimate reality, as the thing-in-itself, it is quite different. "By idea, then, I understand every definite and fixed grade of the objectification of will, so far as it is thing-in-itself, and therefore has no multiplicity." Reality, the thing-in-itself, the *will,* has as its manifestation the world as we experience it, *idea.* "Idea and thing-in-itself are not one and the same," although this may have been true in the philosophies of Kant and Plato, "the idea is for us rather the direct, and therefore adequate, objectivity of the thing-in-itself, which is, however, itself the *will* – the will as not yet objectified, not yet become idea." Visibility of the will is phenomena, our perceptual ideas of the world which we actually experience. Such are the subtle distinctions which Schopenhauer draws between *will* and *idea.*

Mind-Body Problem.

In arriving at a solution to the mind-body problem, Schopenhauer is closer to Spinoza than to the other metaphysicians treated; actually, he finds little disturbing about the matter since will and body are not two different things, but identical. "The act of will and the movement of the body are not two different things objectively known, which the bond of causality unites; they do not stand in the relation of cause and effect; they are one and the same, but they are given in entirely different ways. . . . The action of the body is nothing but the act of the will objectified, *i.e.,* passed into perception . . . This is true of every movement of the body, not merely those which follow upon motives, but also involuntary movements which follow upon mere stimuli, and indeed, that the whole body is nothing but objectified will, *i.e.,* will become idea . . . I shall call the body the *objectivity of will* . . . It is only in reflection that to will and to act are different; in reality they are one. Every true, genuine, immediate act of will is also, at once and immediately, a visible act of the body. And, corresponding to this, every impression upon the body is also, on the other hand, at once and immediately an impression upon the will." This is exemplified in matters pertaining to pleasure and pain; pleasure is that which is in accord with the will, whereas pain is its opposition.

Forces within us, both mental and physical, are will. Will is the inner mechanism responsible for action, movements, and motivation of our being; accordingly, will, which is reality, the ultimate, the thing-in-itself, is not only manifested in nature, but it manifests itself in us as well.

Systematic Pessimism.

Thus far in our adventures in the philosophy of Schopenhauer, Pessimism has been absent; in fact, we have not even encountered intimations of it. His Pessimism lies inherent in the nature of the will. Unlike Hegel's philosophy which placed *reason* at the heart of reality, the Schopenhauerian *will* is a blind, capricious, force which behaves independently of the guidance of reason – it is *irrational* in the same sense that we say, 'love is blind,' that is, the irrational actions which are often prompted from romantic love are inexplicable on the basis of intelligence, and must be rationalized, plausible excuses must be sought, (Freudian rationalization).

This blind irrational force, the *will,* leaves a person ever dissatisfied, and confronts him with a dilemma: either its sensual gratification (this is the most prevalent form of the will), which always results in boredom rather than permanent satisfaction, or a state of unrest in which the instinctual urges of a person are thrown into a disturbing state of frustration. Man is essentially a bundle of unfulfilled instincts, drives, urges, which either remain entirely unsatisfied, or if momentarily fulfilled, produce ennui.

This is the principle which *Sigmund Freud* was later to call 'repetition compulsion,' the ever recurring hungering for sex; the drive can never, according to both Schopenhauer and Freud, be fulfilled, but only temporarily alleviated and satisfied. If the sex drive is deprived of its satisfaction, then a person becomes irritable, unhappy, frustrated; on the other hand, if it is satisfied, then the participants are thrown into a state of boredom – life becomes dull when the sex act is terminated.

The sex life alone does not act in this peculiar manner; what is true of man's sexual nature is typical of his entire being. "The inner being of unconscious nature is a constant striving without end and rest. Willing and striving is its whole being, which may be very well compared to an unquenchable thirst. But the basis of all willing is need, deficiency, and thus pain. Consequently, the nature of brutes and man is subject to pain originally and through its very being. If, on the other hand, it lacks objects of desire, because it is at once deprived of them by a too easy satisfaction, a terrible void and ennui comes over it, *i.e.,* its being and existence itself becomes an unbearable burden to it. Thus its life swings like a pendulum backwards and forwards between pain and ennui." Many Freudian Psychoanalytical ideas are found in Schopenhauer, who antedates Freud, but Freud denies taking them from Schopenhauer, or from Nietzsche, who was heavily influenced in this respect by Schopenhauer. The above paragraph is quite Freudian, particularly regarding his *libido* theory.

The driving force of will manifests itself in man in two major respects: the drive of self preservation, and the drive of the propagation of the species. Man's will to live is relentless, it forces him to hang on to life even under unbearable circumstances, *e.g.*, the atrocities of war, when suffering, humiliation, etc., are beyond endurance. Man's will to reproduce the species is almost equally oppressive; his sex urge has the capacity of driving him to such extreme lengths that he risks reputation, position, and even life, for the sake of sexual gratification. These two forces of will are capable of driving man to the most irrational modes of behavior: The instinct of self preservation is responsible for the desperate and irrational actions issuing from fears and panic which prove damaging to all concerned; the sex drive will often force a man to marry when he is ill-prepared for it; the overwhelming drive consumes him so that he marries despite the impending financial and other hardships he must suffer. "The ceaseless efforts to banish suffering accomplish no more than to make it change its form. It is essentially deficiency, want, care for the maintenance of life. If we succeed, which is very difficult, in removing pain in this form, it immediately assumes a thousand others, varying according to age and circumstances, such as lust, passionate love, jealousy, envy, hatred, anxiety, ambition, covetousness, sickness, etc., etc. If at last it can find entrance in no other form, it comes in the sad, grey garments of tediousness and ennui, against which we then strive in varying ways. If finally we succeed in driving this away, we shall hardly do so without letting pain enter in one of its earlier forms, and the dance begins again from the beginning; for all human life is tossed backwards and forwards between pain and ennui." Such is man's lot and his future.

Man must strive every step of the way through life without ever achieving lasting satisfaction. The nature of the driving force of will is responsible for this; it gives man no rest whatever, except for the brief periods of respite when the drive is momentarily satisfied, such as sex and hunger alleviation, but under such circumstances, man experiences a condition of boredom. If for one moment you think that ennui is not painful, then consider solitary confinement as it is practiced in penal institutions; it is used as a last resort measure because it is the severest punishment known to man, capable of driving him psychotic. Some persons become frantic, even desperate, in their attempt to amuse themselves in order to escape boredom; "when they see a strange, rare animal, they cannot easily confine themselves to merely observing it; they must rouse it, tease it . . . but this need for excitement of the will manifests itself very specially in the discovery and support of card-playing, which is quite peculiarly the expression of the miserable side of humanity." Momentarily, when the will subsides, man becomes free from its harsh taskmaster; in such transitory moments of a quiescent will, a state of happiness may be said to exist. "All satisfaction, or what is commonly called happiness, is always really and essentially only *negative,* and never positive. It is not an original gratification coming to us of itself, but always by the condition which preceded every pleasure . . . Thus the satisfaction or the pleasing can never be more than the deliverance from a pain, from a want; for such is not only every actual, open sorrow, but every desire, the importunity of which disturbs our peace, and, indeed, the deadening ennui also that makes life a burden to us . . . Nothing can ever be gained but deliverance from some sorrow or desire." Thus, happiness is negative in character, not a positive object which may be pursued.

Life is a continuous uphill climb, a never ending obstacle course with brief moments of escape called happiness. This fact is regularly attested to in art, romantic novels, the theatre, etc. where man is depicted as striving in the midst of eternally recurring problems, until at the end, he emerges triumphant and marries the heroine of the play, but at this moment of fleeting happiness, the curtain must be drawn posthaste before another episode, lest it be discovered that new problems will inevitably arise.

Life is such a miserable existence that, not only would a person not want to live his life over again, he would never wish children to be born into this life of pain. Children are born because the sex drive cannot be subdued; when children are born into this world, they are condemned, not to death, but to life — a life of misery. "The life of the great majority is only a constant struggle for this is existence itself, with the certainty of losing at last. But what enables them to endure this wearisome battle is not so much the love of life as the fear of death, which yet stands in the background as inevitable, and may come upon them at any moment. Life itself is a sea, full of rocks and whirlpools, which a man avoids with the greatest care and solicitude, although he knows that even if he succeeds in getting through with all his efforts and skill, he yet by doing so comes nearer at every step to the greatest, the total, inevitable, and irremediable shipwreck, death; nay, even steers right upon it: this is the final goal of the laborious voyage, and worse for him than all the rocks from which he has escaped." Suicide is no solution, man's drive or will to live frustrates that act; furthermore, there is a life after death in which a person must again confront the indestructible will anew there as well as here. Moreover, suicide is a clumsy experiment from which there is no recourse. "Suicide may also be regarded as an experiment — a question which man puts to nature, trying to force her to an answer. The question is this: What change will death produce in a man's existence and in his insight into the nature of things? It is a clumsy experiment to make; for it involves the destruction of the very consciousness which puts the question and awaits the answer." [1]

The only course of salvation open to man is to annihilate all striving of will by shunning the will to live, not life itself; it is wise to shun joys, not sorrows. The greatest good in life or the highest ideal is to achieve a state of Nirvana, an existence of total indifference to the desires and demands of *will*. "True salvation, deliverance from life and suffering, cannot even be imagined without complete denial of the will. Till then, every one is simply this will itself, whose manifestation is an ephemeral existence, a constantly vain and empty striving, and the world full of suffering."

Partial salvation is obtainable through art, creativity (Freudian sublimation), knowledge, a state of being objectively divorced from instinctual desire, such as contemplating Platonic Ideas; for in this way, one obtains an aesthetic experience and can maintain an attitude of objectivity. "But to the great majority of men purely intellectual pleasures are not accessible. They are almost quite incapable of the joys which lie in pure knowledge. They are entirely given up to willing. If, therefore, anything is to win their sympathy, to be *interesting* to them, it must . . . in some way excite their *will*, . . . their existence lies far more in willing than in knowing, — action and reaction is their one element . . . Pure knowing free from will, which certainly, as a matter of fact, is the only pure happiness, which is neither preceded by suffering or want, nor necessarily followed by repentance, sorrow, emptiness, or satiety." However, it is a pity that this form of happiness is not enduring.

There is only one type of morality suited for our miserable existence, an ethics of pity, of compassion. It is advised that instead of condemning a person for his immoral actions, pity him, since he had little choice inasmuch as he was the victim of relentless striving of will to which we all succumb. A morality suited for individual action is that of crushing egoistic self-assertion, annihilating the tyrannous will. "All suffering, since it is a mortification and a call to resignation, has potentially a sanctifying power . . . The whole of life conceived as essentially suffering brings . . . resignation . . . When through some such great and irrevocable denial of fate the will is to some extent broken, almost nothing else is desired, and the character shows itself mild, just, noble, and resigned.

[1] Arthur Schopenhauer, "On Suicide," tr. T. Bailey Saunders.

When, finally, grief has no definite object, but extends itself over the whole of life, then it is to a certain extent a going into itself, a withdrawal, a gradual disappearance of the will, whose visible manifestation, the body, it imperceptibly but surely undermines, so that a man feels a certain loosening of his bonds, a mild foretaste of that death which promises to be the abolition at once of the body and of the will. Therefore a secret pleasure accompanies this grief, and it is this, as I believe, which the most melancholy of all nations has called 'the joy of grief'. ... Only if suffering assumes the form of pure knowledge, and this, acting as a *quieter of the will,* brings about resignation, is it worthy of reverence . . . We cannot help regarding every sorrow, both our own and those of others, as at least a potential advance towards virtue and holiness, and, on the contrary, pleasures and worldly satisfactions as a retrogression from them . . . All true and pure love . . . and even all free justice, proceed from the penetration of the *principium individuationis* [principle of individuation], which if it appears with its full power, results in perfect sanctification and salvation, the phenomenon of which is the state of resignation described above, the unbroken peace which accompanies it, and the greatest delight in death." It appears, that in the final analysis, the Mystic, the Stoic, the religious saint, has succeeded most in the attainment of salvation, and also in moral achievement, provided their spirits are filled with compassion for their fellow men.

Concluding Comments.

Both Schopenhauer and Hegel were confronted with philosophical problems created by Kant; and each, as a result of his grappling with them, arrived at different conclusions. The chief problem entailed the nature of ultimate reality, the thing-in-itself, and specifically, the subject's relationship to the objective world of reality. Hegel resolved the issue by analyzing or tracing the dialectical nature of consciousness as it went through almost endless stages of paradoxical clashes of theses with their corresponding antitheses, until the Absolute was approached, namely, Idea.

Schopenhauer, not too distant from Hegelian thought, discovered an ideal world of *Will,* a capricious, irrational entity which assumed phenomenal appearances in the form of idea or body. Both men noted the world's contradictory elements, its optimistic and pessimistic swings; but Hegel, due to his dauntless and intrepid Spirit, destined to triumph, was attracted to the optimistic, while his one-time colleague, who could see only a totally evil nature, gravitated towards Pessimism.

It might be well to close this evaluation of Schopenhauer's *The World as Will and Idea* with Jean Paul's observation of it: "A book of philosophical genius, bold, many-sided, full of skill and depth, – but of a depth often hopeless and bottomless, akin to that melancholy lake in Norway, in whose deep waters, beneath the steep rock-walls, one never sees the sun, but only the stars reflected; and no bird and no wave ever flies over its surface."

With our treatment of Schopenhauer's philosophy, we ring down the curtain on our wrestlings with metaphysics; the next act takes place when the curtain is raised once more for contemporary schools of philosophy to make their debut.

Part Six: CONTEMPORARY PHILOSOPHY —

Current Schools of Philosophical Thought

CONTEMPORARY PHILOSOPHY:

CURRENT SCHOOLS OF PHILOSOPHICAL THOUGHT

The study of contemporary philosophy may be approached from any one of a variety of ways, such as, treating the integrated systems of various men individually, treating current ideas, or treating contemporary schools of philosophical thought, just to mention a few. The particular approach selected for the present treatment is the last mentioned, contemporary schools of philosophy, with special attention given to chief exponents of each, and to their characteristic ideas and major contributions. It is not within the scope of the present work to offer an exhaustive account of these schools, whether it be the enumeration of the many ideas of the respective schools, or the exhaustive treatment of any specific concept. The purpose of this book is to give the reader an appreciative understanding, so as to initiate him into the world of contemporary philosophical schools of thought.

Some attempt has been made to prevent contemporary philosophy from falling too deeply into a nebulous character; for the reader's benefit, it will be defined as the study of these philosophical *schools* which belong to the twentieth century, whether or not their principal adherents do. Date of birth is of comparatively minor import, for the criteria entitling a philosopher to be considered for treatment consist of whether the man in question founded a current school of philosophy, and whether he lived, wrote, or influenced contemporary thought to a decisive degree.

Modern Philosophy encompasses roughly the period from 1600 to 1900, while Contemporary Philosophy is subsequent to that period, with considerable overlapping. A major portion of Part V was devoted to Modern Philosophy, thus enabling us to treat not only the study of metaphysics, but the scope of Modern Philosophy as well. Nineteenth Century Philosophy was dominated by German Idealism, and was imported to every nation of the Western world, eventually gaining prominence in those countries.

Contemporary Philosophy, however, antithetical to Nineteenth Century Metaphysics, is a decisive revolt against Idealism, particularly that mode generated by Hegel, Absolute Idealism, and its accompanying Rationalism. German Idealism emphasized speculative thought, Rationalism, whereas the sharp cleavage of Twentieth Century Philosophy is a 'revolt against reason' and also against Absolute Idealism. This antithesis is readily seen in philosophies, such as, Pragmatism, with its insistence that only the practical is worthy of consideration; Vitalism, with its sharp attack on reason and the Absolute, by its emphasis on evolutionary change intuitively determined; Personalism, with its claim that 'life is deeper than logic;' Neorealism, with its attack on Idealistic metaphysical reality; Dialectical Materialism, with Marx's disparagement of Hegelians: "The philosophers have only interpreted the world in various ways, the point however is to change it;" [1] and finally, Existentialism, carrying philosophical thought to the opposite extreme from Hegelian Absolutism, to the individual within and his completely irrational subjective existence.

With the exception of a few Idealistic philosophers of stature who managed to survive in the twentieth century, such as Josiah Royce (1855–1916) in America, with his *The World and the Individual* (1901, 1904), Francis Herbert Bradley (1846–1924) in England with his *Appearance and Reality* (1893), and *Benedetto Croce* (1866–1952) in Italy with his *Aesthetics* (1933), Idealism, the roaring lion of another century, has almost reached the status of a sheared lamb; but, ironically, almost every contemporary school of philosophy is tinged with Idealism. If we may rely on the pendulous swings which philosophy has undergone in former ages, it is reasonable to expect Idealism to reappear, in more developed, sophisticated, and synthetic form.

[1] *Theses on Feuerbach.*

XXXIII

PRAGMATISM:

The Philosophy of Practical Consequences

Pragmatism is a school of philosophy which received its initial impetus in the last century in this country under the able pioneering leadership of Charles Sanders Peirce (1839–1914), William James (1842–1910), John Dewey (1859–1952), and abroad by F. C. S. Schiller (1864–1937). The term, originating with Peirce, gained ready acceptance; eventually, however, it underwent significant modifications which to Peirce were no longer indicative of his philosophy; consequently, he coined the term *Pragmaticism* to distinguish his philosophy from all others. Respecting the alteration, he writes in an amusing vein: "So then, the writer, finding his bantling 'pragmatism' so promoted, feels that it is time to kiss his child good-by and relinquish it to its higher destiny; while to serve the precise purpose of expressing the original definition, he begs to announce the birth of the word 'pragmaticism,' which is ugly enough to be safe from kidnappers." [1] Peirce was right, the term was safe from kidnappers; its virtue rested in its noneuphonious tongue-twisting characteristic quality.

Etymologically, James derives the word, Pragmatism, from the Greek *pragma,* meaning action, and traces the words *practice* and *practical* to it; while Peirce prefers the Greek *praktikos* or *pragmatikos,* for they suggest terms more indicative of what the Pragmatist has in mind: *practicism* or *practicalism.* John Dewey, however, favors the term *Instrumentalism* because, to him, theories are "instruments, not answers to enigmas, in which we can rest . . . Any idea upon which we can ride, so to speak; any idea that will carry us prosperously from any one part of our experience to any other part, linking things satisfactorily, working securely, simplifying, saving labor; is true for just so much, true in so far forth, true *instrumentally.* This is the 'instrumental' view

[1] Charles S. Peirce, "What Pragmatism Is," *The Monist,* Vol. 15 (1905).

of truth taught so successfully at Chicago, the view that truth in our ideas means their power to 'work.'"[1]

Peirce, who is under no illusions, does not fancy himself to be the author of Pragmatic thinking; he believes that he is merely applying the sole principle of logic recommended by Jesus: "By their fruits, ye shall know them." Perhaps it was with this very thought in mind that James refers to Pragmatism as "a new name for some old ways of thinking."

1. William James — Pragmatism

The Philosophy of Practical Consequences.

Pragmatism would reject as meaningless, questions which are inconsequential, those which do not issue in concrete results. Scholastic questions, such as: How many angels can stand on the point of a needle? would, for the Pragmatist, be void of significance since it matters little from the standpoint of practicality. In other words, Who cares?

James cites an example of a meaningless question: Does a man go around the squirrel when a squirrel on a tree trunk is revolving about it simultaneously as the man circles the tree, but never reaches the point of the tree vertically positioned with the squirrel? Let James relate it for himself: "A live squirrel [was] supposed to be clinging to one side of a tree-trunk; while over against the tree's opposite side a human being was imagined to stand. The human witness tries to get sight of the squirrel by moving rapidly round the tree, but no matter how fast he goes, the squirrel moves as fast in the opposite direction, and always keeps the tree between himself and the man, so that never a glimpse of him is caught. The resultant metaphysical problem now is this: *Does the man go round the squirrel or not?*" James asserts that the only claim this question has to meaningfulness is its significance from a practical standpoint; if there is none, the question lacks meaning. "I tell this trivial anecdote because it is a peculiarly simple example of what I wish now to speak of as *the pragmatic method.* The pragmatic method is primarily a method of settling metaphysical disputes that otherwise might be interminable. Is the world one or many? — fated or free? — material or spiritual? . . . What difference would it practically make to any one if this notion rather than that notion were true? If no practical difference whatever can be traced, then the alternatives mean practically the same things, and all dispute is idle." Not only are both opinions

[1] Unless otherwise stated, quotations in the section on James are from his *Pragmatism* (London: Longmans, Green and Co., 1907). The quotation cited above is also from the same source.

practically the same due to their impractical nature, but they are meaningless because inconsequential.

According to this philosophy, most arguments in the area of metaphysics are definitely lacking significance, merely because they are inconsequential; they are devoid of practical value. "It is astonishing to see how many philosophical disputes collapse into insignificance the moment you subject them to this simple test of tracing a concrete consequence . . . The universe has always appeared to the natural mind as a kind of enigma, of which the key must be sought in the shape of some illuminating or power-bringing word or name. That word names the universe's *principle,* and to possess it is after a fashion to possess the universe itself. 'God,' 'Matter,' 'Reason,' 'the Absolute,' 'Energy,' are so many solving names. You can rest when you have them. You are at the end of your spiritual quest. But if you follow the pragmatic method, you cannot look on any such word as closing your quest. You must bring out of each word its practical *cash-value,* set it at work within the stream of your experience." Unless an idea can meet the Pragmatic test, it cannot be considered true.

The Pragmatic Theory of Truth.

By definition, truth is the agreement of an idea with reality; if your idea does not correspond with reality, you cannot claim any truth for it. However, the reality in question must be a concrete reality, pregnant with consequences, not an abstract inconsequential quality of the metaphysicians. Pragmatism is essentially a reaction to that metaphysic whose conclusions prove sterile and useless. "Pragmatism, on the other hand, asks its usual question. 'Grant an idea or belief to be true,' it says, 'what concrete difference will its being true make in any one's actual life? How will the truth be realized? What experiences will be different from those which would obtain if the belief were false? What, in short, is the truth's *cash-value* in experiential terms?' " Truth is more than a passive state of existence, it is an active, participating function.

Truth is not singular, it is plural; not all ideas are proper candidates for truth, only those which fructify into action. Only if an idea works, may it be designated true. "It makes itself true, gets itself classed as true, by the way it works . . . Truth *happens* to an idea. It *becomes* true, is *made* true by events. Its verity *is* in fact an event, a process: the process namely of its verifying itself, its veri-*fication.* Its validity is the process of its valid-*ation.*" Thus, we find that truth is neither passive nor is it a single body, but a multiplicity of many diverse truths both coming into being and passing out of existence in some cases.

To illustrate the Pragmatic approach to metaphysical issues, consider for purposes of illustration, the question of the existence of God. Does he or does he not exist? If the belief in God is to you satisfying and is an indispensable aid in your making suitable adjustments to life, then the belief in God is fruitfully rich in consequences, and is definitely for you a true belief. "Her only test of probable truth is what *works* best in the way of leading us, what fits every part of life best and combines with the collectivity of experience's demands, nothing being omitted. If theological ideas should do this, if the notion of God, in particular, should prove to do it, how could pragmatism possibly deny God's existence? She could see no meaning in treating as 'not true' a notion that was pragmatically so successful." But what James fails to explain in this respect is a contradictory situation which may arise between two persons who pragmatically have opposite views in reference to the existence of God. For one person, God's existence is a very practical and significant asset to everyday living, whereas for the other, there is no value for the existence of God. Pragmatically, each has proved his case, but logically, how is it possible for God both to exist and not to exist simultaneously?

By way of summary, it may be pointed out that the scope of Pragmatism is dual: (1) first of all, it is a method, a technique of approaching and resolving what would otherwise be irresolute philosophical issues; (2) its complementary function is a genetic theory of the meaning of truth. "Our account of truth is an account of truths in the plural, of processes of leading, realized *in rebus,* and having only this quality in common, that they *pay* . . . Truth lives, in fact, for the most part on a credit system. Our thoughts and beliefs 'pass' so long as nothing challenges them, just as bank-notes pass so long as nobody refuses them. . . . Truth for us is simply a collective name for verification-processes, just as health, wealth, strength, etc., are names for other processes connected with life, and also pursued because it pays to pursue them. Truth is *made,* just as health, wealth and strength are made, in the course of experience . . . Truth in science is what gives the maximum possible sum of satisfactions . . . We must find a theory that will *work.*" Thus, the workability of an idea is its verification; otherwise it is worse than useless, it is neither true nor is it significant.

Philosophical Dispositions.

James is convinced that an individual's personality plays an important role in determining the metaphysical position which attracts him; philosophical beliefs are psychologically motivated. A person who is predisposed to be tough mentally will gravitate toward an empirical philosophy which is factually grounded, whereas his complement, the sentimentalistically disposed individual, will be attracted toward a Rationalism or Idealism. Bostonians typify the tender-minded, whereas the Rocky Mountain toughs are their opposite in both personality and thought; however, it is our personalities, not our localities, which predispose us to the philosophical ideas to which we adhere. Each considers the other type inferior to self, but actually neither is bad, and most of us are found somewhere between the two extremes with ambivalent tendencies which, at times, are predisposed to one of either direction. "Most of us have, of course, no very definite intellectual temperament, we are a mixture of opposite ingredients, each one present very moderately . . . You recognize these contrasts as familiar; well, in philosophy we have a very similar contrast expressed in the pair of terms 'rationalist' and 'empiricist,' 'empiricist' meaning your lover of facts in all their crude variety, 'rationalist' meaning your devotee to abstract and eternal principles. No one can live an hour without both facts and principles, so it is a difference rather of emphasis . . . Nature seems to combine most frequently with intellectualism an idealistic and optimistic tendency. Empiricists on the other hand are not uncommonly materialistic . . . Rationalism is always monistic. It starts from wholes and universals, and makes much of the unity of things. Empiricism starts from parts, and makes of the whole a collection — is not adverse therefore to calling itself pluralistic. Rationalism usually considers itself more religious than empiricism . . . It is a true claim when the individual rationalist is what is called a man of feeling, and when the individual empiricist prides himself on being hard-headed. In that case the rationalist will usually also be in favor of what is called free-will, and the empiricist will be a fatalist . . . The rationalist finally will be of dogmatic temper in his affirmations, while the empiricist may be more skeptical and open to discussion." William James was also a psychologist as well as a philosopher; he has been described as the most outstanding American psychologist this country has had thus far. These types of which he has been speaking are an indication of the psychologist in him making an appearance, not the philosopher.

James lists the characteristics of each type:

THE TENDER-MINDED	THE TOUGH-MINDED
Rationalistic (going by 'principles')	Empiricist (going by 'facts')
Intellectualistic	Sensationalistic
Idealistic	Materialistic
Optimistic	Pessimistic
Religious	Irreligious
Free-willist	Fatalistic
Monistic	Pluralistic
Dogmatical	Skeptical

How ironic it is that James considered himself one of the 'tough-minded,' since his home and family background are that of the proper Bostonian, whereas his colleague whom he brought from the rough West in its pioneering days, the Idealist Josiah Royce, he regarded as the tender-minded Bostonian.

2. Charles Sanders Peirce — Pragmaticism

Although James, Peirce, and Dewey are credited as co-founders of Pragmatism, Peirce justly deserves the credit as the *father* of this school of thought. Not only did Peirce coin the term *Pragmatism,* but when he was expounding Pragmatism at Johns Hopkins University, Dewey was merely a student under his tutelege, and at that particular time had no concept of Pragmatism, but was deeply immersed in Hegelianism.

Pragmatism is predominantly an American philosophy; the three Pragmatist giants: James, Peirce, and Dewey built the philosophy almost single-handed. Moreover, the lines of the three converge; not only at the point of Dewey's contact with Peirce at Johns Hopkins, but Peirce, for a brief time was James' colleague in the department of philosophy at Harvard University.

Although Peirce referred to himself as a Pragma*ticist* in order to distinguish himself from his fellow Pragmatists, who in his estimation had adulterated Pragmatism to an intolerable degree, his philosophy is usually termed Pragmatism.

A fair amount of Peirce's material is yet relatively inaccessible; in recent years, additional papers have gradually been made available to the public. It was as late as 1931 that Charles Hartshorne and Paul Weiss compiled Peirce's *Collected Papers* (published by Harvard University Press), but even these are far from complete. All of his important work consists of papers, most of which were written for *Popular Science Monthly,* since this was a chief source of income, despite the fact that it was beneath the dignity of his talents. Of his many papers, the most influential, and those from which much of the quoted material found in the present section is taken are: "The Fixation of Belief" *(Popular Science Monthly,* 1877), "How To Make Our Ideas Clear" *(Popular Science Monthly,* 1878), "The Architecture of Theories" *(The Monist,* 1891), "The Doctrine of Necessity" (*The Monist,* 1892), "What Pragmatism Is" *(The Monist,* 1905), "Issues of Pragmatism" *(The Monist,* 1905).

Pragmaticism Defined.

Peirce originally defined Pragmatism as follows: "Consider what effects that might conceivably have practical bearings you *conceive* the object of your *conception* to have. Then, your *conception* of those effects is the whole of your *conception* of the objects."[1] Later, he defined it: "The entire intellectual purport of any symbol consists in the total of all general modes of rational conduct which, conditionally upon all the possible different circumstances and desires, would ensue upon the acceptance of the symbol."[2] Faithful to the mainstream of Pragmatism, Peirce unites thought with action; the significance of an idea, or of a reality, is the nature of the consequences from which understanding of the object is derived.

Peirce is committed to the Pragmatic conclusion "that the whole function of thought is to produce habits of action."[3] Consequently, the meaning of any idea is: "To determine what habits it produces, for what a thing means is simply what habits it involves. Now, the identity of a habit depends on how it might lead us to act, not merely under such as might possibly occur, no matter how improbable they may be. What the habit is depends on *when* and *how* it causes us to act. As for the *when,* every stimulus to action is derived from perception; as for the *how,* every purpose of action is to produce some sensible result. Thus, we come down to what is tangible and practical as the root of every real distinction of thought, no matter how subtile it may be; and there is no distinction of meaning so fine as to consist in anything but a possible difference of *practice.*"[4] For example, in the Christian Eucharist which involves the Doctrine of Transubstantiation, in which it is claimed that the wine undergoes a metaphysical change of properties, if results which affect the senses are absent, then the idea of Transubstantiation is neither clear nor distinct, hence has no claim to validity, since the only meaning which wine can have is that it has certain effects, *i.e.,* sensible effects. "It appears, then, that the rule for attaining the third grade of clearness of apprehension is as follows: consider what effects, which might conceivably have practical bearings, we conceive the object of our conception to have. Then, our conception of these effects is the whole of our conception of the object."[5] The first two grades are: (1) an idea must be *clear;* "a clear idea is defined as one which is so apprehended that it will be recognized wherever it is met with, and so that no other will be mistaken for it."[6] However, clearness must be accompanied by (2) *distinctness;* "a distinct idea is defined as one which

[1] Charles S. Peirce, "What Pragmatism Is" *(The Monist,* 1905); and in "Issues of Pragmaticism" *(The Monist* 1905).

[2] "Issues of Pragmaticism" (*The Monist,* 1905).

[3] C. S. Peirce, "How To Make Our Ideas Clear" *(Popular Science Monthly,* 1878).

[4] *Idem.*

[5] *Idem.*

[6] *Idem.*

contains nothing which is not clear."[1] The third grade of clarification is the highest level, and requires that in order to find the clear meaning of an idea, the concept must be derived from its effects.

Effects are vitally necessary to the significance of an idea; the inner quality of an object is distinguished by its effects; otherwise, if the effects are lacking, "there is absolutely no difference between a hard thing and a soft thing . . . Thus we may define the real as that whose characters are independent of what anybody may think them to be . . . Reality, like every other quality, consists in the peculiar, sensible effects which things partaking of it produce."[2] But, "the only effect which real things have is to cause belief;"[3] and this is precisely the sole function of thought.

Doubt, too, has a function and serves an aim, its purpose is to stimulate thought, and thought consummates in belief. "Action of thought is excited by the irritation of doubt, and ceases when belief is attained; so that production of belief is the sole function of thought."[4] Accordingly, the sole motive, idea, and function of thought is to produce belief.

Belief possesses three properties: "First, it is something that we are aware of; second, it appeases the irritation of doubt; and third, it involves the establishment in our nature of a rule of action, or, say for short, a *habit* . . . Belief is only a stadium of action, an effect upon our nature due to thought, which will influence future thinking. The essence of belief is the establishment of a habit."[5] Not only is thought itself an action, it leads to actions, the principle of which is habit.

Habit is a deeply imbedded concept permeating Peirce's thinking extensively; not only are the laws of nature habits, but personal beliefs are also habits. Peirce devotes his paper "The Fixation of Belief" entirely to the manner in which ideas take hold or fix themselves on the minds of persons, individually and socially, causing them to behave in certain ways. Belief, however, he defines pragmatically, as "that upon which a man is prepared to act."

Belief is a "habit of mind, whether it be constitutional or acquired. The habit is good or otherwise, according as it produces true conclusions from true premises or not . . . The particular habit of mind which governs this or that inference may be formulated in a proposition whose truth depends on the validity of the inferences which the habit determines; and such a formula is called a *guiding principle* of inference.

[1] *Idem.*
[2] *Idem.*
[3] *Idem.*
[4] *Idem.*
[5] *Idem.*

Suppose, for example, that we observe that a rotating disk of copper quickly comes to rest when placed between poles of a magnet, and we infer that this will happen with every disk of copper. The guiding principle is that what is true of one piece of copper is true of another."[1] Habits of mind are not sterile principles which lack consequential import; they exist and come into being because of their practical necessity.

Beliefs penetrate deep into the personality, guiding an individual's line of logical thought and desires as well as his actions. "Our beliefs guide our desires and shape our actions . . . The feeling of believing is a more or less sure indication of there being established in our nature some habit which will determine our actions. Doubt never has such an effect . . . Belief does not make us act at once, but puts us into such a condition that we shall behave in a certain way, when the occasion arises. Doubt has not the least effect of this sort, but stimulates us to action until it is destroyed . . . The irritation of doubt is the only immediate motive for the struggle to attain belief . . . Hence, the sole object of inquiry is the settlement of opinion. We may fancy that this is not enough for us, and that we seek not merely an opinion, but a true opinion. But put this fancy to the test, and it proves groundless; for as soon as a firm belief is reached we are entirely satisfied, whether the belief be false or true . . . For truth is neither more nor less than that character of a proposition which consists in this, that belief in the proposition would with sufficient experience and reflection, lead us to such conduct as would tend to satisfy the desires we should then have. To say that truth means more than this is to say that it has no meaning at all . . . When doubt ceases, mental action comes to an end; and, if it did go on, it would be without a purpose, except that of self-criticism."[2] Consequently, the sum of our thinking in this paragraph has been twofold: (1) the settlement of opinion is the sole object of inquiry, and (2) belief is of the nature of a habit.

The Fixation of Belief.

Inasmuch as a belief is a habit of action; it would logically follow that differing beliefs would give rise to different modes of action; therefore, the process of fixing beliefs becomes a matter of moment. Peirce arrives at four methods of fixing belief: (1) the method of tenacity (dogmatism), (2) the method of authority (pontificating), (3) the a priori method (Rationalism, reasoning independently of or without facts), (4) the scientific method (empirical or factual method; *i.e.*, reasoning from the facts of experience).

[1] Peirce, "The Fixation of Belief" *(Popular Science Monthly,* 1877).
[2] *Idem.*

Each of these methods has its peculiar values, but the scientific method is preferable to the rest. The *method of tenacity* is an ostrich approach which buries its head in the sand on approaching danger, but this practice yields peace of mind and a calm faith; furthermore, it is rich in simplicity, directness, and strength. The method of tenacity is individualistic, while the *method of authority* is social, and creates a warm social feeling because the beliefs are shared as folkways, mores, religious beliefs, etc. which are issued down to the common people from those in authority, such as the Pope's edicts.

The first method is a 'willful' adherence to a belief, whereas the second is an 'arbitrary forcing' of it upon others. The method of authority has the value of controlling and guiding the masses. These former two methods give rise to doubts; accordingly, they must capitulate to the third method, the a priori, in order to alleviate a disturbed mind. The *a priori method* is not only capable of producing an impulse to believe, but decides which propositions shall be accepted as true, by rendering such propositions rational. "The *a priori* method is distinguished for its comfortable conclusions." [1] The a priori method subjects ideas to reason, but does not necessarily square them away with empirical facts; nevertheless, when the scientific method is inapplicable, the a priori method is preferable.

The fourth method, the scientific, is superior to the rest since it does not rely on subjective factors to establish its findings. Its evidence, data, or mode of verification is an appeal to facts, external permanency which minimizes the element of opinion, and by its use "the ultimate conclusion of every man shall be the same, or would be the same if inquiry were sufficiently persisted in. Such is the method of science. Its fundamental hypothesis, restated in more familiar language, is this: There are real things, whose characters are entirely independent of our opinions about them; those realities affect our senses according to regular laws, and, through our sensations are as different as our relations to the objects, yet, by taking advantage of the laws of perception, we can ascertain by reasoning how things really are, and any man, if he have sufficient experience and reason enough about it, will be led to the one true conclusion. The new conception here involved is that of reality." [2] One factor that removes Peirce from the mainstream of Pragmatism into Pragmaticism is his Realism, the belief that things exist objectively in reality, independent of our opinions, and that truth is the acquisition of the knowledge of these things which he terms correct opinion. Unlike other Pragmatists, Peirce does not repudiate the search for ultimate

[1] *Idem.*
[2] *Idem.*

reality, metaphysics, but he is interested in making it relevant; its practicality is a factor to be emphasized.

Although the scientific method is fallible, it does, nevertheless, yield integrity of belief, something to be highly prized. Peirce evaluates each method: "If I adopt the method of tenacity and shut myself out from all influences, whatever I think necessary to doing this is necessary according to that method. So with the method of authority: the state may try to put down heresy by means which, from a scientific point of view, seems very ill-calculated to accomplish its purposes; but the only test *on that method* is what the state thinks, so that it cannot pursue the method wrongly. So with the *a priori* method. The very essence of it is to think as one is inclined to think. All metaphysicians will be sure to do that, however they may be inclined to judge each other to be perversely wrong . . . But with the scientific method the case is different. I may start with known and observed facts to proceed to the unknown; and yet the rules which I follow in doing so may not be such as investigation would approve. The test of whether I am truly following the method is not an immediate appeal to my feelings and purposes, but, on the contrary, itself involves the application of the method. Hence it is that bad reasoning as well as good reasoning is possible; and this fact is the foundation of the practical side of logic." [1] These four methods of fixing belief are, to Peirce, essentially differing systems of logic; he considers of major importance the specific method an individual selects. For the sake of results gained, and especially for the integrity found in the scientific method, Peirce prefers the scientific method over the aforementioned three.

Tychism (Chance), Agapism (Love), and Synechism (Logic).

Although Peirce is a Pragmatist, he is not as extreme in his position as his colleagues, James and Dewey, for he emphatically believes in metaphysical reality, even to the extent of developing his own ontology. In this respect his system is non-Positivistic; indeed, in his "Notes on Positivism," he unequivocally declares Positivism to be entirely false. Elements of unmistakable Idealism are found in his metaphysical views; in "The Architecture of Theories," he writes: "The one intelligible theory of the universe is that of objective idealism, that matter is effete mind, inveterate habits becoming physical laws."

Principal concepts found in his metaphysics are: *tychism* (chance), *agapism* (love), and *synechism* (logic, continuity). *Tychism* is the doctrine that an element of chance exists in the universe, thereby making

[1] *Idem.*

it impossible to determine with finality the world's evolutionary behavior. The concept of tychism is the precursor of Helsenberg's Principle of the Indeterminacy of Matter and Bohr's Principle of Complementarity, a principle in quantum physics which regards laws of nature as statistically determined. In "The Architecture of Theories," Peirce says, "When we come to atoms, the presumption in favor of a simple law seems very slender. There is room for serious doubt whether the fundamental laws of mechanics hold good for single atoms." Peirce, fully aware of the extent to which he has radically departed from the traditional view of laws of nature, laws of science, concludes "The Doctrine of Necessity:" "If my argument remains unrefuted, it will be time, I think, to doubt the absolute truth of the principle of universal law; and when once such a doubt has obtained in living root in any man's mind, my cause with him, I am persuaded, is gained."

Synechism is the principle of continuity whereby the universe acquires habits of action, forms habits, that is, laws of nature; it is also the principle which governs the evolution of life and society, while *agapism* is the principle responsible for the world's rationality and symmetry.

Conceptions of 'First,' 'Second,' 'Third.'

The Peircean concepts of *First, Second,* and *Third* are logical principles applicable to philosophy; principles upon which a metaphysics of cosmic evolution is developed. "*First* is the conception of being or existing independent of anything else. *Second* is the conception of being relative to, the conception of reaction with, something else. *Third* is the conception of mediation, whereby a first and second are brought into relation. To illustrate these ideas, I will show how they enter into those we have been considering. The origin of things, considered not as leading to anything, but in itself, contains the idea of First, the end of things that of Second, the process mediating between them that of Third. A philosophy which emphasizes the idea of the One is generally a dualistic philosophy in which the conception of Second receives exaggerated attention; for this One (though of course involving the idea of First) is always the other of a manifold which is not one. The idea of the Many, because variety is arbitrariness and arbitrariness is repudiation of any Secondness, has for its principal component the conception of First. In psychology, Feeling is First, Sense of reaction Second, General conception Third, or mediation. In biology, the idea of arbitrary sporting is First, heredity is Second, the process whereby the accidental characters become fixed is Third. Chance is First, Law is Second, the tendency to take habits is Third. Mind is First, Matter is Second, Evolution is Third." [1]

[1] Peirce, "The Architecture of Theories" *(The Monist,* 1891).

These conceptions, or Peircean logical principles, are reminiscent of the Hegelian Dialectic, the thesis being First, antithesis representing Second, and synthesis, Third.

3. Ferdinand C. S. Schiller — Pragmatic Humanism

F. C. S. Schiller, the European chief representative of Pragmatism, develops his ideas in two important works, *Humanism: Philosophical Essays* (1903), and *Studies in Humanism* (1907); he credits much of the impetus for his ideas to Peirce and James. Schiller's Pragmatism which is the most radical of the group under consideration because he favors the Relativism of Protagoras, concludes that since nothing is final, man is capable of attaining opinions only, never reality itself. Faithful to Pragmatism he declared that man's practical interests have priority over his speculative or intellectual. Absolute axioms do not exist, unless they are accepted as practical postulates.

True to James, Schiller believes that truth is made, not discovered, for this is precisely the task of Pragmatism; it "essays to trace out the actual 'making of truth,' the actual ways in which discriminations between the truth and the false are effected, and derives its doctrine that when an assertion claims truth, *its consequences are always used to test its claim.* In other words, what follows from its truth for any human interest, and more particularly and in the first place, for the interest with which it is directly concerned, is what established its *real* truth and validity." [1] This concept of truth as related to human interest and consequences, Schiller credits to Peirce.

Two theories which share the same practical consequences must be regarded as identical, for, under such circumstances, the only difference is that they differ in words alone, not truth. Practical interest respecting man as a human being is of paramount importance; this is the significance of Schiller's Humanism. "Human interest, then, is vital to the existence of truth: to say that a truth has consequences and that what has none is meaningless, means that it has a bearing upon some human interest. Its 'consequences' must be consequences *to* some one *for* some purpose. If it is clearly grasped that the 'truth' with which we are concerned is truth *for man* and that the 'consequences' are human too, it is, however, really superfluous to add either (1) that the consequences must be *practical,* or (2) that they must be *good,* in order to distinguish this view sharply from that of rationalism." Eventually, all consequences are practical, including those which affect our nature, for later they will have overt results.

[1] Unless otherwise indicated, quotations in this section are from F.C.S. Schiller, *Studies in Humanism* (London: Macmillan and Co., Ltd., 1907).

Seven Formulations of Pragmatism.

Good consequences, those which fulfill our interests, are deemed true, whereas falsity consists of bad consequences or those less capable of satisfying our purposes. "All testing of 'truth,' therefore, is fundamentally alike. It is always an appeal to something beyond the original claim. It always implies an experiment. It always involves a *risk* of failure as well as a prospect of success. And it always ends in valuation . . . We arrive, therefore, at our first definition of Pragmatism as the doctrine that (1) *truths are logical values,* and as the method which systematically tests claims to truth in accordance with this principle." Implicit in this definition of truth is the necessity of its verification; truths which have not as yet been verified, or if for some reason cannot be, *are not yet truths.*

The most that can be ascribed to truths in such a state is that they are potential truths whose meaning is null and unintelligible, or at least conjectural, and is dependent upon an unfulfilled condition. "To become really true it has to be tested, and it is tested by being *applied.* Only when this is done, only that when it is *used,* can it be determined what it really means, and what conditions it must fulfill to be really true. Hence all truth must have been applied to some problem of actual knowing, by usefulness in which they were tested and verified." This point brings us to the second principle of Pragmatism: (2) *the 'truth' of an assertion depends on its application.* This principle implies that abstract truths cannot be considered truths in the full sense of the word. Truth, being concrete, necessitates a context which renders the statement true, that is, truth depends on who said it, to whom it was said, why, for what purposes, and under what circumstances. Truths lacking practical confirmation may be deemed false; at least this is the case in practice as far as everyday life activity is concerned.

These simple truths are lost to the philosophical intellectualist who has woven for himself a dream world of absolute truths in an absolute reality. The abstract truths of the Absolutist are meaningless, if inapplicable; even mathematical truths are incomplete unless applied to experience. "In short, truths must be used to become true, and (in the end) stay true. They are also *meant* to be used. They are rules for action. And a rule that is not applied, and remains abstract, rules nothing, and means nothing." Accordingly, we arrive at the third principle of the Pragmatist's method: "(3) *the meaning of a rule lies in its application.* It rules, that is, and is true, within a definite sphere of application which has been marked out by experiment." This rule combined with its antecedent permits a fourth rule: "(4) *All meaning depends on purpose,* or that which is tested is always done for some purpose; all Pragmatic activity is significantly purposeful. However, purpose need not be merely logical, often it is psychological; we are motivated psychologically by purpose, particularly in the human mind do we find meaning telic and selective.

Not merely the intellect, but the entire human being is an instrument for effecting adaptation, thus disclosing another major principle of Pragmatism, indeed, its most essential feature: "(5) *All mental life is purposive.* This insistence in reality embodies the pragmatic protest against naturalism, and as such ought to receive the cordial support of rationalistic idealisms." Pragmatism's next principle is to "constitute itself into (6) *a systematic protest against all ignoring of the purposiveness of actual knowing.*" This sixth rule is an injunction against both Idealists and Naturalists, prohibiting them from dehumanizing man's qualities; Naturalists deny freedom, thereby removing that human quality from us, while Idealists dehumanize reason, making of it more than the instrument it is for knowing.

Schiller has a strong tendency towards Voluntarism, and finds a definite place for it in his metaphysic; he believes that Voluntarism (will) entails purpose, hence it is fully in accord with our experience of activity which is always purposive. Metaphysics, for Schiller, is a luxury we can live without, whereas Pragmatism is not a metaphysic, consequently indispensable.

Pragmatism is closely allied to psychology, so close that a principle may be formulated in this respect: (7) Pragmatism is "*a conscious application to epistemology (or logic) of a teleological psychology, which implies, ultimately, a voluntaristic metaphysic.*" Thus we have complete, the seven essential formulations of Pragmatism; although these seven principles may verbally appear different, actually they are alike in meaning, each an expression of the essence of Pragmatism.

Humanistic Pragmatism.

"What is really important, however, is not this or that formulation, but the spirit in which it approaches, and the method by which it examines, its problems. The method we have observed; it is empirical, teleological, and concrete. Its spirit is a beggar thing, which may fitly be denominated Humanism . . . Humanism is really in itself the simplest of philosophic standpoints: it is merely the perception that the philosophic problem concerns human beings striving to comprehend a world of human experience by the resources of human minds."

Schiller is adamant in his stand that man and his activity are rightfully philosophy's central point of concern and proper scope of discussion; he denounces as meaningless that which is divorced from human purposes. Naturalists and Idealists tend to offend in this respect by their concern for that which is irrelevant to man; both schools of thought abuse the Protagorean principle, 'man is the measure of all things.' The principle's significance is Humanistic; whatever leaves man out of account becomes meaningless. The Protagorean principle does not repudiate the external world's reality, nor does it imply that man is the sole reality. "Humanism has no quarrel with the assumptions of common-sense realism; it does not deny what is popularly described as the 'external' world. It has far too much respect for the pragmatic value of conceptions which *de facto* work far better than those of the metaphysics which despise them. It insists only that the 'external world' of realism is still dependent on human experience, and perhaps ventures to add also that the data of human experience are not completely used up in the construction of a real external world." Actually, the reason Realists attack Humanism is not for what it neglects to include, but that which it does; it insists that man's entire integral nature be used as the basis of constructing a philosophy; moreover, the aim and conclusion of philosophy should be for man's complete satisfaction.

The proper advancement of Pragmatism, its proper growth leading to its natural culmination, Humanism, rather than stagnating at the level of epistemology, is to strive to more universal levels. "Humanism will seem more universal. It will seem to be possessed of a method which is applicable universally, to ethics, to aesthetics, to metaphysics, to theology, to every concern of man, as well as to the theory of knowledge." It is possible to constrict Pragmatism at the epistemological level, but to do this would be to arrest human development, and hamper life's interests.

The difference between Pragmatism and Humanism is merely one of degree; though both are methods, one is restricted to the problem of epistemology, whereas the other has wider applications, but neither need be involved in metaphysical questions. As methods, both are necessary for scientific progress, while a metaphysic is purely a luxury, an indulgence devoid of objective validity, an attempt to formulate the 'final synthesis of all the data of our experiences.'

Metaphysics, pretentious and lacking cogency, fancies itself capable of universal validity, but the truth is that *individual* men together with their peculiar experiences derive *individual* truths, not universal ones. Each man, therefore, ends with a philosophy distinctively his own, and believes it to be the one true system; moreover, this is the way that it should be. "Two men, therefore, with different fortunes, histories, and temperaments, *ought not* to arrive at the same metaphysic, nor can they do so honestly; each should react *individually* on the food for thought which *his personal life* affords, and the resulting differences *ought not* to be set aside as void of ultimate significance. Nor is it true or relevant to reply that to admit this means intellectual anarchy. What it means is something quite as distasteful to the absolutist temper, viz. toleration, mutual respect, and practical co-operation." This simply means that an individual should maintain his personal integrity by observing and reporting facts as he honestly understands them to be, rather than submitting to a superfluous tyrannous uniformity. Even two men devoted to the same cause need not think alike; human psychological make-up is such that we cannot see alike, nor will the universe ever appear the same to any two of us.

Although Pragmatism and Humanism are merely methods, they may function as a metaphysic, as a working conception of a science; however, functioning under these conditions should not result in a difference in doctrine, but merely a change in attitude toward them. "Methods may have metaphysical affinities. Thus our last definition of Pragmatism conceived it as derivative from a voluntaristic metaphysic. Humanism, similarly . . . may be affiliated to metaphysical personalism . . . Methods may *point*, more or less definitely, to certain metaphysical conclusions. Thus Pragmatism may be taken to point to the ultimate reality of human activity and freedom, to the plasticity and incompleteness of reality, to the reality of the world-process 'in time,' and so forth. Humanism, in addition, may point to the personality of whatever cosmic principle we can postulate as ultimate, and to its kinship and sympathy with man." Consequently, Pragmatism will not strangulate philosophy with monotonous uniformity; new systems will abound as before, but they will be much more brilliant, colorful, and attractive. The important factor is for metaphysics to submit itself to tests of Pragmatic verification, thereby divesting itself of obscurity and that which has no relevancy or real concern for human life.

The Nature of Truth.

Truth must be viewed in a human and Pragmatic light, for the predication of truth to any statement is a specifically human habit. Truth is a valuation, for "truth is a form of value, and the logical judgment a valuation . . . Truth we may define as logical value, and a claim to truth as a claim to possess such value. The validation of such claims proceeds, we hold, by the pragmatic test, *i.e.* by experience of their effect upon the bodies of established truth which they affect." Various degrees of truth exist; furthermore, truth is often *in the making* as well as already made or established.

Truth is a fabrication, a construction, because it is a human quality; all "*truth is human truth,* and incapable of coming into being without human effort and agency; that human action is physiologically conditioned; that, therefore, the concrete fullness of human interests, desires, emotions, satisfactions, purposes, hopes, and fears is relevant to the theory of knowledge and must *not* be abstracted from." Accordingly, all impersonal truth must be abandoned; independent truth isolated from persons does not exist; claims to impersonal truth can be easily refuted by subjecting them to Pragmatic tests and observing the absurdity of their consequences.

4. John Dewey — Instrumentalism

John Dewey early in his professional career acquired the term *Instrumentalism* to identify his particular mode of Pragmatism, and though his philosophy has been termed *Experimentalism* as well, the designation *Instrumentalism* appears to have predominated from the very beginning. Defining his philosophy, Dewey writes: "Instrumentalism is an attempt to constitute a precise logical theory of concepts, of judgments and inferences in their various forms, by considering primarily how thought functions in the experimental determinations of future consequences."[1] *Instrumentalism is the doctrine that ideas or theories function as instruments of action, and the utility of an idea serves to determine its truth.* In his Gifford Lectures of 1929, *The Quest for Certainty,* Dewey says, "the essence of pragmatic instrumentalism is to conceive of both knowledge and practice as means of making goods — excellencies of all kinds — secure in experienced existence[2] . . . According to experimental inquiry, the validity of the object of thought depends upon the *consequences* of the operations which define the object of thought . . . Conceptions are valid in the degree in which . . . we can predict future events, and can regulate the interactions that . . . take place . . . The test of the validity of any particular intellectual

[1] John Dewey, "Development of American Pragmatism" in *Studies in the History of Ideas* (New York: Columbia University Press, 1925), Vol. II, 351-377. Dewey's *Logic: Theory of Inquiry* in a real sense is the culmination of his ideas on logical theory which were introduced first in his *Studies in Logical Theory* in 1903, and later expanded in *Essays in Experimental Logic,* then summarized in *How We Think* for specific application to the field of education.

[2] John Dewey, *The Quest for Certainty* (New York: G. P. Putnam and Sons and Minton, Balch and Co., 1929), 37.

conception, measurement or enumeration is functional, its use in making possible the institution of interactions which yield results in control of actual experiences of observed objects."[1]

Operationally, a theory or idea must be carried out into practice if it is to have meaning; if the consequences of a theory can be predicted then it possesses *warranted assertibility,* as Dewey terms probability or proof. "The term 'warranted assertion' is preferred to the terms *belief* and *knowledge.* It is free from the ambiguity of these latter terms, and it involves reference to inquiry as that which warrants assertion. When knowledge is taken as a general abstract term related to inquiry in the abstract, it means 'warranted assertibility.' The use of a term that designates a potentiality rather than an actuality involves recognition that all special conclusions of special inquiries are parts of an enterprise that is continually renewed, or is a going concern."[2] Dewey is Peircean in this respect, for he believes that theories are constructed to provide discoveries; in fact, Dewey expresses his indebtedness to Peirce for his theory of inquiry. "The theory, in summary form, is that all logical forms (with their characteristic properties) arise within the operation of inquiry and are concerned with control of inquiry so that it may yield warranted assertions."[3] Logical forms originate in operations of inquiry as well as disclosing themselves during the process of inquiry.

Inquiry, we find to be a theory of investigation, of knowledge, of proof, as well as procedure; conflict or doubt evokes inquiry. In a sense, man would never bother to think if he were free from problems; problems disturb the mind's tranquility, driving it to inquiry, to resolve problematic situations. Without the presence of doubt, there would be no thinking; the steps in the procedure of thought are from doubt to inquiry to belief. "*Belief* may be so understood as to be a fitting designation for the outcome of inquiry. Doubt is uneasy; it is tension that finds expression and outlet in the processes of inquiry. Inquiry terminates in reaching that which is settled. This settled condition is a demarcating characteristic of genuine belief. In so far, belief is an appropriate name for the end of inquiry . . . *Belief* here names the settled condition of objective subject-matter, together with readiness to act in a given way . . . The end of inquiry is settled belief . . . If inquiry begins in doubt, it terminates in the institution of conditions which remove need for doubt. The latter state of affairs may be designated by the words *belief* and *knowledge* . . . I prefer the words 'warranted asserti-

[1] *Ibid.,* 129.

[2] John Dewey, *Logic: Theory of Inquiry* (New York: Henry Holt and Co., 1938), 9.

[3] *Ibid.,* 334.

bility.'"[1] Warranted assertibility, then, is the word for knowledge; one must possess warrant for his assertions, proof for his claims.

But proof is to be understood in terms of consequences, not groundless claims pontifically declared as axiomatic; norms, ideals, must have their practical applications, uses which prove their validity. Ideals, norms, are "needs to be satisfied; consequences to be reached;" they provide the necessary instrumentalities "in accomplishing ends and effecting consequences,"[2] but those which proved ineffective as procedural methods were discarded.

Logic, for Dewey, is 'the theory of inquiry,' and he so subtitles his book on this subject; inquiry is basically 'determination of an indeterminate situation.' Dewey's position is what may be termed *Conditional Pragmatism,* one which allows the "function of consequences as necessary tests of the validity of propositions, *provided* these consequences are operationally instituted and are as such to resolve the specific problem evoking the operations."[3] Reason, that is, reasonableness or rationality, is basically a relation of means and consequences; in setting up an end-in-view, reason requires that the means employed be relevant, applicable, useful to its attainment. Knowledge is never final, but instrumental.

Instrumental theory, a theory of inquiry, "says that knowing begins with specific observations that define the problem and ends with specific observations that can test a hypothesis for its solution."[4] Knowledge is a tool, an intellectual instrumentality, the utensil of civilization, a highly generalized intellectual tool, which the mind uses, and is prepared in advance for all sorts of intellectual emergencies, and when the new problem occurs, it does not have to wait till it can get a special instrument ready. True, the mind abstracts, but this is necessary if the mind is to apply its knowledge to other experiences, for "every concrete experience in its totality is unique; it is itself, non-reduplicable. Taken in its full concreteness, it yields no instruction, it throws no light. What is called abstraction means that some phase of it is selected for the sake of the aid it gives in grasping something else." Abstraction is akin to generalization, and both are vital to successful inquiry; each complements the other, or one may be said to be a negative function and

[1] *Ibid.,* 7.

[2] *Ibid.,* 6.

[3] *Ibid.,* iv.

[4] Except where noted, quotations in the remainder of this section are from John Dewey, "The Significance of Logical Reconstruction," chapter six of *Reconstruction in Philosophy* (New York: Henry Holt and Co., revised edition by The Beacon Press, Boston, 1949). Reprinted by permission of the Beacon Press, copyright © 1949 by Beacon Press.

the other a positive function; generalization is the utilization of an abstraction.

Inquiry is an experimental or functional type of logic, and as such, functions as a theory of truth, as well as a system of verification. "*If* ideas, meanings, conceptions, notions, theories, systems are instrumental to an active reorganization of the given environment, to a removal of some specific trouble or perplexity, then the test of their validity and value lies in accomplishing this work. If they succeed in their office, they are reliable, sound, valid, good, true. If they fail to clear up confusion, to eliminate defects, if they increase confusion, uncertainty and evil when they are acted upon, then they are false. Confirmation, corroboration, verification lie in works, consequences. Handsome is as handsome does. By their fruits shall ye know them. That which guides us truly is true — demonstrated capacity for such guidance is precisely what is meant by truth . . . Now an idea or conception is a claim or injunction or plan to act in a certain way as the way to arrive at the clearing up of a specific situation. When the claim or pretention or plan is acted upon *it guides us truly or falsely;* it leads us to our end or away from it. Its active, dynamic function is the all-important thing about it, and in the quality of activity induced by it lies all its truth and falsity. *The hypothesis that works is the true one:* and *truth* is an abstract noun applied to the collection of cases, actual, foreseen and desired, that receive confirmation in their works and consequences." Accordingly, truth is not static or passive, it is a dynamic, active, growing, utile, consequential, and satisfying value which is arrived at experimentally.

Truth is definable in terms of satisfaction, not mere emotional satisfaction, but "a satisfaction of the needs and conditions of the problem out of which the idea, the purpose and method of action, arises." In this sense, it is both public and objective, as well as useful, but truth defined as utility does not signify personal gain merely, rather "truth as utility means service in making just that contribution to reorganization in experience that the idea or theory claims to be able to make." A road's utility is not that which will profit the builder merely, but its value in functioning as a good road, an effective, useful, convenient means of transportation and communication, etc., "and so with the serviceableness of an idea or hypothesis as a measure of its truth." Such is the Pragmatic theory of truth, viz., that which is true is that which is verified, and that which is verified is that which has been subjected to the test of consequences.

Dewey's Instrumentalism can be, and is, applied to many phases of life: education, morality, religion, etc. *Education,* pragmatically speaking, must be serviceable, useful, applicable, consequential, and one whose objective or end is *growth*, or "the continuous reconstruction of experience;" *morality* is not to be interpreted in terms of abstract axiomatic principles, but growth, for "growth itself is the only moral 'end;'" *religion* must be consequential and relevant, uniting the ideal and actual, and this is precisely Dewey's definition of God – 'union of actual with ideal.'[1]

5. Evaluation of Pragmatism

Pragmatism has contributed considerably to the philosopher's quest by emphasizing an area which was becoming obscure and lost, viz., the practical side. Man is primarily an active, living, growing, purposive, animated, mobile being who must first live life, and only secondly speculate regarding it. Obviously, man's speculations must be relevant to his existence; his purpose for his understanding the world is to control and regulate it for the sake of better living. To effect this, the Pragmatist has stimulated the interest of philosophers of other schools, enlisting their time and effort in productive enterprises, beneficial to man; in this respect, the Pragmatist is also a Humanist whose efforts should be encouraged since they are directed toward far reaching beneficent human values.

The Pragmatist neither denies nor affirms the existence of ultimate reality and dispenses the entire matter as a vain and sterile endeavor, restricting his energies to that which fructifies in productive consequences. However, what the Pragmatist hopefully attempts to avoid, but because of the natural psychological constitution of man cannot, is man's need to comprehend his universe, his environment, for the sheer want of knowing, not merely for the sake of doing. It is as the Personalist Borden Parker Bowne aptly remarked: if man could, he would give up philosophizing.

Man is more than an activity being, he is a knowing being; furthermore, knowing is a form of activity. For example, the knowledge of God, ideals, principles, the universe's substance, metaphysics, etc., has a practical aspect, useful value, consequence, etc., but other than its ordinary application, and what the Pragmatist does not seem to be cognizant of, is the fact that the pure unadulterated knowledge of anything or that to which we refer as 'truth' is of serious consequence, moment, and issues in the most satisfying experience of all, that is to say, knowledge for the sake of knowing is of paramount consequence, value, merely because man is a rational being.

[1] John Dewey, *A Common Faith* (New Haven: Yale University Press, 1934).

Pragmatism, in a sense, is a philosophy of despair, a philosophy which grew up out of a condition in which the search for ultimate reality proved mentally exhausting, too much with which to cope, resulting in an attitude of throwing one's hands up in desperation and hopelessness, as a quitter. The Pragmatist, a valorous one, (and everyone must be a Pragmatist to some degree for the necessity of being one is inescapable, since everyday existence demands it), fulfills a phase of his life by accepting the metaphysical quest as a challenge and as an integral part of human existence.

XXXIV

DIALECTICAL MATERIALISM: *SOCIAL EXISTENCE DETERMINES CONSCIOUSNESS*

For introductory purposes, a fairly complete account of Marxian Dialectical Materialism was offered in Part Three, "Social and Political Philosophy," and additional information was supplied in Part Four, "Philosophy of Religion," consequently, a brief account emphasizing other elements of Dialectical Materialism as developed by *Karl Marx* (1818-1883) and *Friedrich Engels* (1820-1895) should suffice for present purposes.

As a joint effort, the chief works of Marx and Engels are: *Manifesto of the Communist Party, The German Idealogy, Address of the Central Committee to the Communist League,* and a volume containing the *Correspondence of Marx and Engels.*

The following works by Marx contain an introduction by Engels: *Capital: A Critique of Political Economy, Wage Labour and Capital, The Class Struggles in France 1848-1850, The Civil War in France, Critique of the Gotha Programme.*

The following are solely by Marx: *The Bourgeoisie and the Counter-Revolution, The Eighteenth Brumaire of Louis Bonaparte, The British Rule in India, The Future Results of British Rule in India, Speech at the Anniversary of the People's Paper, Inaugural Address of the Working Men's International Association, General Rules of the International Working Men's Association, On Proudhon, Wages Price and Profit, Theses on Feuerbach, Contribution to the Critique of Hegel's Philosophy of Right.*

The remainder were written independently by Engels: *Karl Marx, A Contribution to the Critique of Political Economy, Marx's Capital, The Housing Question, On Authority, On Social Relations in Russia, Dialectics of Nature, Socialism: Utopian and Scientific, The Origin of the*

Family Private Property and the State; Marx and the Neue Rheinische Zeitung, On the History of the Communist League, Ludwig Feuerbach and the End of the Classical German Philosophy, The Peasant War in Germany, The Peasant Question in France and Germany.

Dialectical Materialism

The Communistic ideas of Marx are grounded in the doctrine of *Dialectical Materialism* or, as it is known and taught today as a replacement of religion in the Soviet Union, *Dimat,* a term coined by contracting 'dialectical' and 'materialism.'

Marx's intellectual and educational background shed considerable insight into the development of his philosophical ideas: First of all, he owes an extensive debt to the German Idealistic philosopher Hegel, despite the aspersion he directed at 'the philosopher' who merely *interprets,* when the task is to *change* the world! [1] Marx insisted that the chief emphasis in philosophy should be action, not merely intellectual activity. From Hegel, he borrowed the concept of *Historical Determinism,* the doctrine that the course of history runs a prescribed inevitable pattern (that pattern culminating in Communism), a highly optimistic concept which assures final victory to Communism, and serves also as an excuse in instances where Communist uprisings have failed, the excuse being that the proper moment in history has not yet arrived.

The *Hegelian Dialectic,* the belief that a *thesis* conflicts with its *antithesis* to effect a reconciliation termed a *synthesis,* is the process out of which Dialectical Materialism emerged: the thesis being Hegelian Idealism, clashing with its antithesis, Ludwig Feuerbach's Materialism, and culminating in a reconciliation, the synthesis, Dialectical Materialism. A second reconciliation which Marx attempted to effect on a dialectical basis was a synthesis of science and ethics. He sought to give ethics, particularly social ethics, a scientific foundation, his chief sources of influence in this area being the Positivistic philosophy of *Auguste Comte,* the Positivism and Evolutionary Naturalism of *Herbert Spencer,* and the Evolutionary Naturalism of *Charles Darwin.* Ideas which set the stage for the *Labor Theory of Value* were prompted by the economists *Adam Smith, David Ricardo,* and *Thomas Robert Malthus.*

Dialectical Materialism is essentially a *metaphysics,* its basic tenet being the belief that reality is a continuous transformation in an evolutionary pattern from a *physico-chemical* phase of the universe to a *biological,* its second major stage, terminating in the present *sociological* era. This evolutionary development, however, must not and cannot be

[1] Karl Marx, *Theses on Feuerbach.*

explained on the basis of a mechanistic philosophy, but by dynamic, dialectical transformations. The dialectic is a rational principle, inherent in nature, responsible for the course or turn of events which history takes. The history of man, particularly social and philosophical history, follows the principle of a foregone or predestined plan culminating in world socialism, for this is essentially the doctrine of *Historical Determinism*. Communism, it is believed, will be the inevitable outcome of the history of nations or societies; people may accelerate its rate of progress, or they may retard its normal development, but never prevent its inevitable outcome. Each stage or period of history, owing to its dialectical character, carries within it the "*germs of its own destruction.*"

Historical Materialism and Economic Determinism

Marx argued that material conditions of existence determine the ideologies of people, such as their religious, political, and moral values, rather than their conscious thought and will. "In the social production of their life, men enter into definite relations that are indispensable and independent of their will, relations of production which correspond to a definite stage of development of their material productive forces. The sum total of these relations of production constitutes the economic structure of society, the real foundation, on which rises a legal and political superstructure and to which correspond definite forms of social consciousness. The mode of production of material life conditions the social, political and intellectual life process in general. *It is not the consciousness of men that determines their being, but, on the contrary, their social being that determines their consciousness.*" [1]

At a certain stage in history, material conditions of existence conflict, bringing about an 'epoch of social revolution,' transforming the superstructure of society owing to changes in its economic foundations. When men become conscious of this historical and social conflict, it affects their ideologies, thereby causing them to become disturbed. "In considering such transformations a distinction should always be made between the material transformation of the economic conditions of production, which can be determined with the precision of natural science, and the legal, political, religious, aesthetic or philosophic — in short, ideological forms in which men become conscious of this conflict and fight it out. Just as our opinion of an individual is not based on what he thinks of himself, so can we not judge of such a period of transformation by its own consciousness; on the contrary, this consciousness must be explained rather

[1] Karl Marx, *A Contribution to the Critique of Political Economy.*

from the contradictions of material life, from the existing conflict between the social productive forces and the relations of production." [1] Thus we find the contention of Marx to be that history, as well as a person's ideas, and the culture of his society, religious, ethical, political, are determined by the material conditions of his existence, together with the class struggles which ensue within a given society.

It is not principles or ideologies which keep two social or class factions apart, rather it is the material conditions of their existence, in other words, property, capital and landed property, such as a contrast between city and country people; a person's wealth determines his philosophical, political, and religious outlook. "Upon the different forms of property, upon the social conditions of existence, rises an entire superstructure of distinct and peculiarly formed sentiments, illusions, modes of thought and views of life. The entire class creates and forms them out of its material foundations and out of the corresponding social relations." [2] Persons may fancy that these are their own ideas consciously and independently arrived at, but actually they are prompted or motivated by their material conditions of existence.

From the thesis of Historical Materialism, it is argued that a man's existence determines his thoughts, not his thoughts his existence; his materialistic situation determines his thinking, not his thinking his material condition. Engels in reference to Marx's philosophy asserts: "Now a materialistic treatment of history was propounded, and a method found of explaining man's 'knowing' by his 'being,' instead of, as heretofore, his 'being' by his 'knowing.' " [3] The *being* which determines his knowing is essentially a struggle between two historically developed classes, the proletariat and bourgeoisie, grounded in historico-economic events. "*All* past history, with the exception of its primitive stages, was the history of class struggles; that these warring classes of society are always the products of the modes of production and of exchanges — in a word, of the *economic* conditions of their time; that the economic structure of society furnishes the real basis, starting from which we can alone work out the ultimate explanation of the whole superstructure of juridical and political institutions as well as of the religious, philosophical, and other ideas of a given historical period." [4] Thus we have the doctrine of Historical Materialism explained to us in terms of economic and material conditions of life determining our social, political, religious, moral, and

[1] *Idem.*
[2] Karl Marx, *The Eighteenth Brumaire of Louis Bonaparte.*
[3] Friedrich Engels, *Socialism: Utopian and Scientific.*
[4] *Idem.*

philosophical ideas, that is, our material circumstances determine our philosophies, and when our material circumstances change, our ideologies will concomitantly follow suit.[1]

Inherent in the doctrine of Historical Materialism is the doctrine of ***Class Struggle,*** for the two are inseparable, and present in all historical eras except ancient times. To Engels, this law of Class Struggle was the essence of Communism, and he attributes its founding to Marx. He writes: "Marx who had first discovered the great law of motion of history, the law according to which all historical struggles, whether they proceed in the political, religious, philosophical or some other ideological domain, are in fact only the more or less clear expression of struggles of social classes, and that the existence and thereby the collisions, too, between these classes are in turn conditioned by the degree of development of their economic position, by the mode of their production and of their exchange determined by it."[2] Engels fancied that this law of inherent Class Struggle, as he understood it to be, was as revolutionary and as profound as the law of the Transformation of Energy in physics!

Concluding Comments and Evaluation.

Dialectical Materialism, in academic circles, in the philosophical community, has conspicuously few adherents outside of the 'Iron Curtain' countries; its development has been predominantly Russian, and currently, the Chinese Red leader, Mao Tse-tung, is trying his hand at developing Marxian thought along Leninist lines.

Although Dialectical Materialism originated with Marx, considerable credit is owed to Engels who collaborated with him in a number of works, and developed with him many of the ideas credited to Marx. Dialectical Materialism's foundation was established by Marx and Engels through the latter three-quarters of the nineteenth century; later, others began to develop ideas along the Marxian lines. Chief exponent among these latter was Vladimer Ilich Ulyanov (Nikolai Lenin, 1870-1924), a militant Marxian Communist, among whose voluminous writings (comprising twelve volumes) the best known philosophical work is *Materialism and Empirio-Criticism.* His advocation of world revolution, particularly found in his book *State and Revolution,* provides the impetus for Mao Tse-tung to promote all-out war against the non-Communist world, particularly in the United States, which Tse-tung regards as the stronghold of Capitalism.

Following Lenin, Joseph Stalin (Iosif Vissarionovich Dzhugashvili 1879-1953), was the most vehement exponent of Dialectical Materialism,

[1] See Marx, *Theses on Feuerbach,* III.

[2] Engels, Preface to Marx's *The Eighteenth Brumaire of Louis Bonaparte.*

hence establishing the Marx-Engels-Lenin-Stalin line. Stalin's chief work is *On Dialectical and Historical Materialism* (1940).

Metaphysically, and even philosophically speaking, Dialectical Materialism is neither profound, systematically well developed, nor even a contemporary philosophy. For its metaphysical basis, it draws from philosophies which have been outmoded and buried by philosophers ages ago. Bochenski comments that "on the side of theory they are extremely weak. Not to speak of the almost pre-Socratic level to which dialectical materialism frequently restricts itself." [1] The school's principal value appears to be utilitarian, a political platform of a political party, whose thinking is rigorously regimented along strict dogmatic lines which allow for no progressive thinking on the part of its adherents, and for this reason solely, it can stagnate and die.

In respect to Marxian Socialist political thought, government rule by the *Dictatorship of the Proletariat,* the labor unions, the working class, who are enjoined to unite and thereby succeed in their common goal, has hardly any logic for its support. Instead of electing or even selecting the finest persons most capable of ruling, the laborers rule by dictatorship rights gained through violence. What a reprehensible and ugly thought to entertain, not merely for the Capitalist, but for any serious thinker, and particularly the philosopher, whose very right of philosophizing would be seriously curtailed, if not abrogated outright, because the philosophic quest cannot afford to be involved in vested interests which tend to corrupt its intellectual integrity and impede its honest and free search for truth.

If we may judge from the practice of Marxism by Soviet countries, philosophy would have a dim outlook resembling the era of the *Dark Ages,* for like the Roman Catholic Church, Russia has its "*Index Librorum Prohibitorum*" (Index of Forbidden Books) in which is listed not only books mentioning *God,* such as the Judeo-Christian Bible and the Koran of the Islamic people, but philosophers from Thales to Fichte! This state of affairs is worse than dogmatism, it is unequivocal intellectual suicide, the death of free thought.

[1] I. M. Bochenski, *Contemporary European Philosophy* (Berkeley and Los Angeles: University of California Press, 1957), 71.

XXXV

LOGICAL POSITIVISM:

Verifiability as Sense Observation

Logical Positivism, although a relatively young school, has made sizable strides, and has undergone such major changes and departures that its members have seen fit to designate themselves by new names, ones indicating more closely the nature and objectives of their school. Consequently, a flood of names has been circulating by which thinkers of this general outlook are designated, among which are: Logical Positivism, Neopositivism, Logical Empiricism, Scientific Empiricism, Philosophical Analysis, Logical Analysis, Metaphysical Analysis, Operationalism, Analytic Philosophy, Vienna Circle, Berlin Society for Scientific Philosophy, the Warsaw School, the Cambridge School for Analytic Philosophy, the Cambridge School of Analysis, etc.

The school's inception may be traced to 1924, when the Vienna Circle under Moritz Schlick (1882-1936) [1] conducted seminar meetings consisting of Gustav Bergmann, Rudolph Carnap, Herbert Feigl, Philipp Frank, Otto Neurath, Kurt Gödel, H. Hahn, F. Waismann, most of whom migrated to America. Prior to the era of the Vienna Circle, the school finds its ideas anticipated in Humean philosophy, particularly his views on causality and induction.

Antedating the school's inception in 1924, was the publication in 1921 by *Ludwig Wittgenstein* (1889-1951), the 'Father of Logical Positivism,' of his now classic *Tractatus Logico-Philosophicus,* [2] which has been treated somewhat as a Bible of Logical Positivism. Another notable work is *Alfred J. Ayer's* (1910-   ) *Language, Truth and Logic,* which first appeared in 1936, has since undergone many reprints, and has attained the status of a textbook of Logical Positivism.

[1] Schlick's untimely and tragic death was due to a psychotic student who killed the illustrious professor.

[2] First German edition in *Annalen der Naturphilosophie,* 1921; first English edition in 1922.

The Cambridge School of Analytic Philosophy received its impetus from G. E. Moore, the Neorealist, who himself never quite abandoned Neorealism, yet spawned a sizable number of Neopositivists, and wrote, if not as a Logical Positivist, at least material which was in concord with it. Both Wittgenstein and Moore were troubled with the thought that philosophers were attempting to say the 'unsayable,' what could not be expressed in words or defined; Moore's *indefinability of good* illustrates the point in question. Such considerations as this moved Logical Positivism into the area of Analytic Philosophy, with its emphasis on language clarification; and gave birth to Operationalism, with its insistence upon *operational definitions;* and later, prompted the Vienna School to equate philosophy with methodology, which drifted into a methodology of radical *Scientism,* the belief that scientific method alone issues in validity.

The last score of years or so, philosophy in England has been dominated by Analytical Philosophy with its emphasis on linguistic analysis. The adherents of this school of philosophy object strenously to the misuse of language, and trace most indeterminable philosophical problems to this source. They predicate their philosophy on the belief that a properly formulated question will permit a clear answer; accordingly, the task of philosophy is fundamentally analysis, and the removal of ambiguities, thereby resolving arguments; often the removal of ambiguities reveals the argument to be meaningless. Owing to the fact that the prime objective of philosophy is remedial, linguistic therapy, the removal of ambiguities of language, this philosophy has been referred to as *Therapeutic Positivism.*

Gustav Bergmann (1906-), a member of the Vienna Circle, cites the salient features of Logical Positivism on which agreement seems to be established: "(a) Humean views on causality and induction; (b) the tautological nature of logical and mathematical truths; (c) philosophy as a logical analysis, *i.e.,* as a clarification of the language which we all speak in everyday life; and (d) that such analysis leads to the 'rejection of metaphysics.'"[1]

Neopositivists regard the *analysis of language* as their principle tool in eliminating error and confusion; practically, it has assumed proportions of a methodology and criterion of truth. The importance of the function of language has stimulated the adherents of this school to attempt development of an *ideal language;* its requisites are enumerated

[1] Gustav Bergmann, "Logical Positivism" in *A History of Philosophical Systems,* Vergilius Ferm, Ed., (New York: Philosophical Library, Inc., 1950), 472. The author has taken the liberty of omitting a few words (such as verbs) in this quotation, enabling it to read smoothly as a series.

by Bergmann: It must be "(1) *complete,* (2) *formally constructed,* and (3) it must allow for the *resolution of all philosophical puzzles.*"[1] The Analytic Philosopher's ideal language is not complete in the literal sense, such as are English, German, etc., but is a blueprint or schema, "complete only in the sense that it shows, in principle, the structure and systematic arrangement of all areas of our experience,"[2] by stipulating that an adequate number of observable predicates be used to identify undefined terms.

The criterion of truth to which the Logical Positivist adheres is *public inspection,* that is, verification must possess intersubjectivity, the sense experience of a minimum of two observers; the witness of a single observer is insufficient, for he may confuse reliable reporting of sense with subjective illusions, error.

1. Ludwig Wittgenstein — Logical Atomism

All four of the above mentioned points of Logical Positivism are found in Wittgenstein's *Tractatus Logico-Philosophicus* (1921), according him the pivotal point at which Logical Positivism makes its departure from traditional Empiricism. For many, Wittgenstein is the undisputed dominant figure in the Neopositivistic movement, as well as the primary figure who inaugurated it.

One of Wittgenstein's major efforts is the foundation of an *ideal language,* since he feels that the 'logic of our language is misunderstood.' The aim of his *Tractatus* is "to set a limit to thought, or rather — not to thought, but to the expression of thoughts: for in order to be able to set a limit to thought, we should have to find both sides of the limit thinkable (i.e. we should have to be able to think what cannot be thought). It will therefore only be in language that the limit can be set and what lies on the other side of the limit will simply be nonsense."[3] Wittgenstein's chief stress has been upon the role of language, its use, abuse, and logical function. Language as symbol, if it is to be factually true, must depict a *one to one* relationship as representative of the facts of sense; this *one to one* correspondence of language is a mirroring of the structure of the world.

[1] *Ibid.,* 475.

[2] *Idem.*

[3] Unless otherwise indicated, quotations in this section on Ludwig Wittgenstein are from his *Tractatus Logico-Philosophicus* tr. D. F. Pears and B. F. McGuinness (New York: Humanities Press Inc., and London: Routledge and Kegan Paul Ltd., 1961).

The Later Wittgenstein.

A Viennese, but not a member of the Vienna Circle, yet like others who wanted to escape the Nazi regime, Ludwig Josef Wittgenstein emigrated; in 1928 he received his Ph.D., and in 1930 was made a Fellow of Trinity College, England, where, upon the retirement of G. E. Moore, he was appointed to his chair of philosophy in 1939. Although the *Tractatus* was the only book published by him in his lifetime, he, nevertheless, changed his views to the extent of repudiating the ideas expressed in the *Tractatus.* The *Tractatus* is based upon the doctrine of *Logical Atomism,* the belief that statements are reducible by analysis to their simplest component, the ultimate of analysis, and the apex of linguistic precision, thereby enabling one to construct an ideal language, and reap its concomitant, the elimination of confusion.

Wittgenstein later abandoned the doctrine of Logical Atomism of his *Tractatus* days which flourished during the period of the twenties, and turned to a Pragmatic or Utilitarian approach to language, interpreting language in terms of its use; and in the thirties a dictum of his became popular among the Cambridge School of Analytic Philosophy: *"Don't look for meaning, look for the use."* The doctrine of *Logical Atomism* assumes that simple ultimates exist, and when one arrives at these simple entities, he has disclosed the ideal or perfect language. These simple absolutes, like the axiomatic intuited truths of the Rationalist philosophers, the Cartesian innate ideas, were too Idealistic in nature to be acceptable to Logical Positivists whose criterion of verification was sense observation; accordingly, they were rejected by Wittgenstein, and supplanted by the slogan: *"Look for the use."* The treatment of Wittgenstein's philosophy which follows, the philosophy for which he is best known, is based on his *Tractatus.*

The Earlier Wittgenstein.

Wittgenstein, one time student of Bertrand Russell, has accepted Russell's *Logical Atomism,* [1] the theory that the world is composed of independent facts. Knowledge is a copy, a representation of these atomic facts, for it is impossible to gain knowledge of the world as a whole, but only of limited, bounded parts; this is the fundamental Wittgensteinian thesis. Knowledge of these atomic facts is the most precise or accurate, for they constitute the simple, the smallest part of which the complex is comprised. A proposition asserting an atomic fact is an *atomic proposition,* and is independent of any other atomic proposition, in the

[1] Russell attributes the origination of Logical Atomism to Wittgenstein.

sense that it neither implies, nor is inconsistent with another atomic proposition; but logical inference is *molecular*, it is not simple, nor atomic; it is involved in the construction of *truth-functions*.

Wittgenstein's *Tractatus* is unique in that it is composed of aphorisms, logically arranged by families: (a) logical structure of propositions, (b) inference, (c) epistemology, (d) physics, (e) ethics, (f) philosophy of religion, (or what he terms the 'mystical'). The ingenious characteristic of the book lies in the arrangement of each group by a common main number from one to six,[1] then each specific thought is subdivided as its nature tends to deviate from the main or original natural number one, sometimes extending to the fourth level of specialization; importance of thought rests with those aphorisms whose relative position is closest to the natural number. To illustrate both the unusual Wittgensteinian system and the points discussed above, the following selected quotations are offered:

1 The world is all that is the case.
1.1 The world is the totality of facts, not of things.
1.11 The world is determined by the facts, and by their being *all* the facts.
1.12 For the totality of facts determines what is the case, and also whatever is not the case.
1.13 The facts in logical space are the world.
1.2 The world divides into facts.
2 What is the case — a fact — is the existence of states of affairs.
2.063 The sum-total of reality is the world.
2.1 We picture facts to ourselves.
2.12 A picture is a model of reality.
2.13 In a picture objects have the elements of the picture corresponding to them.
2.131 In a picture the elements of the picture are the representatives of objects.
2.14 What constitutes a picture is that its elements are related to one another in a determinate way.
2.141 A picture is a fact.

Philosophy's objective is not to arrive at theories, but to engage in activity, viz., the logical clarification of thoughts and propositions. An unclear thought, or one which is not grounded in sense data, is repudiated as meaningless. 4.112 reads: "Philosophy aims at the logical clarification of thoughts. Philosophy is not a body of doctrine but an activity. A philosophical work consists essentially of elucidations. Philosophy does not result in 'philosophical propositions', but rather in the clarification of propositions. Without philosophy thoughts are, as it were, cloudy and

[1] Actually, there are seven, but the seventh is an isolated aphorism which reads: "What we cannot speak about we must consign to silence."

indistinct: its task is to make them clear and to give them sharp boundaries." Philosophy's task is to settle disputes pertinent to the limits of natural science; and its relationship to psychology is identical with the relationship it possesses with any other natural science — "the theory of knowledge is the philosophy of psychology." Here, a person must resolve the problem as to whether his study of sign-language corresponds to the study of thought-processes. Perhaps, the reader will recognize this as the philosophy of logic.

Although the propositions of logic are tautologies, that is, they say nothing factual since they are merely analytical, it is not the case with all propositions, for "the totality of true propositions is the whole of natural science," but philosophy is not recognized as a natural science. "The word, 'philosophy' must mean something whose place is above or below the natural sciences, not beside them;" as mentioned, its task is to clarify.

As to value propositions or metaphysics, there are none. Although propositions are of equal value, value *per se* does not exist in the world. "In the world everything is as it is, and everything happens as it does happen: *in* it no value exists — and if it did, it would have no value . . . And so it is impossible for there to be propositions of ethics." Values, not being objects of sense are *non*-sense; if they did exist, they would have to lie beyond the sphere of "what happens to be the case," that is, outside the world. Ethics, and what is the same, aesthetics, is transcendental, therefore cannot be put into words.

Will is not a moral concept, but possesses psychological interest only; and as to death, "the world does not alter, but comes to an end. Death is not an event in life: we do not live to experience death. If we take eternity to mean not infinite temporal duration but timelessness, then eternal life belongs to those who live in the present." In the same manner that our visual field is without limit, our life has no end; there is no guarantee that the soul is immortal. Eternal life is as much a puzzle as our present life.

God does not reveal himself to the world, not in the way facts do, and the "facts all contribute only to setting the problem, not to its solution. It is not *how* things are in the world that is mystical, but *that* it exists." These theological questions must be meaningless because "when the answer cannot be put into words, neither can the question be put into words . . . If a question can be framed at all, it is also *possible* to answer it;" and on the other hand, "skepticism is *not* irrefutable, but obviously nonsensical, when it tries to raise doubts where no questions can be asked. For doubt can exist only where a question exists, a question only where an answer exists, and an answer only where something *can be said.*" The same does not hold true for scientific questions, which incidentally, are the only legitimate ones, and should the time come when every scientific question is answered, the questions of the problems of life will remain unresolved. Life's problems are solved by eliminating the problem itself.

In conclusion, he writes: "There are, indeed, things that cannot be put into words. They *make themselves manifest.* They are what is mystical . . . The correct method in philosophy would really be the following: to say nothing except what can be said, i.e. propositions of natural science — i.e. something that has nothing to do with philosophy — and then, whenever someone else wanted to say something metaphysical, to demonstrate to him that he had failed to give meaning to certain signs in his propositions. Although it would not be satisfying to the other person — he would not have the feeling that we were teaching him philosophy — *this* method would be the only strictly correct one . . . My propositions serve as elucidations in the following way: anyone who understands me eventually recognizes them as nonsensical, when he has used them — as steps — to climb them. (He must, so to speak, throw away the ladder after he has climbed up it). He must transcend these propositions, and then he will see the world aright . . . What we cannot speak about we must consign to silence."

How very interesting and *ironic,* that the very philosophy propounded here cannot adhere to its own specifications and requirements, that is to say, by Wittgenstein's own admission, its foundation rests on *non*sense. Accordingly, he reduces his own book to the level of insoluble pseudo-problems, concluding that it too must be relegated to the realm of things of which we must be *silent.* Thus the conclusion of the treatise is that all propositions are senseless, including those contained in the *Tractatus.*

2. Alfred Jules Ayer — The Oxonian Logical Positivist

The Cambridge School of Analysis.

Turning our attention to the British, and the second great center of Logical Positivism, the Cambridge School of Analysis (the first being on the continent, the Vienna Circle), we find an imposing, irritating, yet stimulating account of Neopositivism offered by Alfred Jules Ayer, a professor at Oxford University, in his *Language, Truth and Logic.* The book, originally written in 1936 when he was a relatively young man for a philosopher, underwent a second edition, considerably modified and toned down in its radical position.

The British Neopositivists gravitated to an extreme position by accepting as the only meaningful language, physics; consequently, this doctrine was called *Physicalism,* virtual Materialism. Furthermore, they sought the unification of all science; in place of having an isolated and abstracted science of biology, one of chemistry, another of physics, etc., they moved to unify them into a single science with a unified language. The entire matter was predicated on the premise that verification is by the senses, that which relates to body and bodies in motion, a doctrine dating back at least to Thomas Hobbes (1588-1679), the first of the British Materialists.

Reducing all meaningful statements and verification to physics or objects of sense perception, eliminates metaphysical realities as valid, and reduces them to the level of pseudo-questions or problems; accordingly, God, soul, immortality, values, moral principles, aesthetic principles, etc., cannot be said to exist, but are brushed aside as sense*less* questions. These metaphysical realities are factually vacuous, consequently cannot be subjected to proof, therefore are meaningless. Metaphysical 'realities' are not rejected as *false,* they are *neither* true nor false, but *non*sense.

The Principle of Verification.

The object of any principle of verification is to provide a criterion to determine whether or not a statement is literally meaningful; only meaningful statements can be spoken of as true or false, the remainder are meaningless. A meaningful statement is a properly constituted *proposition,* of which we may predicate its truth or falsity. Propositional sentences express meaningful statements because they are factual; only factual statements are meaningful. We may now formulate our principle of verification: "A statement is held to be literally meaningful if and only if it is either analytic or empirically verifiable."[1] But verifiability is graded on two levels: weak and strong; "'a proposition is said to be verifiable in the strong sense of the term, if and only if its truth could be conclusively established in experience,' but that 'it is verifiable, in the weak sense, if it is possible for experience to render it probable,'" that is, if the conditions can be prescribed on which the experience may be gained.

Thus we find that a factual content, a sense experience, is necessitated to verify statements, to render them meaningful. "It is only the occurrence of some sense-content, and consequently by the truth of some observation-statement, that any statement about a material thing is actually verified;" or in the case of weak verifiability, statements refer to sense-

[1] Unless otherwise noted, quotations in this section are from A. J. Ayer, *Language, Truth and Logic* (London: Victor Gollancz, and New York: Dover Publications, Inc., 2nd ed., 1946). Reprinted through permission of the publishers.

content, since not all meaningful statements are directly verifiable. "I propose to say that a statement is directly verifiable if it is either itself an observation-statement, or is such that in conjunction with one or more observation-statements it entails at least one observation-statement which is not deducible from these other premises alone; and I propose to say that a statement is indirectly verifiable if it satisfies the following conditions: first, that in conjunction with certain other premises it entails one or more directly verifiable statements which are not deducible from these other premises alone, and secondly, that these other premises do not include any statement that is not either analytic, or directly verifiable, or capable of being independently established as indirectly verifiable." Unless a statement can be verified either directly or in the foregoing sense, it cannot qualify as a literally meaningful statement.

The Elimination of Metaphysics.

The elimination of metaphysical realities as nonsense is predicated on the aforementioned criterion of verification, namely, "we say that a sentence is factually significant to any given person, if, and only if, he knows how to verify the proposition which it purports to express – that is, if he knows what observation would lead him, under certain conditions, to accept the proposition as being true, or reject it as being false." Other propositions are either tautological, as in the case of mathematical or logical propositions, or they are pseudo-propositions.

Certain pseudo-propositions, although not literally significant, are, nevertheless, emotionally significant to the particular individual in question. Such is the case with metaphysical questions involving God, soul, immortality, and matters pertaining to other values, such as, moral principles, aesthetics, etc. We "maintain that no statement which refers to a 'reality' transcending the limits of all possible sense-experience can possibly have any literal significance; from which it must follow that the labours of those who have striven to describe such a reality have all been devoted to the production of *nonsense*." Some Neopositivists add that although it is nonsense, it is an important type of nonsense, but Ayer does not affiliate himself with this kind of 'unheroic' concession, which, to him, is mere hedging and evading the question.

All realities are nonsensical, including scientific realities, such as, power, energy, laws of science, laws of causation, etc., because they are not subject to sense verification, hence are as meaningless as those questions pertaining to God. Scientific realities are not observational or experiential propositions, they are not genuine factual propositions, they are transcendental, therefore are not literally meaningful statements. The only world is the world of appearance, the sense world, beyond this world — to predicate a world of reality — is nonsense. "Consequently, anyone who condemns the sensible world as a world of mere appearance, as opposed to reality, is saying something which, according to our criterion of significance, is literally nonsensical." The world of sense experience is the 'real' world; other than this world, or beyond it, none exists.

Philosophy of Religion.

Religious values, metaphysical in nature, such as the belief in God, soul, immortality, are relegated to the realm of pseudo-propositions, which is to say, they are nonsense. It is not that Ayer assumes a dogmatic Atheistic stand, declaring that God does not exist, he simply insists that questions regarding God are meaningless. "For to say 'God exists' is to make a metaphysical utterance which cannot be either true or false." The Atheist's stand is equally meaningless, "for if the assertion that there is a god is nonsensical, then the atheist's assertion that there is no god is equally nonsensical, since it is only a significant proposition that can be significantly contradicted." Hence, "all utterances about the nature of God are nonsensical." All this merely means is that religious knowledge is impossible; statements pertaining to religion do not constitute valid judgments since they are factually vacuous, literally insignificant.

The Emotive Theory of Values.

All values, moral, religious, aesthetic, etc., do not exist; accordingly, discussion regarding such issues are meaningless. Respecting these matters, we have reached the height of *Value Skepticism,* or even more, *Value Nihilism,* the nonexistence of value. The reason being that value judgments are not judgments at all, for they lack sense content, hence are nonsense.

Ethical considerations are not even matters of opinion as the Ethical Subjectivists attempt to maintain, but are completely devoid of propositional judgments, factual sense content, that is, they are not subject to public sense inspection. When we observe Hitler persecuting the Jews by executing them in his gas chambers, despite the meticulous care with which we observe, we will never be able to *sense* good or evil in the overt act. If, however, we wish to express our repugnance at Hitler's dastardly actions, it is not a moral disapproval which we express, in the sense that we express a moral judgment regarding his immorality, but an evincing or *ejaculation* of our feelings, similar to a psychiatrist's patient experiencing a catharsis.

Many persons on their initial exposure to Ayer's ethical theory, express serious doubts as to whether his Emotive Theory of Ethics is being accurately reported; some are stunned, dumbfounded, and wonder whether they are hearing correctly when Ayer's own words are read to them. Consequently, it seems advisable that instead of offering a second-hand formulation of Ayer's ethical position, he is permitted to speak for himself:

> We begin by admitting that the fundamental ethical concepts are unanalysable, inasmuch as there is no criterion by which one can test the validity of the judgments in which they occur. So far we are in agreement with the absolutists. But, unlike the absolutists, we are able to give an explanation of this fact about ethical concepts. We say that the reason why they are unanalysable is that they are mere pseudo-concepts. The presence of an ethical symbol in a proposition adds nothing to its factual content. Thus if I say to someone, "You acted wrongly in stealing that money," I am not stating anything more than if I had simply said, "You stole that money." In adding that this action is wrong I am not making any further statement about it. I am simply evincing my moral disapproval of it. It is as if I had said, "You stole that money," in a peculiar tone of horror, or written it with the addition of some special exclamation marks. The tone, or the exclamation marks, adds nothing to the literal meaning of the sentence. It merely serves to show that the expression of it is attended by certain feelings in the speaker.
>
> If now I generalise my previous statement and say, "Stealing money is wrong," I produce a sentence which has no factual meaning — that is, expresses no proposition which can be either true or false. It is as if I had written "Stealing money!!" — where the shape and thickness of the exclamation marks show, by a suitable convention, that a special sort of moral disapproval is the feeling which is being expressed. It is clear that there is nothing said here which can be true or false. Another man may disagree with me about the wrongness of stealing, in the sense that he may not have the same feelings about stealing as I have, and he may quarrel with me on account of my moral sentiments. But he cannot, strictly speaking, contradict me. For in saying that a certain type of action is right or wrong, I am not making any factual statement, not even a statement about my own state of mind. I am merely expressing certain moral sentiments. And the man who is ostensibly contradicting me is merely expressing his moral sentiments. So that there is plainly no sense in asking which of us is in the right. For neither of us is asserting a genuine proposition.
>
> But in every case in which one would commonly be said to be making an ethical judgment, the function of the relevant ethical word is purely "emotive." It is used to express feeling about certain objects, but not to make any assertion about them. . .
>
> We can now see why it is impossible to find a criterion for determining the validity of ethical judgments. It is not because they have an "absolute" validity which is mysteriously independent of ordinary sense-experience, but because they have no objective validity whatsoever.[1]

[1] From *Language, Truth and Logic* by A. J. Ayer. Published by Dover Publications, Inc., New York 14, N. Y. and Victor Gollancz, London; reprinted through permission of the publishers. *Op. cit.*

Ayer's contention is that value sentences are not statements, propositions, judgments; therefore it makes no sense to ask whether or not they are true or false. In so doing, a person is merely raising a nonsense question, such as: Ask me a brown question? which, of course, is meaningless. Into the same category, Ayer places questions pertaining to God, values, metaphysical realities, etc. Sentences pertaining to morals are simply 'evincing of feelings,' not value judgments; they are not even statements about a person's feelings, but merely the ejaculation of the feeling itself, and carry no literal significance than emoting expressions, such as, *ugh, ow, oh,* etc.

3. Evaluation of Logical Positivism

Despite objection from certain quarters that the Analytic philosophers have created more confusion than clarification, credit is due the Logical Positivists for their diligent efforts in the area of semantics and logical syntax of language, comprising their attempt to educe a language which expresses our thoughts with a minimum of confusion and error. Though they also assume credit for launching mathematical logic, this is hardly the case, as Bochenski notes: "Mathematical logic must not be identified with neopositivism. Its founders were Platonists – Frege, Whitehead, Russell (at the time *Principia Mathematica* was published), Lukasiewicz, Fraenkel, Scholz, and many others. Nowadays mathematical logic has adherents in almost all schools." [1]

Logical Positivists must be credited with the sincere and noble attempt to bring philosophical speculation in accord with science, freeing it from the occult and shoddy thinking which stems from a disregard of acceptable standards and rules by which to verify facts of experience. Edgar Sheffield Brightman, in his evaluation of Logical Positivists, remarks that they "may well teach us to be precise in our conceptions of experience and of verification." [2] The Neopositivist's attention, centered on methodology, logical and linguistic analysis, the 'meaning of meaning,' has rendered us great service in eliminating, or at least diminishing, vagaries and loose language. Thomas English Hill notes: "The kind of Logical Positivism under consideration properly insists upon the importance of laying clear foundations in linguistic analysis before proceeding to other problems, for, until the meanings involved in a given type of experience are clear, further consideration of its problems is likely to be unavailing; and the emphasis of the Logical Positivists upon this point

[1] I. M. Bochenski, *Contemporary European Philosophy, op. cit.,* 252.
[2] E. S. Brightman, *A Philosophy of Religion, op. cit.,* 5.

has been clearer and stronger than that of any other."[1] The Neopositivists have always striven for better methods and more effective techniques in analysis and language, so much so, that a person could almost conclude that their entire philosophy is reducible to methodology.

The Neopositivist's eagerness to bring all philosophy under the scientist's realm of discourse, scientific method, has eliminated many of the facts of experience. In the area of metaphysics, because they have not found data resembling that which the scientist confronts regularly in his laboratory, the Neopositivists have eliminated this entire area of human existence as a nonentity. The tragedy is their assumption that what is inadmissable data to the natural scientist (the physicist), does not constitute any data whatever. Actually, what the Neopositivists have done is to acquire a dogmatic rule, and have concluded that whatever the rule is incapable of measuring is not only immeasurable, but nonexistent; it is analogous to a narrowminded carpenter who asserts that whatever his yardstick will not measure is neither measurable nor real.

It appears that the Neopositivist eliminates his opposition illegitimately by repudiating as invalid whatever propositions prove a threat to his system; instead of adjusting his system to accommodate new data, he denies their existence, validity, or genuineness, if they are discordant with his system. Yet, how very successful are the many sciences which do not meet the qualifications of the Logical Positivist standard of validity, particularly Psychoanalysis, Analytical, and Individual Schools of Psychology founded by Freud, Jung, and Adler respectively. Furthermore, even in the science of physics, the only science countenanced by many Neopositivists, great use is found for concepts which are used to describe phenomena of a nonphysical nature, or at least a nonsensuous nature, such as those of nuclear physics. Apropos to this point, Russell says: "From all this it seems to follow that events, not particles, must be the 'stuff' of physics. What has been thought of as a particle will have to be thought of as a series of events . . . *Thus 'matter' is not part of the ultimate material of the world, but merely a convenient way of collecting events into bundles.*"[2] Russell's point is a severe blow to Materialistic Neopositivists, if not all Positivists, but the point still remains that events are not publicly observable by sense inspection such as 'matter' is, but must be *intellectually* calculated by a *mind.*

These facts call for broadening the Logical Positivist's yardstick, public sense inspection, to a level where it is reasonably realistic, one which

[1] T. E. Hill, *Contemporary Ethical Theories* (New York: The Macmillan Co., 1950), 25.

[2] Bertrand Russell, *A History of Western Philosophy* (New York: Simon and Schuster, Inc., 1945), 832.

abandons the ostrich's technique of burying its head whenever confronted with conflicting facts, or the technique of the schizophrenic, who when dissatisfied with the real world, creates one to his own liking. Perhaps the best way to describe the error or inadequacy of the Neopositivist is to designate his criterion as committing the *fallacy of restriction,* a negativistic approach to a world which refuses to cooperate or bend to the desired specifications of a person's standard of verification. Whatever gave the Logical Positivist the right to assume that sense experience is the only criterion of truth, or that it is even adequate? Certainly it is not the criterion of the scientist, for ultimately he uses coherence as his test of truth. Whatever the scientist gains by way of knowledge in his experiments must eventually be formulated into a systematic logical whole, consistent and reasonable, rather than what public sense inspection approves; if the scientist depended upon public sense inspection, he would never 'get off the ground' into space.

Perhaps the greatest embarrassment confronting Logical Positivists is the *fact* that their entire philosophy rests upon an irreconcilable and irremovable self-contradiction, viz., the fact that their entire system rests upon a *principle,* a *non*-sense principle, one which is not subject to public sense inspection, the principle being their criterion of verification: 'Only that which is subject to public sense inspection is valid.' This very *principle* of verification cannot be observed by sense, is nonexperiential, yet it is the basis, the entire foundation upon which the Neopositivist's philosophy is posited. Instead of repudiating the principle as nonsense, the Logical Positivist sheepishly replies that he is justified in accepting its validity because he gains excellent results from the principle. However, if this bit of maneuvering is valid for the Positivist, why are not other philosophies entitled to take the same liberty, and utilize principles? Wittgenstein, speaking for the Neopositivist respecting this delicate and embarrassing predicament, writes: "He must, so to speak, throw away the ladder after he has climbed up on it." If we were to throw away every principle, or reject every principle as invalid, we would have to conclude total silence and speak not a word, as Wittgenstein observed and offered as the very last words of his *Tractatus:* "What we cannot speak about we must consign to silence." Hence the outcome of any logically consistent Neopositivist is: *total silence.*

Despite Ayer's objections to the contrary, Francis Herbert Bradley is correct in his assertion that "the man who is ready to prove that metaphysics is impossible is a brother metaphysician with a rival theory of his own." As the preceding paragraph indicates, metaphysics is an inescapable situation; in order to strike critically at another philosophy, a person must argue from some standpoint, and that constitutes his metaphysics.

Perhaps the most debilitating aspect of Ayer's philosophy is his Emotive Theory of Ethics. The extremes to which he has gone in this respect merely for the sake of consistency border on madness. Denying the existence of value judgments subjects his philosophy to the *reductio ad absurdum* argument since it would justify the cruel and vicious actions of Hitler and the Nazis, the actions of Nero, and other sadistic persons. The Neorealist, Bertrand Russell, who has marked leanings toward Neopositivism, notes this discrepancy in the restrictive methods of Neopositivism. Respecting them, he writes: "There remains, however, a vast field, traditionally included in philosophy, where scientific methods are inadequate. This field includes ultimate questions of values; science alone, for example, cannot prove that it is bad to enjoy the infliction of cruelty. Whatever can be known, can be known by means of science; but things which are legitimately matters of feeling lie outside its province."[1] Is this an admission that scientific method is good as far as it goes, but that what is needed, is a method for calculating values? Whether or not it is, one thing is certain, cruelty as demonstrated by the actions of Hitler and the Nazis cannot be dismissed as meaningless and inconsequential; it is incumbent upon the Neopositivists to produce a method which will analyze these *facts* as value judgments, not dismiss them surreptitiously as invalid data.

What must hurt the Logical Positivist who repudiates value judgments the most is the fact that when he disclaims judgments of value, he is in effect discrediting the value of his own position and writings; for example, when Ayer writes a book stating value judgments do not exist, it is in effect saying that his own laborious efforts and book do not possess value, that what he has to say in his book is neither true nor false, and that being the case: Why did he bother to write at all, since it is *valueless* in his estimation?

[1] *Op. cit.*, 834.

XXXVI

NEO-THOMISM:

The Primacy of Act (Existence) Over Potency (Essence)

Neo-Thomists, also referred to as Neo-Scholastics, Scholastics, Thomists, and in metaphysics, Moderate Realists, Classical Realists, or simply Realists (not to be confused with Neorealists), are composed predominantly of adherents of Roman Catholicism. Among the few notable exceptions are: Mortimer J. Adler in the United States, and the Britisher, E. L. Mascall. Contemporary Roman Catholic philosophy may be divided along strict classifications, such as:

I. Roman Catholic Philosophy.[1]
- A. *Augustinianism (Intuitionism, Actualism):*
  1. Johannes Hessen
  2. Peter Wust
  3. Maurice Blondel
- B. *Neo-Scholasticism:*
  1. *Scotism (Franciscans)*
  2. *Suarezianism:*
     - (a) P. Descoqs
     - (b) L. Fuetscher
  3. *Thomism:*
     - (a) Synthetic Group Combining Thomism with Neo-Scholasticism:
       - (1) Joseph Maréchal
       - (2) J. Geyser
     - (b) Molinism
     - (c) Thomism (Proper):
       - (1) Désiré Mercier
       - (2) Ambrose Gardeil
       - (3) Joseph Mausbach
       - (4) Joseph Gredt
       - (5) Antonin D. Sertillanges
       - (6) Gallus M. Manser
       - (7) Martin Grabmann
       - (8) Reginald Garrigou-Lagrange
       - (9) Jacques Maritain
       - (10) Étienne Gilson

[1] Adapted from I. M. Bochenski, *Europäishe Philosophie de Gegenwart* (1947), 239.

Pope Leo XIII in 1879 issued the encyclical *Aeterni Patris,* declaring *Thomism* as the official philosophy of the Roman Catholic Church; accordingly, members of the Thomistic school of philosophy comprise those who endorse the fundamental principles of the philosophy of *St. Thomas Aquinas* (1225-1274). Neo-Thomism, although a designation assumed by any philosopher adhering to St. Thomas' philosophy, is predominantly composed of contemporary Roman Catholic philosophers who have assumed the task of defending and rendering tenable Thomistic philosophy, particularly as it confronts contemporary issues, and those problems created by modern thinkers, such as, Descartes, Kant, Heidegger, and others.

The two men, Étienne Gilson and Jacques Maritain, which we have selected for consideration as representatives of Neo-Thomism make no apology for Thomistic philosophy, and share the opinion that it merely requires restoration and application. Maritain does not even claim to be a Neo-Thomist (New Thomist), but elects to designate himself a *Paleo-Thomist* (Old-Thomist), or simply Thomist. Both of these men have emphasized the Existential nature of Thomistic philosophy, reclaiming Existentialism for St. Thomas.

1. The Twenty-Four Fundamental Theses of Thomistic Philosophy [1]

1. "*Potency and Act so divide being that whatsoever exists either is Pure Act, or is necessarily composed of Potency and Act, as to its primordial and intrinsic principles.*"

Every actual subsisting being — inanimate bodies and animals, men and angels, creatures and Creator — must be either Pure Act — a perfection which is neither the complement of Potency, nor the Potency which lacks further complement — or Potency mixed with Act — something capable of perfection and some perfection fulfilling this capacity. This statement is true both in the existential and in the essential order. In each of these orders the composition of Act and Potency is that of two real, really distinct principles, as Being itself; intrinsic to the existing being or to its essence; into which, finally, all other principles can be resolved, while they cannot be resolved into any other.

2. "*Act, because it is perfection, is not limited except by Potency, which is capacity for perfection. Therefore, in the order in which the Act is*

[1] These theses, translated by P. Lumbreras, were published by the Congregation of Studies on July 27, 1914. *See The Homiletic and Pastoral Review,* Vol. 23, October, 1922–September, 1923, pages 588 ff. and 1040 ff. "Twenty-four Fundamental Theses of Official Catholic Philosophy." Some Thomists regard these theses not as obligatory for Roman Catholic philosophers, but rather as a "safe directive norm." See: Bishop Fidel Martinez, "The Place of St. Thomas in Catholic Philosophy," *Cross Currents,* 1958, 55. The *Theses* are in italics, the remainder constitutes a commentary by P. Lumbreras. Reprinted by permission.

pure, it is unlimited and unique; but in that in which it is finite and manifold, it comes into a true composition with Potency."

Since Act means perfection, perfection belongs to Act by reason of itself; imperfection, then by reason of something else. Limits, therefore, belong to Act but on account of Potency. Consequently, if an Act is pure, it is perfection without limits, and gives no ground for distinction and multiplicity. On the contrary, any finite or manifold Act is mixed with Potency: for it is only as subjected in Potency that it is limited and multiplied according to the capacity of the subject.

3. *"Wherefore, in the exclusive domain of existence itself God alone subsists, He alone is the most simple. Everything else, which participates in existence, has a nature whereby existence is restricted, and is composed of essence and existence as of two really distinct principles."*

If there is any being, the actuality of whose existence — for existent means actual — is not received into the potentiality of essence, such a being subsists of itself, because it is perfection without limits; it is unique, because it excludes composition of any kind; it is the most simple Being: God. All other things, the actuality of whose existence is received into the potentiality of the essence, participate in existence according to the capacity of the essence, which limits in this way the actuality of existence. Essence and existence hold in them the place of Potency and Act in the existential order, and are two real and really distinct principles which intrinsically constitute the compound, the existing being, in the order of existence.

4. *"Being, which derives its name from existence, is not predicated univocally of God and creatures; nor yet merely equivocally, but analogically, by the analogy both of attribution and of proportionality."*

If the actuality of existence is in God a Pure Act and is in creatures an Act mixed with Potency, Being cannot be predicated of God and creatures in an identical way: God is self-existing, creatures have their existence from God. Still, because the effect in some manner reproduces its cause, Being does not belong to God and creatures in a totally different sense. Being, as predicated of God and creatures is an analogous term. Its analogy is first that of attribution, since Being appertains to creatures as far as they have it from God, to whom it appertains by essence; and is secondly that of proportionality, since the actuality of existence is intrinsic to God and creatures as existing beings.

5. *"There is, moreover, in every creature a real composition of subsisting subject with forms secondarily added — that is, accidents; but such a composition could not be understood unless the existence were received into a distinct essence."*

The compound of essence and existence is itself the subject or Potency of a further complement or Act: this Act or complement is but an accidental perfection. The new composition is a real one, as the addition itself is real. It can be observed in every creature. Bodies have quantity, spirits have faculties and operations upon which, furthermore, quality follows; every creature has some relation to the Creator. But this real composition of accidents and subsisting compound lacks a philosophical basis if we put aside the composition of essence and existence. The subsisting being cannot be the subject of accidental Act except in so far as it is Potency; but existence is not Potency. The actuality, then, of existence and that of accident come together in the same substantial essence only because this essence is a Potency really distinct from both Acts.

6. *"Besides the absolute accidents there is also a relative accident, or 'toward something.' For although 'toward something' does not mean, by its own nature, anything inhering in something, frequently, however, it has a cause in things, and, therefore, a real entity distinct from the subject."*

In addition to the absolute accidents – which modify the subject in itself – there is a relative accident – which affects the subject with respect to something else. The proper nature of predicamental relation consists in the very habitude to something else; relation, as relation, does not indicate inherence *in* something, but reference *toward* something. We may think of merely logical relation. This is not always the case. For often we have a real subject, and a real and distinct term, and a real foundation, no one of which, however, is that very habitude which relation means.

7. *"The spiritual creature is as to its essence altogether simple. Yet there remains a twofold composition in it: that, namely, of essence with existence and that of substance with accidents."*

The essence of angels is only Act, for the actuality of the form is not received into the potentiality of matter. Angels, indeed, are but intellectual substances, since to understand is a wholly immaterial operation. The last statement of the thesis has already been justified.

8. *"The corporeal creature, on the contrary, is in its very essence composed of Potency and Act. Such a Potency and Act of the essential order are designated by the names of matter and form."*

Besides the composition in the existential and accidental order, bodies are composed also in the order of essence. Besides, indeed, are extended and active, divisible and yet one, multiplied in individuals while keeping specific unity, subject to substantial changes, which by different and often contrary successive properties are made known. Consequently, there must be in bodies an intrinsic principle as the basis of extension, division, numerical multiplicity, the permanent subject of the substantial change; and another intrinsic principle as the foundation of the activity, unity, specific likeness, the successive phases of the change. The first principle, passive, undetermined, incomplete, potential, the root of extension, the support of the substantial change, is material and substantial. The second, active, determining, completing, term of the substantial change, is substantial and formal. Matter and form, then, constitute the essence of bodily substance: neither one is an essence, a substance, a body: each is but a part of the compound, which is a single essence, a single substance, a single body.

9. *"Neither of those parts has existence, properly speaking; nor is produced or destroyed; nor is placed in a Category except by way of reduction, as a substantial principle."*

Since existence is the Act of essence, neither matter nor form can be granted an existence of its own; the existence belongs to the compound. And because production brings things into existence, and destruction deprives them of it, the term of production or destruction is likewise the compound. Finally, since matter and form are substantial principles, they cannot be collocated among accidents. But neither can they be placed directly in the category of substance, for it is the complete substance which is classed there. They fall, then, into the category of substance by reduction, as principles of substance, as substantial Potency and substantial Act.

10. "*Although extension into integral parts follows corporeal nature, it is not, however, the same for a body to be a substance and to be extended. For substance of itself is indivisible; not certainly after the manner of a point, but after the manner of that which is outside the order of dimension. On the other hand, Quantity, which makes substance to be extended, really differs from substance, and is a veritable accident.*"

To have integral parts – homogeneous, distinct and outside of each other, united together at the extremities – is a proper sequence of matter, one of the essential principles of body. Still, body as a substance implies only essential parts, matter and form – heterogeneous, within each other, united together by compenetration. Substance, of itself, is indifferent to any quantity, and may even exist, miraculously, without any quantity. It is, then, of itself indivisible: not simply as a point – unextended by privation, – but as something devoid of dimension – unextended by negation. Substance is indebted to quantity for its integral parts; but as there is a real distinction between subject-of-existence and extended-into-parts, between the persevering support of successive quantities and these quantities in succession, substance is not really identical with quantity. Faith teaches us that in the Holy Eucharist the substance of bread disappears, but not its quantity. Quantity, therefore, is a genuine accident.

11. "*Matter as subjected to quantity is the principle of individuation or numerical distinction – impossible among pure spirits – whereby individuals of the same species are distinct from each other.*"

The principle of individuation cannot be the essence, for Peter is not humanity; nor some extrinsic mode added to the composite substance, for this mode, if accidental, cannot constitute an individual which is a substance and substantially differs from other individuals, and, if substantial, cannot be received but into some already constituted individual substance; nor the existence, for existence actualizes, does not modify reality and is received, moreover, into a substance which is an individual substance. Though that principle must be intrinsic to the substance, it is not the form because form is a principle of specific and common unity rather than of numerical multiplicity and incommunicability. This principle is matter. Yet not matter of itself, since of itself it is undetermined and capable of being in this and that individual, while the principle of individuation is a determining principle, and renders the subject incommunicable. Matter, as subjected to quantity, is such a principle. For, as related to quantity, it is conceived as divisible into homogeneous parts, and, as related to this quantity, it is conceived as incapable of some other quantity, and, then, as incommunicable to anything else related to different quantity. It is because pure spirits are not composed of matter and form, but are simple forms, Act only which exhausts by itself all the perfection of the essential order, that they cannot be multiplied in the same species: the individuals, indeed, would differ on account of their form, and a difference on the part of the form makes a difference in the species.

12. *"It is also quantity that makes a body to be circumscriptively in one place and to be incapable, by any means, of such a presence in any other place."*

Since quantity makes a body to be extended, and, thus, to have its parts outside of each other, it makes the whole body to occupy some place so that each part of the body occupies a different portion of the place. We have, therefore, some commensuration of the dimensions of the body with the dimensions of the place; and this we call a circumspective presence. But just on account of this commensuration quantity makes a body to be incapable of circumscriptive presence in more than one place; for the dimensions of the body are equal, not greater than the dimensions of the first place, and, since those dimensions are exhausted by this place, it is not possible for the same body to occupy simultaneously a second place. This impossibility is, therefore, a metaphysical one; not even by a miracle can we conceive of any such bilocation.

13. *"Bodies are divided into two classes: some are living, others without life. In living bodies, in order to have intrinsically a moving part and moved part in the same subject, the substantial form, called the soul, requires an organic disposition, or heterogeneous parts."*

Not all bodies are endowed with life: but some are. As living bodies, they have within themselves the principle and the term of their movement. This is to be understood, not as if the whole body, or one and the same part of the body, were both the mover and the moved, but that by nature one part is ordained to give and another part to receive the motion. The different parts, then, must be arranged into some hierarchy, and must be coördinated, not only as regards the whole, but even with respect to each other: all the parts, accordingly, cannot be homogeneous. The soul, substantially informing the organism, informs all the parts, and each of them according to the function each has in the whole.

14. *"Souls of the vegetative and sensitive order, properly speaking, do not subsist and are not produced, but merely exist and are produced as a principle whereby the living thing exists and lives. Since they depend entirely on matter, at the dissolution of the compound, they are indirectly destroyed."*

The substantial form does not subsist in the organic bodies of plants and irrational animals, because it has no operation independent of matter; it is but a principle of substance. A principle, however, that, in giving matter the complement wanted by matter for making up the compound – which properly exists and lives – is called the principle of existence and life. Its relation to production and destruction has been previously explained.

15. *"On the contrary, the human soul subsists by itself, and is created by God when it can be infused into a sufficiently disposed subject, and is incorruptible and immortal by nature."*

The human soul, independent of material conditions for some of its operations, is by itself a simple and complete substance. It is, then, produced from nothing, or created, and created by God, as we shall see. Naturally ordained to inform the human body, it is created when infused into the body. But, since the reception of any form presupposes a convenient disposition in the receiving matter, the infusion of the human soul implies a sufficient disposition of the human body. Such a disposition is not likely to be found in a body recently formed: vegetative and sensible souls would precede the human soul, as the servants precede the master for preparing a lodging worthy of him. Being simple, the human soul cannot be directly destroyed. Being subsisting, it can neither be destroyed indirectly upon the destruction of the compound.

16. *"This same rational soul is so united to the body as to be its single substantial form. By it man is man, and animal, and living, and body, and substance, and being. Soul, therefore, gives man every essential degree of perfection. It communicates to the body, furthermore, the act of existence whereby itself exists."*

Every one is aware of the intrinsic and mutual influence which exists in man between body and soul. Their union is not accidental. Body and soul come together as two constituent principles of a single nature, that of man. The human soul, the substantial form of body, gives matter, the substantial potency of soul, the first substantial act. By itself, then, it informs and determines the undetermined matter to a particular species. It gives to the compound all the perfection which is implied in this species. And it is subsisting, it communicates its existence directly to the compound, indirectly to the body.

17. *"Faculties of a twofold order, organic and inorganic, naturally spring from the human soul. The subject of the organic, to which sense belongs, is the compound. The subject of the inorganic is the soul alone. The intellect, then, is a faculty intrinsically independent of any organ."*

The immediate principles of operation are distinct from the soul: they are accidents, as the operations themselves. But their root is the soul, for they are vital faculties, and the soul is the principle of life. They are divided into two classes, according to the mode in which they spring from the human soul; subsisting by itself, and the form of body. In the latter case we have those faculties whose act is performed by means of bodily organs. Not only the vegetative faculties, but the sensitive likewise, are among them; for their object is extended. As organic faculties, they have for their subject the animated organism, which is neither the soul alone, not the body alone, but the compound. There are some other faculties whose operations are far above matter, and, accordingly, termed inorganic and are subjected in the soul alone. Intellect is such a faculty. Though extrinsically dependent on the imagination and indirectly on the organism, it is intrinsically independent of them.

18. *"Intellectuality necessarily follows immateriality, and in such a manner that the degree of intellectuality is in proportion to the remoteness from*

matter. The adequate object of intellection is being as such; but the proper object of the human intellect, in the present state of union, is restricted to the essences abstracted from material conditions."

Intellectuality means ability to reproduce in oneself the forms of the objects known, without any injury to the proper form. Matter determines forms to be but in this individual: no form can be known except as abstracted from matter; no subject can be intelligent except as independent of matter. A greater intellectuality corresponds to a greater immateriality, and, since matter stands for potency, to a greater act. In the summit of intellectuality the Pure Act is fixed; next, the Act mixed with Potency in the order of existence; then, the Act mixed with Potency in the very order of essence. A form cannot be reproduced except in so far as it is. Being is knowable in itself, and everything is knowable in so far as it is being. Still, the mode of operation is according to the mode of being, and since the being of our soul, in the present condition, communicates with the body, the connatural object of our knowledge is now the forms taken from the matter.

19. *"We, therefore, receive our knowledge from sensible things. But since no sensible thing is actually intelligible, besides the intellect which is properly intelligent we must admit in the soul an active power which abstracts the intelligible forms from the phantasms."*

Our knowledge proceeds, at present, from sensible things. This gives a reason for the union of soul and body. Upon the injury of some organs our mental operation becomes impossible; nor is it by chance that this is associated with sensible images. A sensible image, however, is not intelligible; for intelligible means immaterial. The intellect which properly understands is a passive faculty: it receives the intelligible forms, and does not make the forms to be intelligible. The abstractive faculty, notwithstanding, belongs to the soul alone, for it brings its object to the realm of the immaterial. It is, moreover, an intellectual faculty, for its function is to make something intelligible. It is called the active intellect.

20. *"Through these species we directly know the universal; the singular we know by the senses, and also by the intellect through a conversion to the phantasms; we rise by analogy to the knowledge of the spiritual."*

Since matter individualizes the forms, the forms become universal when abstracted from matter: it is the universal, then, we know directly. The singular implies material conditions and is known directly by the senses, dependent on matter themselves, and indirectly by the intellect, which, in taking the universal from the individuals, perceives the individuals which offer the universal. Starting from the material abstracted essences we arrive at the nature of pure spirits. We affirm of those spirits some positive perfections noticed in the inferior beings, and these we affirm of them in a higher degree, while we deny of them some, or all, the imperfections to which those perfections were associated in the material objects.

21. *"The will follows, does not precede, the intellect; it necessarily desires that which is offered to it as a good which entirely satisfies the*

appetite; it freely chooses among several good things that are proposed as desirable by the wavering judgment. Election, then, follows the last practical judgment; still, it is the will which determines it to be the last."

Will is not prior but posterior to the intellect, in dignity, in origin, in acting. The posteriority in acting is chiefly intended here. Every act of the will is preceded by an act of the intellect; for the act of the will is a rational inclination, and while inclination follows a form, rational inclination follows the intellectually apprehended form. The intellect, in presenting to the will some apprehended good, moves it as to the specification of its act. If the presented good is the absolute or universal good, the will desires it of necessity. If it is good mixed with evil, relative or particular good, it is partially attractive and partially repulsive. The will may desire it, or may not. Once the intellect has settled on the practical excellency of some particular good, the will must accept such an object. Yet, it is the will which freely sustained the intellect in its unilateral consideration; and it is the will which freely wants the process not to be submitted to a further revision.

22. *"That God exists we do not know by immediate intuition, nor do we demonstrate it a priori, but certainly a posteriori, that is, by things which are made, arguing from effect to cause. Namely, from things, which are in movement and cannot be the adequate principle of their motion, to the first mover immovable; from the procession of worldly things from causes, which are subordinated to each other, to the first uncaused cause; from corruptible things, which are indifferent alike to being and non-being, to the absolutely necessary being; from things, which, according to their limited perfection of existence, life, intelligence, are more or less perfect in their being, their life, their intelligence, to Him who is intelligent, living, and being in the highest degree; finally, from the order, which exists in the universe, to the existence of a separate intelligence which ordained, disposed, and directs things to their end."*

Since the proper object of our intellect is the essences of material things, it is clear we have no immediate intuition of God's spiritual essence, and, consequently, neither of His existence. Since the notion we have of His essence is an abstract notion, the existence implied in that notion belongs to the essential order and in no way to the actual. Still, we can demonstrate His existence with a rigorous demonstration which goes from the effects to their ultimate cause. St. Thomas furnishes five proofs, already classical. Things are in movement; whatsoever is moved is moved by something else; above the moved-movers is some immovable-mover. Things are efficient causes of others; they are not the efficient cause of themselves; outside the caused-causes is some uncaused-cause. Some beings did not always exist, some will not always exist: their existence is not essential to them; above beings which do not exist of necessity, is a necessary being. Things are more or less perfect than others; the less perfect has not in itself the reason of the perfection; above things which are limited in their perfection is some being supremely perfect. Things which lack intelligence act for some end; an intelligent being only could adapt and direct them to this end; there is an universal governing intelligence.

23. *"The Divine Essence is well proposed to us as constituted in its metaphysical concept by its identity with the exercised actuality of its existence, or, in other terms, as the very subsisting being; and by the same token it exhibits to us the reason of its infinity in perfection."*

Nothing in the Divine Essence itself can have the character of a constituent, for the Divine Essence is most simple. It is only according to our mode of understanding that we may ask which among the different perfections attributed to God is conceived as first, so as to distinguish God from creatures and to give ground to all the other divine perfections. That first perfection is the real identity of essence and existence: the subsisting being. By that God is distinct from creatures. In that is based any other perfection belonging to Him; for existence means act, and existence which is not received into essence means act without potency, perfection without limits.

24. *"By the very purity of His being God is, therefore, distinguished from all finite beings. Hence, in the first place, it is inferred that the world could not have proceeded from God except through creation; secondly, that the creative power, which directly affects beings as being, cannot be communicated, even miraculously, to any finite nature; and, finally, that no created agent exercises any influence on the being of any effect except through a motion received from the first cause."*

God's essence is God's existence; God is distinct from creatures whose essence is potency for existence. The world proceeds from God as the contingent from the necessary being. It proceeds by means of creation, for no emanation is possible in the pure act. Since creation implies the production of being from non-being, it is contradictory to suppose a creature exercising any causality in creation; it could not exercise that causality which belongs to the principal cause, for being is an universal effect, above the proportion consequently of any particular cause; not that causality which belongs to the instrumental cause, for there is nothing presupposed to creation upon which the instrument could exercise its efficiency. Finally, since every agent, by its act, moves toward the effect, this movement cannot be conceived independently of the first mover. The agent depends on God for its existence, for its powers, for the conservation of that existence and of these powers. It depends also on God for the very exercise of these powers. Because in exercising these powers the agent passes from Potency to Act, its faculties do not move except in so far as they are moved; there must be a motion coming from the immovable mover. This motion is received into the agent previously to the agent's motion; it is properly called *pre-motion*. And since it moves the agent to the exercise of its powers, it is properly called *physical pre-motion*.

The above document was prefaced as follows: "After the Holy Father Pope Pius X, by the *Motu Proprio* 'Doctoris Angelici' published on June 29, 1914, wisely prescribed that in all the schools of philosophy the principles and major propositions of Thomas Aquinas should be sacredly held, not a few masters, appertaining to different institutions, proposed to this Sacred Congregation of Studies for examination some theses which they were accustomed to teach and defend as conformable to the Holy Doctor's principles, especially in metaphysics." Note the arrangement of the above twenty-four theses: the first seven pertain to metaphysics, the next five to cosmology, the following nine to psychology, and the remaining three to philosophy of religion.

2. Étienne Gilson — Systematic Thomism

Étienne Gilson asserts that the only 'gateway' open to a proper understanding of Thomism is to connect a certain metaphysical notion of *Being* with that of the Christian concept of *God*. Both of these concepts will be discussed subsequent to that which claims priority, not on the basis of importance, but for an appreciative understanding of God and Being, namely, methodology, or two royal roads to truth.

Scholastic Method.

Gilson defines Christian philosophy, and by Christian philosophy he specifically has reference to Thomism, as "that way of philosophizing in which the Christian faith and the human intellect join forces in a common investigation of philosophical truth."[1] Both faith and intellect are prime requisites in the search for truth, and in the understanding of Thomas' thinking; it is indispensable and imperative that a person be inculcated with the ability to unite "the light of faith and the light of the intellect." Heretofore, persons have been advised to dispense with faith in their philosophical investigations, but to enter upon an investigation of Thomistic philosophy on this basis will definitely preclude one from ever grasping a proper understanding of this philosophy.

Two royal roads to truth are open to the inquirer: the first is the way of *faith*, revelation, and doctrinal instruction of the Scriptures; the second is the way of the *intellect*, philosophical sciences investigated by human reason. Both are valuable, and provided by God; not that both are necessary, for it is not absolutely necessary for God to arrive at this decision. Either road to truth may be travelled without the other, or both may be trod independently of the other. For example, man's salvation, which is *God*, may be effected through either reason or revelation, but "the same truth cannot be both believed and known by natural reason by the same person and at the same time," for knowledge eliminates the necessity of faith.

[1] Unless otherwise indicated, quotations in this section are from *Elements of Christian Philosophy* by Étienne Gilson. Copyright © 1960 by Doubleday & Company, Inc. Reprinted by permission of the publisher.

Faith is decidedly superior to reason, for its certainty and alacrity of deriving truth; furthermore, certain truths escape detection by knowledge and remain solely objects of faith. "If a certain truth is, of itself and absolutely speaking, an object of faith (as exceeding the grasp of reason), then it cannot possibly become an object of knowledge." These truths constitute a 'body of truth' which must be believed, since they are objects of faith and cannot be known; such may be called *truths of faith.* Perhaps the entire matter may be explained diagrammatically:

THE ENTIRE GAMUT OF TRUTH (‖═══‖)
(*Known Only By God*)

1. *Known By Reason* (——)
(Domain of philosophical Science)

2. *Truths of Faith* (---)
(Domain of Revelation)

3. *Domain of Both Reason and Revelation*
(Overlapping area)

Example of a truth of reason

1. H_2O known as water

Example of truth of faith

2. Knowledge of the Doctrine of the *Trinity*

Example of a truth of both reason or revelation

3. Knowledge of *God* by either faith or philosophical inquiry

Note in the above diagram that certain truths are obtainable by reason alone, others solely by faith, but common ground exists wherein truth is acquired either by faith or reason, such as truth pertaining to God's existence; truth relating to the Trinity issues by sacred doctrine or divine science, and is believed by faith, while the formula for water (H_2O) is known through the intellect, unaided by faith. The extremes of either side of the diagram constitute the area of those truths which are yet unknown to man either by reason or revelation, (but are known only to God). The entire matter is entirely God's doing, that is, God has chosen to reveal to man certain truths which do not transcend reason, others which do exceed human reason, hence "cannot possibly become known to man except by divine revelation . . . Sacred doctrine can treat objects which are the subject matter of philosophical sciences, not indeed as objects of these sciences, but as includable in revelation . . . In this way, sacred doctrine is in the mind as a stamp of the divine science . . . which is the one and simple science of everything."

Scholastic philosophy has been criticized on the basis that it eliminates the free philosophical quest of truth; since truth is given by revelation which the Thomist must accept on faith, why bother to indulge in philosophical investigation? When foregone conclusions are accepted, free thought is extinguished. Gilson responds: "Sacred doctrine resorts to the methods and notions of philosophy in order to make more clear the meaning of its own teaching. In such cases . . . the theologian makes use of human reason, not in order to prove the truth of faith, but merely as a method of exposition. Starting from some article of faith, the theologian argues in order to manifest consequences implied in it and which, therefore, necessarily follow from it. Thus to resort to human reason in expounding the teaching of faith does not do violence to its nature." Natural reason's task is to minister to faith.

Summarily, we may say that there are two orders of true knowledge: (1) 'truths of the intellect,' and (2) 'truths of faith.' The former constitute those which are derived independently by the intellect unaided by revelation; these compose the body of natural science and philosophical knowledge, whereas the latter are revealed truths which exceed the understanding power of the intellect. The latter, as well as the former, involve contingent truths entailing causation; these truths are not calculable solely in terms of rational prediction, but require divine light 'superadded' to mere natural light of the intellect.

The Philosophy of Being.

For the Thomist, three types of Being are acknowledged: (1) *Actual Being,* (2) *Potential Being,* and (3) *God's Being*. The *essences* of things are definable as their quiddity, objects as they are understood by the human intellect, and not as is commonly mistaken, the deepest layer of a material thing, its basic metaphysical structure; for "essences we conceive apart in our minds do not necessarily exist apart in reality." Human nature (essence) and a particular human being's existence are not the same. These abstract essences are attributable to the mind; true, the mind abstracts in order to theorize and understand, but reality is not composed of abstract notions. However, the desired goal of the intellect is to gain a conception of reality as it is in fact. "Now, in analyzing the notion of being, we stressed the fact that, in any being (any *habens esse*), that which has the act of being *(esse)* is the essence. It has also been said that the essence, or quiddity, is that which makes a substance to be a thing *(res);* it is not what makes a thing to be a 'being'; rather, what makes a thing to be a being is its *esse,* or act of being."

In the light of this discussion, we are in a position to appreciate the definition of truth, namely "a perfect correspondence between the knowing intellect and a known *being;*" or to state the classical Scholastic definition: Truth is "the adequation of intellect and thing (*adequatio intellectus et rei*)." Truth, by definition, is inadequate as to granting us a knowledge of reality, since reality is the existence *(esse)* of an object, whereas truth offers us only the essence *(essentia)* or quiddity *(quidditas).*

If by truth is meant the definition of essences of things, then truth does not exist, or to be exact, truth does not define the existence of an object, only its essence. Since man, God, and things are more than mere *essences,* they are existents, then the accepted definition of truth is inadequate until it can define *existences* of objects. "An existent is something that has an *esse* – that is, an act of being of its own – and since the essences of quiddities of sensible objects are the proper objects of human understanding, the second operation of the intellect cannot attain being without, by the same token, attaining the act that lies in it beyond essence." Thus the human intellect must delve deep into the layers of being and reach a layer more profound than the deep seated essence, to the layer of existence. Essences are nevertheless important, for without them existence cannot be. "There is no such *esse* without an essence or quiddity, whose act it is, but *esse* itself is not quiddity." Consequently, valid or genuine truth must consist of the intellect's transcending beyond the essence to existence *per se.* Accordingly, truth does not merely reside in the intellect, it is found in things also. In the light of the present explanation of reality, "metaphysics, the science of being *qua* being, must be understood as the science of that-which-has-an-act-of-being."

One of the profoundest concepts in Thomistic metaphysics is that of "the primacy of act over potency;" Being is dichotomously divided into *act* and *potency.* This dualistic view respecting reality is identified as *Moderate Realism,* and the primacy given act over essence makes it an *Existential* philosophy. In Neo-Thomism, *Being is act,* ultimately and absolutely. Potency is an aspect of Being, otherwise it would be devoid of any reality whatsoever; accordingly, potency or potentiality, must have some share of act or actuality. Essences have potential reality, but unless they possess actuality, they cannot be said to exist. An object or an essence perfects itself by transforming its potentiality into actuality by self-realization or self-actualization; in fact, this is man's moral task or objective in life. God alone, pure act, is free from all potential, is perfect, thereby needs not to realize or actualize himself. Potentiality is most indicative of materiality, whereas the higher the form, spirit, or soul, the greater the actuality. God is "wholly immaterial form . . . God is pure act; a form can be pure act, whereas matter always implies potentiality." Potentiality is laden with purposes, objectives which must be fulfilled in order to derive actuality, and requires a process of self-realization before its actuality can be said to be had.

Evolutionary Gradations of Being.

Thomism formulates a theory of evolution, but not one which has much semblance to the Darwinian mode; rather, it views the world as coming into existence in 'one fell swoop' by an act of God. Not all essences are of equal nature; some are superior to others; each falls on some level of a graded scale from lower to higher Beings, depending upon their respective natures or essences.

The *hierarchy of essences* proceeds from that which is found on the lowest level of Being, such as inanimate objects of the *physico-chemical* world, rocks, sand, etc., to the next higher level of 'causation,' viz., the world of *vegetation;* proceeding upward to another hierarchal level, *man,* a being composed of soul substance as well as material substance; and then again another step upward to *pure forms* (spirits), angels, pure intellectation; finally, we arrive at the pinnacle of the hierarchy, God, the Supreme Being, Pure Act (*Actus Purus*). "God is pure act . . . God is His own *esse,* His own act of being . . . He whose true name is HE WHO IS necessarily is, so to speak, by essence, the very act of being itself in its absolute purity. God does not own it. He *is* it." All beings up to and including man are comprised of matter and form, and by virtue of their materiality are imperfect because matter implies potentiality; until all potentials are actualized, perfection is impossible.

The following chart may prove helpful in illustrating the Act-Potency schematization which is *analogous.* Note well, it arises in Aristotle on *change,* but has been expanded by Thomas and Thomists:

Order of Being[1]

	Esse	Essence	Operation
Act	*Esse*	Form	Accident
Potency	Essence	Matter	Substance

Note that the above applies to all experienced beings; all are composites in several ways of acts and potency. What is act in one order may be potency in another; neither act nor potency is a complete thing.

[1] The author is indebted to Frederick Adelmann, S. J., Ph.D., chairman of the department of philosophy at Boston College, for the above chart.

Social Philosophy.

Neo-Thomistic social or political philosophy is predicated upon the doctrine of the hierarchy of Beings. Social or political equality does not maintain, and ought not to be practiced in a properly ordered society because God did not create men, or for that matter anything in the world, equal; consequently, some persons were made to rule, others to obey. A political society most closely adapted to the Neo-Thomistic hierarchy of Being is Monarchal, a form of polity in harmony with nature, a Monarchal structure with God its supreme head. "God is a Supreme Lawgiver, but all inferior lawgivers are co-operating with God in extending to human societies the legal structure of the created universe. In this view of the world, human laws are derived from the eternal law . . . To the question: whether the inequality of things is from God, Thomas answers in the affirmative, because the very diversity of natures presupposes their inequality . . . The universe is a structure of higher and lower beings, wherein the more perfect beings must act upon the less perfect ones." Correspondingly, in a society, the same principle maintains, namely the better or superior men ruling with the inferior obeying.

A well ordered State is predominantly a *Monarchy,* with sovereign power resting in the hands of a single individual, but within a well-balanced State, definite aspects of *Aristocracy* are found, with a number of persons assisting in authority; furthermore, an element of *Democracy* is also present, in cases where people have the right to choose their leaders. St. Thomas summarizes the matter succinctly: "The best form of government is in a state or kingdom, wherein one is given the power to preside over all, while, under him, are others having governing powers. And yet a government of this kind is shared by all, both because all are eligible to govern, and because the rulers are chosen by all. For this is the best form of polity being partly kingdom, since there is one at the head of all; partly aristocracy, in so far as a number of persons are in authority; partly democracy — *i.e.,* government by the people — in so far as the rulers can be chosen from the people, and the people have the right to choose their rulers."[1] Inequality is a fact of nature, and it is a factor which must be seriously reckoned with in the establishment of a political form of government if one wishes to avoid courting disaster.

Social existence is not a convenience for man, it is a need; "of his own essence, man is a rational animal that needs social life in order fully to develop his rationality." Unlike animal existence in which instruction is unnecesary, man needs a societal life for the sake of instruction so that

[1] St. Thomas Aquinas, *Summa Theologica,* tr. Anton C. Pegis (New York: Random House, 1945) I-II, Q. 105, Art. 1.

he can better and more fully actualize his potential nature. Consequently, God created societies for man's good; all laws, human, natural, divine, issue from God, hence must be obeyed for man's good. "Considered as directing creatures toward their divinely appointed end – the Wisdom of God is called the 'divine law.' The divine law is God himself as creating natures such as they are and act in accordance with their respective essences. As such, the divine law is the source of every other law and, in the first place, of the laws of nature, collectively called 'natural law.'" Since human laws are ultimately derived from eternal law, they ought to be obeyed. Likewise, since natural law proceeds from God, it too holds a claim to obedience.

God.

The central point from which all Neo-Scholastic philosophy emanates is God, the object of theology, philosophy, and man's good. Gilson, satisfied that the existence of God is not self-evident, adduces Aquinas' five arguments as proof of his existence: (1) The Way of Motion, (2) The Way of Efficient Causality, (3) The Way of Possibility and Necessity, (4) The Way of Degrees of Perfection, (5) The Way of Purposiveness.[1]

God alone is perfect, that is, he is 'pure actual existence,' wanting nothing, every potential realized fully; God's essence is his existence. "God is beauty because He is good, God is good because He is being, and since the essence in God is the very act of being *(esse)*, there is nothing to set any limit either on goodness or on being. Therefore, God is perfect and infinite by the very fact that He is Good. For Him, to be God simply is *to be*. And this is the only thing we have been saying thus far, that there is a proper name of God, and that name is: HE IS."

God is *actus purus*, pure actual existence, "a being that is to itself its own being;" his divine being is his essence or nature. "God is pure act, and since in Him there is no potentiality, there can be no essence distinct from the act of being." Consequently, God is not a body, but immaterial; his form is his essence. God is a pure immaterial Being, a self-subsisting form, the First Cause of the world who himself needs not to be caused. "He causes the world to exist by imparting to it an actual existence of its own." Prior to God, there is nothing, either in meaning or in reality, for he is the Prime Mover. Although he creates all else, he is his own act of Being. "God is being, and being is *esse* itself; that is, the very act of being. In God, Who is pure and absolute being, there is nothing other

[1] Since these five proofs have been treated in Part Four, they are merely mentioned at this point.

than this pure act whose name is I AM. Consequently, there is in God no essence distinct from the *esse* He is." All nature is imperfect, it must actualize itself, including human nature, but God, perfect, immaterial, unlimited by potentiality, is pure actuality, whereas all else must realize itself in God. "He Himself is to all things their common end, for He is their efficient cause, their desirable good, and their end."

Man.

Man is an existent Being; furthermore, his existence is primary to his essence; if he had merely essence, he would be *humanity,* rather than *individual* man. Man's nature is human, in essence he is human, but in existence, he is an individual, that is, he possesses a reality which humanity does not, an individual existent essence. Man is not pure spirit, he is a unity of mind and matter; owing to individuating matter from which individuating accidents are derived; man becomes an individual, a reality as a man possessing existence distinct from humanity which is man's essence or nature devoid of existence. "Man is an essence actuated by an act of being."

Man is a unity, not a duality, a substantial unity of matter and form (spirit); man is not a *pure* 'spiritual substance,' only angels are, but man is a spiritual substance unified with a material body. The spiritual substance of man is a human soul, an 'intellectual substance,' and intellectuality is the essential characteristic of man's spirituality. "To know material objects in an immaterial way is an operation in which corporeal matter has no share . . . Intelligibility and knowledge are inseparable from immateriality . . . The intellectual soul of man, then, must be an intellectual substance, a self-subsisting immaterial reality endowed with its own essence and its own act of being . . . A soul is a substance because it is composed of its essence, which is that of a spiritual form, and of its act of being *(esse).* In such an intellectual substance, the essence is its *esse* in the relation of potency to act." What makes the Thomistic concept of the soul unique, at least different from that of Aristotle, is that it is "a spiritual substance composed of potency and act; that is, of essence and existence." Thus the human soul is a substance in its own right, an act of being of its own, comprised of immaterial substance of pure form, unadulterated by matter.

Man's soul is by nature immortal; only God can annihilate a soul, otherwise it endures forever; the soul, being immaterial, simple, and having no parts, cannot disintegrate. The human soul is an *intellectual substance* capable of subsisting independent of the body. 'The human soul,' 'the intellective soul,' and 'the intellective principle' in man are synonymous, designating the same entity. That which distinguishes man from the angels is that his human soul is united with a body, otherwise he would know things by the intellectual principle (soul) alone, hence be an angel, but now he remains a 'rational animal' who knows not only by reason, the intellective principle, but must use his animal characteristics as well, namely, the sense organs, etc.; human knowing is fundamentally an animal function. "The intellectual substance we call 'soul' . . . The real substance, fully constituted in its own species, is neither the human body nor the human soul; it is *man*. The fullness of human nature requires that it be a substantial composite of a body and a soul, along with all the powers that are its instruments inasmuch as it is a knowing and acting substance. Now the same cannot be said of the soul. Unless it has or has had a body, a soul can neither know nor will." Unless the soul has or has had a body, it is "incomplete substance" because it cannot perform the functions of individual man.

Thomistic Ethics.

God created the universe and man; man exists because he is able to act, being is act; *to be is to act.* This action or function of man is purposive; God directs man by final causes, of which man is aware of some. "The act of being of each substance is, by the same token, an act of 'tending to': *esse est tendere.* 'Tendency,' 'inclination,' 'bent' are co-essential to Thomistic being. In other words, Thomas understood beings as always 'bent upon' the pursuit of some end. To begin with, all beings are striving to preserve their own existence; they aim to be, and they instinctively shun all that which puts their being in jeopardy." Furthermore, each Being is bent upon perfecting itself. In respect to ends or goals, nothing remains to chance; there is potency to act, and to act toward a given end.

A Being seeking its end, a desirable and suitable one, is referred to as *fittingness;* "for a being thus to 'fit' another being, as act fits what is in potency to it, is to be its 'good.' There is no more realistic notion of the good than that which makes it consist in the fittingness of a being to the being of something else . . . Goodness is not a 'value' superadded to being or attributed to it by the subject that desires it; goodness is being itself in its ontological relation to another being. Nor is goodness what looks like a good thing but is not; goodness is to be found in that which actually *is* fitting to the real being of another thing." Every agent is by nature seeking his own good, and acts toward that end, namely that which is suited to his nature.

Man's natural desires are good inasmuch as they tend toward that for which he has a natural bent, for *"the good is what all things desire."* The concept of chance has no place in the universe since it cannot account for order, and is discordant with it; all things have been created with a purpose, and have been ordered to act accordingly. Inclination not only tends agents toward their goals, but toward ones which are good for them, as the appetite directs one toward food for the agent's own good. "Having no knowing power of their own, natures can act as though they know what they are doing, but this is true because their first principle has for them the knowledge they lack. The flying arrow does not know its goal, but it reaches its target because it has been directed to it by the archer. In the last analysis, even natures are operating under the guidance of an intellect." This direction or inclination of natures is directly intended and willed by God for their own good. God, however, tends to no end, for he himself is his own end and good, as well as ultimately the good of all else. "Since all natures are being inclined to their own ends by the Prime Mover, God, that to which each of them is being inclined must be what is willed and intended by God. But God has no other end than Himself, and because He Himself is the pure Act of Being, He is supremely good. More exactly, God is the Good Itself, which is His essence, which is in Him *Ipsum Esse*. To say, then, that all things operate with God as their end is tantamount to saying that all things operate in view of the good. Now to operate in view of something is to tend to that thing, and to tend to something as to one's own end is to have an appetite for it. It is to desire it." Note that agents are not forced to their ends directly by God, but rather they by their own inner appetites, inclinations, wants, move themselves to their desired ends which are their goods. The end is merely appointed by God, whereas the craving is the agent's own desire.

God, inasmuch as he made everything with a view to himself, is the ultimate end, good, or object of desire of all creatures. "God has ordained all things to Himself as to their end; hence, all things naturally desire God." Man yearns for God, his supreme good and desire; furthermore, the same holds true for all other created things. The tendency toward God is an inclination to be like him; even the instinct of self-preservation testifies to this matter, the desire to stay alive is the desire for life and existence, that which originates with and is in God.

Human *will* is a *rational appetite* whose end is to imitate God; with it man possesses the power of choice. Man also is endowed with *intellect;* these two (will and intellect) being proper to man alone, are absent in the animal kingdom. Each has its function: "the object of the intellect is being known as being, the object of the will is being desired as good." Endowed with these two superior qualities which are singularly man's, he is enabled in a special way to tend toward God and tend to be like him, to understand God by the intellect, which is man's highest good, for this is man's supernal nature, to will to be like him, since man alone possesses will, choice. "Man seeks God, loves God, and adheres to God by his will. So the ultimate felicity of man is to reach its ultimate end, and since this end is to know God, the ultimate felicity of man consists in an act of knowledge; namely, in knowing God."

When man, by the light of his intellect and the power of choice granted through will, finds his pleasure in a fitting object, it is termed *love.* "In the operations of free choice (*liberum arbitrium*) man chooses by his will among the various goods offered to him by his sense perception and his intellectual knowledge. Through his will, man tentatively experiences a sort of complacency in each one of these possible choices. And, indeed, since each and every one of them is a particular good, the will finds its pleasure in assaying each as a possible object of final choice. This complacency of the will, either provisory or final, in objects that befit the willing being, is called love." Love is not only related to appetite, but inseparable from it; the supreme end of all appetite is God, hence the natural need for the natural love of God.

Love's object is invariably apprehended as good; since the intellect is man's faculty of apprehension, the intellect is man's supernal (divine-like) quality, and assumes absolute superiority, even over the will. Inasmuch as love is an aspect of willing and appetite, (defined as "a modification of the appetite whereby it delights in a certain appetible"), understanding supersedes love, or the intellect is in the ascendency over will. It is precisely for this reason that the end and good of man as an 'intellective soul' is to *understand* God – "the intellectual substance tends to the knowledge of God as its last end." In a certain respect, however, love is superior to understanding; by the intellect we know God mediately, indirectly through his acts, effects, etc., never himself directly, but we can love God directly as he truly is in himself.

3. Jacques Maritain — Existential Thomism

Metaphysics and Epistemology.

Of the two types of Existentialism: (1) one asserts the primacy of existence over essence or natures, and the primacy of the intellect (Thomistic); (2) the other accepts the primacy of existence, but repudiates essences and natures entirely (Satrean). Maritain not only accepts the first, but insists it is the only authentic form of Existentialism. "For if you abolish essence, or that which *esse* posits, by that very act you abolish existence, or *esse*."[1] The second form of Existentialism is repugnant because it posits not only man without a given nature, but also makes God devoid of any nature—an unthinkable notion. According to this philosophical position, the primacy of existence is gained only at the expense of abolishing essence or human nature. Atheistic Existentialism is driven to this untenable position owing to the belief that no God exists to conceive of human nature, therefore none exists; furthermore, Atheistic Existentialism reduces the rest of the world to an unintelligible, incoherent, orderless chaos. In desperation, Existentialists attempt to make Atheism livable, a philosophy by which man can adapt himself to the world.

The intellect is an indispensable aspect of existence, since existence itself is reached through the intellect. The intellect discovers facts rather than deducing them, and in this manner acquires truth. "Truth follows upon the existence of things, i.e. of those trans-objective subjects with which thought stands face to face. Truth is the adequation of the immanence in act of our thought with that which exists outside our thought." True knowledge is a type of super-existence in which I can enter or become the other object which exists; hence, knowledge is deeply immersed in existence.

Knowledge is attained through the *senses* and *intuition;* sense delivers to us the object as existing, while intuition, true knowledge, is the intellect's grasp of Being. "The intellect, laying hold of the intelligibles, disengaging them by its own strength from sense experience, reaches, at the heart of its own inner vitality, those natures or essences which, by abstracting them, it has detached from their material existence at a given point in space and time." Thus we find the intellect's function of judgment is an existential one.

The object of man's intellect is abstract perception, but not perception of eternal objects in a fanciful intelligible universe separate from existence, such as that found in Platonic Idealism. "The metaphysician knows that his task is to search for the ultimate foundation of the intelligibility of things as of every other quality or perfection of being. He finds it in the pure Act, and understands that in the final analysis there would be no human nature if the divine Intellect did not perceive its own Essence, and in that Essence the eternal idea of man, which is not an abstract and universal idea, as our ideas are, but a creative idea. What we perceive, however, is not this divine idea; it is not in this intelligible heaven that we grasp human nature. The intelligible heaven in which

[1] Unless otherwise indicated, quotations in this section are from Jacques Maritain, *Existence and the Existent,* tr. Lewis Galantiere and Gerald B. Phelan (New York: Pantheon Books, Inc., 1948). Reprinted by permission of Random House, Inc.

we grasp and manipulate essences and natures is within ourselves, it is the active immanence of our immaterial thought. In that path which the intellect cuts through reality and sense experience in order to obtain its sustenance, that is to say, in abstractive perception, what the intellect lays hold of is the natures of essences which are in existents or things or subjects (but not in the state of universality or intelligibility in act), which themselves are not things, and which the intellect strips of existence by immaterialising them. These are what, from the very beginning, we call intelligibles, or objects of thought." Judgment's function is dual: it is existential on the one hand by affirming existences; and, on the other, restores essences, intelligibles, objects of thought to existence by transposing simple essences of objects of thought to the plane of things which possess existence, actuality. However, existences are not essences and must not be so confused; existence is more basic, fundamental, primal to the mere intelligible object or essence, it is an act, a trans-objective act, a super-intelligibility of existence and actually given.

True Being, existent Being, is attained through *intellectual intuition;* in this manner the existent reality itself is reached; otherwise, a de-realized Being or pseudo-Being of other philosophies results. By 'authentic intellectual intuition' one 'takes the leap' from the sense of essence to the act of existing. "What counts is to have seen that existence is not a simple empirical fact but a primitive datum for the mind itself, opening to the mind an infinite supra-observable field — in a word, the primary and super-intelligible source of intelligibility." Ideas which intelligence apprehends are essences, not existences, for existences are distinct from essences. We acquire essences by simple apprehension, but the act of existence is derived through judgment; ideas are formed of essences, while judgments are of existences.

Nevertheless, existences cannot be detached from essences, for they both constitute one and the same Being; and it is Being which is the object of metaphysics, not as sensible things, nor as material things, but as Being. Being (as the object of metaphysics) is not a universal, and must not be so regarded; it is reality par excellence, but existence must be the existence of something, namely essence, hence for this reason cannot be detached from essence: thus every being directly experienced has essence and existence simultaneously. Accordingly, we may define Being as *"that which exists or is able to exist, that which exercises or is able to exercise existence."* The two fuse in unity by "the incomprehensible unity of *Him Who is.*"

How do we gain knowledge of these realities? By *intuition,* by the intellect, or by *reason,* which gives us knowledge discursively. "The thesis of the real distinction between essence and existence in all that is not God — in other words, the extension of the doctrine of potency and act to the relation between essence and existence, is directly connected with this intuition. This is, in truth, a thesis of extreme boldness, for in it potency (essence, or intelligible structure already achieved in its own line of essence) is completed or actuated by an act *of another order* which adds absolutely nothing to essence as essence, intelligible structure, or quiddity, yet adds everything to it in as much as it posits it *extra causas* or *extra nihil.* We can understand nothing of this if we confine ourselves within a purely essentialist perspective, if we do not see that the very intelligibility of the essences — I say, in things, not in our mind, where they are separated from things — if we do not see that the very intelligibility of essences is a certain kind of ability to exist . . . Knowability or intelligibility, essence, is to be understood in its relationship to the act of existing." The act of existing is not an essence, but the actuality of every form or nature. Existence at its height is to be found in God, who is "the very act of existing, subsistent by itself, namely, Being itself." Thus the heart of the metaphysics of Neo-Thomism is predicated on 'the primacy of the act of existing,' not essence but existence; and to exist, existence par excellence, is *act.*

Thomistic Personalism.

Neo-Thomistic philosophy differentiates between *persons* and *individuals;* "personality is the subsistence of the spiritual soul communicated to the human composite;" [1] while the individual is the material pole of a human being, a mere 'shadow of personality.' The spiritual pole constitutes true personality, for this is the realm of the intellect and will.

Individuality is grounded in matter, the terrestrial, and consequently is spatially and temporally limited. "Matter itself is a kind of non-being, a mere potency or ability to receive forms and undergo substantial mutations; in short, avidity for being." However, all matter contains Being of some nature, pure potency, metaphysical energy, form, or soul, which actualizes itself. In the case of the human being who is one substance, both carnal and spiritual, the human soul is united with matter. "Soul and matter are the two substantial co-principles of the same being, of one and the same reality, called man." Souls animate bodies.

As individuals, each of us constitutes a fragment of the universe, a determinate being in a physical world, but as persons we are spiritual souls with the capacity of creative unity, independence and liberty. When

[1] Unless otherwise indicated, quotations in the section entitled: "Thomistic Personalism" are from Jacques Maritain, *The Person and the Common Good,* tr. John J. Fitzgerald (New York: Charles Scribner's Sons, 1947); and *The Review of Politics,* (1946).

we love, we love the person himself, not merely qualities of personality. "Love is not concerned with qualities. They are not the object of our love. We love the deepest, more substantial and hidden, the most *existing* reality of the beloved being. This is a metaphysical center deeper than all the qualities and essences which we can find enumerated in the beloved." Love strikes the center of the real person himself, a center laden with existence, bounty, and action; love offers self as a gift and receives another self in return.

Accordingly, we find that Thomistic Personalism emphasizes metaphysical distinctions between individuality and personality, yet the two are metaphysically real aspects of a human being, not two separate entities. "Our whole being is an individual by reason of that in us which derives from matter, and a person by reason of that in us which derives from spirit." The materiality of individuality does not imply that it is something evil in and of itself; actually, it is good since it is part of our very created existence, and more so when properly related to personality, but "evil arises when, in our action, we give preponderance to the individual aspect of our being . . . Man will be truly a person so far as the life of the spirit and of liberty reigns over that of the sense and passions." If a person allows himself to develop material individuality, he will gravitate toward the ego, which is selfish and detestable.

The person, on the other hand, aspires toward spiritual growth of the generous self, and is oriented upward to saintly pursuits. "The human person is ordained directly to God as to its absolute ultimate end . . . The deepest layer of the human person's dignity consists in its property of resembling God – not in a general way after the manner of all creatures, but in a *proper* way. It is the *image of God.* For God is a spirit and the human person proceeds from Him in having as principle of life a spiritual soul capable of knowing, loving and of being uplifted by grace to participation in the very life of God so that, in the end, it might know and love Him as He knows and loves himself." God, the sovereign person, pure and absolute super-existence, by virtue of his intellection and love, is neither individuality nor corporeality, but personality of the deepest and highest dimensions of Being.

Neo-Thomistic Ethics.

Neo-Thomistic ethics is based upon *natural law* and the *intellect;* the intellect by reason is "the measure of human actions," and "Natural Law for man – is moral law." [1] Natural law is moral law, for man may choose

[1] Quotations in this section on "Neo-Thomistic Ethics" are from Jacques Maritain, "Natural Law and Moral Law," tr. D. A. Gallagher, in *Moral Principles of Action,* Ruth Nanda Anshen, ed., (New York: Harper and Brothers, 1952).

to disobey it; furthermore, practical reason necessitates natural law as a yardstick, a rule by which to measure. "Natural Law is the normality of functioning of the human being;" to disobey natural law is to frustrate, distort, or pervert one's human nature.

Two essential components of natural law are: (1) *ontological,* ideal order which regulates human morality, normalcy of functioning of human nature; and (2) *gnoseological,* moral or natural law as known, naturally known, known through inclination, known by congeniality or connaturality, rather than through the usual modes of reasoning and knowledge. Natural law presents itself to practical reason, not conceptual or discursive judgments (the rational exercise of reason), but proceeds rather "from *connaturality or congeniality* through which what is consonant with the essential inclinations of human nature is grasped by the intellect as good; what is dissonant, as bad . . . The motive power on which they depend is not reason, demonstration, *logos,* but nature and nature's root inclinations. Thus it is that Natural Law is, in the fullest sense of this word, *unwritten* law." The inclinations are vitalistic, dynamistic tendencies which are inexpressible conceptually, therefore they are said to be known through inclinations or principles 'immediately known.'

These tendencies are more than mere animal propensions, they are rational human inclinations as well, though found in the 'non-conceptual' sphere of the mind, in an unconscious or preconscious state, but nevertheless, consonant with reason. Natural inclinations operate on a 'self-evident principle,' that is, a person is naturally cognizant that evil is to be eschewed, and good pursued. Truly authentic inclinations have become laws and regulations supported by conscience, while warped, perverted, or devious inclinations have been repudiated, yet at times, intermingled with the authentic.

The foundation of law, civil, natural, etc. is grounded in *eternal law,* whose author is God, governing by divine reason and so ordering natural law. "Eternal Law is one with the eternal wisdom of God and the divine essence itself." Natural law is based on reason, 'Subsistent Reason,' not human reason, and it is for this reason that human natural bent or inclination leads one to an end which proves to be good for him. "The law, in effect, is essentially an ordinance of reason *(ordinatio rationis),* so that without an ordering reason there is no law . . . Indeed, in the case of Natural Law, human reason has no share in the initiative and authority establishing the Law, either in making it exist or in making it known. How then does it know Natural Law? It knows it through inclination, by connaturality — through the inclinations of nature, which is the work of God, and not by its own rational effort . . . The author of Natural

Law is exclusively the divine reason . . . Natural Law is a participation in the Eternal Law . . . If God does not exist, the Natural Law lacks obligatory power . . . The Eternal Law is not written upon paper, it is promulgated in the divine intellect and is known in itself solely by God and those who see Him in His essence." Natural law obtains its rational nature from divine reason, the same reason which is responsible for man's natural inclinations and human reason, which responds to the natural.

4. Evaluation of Neo-Thomism

The fundamental value of Thomistic philosophy appears to lie in the measure of mental security that it offers, and it seems to be for this reason that some of its outstanding adherents were initially attracted to it. Maritain, as one case in point, was neither Thomistic nor Roman Catholic originally, but was drawn to its thinking along with his wife Raïssa.

But the sense of mental security is gained at the cost of free philosophic inquiry, for a person's conclusions are predetermined before his philosophical investigations commence. Some persons regard this fact as the essence of Scholasticism, or of the Scholastic method, objecting that the philosophic quest can never be genuine, in the free spirit of inquiry in the quest of truth, on Scholastic premises, but rather a person must sacrifice his intellectual freedom in exchange for the alleviation of doubts prompted by open philosophical inquiry. Accordingly, a Scholastic falls squarely under Husserl's injunction (the motto of this book): "But when all is said, this work of mine can help no one who has already fixed his philosophy and his philosophical method, who has thus never learnt to know the despair of one who has the misfortune to be in love with philosophy." [1]

On one basis, and one basis only, can a person escape this stricture levied at Scholastic philosophy, and that is if he independently, coincidentally, arrives at Thomistic conclusions resulting from his own free philosophical inquiry; and thereby allies himself with this school of kindred spirit.

A second difficult tenet of Neo-Thomism, one rationally unacceptable, is the claim that reality is knowable by *intuition*, that our minds and sensations can somehow penetrate through phenomena to their inner realities, withdraw their hidden inner Beings, and convey them to our

[1] Edmund Husserl, *Ideas: General Introduction to Pure Phenomenolgy*, tr. W. R. Boyce Gibson (New York: The Macmillan Co., 1931), preface.

minds.[1] That intuition is any criterion whatever, remains to be proved; and to offer intuition as a criterion appears to be a desperate last resort attempt, as if to say, 'I cannot prove reality, but I just know it must be.' The metaphysical Realism of this school rests upon intuition as its criterion of truth, (and revelation), but it is incumbent upon the Neo-Thomist to prove intuition as a valid criterion of truth; thus far, he has been unsuccessful.

Neither the concept of the *soul* nor the concept of *God,* as viewed by the Neo-Thomist, seems satisfactory. The soul is an intellectual substance lacking individuality, consequently in a life after death, the soul alone survives, that is, not only does the body perish, but that which makes of an individual a person: his memories, his mind, his self. Only his soul survives, a substance possessing intellect, an 'intellective soul,' an 'intellective principle,' nothing more. If this 'intellective principle' is all that survives, then immortality is not worth the having, it is not a personal immortality; whatever that soul is in any future life, it cannot be regarded as *I* or *you;* that 'intellective principle' may just as well be someone else, for all it practically matters.

The Thomistic ethic makes it morally mandatory for one to obey the laws of nature, the natural bent a person has within. On the basis of this premise a person would not only be allowed to repudiate some important Christian and Western moral principles, sanctioned for centuries, such as the Western regard for monogamy, but Thomism would, by implication, dictate the practice of polygamy as moral, since man, as psychologists have amply proved, is polygamous by nature. Within man's nature are many natural dispositions which call for curbing, such as those which are found in the Freudian *Id;* man has an impetus for selfish and destructive measures. If we were to accept the Neo-Thomistic injunction and follow these inclinations through to their desired objectives, sadistic results, injuries, destruction, havoc, etc., would be the outcome. Nazi-like inclinations would find sanction under this ethic,

[1] Regarding *intuition,* Frederick Adelmann, S.J., Ph.D. comments: "This is rather undeveloped and unclear among Thomists. However, in general this can be said: intuition from its very etymology means see-ing. There are no innate ideas for Thomists, who draw their data from reality through the senses. But the human intellect has a natural tendency and power to grasp directly its object: "being", a sense-ing experience. This generates the first principles of knowledge, which are thus self-evident and certain, *i.e.,* the principles of contradiction and of causality.

It is to be noted that these principles are not reasoned to through some kind of syllogistic process but that they form the first premise of all reasoning processes.

If this position is not held, then all reasoning culminates in mere probability and can be pushed back in the other direction in an infinite regression. For example, when one says that the whole is greater than any one of its parts, this is self-evident and intuited from the power of the mind looking at being face to face in a sensed experience."

unless curbed by reason independent of and in conflict with natural bent.

As for the concept of God, an '*Actus Purus*' (Pure Act) is definitely not the impression a person gains of him in the Judeo-Christian Scriptures; it is certainly not the God of which Jesus speaks, yet this is the presumption that we are asked to believe by Gilson; he speaks of his philosophy and that of St. Thomas' as the Christian philosophy and so entitles his book: *Elements of Christian Philosophy.*

Furthermore, *Pure Act,* namely a Being free from all potentiality, is difficult to accept as the definition of God's perfection. To assert that God is wanting in nothing, consequently has nothing to do, and this fact constitutes the nature of his perfection, is unacceptable. It is as objectionable as Aristotle's God (from which this is taken) who has nothing else to do but to contemplate himself, since he is perfect, wanting in nothing. The *need* to do something in Thomism and Aristotlelianism implies imperfection, but what is wrong with submitting the concept of God's perfection as *inexhaustible perfectibility?* The Personalitic philosopher of religion, Edgar Sheffield Brightman, does so with satisfactory results, coherently ordered. A Pure Act is too constricting or limiting upon God, and reduces him to a status less than that of a person who has a beautiful life of possibilities ahead, laden with potentialities ready to be realized. A person who has absolutely nothing to do is in a worse state than death or annihilation itself.

Rather than concluding with these disparaging remarks, it should be noted and emphasized that Neo-Thomism has many fine features to commend it, among which is its suitability as a philosophy of life, one by which to live, and people have lived by it for centuries.

In defence of Thomism, Frederick Adelmann S. J., Ph.D. argues: "It would seem to me that any philosopher in the concrete situation brings to his philosophizing some necessary commitments. In the one case these may be the commitment of the Christian to set beliefs that God does exist; it might be the commitment of the atheist to the belief that He does not exist; it might be the commitment of the agnostic that the problem cannot be solved. Even the philosopher who begins with a recognition of common sense experiences that have brought him to the threshold of his philosophizing has made a commitment to the validity of this human situation. At any rate, it seems to me that every individual as he begins to philosophize brings to that natural activity some previous commitment. None of these positions of commitment should, however, enter in as positive ingredients to his actual process of philosophizing. His conclusions should be based on rigorous demonstration that should stand or fall upon the validity of the intrinsic process itself."

XXXVII

NEOREALISM:

Objects of Cognition and Sense as Real in Their Own Right

One might say that *Neorealism* was launched during the spring of 1910 when a half dozen professors of philosophy, dissatisfied with existing systems, particularly Idealism and Materialism, assembled to inaugurate one to their own liking, or at least to find areas of agreement on which to establish a basis for one. The men in question were: *Ralph Barton Perry* (1876-1957) of Harvard University, *Walter T. Marvin* (1872-1944) of Rutgers University, *Edward G. Spaulding* (1873-1940) of Princeton University, *Edwin B. Holt* (1873-1946) of Harvard University, *Walter B. Pitkin* (1878-1953) of Columbia University, and *William Pepperell Montague* (1873-1953) of Columbia University. Each contributed to a volume on the new philosophy entitled: *The New Realism* (1912), but prior to this publication, they jointly published in *The Journal of Philosophy:* "A Program and First Platform of Six Realists."

A second group of Realists, who elected to call themselves *Critical Realists,* met approximately around 1920 in a concerted effort to launch their own program in a book entitled: *Essays in Critical Realism.* For all practical purposes, Critical Realism is identical in all major respects with Neorealism, except for one major point of departure respecting epistemology; whereas the Neorealists were *Epistemological Monists,* the Critical Realists were *Epistemological Dualists;* (more will be said of this discrepancy later). The Critical Realists consisted of: *George Santayana* (1863-1952) of Harvard University, *Charles Augustus Strong* (1862-1940) of Columbia University, *Arthur Kenyon Rogers* (1868-1936) of Yale University, *Arthur O. Lovejoy* (1873-) of Johns Hopkins University, *James Bissett Pratt* (1875-1944) of Williams College, *Durant Drake* (1878-1933) of Vassar College, and *Roy Wood Sellars* (1880-) of the University of Michigan. Numbered among the European Neorealists are: *George Edward Moore* (1873-1958), *C. Lloyd Morgan* (1852-1936), *Alfred North Whitehead*[1] (1861-1947), *T. Percy Nunn* (1870-1944), *Bertrand Russell* (1873-), *Samuel Alexander* (1859-1938), *Charlie Dunbar Broad* (1887-), *John Laird* (1887-1945), *C. E. M. Joad* (1891-1953), *H. H. Price* (1899-), *A. C. Ewing* (1899-), and *Gilbert Ryle* (1900-).

1. Ralph Barton Perry — American Neorealism

The Platform of Neorealism.

Metaphysically, major divergencies existed among the Neorealists, little was shared in common, but they did, however, agree on epistemology; and this epistemological method is summarized by William Pepperell Montague as follows:[2]

> 1. Philosophers should follow the example of scientists and co-operate rather than work alone. The co-operation which we were to practice consisted in each man showing his essay to the others, taking account of their suggestions, and securing not unanimous agreement with every proposition, but general assent to the essay as a whole. . .
>
> 2. Philosophers should follow the example of scientists in isolating their problems and tackling them one by one. We were to follow this precept by isolating the epistemological problem and studying the cognitive relation obtaining between the knower and apprehended and any object that he knows or apprehends without prejudging or even raising the question as to the ultimate nature of the apprehending subjects or of the apprehended objects. . .
>
> 3. Some at least of the *particulars* of which we are conscious exist when we are not conscious of them.
>
> This was the ordinary particularistic or *existential* realism of common sense.
>
> 4. Some at least of the *essences or universals* of which we are now conscious subsist when we are not conscious of them.
>
> This was Platonic or *subsistential* realism.
>
> 5. Some at least of the particulars as well as the universals that are real are apprehended directly rather than indirectly through copies or mental images.
>
> This was the *presentative* realism of Reid as contrasted with the representative realism or epistemological dualism of Descartes and Locke.

Epistemological Monism and Dualism.

As previously mentioned, it was primarily epistemology that sent the Realists in divergent trends; the Neorealists, Epistemological Monists,

[1] Whitehead is also a Platonist, Panpsychist, and Leibnizian; Russell has shifted to Logical Positivism and Scientism; Ryle is also considered a member of the Analytic School of Philosophy.

[2] *Philosophy*, Vol. 12, No. 46, 140 ff.

asserted that the knower and the object of his knowledge were one and the same; the knower merely reflected his surroundings as a mirror. In this respect, their psychological outlook was essentially Behaviorism; many of the Realists were Behaviorists, as was their chief American exponent, Ralph Barton Perry.

If the knower and the thing known are one and the same, crucial problems emerge, particularly those which entail facts which occurred in past time, such as historical data. Take for example the fact, 'Napoleon fought in the Battle of Waterloo;' if Epistemological Monism is valid then how is it possible to reflect, as a mirror, knowledge of this fact occurring prior to the time of our generation. It simply cannot be done; consequently, Critical Realists came to the rescue of Neorealism by offering a solution in the form of Epistemological Dualism, the belief that knower and the object of his knowledge are two different and distinct entities. Dualists concluded that my knowledge at the present moment of Napoleon and the fact of his existence are not the same, but different objects entirely.

Critical Realists charged the Neorealists with Naive Realism, the doctrine that 'things are precisely as they appear to the senses;' an unsophisticated belief such as this is hardly countenanced in a modern scientific era. The Neorealist, Montague, writes: "They regarded our New Realism, with its attempt to interpret existent objects as directly presented to the mind (rather than as indirectly represented through images or copies), as a form of Naive Realism – (which indeed it was), and they chose the word 'Critical' as suitably antithetic to the 'Naiveness' of which we their predecessors had been guilty . . . This dualistic epistemology is very simple and clear. Its tenets are the following: 1. The world is composed of at least two sets of entities: (*a*) material things; and (*b*) mental states or ideas. 2. The ideas alone are given or presented as objects in consciousness and in that sense are *immediately* known, being inferred as the direct or indirect causes of the ideas. 3. The inferred material objects are always numerically or existentially non-identical with the immediately presented objects of ideas from which they are inferred; and they are furthermore at least partially different in kind or nature from the latter."

One important and probably the crucial reason why the Neorealists preferred Epistemological Monism to Dualism is that they eschewed an inherent implication of Epistemological Dualism, namely, that the only universe which the knower receives (or ever can receive), is a *copy,* and *not* the real world; a fact which would prove devastating to Realism. The Epistemological Monist, Montague, asserts that "the truth of such a conclusion would mean that the whole perceptual world is inside the percipient and that it is at best no more than a copy of the external world of physical entities." Obviously, the Neorealist is illcontent with merely being in possession of *mental images* or copies of the real world, he, being a Realist, requires direct knowledge of any objectively *real* universe which is in essence nonmental and nonpsychological. Epistemological Monism avoids this problem much more acceptably than does Dualism, but on the other hand, Monism creates other problems as the one previously noted respecting historical or past events.

The Epistemology and Metaphysics of Neorealism.

Primarily, Neorealism's epistemological doctrine is one which seeks to define the relation between the individual's knowing process and the thing known. It concludes in *Epistemological Monism* based on the doctrine of *Naive Realism,* the belief that reality of things is exactly as the senses record them to be. The theory of Naive Realism "conceives of objects as directly presented to consciousness and being precisely what they appear to be. Nothing intervenes between the knower and the world external to him. Objects are not represented in consciousness by ideas; they are themselves directly presented. This theory makes no distinction between seeming and being; things *are* just what they *seem.*" [1] Knowledge or thought is merely the outside world entering personality as a light which streams through the sense organs.

The chief difficulty with Naive Realism is that it has no way of accounting for error, inasmuch as the senses record exactly what is fed to them from the external world. But since everyone is doubtless aware of being in error sometime or other, from whence then does error issue? Apparently from the internal world of personality which interferes with sense data. "Unreal events that are in conflict with the experience of one's fellows, and even with one's own more inclusive experience, must be banished completely from the external world. Where, then, shall they be located? What is more natural than to locate them inside the person who experiences them? For it is only upon him that the unreal object produces an effect." Errors may be likened to desires and other subjective experiences which are regarded to exist purely within the individual who is undergoing that particular experience. One mind, and one mind only, has a fancy, dream, illusion, etc., but senses gather experiences which are common to all who happen to share in any particular sense object.

The Naive Realist believes that he is actually sensing the real world,

[1] Quotations in the remainder of this section are from *The New Realism,* the joint effort of Edwin B. Holt, Walter T. Marvin, William Pepperell Montague, Ralph Barton Perry, Walter B. Pitkin, and Edward Gleason Spaulding (New York: The Macmillan Co., 1912).

and not that he is receiving merely a mental picture of it through his psychological sensations; a person does not make contact with the real world through intermediaries, such as the sense of sight, but directly— not a *re*presentation of the real world through the senses, but a *presentation* of it directly. Either the senses give us the thing-in-itself or there is none to be had, none exists. Epistemological Dualism, the *re*-presentative theory of knowledge, asserts that sense data is merely mental images of what really exists; and the real world, which at best, can only resemble these ideas, has the decided advantage of accounting adequately for error and illusion by regarding them as erroneous ideas. That is to say, at times, our picture or sensation of the real world is inaccurate, because we are receiving the outside world second-hand, hence error is due to inaccurate transmission of the facts of reality. The difficulty created by Epistemological Dualism is that we can never directly experience the external world, but depend upon the trustworthiness of our sense of it (image of it). "The only external world is one that we can never experience, the only world that we can have any experience of is the internal world of ideas . . . We are met by the difficulty that the world we infer can only be made of the matter of experience, that is, can only be made up of mental pictures in new combinations . . . The only things according to this view that can be experienced are our mental states." Consequently, we are devoid of any basis for concluding that there exists any externally real universe whatever, and if one did exist, that it is what our senses represent it to be; for all we know, it may be a ghastly world, akin to the weirdest fantasies ever conjured by the mind of man.

Moreover, Epistemological Dualism gives license to Berkeleyan Idealism (the belief that reality is spiritual) and Subjectivism (reality is merely man's subjective opinion) by allowing the existence of ideas which are not necessarily correlated by a correspondingly real world external to us. Each person's world is essentially his own mental world as he pictures reality to be; there is no guarantee that it correlates with the real world. Accordingly, *Solipsism* may be argued, the doctrine that "each fragmentary self will have to assume that its own experience constitutes the entire universe;" my mental picture of the world may be the only world in existence, therefore, I alone, along with my own ideas or experiences, exist.

Thus, for any objectively valid philosophy, it is necessary to rid ourselves of Solipsism, and every form of Subjectivism. This, the Neorealist seeks to accomplish by avoiding Epistemological Dualism, and all forms of *re*presentative theories of epistemology, thereby making direct access to reality unimpeded by intermediaries which lead to Idealism, Subjectivism, or Solipsism. This is effected by the Neorealist's *Relational Theory* *of Knowledge,* a return to "that primordial common sense which believes in a world that exists independently of the knowing of it, but believes in a world that that same independent world can be directly presented in consciousness and not merely represented or copied by 'ideas.' In short, the new realism is, broadly speaking, a return to that naive or natural realism." Thus we find the New Realism, in epistemology, is merely the old Realism with a new name; yet this is not quite the case, for Naive Realism is modified to make it compatible with the Theory of Relativity.

Major Tenets of Neorealism.

Major tenets of Neorealists may be outlined as follows:

1. The Emancipation of Metaphysics from Epistemology.
2. The Method of Analysis.
3. Metaphysical Pluralism.
4. The Rejection of Subjectivism.
5. Epistemological Monism.
6. Platonic Realism.
7. Naive Realism.
8. Neutral Entities.
9. The Ego-Centric Predicament.

(1) *The Emancipation of Metaphysics from Epistemology.*

By emancipating or rescuing metaphysics from epistemology "means that the nature of things is not to be sought primarily in the nature of knowledge;" [1] but from this it should not be concluded that a Realist may not elect to have a philosophy in which moral or spiritual realities truly exist. The Realist merely insists that epistemology should not presume a right of priority over objects; because I do not have knowledge that something exists does not imply that it does not, nor does it mean because I gain knowledge of an object, it comes into being by virtue of that fact. Knowledge of reality, and objects of reality are two separate and independent entities in the sense that knowledge does not bring reality into existence. If I never get to know an object, and if no one else ever does either, this does not signify that the object does not exist; this is the sense in which it is meant that metaphysics is to be emancipated from epistemology. The existence of an object is not dependent upon its knowledge, upon its being known, *esse* is not *percipi.*

[1] Unless otherwise indicated, quotations in this section on Neorealism are from *The New Realism, op. cit.*

(2) *The Method of Analysis.*

Explanation consists in analyzing an object into its smallest component parts; when a person can define each component part in its proper relationship to all others, he has in effect explained the meaning or nature of the object. "A neo-realist recognizes no ultimate immediacies nor non-relational nor indefinable entities, except the simples in which analysis terminates. The ultimate terms of knowledge are the terms that survive an analysis that has been carried as far as it is possible to carry it; and not the terms which possess simplicity only because analysis has not been applied to them." The Neorealist's system of explanation, viz., analysis, is scientific in nature; in fact, the Neorealist repudiates philosophies which diverge from science or that reduce scientific facts and laws to mere abstractions or instrumental artifacts.

(3) *Metaphysical Pluralism.*

Neorealists tend to believe that ultimate reality is composed of a number of entities. "The evidence at present available indicates that while all things may perhaps be related, many of these relations are not constitutive or determinative; that is, do not enter into the explanation of the nature or existence of their terms." Metaphysical Monism, the belief that ultimate reality is a single entity assumes that relationships between any two objects must therefore be internal since the two are basically one and the same object, but Realism rejects this conclusion as not being in accord with experience; the average person's experience is that interaction is external.

(4) *The Repudiation of Subjectivism.*

Knowledge is not subjective, but as real as objects themselves; "when knowledge takes place, there is a knower interacting with things . . . The knower . . . must take its place in one manifold with the things it knows." Furthermore, knowledge implies knowledge of something other than itself. "In all this it is presupposed that if there is to be knowledge, there must be something there to be known, and something there to know . . . In the first place being known is something that *happens* to a prëexisting thing. Then, in the second place, when the knowing takes place, these characters are at least for the most part undisturbed." Knowledge is not a matter of opinion, it is a real entering into facts themselves, so that a person derives the essence of the object by his sense, that is, he makes sense contact with ultimate reality. Knowledge is an extra-mental reality.

(5) *Epistemological Monism.*

The belief that the knower and the object of his knowledge are one and the same, Epistemological Monism, is a tenet of Neorealists. This tenet is necessary in order to maintain Neorealism as a coherent whole, an integrated system, for if dualism were the case, Neorealism would be critically weakened; to isolate ideas from real objects casts serious doubt as to whether objects do in fact exist. "In immediate and intimate connection with this doctrine of the independence of things known and the knowing of them stands another special doctrine — to the effect that the content of knowledge, that which lies in or before the mind when knowledge takes place, is numerically identical with the thing known. Knowledge by intermediaries is not denied, but is made subordinate to direct or presentative knowledge . . . In the end all things are known through being themselves brought directly into that relation in which they are said to be witnessed or apprehended. In other words, things when consciousness is had of them become themselves contents of consciousness; and the same things thus figure both in the so-called external world and in the manifold which introspection reveals."

(6) *Platonic Realism.*

A Neorealist is a Platonic Realist as well because "he accords full ontological status to the things of thought as well as to the things of sense, to logical entities as well as physical entities, or to subsistents as well as existents." The Neorealist method of analysis merely grants him access to reality, it does not alter or transform reality, hence it is true that the eternal Ideas of Plato genuinely subsist as he believed them to be.

(7) *Naive Realism.*

(Inasmuch as Naive Realism has been sufficiently discussed, we shall dispense with it here, and refer the reader to the section "The Epistemology and Metaphysics of Neorealism").

(8) *Neutral Entities.*

Although reality appears at times mental in nature, and at other times material, ultimately, exhaustive analysis would indicate that it is a *tertium quid,* a tertiary quality, a *neutral entity.* Holt says that "the entities (objects, facts, etc.) under study in logic, mathematics, and the physical sciences are not mental in any usual or proper meaning of the word 'mental.'" "In other words, the elements of the introspective manifold are in themselves neither peculiarly mental nor peculiarly mine; they are *neutral and interchangeable,"* [1] says Perry. In the final analysis, entities are neither mental nor physical, but neutral.

(9) ***The Ego-Centric Predicament.***

Perry, who gave birth to the Ego-Centric Predicament, defines it as "the argument that because entities are content of consciousness they can not also transcend consciousness; it also implies that, so far as based on such subjectivistic premises, the idealistic theory of a transcendent subjectivity is gratuitous." Idealists have seized upon this theory in substantiation of their own position, arguing that if all knowledge (every fact, reason, thought, idea, etc.) is mental or of the nature of mind, then reality must be of the same substance, or of an equivalent nature, otherwise it cannot be known. Even if reality were material, before it can enter the mind of man, it must be converted into a spiritual or conscious nature. We, as persons cannot gain any object of the universe without its first either *being* of the nature of mind, or else *converted* into the nature of mind. "*No thinker to whom one may appeal is able to mention a thing that is not idea,* for the obvious and simple reason that *in mentioning it he makes it an idea* . . . In other words, one cannot conceive things to exist apart from consciousness, because to conceive is *ipso facto* to bring within consciousness . . . No one can report on the nature of things without being on hand himself. It follows that whatever thing he reports does as a matter of fact stand in relation to him, as his idea, object of knowledge, or experience . . . It is necessary to have a name for this situation just as it stands. It will be convenient to call it '*the ego-centric predicament.*'" [2] Epistemologically or logically, we have no grounds for proving that reality is of any nature other than mind, but the Neorealist voices vehement objections to its being of the nature of mind, spiritual or conscious.

2. George Santayana — Critical Realism

Critical Realists, following the example set by Neorealists, engaged in their own cooperative endeavor to publicize a philosophy very much allied to Neorealism, with but one crucial departure, Epistemological Dualism. The cooperative work of the Critical Realists which included: *Durant Drake* (1878-1933), *Arthur O. Lovejoy* (1873-1962), *James Bissett Pratt* (1875-1944), *Arthur Kenyon Rogers* (1868-1936), *George San-*

[1] Ralph Barton Perry, *Present Philosophical Tendencies* (New York: George Braziller, Inc., and London: Longmans, Green, and Co., 1912), 277.
[2] *Ibid.*, 129.

tayana (1863-1952), *Roy Wood Sellars* (1880-), and *Charles Augustus Strong* (1862-1940), was published in 1920 under the title: *Essays in Critical Realism.*

Ontologically, except for a bent toward Naturalism, the metaphysics of the six Critical Realists flows in divergent directions; at least they reserved this right for themselves individually. Mutual agreement is found primarily on the epistemological issue. Although termed *Critical* Realism, there exists no reference to Kantian Critical philosophy; if the word *critical* has reference philosophically, it implies a critical rather than a naive approach to Realism in respect to the epistemological problem. Montague comments regarding the Critical Realists: "So far as I can see their contributions to epistemology are mainly confined to a refutation of the *monistic objectivism* of the New Realists and to a restatement in slightly different form of the dualistic or representative theory of perception." [1]

Durant Drake and Apologetic Realism.

Durant Drake staunchly defends the Realist's stand in *Essays in Critical Realism,* declaring that Realism must be true because it is instinctive for us to believe in it. He writes: "What right have we to believe in the existence of physical objects. The answer, in a word, is that our instinctive (and practically inevitable) belief in the existence of the physical world about us is pragmatically justifiable . . . Everything is *as if* realism were true; and the *as if* is so strong that we may consider our instinctive and actually unescapable belief justified . . . Consistency demands either universal scepticism or a fearless and full-fledged realism." [2] It may be commented that it seems an inapt situation that Drake, or for that matter the other Realists, is unable to find logical proof for reality, except to take refuge in *instinct;* later we shall find other Realists adding that we know reality *intuitively.* If we depended upon instinct as the criterion of truth, we could arrive at some grotesque conclusions, as well as some good ones, such as, God, soul, immortality.

The Philosophy of Santayana.

Santayana, born of Spanish parentage in 1863, came to Boston, Massachusetts at the age of nine. Despite the fact that on his arrival in America he had no knowledge of English, he rose to a position of prominence in the literary world; appreciation of his talent and mastery of literary expression transcends philosophical circles to the field of literature.

[1] Montague, *op. cit.*
[2] Durant Drake, "The Approach to Critical Realism," in *Essays in Critical Realism* (London: Macmillan and Co., Ltd., 1920).

Notwithstanding his Atheistic belief, he remained loyal to Roman Catholicism, the faith in which he was entrenched from birth, but he dismissed religion "as a work of human imagination," a kindly illusion, bad physics, superstitions, magic, myth, a misrepresentation of material conditions; theology is merely untrue science, and religion, great fairy tales of the conscience.

Later, he began to query whether the real world was not itself a work of the imagination as well as the spiritual world of religion. Santayana's Skepticism was both penetrating and enduring; he questioned the validity of all systems, including science. Accepting a philosophy or religion is merely a matter of which "imaginative system will you trust. My matured conclusion has been that no system is to be trusted, not even that of science in any literal or pictorial sense; but all systems may be used and, up to a certain point, trusted as symbols." [1] His inclination toward a philosophy of Naturalism was clear and decisive from the begining, and on this premise he sought to base all other aspects of his philosophy; if Naturalism yielded at all, then it momentarily capitulated to Solipsism or Skepticism — as it was, his thinking pendulated from one to the other. "We must oscilate between a radical transcendentalism, frankly reduced to a solipsism of the living moment, and a materialism posited as a presupposition of conventional sanity. There was no contradiction in joining together a scepticism which was not a dogmatic negation of anything and an animal faith which avowedly was a mere assumption in action and description." This vascillation he felt was justifiable on the grounds that it rendered his philosophical position coherent with the facts of immediate experience and the natural world.

Santayana's *Naturalism,* based on a philosophy of Metaphysical Materialism, was not a product of his logical thinking, but, as he put it, "an everyday conviction which came to me . . . from experience and observation of the world at large, and especially of my own feelings and passions. It seems to me that those who are not materialists cannot be good observers of themselves: they may hear themselves thinking, but they cannot have watched themselves acting and feeling; for feeling and action are evidently accidents of matter . . . The recognition of the material world and of the conditions of existence in it merely enlightens the spirit concerning the source of its troubles and the means to its happiness or deliverance: and it was happiness or deliverance, the supervening supreme expression of human will and imagination, that alone really concerned me. This alone was genuine philosophy; this alone was

[1] Unless otherwise noted, quotations in this section are from George Santayana, "Brief History of My Opinions," in *Contemporary American Philosophy,* G. P. Adams and W. P. Montague, editors (London: George Allen & Unwin Ltd.).

the life of reason." The life of reason so engaged the mind and spirit of Santayana that he wrote a five volume work under that title.

The life of reason for Santayana was an adjustment or an adaptation to life based on Herbert Spencer's definition, namely, an adjustment of inner to outer relations, "an adaptation of fancy and habit to material facts and opportunities." The subjective state of the human mind fascinated him, and he devoted his entire life to describing the inner life, imaginations, 'nature bred in the human mind.' "I assumed throughout that the whole life of reason was generated and controlled by the animal life of man in the bosom of nature. Human ideas had, accordingly, a symptomatic, expressive, and symbolic value: they were the inner notes sounded by man's passions and by his arts: and they became rational partly by their vital and inward harmony — for reason is a harmony of the passions — and partly by their adjustment to external facts and possibilities — for reason is a harmony of the inner life with truth and with fate." The same holds true for science, its validity rests on its ability to aid man in making suitable adjustments to life. "In science there was an element of poetry, pervasive, inevitable, and variable: it was strictly scientific and true only in so far as it involved a close and prosperous adjustment to the surrounding world, at first by its origin in observation and at last by its application in action. Science was the mental accompaniment of art." In this respect, Santayana is emphatically Pragmatistic, and discloses that element of his philosophy in discussions, entitled: "Normal Madness," found in his *Dialogues in Limbo.*

Epiphenomenalism and Behaviorism play an integral role in Santayana's Realism; Epiphenomenalism is the belief that spiritual and mental qualities are not genuinely real in their own right, but are by-products produced by, and dependent for their existence upon, a basic reality, viz., matter. Consciousness, spirit, mind, etc., are all attendant upon matter as their cause and ground, hence the dissolution or destruction of matter concomitantly destroys its epiphenomena: mind, spirit, consciousness, etc. Behaviorism is a psychological school of thought which rests on the premise that mind, consciousness, spirit, etc. are epiphenomena, therefore are reducible to body or material substance. Introspective data (mind, spirit, etc.) are invalid data owing to their inability to be publicly observed, consequently not subject to measurement.

Santayana regards consciousness merely as an epiphenomenal emergence of animal bodies. "A psyche, or nucleus of hereditary organisation, gathers and governs these bodies, and at the same time breeds within them a dreaming, suffering, and watching mind . . . An interesting and consistent complement to these discoveries is furnished by behaviourism, which I heartily accept on its positive biological side: the hereditary life of the body, modified by accident or training, forms a closed cycle of habits and actions. Of this the mind is a concomitant spiritual expression, invisible imponderable, and epiphenomenal, or, as I prefer to say, hypostatic: for in it the moving unities and tensions of animal life are synthesised on quite another plane of being, into actual intuitions and feelings." All spiritual life, for Santayana, is as natural as any which we regard natural; it is a 'natural miracle;' thus unfolds the role of Naturalism in this man's philosophy.

Essence, which constitutes the heart or ontology of Santayana's metaphysical thought, and to which he devoted an entire book, *The Realm of Essence,* is defined as internal objects of consciousness. "A pure and radical transcendentalism will disclaim all knowledge of fact. Nature, history, the self, become ghostly presences, mere notions of such things; and the being of these images becomes purely internal to them; they exist in no environing space or time; they possess no substance or hidden parts, but are all surface, all appearance. Such a being, or quality of being, I call an essence; and to the consideration of essences, composing of themselves an eternal and infinite realm, I have devoted much attention." The ontology of essences includes Plato's Ideas; but the Materialist, Santayana, does not permit essences ultimately real classifications; at best, they are nature's epiphenomena, and with matter, these eternal ideals must perish.

Skepticism and Animal Faith are the courts of last appeal in Santayana's Naturalism; logically speaking, we can prove nothing, consequently must, on this level, remain Skeptics, for all epistemological effort proves futile; but on the animal level of our hopes and fears, our cravings and desires, we can conclude a world of material substance, a world of reality. "When all the data of immediate experience and all the constructions of thought have thus been purified and reduced to what they are intrinsically, that is, to eternal essences, by a sort of counterblast the sense of existence, of action, of ambushed reality everywhere about us, becomes all the clearer and more imperious. This assurance of the not-given is involved in action, in expectation, in fear, hope, or want; I call it *animal faith.*" Reality, material substance which underlies all phenomena, is known by animal faith, instinct, intuition; our *instinct* tells us the world is ultimately material; we *intuit* that it is substantially real. The centuries old mystery regarding the ultimate nature of substance, Santayana fancies to have solved, having reduced to matter that which is known by instinct. It appears, that with Santayana, we revert to the times of the ancient Greek philosophers; actually, this is not too surprising since the Critical Realist, Santayana, was deeply and permanently influenced by the thinking of Hellenic philosophers.

3. G. E. Moore — European Neorealism

George Edward Moore's classic paper "The Refutation of Idealism" marked the birth of the era of Neorealism in Europe where he exerted more influence on British thought than any other English philosopher, despite the imposing presence there of Bertrand Russell, considered *the* philosopher, in the eyes of many. However, with the exception of *Principia Mathematica,* Russell has not contributed a systematized philosophy, nor has he founded a new school of philosophy; he has been more of a satirist, critic, iconoclast, or a modern Voltaire, as some have referred to him.

One of G. E. Moore's major contributions to Neorealism assumes the form of an attack on the fundamental thesis of Idealism, particularly that of the Berkeleyan mode which reduces the real world to the nature of mind. "Modern Idealism, if it asserts any general conclusion about the universe at all, asserts that it is spiritual . . . It is certainly meant to assert (1) that the universe is very different indeed from what it seems, and (2) that it has quite a large number of properties which it does not seem to have."[1] For example, chairs are definitely different from us human beings, at least our experience tells us so, but Idealism would have us think that they are like us, spiritual. If chairs are spiritual, then they are of the nature of consciousness, but our experience indicates otherwise; to us they appear lifeless and unconscious.

The Idealistic thesis which Moore proposes to destroy is Berkeley's *esse* is *percipi* (to be is to be perceived). "Accordingly, whatever *esse* is *percipi* may mean, it does *at least* assert that whatever is, is *experienced* . . . I beg, therefore, that *percipi* may be understood, in what follows, to refer to what is *common* to sensation and thought . . . 'That what makes [any piece of fact] real can be nothing but its presence as an inseparable aspect of a *sentient experience.*'" Moore does not purport to refute all forms of Idealism, but merely the Berkeleyan formulation and definition.

To assert that *esse* is *percipi,* is to say that *esse* implies *percipi;* consequently, whenever *esse* is present, then *percipi* must also be. Let x stand for *esse,* then "it will be convenient if, for the future, I may be allowed to use the term '*esse*' to denote x *alone* . . . What is worth dispute is whether *percipi* is necessarily connected with x. We have therefore discovered the ambiguity of the copula in *esse* is *percipi,* so far as to see that this principle asserts two distinct terms to be so related, that whatever

[1] Unless otherwise noted, quotations in this section devoted to G. E. Moore are from his "The Refutation of Idealism" in *Mind,* N.S. Vol. 12, (1903).

has the *one,* which I call *esse,* has *also* the property that it is experienced." Whatever is experienced must necessarily exist; or, the object of our experience is inconceivable apart from the thinking subject who entertains the thought.

Moore asserts that Idealists claim that an object of our thought and the experiencing subject are necessarily connected; the two are not distinct entities; for example, the color green in an object and the experience of green are equated as one and the same in the mind of the Idealist, and it is precisely this failure to distinguish the two as separate entities with which Moore takes issue. "The facts present themselves as a kind of antinomy: (1) Experience *is* something unique and different from anything else; (2) Experience of green is entirely indistinguishable from green; two propositions which cannot both be true." Idealists attempt to subscribe to both antithetical ideas by reasoning from one at times, then oscillating to the other when convenient to their line of argument. Moore is aware that many Idealists would object to this charge as unfounded, maintaining that it does not hold true in all forms of Idealism.

Moore's Neorealism accounts for objects which are distinct from us, the subjects, thinking them, on the basis of what he terms an 'organic unity,' a *Gestalt,* an organic whole which cannot be divided without destroying the reality itself. A subject connected with its object is one such organic unity, and to sever the two is an 'illegitimate abstraction' which damages both. Something is always lost in translation from the whole to the analysis of the individual parts; for example, water has the quality of wetness, but to analyze it into its component parts, hydrogen and oxygen, would eliminate wetness, for neither hydrogen nor oxygen possesses the property wetness. Similarly, this principle holds true with the thinking *subject* and the *objects* of the external world which he (the subject) thinks about. "A distinction is asserted; but it is *also* asserted that the things distinguished form an 'organic unity.' But forming such a unity, it is held, each would not be what it is *apart from its relation to the other.* Hence to consider either by itself is to make an *illegitimate abstraction.* The recognition that there are 'organic unities' and 'illegitimate abstractions' in this sense is regarded as one of the chief conquests of modern philosophy . . . For as the whole can, nay *must,* be substituted for the part in all propositions and for all purposes, this can only be because the whole is absolutely identical with the part. When, therefore, we are told that green and the sensation of green are certainly distinct but yet are not separable, or that it is an illegitimate abstraction to consider the one apart from the other, what these provisos are used to assert is, that though the two things are distinct yet you not only can but must treat them as if they were not."

Applying the implications of these principles of organic unity and illegitimate abstraction to the particular issue before us would indicate that *Being* and *being experienced* are connected; and for human beings, whatever *is* is also experienced, but there is no logical justification for concluding Being and being experienced to be identical. "We have then in every sensation two distinct elements, one which I call consciousness, and another which I call the object of consciousness." The two must be distinguished, otherwise you will confront the disturbing problem of not being able to differentiate between the sensation of blue and the sensation of green; both are sensations of color, yet they must possess an inherent difference, or the whole world would be an unintelligible confusion of indistinguishable sensations.

Our difficulty is created by the fact that whenever a sensation such as blue appears, it is invariably accompanied by consciousness. This can mean only one of two things: either both the sensation of the real object itself together with the subject's consciousness (sensation, idea) of it exists, or else only the consciousness exists (Solipsism). Moore elects to believe the former: "for we can and must conceive the existence of blue as something quite distinct from the existence of the sensation. We can and must conceive that blue might exist and yet the sensation of blue not exist." The object of sensation is truly real; this does not mean that sensation is not, but it does mean that the two should be distinguished, and that the former is objectively real. "The point I had established so far was that in every sensation or idea we must distinguish two elements, (1) the 'object,' or that in which one differs from another; and, (2) 'consciousness,' or that which all have in common — that which makes them sensations or mental facts. This being so, it followed that when a sensation or idea exists, we have to choose between the alternatives that either object alone, or consciousness alone, or both exist; and I showed that of these alternatives one, namely that the object only exists, is excluded by the fact that what we mean to assert is certainly the existence of a mental fact. There remains the question: Do both exist? Or does the consciousness alone? And to this question one answer has hitherto been given universally: That both exist."

One must not conclude that the object of sensation is its content, such as blue is the content of the sensation blue, for this implies that it is merely a quality of a sensation, rather than a reality in its own right. "This answer follows from the analysis hitherto accepted of the relation of what I have called 'object' to 'consciousness' in any sensation or idea. It is held that what I call the object is merely the 'content' of a sensation or idea. It is held that in each case we can distinguish two elements and two only, (1) the fact that there is feeling or experience, and (2) *what* is felt or experienced; the sensation or idea, it is said, forms a whole, in which we must distinguish two 'inseparable aspects,' 'content' and 'existence' . . . This analysis is false." It is false because to make the object, *e.g.*, blue, the content of sensation is to reduce it to a mere quality, and divorce it from being a reality *sui generis.* Blue is really blue, blue out there, external to us, whether or not sensations are ever gained of it.

Awareness is an important factor and plays a major role in Moore's Neorealism; by it he seeks to prove the reality of sense objects. Reduced to simple terms, he claims that we can become *aware* of mental or internal thoughts as well as external sense content; when I am aware of a thought, I do not say that the thought is part of my awareness, I experience it separately. The same holds true for objects of sense; when I am aware of an object of sense such as blue, the conscious awareness is not blue *per se* to me; I distinguish between them. I am not aware of the blue as being my consciousness itself. "It being the case, then, that the sensation of blue includes in its analysis, beside blue, *both* a unique element 'awareness' *and* a unique relation of this element to blue . . . Blue is probably not part of the content of the sensation at all . . . If it were true, then, when the sensation of blue exists, there exists a *blue awareness* . . . Blue is, in this case, a *content* of consciousness or experience. Whether or not, when I have the sensation of blue, my consciousness or awareness is thus blue, my introspection does not enable me to decide with certainty . . . But whether it is or not, the point is unimportant, for introspection *does* enable me to decide that something else is also true: namely that I am aware *of* blue, and by this I mean, that my awareness has to blue a quite different and distinct relation. It is possible, I admit, that my awareness is blue *as well* as being *of* blue; that it has to blue the simple and unique relation the existence of which alone justifies us in distinguishing knowledge of a thing from the thing known, indeed in distinguishing mind from matter. And this result I may express by saying that what is called the *content* of a sensation is in very truth what I originally called it — the sensation's *object.*" Our awareness tells us that we are aware of something other than consciousness, we are aware of an externally real object, not merely a content of a sensation.

Thus, we arrive at the chief significance and contention of the Neorealist, namely, that facts of experience are genuinely and objectively real, independent of the subject in whose consciousness the facts of experience are transpiring. It is primarily a repudiation of Berkeleyanism, a rejection of the belief that without consciousness, the objects or factual world which is conveyed to us via experience cannot, or does not, exist.

4. Bertrand Russell — The Philosophy of Logical Atomism

Earlier, it was mentioned that Russell's philosophy offers neither an integrated system nor a school of thought, consequently the following discussion of his philosophy may appear atomistically disconnected. C. D. Broad, Russell's colleague, was correct in his remark: "As we all know, Mr. Russell produces a different system of philosophy every few years." There are, nevertheless, certain definite contributions which the brilliant and capable Russell has offered as indicative of his own philosophical outlook, and these will be presented for examination: (1) Two stages in Russell's evolutionary philosophical growth, (2) Logical Positivism and Scientism, (3) Skepticism and Agnosticism, (4) The Doctrine of Logical Atomism, and (5) Mathematical Logic.

Two Stages in Russell's Evolutionary Growth in Philosophy.

Bertrand Russell, considered *the philosopher* by many contemporary Logical Positivists, and regarded as a modern Voltaire by others, an iconoclast par excellence, is an antireligious radical and Agnostic. Russell's interests can be arranged dichotomously: the first division is that between mathematical logic and theoretical philosophy, and the second between his earlier philosophical interests, definitely Leibnizian and Platonic, contrasted with his later philosophical outlook which was markedly Positivistic and Agnostic. Characteristic of the former division is the fact that his classic *Principia Mathematica,* one of the most influential works of the present century, and his thinking of that time were decidedly Platonic. In "My Mental Development," he mentions that he was a *Platonic Realist.* His regard for universals was elevated to a point where he placed philosophy on the plane of a deductive science.

Logical Positivism, Scientism, and Skepticism.

The later Russell, the Russell of the present day, has lapsed almost completely into Logical Positivism; he is an avowed adherent of Scientism, the belief that the methods of science alone give valid knowledge, or that knowledge beyond the scope of science is invalid. "In the welter of conflicting fanaticisms, one of the few unifying forces is scientific truthfulness . . . To have insisted upon the introduction of this virtue into philosophy, and to have invented a powerful method by which it can be rendered fruitful, are the chief merits of the philosophical school of which I am a member."[1] Since nonscientific judgments are unverifiable,

[1] Russell, *History of Western Philosophy, op. cit.,* 836.

Russell is reduced to Skepticism in nonscientific realms, such as, ethics, religion, etc.

In his *Religion and Science* (1935), he concludes: "That while it is true that science cannot decide questions of value, that is because they cannot be intellectually decided at all, and lie outside the realm of truth and falsehood. Whatever knowledge is attainable, must be attained by scientific methods; and what science cannot discover, mankind cannot know." His Scientism is complete, as expressed in the preceding statement; this means that moral values, as well as other nonscientific facts, are unknowable and that mankind must remain forever in ignorance concerning them, unless they can be brought within the scope of scientific method, and that is out of the question. "Questions as to 'values' — that is to say, as to what is good or bad on its own account, independently of its effects — lie outside the domain of science, as the defenders of religion emphatically assert. I think that in this they are right, but I draw the further conclusion,which they do not draw, that questions as to 'values' lie wholly outside the domain of knowledge." [1] Moral and religious matters are merely emotive in nature and value; when discussing such issues, we are merely giving vent to our emotions, rather than expressing matters of fact to which we may ascribe truth.

Russell comments on his doctrine of *Skepticism:* "It is undesirable to believe a proposition when there is no ground whatever for supposing it true," [2] then presents its three salient points: "(1) that when the experts are agreed, the opposite opinion cannot be held to be certain; (2) that when they are not agreed, no opinion can be regarded as certain by a non-expert; and (3) that when they all hold that no sufficient grounds for a positive opinion exist, the ordinary man would do well to suspend his judgement." [3] Russell believes that despite the mild tone of these principles, they are capable (if accepted) of revolutionizing human life.

Mathematical Logic.

Perhaps Russell (with his one-time colleague, Alfred North Whitehead) will be best remembered for his monumental feat, *Principia Mathematica* (Vol. I, 1910; Vol. II, 1912; Vol. III, 1913). Russell originally entered philosophy through mathematics, a fact to which he attests in his article "Logical Atomism." The ambitious task that he and Whitehead confronted in *Principia Mathematica* was to uphold the claim that pure

[1] Bertrand Russell, *Religion and Science* (London: Oxford University Press, 1935), 230.

[2] Bertrand Russell, *Sceptical Essays* (London: George Allen & Unwin; New York: Barnes & Noble, 1928, 1956), 9.

[3] *Ibid.*, 10.

mathematics was derived from axioms of formal logic; mathematical concepts are reducible to logical concepts. In *The Principles of Mathematics* (1903), Russell contends: "Mathematics and logic are identical . . . The present work has two main objects. One of these, the proof that all pure mathematics deals exclusively with concepts definable in terms of a very small number of fundamental logical concepts, and that all its propositions are deducible from a very small number of fundamental logical principles." Then he proceeds to define pure mathematics as "the class of all propositions of the form '*p*' implies '*q*,' where *p* and *q* are propositions containing one or more variables, the same in the two propositions, and neither *p* nor *q* contain any constants except logical constants." Mathematics becomes, according to this claim, an offshoot of logic.

Principia Mathematica predicates (a) that mathematical discourse is reducible to logical terms; (b) that the concepts of logic grant a clarity superior to those of mathematics, and are capable of eliminating puzzling paradoxes of mathematics merely by transposing them into logical terms; (c) that greater logical certainty is had owing to basic mathematical assumptions, such as, infinite classes.

The symbols used in *Principia Mathematica* were based somewhat on those developed by the Italian mathematician, *Giuseppe Peano* (1858-1932); the premise that pure mathematics is merely a prolongation of logic was offered by *Gottlob Frege* (1848-1925) of Jena, whose ideas, in turn, were inspired by Peano's axioms.

Although mathematical logic as a 'pure science' is sometimes left to mathematicians rather than philosophers, its problems, assumptions, and metaphysical premises are philosophical; furthermore, the philosopher is interested in conclusions at which the mathematician arrives, particularly those of a paradoxical nature.

> One such paradox arose in connection with the definition of number in Principia Mathematica. The notion of 'class of all classes' was the cause of it. For evidently the class of all classes is itself a class, and therefore belongs to the class of all classes; it thus contains itself as one of its members. There are, of course, many other classes that do not have this property. The class of all voters does not itself enjoy the benefits of universal suffrage. The paradox now arises when we consider the class of all classes which are not members of themselves.
>
> The question is whether this class is a member of itself or not. If we suppose that it is a member of itself, then it is not an instance of a class that does include itself. But in order to be a member of itself, it must be of the kind that is being considered in the first place, that is, not a member of itself. If, on the contrary, we assume that the class under discussion is not a member of itself, then it is not an instance of a class

> that does not include itself. But in order to be no member of itself, it must be one of the classes in the class about which the original question was asked, and so it is a member of itself. In either case we reach a contradiction.
>
> The difficulty can be removed if we note that one must not treat classes on quite the same footing as classes of classes, just as normally one would not speak of men on the same level as of nations. It then becomes evident that we should not talk about classes that are their own members so glibly as we did in setting up the paradox.[1]

Although paradoxes such as the foregoing have been approached in various ways, no consensus has been reached on their disposition; they continue to remain a problem. However, they have opened new vistas, and have had the effect of summoning the attention of philosophers to expend their efforts in scrutinizing this area.

Logical Atomism.

Russell's philosophy of *Logical Atomism* is an attempt to reduce concepts to their lowest logical components by way of analysis, with the hope that the clarity and simplicity resulting therefrom will prove elucidating, thus diminishing, if not completely removing, all errors. "The reason that I call my doctrine *logical* atomism is because the atoms that I wish to arrive at as the sort of last residue in analysis are logical atoms and not physical atoms. Some of them will be what I call 'particulars'— such things as little patches of color or sounds, momentary things— and some of them will be predicates or relations and so on. The point is that the atom I wish to arrive at is the atom of logical analysis, not the atom of physical analysis."[2] Logical Atomism is an attempt to arrive at an *ideal language,* one free from ambiguities.

Russell's *Principles of Mathematics* proved that an analysis of mathematics revealed its base to be logic, strict formal logic; logical atomism is, in a sense, the inverse, that of reducing a logical doctrine to mathematical philosophy. "The logic which I shall advocate is atomistic, as opposed to the monistic logic of the people who more or less follow Hegel. When I say that my logic is atomistic, I mean that I share the common-sense belief that there are many separate things; I do not regard the apparent multiplicity of the world as consisting merely in phases and unreal divisions of a single indivisible Reality."[3] Each atomic logical term, according to this pluralistic concept of the universe, may stand for a single isolated fact. The matter would be greatly facilitated if the phil-

[1] Bertrand Russell, *Wisdom of the West,* 283. Copyright © by Rathbone Books Ltd., London, 1959. Reprinted by permission of Doubleday & Co., Inc.

[2] Bertrand Russell, "Philosophy of Logical Atomism" in *Monist,* (1918).

[3] *Idem.*

osophy of Realism were predicated as the basis of this philosophy. Each experience would represent a fact, that is to say, particular sense data serve as ultimate constituents of the universe. An isolated sense datum would represent an ultimate atomic fact; when each atomic fact is given a term, then our ideal language will have been constructed.

Logical Atomism, and its intimation of an ideal language, actually originated with Ludwig Wittgenstein, Russell's former student, not with Russell himself. However, Russell developed the system and remained faithful to it, whereas Wittgenstein eventually repudiated it. Although Russell confesses that he learned the philosophy of Logical Atomism from Wittgenstein, the doctrine was inherent in his *Principia Mathematica.*

5. Evaluation of Neorealism

Neorealists have voiced an opinion which most of us unquestionably share, namely the belief that there exists a genuinely real and objective world; this contention maintains for the Idealist and others as well as for the Realist; only the Skeptic and Solipsist would not share in this belief. What the Realist, and for that matter any other philosopher, has failed to do, is to prove the precise nature of the external world, not merely the phenomenal world, but particularly the ultimately real one.

The nearest that philosophers have come to it is to show that it is of the nature of mind, consciousness, spiritual; the very thing which the Neorealists are earnestly, but vainly, trying to disprove. The Neorealist, through a prime spokesman, Ralph Barton Perry, seeks to invalidate an Idealistic or spiritual universe through the *"Ego-Centric Predicament"* argument, viz., the belief that all knowledge, experience, facts, reasoning, etc. concerning the world around us, whatever its nature may ultimately be, must first be reduced to the nature of consciousness before it can enter the mind of man, for only that which is spiritual, mental, of the nature of consciousness, can possibly find its way into human knowledge and personality. We are persons, spiritual beings, with a life and existence composed of the nature of consciousness, mind; consequently, whatever enters our existence *must be* of, or else must be reduced to, the nature of mind. In other words, if the real world is other than the nature of mind, it is impossible for us to know it in those terms, for we have no organ by which to know that which is nonmental; it must first be converted into the nature of mind, (consciousness) before the human being can experience it. Accordingly, what was initially intended to be an argument designed to defeat Idealism, turns out to be evidence in its support.

The Neorealist reduces ultimate reality to neutral substance, not mind nor matter, but a *neutral entity* which at times appears mental, and at other times, material. He justifies this conclusion on the basis of *analysis,* that is, a thoroughgoing analysis will indicate, he claims, that matter and mind are of a substance akin to mathematical principles, Platonic subsistents, a *tertium quid,* an entity, neutral to both mind and matter, and more basic than either.

The Neorealist's criteria of truth, instinct and intuition, are far from acceptable; if we depended upon instinct or intuition to gain knowledge in scientific research respecting outer space or medicine, we would be paralyzed in our efforts, and would be arrested in scientific development at the level of the savage. Yet, some Neorealists (e.g., Santayana) feel perfectly justified in asserting that we know substance exists, and its nature is matter, on the basis that instinct tells us so. Rather than an argument worthy of respectful consideration, this sounds more like a defeated man in his last efforts of desperation, seeking a refuge in which to hide.

G. E. Moore's argument, which is decidedly superior to the others, has not successfully substantiated the Neorealist's position; his case rests finally on the argument as he formulates it: "I am as directly aware of the existence of material things in space as of my own sensations," but this is not so; we do not experience matter as such; we experience an image which never leaves our bodies, an image we *assume* is a true copy of a material object in an outer world; and even this assumption is critically weakened by the fact that our images of the outer world are often proved inaccurate, if not entirely misleading.

In the final analysis of Neorealism, the most that can be said is that although a strong sympathy can be felt for this position, it is incapable of establishing its case.

XXXVIII

PERSONALISM:

The Key to Reality Is Personality

Contemporary Personalism may be defined as the philosophy which maintains that *personality* is of infinite intrinsic value, and the key to the meaning of reality. Traditional Personalism is Theistic; most Personalists believe in the existence of God who serves as the ground or explanation of the nature of the universe. As Pragmatism, Personalism, too, is essentially an American philosophy; the term was used as early as 1863 by *Amos Bronson Alcott* (1799-1888) who defined it as "the doctrine that the ultimate reality of the world is a Divine Person who sustains the universe by a continuous act of creative will." In recent years, the word is coming more to mean the doctrine which emphasizes man's significance, uniqueness, and inviolability.

Systematic Personalism is attributable to *Borden Parker Bowne* (1847-1910) who referred to himself as "a Personalist, the first of the clan in any thoroughgoing sense," and applied it to various areas of philosophy: (1) to *ethics,* to mean that the universe is friendly to values; values are real owing to the personal nature of the universe; (2) to *metaphysics,* to imply the personal nature of the World Ground (cosmos); (3) to *epistemology,* to mean that knowledge is grounded and mediated in and through personality; the World Ground is the source of all knowledge and thought; (4) to *logic,* to signify that 'life is deeper than logic,' in a pragmatic sense.

Edgar Sheffield Brightman (1884-1953), a leading contemporary and vigorous exponent of Personalism, defines it as "a philosophical system in which persons (or selves) are the sole (or dominant) metaphysical realities, as well as the only ultimate intrinsic values."[1] By personality is meant an "individual substance of a rational nature," not a psychophysical organism. As to the main ideas of Personalism, Brightman says that

[1] *Encyclopedia of Religion,* ed., Vergilius Ferm (New York: Philosophical Library, Inc., 1945).

it "proposes a psychology (self psychology, gestalt), a logic (synoptic method, coherence of total personality as criterion of truth), an epistemology (activity of mind in knowledge, dualism of idea and object), and a metaphysics (the universe a society of persons)." [1]

Personalism, as was the case with Pragmatism, is a new term for old ways of thinking "which grows out of the attempt to interpret the self as a part of the phenomenological experience," [2] says *Ralph Tyler Flewelling,* a leading contemporary Personalist. Personalistic thinking can be traced to as early as the philosophical thinking of Heraclitus (563-470) and Anaxagoras (500-430), but the term itself was first used in the era of Modern Philosophy by *Friedrich Schleiermacher* (1768-1834) in his *Reden* (*Discourses,* 1799, p. 56, 57), synonymously with Theism. Its initial appearance in America was in 1863 by Alcott, and then again a few years later, in 1868, when *Walt Whitman* entitled an essay "Personalism." In 1903, the French philosopher, *Charles Bernard Renouvier* (1815-1903), wrote a book entitled *Le Personalisme* (*Personalism,* 1903); *Borden Parker Bowne* wrote his *Personalism* in 1908; *Albert Cornelius Knudson* (1873-1953), his *The Philosophy of Personalism* in 1927; and in 1918 the organ of the school appeared from the University of Southern California, *The Personalist,* followed by its Spanish sister, *Luminar,* published in Mexico City.

Although Personalism is predominantly a Theistic philosophy, variations of it do exist in the form of (1) Atheistic Personalism, chiefly represented by the British philosopher *John M. E. McTaggart* (1866-1925); (2) *Pantheistic Personalism* whose foremost proponent is the German philosopher William Stern (1871-1938), author of *Person und Sache* (*Person and Thing,* 1906, 1918, 1924, 3 vols.), subtitled *Critical Personalism;* (3) *Relativistic Personalism,* typified by the system of *Charles B. Renouvier;* (4) *Finalistic* or *Teleological Personalism* (Personal Idealism) of *George H. Howison* (1834-1916) who taught that God was not First Cause of the universe, but its Final Cause, and that persons are coeternal with him; (5) *Absolutistic Personalism,* represented by Neo-Hegelians; and (6) *Typical Theistic Personalism,* the mainstream of Personalism, which we shall refer to as traditional, or merely *Personalism.*

Personalists are dichotomously divided in their views on the phenomenal world; some adhere to *Panpsychism,* the belief that phenomena are of the nature of activity, force, psychic in some respect; others are *Occasionalists,* who believe that the laws of nature are the orderly, habitual ways of the behavior of God, and that nature is devoid of inherent forces

[1] *Idem.*

[2] *Dictionary of Philosophy,* ed., Dagobert Runes (New York: Philosophical Library, Inc., n.d.).

or powers called *cause;* cause is merely the 'orderly and continuous intervention of God.'

In respect to epistemology, the Personalist's creed is: (1) Epistemological Dualism — thought and thing are distinct entities, (2) the reliability of reason as criterion of truth, (3) thought as creative activity, and (4) the primacy of practical reason, that is, scientific technological knowledge subserves moral goals. The reader will recognize some of these epistemological ideas as shared with other schools of philosophy.

1. Albert Cornelius Knudson — Systematic Methodological Personalism.

Personalism Defined.

Albert Cornelius Knudson defines Personalism as *"that form of idealism which gives equal recognition to both the pluralistic and monistic aspects of experience and which finds in the conscious unity, identity, and free activity of personality the key to the nature of reality and the solution of the ultimate problems of philosophy."* [1] Thus we find that Personalism's basic principle is the 'self-sufficiency of personality' in explaining metaphysical issues. The ontologically real is personality as well as personality being the key to reality — only persons (including the Supreme Person, God) are metaphysically real, whereas the nature of the material world is merely phenomenal.

Six Major Tenets of Personalism.

Knudson concisely summarizes the metaphysics of Personalism under six major tenets:

> First, personalism holds that *reality is concrete and individual.* It thus leans towards pluralism and natural realism. It does so in the interest of the reality and independence of the finite person and also in the interest of a more distinct and clearly defined conception of the infinite than has prevailed in many philosophies.
>
> Second, it stresses the *unity of the world and the worldground.* In this respect it leans toward monism and absolutism, thus satisfying the religious demand involved in the feeling of absolute dependence and also the intellectual demand for a universe as distinguished from a "multiverse."
>
> Third, it maintains that *reality in its essential nature is active.* In other words, it interprets substance in terms of causality. It thus falls in line with modern physical theory and also with the modern tendency to con-

[1] Unless otherwise indicated, quotations in the section on Knudson are from his *The Philosophy of Personalism* (Boston: Boston University Press; Nashville: The Abingdon Press, 1927). Reprinted by permission of Boston University Press.

ceive of the *soul as a mental agent* rather than as mere substance.

Fourth, it takes an important step beyond modern energetics and contends that energy or causality must ultimately be interpreted in terms of *volition*. Here personalism breaks with the realistic systems of the past and becomes idealistic.

Fifth, it holds that *matter is phenomenal,* and that in a more thoroughgoing sense than any realistic theory would admit. This follows necessarily from its interpretation of causality. Not only does personalism deny extramental existence to the extended matter of sense experience but also to its dynamic ground. It conceives of the whole material world as the ceaseless product of the divine energizing. Indeed, in its thoroughgoing form it holds to the *complete ideality of space and time.*

Sixth and finally, it contends that *personality is the key to ultimate reality.* Abstract thought leads to fundamental antinomies such as those between identity and change, the One and the Many, freedom and necessity. A solution of these antinomies is possible only in personal experience. Here we have in very fact, however we may account for it, a union of personal identity with change, of conscious unity with multiplicity of experience, and of freedom or self-control with uniformity or necessity. If we, therefore, conceive of ultimate reality as personal, we have in that conception an answer, and the only adequate answer, to the fundamental questions of speculative thought.

1. *The Individuality of Reality.*

A major tenet and an indispensable basic premise of Personalism is its emphasis upon individuality, as opposed to generalizations and universals; the individual exists, individual persons, and individual things. "Personalism begins its theory of reality with the affirmation that metaphysical existence can be predicated only of that which is individual and concrete. The universal and abstract are essential as ideas; without them thought would disintegrate. In making a statement about a thing we are required to use a universal; and all things, we assume, have qualities of one kind or another. But these qualities and universals have themselves no thing-like existence. There are individual trees but no tree in general. There are white objects but no independent self-existent whiteness." This conclusion is the apparent one which we receive from common sense, and most persons would never consider objects in the world to be otherwise, but Platonic Realists and others consider reality to be universal abstract objects divorced from particular objects which merely serve as their transient copies.

The issue as to whether particular objects or their universal abstract counterparts are real has been debated since the Platonic era, and continues to present times. The belief in the reality of universals met its antithesis in *Nominalism,* the doctrine that universals are merely names for a particular class of objects; later, a synthesis between these two opposing doctrines was found in *Conceptualism,* the theory that the reality of universals exists in the mind of man as concepts, but do exist in nature, and, as ultimate realities, in the mind of God.

The *principle of individuality* found in Personalism is derived from Leibnizian Panpsychism, which, through its concept of Monads, divested individuality of its universal garb, and gave it an Idealistic quality of its own. Leibniz' *Monadology* stressed the uniqueness of the individual Monad, and its absolute separateness from any other objects, thus enjoying for each Monad a reality of its own and in its own right, for the Monads are individual, and have no 'windows through which anything can come in or go out.' Individual *substance* is not a passive *thing,* but activity, possessing the power of action, personalities in their own right, *sui generis.* Hence persons, who constitute ultimate reality, are selves, with unique existences; each is a world within itself, impenetrable by any other person or thing, possessing its own individual character, its own individual nature, and is capable of imputing value to every other object because values lie exclusively in and for persons alone. Without personality, there can be no value whatever; value is personal.

2. *The Unity of the World and World Ground.*

This tenet of Personalism ranks second only to the principle of individuality, and at times has been confused with it. Unity is the concept which emphasizes "the unique relation of the Absolute to the world or the unique characteristic of ultimate reality . . . The world is one as well as many." The concept of unity is valuable in bringing about syntheses from antithetical concepts which were irreconcilable by other principles employed in the past. For example, it resolves the monistic-dualistic dispute because Personalism regards personality as a *unitas multiplex,* a multiple unity (W. Stern) capable of including both. The same holds true for *being* and *action, change* and *permanency.*

Unity is achieved through reason thereby satisfying the rational demand for unity. "Sense-experience is manifold and pluralistic; but reason is unitary and systematic." Without the World Ground (the unity of reason), 'tychism' (Peirce's philosophy of a world of chance) would result. "On this basis things are as they happen to be. There is no necessity, rational or otherwise, lying back of them. There might happen to be a God, but there is nothing in the structure of the universe that requires such a being. This viewpoint makes possible an ultimate pluralism, but it also involves the abnegation of reason." Both Monism and Pluralism are empirically true, but reason requires fundamental unity in a world of diversity, and this is achieved only through invoking the concept of personality, that which is capable of effecting unity in diversity.

3. ***Reality as Activity.***

"Personalism is activistic. It holds that reality consists in the power of action." In this respect, Personalism differs from certain forms of Idealism, Sense Metaphysics, and Pantheism. It opposes Sense Metaphysics because Personalism does not accept the reality of Being as found in sense qualities, but discovers reality in its activity. Sense Metaphysics views reality as a passive, inert material substance, whereas Personalism stresses the innate activity of matter, its force. Sense Metaphysics claims that matter must first *be* (exist), before it can act, while Personalism maintains that matter or its reality is activity; to act is to be, not to be and then you may possibly act.

Activity requires agency, and both are found in personality. "The real thing is always an agent acting in certain ways. Apart from the agent there is no activity, and, on the other hand, there is no agent without activity. Activity penetrates to the very core of being, and constitutes its essential nature." Reality is, and must always be, a single and unitary agent, otherwise, Being or matter is but an empty and incoherent abstraction.

4. ***Volitional Causality.***

"Reality is something we must accept; we cannot deduce it. But if it is to perform its function in the system of thought, and have any definite meaning, it must be conceived as cause." But cause is to be understood as real, objective to thought; although it is apprehended by thought, cause is distinct from it. This conclusion distinguishes Personalists who are Activists from Absolute Idealists who desist from drawing any distinction between cause and thought.

"Having defined reality as causality, or the power of action, we now proceed to determine more precisely how causality is to be conceived. In doing so we discover that personalism differentiates itself rather sharply from other types of activism. Activism as such may take many different forms. It may be dualistic or monistic; it may be realistic or idealistic. In our exposition thus far of personalism as a theory of reality we have found it leaning toward realism, and this remains one of its permanent characteristics as over against absolute idealism. Its activism refuses to be dissolved into a mere thought-process." But Personalism has strong Idealistic leanings as well. "Its idealism, however, is concrete and spiritual rather than abstract and logical, and so retains a realistic element."

Reality, and by that word is meant substance, must be interpreted in causal terms, of which there are three major concepts: (1) Positivistic, (2) Rationalistic, and (3) Voluntaristic. The first, stemming from Hume, reduces cause to an illusion; the second, Spinozistic and Hegelian, is deterministic, and reduces cause to necessity, or it is teleological in the Aristotelian sense, thus is externally restrictive, lacking autonomy; the third, Personalistic, is volitional and dynamic. "All concrete existence is contingent, and owes its origin to the divine purpose. It is an act of will. And it is in this realm of the volitional and dynamic that causality finds its true meaning." It is not a capricious will, however, but one which accedes to the principle of sufficient reason. The 'voluntaristic theory of causality' is attributable to Leibniz because it was he who emphasized the teleology, individualism, contingency, and spiritual interpretation of cause together with the causal interpretation of substance. "Passive substance, whether material or immaterial, cannot fulfill the function of reality. Reality must explain appearance, and this it can do only insofar as it is causal in the dynamic sense of the term. But dynamism is invisible. It cannot be represented to the imagination, and it can be given concrete and definite meaning only in the form of volitional causality. This we experience. We are conscious of ourselves as willing and struggling beings. But beyond this experienced fact we have no idea what causality would mean. Impersonal force is to us inconceivable. We must, therefore, think of all force or power or cause as personal or spiritual." The 'volitional theory of cause' functions as a synthesis to fuse a priorism with empiricism; such is the foundation of modern Voluntarism, which includes Existentialism. It is of interest that Edgar S. Brightman considers Existentialism a form of Personalism. [1]

5. *The Phenomenality of Matter.*

From the preceding tenets which concluded the nature of reality to be causal, and the nature of causality to be volitional, we infer the phenomenal nature of matter, both in its passive aspect as a derivative of sense experience and in its dynamic aspect providing scientists with their subject matter. Unlike Absolute Idealism, Personalism or Spiritualism is "realistic in the sense that it maintains that existence is something other and deeper than thought. To set a thing in reality means more than simply to think it. It implies a deed, a creative act. How creation is possible we do not know, but the term at least brings out the distinctiveness of reality and the mystery that surrounds it. The soul is more than a thought-process; it is the source of thought rather than its product. Real existence is personal, not simply ideational; it is spiritual, not merely

[1] See his article "Personalism" in *Twentieth Century Encyclopedia of Religious Knowledge,* ed. Lefferts A. Loetscher (1955).

logical. In thus emphasizing the concrete, the extralogical, the volitional character of reality personalism retains a realistic element that the absolute idealist seeks to dissolve away." Equally objectionable to Personalism is Positivism, or Postivistic Idealism, in its dissolution of reality by reducing it to the subjectivity of consciousness, instead of a reality of its own. "As opposed to these types of thought it denies all extramental existence and affirms the complete phenomenality of matter."

For the Personalist, reality is deeper than consciousness, and abides its passing states of change; moreover, reality can be measured and apprehended by the mind of individual persons. The phenomenality of matter is not unique with Personalism; the theory is shared with Positivists and Absolute Idealists alike, but for the Personalist, "soul is the essence of all existing things; materiality is simply their phenomenal form;" thus physical nature becomes the instrument of spiritual nature. Furthermore, Personalists reject "the metaphysical reality of space and hold that it is as phenomenal as the matter supposed to be contained in it. Apart from experience space has no existence. The spatial world is an effect in us and in thinking beings in general. We need a real space to see things in as little as we need a real space to dream things in. Both the reactions of the sensibility and the activities of the mind are spaceless, and it is these that give rise to the knowledge of space. Space, then, is simply the form of objective experience, and in and by itself is a bare abstraction. Without spatial objects there would be no space. Its phenomenality, therefore, is a corollary of the phenomenality of matter."

The ideality of time, however, creates certain problems, for unlike nonspatial experiences, persons have never had nontemporal experiences. For time to be ontologically real, it must be *active,* but this is hardly the case; furthermore, if time were real, nothing else could exist except that which is in the present, but there cannot be any present since time is in constant flight. Time, therefore, is not ontologically real, "but a temporal relation, like the spatial, we must regard as merely the form under which we conceive the cosmic process. This process is grounded in the divine activity . . . Just as the spatial form of experience has its ground in an immaterial and nonspatial agency, so it is quite possible that the temporal order may be maintained by an activity that has in itself no before and after. Temporality does not require a temporal cause." It is as Bowne claimed: "The successive can exist only for the nonsuccessive." Therefore Personalists maintain, "God is a nontemporal Being, and yet he founds change. This is possible because he is a Person. A free being can initiate change without being himself involved in it. This is the mystery of personality and its most distinctive characteristic."

As to the role and nature of time in respect to the universe, it is as Augustine conceived, and subsequently formulated as a saying: "God made the world not *in* time but *with* time." Temporal relations therefore coexist with cosmic processes, yet apart from them are unreal.

6. ***Personality as the Key to Reality.***

"The metaphysics of personalism may be summed up in the statement that *personality is the key to reality.* All that has thus far been said about the individuality of the real, about a basal unity, about causality, and about the phenomenality of space and time, has pointed toward this truth. It is in personality that individuality finds its only adequate realization. It is personality alone that has the characteristics necessary to a basal unity. It is in personal agency that we have the source of the idea of causality and its only self-consistent embodiment. It is the reality of personality that constitutes the foil to the phenomenality of matter, space, and time and renders it intelligible. From every point of view it is thus evident that in personality we have the crown of the personalistic system, the keystone in its arch, the masterlight of all our metaphysical seeing."

The reality of personality is certainly not a new concept initiated by contemporary Personalism, it stems from antiquity, but in ancient philosophy, its reality was viewed as a *substance* rather than an *activity.* Augustine was the first to stress the certainty of self-existence, and Descartes reiterated it with emphasis: To think implies existence — *Cogito, ergo sum* (I think, therefore I am). Leibniz queried: "I should like to know how we could attain to a knowledge of reality if we or our souls were not real." Fichte, too, had his argument: "However it may be with the reality of a sensible world external to me, I myself am real; I take hold on reality here; it lies in me, and is there at home." Perhaps, we can modify or attempt to infer from the Fichtean statement the following: How can a real world external to me of which I possess knowledge exist, unless I too exist?

The Personalistic definition of self or soul is not mere substance, but activity with its own self-conscious unity and freedom; personality becomes the norm of Being — *personality is the key to reality.* "This doctrine is fundamentally empiricistic. Personality is something given. We do not create it, nor do we know how it is created. It is an ultimate fact, but as such it contains the 'key to the whole puzzle about reality,' so far as this puzzle admits of solution." Personality provides the only adequate ground for explaining many of our persistent philosophical problems, for it combines unity with diversity, identity with change, unity with plurality, etc., hence personality is the only adequate resolution of antinomies. These are not idle claims, nor speculative ones either, they are facts of experience. Mysterious as the case may be, personality provides "conclusive evidence that in reality the problem of unity and diversity are somehow solved. Our self-experience, and it alone, gives us the solution. It is, therefore, no 'arbitrary refuge' to which we resort when we make personality our ultimate and irreducible datum." Our claims are justified and verified by the data of everyday experience common to everyone.

2. Edgar Sheffield Brightman — Personalistic Value Theory

Values as Existing in and for Persons.

Values, for a Personalist, are not free floating objects in thin air, but are grounded in personality, both human and divine. In the Supreme Person, values exist as *norms*, true values, values as they ought to be, values for a coherently ordered and rational mind. Without persons, there can be no values whatever; persons impute values to objects since they alone are evaluators; and in the light of this fact, Brightman derives his definition of personality: "Person is defined as a complex unity of self-consciousness that is able to develop ideal values and to act in itself and to interact with others."[1] Persons, and only persons, actually experience values. Without value, even substance, or more accurately, Being loses its meaning, for Being also is intelligible only in terms of true value, the realm of 'goods that ought to be.' We cannot know the true nature of Being without reference to the nature of will, or "we cannot know being without knowing what ought to be."

Value Defined.

As to a definition of values, it "means whatever is actually liked, prized, esteemed, desired, approved, or enjoyed by anyone at any time. It is the actual experience of enjoying a desired object or activity. Hence, value is an existing realization of desire."[2] Although it is true that anything which is desired is a value, this does not imply that anything desired is desir*able*, that is, *ought* to be desired, that which is consistent with a coherently reasoned desire, that which an omniscient mind (God) would desire. In other words, not all values are of intrinsic worth; if they are

[1] Edgar Sheffield Brightman, *Person and Reality — An Introduction to Metaphysics*, edited by Peter Anthony Bertocci. Copyright © 1958 The Ronald Press Company. Unless otherwise noted, quotations in section 2 are from the above work.

[2] Brightman's definition of value as it is found here in *Person and Reality* is identical to those found in another of his books: *Philosophy of Religion (op. cit.)*, and consistent with those found in *Moral Laws* (1933), and *Nature and Values* (1945).

actually desired, they are *value-claims,* but become true values only when they are in accord with *norms,* values as they exist for the Supreme Person, God.

Norms and Values.

Values are private; they exist for some particular person; they "have their being solely in the shining present of the self or person who experiences them." They "reside in the shining present of the experient. All values, then, are inherently private, subjective, personal experiences . . . Norms, however, are public." Assertions for norms are warranted; they are "rationally defensible as well as empirically grounded;" accordingly they must possess objectivity, validity, and truth. Human values are attempts at gaining norms and for the most part are rough approximations of true norms, truth. Unless the existence of objectively valid norms is conceded, "experience remains groping with no hope that the most prolonged series of trials and errors would lead to or toward the truth."

Respecting the objectivity of values, they, "as human experiences, are not objective; norms, developed by coherent criticism of human experience of value, are objective and are valid for all persons. But their objectivity, we suggest, consists in the fact that the cosmic Mind knows them to be norms, or, better, purposes that human beings should achieve coherent value-realization only through living in accordance with them. Since the norms are rational truth, it follows that ultimately they cannot be changed either by the human mind or the cosmic Mind."[1] Norms are eternal objects, but this does not mean that they float about ungrounded by personality, for their existence is a "life within the context of a cosmic Mind." In human experience, norms assume the form of principles, objective and ideally true for all persons.

3. Borden Parker Bowne — The Refutation of Impersonalism

Borden Parker Bowne is, in many Personalistic circles, recognized as the founder of Personalism, at least systematic Theistic Personalism as it is widely adhered to in America. Even Bowne regarded himself as the first of the clan of Personalists which encompassed many schools, such as, Theistic Idealism, Transcendental Empiricism, Idealistic Realism, and Realistic Idealism. Bowne's chief influence, setting the stage for his thinking, was Rudolph H. Lotze (1817-1881), who, although regarded as a Personalist, was a German Idealist who taught a *self-psychology,* a concept which played a definite role in the tenets of Personalism.

[1] Edgar Sheffield Brightman, *Person and Reality — An Introduction to Metaphysics,* edited by Peter Anthony Bertocci. Copyright © 1958 The Ronald Press Company.

William Ernest Hocking (1873-) said of Bowne's militant attack against impersonalism: "There is no more powerful and convincing chapter in American metaphysical writing than that of Bowne on 'the failure of impersonalism.'"[1] Bowne's refutation of impersonalism is directed at all forms, but particularly against Naturalism with its Positivistic tendencies, and Absolute Idealism which has sacrificed the individual person for the impersonal Pantheistic Absolute.

Impersonalism seduces two types of individuals: the first is the 'sense-bound mind' with his superficial and naive outlook on the nature of things; the second is the type who commits the 'fallacy of the abstract,' by explaining explanations by still more abstract explanations, terminating in infinite regress. Naturalists fall prey to the former, whereas Absolute Idealists are victimized by the latter.

Scientific Naturalism is not under attack here, but philosophical, a Common-Sense Realism which seeks to explain higher forms of experience, including even life and society, in terms of force and matter, impersonal force ruled by mechanical laws. When these people complete their investigations, the world is reduced to one beyond all experiential recognition; no such world actually exists, except 'among the abstractions of physicists.' The scientific world of abstract laws of nature (light waves, sound waves, etc.) is not the world of personal experience which we daily enjoy; the scientific impersonal world is one of scientific machines, one arrived at by quantitative measurement to the complete disregard for the qualitative aspects of experience, such as human experience, the world encountered by personality. The scientific world is reduced to one of abstract theoretical explanations, void of sense qualities to the point that the "real world becomes less and less accessible and less and less worth knowing . . . The most important part of experience is not explained at all, but is handed over to a kind of subjective experience somewhere in consciousness, while the theoretical explanation applies only to abstractions. Thus we invert the true order of fact. We discredit the real experience, or ignore it, and triumphantly solve an imaginary problem. . . . We are shut up by this way of thinking to transfigured realism and all its fictitious problems, with the result that the world we experience becomes more and more subjective."[2] The major failure of this form of impersonalistic thinking is that it terminates in a world of reality composed of impersonal laws of science, whereas the actual world, the one in which we live, is composed, not of universals, but of particular objects; our everyday experience is confronted with individual objects, not uni-

[1] *Methodist Review* (1922).

[2] Except where noted, quotations in this section are from Borden Parker Bowne, *Personalism* (Boston: Houghton Mifflin Co., 1908).

versal abstract principles solely. Hence science is failing to account for a most important phase of human experience, viz., human existence with its multifarious experiences which exceeds universal abstract laws. Law *per se* is merely classification, but persons do not live in abstract classifications; they live in concrete individual circumstances with concrete individual objects, so personal and individual as to defy classification, except in a very general way. It is a fallacy to assume that the nature we have in common is reducible to generalizations or laws of science, for I personally and individually am not a law of science, an abstract generalization; I am an individual personality, primarily, and must be so regarded. I am more than the causes which motivate me; they are abstract universal generalizations, while I am a particular individual personality. Individual persons exist, not universal man; a unique person exists, not a 'text-book' man which is supposed to be the true you or me. The 'text-book' man is only remotely any particular individual, whereas the real person is individual, unique, and existently real.

The fallacy committed here, notes Bowne, is analogous to abstracting language from intelligence, then adducing language as the explanation of intelligence. No such world or man of the impersonalistic philosophers exists, except in the abstractions of physicists and psychologists.

As to the nature of causation, that too must be personal; "unless we assume a mover without, we must posit moving forces within;" the only adequate reasonable and coherent account of anything must be sought in a world of *power,* of forces, of experience. Abstract cause is not experienced, but *volitional causality* is; volitional causality is a present, dynamic, and active force operative in the world, not one which is posited by the *fallacy of the universal.* It is because of the fallacy of the universal which *mistakes logical processes for ontological ones* that "classification has passed for identification, phenomena have been made into things, and sequence has been mistaken for causality."

In conclusion, we may say that impersonalism is a failure (1) because we are not abstract intellects; as the Absolute Idealists fancy, nor are we abstract wills, we are unique living individual persons who possess *substantial* reality, and (2) because impersonalism confuses the person with a physical organism. An organism as an impersonal entity cannot produce personality; the personal does not issue from the nonpersonal. "Personality can never be construed as a product or compound; it can only be experienced as a fact. It must be possible because it is given as actual. Whenever we attempt to go behind this fact we are trying to explain the explanation." The self-conscious existence of personality is the truly ultimate fact. "The essentially impersonal can never by any logical process other than verbal hocus-pocus, which is not logical after all, be made the sufficient reason for a personal development." Only a supreme Person can produce and sustain a personal spirit such as a human being. How God effects this is admittedly unknown, but that persons are a *fact* is obvious. Furthermore, the definition of personality is also known: "The essential meaning of personality is selfhood, self-consciousness, self-control, and the power to know . . . Any being, finite or infinite, which has knowledge and self-consciousness and self-control, is personal; for the term has no other meaning." (3) "Impersonalism appears as doubly a failure. If we ask for the positive foundation of its basal conceptions, we find that there is none. They are empty forms of thought to which no reality can be shown to correspond, and upon criticism they vanish altogether. If we next ask what insight impersonalism gives into the problems of experience, we find nothing but tautology and infinite regress. Such a theory surely does not pay expenses. *The alternative is personalism or nothing.*"

4. Evaluation of Personalism

Personalism has thus far appeared to be the most satisfying of the philosophies heretofore discussed; it meets confronting problems with more adequate explanations. For the first time, personality, which was fast becoming lost to the sight of philosophy (almost since the time of Socrates and Jesus), has once again regained its birthright. Later, we shall find Existentialists and Phenomenologists giving more attention to it, but no philosophy has accorded more credence to the reality of personality than the philosophers of Personalism. None has imputed to persons a sacredness, and an infinity of intrinsic value as have Personalists.

Personalism also serves as a philosophy which can be incorporated into other philosophies, filling in embarrassing gaps which otherwise would damage the coherence of such systems. For example, Moritz Schlick, the Logical Positivist who founded the Vienna Circle, regards himself as a Personalist in philosophy of religion, limiting his Positivism to scientific inquiry.

As all philosophies have their weak points, so does Personalism; its major weakness is its failure or inability to explain the precise nature by which persons come into existence. We know they are here, but we would also like to know how they come to be. Granting this as a weakness, we must not lose sight of the fact that finite man has never been able, and probably will never be able to grasp an absolute and exhaustive understanding of the totality of reality, but must rest content with acquiring the most coherent philosophy accessible at the time, that is, the philosophy which most adequately explains the facts of experience afforded man. At the present time, Personalism appears to be one of the strongest contenders for that enviable position, if not paramount to the rest.

XXXIX

VITALISM:

The Autonomy of Life

(*Including the Philosophy of ORGANISM*)

Vitalism, a doctrine which gives priority to life over either reason or the laws of physics and chemistry, asserts that life is autonomous or self-determined; vitalistic powers are active in organisms which are independent of physico-chemical laws or forces. Vitalism is a philosophy which generated as a revolt, a revolt against reason, particularly in its Absolute Idealistic form.

Prominent characteristics common to Vitalism are: (1) reality is regarded as a life-impulse; (2) *actualism,* life, movement, or the philosophy of becoming; (3) the concept of reality as organic; (4) its emphasis on irrationalism or attack on reason; (5) its Pragmatic outlook; (6) its evolutionary perspective; (7) Ontological Idealism *i.e.,* the vitally real is viewed in spiritual terms.

Vitalism is essentially the doctrine that life and the organic universe is inexplicable in physico-chemical terms, for these sciences are restricted to laws of mechanics, but the laws of mechanical necessity do not maintain for living organisms; they do not hold true for conscious life. Physics and chemistry will never give us the *key to life,* for natural systems of life cannot be enfolded into the artificial systems of science, since *life* is not inert matter, nor can it be explained in rational terms, but in nonrational ones, such as *intuition,* life force, consciousness. "A physico-chemical explanation of the motions of the amoeba, and *a fortiori* of the behavior of the Infusoria, seems impossible to many of those who have closely observed these rudimentary organisms . . . The tendency to explain everything by physics and chemistry is discouraged rather than strengthened by deep study of histological phenomena . . . 'The study of the cell has, on the whole, seemed to widen rather than narrow the enormous gap that separates even the lowest forms of life from the inorganic world.'"[1] This being the case, a mechanistic conception of life and the world proves false, for life remains indeterminate to rational laws of mechanics, free to choose its own course of development and progress.

1. Henri Bergson — Élan Vital in Real Duration

Henri Bergson (1859-1941), the brilliant star of the philosophy of Vitalism, is regarded by some as France's greatest philosopher since the time of René Descartes; so outstanding is he that Vitalism is often identified with his name, and the school of philosophical thought is termed *Bergsonism.* France's three bright lights form a triune despite their respective divergent tendencies: (1) Descartes and Rationalism, (2) Auguste Comte (1798-1857) and Positivism, and (3) Bergson and Intuitionism. It provides an interesting comparison that Bergson, a contemporary of John Dewey, born the same year (1859), and the author of the Introduction of the French edition of William James' *Pragmatism,* disavows Pragmatism, yet holds in common with that school of thought: (a) the priority of change over permanence, (b) the importance of time, (c) the doctrine of the freedom of the will, (d) the Utilitarian or Instrumental value of concepts and percepts enabling more effective action by man. Bergson severs intellectual relations with these two men, particularly in respect to his criterion of truth, Intuitionism, and his denial of the validity of Instrumentalism, on the grounds that concepts and percepts, at times, distort experiences of reality, rather than clarify them as useful instruments.

Bergson produced four major and very influential books: his doctoral dissertation, *Time and Free Will* (1889), *Matter and Memory* (1896), his classic *Creative Evolution* (1907), and *The Two Sources of Morality and Religion* (1932) which gave the world his long awaited philosophy of religion; to these four may be added as supplementary: *Introduction to Metaphysics* (1903), *Mind-Energy* (1920), and the very minor work, a philosophy of comedy, *Laughter: An Essay on the Meaning of the Comic* (1911).

Intelligence, Instinct, and Intuition.

Bergson's masterpiece, *Creative Evolution,* provides the basis of Vitalism, explaining philosophy in terms of an *Élan Vital* (Vital Impulse,

[1] Unless otherwise indicated, quotations in this section, and the one to follow are from Henri Bergson, *Creative Evolution,* tr. Arthur Mitchell (New York: Henry Holt and Co., 1911).

Vital Impetus) *in real duration,* genuine time. The Vital Impulse, Bergson discloses to be God in action, who, like an artist, unhampered by the laws of mechanics (determinism) or teleology (uncommitted to any purpose), creates the world by a consciousness which is not only deeper than reason, but free from its restrictions. Reason is merely a tool, a handmaiden, the product of matter, in whose hands life remains inexplicable and inexorable.

The *Élan Vital* travelled two courses in the evolution of life: (1) the arthropod culminating its journey in insect life, and (2) the vertebrate, terminating in man. Each, together with plant life, possesses its corresponding vital impulsion: (a) torpor (lethargy) in plants, (b) instinct reaching its pinnacle in the life of insects, and (c) vertebrate life wherein two divergent paths appear, one leading to instinct, and another to intelligence. Both instinct and intelligence originate from a common source, and though complementary and antagonistic, do retain something of their common origin, for there is a semblance of intelligence in instinct. The origin of intelligence may be traced to the appearance of tools, weapons, etc.; although nonintelligent creatures possess tools, theirs cannot be severed from the body, are actually part of the organism, and by a corresponding instinct, they know how to use them. "*Instinct perfected is a faculty of using and even of constructing organized instruments; intelligence perfected is the faculty of making and using unorganized instruments.*" Instinct and intelligence operate as two divergent solutions to identical problems, but intelligence functions on a conscious level, while instinct behaves unconsciously; intelligence conceives of relations, form, whereas instinct perceives matter; intelligence constructs artificial or unorganized instruments, instinct organized ones; intelligence treats things mechanically, instinct organically; intelligence deals with the inert, discontinuous, immobile, mechanical, with a natural inability to comprehend life, but instinct understands life. "Instinct is sympathy. ... Intelligence and instinct are turned in opposite directions, the former towards inert matter, the latter towards life . . . It is to the very inwardness of life that *intuition* leads us — by intuition I mean instinct that has become disinterested, self-conscious, capable of reflecting upon its object, and of enlarging it indefinitely." At times, intuition may grasp an insight when intelligence fails us.

Intuition gives insights beyond the reach of intelligence; by intuition the categories of life are appreciated, not as the age-old problem of one and the many, neither as mechanical causality nor teleological finality, but by a vital process which falls into neither mold.

The Élan Vital in Real Duration.

The fundamental thesis of Bergsonian philosophy is the doctrine of a Vital Impulse (*Élan Vital*), a principle operating in real duration, real time. All existence is in time, in process; and in man, continuity is gained through memory tying the past with the present. "The truth is that we change without ceasing, and that the state itself is nothing but change . . . For an ego which does not change does not endure . . . Duration is the continuous progress of the past which gnaws into the future and which swells as it advances . . . For a conscious being, to exist is to change, to change is to mature, to mature is to go on creating oneself endlessly . . . . The universe *endures* . . . Duration means invention, the creation of forms, the continual elaboration of the absolutely new . . . Like the universe as a whole, like each conscious being taken separately, the organism which lives is a thing that endures . . . *Wherever anything lives, there is, open somewhere, a register in which time is being inscribed.*" Time is irreversible; all reality is in process, all is in *real* time. Life, as is true of all conscious activity, is unceasing creation, invention.

The doctrine of the Vital Impulse repudiates all mechanistic explanations, those which regard the world as a machine; and all finalistic explanations, those which predicate the creation of the world based on a 'preconceived plan with a view to a certain end,' the world being merely an imitation of a model, the realization of an idea. "We must get beyond both points of view, both mechanism and finalism . . . An artist of genius has painted a figure on his canvas. We can imitate his picture with many-colored squares of mosaic. And we shall reproduce the curves and shades of the model so much the better as our squares are smaller, more numerous and more varied in tone. But an infinity of elements infinitely small, presenting an infinity of shades, would be necessary to obtain the exact equivalent of the figure that the artist has conceived as a simple thing, which he has wished to transport as a whole to the canvas, and which is the more complete the more it strikes us as the projection of an indivisible intuition. Now, suppose our eyes so made that they cannot help seeing the work of the master of a mosaic effect. Or suppose our intellect so made that it cannot explain the appearance of the figure on the canvas except as a work of mosaic. We should then be able to speak simply of a collection of little squares, and we should be under the mechanistic hypothesis. We might add that, beside the materiality of the collection, there must be a plan on which the artist worked; and then we should be expressing ourselves as finalists. But in neither case should we have got at the real process, for there are no squares brought together."

God, through the Élan Vital in *real duration*, creates, develops, an ongoing organismic world which is in the process of yet being made; this God does, not with mechanical necessity, laws of science which limit his activity, nor with a preconceived purpose which is almost as equally confining, but this he accomplishes as an artist, creating each step of the way without restrictions of any kind. God has no blueprint for the world and its future; he is an author or poet who autonomously proceeds in the evolutionary creation of the world.

Free Will and Consciousness.

A dominant characteristic of life is consciousness; it is consciousness that directs the course of life on its evolutionary progress upwards, as it did in the case of acquiring intelligence for man. Not all consciousness is alike, since it differs according to the evolutionary level of progress or development; a comcomitant relationship exists between an organism's consciousness and its power of choice, "for consciousness corresponds exactly to the living being's power of choice . . . consciousness is synonymous with invention and with freedom." Invention in the animal is merely a variation of a routine, but in man, consciousness becomes more than invention, it becomes freedom. The entire history of life has been a ceaseless effort of consciousness to raise matter to triumph over mechanism, the determinism of nature to freedom.

Man, a machine, an automatism, has achieved a level of superiority in which he has acquired for the sake of consciousness, an immaterial body, namely language, a factor he owes to another level of superiority, social life. Man has become the pinnacle of evolutionary progress; paramount over all other species. "While at the end of the vast spring-board from which life has taken its leap, all the others have stepped down, finding the cord stretched too high, man alone has cleared the obstacle. It is in this quite special sense that man is the 'term' and the 'end' of evolution. Life, we have said, transcends finality as it transcends the other categories. It is essentially a current sent through matter, drawing from it what it can." Organic life has striven upwards, but it is only in human form that it has reached the level of freedom; consciousness has stagnated everywhere but in man, the only being who registers free will.

In man the vital movement continues to progress indefinitely. Consciousness which wrought man, did it at the cost of abandoning a part of itself, the nonhuman kingdom. "Consciousness, in man is pre-eminently intellect. It might have also been, it ought, so it seems, to have been also intuition. Intuition and intellect represent two opposite directions of the work of consciousness: intuition goes in the very direction of life, intellect goes in the inverse direction, and thus finds itself naturally in accordance with the movement of matter." Another direction of evolution, a different type of evolution, could have directed humanity either to still more intellect or perhaps more intuition, an intuition greater than intellect. The probability is that consciousness, in its attempt to conquer matter and self, exhausted its consciousness, its energy, its power, on intellect; consequently, intuition is an almost extinguished lamp following an evolutionary path which diverges from that of the intellect.

Notwithstanding the fact that consciousness undergoes the vicissitudes of its organism, the organism which it animates, it is nevertheless distinct from it; the destiny of consciousness is not, does not fall with, that of cerebral matter despite the interdependency of brain and consciousness. "Consciousness is essentially free; it is freedom itself; but it cannot pass through matter without settling on it, without adapting itself to it; this adaptation is what we call intellectuality." Bergson believes that there exists the possibility that consciousness will lead the evolutionary progress ahead so successfully that it will remove even the obstacle of *death* itself. "The animal takes its stand on the plant, man bestrides animality, and the whole of humanity, in space and in time, is one immense army galloping beside and before and behind each of us in an overwhelming charge able to beat down every resistance and clear the most formidable obstacles, perhaps even death." This feat can be accomplished by all living beings holding together in one concerted effort, yielding to the same tremendous push of consciousness, piercing right through matter.

The Dualism of Mind and Matter.

In his treatise, *Matter and Memory,* Bergson admits to dualism, affirming both the reality of spirit together with the reality of matter; the relationship of one to the other is determined through memory. Mind and matter, as real, are predicated on the basis of common sense, but this does not imply that Bergson is an Idealist or a Realist, for he believes that each of these positions is excessive. Matter is more than the perception which we have of it, more than mere representation, but on the other hand, it is not the 'thing' the Realists claim it to be; rather, "matter, in our view, is an aggregate of 'images.' And by 'image' we mean a certain existence which is more that that which the idealist calls *representation,* but less than that which the realists calls a *thing* – an existence placed half-way between the 'thing' and the 'representation.' This conception of matter is simply that of common sense." [1] Common sense tells

[1] Quotations in this section, "The Dualism of Mind and Matter," are from Henri Bergson, *Matter and Memory* tr. Nancy Margaret Paul and W. Scott Palmer (New York: The Macmillan Co., 1911).

us that an object exists in itself; moreover, it informs us that the object perceived by us is pictorial, it is an image which we gain of it, a *self-existing image.*

The mind-body problem has not heretofore been satisfactorily answered; the body is not an instrument of the soul nor is the soul a mere *epiphenomenon* of the body; *psychophysical parallelism* likewise is rejected. These latter two doctrines regard thought as the function of the brain merely, consciousness as the brain's epiphenomenon, void of any reality of its own — as if fancying that we could "penetrate into the inside of a brain at work and behold the dance of the atoms which make up the cortex.' Psychophysical parallelism assumes fundamentally the same conclusion, viz., if "we possessed the key to psycho-physiology, we should know every detail of what is going on in the corresponding consciousness." Although these two views are most commonly held by philosophers, they are to be seriously questioned, for they are factually unwarranted. "That there is close connexion between a state of consciousness and the brain we do not dispute. But there is also a close connexion between a coat and the nail on which it hangs, for, if the nail is pulled out, the coat falls to the ground. Shall we say, then, that the shape of the nail gives us the shape of the coat, or in any way corresponds to it? No more are we entitled to conclude, because the physical fact is hung on to a cerebral state, that there is any parallelism between the two series psychical and physiological." Connection of mind and body is a fact, but epiphenomenalism and psychophysical parallelism are only hypothetical theories, not proof.

Mind and matter are related to one another by memory which is "the intersection of mind and matter." Memory is not to be regarded as a function of the brain, it differs in kind, not merely in degree. Memory is "spirit in its most tangible form," the domain of spirit; moreover, the psychical state, the mental state, is immensely wider than the cerebral, the brain state. A person "endowed with a superhuman intellect, did he possess the key to psycho-physiology, he would know no more of what is going on in the corresponding consciousness than we should know of a play from the comings and goings of the actors upon the stage." The cerebral state does not hold a constant relation to the mental; there are differing tones or levels of mental life, planes of consciousness, that is, psychic life has different degrees of attention, varying heights of existence.

These ideas give us a basis of explaining personality disorders in terms of a breaking of the tie which holds the psychic to its concomitant motor existence, hence weakening one's attention to life without. Memory images of words and aphasia cannot be localized; the phenomenon of neurosis has proved that loss of memory is of psychic origin and nature.

The conclusion to which we are entitled is that matter and spirit, both independently real, interact; their point of determination is memory, the domain of pure spirit whose psychic life is constituted in ascending levels. "Spirit borrows from matter the perceptions on which it feeds, and restores them to matter in the form of movements which it has stamped with its own freedom." Matter and life are coexistent and interdependent; mind is consciousness, and the essence of consciousness is memory.

Philosophy of Religion and Ethics.

Bergson postulates two differing types of ethics: (1) a *closed morality*, one in which behavior is instinctively and automatically performed as a result of adhering to society s conventions, demands, etc., and (2) an ***open morality***, a free, progressive, autonomous, inner motivated morality indicative of saints, heroes, etc. These two differ not merely in degree, but in kind.

The dualism found in both the fields of ethics and religion is typical of the dualism which permeates all phases of Bergson's philosophy, reaching its ultimate dualism in life and matter. Life, dynamic, girded with force and will, understood by intuition, struggles upward through and beyond matter, striving for immortal life; while matter, congealed residue of creation, subject to nature's laws and intelligence, is gradually eroding. Ethics and religion, too, are dual; a morality may be *closed* or *open*, a religion may be *static* or *dynamic*.

Closed morality is a coerced one whose obligatory impetus comes from the pressure of society, duties performed on the level of mere habit, practice, a clear cut and precise formula to be followed, one prescribed by society. A closed morality is an impersonal one comparable to the natural forces of habit and instinct, motivated by self-preservation. *Open morality* springs from the depths of the heart, expresses a certain emotional warmth, full of enthusiasm, one which makes for advancement and progress, embraces humanity and love of neighbor, is heroic. "Now heroism cannot be preached, it has only to show itself, and its mere presence may stir others to action. For heroism itself is a return to movement, and emanates from an emotion — infectious like all emotions — akin to the creative act. Religion expresses this truth in its own way by saying that it is in God that we love all other men. And all great mystics declare that they have the impression of a current passing from their soul to God, and flowing back again from God to mankind."[1] Closed morality is a purely static one functioning on an infra-intellectual level of habit and instinct, beneath the level of intelligence; whereas open morality is purely dynamic, a supra-intellectual one, above the level of intelligence, motivated by inspiration, intuition, emotion, etc. Somewhere between the two, intelligence is to be found.

Static Religion, the result of intelligence's 'myth-making function' *(fonction fabulatrice), "is a defensive reaction of nature against what might be depressing for the individual, and dissolvent for society, in the exercise of intelligence."* Man, terrified as the only being aware of his impending death, is driven to the creation of myths. "Man is the only animal whose actions are uncertain, who hesitates, gropes about and lays plans in the hope of success and the fear of failure. He is alone in realizing that he is subject to illness, alone in knowing that he must die. The rest of nature goes on its expanding course in absolute tranquility." Animals and plants, unlike man, "rely on the passing hour as they would on eternity. We drink in something of this unshakable confidence during a country walk, from which we return quieted and soothed." Man pays a heavy price for his intelligence: myth-making, selfish preoccupations, instead of attending to the common good, etc.

Dynamic Religion, the mysticism of St. Paul, St. Francis, St. Teresa, etc., is prompted by the *Élan Vital,* whereby the human will is identified with that of the divine. The soul listens to a voice calling, feels an indefinable presence, "then comes a boundless joy, an all-absorbing ecstasy or an enthralling rapture: God is there, and the soul is in God. Mystery is no more. Problems vanish, darkness is dispelled; everything is flooded with light . . . Joy is boundless . . . *Now* it is God who is acting through the soul, in the soul; the union is total, therefore final . . . Let us say that henceforth for the soul there is a superabundance of life. There is a boundless impetus. There is an irresistible impulse which hurls it into vast enterprises." The mystic has nothing which distinguishes him outwardly, but within is a superabundance of vitality, an elevation which is free from pride; moreover, instead of pride there is humility, for he has been 'alone with The Alone,' a soul absorbed in God; and now he must attend to his apostolate, express the inexpressible "truth flowing into his soul from its fountainhead like an active force," for he cannot contain himself, but must spread abroad like the sun diffusing its light, "for the love which consumes him is no longer simply the love of man for

[1] Quotations in this section entitled: "Philosophy of Religion and Ethics" are from Henry Bergson, *The Two Sources of Morality and Religion* (New York: Henry Holt and Co., Inc., 1935).

God, it is the love of God for all men. Through God, in the strength of God, he loves all mankind with a divine love." The mystic embraces all humanity with an indivisible undissimulated love.

The mystic's love of humanity is not a natural love, such as love for family or fatherland, nor is it an extension of an instinct, nor something originating in a philosopher's idea. It does not proceed from the senses, nor from the mind, but implicitly from both and more. "For such a love lies at the very root of feeling and reason, as of all other things. Coinciding with God's love for His handiwork, a love which has been the source of everything, it would yield up, to anyone who knew how to question it, the secret of creation. What it wants to do, with God's help, is to complete the creation of the human species and make of humanity what it would have straightaway become, had it been able to assume its final shape without the assistance of man himself. Or, to use words which mean . . . the same thing in different terms: its direction is exactly that of the vital impetus: it *is* this impetus itself, communicated in its entirety to exceptional men who in their turn would fain impart it to all humanity and by a living contradiction change into creative effort that created thing which is species, and turn into movement what was, by definition, a stop." The mystic, imbued with the vital impetus, is charged with transforming humanity by infusing part of self to others.

In *The Two Sources of Morality and Religion,* Bergson goes beyond the conclusions reached in his *Creative Evolution* by viewing the nature of God as *love;* "divine love is not a thing of God: it is God Himself;" and by this creative love, creative emotion, the world was able to come into being, for the world is a manifestation of God's love. Mysticism suggests, for the philosopher's edification, "a universe which is the mere visible and tangible aspect of love and of the need of loving, together with all the consequences entailed by this creative emotion: I mean the appearance of living creatures in which this emotion finds its complement; of an infinity of other beings without which they could not have appeared, and lastly of the unfathomable depths of material substance without which life would not have been possible.' The mystics have triumphed over materiality by resisting matter, reaching God, and blazing a trail for the remainder of mankind to follow.

The mystic's intuition can give us joy, a joy found in simplicity of life, and a vision of the life beyond, but this must be accomplished by a thoroughgoing spiritual reform, one which copes with obstacles that we set up 'against our civilization.' "But whether we go bail for small measures or great, a decision is imperative. Mankind lies groaning, half crushed beneath the weight of its own progress. Men do not sufficiently realize that their future is in their own hands. Theirs is the task of determining first of all whether they want to go on living or not. Theirs is the responsibility, then, for deciding if they want merely to live, or intend to make just the extra effort required for fulfilling, even on their refractory planet, the essential function of the universe, which is *a machine for the making of gods.*" Thus from the mystic we learn the existence of God, survival beyond death, and becoming gods, for God made the world of such a nature that it can make of us gods, too.

Synopsis of Bergson's Vitalism.

Bergson, a Vitalist, who considers the primacy of life to take precedence over physico-chemical laws, postulates as the basis of his philosophy, *creative evolution.* Creative evolution is a temporal, indeterminable, developmental process travelled by the *Élan Vital,* a vital impulse, God operative in the world. The structure of the *Élan Vital* is nonindividual, yet common to every member of the species. In plants, it is unconscious; it is free, possessing a will of its own, thus makes its own decisions. The *Élan Vital* in the process of time developed two kinds of consciousness: (a) *instinct,* and (b) *intelligence;* instinct may be regarded as a form of immediate intuition or sympathy, while intelligence makes action possible. Reason, unable to penetrate duration, is static, hence man reasons spatially, that is, he merely classifies when reasoning, as is indicative of syllogistic reasoning; *e.g.,* *A* is (in the class) *B,* and *B* is (in the class) *C,* therefore *A* is (in the class) *C.* Euler's diagrammatic logic illustrates this point:

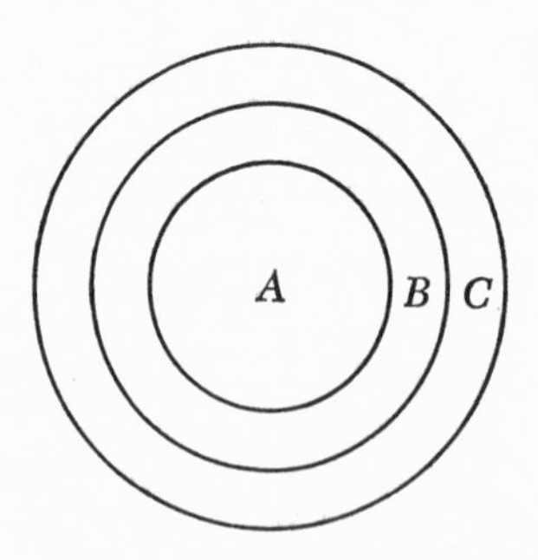

Man's inner life is not subject to causal laws, his nature is free, yet reason is incapable of understanding this fact, for its capacity is limited to thinking in terms of cause and effect; however, we possess free will and are intuitively aware of the fact that we do. Not only is the evolutionary world free to choose its own course, man also is free to design his own future by his personal actions and choices.

Mechanism and Materialism are both objectionable; life, an opposite current to both, builds organism out of matter. Teleology, too, is repudiated, for finalism is merely mechanism, or determinism, in reverse. The real world, an organismic world, indeterminate either in the light of its past or in the light of its future, is free to build as it chooses by the *Élan Vital,* while matter, subject to entropy, is degenerating.

The world, a 'machine for making gods,' has by the *Élan Vital* led mankind in progress, mentally and spiritually, upward in its conquering of obstacles, to the point where it may one day overcome even death itself.

XL

PANPSYCHISM AND ORGANISM:

The Philosophy of Alfred North Whitehead

It is difficult to label Alfred North Whitehead (1861-1947) by neatly pigeonholing him into a category, for there are many definite strains of a wide variety of schools of thought in his philosophy of *Organism,* as he chooses to designate his philosophical thought. He is considered an English Neorealist, a Platonist, an Aristotelian, a Panpsychist, and shares important ideas in common with Leibniz, Spinoza, and Kant. It would be unfair to regard his system as an eclectic one, merely a compilation of numerous other philosophies, because his is highly original, and in certain respects, unique. Basically, his philosophy is not difficult to understand, but the novel nomenclature he employs will definitely give the novice the feeling that it is; however, Whitehead, as is true of other philosophers, felt constrained to develop a terminology which would not be confused with other philosophies, and to guard against his words being given a meaning which he did not want to convey.

Terminology.

Whitehead's ideas are found principally in his: *Science and the Modern World* (The Lowell Lectures, 1925), *Adventures of Ideas* (1933), and his classic *Process and Reality* (The Gifford Lectures, delivered at the University of Edinburgh in the 1927-1928 season, and published in 1929). Perhaps, a helpful beginning would be to supply the reader with a brief glossary of terms:

PROCESS. Time is the form of process, and process is the form of time. Permanence does not exist. The *principle of process* is the understanding of *Being* as it is constituted by *Becoming.*

REALITY. Realism. Platonism. Panpsychism. Metaphysical Pluralism. The world is made up of many *actual entities,* or what is the same, *actual occasions.* "Reality is just itself, and it is nonsense to ask whether it be true or false."[1]

TRUTH. "Truth is a qualification which applies to Appearance alone . . . Truth is conformation of Appearance to Reality."[2] "The truth itself is nothing else than how the composite natures of the organic actualities of the world obtain adequate representation in the divine nature."[3]

ACTUAL OCCASIONS. Actual entities. "The final things of which the world is made up. There is no going behind actual entities to find anything more real. They differ among themselves: God is an actual entity, and so is the most trivial puff of existence in far-off empty space." These vary in gradation, importance, and function, but are on the same level of actuality. "The final facts are, all alike, actual entities; and these actual entities are drops of experience, complex and interdependent." Like Leibniz' *Monads,* each occasion has nothing to do with any other. *Actual Entity* is Whitehead's term for substance. See *event* (Whitehead's earlier term for *occasion*).

ACTUALITY. "The ultimate entry into the concrete."

PREHENSION. The relation of many entities into a single unity; the awareness of other actual occasions; such constitutes organic pluralism. Prehensions are the *concrete facts of relatedness,* one of the Whiteheadian categories of existence.

RELATION. Synonymous with *Prehension.* Each actual occasion is related to the rest of the universe by feeling, a telepathic rapport.

RELATIONAL ESSENCE. "An eternal object, considered as an abstract entity, cannot be divorced from its reference to actuality generally; though it is disconnected from its actual modes of ingression into definite actual occasions."[4]

INGRESSION. The mode by which an eternal object's potentiality is realized.

FEELING. Consciousness, devoid of reasoning; any immediate psychological experience, provided reasoning is absent.

EXPERIENCE. Equivalent to feeling.

NEXUS (plural *NEXUS*). One of the categories of experience, a 'Public Matter of Fact.' A society of occasions. Any "fact of togetherness

[1] Alfred North Whitehead, *Adventures of Ideas* (New York: The Macmillan Co., 1933).

[2] *Ibid.*

[3] Except where otherwise noted, quotations in this chapter on Whitehead's philosophy are from his *Process and Reality* (New York: The Macmillan Co., 1929).

[4] Alfred North Whitehead, *Science and the Modern World* (New York: The Macmillan Co., 1925).

among actual entities is called a 'nexus' . . . The ultimate facts of immediate actual experiences are actual entities, prehensions, and nexūs."

PERSONALITY. A person consists of perishing actual occasions; he is related to others in a society, and governed by subjective aims. There is no permanent unchanging substance.

PURPOSE. Subjective aims (values).

IMPORTANCE. Definition of value. Value is that which is purposed; coordinated with, and a contribution to, the whole.

HISTORY. Complex society of societies.

EPOCH. A time span. "A duration, as the field of the realised in the actualisation of one of its contained events, is an epoch, *i.e.*, an arrest." [1]

EVENT. "The grasping into unity of a pattern of aspects . . . Event is the life history of the pattern." An event is an actual occasion. "Duration is the whole of nature simultaneous with the event." [2] See occasion.

GOD. The Supreme Being; a single entity, yet possesses a dipolar nature: (a) *Primordial* — eternal, conceptual, infinite, free, complete, actually deficient, and unconscious. (b) *Consequent* — actual, feeling, consequential, conscious, determined, incomplete, everlasting, goodness.

TIME. Real duration, with neither beginning nor end.

PRIMORDIAL OBJECTS. Eternal, ingredient, and potentials (when they enter particular objects).

CREATIVITY. The principle of novelty. "An actual occasion is a novel entity diverse from any entity in the 'many' which it unifies. Thus 'creativity' introduces novelty into the content of the many."

UNIVERSALS. God's primordial nature; eternal objects.

FALLACY OF MISPLACED CONCRETENESS. "The accidental error of mistaking the abstract for the concrete." [3]

ONTOLOGICAL PRINCIPLE. "Every condition to which the process of becoming conforms in any particular instance, has its reason *either* in the character of some actual entity in the actual world of that concrescence, *or* in the character of the subject which is in process of concrescence. This category of explanation is termed the 'ontological principle.' It would also be termed the 'principle of efficient, and final, causation' . . . This ontological principle means that actual entities are the only *reasons;* so that the search for a *reason* is to search for one or more actual entities."

[1] *Ibid.*
[2] *Ibid.*
[3] *Ibid.*

"The ontological principle can be summarized as: no actual entity, then no reason."

CONCRESCENCE. "The name for the process in which the universe of many things acquires an individual unity in a determinate relegation of each item of the 'many' to its subordination in the constitution of the novel 'one.'" It is the process of an entity becoming an actuality.

PHILOSOPHY. "Speculative Philosophy is the endeavour to frame a coherent, logical, necessary system of general ideas in terms of which every element of our experience can be interpreted."

"Philosophy is the self-correction by consciousness of its own initial excess of subjectivity." The function of philosophy is the 'systematization of civilized thought.'

METAPHYSICS. "The description of the generalities which apply to all the details of practice."

RELIGION. "The translation of general ideas into particular thoughts, particular emotions, and particular purposes; it is directed to the end of stretching individual interest beyond its self-defeating particularity . . . Religion is an ultimate craving to infuse that non-temporal generality which primarily belongs to conceptual thought alone."

The Philosophy of Organism.

The philosophy of Organism is that of an integrated system coherently ordered in which *actual entities,* or *actual occasions,* compose the actual world; the entire universe is a process, the process of becoming actual entities. These creatures, (actual entities), come into existence by an ontologically ultimate, called *creativity;* "in the philosophy of organism this ultimate is termed 'creativity'; and God is its primordial, nontemporal accident." Actual entities, composed of Cartesian substance, are in process of becoming, being, perishing, as well as in a state of relatedness. "This is the doctrine that the creative advance of the world is the becoming, the perishing, and the objective immortalities of those things which jointly constitute *stubborn fact.*" Unlike earlier philosophies, this one postulates the *relatedness* (prehension) of actualities as the more dominant category, ascendant over quality; actual entities differ more markedly in their *relatedness,* than in quality.

In the philosophy of Organism, there are four types of categories: (1) *The Category of the Ultimate,* (2)*Categories of Existence,* (3) *Categories of Explanation,* and (4) *Categoreal Obligations.*

The Category of the Ultimate consists of (1) *Creativity,* (2) *Many,* and (3) *One;* these three are ultimate notions responsible for *thing, be-*

ing, entity (synonymous concepts). Creativity, the universal of universal, is the principle of *novelty,* which with the *many* and the *one* make a variegated universe into one organism. The course by which this is effected is *togetherness,* an ultimate notion embodied in *concrescence,* whereby various entities are 'together' in one actual occasion.

The Categories of Existence are: (1) *Actual Entities* or *Actual Occasions* (Final Realities, *Rés Verae*); *Prehensions,* (Concrete Facts of Relatedness); (3) *Nexūs* (Public Matters of Fact); (4) *Subjective Forms* (Private Matters of Fact); (5) *Eternal Objects* (Pure Potentials for the Determination of Fact or Forms of Definiteness); (6) *Propositions* (Matters of Fact in Potential Determination, Impure Potentials for the Specific Determination of Matters of Fact, Theories); (7) *Multiplicities* (Pure Disjunctions of Diverse Entities); (8) *Contrasts* (Modes of Synthesis of Entities in one Prehension). The Categories of Explanation total twenty-seven, and there are nine *Categoreal Obligations.*

Actual Entities.

In the philosophy of Organism, the world is made up of *actual entities* (actual occasions); God, too, is an actual entity. These are final facts, behind or beyond them nothing exists; they may be viewed as 'drops of experience.' The relationship of occasion to prehension is synonymous while power, the notion of which Locke spoke in reference to laws of causation, is a principle. The reason, explanation for things, is to be found in their actual entities; without actual entity, reason fails.

Prehensions.

The concrete facts of relatedness, termed prehensions, consist of three factors: (a) the prehending subject, the actual entity wherein prehension is a concrete element; (b) the prehended datum; and (c) the 'subjective form,' the manner in which the subject prehends the datum. "An occasion is a subject in respect to its special activity concerning an object; and anything is an object in respect to its provocation of some special activity within a subject. Such a mode of activity is termed a 'prehension.' Thus a prehension involves three factors. There is the occasion of experience within which the prehension is a detail of activity; there is the datum whose relevance provokes the origination of this prehension; this datum is the prehended object; there is the subjective form, which is the affective tone determining the effectiveness of that prehension in that occasion of experience." [1] The relationship of occasion to prehension is synonymous with that of 'recipient' to 'provoker,' or subject to object.

[1] *Adventures of Ideas, op. cit.*

Nexus.

Because actual entities prehend each other, constituting a genuine togetherness of real, individual, particular facts (actual entities), there is said to be *togetherness,* not merely an illusory relationship, but a real, individual, fact of togetherness. Prehension is as real a fact as is an actual entity; it is real, individual, and particular, comparable to the case of actual entities; for Whitehead, relations are *real,* more dominant than are qualities of which other philosophers speak. *Nexūs* are particular facts of togetherness which maintain among actual entities, public matters of fact, a society of occasions. "The ultimate facts of immediate actual experience are actual entities, prehensions, and nexūs. All else is, for our experience, derivative abstraction." These three constitute the concrete facts of experience, and provide the basis for explaining all abstract entities; moreover, should a person reverse the order of explanation by accidentally or erroneously assuming the abstract to be the concrete, he is guilty of the *fallacy of misplaced concreteness.*

Concrete particular facts cannot be constructed out of universal abstractions; otherwise: "How can concrete fact exhibit entities abstract from itself and yet participated in by its own nature? . . . Philosophy is explanatory of abstraction, and not of concreteness. It is by reason of their instinctive grasp of this ultimate truth that, in spite of much association with arbitrary fancifulness and atavistic mysticism, types of Platonic philosophy retain their abiding appeal; they seek the forms in the facts. Each fact is more than its forms, and each form 'participates' throughout the world of facts. The definiteness of fact is due to its forms; but the individual fact is a creature, and creativity is the ultimate behind all forms, inexplicable by forms, and conditioned by its creatures." *Creativity* is an ontologically ultimate, beyond which there is no reality.

Creativity.

Creativity, the Category of the Ultimate, is the most fundamental nature of reality, God's most basic Being. It constitutes the 'principle of *novelty,*' the principle whereby new entities enter the world. Actual entities are produced by the 'principle of novelty,' *Creativity.* Since actual entities are in process, the process of becoming, and, as an event, perishing, Creativity must constantly produce them. Creativity, as a principle of novelty, produces actual entities as individuals, distinct from each other. Although each belongs to the organic whole, as would be expected from a philosophy of Organism, yet each is distinct; the Category of the Ultimate also provides for this, since the 'one' and the 'many' are two other notions in the Category of the Ultimate.

There are, however, no novel eternal objects, that is to say, eternal objects are neither in process nor are they created, but are co-eternal with the primordial nature of God. A fuller treatment of the *primordial* will be offered in the section treating Whitehead's concept of God.

Creativity is a 'factor of activity', the originator of occasions, the initial phase of every new occasion. "It can thus be termed a 'real potentiality.' The 'potentiality' refers to the passive capacity, the term 'real' refers to the creative activity . . . This basic situation, this actual world, this primary phase, this real potentiality — however you characterize it — as a whole is active with its inherent creativity, but in its details it provides the passive objects which derive their activity from the creativity of the whole. The creativity is the actualization of potentiality, and the process of actualization is an occasion of experiencing. Thus viewed in abstraction objects are passive, but viewed in conjunction they carry the creativity which drives the world. The process of creation is the form of unity of the Universe." [1] The universe conjunctively is one actual occasion, however, the principle by which the disjunctive universe became one is by creativity. The Category of the Ultimate, namely Creativity, supplants Aristotle's category of 'primary substance.'

Process, Concrescence, and Organism.

The philosophy of Organism is predicated on the 'organic theory of nature,' a doctrine which regards nature, and its understanding, not as isolated entities, but as a whole in process. "The notion of 'organism' is combined with that of 'process' in a twofold manner. The community of actual things is an organism; but it is not a static organism. It is an incompletion in process of production. Thus the expansion of the universe in respect to actual things is the first meaning of 'process'; and the universe in any stage of its expansion is the first meaning of 'organism.' In this sense, an organism is a nexus . . . Each actual entity bears in its constitution the 'reasons' why its conditions are what they are." The previous sentence is reminiscent of Leibniz' principle of sufficient reason.

Occasions, no two of which have identical actual worlds, are constantly in transitional states, states of becoming, and consequently, states of 'perpetual perishing,' owing to their nature of flux or fluency, (their temporal constitution). Occasions, being in a state of perpetual process, are constantly in states of *transition,* by which they strive to achieve their subjective aim, final cause. "Concrescence moves towards its final cause, which is its subjective aim; transition is the vehicle of the efficient cause, which is the immortal past . . . 'Concrescence' is the name for the proc-

[1] *Adventures of Ideas, op. cit.*

ess in which the universe of many things acquires an individual unity in a determinate relegation of each item of the 'many' to its subordination in the constitution of the novel 'one.'" Each entity, thing, strives to be, or is one of the *many;* each seeks to find a niche for itself in each instance of concrescence. There are not found both novel things and concrescence; novelty is the process of concrescence. "'Actuality' means nothing else than this ultimate entry into the concrete . . . An instance of concrescence is termed an 'actual entity' — or, equivalently, an 'actual occasion.' . . . An actual occasion is a concrescence effected by a process of feelings . . . An actual occasion is nothing but the unity to be ascribed to a particular instance of concrescence. This concrescence is thus nothing else than the 'real internal constitution' of the actual occasion in question." Actual occasions are substantially unanalyzable, for on analysis they will be found to be operations, and the term used to designate the generic description of such operations, is *feeling.*

Philosophy of Religion.

God possesses two definite and dipolar characteristics: (a) *primordial* and (b) *consequent.* "Viewed as primordial, he is the unlimited conceptual realization of the absolute wealth of potentiality. In this aspect, he is not *before* all creation, but *with* all creation." This aspect of God's nature is 'deficiently actual,' that is, he lacks actuality; this phase of his nature is purely conceptual, therefore devoid of consciousness. God's *primordial* nature is an abstraction; this "side of God's nature is constituted by his conceptual experience. This experience is the primordial fact in the world, limited by no actuality which it presupposes. It is therefore infinite, devoid of all negative prehensions. This side of his nature is free, complete, primordial, eternal, actually deficient, and unconscious." The primordial nature of God belongs to the realm of concepts, universals, eternal objects, that portion of him which is responsible for the principle of concretion.

While the primordial nature of God is conceptual, he does possess another, a *consequent,* which represents the activity of God in the world which is "the weaving of God's physical feelings upon his primordial concepts." This side of God's nature "originates with physical experience derived from the temporal world, and then acquires integration with the primordial side. It is determined, incomplete, consequent, 'everlasting,' fully actual, and conscious." The *goodness* of God is attributable to his consequent nature, God's concern that nothing be lost. God's consequent nature is his objectification in the world, sharing with each new creation 'its actual world;' concrescent creatures are objectified in God.

The doctrine of *valuations*, however, is found in the primordial nature of God; they consist of conceptual feelings, composing his primordial nature, and herein is to be found God's *subjective aim*, 'subjective forms of valuation,' that is to say, the purposes of God. God is each person's subjective aim, value, purpose; he is the eternal 'urge of desire,' 'object of desire,' etc. God's subjective aim, stemming from his primordial nature, eventuates in his consequent nature, in unaffected transition. "The wisdom of subjective aim prehends every actuality for what it can be in such a perfected system — its sufferings, its sorrows, its failures, its triumphs, its immediacies of joy — woven by rightness of feeling into the harmony of the universal feeling, which is always immediate, always many, always one, always with novel advance, moving onward and never perishing . . . The image under which this operative growth of God's nature is best conceived, is that of a tender care that nothing be lost." More than a creator of the world, God is the savior of the world. "He saves the world as it passes into the immediacy of his own life. It is the judgment of a tenderness which loses nothing that can be saved . . . He does not create the world, he saves it: or, more accurately, he is the poet of the world, with tender patience leading it by his vision of truth, beauty, and goodness." Another image of God's consequent nature is his infinite patience by which he tenderly saves; in the turmoil of this intermediate world, he is completing his own nature. Coordinating the world, and limited by his own consequent nature, God strives in the process of becoming and through prehension, to enrich both himself and the world.

God is both transcendent and immanent in the world, its principle of harmony, order, and value, its very guarantor of value, and as such, wages a fight against evil, an evil which is not of his own doing or will, and which he has not been able to eradicate, yet is continuously battling, and will eventually become its victor. God and man, man who suffers, as allies fight together to overcome the world's evils. "God is the great companion — the fellow-sufferer who understands."

Evaluation of the Philosophy of Bergson and Whitehead

Unquestionably, we have in Bergson and Whitehead, two men whose philosophies have made, and will continue to make, lasting impressions on the philosophical world. Bergson has already many followers; the name *Bergsonism* now stands for a school of philosophical thought with many adherents, particularly in Europe, and especially in France. His philosophy, a *life-philosophy,* has been linked with several schools of thought, such as, Personalism, Voluntarism, Spiritualism, etc., as a supporting philosophy.

Both of these men have departed from traditional thought, and have offered original philosophies; both are alike in presenting evolutionary philosophies, philosophies of Organism. Differences are noticeable in the criteria of each: Bergson is strongly Intuitionistic, and exhibits a repugnance for Rationalism, while Whitehead prefers Leibniz' principle of sufficient reason, rather than sharing Bergson's philosophy of Irrationalism.

Bergson's disdain for, or at least revolt against, reason is plainly visible in his arguments, (in the sense that they lack rational cogency, but are rich and attractive in emotive appeal). He vehemently attacked what William James termed 'the beast, Intellectualism.' His logic in support of his various contentions is often the argument by analogy, which, for a number of logicians, carries no more value than an illustration, but how effectively Bergson employs it! To mention one, the reader will recall the analogy of the nail coat hanger to prove that mind and body are separate substances; although the coat depends on the nail hanger for support, the destruction of the nail does not involve that of the coat. How vividly this illustration stands out in the mind, and how convincingly his point is made, yet from the standpoint of some logicians, it is supposedly deficient in logical strength.

It is interesting to note, in this and other respects, that a person can never reject *reason* and survive intellectually. Bergson, the anti-Rationalist, too, must pay it homage, for in support of his philosophy he must use all the persuasiveness reason can rally to bear upon the validity of his philosophical position. Even his intuitionism requires the support of reason; reason ultimately must be recognized as the explanation of all things including itself.

Bergson's metaphysical Dualism and Metaphysical Realism come surprisingly close to Thomism. Many leading Roman Catholic thinkers were influenced by Bergson: Jacques Maritain, a foremost Neo-Thomist; Claude Debussy, the brilliant French composer of music; George Bernard Shaw, literary genius; Marcel Proust, and others. So popular was he in his day that books, such as *Bergson for Beginners,* as well as technical treatises on his philosophy made their appearance. So beautifully did he write that the Nobel Prize for literature was bestowed upon him in 1928.

Bergson's mysticism appears a little extreme, more emotive than logical; he has sided with the mystic, rather than the scientist. His optimism respecting the capability of conscious life to overcome even death itself seems too roseate to share. His emphasis on *real duration* is overplayed, even to the extent of saying, *Je dure donc je suis* (I endure therefore I am) to paradigm his fellow countryman, Descartes.

The most serious objection to Evolutionary philosophies, and one of which Max Scheler, the Phenomenologist, takes note, is the *error of assuming that lower forms of species are capable of explaining higher forms* merely by simple comparison, hence committing a genetic fallacy. If higher forms are genuinely higher, then they possess characteristics or qualities which are singularly theirs alone, and consequently can never adequately be explained merely on the basis of lower forms of existence. For example, if we as persons are truly human spirits or human souls, then it makes absolutely no difference where, how, or when we obtained this quality, the fact is that we possess it; from whence it originates, or tracing it to its origin, does not diminish its luster, value, or reality one iota. If I am a human person, endowed with qualities characteristic of human beings, such as, being a soul, spirit, etc., whether I received it from animal ancestry or God, it makes no difference whatever as to the genuineness of my spiritual nature; I will in either case possess it; and, if it is an eternal nature, it will remain eternal whether it came from God, the ape, or anywhere else. Logically, the nature of man as a soul would maintain its full reality, significance, worth, and dignity, even if we could create a human being in a scientific laboratory; the Theist would merely regard this feat as a cooperative activity between man and God, (considering it impossible without God's participation). Even on a non-Theistic basis, or one where God withholds all cooperation, if man is a genuine soul capable of surviving to immortality, it matters little how he came into existence, the fact would still remain that he is a man, a soul, and an eternal one.

XLI

PHENOMENOLOGY:

The Descriptive Analysis of Subjective Processes

(*The Philosophy of Essence*)

Phenomenology, as a Twentieth Century school of philosophy, is attributable to *Edmund Husserl* (1859-1938), brilliant logician, who sought to place science and philosophy on a firmer footing by freeing them from former biases, and starting anew without preconceived notions of any kind. It is imperative to distinguish Phenomenology from Phenomenalism, the belief that appearances alone exist, *i.e.*, beyond phenomena, there is no reality; David Hume's philosophy exemplifies the philosophy of Phenomenalism well.

Phenomenology distinguishes itself from other philosophies in a number of ways, but particularly in (1) its search for essences, the ideal intelligible structure of phenomena; and (2) the procedure of attending and grasping that which is itself immediately presented to consciousness without bias. Thus we find that Phenomenology is more than a philosophy; it comprises a methodology as well. The growth of Phenomenology has been steady and fruitful; the Neorealism of both the American and British, particularly that of G. E. Moore, received its impetus from Phenomenology, as did the Existentialism of Heidegger and Sartre. The value theory of Nicolai Hartmann, as well as others, gained its stimulus from Phenomenology, each making specific applications of the method, such as, Max Scheler to the fields of anthropology, axiology, and philosophy of religion; Theodore Lipps, to the field of aesthetics; Rudolph Otto, to the field of philosophy of religion; and Karl Mannheim, to the study of sociology.

The chief organ of this school was, until 1930, the *Jahrbuch für Philosophie und phänomenologische Forschung* (*Yearbook for Philosophy and Phenomenological Research*) under the editorship of Edmund Husserl in collaboration with Moritz Geiger (1880-1937), Martin Heidegger (1889-

), Alexander Pfänder (1870-1941), Adolph Reinach (1883-1917), and Max Scheler (1847-1928), Husserl's *Ideen zu einer reinen Phänomenologie und phänomenologischen Philosophie* (*Ideas Pertaining to a Pure Phenomenology and to a Phenomenological Philosophy*) translated into English under the title, *Ideas: General Introduction to Pure Phenomenology,*[1] initiated the first edition of the Yearbook, a journal of eleven volumes which continued in publication from 1913 to 1930. In 1933, upheaval provoked by Hitler's reign of terror, prompted many of the Phenomenologists to migrate to other nations, including America where under the leadership of Marvin Farber (1901-) and some American Phenomenologists, they founded in 1939 the International Phenomenological Society which began publication of their quarterly journal, *Philosophy and Phenomenological Research,* in 1940.

1. Edmund Husserl — Transcendental Phenomenology

Summary of Husserl's Phenomenology.

Transcendental Phenomenology is an attempt to get at 'the things themselves,' essences, which Husserl terms *eidos,* the Greek word signifying: shape, form, figure, but which in this philosophy denotes the intelligible structure of *things themselves* which are intuited by consciousness, the ego or *cogito.* 'The things themselves' are what is given in a person's consciousness, what is perceptible in consciousness, by everyone's consciousness; and the object of that perception is called phenomenon, while the study of its essence is termed Phenomenology.

The object of Phenomenology is to determine the essence, the *eidos,* the logical structure of the things themselves, "the realm of essential structures of transcendental subjectivity immediately transparent to the mind,"[2] by the method of *epoche,* a Greek term signifying a suspension of judgment (used by the Skeptic philosophers), a method akin to Cartesian doubt. *Epoche,* abstention or suspended judgment, is achieved through *bracketing,* a technique or method of reduction whereby certain elements in the things themselves which are given in consciousness are held in brackets, severing them from the subject's field of consciousness. By the historical *epoche,* all preconceived notions, biases, dogmas of science, are set aside, held there in abeyance, permitting 'eidetic reduction,' allowing one to derive essences from the things themselves, such as

[1] Translated by W. R. Boyce Gibson.

[2] Edmund Husserl, *Ideas: General Introduction to Pure Phenomenology,* tr. W. R. Boyce Gibson (New York: The Macmillan Co., 1931).

pure essence, a derivative of formal mathematics (not applied mathematics). Bracketing is, therefore, what is bracketed in existence with the exception of *transcendental reduction,* which brackets out all except pure consciousness and that which is given to it, its object, its intentionality, its objective referrent.

Intentionality, that to which consciousness refers, whatever the subject is conscious *of,* the correlative of consciousness, is the object presented to consciousness. The intelligible structure of this object is the goal of Phenomenology, for this constitutes essence or *eidos,* reality, ontological reality, for which we are in search. Reality, then, is a stream of experiences, ideal in its objective nature, and called the *noema* (experienced object, data of pure intention), while ideal in its subjective nature, *noesis,* (the act of experiencing); *noema* is what appears in *noesis.*

Phenomenology, the science of essences, is an a priori science, which culminates in philosophical Idealism. Phenomenological Psychology, unlike Transcendental Phenomenology, is a science of experience, a science of facts in the Humean sense of the word, and it treats phenomena as real existence of real subjects who belong to the spatio-temporal world. "As over against this psychological 'phenomenology,' *pure or transcendental phenomenology will be established not as a science of facts, but as a science of essential Being* (as 'eidetic Science); a science which aims exclusively at establishing 'knowledge of essences' (Wesenserkenninisse) and *absolutely no 'facts.'* The corresponding Reduction to the pure 'essence,' or, in respect of the judging thought, from factual ('empirical') to 'essential' universality, is the *eidetic Reduction.*"[1] Edmund Husserl regarded his Pure or Transcendental Phenomenology as a new science, a First Philosophy, 'a science of essential being — an a priori science' which deals directly with the *things themselves,* obtaining their essences. Transcendental Phenomenology is neither an empirical science nor is it founded on empirical facts, but rather on essences, the intelligible structure of things, similar to that which is called pure logic or pure mathematics. Accordingly, Transcendental Phenomenology is an a priori science whose subject matter is *eidetic,* 'universals' in somewhat of a Platonic sense, which are intuited.

Eidos and Essence.

To appreciate the meaning of what has been said, it will help to mention the historical background of Phenomenology, and the sources from which many of its ideas have sprung: Platonic Ideals, the Cartesian

[1] *Ideas.*

Cogito, Franz Brentano's (1838-1917) concept of 'intentional,' Locke, Berkeley, and Hume's Empiricism. Husserl's Phenomenology is fundamentally a 'philosophy of essence;' essence (*Wesen*) is the *ideal intelligible structure* of phenomena, rather than the phenomena *per se.* In this respect, though it deals with phenomena as data, it is not a philosophy of Phenomenalism, since Phenomenology goes beyond phenomena to extracting its *essence.* Nonmaterial essence, *eidos,* (the Greek for shape, form, figure), is intuited by human consciousness, and resembles Plato's Idea. "I therefore make use, as a foreign expression, of the terminology unspent *Eidos,* and as a German expression of a term whose equivocations are harmless, though at times vexatious, the word *Wesen* (Essence or Essential Being). I would have been pleased to dispense with the heavily laden word Real, if only I could have found a suitable substitute."[1] Thus, *eidos* and *essence* are synonymous terms, and constitute the object of our philosophical search.

From David Hume, Husserl acquired the first systematic 'sketch' of a pure Phenomenology, but Hume treated the entire matter from the standpoint of psychology, as did Berkeley, and also Locke with his concept of 'white paper' to represent the soul; however, unlike Husserl, the treatment of these men merely classifies 'sense data,' and identifies reality as the content of our representations, rather than transcendental essences.

Descartes is credited with first disclosing 'Transcendental Subjectivity' by the introduction of his "*cogito, ergo sum*" (I think, therefore I am), thereby giving reality a conceptual content or structure.

Intentionality, Phenomenological Idealism, Noesis, and Noema.

Franz Brentano's contribution to Transcendental Phenomenology consisted in isolating mental acts from nonmental ones, yet maintaining mental acts refer to things other than themselves; to this process, he gave the term *intentional,* that is, having reference to something external. Brentano spoke of three classes of psychic phenomena: (1) image, (2) judgment, and (3) emotion, interest, or love, each having its intention, its corresponding object in the external world.

Husserl utilized this concept of intention to designate the consciousness of objective essences which the mind intuits. "Conscious processes are also called *intentional;* but then the word intentionality signifies nothing else than this universal fundamental property of consciousness: to be consciousness *of* something . . . This being-in-consciousness is a *being-in of a completely unique kind:* not a being-in-consciousness as a really intrinsic component part, but rather a being-in-it 'ideally' as some-

[1] *Ideas.*

thing *intentional,* something appearing — or, equivalently stated, a being-in-it as its immanent *'objective sense'.* The 'object' of consciousness, the object as process, does not come into the process from outside; on the contrary, it is included as a sense in the subjective process itself — and thus as an *'intentional effect' produced by* the synthesis of consciousness."[1] The task of the Phenomenologist is to describe consciousness concretely, its many facts, which heretofore have not been explored. Facts intuited by consciousness are *facts of synthetic structure,* which have both a subjective or experiential quality (act of perceiving) and an objective *experienced* nature (that which is perceived); the former is designated *noesis* (perceiving), and the latter *noema* (that which is perceived). These two, *noesis and noema,* are synthesized into a single unity as a concrete integral whole. There exists a duality in the thought of Husserl; *noesis,* the act of perceiving, is psychological, subjective, mental, whereas *noema* is the object of our perceiving, that which is perceived. For example, *noesis* is the act of our perceiving the color red, our seeing redness; while *noema* is the redness itself, the essence of redness. Since these two combined constitute the reality of the universe, and since both are of the nature of *mind,* (Idea), Husserl's Phenomenology may be classified as a form of Idealism, akin to the Platonic mode. "Carried out with this systematic concreteness, phenomenology is *eo ipso 'transcendental idealism,'* though in a fundamentally and essentially new sense. It is not a psychological idealism . . . We have here a transcendental idealism that *is* nothing more than a consequentially executed self-explication of my ego as subject of every possible cognition, and indeed with respect to every sense of what exists, wherewith the latter might be able to *have* a sense for me, the ego . . . *The proof of this idealism is therefore phenomenology itself.*"[2]

The concept of *noesis* and *noema* is not restricted to perceptions of physical objects merely; in fact the physical object *per se* lacks *noema,* it is rather its structural form, it essence; *noesis* and *noema* may also be applied to valuing, and objects of value, such as moral values, religious values, aesthetic values. A religious experience or a moral experience is a *noesis,* while its object, God or goodness, is *noema.* Take an aesthetic experience as an example; *noesis* would be the actual appreciating or perceiving of music, while the music itself, its structure, its essence, is *noema.* Thus the valuing of the music is *noesis,* whereas the value of the music its *noema.*

[1] Edmund Husserl, *Cartesian Meditations: An Introduction to Phenomenology,* tr. Dorion Cairns (The Hague: Martinus Nijhoff, 1960).

[2] *Ibid.*

Epoche, Bracketing, and Reduction.

A *Phenomenologist* begins with consciousness, pure experience, in which he finds phenomena, actually his own life's experiences. At this point he must practice an *epoche* (abstention), suspend judgment concerning the objective world by placing it in *brackets.* "Our comprehensive *epoche,* as we say, the world between brackets, excludes the world which is simply there! from the subject's field, presenting in its stead the so-and-so-experienced-perceived-remembered-judged-thought-valued-etc., world, as such, the 'bracketed' world. Not the world or any part of it appears, but the 'sense' of the world."[1] Phenomenological experience is a suspension of appearance to the bracketed objects themselves.

The practice of *epoche,* bracketing elements in the *given,* allows for eidetic reduction, extraction of essences, whereby the *noetic* (experiencing *per se*) and the *noematic* (experienced) are reduced to two parts. Phenomenological experience is internal, the bracketing entails or is of objective phenomena: the former considered *noesis,* and the latter *noema; noema* appears in *noesis.*

By the method of reduction, we are able to extend our own self-experience to that of other selves, not only experiencing other selves, but society also. Moreover, as a group, we may perform *inter-subjective* reductions, whereby my individual experience may be universalized to maintain for you, or that my individual experiences, intentionalities, consciousness of objects, essences, will be found to be the same for you. "And, further, that society, which we experience in a common consciousness, may be reduced not only to the intentional fields of the individual consciousness, but also by means of an inter-subjective reduction, to that which unites these, namely the phenomenological unity of the social life."[2]

Eventually, we may accomplish *eidetic reduction,* severing everything which is not pure consciousness, and bracketing it; with existence bracketed in this manner, the remainder or the result of this reduction is the essence, *eidos,* the intelligible structure of the object given the subject. This *eidos* or essence is the intentional counterpart of consciousness, the object outside of consciousness which refers to the consciousness. Consciousness, by intuition, is able to receive its intentional object, the essence without, and bring it within as its intentional object, for this is precisely the process of *Transcendental Phenomenology.*

[1] Edmund Husserl, "Phenomenology" in *Encyclopedia Britannica,* 14th ed.
[2] *Ibid.*

2. Max Scheler —Phenomenology Applied

An original thinker, not very well known to Americans, but an influential member of the Phenomenological school of philosophy, second only to Husserl, is *Max Scheler.* Heidegger, out of respect and admiration for Edmund Husserl, dedicated his classic, *Being and Time,* to him, but another fine work, *Kant and the Problem of Metaphysics,* he dedicated "to the memory of Max Scheler." Scheler, at the height of his career, died in 1928 at the age of 54 as he was about to assume academic responsibilities at Frankfurt.

Scheler's originality in thought led him to pursue one philosophical thought after another, consequently it is difficult to identify his philosophical position since, like a travelling stream, it is in a state of flux. Two definite modes of thought are readily perceptible, and probably three: the first period of his thinking was dominated by the influence of his teacher, Rudolph Eucken (1846-1926), and Kantian philosophy. The second period, marked by an affinity for Personalism, Theism, and Christianity, saw the publications of his greatest books: (1) *Formalismus in der Ethik und die materiale Wertethik* (*Formalism in Ethics and the Non-Formal Ethic of Value*), a work regarded as his greatest, and first published in the *Yearbook for Philosophy and Phenomenological Research* (1913), (2) *Ressentiment* (1912, 1915), (3) *The Nature of Sympathy* (1913, 1st ed.), and (4) *Of the Eternal in Man* (1920). The third and last period, unfinished owing to his untimely death, saw the marked beginnings of a change from Theism to Pantheism, as evidenced in his *Man's Place in Nature* (1928), published the year of his death.

Scheler's influence issued from a number of streams; Kant and Eucken were mentioned; heaviest influence was the Phenomenology of Husserl whose indelible mark never left him, and the Phenomenology of Franz Brentano (1838-1917). During his Theistic period, he was strongly influenced by St. Augustine, Pascal, Cardinal Newman, and St. Francis; gradually he veered with ever greater acceleration toward Friedrich Nietzche (1844-1900) to such an extent that he was labeled by Ernst Troeltsch, the *Catholic Nietzsche.* The Vitalism of Henri Bergson and Wilhelm Dilthey (1833-1911) was with him to the end, so much so, that Bergson's concept of the universe as "a machine for the making of gods" became his philosophy, except that for the Theist Bergson, the *Élan Vital* comes from God, whereas for the one-time Theist and now Pantheist, Scheler, it is God.

Epistemology and Phenomenology.

Man, possessing the means of knowledge, perceives the source of all things, the metaphysically real, the Absolute; furthermore, his individuality acquires for him a "living share in the source of all things." [1]

Man is capable of threefold knowledge: (1) *knowledge of control,* (2) *knowledge of essence,* and (3) *knowledge of metaphysical reality and salvation.* By the first, man gains power over nature, society, and history, such as is found in experimental or specialized sciences; basically, it consists of a knowledge whereby man can control nature by deriving its laws which, for Scheler, are purely statistical, laws of fortuitous realities, laws of coincidence.

(2) *Knowledge of essence* is that which Phenomenologically inquires: " 'What is the world, what is, e.g., each so-called 'body,' each 'living being'; what is the *essence* of plant, animal, man, etc., in its invariable structure and essential qualities?' In a similar way it asks: 'What is 'thought,' what is it to feel 'love' or 'beauty' quite independent from the fortuitous temporal stream of consciousness of this or that man in whom these activities *de facto* appear?" Knowledge of essence is recognizable as Husserl's Phenomenology, or what Aristotle termed *First Philosophy,* ontology of the nature of the world and man. Knowledge of essence is an attempt to eliminate dogmatic attitudes on the part of scientists who rely on sense knowledge; instead, knowledge of essence replaces sense knowledge "by a *loving* attitude which seeks out the basic phenomenon and ideas of the world." Furthermore, it "disregards the real existence of things," the fortuitous circumstances furnished by sensory perception, and gains "knowledge of essence from things imagined. I am able, for instance, to see beyond movements on a movie screen or a good painting of a dog and to grasp, in addition, the ultimate components which pertain to the essence (*essentia*) of motion and to every 'living being,' etc." Although knowledge of essence is not independent of all experience, it is nevertheless free from the "*quantum* of experience or of so-called 'induction;' " that is to say, it is prior to induction since knowledge of essence can be gained from statistical count. Knowledge of essence grants one validity from the initial particular instance, from the first case considered, comparable to a priori knowledge of the principles of pure mathematics; for example, $2 + 2 = 4$ is known intuitively from the first individual case

[1] Unless otherwise indicated, quotations in this section entitled: "Epistemology and Phenomenology" are from: Max Scheler, "Philosopher's Outlook" in *Philosophical Perspectives,* tr. Oscar A. Haac. Reprinted by permission of the Beacon Press, copyright © 1958 by Beacon Press. Translated from the German edition in the series, Dalp Taschenbucher, Vol. 301 (Bern: A. Franke, and Munich: L. Lehnen, 1954).

cited. "This knowledge is valid also for being *by itself and in itself.* It has a 'transcendental' dimension, and thus becomes the jumping-off point for all 'critical metaphysics.'" We may conclude that knowledge of essence in a *First Philosophy* is the "true knowledge of reason, . . . a priori knowledge of *essence,*" and it becomes, to use Hegel's expression "the window into the absolute," by furnishing us with axioms of *essential* nature. "*The supreme aim informing a metaphysical outlook* through philosophy is, therefore, to conceive and consider absolute being through itself *in such a way* that it corresponds and is appropriate to the *essential* structure of the world as discovered in 'first philosophy,' to the real *existence* of the world as it appears to us in its resistance to our drives, and to all fortuitous circumstances." Ultimate Being, may be said to have two mental attributes: *ideating spirit* and *rational power,* both of which account for the world's *essential* structure; furthermore, it must contain an *irrational driving force,* responsible for irrational existence, the images which we see. These two attributes form the world, that historical phenomenon in time.

(3) *Knowledge of metaphysical reality and salvation,* the third type accessible to man, is knowledge of life, matter, and the Absolute. The first two constitute metaphysics of the first order; metaphysics of the second order is metaphysics of the Absolute. Knowledge of salvation "is the knowledge by which the nucleus of our person seeks to partake in ultimate being and the very source of all things."[1] Between metaphysical problems of the first and second order there lies another, *philosophical anthropology.* Each of these disciplines raises and attempts to resolve pertinent questions appropriate to its respective realm. Metaphysics of the first order queries: What is life? What is matter? Metaphysics of the second order inquires as to the metaphysics of the Absolute, God; while philosophical anthropology is in quest of: What is man? Kant was the first to cope with the third problem by postulating that all concrete Being, the outer and inner world, is explicable only in relation to man, Being depends on man's being. The entire outer world must be studied in man, "and for this reason the *being of man as microtheos is also the primary access to God.*" Apropos to this point, Husserl concludes his *Cartesian Meditations* quoting St. Augustine: "Do not wish to go out; go back into yourself. Truth dwells in the inner man."

Knowledge of salvation, of God, is not theoretical, but a personal and active commitment to God, and to a progressive self-realization. Man, a collaborator with God, is also an organic unit of spiritual acts, for this

[1] Max Scheler, "The Forms of Knowledge and Culture" in *Philosophical Perspectives, op. cit.*

identifies him as a person, a unique, individual, infinite spirit. "Man is thus not the imitator of a 'world of ideas' or 'providence' which arose spontaneously, or was already present in God before the creation, but he is *co*-creator, *co*-founder, *co*-executor of a stream of ideas which *develop* throughout world history and with man. Man is the only locus in which and through which original being grasps and recognizes itself, but man is also the being in whose free *decision* God can *realize* and sanctify his pure essence. It is man's destiny to be more than 'serf' and obedient servant, more also than merely the 'child' of a ready-made and completed God. In his being as man, a condition involving decisions, man bears the higher dignity of an ally and even collaborator of God. Amid the storms of the world, man must carry before everything the flag of dignity, the flag of the '*Deitas*' [divinity] which realizes itself only in the course of world history." Man's spiritual person is a unique self-concentration of the spirit of the divine.

Former concepts of man, such as the following, have been much too narrow and restricted: the classic concept of man as *animal rationale*, Nietzsche's Dionysian man and superman, Linné's *homo sapiens*, La-Mettrie's *l'homme machine*, Machiavelli's man interpreted in the light of power, the Freudian *libido*, Marx's economic being, or even 'fallen man' Adam. These concepts are not only too narrow, they regard man as a *thing;* moreover, they fail to consider the whole man. "Man is not a thing. He is a direction of the *movement of the universe* itself, even of its source. Man is 'microcosm and a being filled with spirit.' "[1] An absolutely total man, the ideal, has realized every one of his essential capabilities. "Indeed, he is as far from us as God, who in so far as we grasp his essence in spirit and life, is nothing but the *essentia* [essence] of man, only in infinite form and fullness." Nevertheless every period of history has its '*relatively total man,*' the maximum of total humanity possible under the circumstances, a participation of the highest in human existence; and we, too, have shared in this to a relative degree.

Philosophical Anthropology.

Scheler defines philosophy as "an attempt to attain a kind of knowledge in which facts are *no longer relative because they depend on life, not* relative to its range of values."[2] Such knowledge is knowledge of *essence;* the scientist, on the other hand, avoids ultimate reality, and studies the world 'related to existence.' Philosophy's standards of measurement are

[1] Max Scheler, "Man in the Era of Adjustment" in *Philosophical Perspectives*, *op. cit.*

[2] Max Scheler, "The Forms of Knowledge and Culture," *op. cit.*

twofold: (1) the a priori level which pertains to a priori truth or falsity of essences, and (2) the level of absolute Being found in objects of knowledge. The first relates to knowledge of culture; "the cultured person is one who has acquired in the world a *personal structure,* an inclusive concept of ideally mobile patterns super-imposed on each other, in order to arrive at *one single* way to view the world, to think, comprehend, judge, and deal with the world and *any* of its fortuitous manifestations – patterns *anterior* to fortuitous experience, their personal 'world.'" The second pertains to knowledge of salvation, the search for the absolutely real in all things, their existence, essence, and value; thus, it is metaphysical knowledge, whereas the first is ontological, a First Philosophy which studies the a priori structural essence of the world.

Knowledge is never 'knowledge for knowledge sake,' but has a concrete aim and purpose, namely, a process of growth, change. The purposes of growth which knowledge serves are threefold: (1) *Knowledge of culture* (knowledge of essence), growth and complete development of the person as a knowing being; (2) *knowledge of salvation or grace,* knowledge for the sake of God, and (3) *knowledge of control or achievement,* scientific knowledge.

Culture is not a category of knowledge or experience, but a category of being, the end result of shaping or molding the total being of man; culture is growth, a process of growth to manhood, to self-deification. If man fails in this respect, he, as a mere vitalistic being, will become 'a dead-end road of nature,' but as spirit, he can free himself from nature's driving forces and become *'the vital being capable of spiritual acts,'* qualitatively removed from being a mere animal. Man distinguishes himself from the animal primarily by possessing a priori insight; as to freedom of will, this he lacks in the usual sense of the word; free will is a negative power used to sublimate our instinctual urges, to control impulses or drives.

Inner psychophysical life is composed of stages or levels of existence; the first, and lowest, is vital feeling, drive, or impulse, in which consciousness, sensation, and representation are absent. Although it may be the lowest and found in plant and animal life as well as in man, it is nevertheless the power behind the highest spiritual level, the potency undergirding activity; furthermore, the spirit or soul obtains whatever potency it possesses from lower impulses and urges.

The second stage of psychic life is instinctual, a drive which manifests itself in the form of growth and reproduction in plant and animal, but serves in a more extended capacity in man. Judging by plant life, the basic drive is toward reproduction and death, not a will to power as Nietzsche purported.

Out of instinct, two modes of behavior arise (the third and fourth stages): *habit* and *intelligence.* Habit is basically *associative memory,* what Pavlov termed 'conditioned reflex,' association; intelligence is sudden insight, anticipatory responsiveness to new situations, independent of trial and error, capable of solving drive-determined situations; and differs from associative memory in its capability of grasping and mastering new or atypical situations. The fifth stage is *choice,* also common to both man and animal, for animals select among impulses rather than merely being motivated by the strongest one.

The unique nature of man consists in the sixth and final stage of psychic life, in his being a *person* with abilities exceeding intelligence and even choice; animals have the capacity to make choices, but only man has the ability to *discriminate between values.* A person is a spirit, capable of reasoning conceptually, intuiting essences, performing "voluntary and emotional acts such as kindness, love, remorse, reverence, wonder, bliss, despair and free decision." [1] A spiritual being, a person, neither possesses self-consciousness nor objectivity; furthermore, he can forfeit his own life. Man enjoys a free will which is capable of outlasting the pressure of drives throughout their changing states; he is as Nietzsche noted: "Man is an animal that can make promises." An animal will never become a psychologist or physiologist, nor can the animal develop categories of thing and substance, and it lacks unified space, space compiled or inituited from tactile space, visual space, auditory space, kinesthetic space, etc. "Man can be either more or less than an animal, but never an animal," because of his capacity to isolate drives from instincts, separate pleasure from enjoyment, become ascetic, sublimate.

Although laws of the universe remain constant, man does not; he can transform, "go beyond himself as an organism . . . Man as a spiritual being is a being that surpasses himself in the world." Man, a dynamic being, "the spiritual center of activity, which we have called the person in man, is not a substance but a hierarchical structure of acts, in which one of them assumes direction and guidance in accordance with the goal of a value or idea with which the individual happens to 'identify himself.'" Materialism and Naturalism have fallen into a grave error, that

[1] Unless otherwise noted, quotations in the remainder of this section on "Philosophical Anthropology" are from Max Scheler, *Man's Place in Nature,* tr. Hans Meyerhoff. Reprinted by permission of the Beacon Press, copyright © 1958 by Beacon Press. Translated from the German edition in the series, Dalp Taschenbucher, Vol. 301 (Bern: A. Francke, and Munich: L. Lehnen, 1954).

of assuming higher forms of being develop genetically from the lower; yet, on the other hand, it is equally erroneous to assume that higher forms of being cause the lower, such as Vitalism or Idealism assume; mechanism and teleology alike, are false.

Higher values are weaker than the lower because higher forms of existence depend on the lower, while the lower tend to be less dependent relatively to the higher – from plant to animal to man. Spirit or person relies upon energies of lower existence for power. "Spirit, originally impotent, and the demonic drive originally blind to all spiritual ideas and values, may fuse in the growing process of ideation, or spiritualization, in the sublimation of the drives and in the simultaneous actualization, or vitalization, of the spirit . . . Spirit is originally devoid of power and efficacy, and the more this is so, the purer it is . . . 'To begin with, the lowest forms are the most powerful, and the highest the most impotent.' Every higher form of being is relatively impotent with respect to the lower: it is realized, not through its own power, but through the energy of the lower forms . . . Spirit can *acquire* energy through the process of sublimation . . . But, to begin with and inherently, the spirit has no energy of its own." This is a most remarkable and unique doctrine in Scheler's philosophy, the belief that the higher form, the person, is devoid of energy and must acquire it somehow from his baser nature. However, the person does determine essences, and has access to the region of the essential world, one which is realized through a principle, (a *vital principle* or image-producing *vital fantasy*) indicative of the *Ground of Being.*

Pantheism.

Of the two basic forces in nature, the most powerful, the centers of energy, are found in the inorganic world, but are blind in their primitive manifestations. Owing to biological necessity, these blind lawless forces are subjugated by man to law. Eventually, reason interprets regularity as natural law; consequently, natural laws merely possess statistical validity, rythmical processes. Higher forms of existence, devoid of any energy of their own, borrow whatever they possess from the lower – a process known as sublimation. "Sublimation would then designate the natural process by which energies of a lower sphere of being, in the course of evolution, are made available to higher forms of being and becoming. For example, the energy exchange among electrons would give rise to the structure of the atom, or, the energies in the inorganic world would be pressed into service on behalf of life. The evolution of man would then represent the last act of sublimation in nature, at least until now."[1] The power process is effected by instinctual energy being transformed into spiritual activity; the person, *per se,* is impotent. Spirit and will lack power, merely serving to guide the organism's instinctual and vital powers.

Becoming human is the highest stage of sublimation, the "intimate fusion of all the essential stages of nature." Thus man must learn to live with himself, his baser drives and perverse inclinations; rather than fighting them, he must invest the energy derived therefrom and channel it into useful, wholesome, and worthwhile endeavors.

Man's development is an ongoing process which cannot stop short of its goal, the highest form of Being – the *World-Ground, deitas,* its *causa sui* (its own cause), that which accounts for reality. The World-Ground also lacks energy, creative power, and is, moreover, in process of realizing its deity, its values, and its ideas. "In order to realize its *deitas,* or its inherent plenitude of ideas and values, the Ground of Being was compelled to release the world-creative drive. It was compelled, as it were, to pay the price of this world process in order to realize its own essence in and through this temporal process . . . It realizes its eternal *deitas* in the processes of world history and in or through man. In fact, this process, essentially timeless, but manifesting itself in time for our finite experience, can approach its goal – the self-realization of the Godhead – only to the degree to which what we call 'world' becomes the perfect body of the eternal substance."

Man, threatened by *pure nothingness,* inquiring as to his place in the universe, discovering both his existence and a world, turns to religion as a protection against nihilism. But man's highest Ground of Being, God, is not Theistic, a spiritual personal omnipotent Being, but a Ground of Being which "comprehends and realizes itself directly in man, who, as spirit and as life, is but a partial mode of the eternal spirit and drive. . . . The original Being becomes conscious of itself in man in the same act by which man sees himself grounded in this being." Man's fulfilling of his nature is an active commitment to the ideal demand of God (Ground of Being), and "in and through this fulfillment, *man cooperates in the creation of God,* who emerges from the Ground of Being in a process whereby spirit and drive interpenetrate increasingly." Man's self-realization is a self-deification, a cooperative interplay between two attributes of Being: spirit and drive, man being their focus of intersection and unity.

The evolution of the world is the story of an incomplete God, God

[1] Unless otherwise noted, quotations in this section, "Pantheism," are from Max Scheler, *Man's Place in Nature, op. cit.*

in the process of becoming, progressing toward his realization. "The logos 'according to' which the world comes into being becomes in man an act in which he can cooperate. Thus, according to this view, the birth of man and the birth of God are, from the outset, reciprocally dependent upon each other . . . The final actual 'reality' of this Being in itself is not capable of objectification any more than the being of another person. One can take part in its life and spiritual actuality only through participation, through an act of commitment or active identification. Absolute Being does not have the function to protect or to complement man's weakness and needs which always want to make an 'object' out of this being." If anyone takes objection to this religious philosophy on the grounds that it does not aid or comfort man, then "my answer is that metaphysics is not an insurance policy for those who are weak and in need of protection." But there is a type of support, one which issues from the "total process of realizing values in world history in so far as this process has moved forward toward the making of 'God.' But we must not wait for theoretical certainties before we commit ourselves. It is the commitment of the person himself that opens up the possibility of 'knowing' this Being in itself." Man is the link between this Being in itself, for he dwells within this Being, and base drives. Man finds his determination in recognizing this fact; moreover, the highest Being itself is dependent upon the cooperation of man to find its own determination. Spirit and drive, incomplete in themselves, must be realized together in the process of the history of man and the evolution of life.

Ethics and Value Theory.

Scheler presents a hierarchal doctrine of values, one ordered on a four-fold scale of two divisions. The first ascending scale of four consists of (1) *pleasure values,* (2) *vital* or *welfare values,* (3) *spiritual* or *cultural values,* and (4) *sacred, religious,* or *values of the holy.* The first, relative to the individual, are either *agreeable* or *disagreeable,* pleasant or unpleasant; the second promote life, health, well-being, vitality, etc., therefore are called *life* or *vital* values; the third group comprise *beauty, justice,* and *truth;* while the fourth, and highest, is composed of *sacred values of holiness.* The higher values exercise primacy over the lower, consequently when necessary, the lower are sacrificed in the service of the higher, on the altar of sanctity.

A second scale of evaluating relates to their depth, durability, and primacy; by right of independence, each is judged according to four principles: (1) enduring values are preferable to mutable, changing, perishable ones; (2) those shared by a greater number of persons are preferable to those enjoyed by fewer; (3) if one value is dependent upon another for its existence, then the foundation value is deemed superior; (4) the depth of satisfaction is the last rule by which to determine the relative importance of values.

Not only is Scheler's scale of values aristocratically ordered, but the concept of inequality maintains for persons as well. Persons may not only embody values of different relative worth, but persons themselves are not of equal stature, differing according to hierarchal rank. Respecting Democracy, it is an invalid social philosophy of bourgeois origin.

Scheler's value theory comprises a synthesis between Relativism and Absolutism. He is aware of heterogeneous societies and persons entertaining different systems of values, such as monogamy being the acceptable moral practice in the Western World, and polygyny its counterpart in the Middle East, yet both are true, despite their reciprocal rejection of each other. "I am also convinced that those conflicts of opinion as to the moral value of sympathy and love (between Schopenhauer and Nietzsche, for instance, or between the rival exponents of social progress and racial superiority), which have so greatly aroused the interest of the educated public, are due far less to differences of standards in evaluating these emotions, than to an inadequate conception and analysis of the relevant phenomena themselves."[1] Rival positions differ in relation to the Absolute only in relation to perspective, and here, the relativity of values ends. Only God, the Value of Values, from his heavenly vantage point, perceives with accuracy the entire truth respecting values as absolute.

Values, in reality, are facts — value facts, not merely valuations; there exists a realm of values into which we enter and experience. Values are genuine phenomena, real objective entities, and are the a priori ground of emotions, but differ completely from states of feeling since values are in quality ideal objects given to us, not by reason, but by feeling, emotion, yet they possess qualities common to other ideal objects such as color sound, etc. Values are known by Pascal's *ordre du couer, logique du couer, raison du couer* (order of the heart, logic of the heart, reason of the heart).

Values have both *aim* and *end;* a conscious aspect requiring realization is the aim, while the nonmental goal or process of aspiration is their end. Man is a value being; he seeks and aspires to values as well as experiencing them directly; values are not feelings, emotions; they are facts which man pursues. Pleasure is not man's goal, even when he pursues it, but values are; when a man seeks pleasure, he does so under the

[1] Max Scheler, *The Nature of Sympathy,* tr. Peter Heath (London: Routledge and Kegan Paul, 1945).

apprehension that it possesses value. Unlike feelings, values have a real essence, a structure held intact by a priori laws.

Up to this point we have been classifying values according to objective or external relationships, but they permit of still another classification in respect to their subjects (persons). Personal values, those relating to the individual himself, are, in essence, superior to those attached to things; consequently, persons ultimately are good or evil. Ethical values are unequivocally personal, since they are specifically acts of a person.

Besides his classic work in value theory, *The Formalistic Principle in Ethics and the Non-Formal Ethic of Value,* Scheler wrote two other important books in the field of ethics: *The Nature of Sympathy,* an evaluation of Schopenhauer's Ethics of Sympathy, and *Ressentiment,* an evaluation of Nietzsche's Slave Ethic.

Ressentiment, French for resentment, a term first used by Friedrich Nietzsche in a special capacity, later became a *terminus technicus,* signifying a state resulting from repressed emotions of hostility and rancor against one's superior before whom a person feels impotent, because he cannot express the anger which his superior incites. Scheler identifies *ressentiment* as a "self-poisoning of the mind which has quite definite causes and consequences. It has a lasting mental attitude, caused by the systematic repression of certain emotions and affects which, as such, are normal components of human nature. Their repression leads to the constant tendency to indulge in certain kinds of value delusions and corresponding value judgments. The emotions and affects primarily concerned are revenge, hatred, malice, envy, the impulse to detract, and spite. Thirst for revenge is the most important source of *ressentiment*."[1] The essential distinguishing features of revenge are (1) the repression of anger owing to impotence, otherwise a person would attack his foe, and (2) the conscious desire to retaliate, 'tit for tat.' If an individual were strong enough to fight back against his foe at the moment of attack, his feelings of hostility being given vent, thereby dissipating, would not permit *ressentiment* to incubate within the personality.

Scheler objects to Nietzsche's designating Christian values as *ressentiment* values, though bourgeois morality from the thirteenth century to the time of the French Revolution is rooted in *ressentiment.* "The more I reflected on this question, the more clearly I realized that the root of Christian love is entirely *free* of *ressentiment*;"[2] *but the* 'universal love of mankind,' a love which does not spring from man's ideal spiritual self

[1] Max Scheler, *Ressentiment,* tr. William W. Holdheim (New York: The Free Press, a division of the Crowell-Collier Publishing Co., 1961).
[2] *Ibid.*

is rooted therein. The latter is merely modern sentimentality which holds in contempt higher values including God, and constitutes an inversion of the scale of true values, an ultimate denial of love. Universal love of mankind, a bourgeois morality grounded in Democracy, the error that all men are equal, stems from a confusion of organ and tool, which places Utilitarian (pleasure values) above cultural and vital values (their superiors), consequently creating a subversion of values prompted by *ressentiment,* a phenomenon indicative of the philosophy of decadence.

In *The Nature of Sympathy,* Phenomenology of love is worked out, the main thesis of which purports that by *sympathy* and *love,* (not the argument by *analogy* and *empathy*), transcending *Solipsism* and *ego-centrism,* we prove the existence of other persons, not only as valuable, but as real.

Love is defined as a movement toward positive value, "that movement wherein every concrete individual object that possesses value achieves the highest value compatible with its nature and ideal vocation; or wherein it attains the ideal state of value intrinsic to its nature." [1] Hatred, on the other hand, is moving in the reverse direction. *Sacred love* is neither perversion, resentment, nor illusory sublimation, but characterized by those persons who when "imbued with it do not chafe and struggle against suffering and death, but embrace it willingly and gladly. They are not men who no longer value life — for in that case how could they sacrifice it? They love it well, but esteem it less than some other and greater thing. They endure suffering indeed, not because they are inured to it, but because the love and loyalty they evince for what is holy to them crowns their suffering with a beautitude before whose radiance all the joy and happiness of life pale into insignificance and seem of little worth."[2] The philosophy of Naturalism and Psychoanalysis fail in their naturalistic explanations of the phenomenon of sacred love by offering very limited interpretations in terms of perverted life impulse or illusory sublimation of the libido.

Love is an emotion, a movement, an act, not a feeling, particularly not a fellow-feeling. Love is effortless, following a law diametrically opposed to the *law of effort.* Acts of love differ, and their differences may be characterized according to a 'three-dimensional classification:' *forms, modes* and *kinds.* "Corresponding to the basic division of all acts into vital acts of the body, purely mental acts of the self, and spiritual acts of the person, we also find love and hatred existing in three *forms:* spiritual love of the person, mental love of the individual self, and vital or pas-

[1] *The Nature of Sympathy, op. cit.*
[2] *Ibid.*

sionate love. Although vital, mental and spiritual acts are intrinsically different in themselves, and are felt as different, without prior reference to their source, they do have an essential affinity with these sources, namely the body, the self and the person. At the same time, these emotional act-forms also have an essential reference to particular kinds of *value* as their noematic counterparts; vital acts to the values of the 'noble' and the 'mean' or 'base'; mental acts to the values of knowledge and beauty (cultural values); and spiritual acts to the values of the 'holy' and the 'profane'. The highest form of love is accordingly that which relates to objects (or persons), having the intrinsic value of holiness; mental love is that which the self has for cultural values of any kind; while vital love relates to the 'noble'. Objects whose value is simply that of being 'pleasant', engender neither love nor hatred;"[1] since they do not contribute to the enhancement of value, they are not suitable objects of love, accordingly 'sensual love' is a misnomer, no such thing exists.

As to different kinds of love, such as mother-love, love of country, love of home, etc., these are *'qualities in the acts themselves,'* experiential without a corresponding object; for example, a person can experience nostalgia and be homesick with no home to which to go; or a woman can experience mother-love, with no children on whom to shed it, etc. Modes of love are merely *'conjunctions* of acts of love,' such as social dispositions, feelings of sympathy, etc. Here, it is the attitude which is under consideration, not the object's worthiness to be loved; these modes are expressed in terms of kindness, goodwill, fondness, amiability, etc.

In respect to *sacrificial love,* a person is entitled to, and morally compelled to, love sacrificially when the act performed sacrifices a love lower on the scale of values for one which holds a position of ascendency. For example, sexual love, a vital form of love, occupies the second position on the scale of four gradations of value, accordingly it is justifiable, and even morally incumbent upon a person, to renounce sex love for the ascetic live, provided the value gained occupies a relatively higher position on the value scale. If a life of renunciation and asceticism will fructify into a complete development of one's spiritual personality or personal religious salvation, then for the sake of these supreme personal values, sex love should definitely be sacrificed, since spiritual values enjoy a position second only to sacred values, while religious values reign supreme. "To renounce true love for the sake of God is a still finer and more glorious sacrifice . . . Life and all its values may and should indeed be sacrificed none the less, firstly for the sake of a nobler life, and secondly for ends and values of a purely spiritual and religious kind. But such

[1] *Ibid.*

a sacrifice should never be undertaken for utility's sake, nor even for that of 'science' so far as the latter continues to be governed by the principle of an ulterior motive. There are 'martyrs' to philosophy, the *gaya scienza,* and martyrs to faith, who deservedly rouse our admiration. Martyrs to 'science', however, are not sublime, but ridiculous." [1] We may conclude by asserting that genuine love is strictly for persons, and is not value for value's sake; in this respect, Scheler is a Personalist. Love, being essentially a movement, directs us to its highest level of ideal value, the love of God; yet, not as mere passive feeling, but as active participation in his love for his world, "an emotional identity with the living universe," [2] for it is in his creation that God is revealed as love and its source. Furthermore it is here that man finds his Ground of Being.

3. Evaluation of Phenomenology

Phenomenology is unquestionably one of the most difficult philosophies to grasp, consequently has little promise of becoming popular with the masses; perhaps Scheler had this thought in mind when quoting Plato: "The masses will never become philosophers." If the masses ever do become philosophers (and in a sense we are all philosophers whether we like it or not, and whether or not we are aware of it, since even the person who refuses to philosophize has assumed a philosophical position), they will be incapable of philosophizing Phenomenologically.

Perhaps we may say, with a fair degree of support, that Phenomenology is a philosopher's philosophy, for it has sired profound philosophical concepts, ones which have opened new inroads in the field, as well as creating a sharp and decisive rupture with past philosophies. It may be said with but little degree of error that Phenomenology marks the transitional period from Modern Philosophy to Contemporary Philosophy, not because of its chronological position in the history of philosophy, but for the revolutionary ideas which it has spawned, ones to be grappled with, and which have created new departures in philosophical thinking, and have caused a permanent rift with the past. Existentialism is definitely one offspring sired by Phenomenology — both Heidegger and Sartre in their classic works: *Being and Time,* and *Being and Nothingness,* authored respectively, have admittedly acknowledged themselves as using the Phenomenological method; in fact, Sartre subtitles his book: *An Essay on Phenomenological Ontology,* while Heidegger's treatise was published originally in *The Yearbook for Phenomenology and Phenomenological Research,* edited by Husserl.

[1] *Ibid.*
[2] *Ibid.*

Phenomenology has introduced into the philosopher's scope: (1) a new method, (2) Neo-Idealism, (3) an Axiological Absolutism, (the objective reality of values), and (4) a return to personality which may possibly be designated Neo-Personalism.

The greatest weakness of Phenomenology is its inability to resolve with complete adequacy problems it has set to solve; being a philosophy of *essence,* it never did deliver into the hand of the philosopher real *existence,* the genuine Being of which we are in search, rather it proposed some remote Absolute being dwelling in some far off transcendental sphere remote from human experience and personal contact. Consequently, the problem to be solved, namely a wedlock between transcendental essence (ultimate reality) and phenomenal reality, never culminated. Existentialism, in its approach to a solution of this seemingly irresolute problem, emphasizes inner existence, inner phenomenal experience, but at the expense and loss of essence.

In deference to honesty, the philosopher must confess that a systematic philosophy has not as yet been found which solves these human, cosmic, and theological problems adequately and fully, yet the philosopher's quest must go on, for with every new generation or era more light is cast, and from newer angles, on these vexing problematic issues. Perhaps Scheler was correct in his assessment of value relativity in relation to value absolutism — discrepant viewpoints merely constitute different angles by which insight is gained into the Absolute, different windows by which to peer in at the truth. This is precisely what philosophy has been, the addition of newer, larger, and brighter windows shedding light on the truth which the world has in store for man. Is not man, after all, the universe's sole thinking, self-conscious, reflective being, who in this respect is either unique, or else resembles his maker, God?

XLII

EXISTENTIALISM:

Existence Precedes Essence

The salient features which should be incorporated into any definition of Existentialism are: (1) existence precedes essence, subjective existence has priority over essence or substance, if any essential substance there be; (2) a person's essence is his subjective state of existence; (3) freedom and contingency constitute the essential make-up of man's existence; (4) a person is devoid of any basic human nature; he is what he makes of himself by his own free choice, he creates himself; (5) the concomitant sense of dread which accompanies the awful sense of responsibility for making decisions which shape reality; (6) an introspective Humanism, or in the case of religious Existentialism, the role played by the subjective aspects of a human person in relation to God; (7) truth is found in paradox; (8) the existent is not rational; (9) (in the case of some Existentialists), an existence without essence.

1. Sören Kierkegaard — Theistic Existentialism

Sören Kierkegaard (1812-1855),[1] father of Existentialism, was the first to use *existence* in the current connotation employed by Existentialists. Although Kierkegaard, or S. K. as he is often referred to, and even called Either/Or by his fellow Danes,[2] (after the title of a classic work of his), died over a hundred years ago, his philosophy was little known in English-speaking countries until relatively recently, when translations of his books began to flow steadily out of the printer's shop, and are yet in the making.

The major tenets of Kierkegaardian philosophy are: (1) subjectivity is truth; (2) truth is found in paradox; (3) ethics of self-realizationism,

[1] Pronounced Sû'ren Kɪr'kĕ gôr.

[2] In *The Instant*, No. 1, S. K. writes: "Should I not understand it who am known to all, even to the children in the street, by the name of 'Either/Or?' "

which progresses from the aesthetic stage of life to the ethical stage, and culminates in the religious; (4) reality of the *individual;* (5) the *moment* (of decision); (6) the *choice:* either/or; (7) a person *can* do what he wills; (8) the *leap* (of faith) in fear and trembling; (9) anti-Hegelianism and anti-Rationalism; (10) emphasis upon *existence*; (11) passion (not reason) as the criterion of existence; (12) the 'infallible law' (as an *idée fixe*) – guilt and punishment; (13) self-transparency (in the psychological sense); (14) the crowd as 'untruth;' (15) repetition – 'forward-looking recollection;' (16) possibility and freedom; (17) the concept of dread as 'dizziness;' (18) the concept of *despair as sin;* (19) faith (not virtue) as the opposite of sin.

Many of Kierkegaard's works were pseudonymous, written under such names as, Johannes Climacus and Virgilius Haufniensis; among them are to be found most of his major contributions to philosophical thought: *Either/Or* (1843), *Fear and Trembling* (1843), *Repetition* (1843), *Philosophical Fragments* (1844), *The Concept of Dread* (1844), *Stages on Life's Way* (1845), and *Concluding Unscientific Postscript* (1846 – S.K.'s greatest philosophical work). As suggested by the title of the last mentioned book, this was to terminate his literary or philosophical career, but as it turned out, a new stage of life was about to commence with another series of major works, somewhat inferior in philosophical value to the former. Among the major works written subsequent to the first period, (with the exception of *The Journals* which constitute a diary laden with philosophical ideas written from 1834 to 1845), are: *Edifying Discourses* (18 of them published at various times since the publication of *Either/Or*), *The Present Age* (1846), *The Point of View for My Work as an Author* (1848), *The Individual* (1849),[1] *The Sickness unto Death* (1849), *Training in Christianity* (1850), *Two Discourses at the Communion on Fridays* (1851), *The Attack upon Christendom* (1854-1855),[2] *For Self-Examination* (1851), *Judge For Yourself!* (1851-1852), *God's Unchangeableness* (1855).

Anti-Hegelianism.

In Kierkegaard we find a new departure in philosophical thought; S. K. attempts to dethrone Hegel, regarded as *the philosopher,* the seemingly omnipotent who practically held control of philosophical thinking in the palm of his hand. Taken as a whole, S. K.'s philosophy is a direct antithesis to Hegelianism: (1) Hegel declared, 'the truth is the whole,' while

[1] *The Individual* was published in conjunction with *The Point of View for My Work as an Author* in 1859, posthumously.

[2] These attacks are upon Christendom, not upon Christianity or Jesus Christ; these were originally newspaper articles entitled: "The Instant."

Kierkegaard contradicted, 'the individual is truth;' (2) Hegel made truth absolute and objective, whereas S. K. claimed 'subjectivity is truth; (3) Hegel's dictum proclaimed 'the real is the rational,' but S. K. insisted 'truth is a paradox;' (4) Hegel saw the truth as a synthesis, reconciling thesis with antithesis, but S. K. responded with his philosophy of *Either/or* which legitimatized contradictory propositions, a paradox which necessitates 'the leap' of faith, the acceptance of that which is logically disconnected; furthermore, S. K. condemned 'syntheses' as hellborne compromises – "Both-and is the way to Hell;" (5) 'essence' composed Hegel's reality but *existence* was S. K.'s; (6) reason and coherence were Hegel's criteria of truth, but S. K. controverted with 'intensity of passion' (feeling) as criterion.

The antithetical ideas of the two men do not terminate here, but continue; the following is a list of Kierkegaardian-Hegelian antinomies:

HEGEL	KEIRKEGAARD
1. Communication as direct	1. Indirect Communication Maiuetic (Socratic Midwifery) Reduplication, Double Reflection.
2. Objectivity (disinterestedness	2. Subjectivity (inwardness, intense feeling, passion, pathos).
3. Immanence	3. Transcendence
4. Necessity	4. Freedom
5. The System	5. Paradox
6. Speculation	6. Existence
7. Mediation	7. The Leap
8. The Universal	8. The Particular and Individual
9. Recollection	9. Repetition
10. Openness	10. Concealment
11. Immediacy	11. Mediacy or Reflection
12. Actuality	12. Possibility
13. Absolute	13. Relative

Kierkegaardian Existentialism.[1]

Rather than eliminate thought entirely, thought and existence are fused together in Kierkegaardian Existentialism; without inwardness, subjectivity, genuine knowledge is impossible. Experience (existence) is primarily inwardness, introspection, a peering into the individual's existence; in this effort, reason is grossly handicapped, whereas feeling is

[1] In order to facilitate details involved in documentation, the following system and key will be implemented:

EO – *Either/Or,* tr. David F. Swenson and Lillian Marvin Swenson (Princeton: Princeton University Press, 1944).

PH – *Purity of Heart,* tr. Douglas V. Steere (New York: Harper & Row, Publishers, Inc., 1938).

SD – *Sickness unto Death,* tr. Walter Lowrie (Princeton: Princeton University Press, 1941).

capable of delving deep into the recesses of the human being. Reason, a suitable instrument for acquiring facts and universal concepts, fails in gaining access to internal subjectivity. "Existence involves first and foremost particularity, and this is why thought must abstract from existence, because the particular cannot be thought, but only the universal." For extracting existential data which by nature is always particular, feeling, intense feeling in the form of emotion, passion, is the suitable criterion. A person can actually gain universal principles upon which to construct a system by *inwardness*, viewing via feeling the internal existential being which maintains for all individuals. For example, my grief, my anxiety, though individual, and never subject to being imparted to another as one can and does do with reason, is identical to the same pathos, etc. that another feels; therefore, whatever thoughts I may gain respecting the truth of my feelings hold true for any other individual person. Reason never gives us direct knowledge of existence or actuality, only universals or essences, yet man exists as an actuality, not as a universal essence. The Hegelian "systematic idea is the identity of subject and object, the unity of thought and being. Existence, on the other hand, is their separation. It does not by any means follow that existence is thoughtless; but it has brought about, and brings about, a separation between subject and object, thought and being . . . This objective thought has no relation to the existing subject."(CP) Objective thought takes away man's individuality, and makes of him a universal entity, an impersonal essence; such Hegelian Absolutism inevitably terminates in Pantheism, thereby sacrificing everything individually personal, including the individuality of God.

Neither the essence of man nor universal man creates systems respecting reality, individual existing human beings do. Is man a human being, an existent, an actuality; or is he an abstract universal essence, an impersonal system? "Is he a human being, or is he speculative philosophy

---

FT — *Fear and Trembling,* tr. Walter Lowrie (Princeton: Princeton University Press, 1941).

PF — *Philosophical Fragments,* tr. David Swenson (Princeton: Princeton University Press, 1936).

CP — *Concluding Unscientific Postscript,* tr. David Swenson (Princeton: Princeton University Press, 1941).

J — *Journals,* tr. Alexander Dru (London: Oxford University Press, 1939).

AC — *Attack Upon Christendom,* tr. Walter Lowrie (Princeton: Princeton University Press, 1944).

CD — *Concept of Dread,* tr. Walter Lowrie (Princeton: Princeton University Press, 1944).

PV — *Point of View for My Work as an Author,* tr. Walter Lowrie (London: Oxford University Press, 1939).

IN — *The Instant* in *Attack Upon Christendom,* tr. Walter Lowrie (Princeton: Princeton University Press, 1944).

in the abstract? But if he is a human being, then he is also an existing individual. Two ways, in general, are open for an existing individual: *Either* he can do his utmost to forget that he is an existing individual, by which he becomes a comic figure, since existence has the remarkable trait of compelling an existing individual to exist whether he wills it or not . . . *Or* he can concentrate his entire energy upon the fact that he is an existing individual. It is from this side, in the first instance, that objection must be made to modern philosophy; not that it has a mistaken presupposition, but that it has a comical presupposition, occasioned by its having forgotten, in a sort of world-historical absent-mindedness, what it means to be a human being. Not indeed, what it means to be a human being in general; for this is the sort of thing that one might even induce a speculative philosopher to agree to; but what it means that you and I and he are human beings, each one for himself." (CP) In Hegelian philosophy, man loses his existential nature and acquires that of an abstract essence devoid of ethics, for only an existent man is ethical; furthermore, in Hegelianism, the Absolute is existential rather than man. But individuals do not exist metaphysically, they exist actually.

An existential *system* (not an existential being such as man) is impossible since human moments of existence are free from any rational abstract system, indeed, man is essentially freedom, existence, and passion, none of which is explicable by reason, essences, or systems. "Existence is a system — for God; but it cannot be a system for any existing spirit. System and finality correspond to one another, but existence is precisely the opposite of finality. It may be seen, from a purely abstract point of view, that system and existence are incapable of being thought together; because in order to think existence at all, systematic thought must think it as abrogated, and hence as not existing. Existence separates and holds the various moments of existence discretely apart; systematic thought consists of the finality which brings them together."(CP) But with respect to existent man, nothing is complete, nothing final; in his freedom, he strives persistently to realize himself as an individual, as an actuality.

Kierkegaard does not repudiate thought, rather he seeks to identify its place in the scheme of things, that is, its existential relationship, the fusion or juncture of thought with existence. Man both thinks and exists; this is the nature of individuals, but society and metaphysical systems do neither. "God does not think, He creates; God does not exist, He is eternal. Man thinks and exists, and existence separates thought and being, holding them apart from one another in succession." (CP) Metaphysical systems are illusions, not actualities; they appear to be so from the point of reason, not in existential actuality.

Subjectivity as Truth.

In contrast to Hegel's contention that the "truth is the whole," Kierkegaard argues that truth is individual, belonging to the existent subject; it is subjectivity (not subjective). "Subjectivity is truth, subjectivity is reality." (CP) Inner light regarding subjectivity is acquired through passion or an *intensity of feeling;* this vehicle also grants us a relationship with God, and provides us communication with other individuals. An individual is a subject, and for this reason he can relate to himself; moreover, he can relate to, and only to, other subjects, namely to other individual persons and to God, for he too is a subject. "God is a subject, and therefore exists only for subjectivity in inwardness." (CP) Such individual relationships are wrought through intense feeling, passion, not reason; we don't know by reason, that is, we cannot prove by logic the existence of other persons or God; we know them by passion, "and passion is also the highest expression of subjectivity." (CP)

We are now prepared for a definition of truth as 'subjectivity' and as 'the tension of subjective inwardness.' "Here is such a definition of truth: *An objective uncertainty held fast in an appropriation-process of the most passionate inwardness is the truth,* the highest truth attainable for an *existing individual* . . . The truth is precisely the venture which chooses an objective uncertainty with the passion of the infinite." (CP) Objectively, no metaphysical entity can be proved; the result of such an endeavor is uncertainty, paradox, never truth. Passion alone issues in certainty; for example, a rational investigation of the truth respecting the existence of God eventuates in mental disturbance and anxiety, the fruits of objective uncertainty.

A careful examination of the preceding definition of truth will reveal that it is identical with *faith!* Truth is not passive, objective, nor abstract; it is individual, inward intensity of feeling, subjectiveness (not subjective in the sense of reducing truth to a matter of mere opinion). The above definition of truth is an equivalent expression for faith. Without risk there is no faith. Faith is precisely the contradiction between the infinite passion of the individual's inwardness and the objective certainty."(CP) By objective reason we cannot prove the existence of God, but by inwardness, intense feeling, we can.

Rationally, the preceding may seem paradoxical, but objectively, (and reason is objective), truth is a paradox. "When eternal truth is related to an existing individual, it becomes a paradox."(CP) Truth is always a paradox for existent individuals, but from the standpoint of the eternal, that is, from God's vantage point or viewpoint, the paradoxical nature of truth vanishes, and it is seen in its purity as rational. Human beings will never be able to comprehend the truth as it objectively exists, for they are limited to persistent striving after truth. "When subjectivity, inwardness, is the truth, the truth objectively defined becomes a paradox; and the fact that the truth is objectively a paradox shows in its turn that subjectivity is the truth. For the objective situation is repellent; and the expression for the objective repulsion constitutes the tension and the measure of the corresponding inwardness. The paradoxical character of the truth is its objective uncertainty; this uncertainty is an expression for the passionate inwardness, and this passion is precisely the truth . . . The eternal and essential truth, the truth which has an essential relationship to an existing individual because it pertains essentially to existence . . . is a paradox. But the eternal essential truth is by no means in itself a paradox; it becomes paradoxical by virtue of its relationship to an existing individual. The Socratic ignorance is the expression for the objective uncertainty; the inwardness of the existing individual is the truth . . . Socratically the eternal essential truth is by no means in its own nature paradoxical, but only in its relationship to an existing individual."(CP) Accordingly, 'earthbound' individuals see only paradoxes when they attempt objectively to reason their way through to truth or metaphysical reality; God alone escapes the paradox of objective reason. Man must be content with inwardness, arriving at the truth through intense feeling, faith.

These paradoxes of reason become most poignant when religious truths are considered, as for example, the 'Absolute Paradox,' Christ — the God-man, namely, the paradox of God in time, history. This momentous paradox has become an offense to reason, a scandal; its only explanation is the inwardness of intense feeling — *faith*. God, himself, has provided the conditions for man's understanding the Absolute Paradox; it is a 'new organ' of apprehension, faith. S. K. offers as the 'moral' of *Philosophical Fragments,* a "new organ: Faith; a new presupposition: the consciousness of Sin; a new decision: the Moment; and a new Teacher: God in Time."(PF)

The Individual.

Hegel defined individual man in terms of social man, society; and society in terms of the World-Spirit or Absolute, thereby reducing individual man in his solitude close to a nonentity. S. K. repudiates vehemently these Hegelian conclusions by positing individual man as reality, society as 'untruth,' and faith or inward passion as the criterion of truth to replace Hegel's role of reason, objectivity, and coherence theory of truth. Existential truth, claims S. K., does not lend itself to systematization or mediation as Hegel fancied with his logic of synthesis; rather, existential truths are elements in *moments,* as we find them in individual existence. "Speculative philosophy never gets into its head, and it can only universalize the particular man fantastically."(SD)

The *individual* becomes, or is, a category for understanding all truth and reality; reality must be understood in the light of individual existence, never by abstract thought of an impersonal system. " 'The individual' is the category through which . . . our age, our race and its history must pass . . . My duty is . . . to help the masses trying to go through the narrow pass, 'the individual,' through which, be it noted, no one can ever go without first becoming 'the individual.' Yet had I to crave an inscription on my grave I would ask for none other than 'the individual' . . . I bind myself to make every man whom I can include in the category 'the individual' into a Christian or rather, since no man can do that for another, I vouch for his becoming one. As 'that individual' he is alone, alone in the whole world, alone — before God: then it will be easy to obey."(J) The individual is the category of the spirit, a decisive Christian category. A person must order his life and live it, never losing sight of the fact that he is primarily and essentially an existent individual; you must "live in such a way that you are conscious of being an "individual.' "(PH) The concept of 'the individual was so fundamental to the philosophical outlook of Kierkegaard that not only did he crave it for an inscription on his grave, he dedicated his *Purity of Heart Is to Will One Thing* "to 'that solitary individual.' "(PH)

Man functions as an individual, he grows as an individual, develops as an individual, makes choices as an individual, suffers as an individual, experiences intense feelings as an individual, dies only as an individual, faces God, alone, as an individual. "In eternity, the individual, yes, you, my listener, and I as individuals, will each be asked solely about himself as an individual, and about the individual details in his life."(PH) Except in the light of this category, that of the individual, man cannot be understood.

Human existence is always individual in character, never social; the social, or as S. K. is fond of terming it, the *crowd,* is an 'inhuman quality;' in it one loses his identity. "The 'crowd' is the untruth . . . A crowd in its very concept is the untruth . . . 'Crowd' stands for number, the numerical, a number of noblemen, millionaires, high dignitaries, etc — as soon as the numerical is involved it is 'crowd', 'the crowd' . . . For 'crowd' is an abstraction and has no hands: but each individual has ordinarily two hands."(I) In a crowd, individuals lose their identity; they are reduced to mere specimens. Some cowardly individuals purposely seek refuge by hiding anonymously in a crowd, where their identity will be lost and their dastardly acts performed incognito. The crowd is 'untruth' whereas all truth relates itself to the individual – "no witness for the truth dare become engaged with the crowd . . . The communicator of truth can only be a single individual."(I) It is impossible to edify or be edified, to love or be in love, *en masse*. The crowd is even guilty of "tricking God out of his rights as the proprietor of Christianity."(I) To S. K. the crowd was repugnant, and some of his harshest strictures were reserved for the 'crowd' – "for many fools do not make a wise man, and the crowd is doubtful recommendation for a cause. Yes, the larger the crowd, the more probable that that which it praises is folly, and the more improbable that it is truth, and the most improbable of all that it is any eternal truth. For in eternity crowds simply do not exist."(PH) S. K.'s aversion for the life of the crowd dovetails with his dislike of popularity, for they both emanate from the same 'untruth.'

Man, Despair, Faith, and the Paradoxical Nature of Truth.

We have discussed the nature and importance of man as an individual; now we are prepared for a definition of man. Kierkegaard offers a very complex definition of man, but the knowledge of it is a prerequisite for understanding other concepts, particularly passion, despair, and faith, since these are integrally interwoven in his philosophy. "Man is spirit. But what is spirit? Spirit is the self. But what is the self? The self is a relation which relates itself to its own self, or it is that in the relation [which accounts for it] that the relation relates itself to its own self; the self is not the relation but [consists in the fact] that the relation relates itself to its own self. Man is a synthesis of the infinite and the finite, of the temporal and the eternal, of freedom and necessity, in short it is a synthesis. A synthesis is a relation between two factors. So regarded, man is not yet a self."(SD) Man is in the making still; he must actualize himself, make real the possibilities which are his. Ethically, self-realization is the goal posited for man, but infinite possibilities lie before the individual.

Thus, the self we find is a relation to its own self; in a sense, we at times speak of ourselves in the third person, "but in eternity, you are the individual, and conscience when it talks with you is no third person, any more than you are a third person when you talk of conscience. For you and conscience are one. It knows all that you know, and it knows that you know it . . . You relate yourself to yourself as an individual with eternal responsibility."(PH) These eternal responsibilities, coupled with a poignant conscience, one which arouses guilt with its concomitant dread, is at the root of all despair, and constitutes the 'sickness unto death.'

The Kierkegaardian concept of despair is such a unique thought, most beautifully expressed, that anything short of a verbatim quotation of it would cause it to lose its splendor, if not damage it critically; consequently, it is offered in S. K.'s own words:

Despair is "The Sickness unto Death."(SD)

The concept of the sickness unto death must be understood, however, in a peculiar sense. Literally it means a sickness the end and outcome of which is death. Thus one speaks of a mortal sickness as synonymous with a sickness unto death. In this sense despair cannot be called the sickness unto death. But in the Christian understanding of it death itself is a transition unto life. In view of this, there is from the Christian standpoint no earthly, bodily sickness unto death. For death is doubtless the last phase of the sickness, but death is not the last thing. If in the strictest sense we are to speak of a sickness unto death, it must be one in which the last thing is death and death the last thing. And this precisely is the despair.

Yet in another and still more definite sense despair is the sickness unto death. It is indeed very far from being true that, literally understood, one dies of this sickness, or that this sickness ends with bodily death. On the contrary, the torment of despair is precisely this, not to be able to die. So it has much in common with the situation of the moribund when he lies and struggles with death, and cannot die. So to be sick unto death is, not to be able to die – yet not as though there were hope of life; no, the hopelessness in this case is that even the last hope, death, is not available. When death is the greatest danger, one hopes for life; but when one becomes acquainted with an even more dreadful danger, one hopes for death. So when the danger is so great that death has becomes one's hope, despair is the disconsolateness of not being able to die.

It is in this last sense that despair is the sickness unto death, this agonizing contradiction, this sickness in the self, everlastingly to die, to die and yet not to die, to die the death. For dying means that it is all over, but dying the death means to live to experience death; and if for a single instant this experience is possible, it is tantamount to experiencing it forever. If one might die of despair as one dies of a sickness, then the eternal in him, the self, must be capable of dying in the same sense that the body dies of sickness. But this is an impossibility; the dying of despair transforms itself into a living. The despairing man cannot die; no more than "the dagger can slay thoughts" can despair consume the eternal thing, the self, which is the ground of despair, whose worm dieth not, and whose fire is not quenched. Yet despair is precisely *self*-consuming, but it is an impotent self-consumption which is not able to do what it wills; and this impotence is a new form of self-consumption, in which again, however, the despairer is not able to do what he wills, namely, to consume himself. This is despair raised to a higher potency, or it is the law for the potentiation. This is the hot incitement, or the cold fire in despair, the gnawing canker whose movement is constantly inward, deeper and deeper, in impotent self-consumption. The fact that despair does not consume him is so far from being any comfort to the despairing man that it is precisely the opposite, this comfort is precisely the torment, it is precisely this that keeps the gnawing pain alive and keeps life in the pain. This precisely is the reason why he despairs — not to say despaired — because he cannot consume himself, cannot get rid of himself, cannot become nothing. This is the potentiated formula for despair, the rising of the fever in the sickness of the self.

A despairing man is in despair over something. So it seems for an instant, but only for an instant; that same instant the true despair manifests itself, or despair manifests itself in its true character. For in the fact that he despaired of something, he really despaired of himself, and now would be rid of himself . . .

To despair over oneself, in despair to will to be rid of oneself, is the formula for all despair . . .

Thus it is that despair, this sickness in the self, is the sickness unto death. The despairing man is mortally ill. In an entirely different sense than can appropriately be said of any disease, we may say that the sickness has attacked the noblest part; and yet the man cannot die. Death is not the last phase of the sickness, but death is continually the last. To be delivered from this sickness by death is an impossibility, for the sickness and its torment . . . and death consist in not being able to die.

This is the situation in despair. And however thoroughly it eludes the attention of the despairer, and however thoroughly the despairer may succeed (as in the case of that kind of despair which is characterized by unawareness of being in despair) in losing himself entirely, and losing himself in such a way that it is not noticed in the least — eternity nevertheless will make it manifest that his situation was despair, and it will so nail him to himself that the torment nevertheless remains that he cannot get rid of himself, and it becomes manifest that he was deluded in thinking that he succeeded. And thus it is eternity must act, because to have a self, to be a self, is the greatest concession made to man, but at the same time it is eternity's demand upon him.[1]

Despair is a universal characteristic, richly Christian to such an extent that he who has not experienced despair, or is not in despair, cannot possibly claim that designation for himself. Despair can be of major service to the individual who is consciously aware of the existence of his despair within; its import is decisive. "It is in this sense that consciousness is decisive. Generally speaking, consciousness, i.e. consciousness of self, is the decisive criterion of the self. The more consciousness, the more will, and the more will, the more self. A man who has no will at all is no self; the more will he has, the more consciousness of self he has also." (SD) Here, we obtain a deeper insight into the nature of self, a

[1] Sören Kierkegaard, *Sickness Unto Death,* tr. Walter Lowrie (Princeton: Princeton University Press, 1941). Reprinted from *Sickness Unto Death* by Sören Kierkegaard by permission of Princeton University Press.

self-conscious existence in which an individual's will operates decisively; in fact, the greater or more actively it functions, the more fully is the self realized, hence the explanation of the earlier definition of man as 'not yet a self.'

Despair need not be permanent and can be eradicated from the personality; actually, it is expunged from the individual who is in wholesome spiritual health. "Every human existence which supposedly has become or merely wills to become infinite is despair. For the self is a synthesis in which the finite is the limiting factor, and the infinite is the expanding factor. Infinitude's despair is therefore the fantastical, the limitless. The self is in sound health and free from despair only when, precisely by having been in despair, it is grounded transparently in God."(SD) To be transparent denotes an existence of complete spiritual or psychological nakedness, nakedness before God, self, and man; an existent individual who has hidden nothing from God, self, or man, is free from complexes and hides behind none; this is the individual who has successfully heeded the Socratic injunction: *Know thyself*. If a person fails in this respect, does not, or cannot recognize himself because of the many layers of complexes which encrust him and prevent his peering within, in losing this inwardness, he loses his own self. "The greatest danger, that of losing one's own self, may pass off quietly as if it were nothing; every other loss, that of an arm, a leg, five dollars, a wife, etc., is sure to be noticed."(SD) But if one pauses to look inward, to become self-conscious, he can discover the self, for "the self is a reflection, and imagination is reflection, it is the counterfeit presentment of the self, which is the possibility of the self."(SD) Though imagination is not a genuine self, but merely a feigned substitution, it can be the vehicle whereby possibilities are suggested to the self for its development.

One conclusive manner by which to lose your very self is to become one with the crowd, and unless a person exercises caution he will be seduced into becoming one with the crowd, for the temptation is great, "particularly for one who does not dare to believe in himself, finds it too venturesome a thing to be himself, far easier and safer to be like the others, to become an imitation, a number, a cipher in the crowd."(SD) Many material advantages are to be gained by siding with the crowd, but the cost is great—the loss of self!

The *self* is an achievement, a fulfillment of possibilities; in the accomplishment or realization of this potential, man gains unity, that is, a self; actually, that is not the case with most persons, for they have been unable to realize their selves. The fact is that existential man is at variance with himself, a split personality, a disunity composed of disjointed pieces as in a mosaic, irrationally existential. This disruption of human nature is caused by corruption owing to *despair* (when speaking as a psychologist), but religiously speaking, it is what the Church designates *sin.* Despair is sin. "Sin is this: *before God, or with the conception of God, to be in despair at not willing to be oneself, or in despair at willing to be oneself.* Thus sin is potentiated weakness or potentiated defiance: sin is the potentiation of despair."(SD) If despair is sin, and it has affected and infected every person, then the only remedy is Christianity which offers the cure from sin.

S. K. notes that "the consciousness of sin is the *conditio sine qua non* of Christianity;"(J) if it were not for sin, Christianity would be obsolete. A person can readily detect conviction of sin by analyzing himself for its symptoms of despair; they are: (1) unwillingness to be himself, (2) willing despairingly to be himself, (3) being in a state of despair, unconscious of having a self, and an eternal self, (4) tearing himself away from the power which constituted the self. All of the foregoing are symptomatic of sin or, which is the same, despair, the remedy of which is the opposite — *faith.* It is interesting to note that the opposite of sin is not *virtue,* but faith; also, the opposite of despair is not *optimism* or hope, but faith.

Sin is despair, but faith is "the self in being itself and in willing to be itself grounded transparently in God. But too often it has been overlooked that the opposite of sin is not virtue, not by any manner or means. This is in part a pagan view which is content with a merely human measure and properly does not know what *sin* is, that all sin is before God. No, *the opposite of sin is faith* . . . And for the whole of Christianity it is one of the most decisive definitions that the opposite of sin is not virtue but faith."(SD) Thus we have our opposites: sin/faith' despair/ faith; paradoxical it is, but truth is paradox from the viewpoint of us who are 'earthbound;' only God, or those who can peer at truth from the side of eternity can see it rationally, (which it is in reality, but not existentially).

Despair vanishes only by self-identity, the willingness to accept oneself, and this is effected by faith, the antinomy of despair. " 'By relating itself to itself, the self is grounded transparently in the Power which constituted it.' And this formula again, as has often been noted, is the definition of faith."(SD)

Faith is an integral aspect of the Kierkegaardian criterion of truth: truth is inwardness, subjectivity is truth, truth is arrived at by intense feeling, passion; but faith is both inwardness and *passion.* It is important to appreciate faith understood as passion in order to grasp the full significance of Kierkegaardian inwardness, subjectivity, passion, etc., as the criteria of truth. One reason for the vital necessity of faith is that eternal truth assumes the form of a paradox to the existential individual, and it must be grasped, understood, appreciated by faith, for it does not cohere in a *rational* system objectively. "When the eternal truth is related to an existing individual, it becomes a paradox. The paradox repels in the inwardness of the existing individual, through the objective uncertainty . . . But since the paradox is not in the first instance itself paradoxical (but only in its relationship to the existing individual), it does not repel with a sufficient intensive inwardness. For without risk there is no faith, and the greater the risk, the greater the faith; the more objective security, the less inwardness (for inwardness is precisely subjectivity), and the less objective security, the more profound the possible inwardness. When the paradox is paradoxical in itself, it repels the individual by virtue of its absurdity, and the corresponding passion of inwardness is faith. But subjectivity, inwardness, is the truth . . . But there can be no stronger expression for inwardness than when the retreat out of existence into the eternal by way of recollection is impossible: when, with truth confronting the individual as a paradox, gripped in the anguish and pain of sin, facing the tremendous risk of the objective insecurity, the individual believes. But without risk no faith."(CP) Objective systems, reasons, cannot issue certainty; reason is an inappropriate road to certainty, for it offers only paradoxes, doubts, mental discomposure, because objectivity is absurd, paradoxical in nature. "When Socrates believed that there was a God, he held fast to the objective uncertainty with the whole passion of his inwardness, and it is precisely in this contradiction and in this risk, that faith is rooted. Now it is otherwise. Instead of the objective uncertainty, there is here a certainty, namely, that objectively it is absurd; and this absurdity, held fast in the passion of inwardness, is faith."(CP) These seeming paradoxes hold true for the reason that *subjectivity is true;* viewed from the standpoint of objectivity, inward truths are paradoxical, but seen from the standpoint of subjectivity with the criteria of inwardness, intense feeling, faith, passion, they are quite acceptable, and grant the individual an inward sense of certainty, vanquishing all doubt and despair.

Self-Realization Ethics.[1]

The highlights of the 'dialectical' ethics of Kierkegaard are: (1) an ethics of Pessimism; (2) the preference of suffering over sin; (3) man, an egoist by nature, regenerated through despair; (4) Self-Realizationism, *i.e.*, the transformation of potentialities into actualities; (5) three stages of the ethical dialectic: (a) aesthetic, (b) ethical, and (c) reli-

[1] Adapted from William S. Sahakian, *Systems of Ethics and Value Theory* (New York: Philosophical Library Inc., 1963), 294.

gious; (6) life confronts a person with an either/or choice from which there is neither escape nor evasion (both/and is the way to hell); (7) purity of heart is to will one thing, namely, the good in truth; (8) self-acceptance and the primacy of will.

The moral sphere of existence is *inwardness*, the realm where in passionate intensity, the individual in freedom makes 'the choice.' Moral truth, as well as all other truth is subjectivity, the region in which existent man acts decisively; inward decisive actions produce their overt concomitant consequences. Ethics is primarily one of self-realization, the developing of an inner self, for "a self, every instant it exists, is in process of becoming, for the self, *kata dunamin*, does not exactly exist, it is only that which it is to become."(SD) Development of the individual transpires before God in full transparency; "to know that one exists before God, and not go mad or be brought to naught," demands *courage to exist*. Man must be transparent both to himself and others; "one becomes the normal man by becoming stark naked,"(EO) that is to say, an individual must 'know himself' in the Socratic sense. He must go beyond the Socratic injunction, 'know thyself' which is pure self-consciousness, to 'choose his self,' that is, to have "a reflection about oneself which is itself an action, and therefore I have purposely used the expression 'choose yourself' instead of 'know yourself.'"(EO) "Subjectivity in all its fulness, and inwardness in all its infinite richness, can just as truly be indicated by the words 'know yourself'."[1]

The moral life of self-realization progresses along three stages: (a) the aesthetic, (b) the ethical, and (c) the religious. Each of these three stages of existence is, in a sense, an avenue men trod hoping to gain self-realization; persons do not necessarily proceed from the aesthetic to ethical to religious respectively; they may remain within a single channel, such as the aesthetic, desirous of attaining self-realization herein solely, while others may attempt both the aesthetic and ethical concurrently, but this latter effort inevitably proves futile. S. K. was wroth with those who adulterated, by admixture, two avenues (those who sought to trod both roads.) Concerning this situation, he writes: "For what is either/or, if I am to say it, who surely must know? Either/or is the word before which the folding doors fly open and the ideals appear — O blissful sight! Either/or is the token which insures entrance into the unconditional — God be praised! Yea, either/or is the key to heaven! On the other hand, what is, was, and continues to be man's misfortune? It is 'to a certain degree,' the invention of Satan or of paltriness or of cowardly shrewdness . . . This thing of 'to a certain degree' is theatrical, it grasps an

[1] Sören Kierkegaard, *Concept of Irony*, in T. H. Croxall, *Kierkegaard Commentary* (New York: Harper and Brothers, 1956), 22.

illusion . . . What is in God's service is either/or . . . I who am called 'Either/Or' cannot be at the service of anybody with both-and."(IN) Then he adds, the New Testament "inspires me with an indescribable horror of both-and."(IN) He adds elsewhere, "Both-and is the way to hell."

Man may find his self-realization in either path (aesthetic or ethical); he cannot embrace both successfully. "My friend, What I have so often said to you I say now once again, or rather I shout it: Either/or, *aut/ aut.*"(EO) This absolute disjunctive choice is followed up with Kierkegaardian pessimism, since his Existentialism regards either choice a vain endeavor, for he writes: "Yes, I perceive perfectly there are two possibilities, one can either do this or that. My sincere opinion and my friendly counsel is as follows: Do it/or don't do it – you will regret both."(EO) Each decision is a risk, and fraught with uncertainty, but the individual must decide, alone and for himself.

What is precisely the nature of the two 'disjunctive conjunctive' choices? The aesthetic life is chiefly composed of *Eudaemonism,* physical well-being and happiness, or *Hedonism,* the pursuit of pleasure and physical satisfaction; the ethical life is dominated by *remorse,* pathos, and the repudiation of pleasure. "The ethicist is not decked out with a superior dialectical skill; on the contrary, the estheticist appears to be unquestionably the more brilliant mind . . . Hence it becomes clearer precisely in what the ethicist differs from the estheticist, namely in the quality of his pathos, and in his more calm and secure assurance with respect to the problems of life; a moral and existential superiority is not confused with a merely intellectual giftedness; the choice offered becomes a choice of character, not of brains." [1] Regardless of which course a person chooses in life, he will never be completely free of elements of the other; as for S. K., he does not commit himself to a preference, declaring which of the two is superior, but rests that matter with the reader who must choose, and choose decisively!

Although Kierkegaard's classic work, *Either/Or,* is concerned only with the aesthetic and ethical lives, with a volume devoted to each, the highest stage of existence is the religious, which, while it 'dethrones' the aesthetic life, it does not abolish it completely. As to the religious stage displacing the ethical life as well, this could hardly be the case since the two are neither antithetical nor even conflicting in any serious manner.

The religious mode of existence consists of *purity of heart,* the sole object of an individual's will; it constitutes the superior form of existence, superseding both the aesthetic and ethical in stability and value. At the

[1] David Swenson, Introduction to *Philosophical Fragments* (Princeton: Princeton University Press, 1936), xvi–xvii.

religious stage of life, an individual achieves purity of heart, simplicity of soul, unalloyed with impure motives. "Purity of heart is to will one thing, viz., the will of the good in truth, i.e., one's choice must be in simplicity, with singlemindedness and without dissimulation of spirit. Purity of heart is assisted by 'eternity's emissaries to man,' viz., remorse, repentence, and confession, but one may encounter deterrents such as double-mindedness, enticement, *e.g.*, reward, discouragement provoked by illness, intimidation, *e.g.*, punishment, and other ulterior motives. The manifold cost of willing one thing is complete commitment and loyalty to the service of the good, sacrificial suffering without evasiveness. The task of him who would will only one thing is attentiveness to duty, living as an individual, the search and pursuit of one's occupation and calling, and assuming a right relationship with God." [1]

2. Jean-Paul Sartre — Atheistic Existentialism

Humanistic Existentialism.

Jean-Paul Sartre (1905-   ) is an Atheistic Existentialist who occasionally refers to his system as Humanism; in fact, he wrote a book, *Existentialism Is a Humanism.* He regularly professes his Atheistic stand and posits reasons for his preference; he writes: "Atheistic existentialism, which I represent, is more coherent. It states that if God does not exist, there is at least one being in whom existence precedes essence, a being who exists before he can be defined by any concept, and that this being is man, or, as Heidegger says, human reality." [2] Existentialism is Humanistic because it never exceeds the bounds of the human situation; whatever is discussed relates to human life; "by existentialism we mean a doctrine which makes human life possible and, in addition, declares that every truth and every action implies a human setting and human subjectivity." Existentialism, therefore, is Humanism, or a form of Humanism, but this unequivocally does not mean Naturalism, for Naturalism can imply the law and behavior of the jungle, whereas Existentialism is pregnant with human concern.

Furthermore, Existentialism is Humanistic in the sense that individual subjects alone exist, not just myself alone, but you and a society of social existents (subjects); beyond existent persons, nothing remains. "There is no universe other than a human universe, the universe of human sub-

[1] William Sahakian, *Systems of Ethics and Value Theory, op. cit.,* 303.

[2] Unless otherwise indicated, quotations in this section pertaining to Jean-Paul Sartre are from *Existentialism,* tr. Bernard Frechtman (New York: Philosophical Library, Inc., 1947).

jectivity. This connection between transcendency, as a constituent element of man . . . and subjectivity, in the sense that man is not closed in on himself but is always present in a human universe, is what we call existentialist humanism. Humanism, because we remind man that there is no law-maker other than himself, and that in his forlornness he will decide by himself; because we point out that man will fulfill himself as man, not in turning toward himself, but in seeking outside of himself a goal which is just this liberation, just this particular fulfillment." Thus Existentialism is Humanistic in that God is eliminated from the picture, and man stands alone without assistance of any kind except that which he is able to furnish for himself. The fact that God does not exist is most distressing, and creates a most demanding state of affairs on the Atheist who must shoulder his responsibilities alone, but even if God did exist, that fact would not change matters since man's existential situation and responsibility would remain the same. In such a state of abandonment, man experiences a deep sense of forlornness, anguish, nausea, or despair in complete isolation.

The main tenets of Sartre's Existentialism are: (1) existence precedes essence; (2) subjectivity is the starting point of all philosophizing; (3) a person in his solitariness must confront a universe devoid of purpose; (4) one is personally responsible for his actions, and for what he makes of himself; (5) external to individual persons, no values exist; (6) no purpose exists for human nature to fulfill, since there is no given human nature; (7) man, by his choices, creates himself, consequently, he can make whatever type of person of himself that he chooses; (8) man chooses the values which go to make up his personality; (9) the essence of man is subjectivity, freedom, and anguish; (10) man's engagement, that is, he is committed to action, to life, to involvement in social and personal circumstances.

Existentialism Defined.

Sartrean Existentialism may be defined as: *existence precedes essence.* The significance of this dictum is penetrating; not only does it grant priority of existence over essence in time, in importance, and in reality, but if any essence there be, it was created by existence. Moreover, it connotes that human nature is a product of a person's existence, that is to say, at birth man lacks that which is called human nature (essence). There is, and was, no mold into which man was poured which gives him a nature, a type or constitution which psychologists may describe and classify. Man creates himself; what he is, he himself made. Sartre queries rhetorically: "What is meant here by saying that existence precedes essence? It means that, first of all, man exists, turns up, appears on the scene, and, only afterwards, *defines himself.* If man, as the existentialist conceives him, is indefinable, it is because at first he is nothing. Only afterwards will he be something, and he himself will have made what he will be. Thus, *there is no human nature,* since there is no God to conceive it. Not only is man what he conceives himself to be, but *he is also only what he wills himself to be* after this thrust toward existence. *Man is nothing else but what he makes of himself.* Such is the first principle of existentialism." Thus we find that human nature does not exist; what is describable as human nature is that into which a man developed himself by his own initiative, whether for good or bad. If man does have any essence, it is what was manufactured by his bare existence through the instrument of his will. Every man is self-made, you are what you decided for yourself. An abstract nature, an essence which is independent of, or prior to, man's existence simply does not exist, nor does a general human condition exist.

Will, Responsibility, and Subjectivity.

The inner world of man is of major significance to the Existentialist, for this basically is his world of reality, inner subjective experiences. Subjectivity is real, and the truth is subjectivity; whatever essence exists is subjective. Man making himself the being he is, is what Sartre means by *subjectivity;* this assertion constitutes part of his first principle of Existentialism. Subjectivity is "the name we are labeled with when charges are brought against us. But what do we mean by this, if not that man has greater dignity than a stone or table? For we mean that *man first exists,* that is, that man first of all is the being who hurls himself toward a future and who is conscious of imagining himself as being in the future. Man is at the start a plan which is aware of itself, rather than a patch of moss, a piece of garbage, or a cauliflower; *nothing exists prior to this plan*; there is nothing in heaven; *man will be what he will have planned to be.* Not what he will want to be. Because *by the word 'will' we generally mean a conscious decision,* which is subsequent to what we have already made of ourselves. I may want to belong to a political party, write a book, get married; but all that is only a manifestation of an earlier, more spontaneous choice that is called 'will.' But if *existence really does precede essence, man is responsible for what he is.* Thus, existentialism's first move is to make man aware of what he is and to make the full responsibility of his existence rest upon him. And when we say that a *man is responsible for himself,* we do not only mean that he is responsible for his own individuality, but that *he is responsible for all men.*" Man's choices affect everyone, he not only makes himself, he makes the world which is always in the making; never is there anything static regarding existence.

Man's responsibility is binding both upon himself and upon all mankind; his choices regularly affect others as well as himself, if for no other reason, then for the fact that he continuously lives in a society. Man not only creates his own image, but the entire age in which he lives; his particular epoch is his individual responsibility. If *"existence precedes essence,* and if we grant that we exist and fashion our image at one and the same time, the image is valid for everybody and for our whole age. Thus, our responsibility is much greater than we might have supposed, because it involves all mankind. If I am a workingman and choose to join a Christian trade-union rather than be a communist, and if by being a member I want to show that the best thing for man is resignation, that the kingdom of man is not of this world, I am not only involving my own case — I want to be resigned for everyone. As a result, my action has involved all humanity. To take a more individual matter, if I want to marry, to have children, even if this marriage depends solely on my own circumstances or passion or wish, I am involving all humanity in monogamy and not merely myself. *I am responsible for myself and for everyone else. I am creating a certain image of man of my own choosing. In choosing myself, I choose man."* Consequently, since man does not live alone, he is his brother's keeper; not because he is a social being, but because his actions involve others as well as himself.

Subjectivism possesses a dual connotation in Existentialist philosophy, and Existentialists are often criticized for it; one connotation is integrally basic to its system, the other ancillary. "Subjectivism means, on the one hand, that *an individual chooses and makes himself;* and, on the other, that *it is impossible for man to transcend human subjectivity.* The second of this is the essential meaning of existentialism. When we say that *man chooses his own self,* we mean that every one of us does likewise; but we also mean by that that *in making this choice he also chooses all men.* In fact, in creating the man that we want to be, there is not a single one of our acts which does not at the same time create an image of man as we think he ought to be. *To choose to be this or that is to affirm at the same time the value of what we choose,* because *we never choose evil. We always choose the good,* and *nothing can be good for us without being good for all."* For precisely this reason, namely that our choices more than affect us indelibly, they have a permanent effect on others; moreover, their consequences may continue indefinitely, so that the mere thought of being a person wielding power with such devastating potential, casts us in anguish.

Anguish, Abandonment, and Despair.

We dread the thought of being persons, for we as individuals must make choices, not as a group wherein we may hide, huddle together, or shift responsibility from one to another — or even share responsibility. "When we speak of forlornness, a term Heidegger was fond of, we mean only that God does not exist and that we have to face all the consequences of this." The state in which we find ourselves is as if God deserted us — his nonexistence is equivalent to desertion, abandonment.

I, alone in my human subjectivity, must make these everlasting choices which affect everyone; I must do it alone, and shoulder the responsibility as an isolated solitary individual. Consequently, I am cast into anguish, forlornness, despair, for no one can help; I have been completely abandoned, I remain alone within my subjective self — and then choose. I am left alone, without even God to help. "This helps us understand . . . the actual content of such rather grandiloquent words as anguish, forlornness, despair . . . First, what is meant by anguish? The existentialists say at once that *man is anguish.* What that means is this: *the man who involves himself and who realizes that he is not only the person he chooses to be, but also a law-maker who is, at the same time, choosing all mankind as well as himself, can not help escape the feeling of his total and deep responsibility.* Of course, there are many people who are not anxious; but we claim that they are hiding their anxiety, that they are fleeing from it. Certainly, many people believe that when they do something, they themselves are the only ones involved, and when someone says to them, 'What if everyone acted that way?' they shrug their shoulders and answer, 'Everyone doesn't act that way.' But really, one should always ask himself, 'What would happen if everybody looked at things that way?' There is no escaping this disturbing thought except by a kind of double-dealing. A man who lies and makes excuses for himself by saying 'not everybody does that,' is someone with an uneasy conscience, because *the act of lying implies that a universal value is conferred upon the lie.*" The immoral man is either fooling himself with a mask of complexes or else he must stand squarely and face anguish in guilt and remorse; the only other recourse is to choose aright. It is the horrifying thought of being confronted with the choice that is so terrifying; consequently, there is no escape from anguish — it is evident under any garb of concealment.

The substance of which man is composed, assuming that he has a substance, is *anguish.* Sartre writes in *Being and Nothingness*s "It is certain that we can not overcome anguish, for we are anguish." Consequently, we can neither hide from it nor avoid it; a feeble and vain attempt to fight it is the most that can be done; or else to mask it. How is it possible under the stress and demand of this life in which we have involved everyone else with us to escape anguish. "For every man, everything happens as if all mankind had its eyes fixed on him and were guiding itself by what he does. And every man ought to say to himself, 'Am I really the kind of man who has the right to act in such a way that humanity might guide itself by my actions?' And if he does not say that to himself, he is masking his anguish." A sense of deep responsibility or the state of anguish can create a feeling of nausea; in fact, existence is *nausea.*

Man as Freedom and Futurity — the Concept of Involvement.

If man had an essence, it would be *freedom,* but man lacks a nature, he is without a constitution — he consists of freedom; "man is free and . . . there is no human nature for me." This freedom of which man is composed is directly responsible for making him whatever character he happens to be; man freely decides what he shall be. He never really is, he is continually in the making of himself as an artist who freely creates a picture according to his own will and choosing. Man is devoid of any human nature which he may fulfill, he makes himself, or as the Existentialist would say, chooses himself as he goes through life. "There is no reality except in action . . . Man is nothing else than his plan; he exists only to the extent that he fulfills himself; he is therefore nothing else than the ensemble of his acts, nothing else than his life . . . A man is involved in life, leaves his impress on it, and outside of that there is nothing." Man is involved, involved in life; he *is* his life, existence; for example, no love exists except the act of being in love, no genius exists except the action of being a genius; this is entirely done by choice, man's freedom which is the essence of his existence. Consequently, the great man makes himself great, the coward makes himself cowardly, the hero heroic. Each man may choose to alter himself since his life is in the making, never made; the hero may by his actions choose at any time to become a coward, and the coward a hero. Existentialism "defines man in terms of action," it is not an "attempt to discourage man from acting, since it tells him that the only hope is in his acting and that action is the only thing that enables man to live. Consequently, we are dealing here with an ethics of action and involvement." In so doing, Existentialism imputes to man a dignity inasmuch as it does not reduce him to an object as do other philosophies, particularly Materialism.

Thus we find man, whose existence is *freedom,* choosing for himself what he will realize by an *involvement* with life and the universal '*human condition.*' Accordingly, it is not man's essence (being or substance) which gives him, or makes possible for him, an existence; *he is "an existence which chooses its essence.*" Choose, he must, for it is impossible to go through life without choosing and without accepting full responsibility for decisions. "Man is in an organized situation in which he himself is involved. Through his choice, he involves all mankind, and he can not avoid making a choice . . . Man makes himself. He isn't ready made at the start. In choosing his ethics, he makes himself, and force of circumstances is such that he can not abstain from choosing one. We define man only in relationship to involvement." By involvement is meant man's obligation to assume moral responsibilities in life, individual and social. He must enter his human condition, the situation which confronts him, and the social scene in which he participates, makes decisions, and takes sides — he must 'stand up and be counted.'

Man's moral responsibility is weight, so heavy as to incur *nausea;* alone, forlorn, and abandoned by God, or at least without God owing to Sartre's Atheism, man must order his life on his own initiative and responsibility by making his own free choices, for this is the nature of his substance (provided he had one). "We have defined man's situation as a free choice, with no excuses and no recourse, every man who takes refuge behind the excuse of his passions, every man who sets up a determinism, is a dishonest man." Man cannot hide behind his passions, using them as an excuse for reprehensible behavior, because he is held responsible for choosing the type of man he is. Those who make excuses for their deleterious behavior are either 'cowards' or 'stinkers,' the former if they use determinism as their excuse for inability, and the latter if they resort to the argument that their existence was necessary, that is, they did not choose to exist (to be born).

Existent man is a creator of values; not only does he make himself, he defines and establishes values by virtue of his freedom. Since God does not exist, man must create values. "Life has no meaning *a priori.* Before you come alive, life is nothing; it's up to you to give it a meaning, and value is nothing else but the meaning you choose." Man's freedom is the basis of all values; he more than constructs values, he builds a human community.

Being and Nothingness.

Whether Sartre is an Idealist or Realist, it is difficult to say; logically, an Existentialist cannot be either, for he believes in an *existence without essence;* but when Sartre speaks of a *Being-in-itself,* the implication is an essence without, external to subjective existence, something corresponding to the Cartesian property which substance possesses, *extension;* and when at times Sartre discusses *Being-for-itself,* it correlates with Hegel's *Idee* (Thought).

In *Being and Nothingness* (1943), Sartre's classical work, he is definitely involved in metaphysical reality, attempting to resolve the ontological problem of the essence of reality. Being assumes two forms: (1) Being-in-itself *(Être-en-soi)*, the phenomenon which confronts man, nonconscious in nature; and (2) Being-for-itself *(Être-pour-soi)*, a consciousness without Being (essence), but with a desire for Being; since this consciousness possesses only existence but lacks Being, it is Nothingness (that which is devoid of Being yet supported by Being, and enters the world by the Being-for-itself). Apparently, for Sartre, two forms of Being exist, since these two Beings are characteristically opposed; postulating the existence of the former makes Sartre a Materialist; and the latter, an Idealist.

Consciousness is reduced to Nothingness when confronted with Being-in-itself, which is equivalent to saying that human existence is nothingness; man is nothing, man is without nature, possessing no essence. This Nothingness, called man, not satisfied with his existence, desiring essence or Being, strives toward being God. "The fundamental value which presides over this project is exactly the in-itself-for-itself; that is the ideal of consciousness which would be the foundation of its own being-in-itself by the pure consciousness which it would have of itself. It is this ideal which can be called God. Thus the best way to conceive of the fundamental project of human reality is to say that man is the being whose project is to be God . . . God, value and supreme end of transcendence, represents the permanent limit in terms of which man makes known to himself what he is. To be man means to reach toward being God. Or if you prefer, man fundamentally is the desire to be God . . . It appears here that the initial project of being God, which 'defines' man, comes close to being the same as a human 'nature' or an essence.'"[1] Sartre's metaphysics is ambiguous and paradoxical, but this need be no deterrent to him since he conceives of existence as both ambiguous and paradoxical.

Risking danger of oversimplification, it may be said that Being-for-itself is the human being, the existent person, while Being-in-itself is the external phenomenal world. The person *per se* is devoid of essence; his essence is what he *was*, not what he is; it constitutes his past. "Man continually carries with him a pre-judicative comprehension of his essence, but due to this very fact he is separated from it by a nothingness. Essence is all that human reality apprehends in itself as *having been* . . . Essence is what has been." The only *you* which can possibly exist is a 'has-been.'

[1] Quotations in this section pertaining to *Being and Nothingness* are from Jean-Paul Sartre's book by the same title, translated by Hazel E. Barnes (New York: Philosophical Library Inc., 1956).

Keeping in mind that God does not exist, consequently no intelligent Cosmic Mind either planned or created the world; it is, it exists for no reason at all; accordingly, facts do not permit of an explanation, things happen to be as we find them without 'rhyme or reason.' "Uncreated, without reason for being, without any connection with another being, Being-in-itself is *de trop* for eternity. Being is. Being is in-itself. Being is what it is. There are three characteristics which the preliminary examination of the phenomenon of being allows us to assign to the being of phenomena." If any ontological reality exists, it is Being-in-itself.

A synthesis of Being-for-itself uniting with Being-in-itself is responsible for the world as we know it, a chaotic, disturbed, agitated existence. "The For-itself and the In-itself are reunited by a synthetic connection which is nothing other than the For-itself. The For-itself, in fact, is nothing but the pure nihilation of the In-itself; it is like a hole of Being at the heart of Being . . . The For-itself is like a tiny nihilation which has its origin at the heart of Being; and this nihilation is sufficient to cause a total upheaval to *happen* to the In-itself. *This upheaval is the world.*" This upheaval is analogous to an atomic blast which can demolish the world by the annihilation of a single atom which according to atomic physics is capable of disturbing the world to catastrophic proportions; the annihilation of Being-for-itself represents the annihilated atom. The only reality Being-for-itself possesses is the nihilation of Being.

3. Martin Heidegger — The Philosophy of Existence

Martin Heidegger (1889-) and his Existential philosophy have been a source of contention among his European colleagues; some praise him unrestrainedly, while others hold him in contempt. Georges Gurvitch regards him merely as a Nazi, "not an honest thinker, but an able constructor and calculator bereft of ethics and intellectual scruples;"[1] Logical Positivists ridicule his philosophy, especially elements such as, "Nothingness makes nought" *(das Nichts selbst nichtet);* while ardent admirers hold his philosophy in high respect, such as Emmanuel Levinas who in debate defended Heidegger saying: "We will come to realize that there is only one existentialist or philosopher of existence, and that this one and only existentialist is neither Kierkegaard, nor Nietzsche, nor Socrates, nor even — despite all the talent deployed — some one of the successors of Heidegger. The only existentialist is Heidegger himself. . . . Heidegger restored pathetic thoughts to the categories of the pro-

[1] John Wahl, *A Short History of Existentialism,* tr. Forrest Williams and Stanley Maron (New York: Philosophical Library, Inc., 1949), 38.

fessors."[2] Whatever Heidegger is, on one thing we may rely, he is widely read and discussed among philosophers, and will increase, if not in popularity, at least in being discussed and treated in philosophical literature. His philosophy may not be here to stay, but it is very much present at the moment, and cannot be ignored.

Heidegger is one of the most difficult philosophers to comprehend, especially for the philosophical novitiate. His *Being and Time* (1927), already regarded a philosophical classic, has assigned for itself the difficult question of the meaning of *Being*. The book is difficult reading even for professional Existentialist philosophers; the language employed is new or used with connotations which differ from general accepted usage; some very important ideas are vague, not only in Heidegger's verbal expression of them, but in his own mind, for they are not as yet completely or coherently worked out by him.

Summary of Heideggerian Existentialism.

Human existence, in the form of *Dasein,* is grounded in and dominated by anxiety, primarily for the reason that human existence is finite; man continually anticipates and must eventually experience death. Mortal man is the only Being cognizant of his existence, and by virtue of this fact, the only one with existence (Dazein); he is anxiety-laden owing to his mortality, finitude, and impending death, seeking 'salvation' in wisdom, that is, the acceptance of what is.

Philosophy is defined, not traditionally as the 'love of wisdom,' but as the *wisdom of love.* Such an acceptance by Dasein (the human being) of his existent mortal situation, renders man truly authentic, which is to say, reveals oneself as his self, as he truly is. To be authentic is to be true, to reveal Being as it is in truth; otherwise, inauthenticity will disguise a person's reality and essence from himself, rendering him incapable of revealing reality as it truly is.

Dasein (man), destitute of God, religion, and metaphysical reality, flung into the world as he finds it, perched on the abyss of Nothingness, experiences a sense of abandonment, anxiety, forlornness. Without any reason or explanation for it, man finds himself in the world, such as it is, and such as he is, knowing only that he lives for the end of dying (the state of Nothingness); consequently, this paralyzes and limits both his possibilities and future, despite the fact that he is a *'being-for-the-future.'* Desiring immortality, when there is none to be had, is man's agonizing situation. Knowing this to be his precarious situation, his life subject at any moment to forfeiture, his existence is continuously undergirded with anxiety, anguish, and forlornness.

[2] *Ibid.,* 48–49.

Phenomenological Method.

Heidegger and Sartre both claim that their entire approach has been a Phenomenological one; in fact, Sartre subtitles his *Being and Nothingness, An Essay on Phenomenological Ontology,* while Heidegger dedicates his *Being and Time* to the outstanding Phenomenologist, Edmund Husserl. The Phenomenological method of investigation, and for Heidegger it remains a method only, not a philosophy, treats 'things themselves.' As a method, it restricts itself to the task of delineating the *how* of research, not *what* objects are to be involved in research. It is a method which leads one to *things themselves,* or "the way we come to terms with the things themselves;"[1] and as such, it is not a technical device. "Thus the term 'phenomenology' expresses a maxim which can be formulated as '*To the things themselves!*' It is opposed to all free-floating constructions and accidental findings; it is opposed to taking over any conceptions which only seem to have been demonstrated; it is opposed to those pseudo-questions which parade themselves as 'problems'. . . . Yet this maxim, one may rejoin, is abundantly self-evident, and it expresses, moreover, the underlying principle of any scientific knowledge whatever." 'To the things themselves' is a byword or slogan for Husserl's Phenomenology; for Husserl it signifies *things* which words may be found to identify, provided their significations are accurately intuited.

Being and Existence.

One of the most difficult concepts to grasp in Heidegger's philosophy is the concept of Being, a notion which entails a variety of meanings: (1) the Being of animals, (2) the Being of mathematical principles or forms, (3) the Being of tools and instruments, (4) the Being of things seen or scenes, (5) the Being of man. Although there are at least five forms of Being as indicated above, none of them with the exception of man *exists.*

Man alone exists, ("the substance of man is existence"), and through the existence which man possesses, Heidegger hopes to reach ultimate reality, the ontologically real. Human existence, which Heidegger terms *Dasein,* "is an entity whose Being has the determinate character of existence." Thus we see the reason Heidegger disclaims being an Exis-

[1] Except where indicated, quotations in this section devoted to Martin Heidegger are from his *Being and Time* (*Zein und Zeit,* 1927), translated by John Macquarrie and Edward Robinson (London: SCM Press, Ltd., 1962, and New York: Harper & Row, Publishers, Inc.). Quotations from his "On the Essence of Truth" and "What is Metaphysics?" will be abbreviated *Truth* and *Metaphysics* respectively; these latter two were translated by R. F. C. Hull and Alan Crick jointly; both were included along with other essays in a book entitled, *Existence and Being* (London: Vision Press Ltd., and Chicago: Henry Regnery Company, 1949).

tentialist, for he believes in an ontologically real Being, and *existence* directs us to it.

Nevertheless, Heidegger is an Existentialist; his Existentialism lies in his insistence that *Dasein* (human existence) is the origin from which our investigations begin, and Being must be approached from this orientation, for there is no other for man. Animals, vegetables, minerals, may be, but only persons exist; "the term 'existence', as a designation of Being, will be allotted solely to Dasein . . . The essence of *Dasein's 'essence' lies in its existence.*" Hence, it is in man's existence that he is *ontological* (real), whereas other Beings are merely *ontic* (factual). "I am myself the entity which we call Dasein . . . Dasein understands itself as Being-in-the-world . . . No matter how far removed from an ontological concept the distinction between existence and Reality may be, no matter even if Dasein proximately understands existence as Reality, Dasein is not just present-at-hand but has already *understood itself.*" This concept of Dasein (human existence) gives formal structure to human nature, thus freeing this philosophy from being designated Existentialism.

Nevertheless, respecting the two characteristics of Dasein, existence and essence, there maintains a "priority of *'existentia'* over *'essentia.'*" The character of Being possesses two possibilities, that of being *existentialia* or *categories,* that is, an entity is either a *who* or a *what;* if it is a 'who' then it possesses existence, but if it is a 'what,' it has *'presence-at-hand.'* "In determining itself as an entity, Dasein always does so in the light of a possibility which it *is* itself and which, in its very Being, it somehow understands. This is the formal meaning of Dasein's existential constitution. But this tells us that if we are to interpret this entity *ontologically,* the problematic of its Being must be developed from the existentiality of its existence. This cannot mean, however, that 'Dasein' is to be construed in terms of some concrete possible idea of existence. . . . Dasein should not be interpreted with the differentiated character *[Differenz]* of some definite way of existing, but that it should be uncovered *[aufgedeckt]* in the undifferentiated character which it has proximally and for the most part. This undifferentiated character of Dasein's everydayness is *not nothing,* but a positive phenomenal characteristic of this entity. Out of this kind of Being – and back into it again – is all existing, such as it is. We call this everyday undifferentiated character of Dasein *'averageness.'*" Dasein is personal, and must be referred to with personal pronouns; furthermore, Dasein has *authenticity,* or is *authentic,* when a person is true to himself, possesses *transparency,* that is, is not hiding behind complexes which disguise him or prevent his making choices truly indicative of himself.

Existence and Temporality.

Dasein (man's existence) was thrown into the world; he is an existent who *has* to exist; as finite being, his future is Nothingness, death. He is a *being for death,* lives and is born for this end; "*Being-towards-death* belongs to Dasein's Being . . . Being-towards-death is possible only as something *futural* . . . By the term 'futural,' we do not here have in view a 'now' which has *not yet* become 'actual' and which sometimes *will be* for the first time. We have in view the coming *[Kunft]* in which Dasein, in its ownmost potentiality-for-Being, comes towards itself. Anticipation makes Dasein *authentically* futural." Man, whose '*authentic temporality is the future,*' looks forward to the future, to death, since this is the inevitable end of finitude.

True existence differs from merely remaining in the realm of things-seen or things-used, it consists of living *authentically* in the domain of *existence.* A person may drift through or be carried by the currents of society, and thereby never truly leave the *everyday* world, the sphere of '*the anyone*' or '*the domain of Everyman.*' In this domain we lose ourselves in the crowd, and are unconscious of our own existence, until by the experience of anguish, we confront the Nothingness from which our Being, and all else, erupts. "Pure Being and pure Nothing are thus one and the same." [1]

Being as man must face it, is composed of *care* and *temporality;* care, because all that is afforded man is death, anguish, guilt, etc.; "the existential phenomena of death, conscience, and guilt are anchored in the phenomenon of care." Merely by existing, man 'takes over Being-guilty,' for this is his nature.

Existence and Nothingness.

Nothingness, the nature of reality, is the quest of the philosopher interested in metaphysics. Science ignores the study of *Nothing* by dismissing it as *that which is not,* but "we postulate Nothing as something that or other somehow 'is' — as an entity (*Seiendes*) . . . Nothing is the negation *(Verneinung)* of the totality of what-is: that which is absolutely not." [2] By dread (*Angst*), is not meant anxiety or fear, for the former relates to nervousness, and the latter to a rational fear *of* or *about* an object of which we are cognizant; by *dread* we mean an ill-defined threat from nowhere, emanating from the world, whereas anxiety *(Sorge)* is the Being of human existence. "In dread, as we say, 'one feels something uncanny.' What is this 'something' *(es)* and this 'one'? We are unable

[1] *Metaphysics.*
[2] *Metaphysics.*

to say what gives 'one' that uncanny feeling. 'One' just feels it generally *(im Ganzen)*. All things, and we with them, sink into a sort of indifference. But not in the sense that everything simply disappears; rather, in the very act of drawing away from us everything turns towards us. This withdrawal of what-is-in-totality, which then crowds round us in dread, this is what oppresses us. There is nothing to hold on to. The only thing that remains and overwhelms us whilst what-is slips away, is this 'nothing.' Dread reveals Nothing. In dread we are 'in suspense' . . . In the trepidation of this suspense where there is nothing to hold on to, pure *Da-sein* is all that remains. Dread strikes us dumb. Because what-is-in-totality slips away and thus forces Nothing to the fore . . . The fact that when we are caught in the uncanniness of dread we often try to break the empty silence by words spoken at random, one proves the presence of Nothing . . . We ourselves confirm that dread confirms Nothing – when we have got over our dread . . . What we were afraid of was 'authentic' Nothing. And indeed Nothing itself, Nothing as such, was there. With this key-mood of dread, therefore, we have reached that event in our *Da-sein* which reveals Nothing."[1] Thus, we discover the world to be constructed of Nothing, and it is to Nothingness that Dasein (a human being) has to look forward; a dreadful thought, to be sure, but it was precisely dread which revealed this truth to us, "'Nothing is revealed in dread.'"[2]

The very meaning of our existence is to be cast into Nothingness; "*Da-sein* means *being projected into* Nothing;"[3] the essence of this Nothingness is nihilation.

By the understanding, and to understand means to 'project;' we are able to *project* into Nothingness, thereby relating to it. "It is only through 'projecting into Nothing' that our *Da-sein* relates to what-is, in other words, has any existence, and if Nothing is only made manifest originally in dread, should we not have to be in a continual suspense of dread in order to exist at all?"[4] Not only is our existence saturated with dread and leads us to a world of Nothingness as reality, but we are *Beings-unto-death* who must look forward to death as the culmination of our existence; beyond death, there is neither God nor existence.

The Nature of Truth As Freedom.

Besides writing a classic book, *Being and Time* (1927), Heidegger wrote two very important and widely discussed essays (addresses,

[1] *Metaphysics.*
[2] *Metaphysics.*
[3] *Metaphysics.*
[4] *Metaphysics.*

lectures), or as they are sometimes called, 'tracts,' entitled: (1) "What is Metaphysics?" (1929), and (2) "On the Essence of Truth" (1930). The former two writings having been discussed, it remains now to treat "On the Essence of Truth."

Heidegger declares the essence of truth to be *freedom,* not traditional concepts of truth, such as: (a) the true is the real, (b) a statement is true when what it means and says agrees with the thing of which it speaks, (c) correspondence of a thing with the idea of it, (d) truth is the approximation of perception to thing (object). Rather, "*the essence of truth is freedom* . . . Freedom is the *essence* of truth itself. 'Essence' is understood here as the basis of the inner possibility of whatever is accepted in the first place and generally admitted as 'known.'"[1]

By the essence of truth is meant the rightness of a statement, namely, *freedom,* which must appear strange to us; but freedom is not to be construed as caprice, license, doing what one pleases, though "truth is brought down to the subjective level of the human subject. Even if this subject can attain to some kind of objectivity, it still remains human in its subjectivity and subject to human control."

Truth as *rightness* requires freedom, for "freedom is the basis of the inner possibility of rightness only because it receives its own essence from that thing of earlier origin: the uniquely essential truth." Freedom is defined as "freedom to reveal something overt lets whatever 'is' at the moment *be* what it is. Freedom reveals itself as the 'letting-be' of what-is. . . . 'We let it be' means: not touching it again, not having anything more to do with it. 'Letting be' here has the negative sense of disregarding something, renouncing something, of indifference and even neglect."

The Greek for truth, *aletheia,* may be translated 'unconcealment' or 'revealment;' freedom is the *letting-be* of truth pour forth. "In this manner 'letting-be' exposes itself *(setzt sich aus)* to what-is-as-such and brings all behaviour into the open *(versetzt ins Offene).* 'Letting-be,' i.e. freedom, is in its own self 'ex-posing' *(aus-setzend)* and 'ex-sistent' *(ek-sistent).*" In this light, freedom related to truth is an 'exposition' of "the revealed nature of what-is . . . Freedom is a participation in the revealment of what-is-as-such . . . Freedom, so understood as the letting-be of what-is, fulfills and perfects the nature of truth in the sense that truth is the unconcealment and revealment of what-is . . . a revelation through which something 'overt' comes into force. All human behaviour is an exposition into that overtness. Hence man *is* in virtue of his ex-istence . . . Ex-istent freedom, being the essence of truth, is not a property of man . . . it being

[1] Unless otherwise noted, quotations in this section: "The Nature of Truth as Freedom" are from Heidegger's "On the Essence of Truth," *op. cit.*

rather the case that man only ex-ists as the property of this freedom." In this way man becomes historical man, capable of history, whereas nature has no history.

In conclusion, we may say that the essence of truth is revealed as freedom, since freedom is the very participation of the revealment of truth, of *what-is-in-totality,* whereas untruth is concealment, *dis-essence,* or that which precedes essence. Untruth is error, an element inherent in the human structure. "Man errs. He does not merely fall into error, he lives in error . . . Error is part of the inner structure of *Da-sein,* in which historical man is involved." Radical as this view respecting truth is, namely, the essence of truth as freedom, Heidegger regards it as far superior to traditional philosophical thinking which fails to consider the *essence of truth,* but rather considers *truth of essence,* and conceives of essence as Being, *what-is-in-totality.*

4. Evaluation of Existentialism

Most persons will concede that Existentialists have provided us with a new emphasis in philosophy, not that what they offer is new, but its stress, its elaborations, and its manifold ramifications, unquestionably are. Existentialists have opened or re-opened a new world within, subjective existence which has scarcely been treated by philosophers since Socrates; moreover, they have brought to focus once again the needed emphasis upon individual responsibility and freedom, which was becoming rapidly forgotten in a world which was relegating moral responsibility to the realm of pseudo-factuality. Furthermore their stress on the role which 'possibility' plays in the life of man is more than challenging; it is an encouraging thought which should inevitably lead to optimism, despite the pessimistic outlook and conclusions of the Existentialist. How can a person be other than optimistic with the thought that his life is laden with numerous possibilities to which he has direct access and control by individual choice! To ask for more would be to place heaven beneath earthly existence.

Looking at the other side of the ledger, we find some serious difficulties inherent in Existentialism, chief among which is the obvious repudiation of reason, despite the assertion to the contrary by a number of persons sympathetic to this philosophy. The critic of reason may justifiably indicate the limitations of reason, but to take 'the leap' to the extent of denying it any validity, by assuming that all truth is reducible to subjectivity, is intellectual suicide as well as the annihilation of every philosophical system including Existentialism. The critic of reason invariably places himself in the delicate and logically embarrassing position of having disproved the validity of reason by an appeal to reason as criterion. To assert that reason is not a valid test of truth makes it incumbent upon the person claiming such to prove his case; either he must effect this by employing reason, or he must appeal to a nonrational or irrational criterion of truth, which of course is absurdity. Consequently, a person is obligated to accept reason or a rational criterion of truth to prove his own position, and must do so even to attack reason if he is so inclined. But what he may not do without intellectual suicide is to deny its validity. Accordingly, every philosophy, including Existentialism, the philosophy of Irrationalism, cannot dispense with reason without self-destruction.

A second serious stricture which Existentialists will have to take notice of, and modify their philosophy accordingly, is the overemphasis on pessimistic elements of existence. Granted there are decidedly unpleasant existential facts confronting every individual, but to relegate a disproportionate place of importance to them, to the extent of rendering every other existential fact out of perspective, is to treat facts of existence in a seriously biased manner which will never allow legitimate conclusions. The point which we wish to stress here is that *hope, confidence, optimism*, etc. are existentially factual and existentially valid as dread, despair, abandonment, and other concepts emphasised by Existentialists, if not decidedly more so; at least more persons live and succeed in life more by hope and confidence than by despair and abandonment.

Existential literature too regularly gives the reader the feeling that the author is living and observing the world with glasses coated with gloom, rendering him incapable of seeing it in any other light. To appreciate Existentialism, it almost appears that a person would have to have a heavy dose of depression, otherwise he will find it most difficult to make Existential philosophy cohere with his delightful experiences of life, or even his common everyday experiences. As one critic expressed it, 'Has the Existentialist never looked into the infant's smiling face?'

At times it is true of Sartre, but typical and emphatically true of Heidegger, that death and 'Nothingness' are of paramount importance; in fact, Heidegger regards us as *Beings-flung-towards-death (Zum Tode Sein)*, but to be destined for death, or even to be delivered up to its clutches, ignores the fact that life is laden with values: moral, human, cultural, religious, scientific, aesthetic, etc.

Part Seven: PHILOSOPHERS: IN OUTLINE

PHILOSOPHERS: IN OUTLINE[1]

(Arranged Chronologically according to Schools of Philosophical Thought)

Outline of Ancient Philosophy

I. THE PROBLEM OF MATTER: THE IONIAN PHYSICISTS (600–528 B.C.)

A. Thales (624–546). Eclipse, 585. Miletus.
B. Anaximander (610–546). Miletus submits to Persia, 546.
C. Anaximenes (585–528).

II. THE PROBLEM OF NUMBER: THE PYTHAGOREANS (500 on)

A. Pythagoras of Samos (c. 580–497). Croton.
B. Philolaus (Contemporary of Socrates). Thebes.

III. THE PROBLEM OF IDENTITY AND CHANGE (540–370)

A. *Thesis*. All is one: The Eleatics. (of Elea).
  1. Xenophanes, "The theological Eleatic" (c. 570–475).
  2. Parmenides, "The metaphysical Eleatic" (c. 540–470).
  3. Zeno, "The dialectical Eleatic" (c. 490–430).
  4. Melissus.
B. *Antithesis*. All is change: Heraclitus of Ephesus (c. 544–484).
C. *Synthesis*. Being is both Identity and Change: The Mediating Systems (470–370).
  1. Empedocles (495–435). Agrigentum, Sicily.
  2. Anaxagoras of Clazomene (499–428). Athens.
  3. The Atomists:
    a. Leucippus of Abdera (5th century).
    b. Democritus of Abdera (460–370).

IV. THE PROBLEM OF MAN (450–400)

A. The Sophists.
  1. Protagoras of Abdera (481–411).
  2. Gorgias (483–375). Sicily.

[1] Arranged originally by Edgar S. Brightman, and used by permission of Mrs. E. S. Brightman; revised and enlarged by the author, plus several new sections added, including the extended one entitled "Contemporary Philosophy." This "Outline of Philosophers" is copyrighted by William S. Sahakian (1963).

3. Hippias.
4. Prodicus.

B. Socrates (470–399). Athens.
C. The Lesser Socratics.
1. Euclid of Megara (c. 450–380). Megarian.
2. Aristippus of Cyrene (435–355). Cyrenaic.
3. Antisthenes of Athens (445–365). Cynic.

V. THE PROBLEM OF SYSTEMATIC PHILOSOPHY (399–322)

A. Plato (427–347). Athens.
B. Aristotle (384–322). Athens.

VI. THE PROBLEM OF SALVATION (ETHICAL AND RELIGIOUS): HELLENISTIC AND ALEXANDRIAN (300 B.C.–529 A.D.)

A. Stoics. Stoa in Athens.
1. Zeno (336–264).
2. Cleanthes (300–220).
3. Chrysippus (280–210).
4. Epictetus (50–120 A.D.).
5. Marcus Aurelius (121–180).

B. Epicureans. Garden in Athens.
1. Epicurus (341–271).
2. Lucretius (96–55).

C. Skeptics. Mostly Athens.
1. Academic:
a. Arcesilaus (315–241).
b. Carneades (215–130).
2. Pyrrhonic:
a. Pyrrho (365–275).
b. Timon of Phlius and Athens (320–230).
3. Sensationalistic:
a. Aenesidemus (fl. 10 B.C.).
b. Sextus Empirious (fl. 180–210).

D. Eclectics. Rome.
1. Cicero (106–43).
2. Seneca (4–65 A.D.).

E. Christianity.
1. Jesus (4 B.C.–30 A.D.).
2. Paul (d. 64).
3. Tertulian (fl. 180).
4. Irenaeus (fl. 180).
5. Clement (fl. 180).
6. Origen (d. 254).
7. Augustine (354–430). *Cogito, ergo sum* (I think, therefore I am).

F. Neo-Platonists:
   1. Philo of Alexandria (30 B.C.–50 A.D.). Jewish theologian.
   2. Plotinus (204–269).
   3. Porphyry (230–300).
   4. Jamblichus (d. 330).
   5. Proclus (411–485).
      (Justinian closed the Academy in 529).

Outline of Medieval and Modern Philosophy

I. THE MIDDLE AGES (529–1453)

A. *The Platonic Period.* 529–1200.
   1. Dionysius the Areopagite (Neoplatonic). (500).
   2. John Scotus Erigena (c. 810–877). Irish; taught in Paris; Pantheist.
   3. Roscellinus (c. 1050–1121). Nominalistic heretic.
   4. Anselm of Canterbury (1033–1109). Platonic Realist.
   5. Peter Abelard (1079–1142). Conceptualist.
   6. Bernard of Clairvaux (1091–1153). Mystic.
      (Founding of universities, Gothic architecture, Crusades).

B. *The Aristotelian Period.* (1200–1453).
   1. Arabian philosophers who preserved and interpreted Aristotle:
      a. Avicenna (980–1037).
      b. Averroës (1126–1198).
      c. Al-Ghazali (1059–1109). A sort of orthodox Hume, was skeptical of philosophy.
      d. Maimonides (1135–1204). The great Jewish philosopher; he was influenced by the Arabs.
   2. Albertus Magnus (1193–1280). Teacher of St. Thomas.
   3. Thomas Aquinas (1225–1274). *Doctor Angelicus.* Greatest Scholastic.
   4. John Duns Scotus (1265–1308). *Doctor Subtilis.* Voluntarist.
   5. William of Occam (1280–1347). Nominalist. Occam's razor.
   6. Mystics:
      a. Bonaventura (1221–1274).
      b. Meister Eckhart (1260–1327).
   7. Roger Bacon (1214–1294). Franciscan, scientist.
   8. Nicolas of Cusa (1401–1464). *Docta Ignorantia.* (1453, fall of Constantinople).

II. THE RENAISSANCE (1453–1690)

A. *The Humanistic Period.* 1453–1600.
   1. Leonardo da Vinci (1452–1519). Scientific, artistic genius.
   2. Nicolas Copernicus (1473–1543). Heliocentric theory.
   3. Pico della Mirandola (1463–1494). Last schoolman.

4. Theophrastus of Hohenheim (Paracelsus), (1493–1541). Alchemist.
5. Nicolo Machiavelli (1469–1527). *The Prince,* (*Il Principe,* 1532).
6. Philip Melanchthon (1497–1560). Aristotelian, reformer.
7. John Calvin (1509–1564). *Institutes of the Christian Religion, (Institutio Christianae Religionis),* 1559.
8. Giordano Bruno (1548–1600). Monads. Burned at the stake.
9. Tommaso Campanella (1568–1639). *City of the Sun,* 1623 (*Civitas Solis*).
10. Jacob Boehme (1575–1624). Mystical cobbler of Görlitz.

B. The Natural Science Period (1600–1690).
1. Francis Bacon (1561–1620). *Novum Organum,* 1620.
2. Galileo Galilei (1564–1642). *"E pur si muove."*
3. Hugo Grotius (1583–1620). *De Jure Belli et Pacis.*
4. Thomas Hobbes (1588–1679). Materialist. Double Truth Theory. *Leviathan,* 1651.
5. Isaac Newton (1642–1727). *Mathematical Principles of Natural Philosophy,* 1687.

III. THE ENLIGHTENMENT (1690–1781)

(Including thinkers before 1690)

A. *Continental Rationalism:*
1. René Descartes (1596–1650). *"Cogito ergo sum."*
2. Occasionalists:
   a. Arnold Geulincx (1625–1669).
   b. Nicole Malebranche (1688–1715).
3. Benedict Spinoza (1632–1677). *Ethics,* (Ethica), 1677.
4. Gottfried Wilhelm Leibniz (1644–1716). *Monodology,* (*Monadolgia*), 1714.
5. Christian Wolff (1679–1754). Systematizer of Leibniz.

B. British Empiricism (and Enlightenment):
1. Francis Bacon (1561–1620). (above).
2. Thomas Hobbes (1588–1679). (above).
3. John Locke (1632–1704). *An Essay Concerning Human Understanding,* 1690.
4. William Wollaston (1659–1724). *The Religion of Nature Delineated,* 1722.
5. Bernard de Mandeville (1670–1733). Machiavellian view of human nature. *Fable of the Bees,* 1705. Defends selfishness.
6. John Toland (1670–1722). *Christianity Not Mysterious,* 1696. First to coin the term *Pantheism,* and to be called *freethinker.*
7. Anthony Ashley Cooper (Earl of Shaftesbury, later called Lord Ashley) (1671–1713). Repudiates Hobbesian Egoism. *Inquiry concerning Virtue and Merit,* 1711.
8. Samuel Clarke (1675–1729). *Discourse Concerning the*

Being and Attributes of God (Boyle Lectures of 1704–1705).

9. Anthony Collins (1676–1729). *Discourse on Freethinking,* 1713. Necessitarianism.
10. George Berkeley (1685–1753). *A Treatise Concerning the Principles of Human Knowledge,* 1710.
11. Joseph Butler (1692–1752). *Fifteen Sermons upon Human Nature,* 1726, 1729; *The Analogy of Religion,* 1736.
12. Francis Hutcheson (1694–1747). Emotional Intuitionism. First to use the dictum: "The greatest good for the greatest number." *System of Moral Philosophy,* 1755.
13. David Hartley (1705–1757). *Observations on Man,* 1749.
14. David Hume (1711–1776). *A Treatise of Human Nature,* 1739.
15. Adam Smith (1723–1790). *Laissez faire. Wealth of Nations,* 1776.
16. Joseph Priestley (1733–1804). *Disquisitions Relating to Matter and Spirit. Laissez faire.*
17. William Paley (1743–1805). *Natural Theology,* 1802.

C. *The French Enlightenment:*

1. Blaise Pascal (1623–1662). Religious wager. Pensées, 1670.
2. Pierre Bayle (1647–1706).
3. Francois Salignac de la Mothe-Fénelon (1651–1715).
4. Bernard le Bovier de Fontenelle (1657–1757).
5. Charles Louis de Secondat (Baron de la Brède et de Montesquieu) (1689–1755).
6. Voltaire (Francois-Marie Arouet) (1694–1778). Satirist. Deist. *Écrassez l'infame.*
7. Julien Offray de Lamettrie (1709–1751). *Man a Machine (L'homme machine),* 1748.
8. Jean Jacques Rousseau (1712–1778). Swiss. *Social Contract (Du contract social),* 1762.
9. Denis Diderot (1713–1784). *Encyclopédie.*
10. Étienne Bonnot de Condillac (1715–1780). Sensationalist.
11. Claude Adrien Helvétius (1715–1771).
12. Jean Le Rond D'Alembert (1717–1783).
13. Dietrich von Holbach (Paul Henri Thiry, Baron D'Holbach) (1723–1789).

D. *The German Enlightenment:*

1. Christian Wolff (1679–1754). (above).
2. Johann Christian Edelmann (1698–1767).
3. Frederick the Great (1712–1786). *Nach seiner fasson.*
4. Alexander Gottlieb Baumgarten (1714–1762).
5. Johann Joachim Winckelmann (1717–1768).
6. Gotthold Ephraim Lessing (1729–1781).
7. Moses Mendelssohn (1729–1786). Jewish.
8. Johann Gottfried von Herder (1744–1803).
9. J. N. Tetens (1736–1805). Psychologist.

E. *The Italian Enlightenment* (including other Italians):
   1. Pierre Gassendi (1592–1655). *The Philosophy of Epicurus,* 1649.
   2. Giovanni Battista Vico (1668–1744). *Principles of a New Science (Una scienza nuova),* 1725.
   3. Antonio Rosmini-Serbati (1797–1855). Idealist. *New Information on the Origin of Ideas,* 1830.
   4. Vincenzo Gioberti (1801–1852). *Introduction to the Study of Philosophy,* 1840, (*Introduzione alla Filosofia*).

F. *Early American Philosophy:*
   1. Roger Williams (1604–1684).
   2. Increase Mather (1639–1723).
   3. Cotton Mather (1663–1728).
   4. Samuel Johnson (1696–1772). *Elementa Philosophica,* 1752.
   5. Jonathan Edwards (1703–1758). Outstanding Calvinist. *Sinners in the Hands of an Angry God; Freedom of the Will,* 1754.
   6. John Woolman (1720–1772). *The Journal; Remarks on Sundry Subjects.*

G. *The American Enlightenment:*
   1. Benjamin Franklin (1706–1790). *Autobiography,* 1868; *Poor Richard's Almanack* (26 vols. 1732–1757).
   2. John Witherspoon (1723–1794). *Lectures on Moral Philosophy; Works,* 1800.
   3. Ethan Allen (1737–1789). *Reason, the Only Oracle of Man; or a Compendious System of Natural Religion,* 1784.
   4. Thomas Paine (1737–1809). *Common Sense,* 1776; *The Age of Reason,* 1794, 1796; *Rights of Man,* 1791, 1792.
   5. Thomas Jefferson (1743–1826). Declaration of Independence. Deist. *Autobiography,* 1821.
   6. William Hamilton (1757–1804). Hobbesian.
   7. Elihu Palmer (1764–1806). Deist. *Posthumous Pieces; Works,* 1824.

IV. AMERICAN TRANSCENDENTALISM

A. William Ellery Channing (1780–1842). *Unitarian Christianity.*
B. Orestes Augustus Brownson (1803–1876).
C. Ralph Waldo Emerson (1803–1882). *Nature,* 1836; *American Scholar Address,* 1837; *The Divinity School Address,* 1838; *Essays: First Series,* 1841; *Second Series,* 1844; *Representative Men,* 1850; *Conduct of Life,* 1860; *Society and Solitude,* 1870.
D. Theodore Parker (1810–1860). *The World of Matter and the Spirit of Man; The Transient and the Permanent in Christianity,* 1841 *Works* 1853–1872. Abolitionist.
E. James Freeman Clarke (1810–1888).
F. Henry David Thoreau (1817–1862). *Walden, or Life in the Woods,* 1854; *Civil Disobedience; Works,* 1906.
H. Walt Whitman (1819–1892). *Leaves of Grass,* 1855; *Democratic Vistas,* 1871.

V. SCOTTISH PHILOSOPHY

A. Francis Hutcheson (1694–1746).
B. Thomas Reid (1710–1796). Naive Realist. Common Sense School.
C. David Hume (1711–1776). Phenomenalist. Empiricist. (above).
D. Adam Smith (1723–1790).
E. Dugald Stewart (1753–1828).
F. Thomas Brown (1778–1820). Naive Realist. Common Sense School.
G. William Hamilton (1788–1820). Logician.
H. James Frederick Ferrier (1808–1864). Idealist. Coined the term *epistemology*.
I. James McCosh (1811–1894). Naive Realist.

VI. KANTIAN CRITICISM

(A synthesis of Continental Rationalism and British Empiricism).
A. Immanuel Kant (1724–1804). *The Critique of Pure Reason, (Die Kritik der reinen Vernunft),* A 1781, B 1787.

VII. POST-KANTIAN IDEALISM

A. *The Optimistic (Melioristic) Idealists*:
   1. Johann Gottlieb Fichte (1762–1814). *The Science of Knowledge. Grundlage der gesammten Wissenschaftslehre,* 1794.
   2. Georg Wilhelm Friedrich Hegel (1770–1831). *The Phenomenology of Spirit, (Die Phänomenologie des Geistes),* 1807.
B. *German Romanticists:*
   1. August Wilhelm Schlegel (1767–1845).
   2. Friedrich Schleiermacher (1768–1834).
   3. Novalis (Friedrich Philipp von Hardenberg) (1772–1801).
   4. Friedrich Schlegel (1772–1829). Brother of A. W. Schlegel.
   5. Jacob F. Fries (1773–1843). Kant's successor at Königsberg.
   6. Friedrich W. J. Schelling (1775–1854).
C. *The Pessimistic Idealists:*
   1. Arthur Schopenhauer (1788–1860). *The World as Will and Idea, (Die Welt als Wille und Vorstellung),* 1819.
   2. Eduard von Hartmann (1842–1906). *Philosophy of the Unconscious, (Die Philosophie des Unbewussten),* 1869.

VIII. POST-HEGELIAN PHILOSOPHY

A. *Reaction against Idealism:*
   1. Johann Friedrich Herbart (1776–1841). Realist.

2. Ludwig Feuerbach (1804–1872). Materialist.
3. Jacob Moleschott (1822–1893). Materialist.
4. L. Büchner (1824–1899). Materialist.
5. Ernst Haeckel (1834–1919). Materialist. *The Riddle of the Universe,* (*Die Welträtsel*), 1899.

Outline of Contemporary Philosophy

I. NEO-KANTIANISM

A. Alfonso Testa (1784-1860). Italian.
B. Noah Porter (1811-1892). *The Human Intellect,* 1868. American.
C. Charles Renouvier (1815-1903). French Kantian Idealist.
D. Hermann Helmholtz (1821-1894). Physiological movement.
E. Albrecht Ritschl (1822-1889).
F. Kuno Fischer (1824-1907). *History of Modern Philosophy,* 1854-1877.
G. Friedrich Lange (1828-1875). The physiological movement. *History of Materialism,* 1866.
H. Otto Liebmann (1840-1912). "Back to Kant."
I. Hermann Cohen (1842-1918). Founder of the Marburg School. *Kant's Theory of Experience,* 1871.
J. Alois Riehl (1844-1924). Kantian Realist. Emphasized "things-in-themselves."
K. Johannes Volkelt (1848-1930). Maintained the possibility of critical metaphysics.
L. Hans Vaihinger (1852-1933). Idealistic Positivism. *The Philosophy of 'As If,'* 1911.
M. Paul Natorp (1854-1924). *The Logical Basis of the Exact Sciences,* 1910; *Platons Ideenlehre,* 1903.
N. Rudolph Stammler (1856-1938). Philosopher of law in the Marburg School.
O. Alessandro Chiapelli (1857-1932). Italian.
P. Georg Simmel (1858-1918). Maintained the psychological and relative nature of the a priori in Kant.
Q. Karl Vorländer (1860-1928). Synthesized Kantian and social ethics.
R. Hans Cornelius (1863-1947). In the psychological school; moved closer to Positivism.
S. Ernst Cassirer (1874-1945). *Problem of Knowledge,* 1906; *An Essay on Man,* 1944.
T. Richard Hönigswald (1874-1947). Kantian Realist. Emphasized "things-in-themselves."
V. José Ortega y Gasset (1883-1955). *The Revolt of the Masses,* 1930. Spanish. "Philosopher of the agora." "Generation of 98." Later left Neo-Kantianism.

II. NEO-HEGELIANISM

A. *In Germany:*
1. William Dilthey (1833-1911). *Introduction to the Sciences of the Spirit,* 1883.
2. Wilhelm Windelband (1848-1915). Founded the Baden School. *Präludien,* 1884; *A History of Philosophy,* 1893; *History and Natural Science,* 1894.
3. Hugo Münsterberg (1863-1916). Came to Harvard University in 1897.
4. Heinrich Rickert (1863-1936). *The Limits of Natural Scientific Conceptions,* 1896.
5. Emil Lask (1875-1915). Close to Phenomenology.
6. Bruno Bauch (1877-1942). Attempted to synthesize the Marburg and Baden Schools.

B. *In Great Britain:*
1. Edward Caird (1835-1908). Critical Philosophy of Kant, 1889.
2. Thomas Hill Green (1836-1882). *Prolegomena to Ethics,* 1883. Self-Realizationism. Personalist.
3. Francis Herbert Bradley (1846-1924). *Appearance and Reality,* 1891.
4. Bernard Bosanquet (1848-1923). Objective Idealist. *Logic or the Morphology of Thought,* 1888.
5. John McTaggart Ellis McTaggart (1866-1925). *Some Dogmas of Religion,* 1906.

C. *In the United States:*
1. Josiah Royce (1855-1916). *The World and the Individual,* 1900; *The Religious Aspect of Philosophy,* 1885.
2. James E. Creighton (1861–1924). Editor of the *Philosophical Review.* Active in *Kantsudien* (*Kant Studies*), a journal. A founder of the American Philosophical Association.
3. Mary W. Calkins (1863-1930). One of the rare women in philosophy. Wellesley College Professor. *Persistent Problems in Philosophy,* 1907.

III. DIALECTICAL MATERIALISM

A. Karl Marx (1818-1883). Hegelian Leftist. Founder of Dialectical Materialism. *Das Kapital,* 1867; *Manifesto of the Communist Party,* in collaboration with Engels, 1848.

B. Friedrich Engels (1820-1895). Formulator of Dialectical Materialism.

C. Edward Bernstein (1850-1932).

D. Daniel DeLeon (1852-1914).

E. Karl Kautsky (1854-1938).

F. Georgi Plekhanov (1856-1918).

G. Jean Jaurès (1859-1914).

H. Rosa Luxemburg (1870-1919).

I. Nikolai Lenin (Vladimir Ilich Ulyanov) (1870-1924). Expounder of the doctrines of Marx and Engels for the Communist Party. *State and Revolution,* 1917; *Materialism and Empirio-Criticism,* 1909.
J. Leon Trotsky (1877-1940). *Literature and Revolution,* 1924.
K. Joseph Stalin (Iosif Vissarionovich Dzhugashvili), (1879-1953). Systematized Marx along Lenin lines. *On Dialectical and Historical Materialism,* 1940.
L. Mao Tse-tung (1893-). Chinese Communist; Leninist.

IV. THE DIALECTICAL SCHOOL

A. Gaston Bachelard (1881-). French.
B. Ferdinand Gonseth (1890-). Leading spokesman. School's journal: *Dialectica* (founded in 1947; Zurich).

V. EVOLUTIONARY NATURALISM

A. Charles Darwin (1809-1882). *Origin of Species,* 1859-1872; *The Descent of Man,* 1871.
B. Herbert Spencer (1820-1903). *First Principles,* 1860-1862.
C. Thomas Henry Huxley (1825-1895). Coined the terms: Agnosticism and Epiphenomenalism. *Man's Place in Nature,* 1863 *Agnosticism,* 1889.
D. Chauncey Wright (1830-1875). *Philosophical Discussions,* 1877.
E. Ernst Haeckel (1834-1919). *Riddle of the Universe,* 1899.
F. John Fiske (1842-1901). *Through Nature to God,* 1899. *Idea of God,* 1885.
G. Friedrich Wilhelm Nietzsche (1844–1900). Superman. Will to Power. Master Morality vs. Slave Morality. *Thus Spake Zarathustra,* 1883-1892.
H. C. Lloyd Morgan (1852-1936). *Emergent Evolution,* 1922-1923.
I. Samuel Alexander (1859–1938). *Space, Time, and Deity,* 1920. Nisus. Space-Time.
J. Henri Bergson (1859-1941). Vitalist. Intuitionist. *Creative Evolution,* 1907.
K. Roy Wood Sellars (1880-). *Evolutionary Naturalism,* 1922.

VI. PRAGMATISM

A. Charles Sanders Peirce (1839-1914). Coined the term 'Pragmatism;' later changed it to 'Pragmaticism' to differentiate his system from any other. "How to Make Our Ideas Clear," 1878; "The Fixation of Belief," 1877.
B. William James (1842-1910, *Pragmatism,* 1907. Regarded as a founder of Pragmatism along with Peirce and Dewey.
C. John Dewey (1859-1952). Dean of American Philosophers. *Reconstruction in Philosophy,* 1920; *The Quest for Certainty,* 1929.
D. George Herbert Mead (1863-1931). Social Behaviorist. *Philosophy of the Act,* 1938.

E. Ferdinand C. S. Schiller (1864-1937). *Humanism,* 1903.
F. Clarence I. Lewis (1883-1964). *Mind and the World Order,* 1929.
G. Sidney Hook (1902-).

VII. VITALISM (BERGSONIAN VOLUNTARISM):

A. Léon Ollé-Laprune (1839-1899).
B. Friedrich Nietzsche (1844-1900). (above).
C. Jean de Gaultier (1858-1942).
D. Henri Bergson (1859-1941). (above).
E. Lucien Laberthonnière (1860-1931).
F. Alejandro Korn (1860-1936). Latin America.
G. Maurice Blondel (1861-1948).
H. Edouard Le Roy (1870-).
I. Maurice Pradines (1878-).
J. José Vasconcelos (1882-). Latin America.
K. Antonio Caso (1883-1946). Latin America.

VIII. CLASSICAL POSITIVISM (INCLUDING UTILITARIANISM)

A. Jeremy Bentham (1748-1832). Utilitarian.
B. Auguste Comte (1798-1857). Founder of Sociology. Father of Positivism. Phenomenalist. *A General View of Positivism,* 1848.
C. Carlo Catteneo (1801-1869). Italian Positivist.
D. John Stuart Mill (1806-1873). Utilitarian. Coined the term *Utilitarianism.*
E. Giuseppe Ferrari (1812-1876). Italian Positivist.
F. Gabino Barreda (1818-1881). Mexican Positivist.
G. Herbert Spencer (1820-1903). Evolutionary Naturalist and Utilitarian. (above).
H. Roberto Ardigo (1828-1920). Influential Italian Positivist.
I. Henry Sidgwick (1838-1900). Utilitarian.
J. Ernst Mach (1838-1916). Phenomenalist. Austrian.
K. Eugenio Maria de Hostos (1839-1903). Puerto Rico. Positivist.
L. Richard Avenarius (1843-1896). Swiss Positivist.
M. Enrique José Varona (1849-1933). Cuban Positivist.
N. Enrico Morselli (1852-1929). Italian Positivist.
O. Jules Henri Poincaré (1854-1912). Positivist. *Science and Hypothesis,* 1902.
P. Karl Pearson (1857-1936). Positivist.
Q. Joseph Petsoldt (1862-1929). Positivist. *Annalen der Philosophie.*
R. Theodor Ziehen (1862-1950). Positivist.
S. González Ingenieros (1877-1925). Positivist. Argentina.

IX. LOGICAL POSITIVISM (INCLUDING ANALYTIC PHILOSOPHY)

A. Charles Ernest Voullemin (1865-). French.
B. Heinrich Gomperz (1873-).

C. Hans Hahn (1879-1934). Vienna Circle.
D. Moritz Schlick (1882-1936). Founder of the Vienna Circle.
E. Otto Neurath (1882-1945). Member of Vienna Circle.
F. Philipp Frank (1884-). Vienna Circle.
G. L. Susan Stebbing (1885-1943).
H. Ludwig Wittgenstein (1889-1951). Father of Logical Positivism. Logical Atomism.
I. Louis Rougier (1889-). French.
J. Hans Reinchenbach (1891-1953).
K. Rudolph Carnap (1891-). Vienna Circle.
L. Edgar Zilsel (1891-).
M. C. A. Mace (1894-).
N. Felix Kaufmann (1895-).
O. Gilbert Ryle (1900-). Highly influential in England. *The Concept of Mind,* 1949.
P. Ernest Nagel (1901-). U.S.
Q. Alfred Tarski (1901-).
R. Herbert Feigl (1902-). Vienna Circle.
S. Karl Popper (1902-).
T. John Wisdom (1904-). British. Therapeutic Positivism.
U. Gustav Bergmann (1906-). Vienna Circle.
V. Kurt Gödel (1906-). Vienna Circle. Incompleteness Theorem.
W. Alfred Jules Ayer (1910-). British. *Language, Truth and Logic,* 1936.
X. F. Waismann was also a member of the Vienna Circle.

The influential representatives of Logical Positivism are predominantly German, a fair number of whom have migrated to the United States.

Chief Organ: *Erkenntnis,* and later: *Journal of Unified Science.*

X. NEO-SCHOLASTICISM (INCLUDING NEO-THOMISM)

A. Désiré Mercier (1851-1926). Founder of the Institut Supérieur de Philosophie at Louvain University, an outstanding center of Neo-Thomism.
B. Ambrose Gardeil (1859-1931).
C. Joseph Mausbach (1861-1931). German School.
D. Maurice Blondel (1861-1948). Augustinian. (above).
E. Joseph Gredt (1863-1940). Systematizer of the School.
F. Antonin Gilbert Sertillanges (1863-1948). Outstanding.
G. Gallus M. Manser (1866-1950). The German School. Swiss.
H. Martin Grabmann (1875-1949). German School.
I. Réginald Garrigou-Lagrange (1877-). French.
J. Joseph Maréchal (1878-1944).
K. Léon Noël (1878-).
L. Pierre Rousselot (1878-1915).
M. Peter Hoenen (1880-).
N. Jacques Maritain (1882-). The foremost living Neo-Thomist. Former Professor at Princeton University.